A Little Treasury

of Modern Poetry

A Little Treasury
of Modern Poetry

ENGLISH & AMERICAN

Third Edition

Edited with an Introduction by

OSCAR WILLIAMS

CHARLES SCRIBNER'S SONS
New York

COPYRIGHT NOTICES AND ACKNOWLEDGMENTS

Grateful acknowledgment is made to the following poets, their copyright
owners and their publishers for permission to reprint certain poems in this
anthology:

GEORGE ALLEN & UNWIN LTD. for "Song" and "The Peasants" from *Ha! Ha!
Among the Trumpets* by Alun Lewis.

ARCHON BOOKS for prose statements from *The Lion Hunt: A Pursuit of
Poetry and Reality* by John Holloway, copyright 1964.

ASTOR-HONOR, INC. for "How Still the Hawk" and "Winter Encounters"
from *Seeing Is Believing*, copyright © 1960 by Charles Tomlinson.

ATHENEUM PUBLISHERS for "The End of the Weekend" from *The Hard
Hours*, copyright © 1959, 1967 by Anthony E. Hecht. This poem originally
appeared in the *Hudson Review*. For "Japan" and "Samuel Sewall" from
A Summoning of Stones, copyright 1954, © 1967 by Anthony E. Hecht.
For "The Woman at the Washington Zoo" from *The Woman at the Washington Zoo* by Randall Jarrell, copyright © 1960 by Randall Jarrell. All
reprinted by permission of the publisher.

ATLANTIC-LITTLE, BROWN AND CO. for "A Choice of Weapons," copyright
© 1956 by Stanley Kunitz and "Foreign Affairs," copyright © 1958 by
Stanley Kunitz (this poem appeared originally in *The New Yorker*), both
from *Selected Poems: 1928–1958*.

BASIC BOOKS, INC. for prose statements by Conrad Aiken, John Brinnin, Gregory Corso, James Dickey, Robert Duncan, Richard Eberhart, Vassar Miller, May Swenson, and Richard Wilbur from *Poets on Poetry*, edited by Howard Nemerov, copyright © 1966 by Howard Nemerov, Basic Books, Inc., Publishers, New York.

BEACON PRESS for prose statements from *I Wanted to Write a Poem* by William Carlos Williams, copyright © 1958 by William Carlos Williams. Reprinted by permission of the publisher.

BASIL BLACKWELL & MOTT LTD. for prose statements from *A Hope for Poetry* by C. Day-Lewis. Reprinted by permission of the publisher.

THE BOBBS-MERRILL COMPANY, INC. for "Blindman's Buff" and "Vale" from *New and Selected Poems,* copyright © 1967 by Peter Viereck, reprinted by permission of the publisher.

JONATHAN CAPE LTD. for "Leisure" and "Sheep" from *The Complete Poems by W. H. Davies.* Reprinted by permission of Mrs. H. M. Davies and Jonathan Cape Ltd. For "Naming of Parts" and "Chard Whitlow" from *A Map of Verona* by Henry Reed. Reprinted by permission of Henry Reed and Jonathan Cape Ltd.

CHATTO & WINDUS LTD. for twelve poems by Richard Eberhart from *Collected Poems by Richard Eberhart.* For eight poems by William Empson from *Collected Poems* by William Empson. For ten poems by Wilfred Owen from *Collected Poems* by Wilfred Owen. For "Procne" and "The Flight into Egypt" from *Poems* by Peter Quennell. For "Dead Man's Dump" from *Collected Poems* by Isaac Rosenberg.

JOHN CIARDI for "Ode for the Burial of a Citizen" from *Other Skies,* copyright 1944, 1945, 1946, 1947 by John Ciardi, for "To Judith Asleep" from *I Marry You* by John Ciardi, copyright 1958 by Rutgers, The State University, for "The Gift," from *39 Poems* by John Ciardi, copyright 1959 by Rutgers, The State University, for prose statements by John Ciardi from *Poet's Choice,* edited by Paul Engle and Joseph Langland. Reprinted by permission of the author and the Dial Press, Inc.

CITY LIGHT BOOKS for "Supermarket in California" from *Howl and Other Poems* and "To Aunt Rose" from *Kaddish and Other Poems* by Allen Ginsberg, copyright © 1968 by Allen Ginsberg, reprinted by permission of the publisher.

THE CLARENDON PRESS, OXFORD for eight poems by Robert Bridges from *Poetical Works of Robert Bridges,* Vol. II, reprinted by permission of the publisher.

COLLINS-KNOWLTON-WING, INC. for thirteen poems by Robert Graves from *Collected Poems 1955,* copyright © 1955 by Robert Graves. For prose statements by Robert Graves from *Oxford Addresses on Poetry,* copyright © 1962 by Robert Graves. Reprinted by permission of Collins-Knowlton-Wing, Inc.

CORINTH BOOKS, INC. for "I, Maximus of Gloucester, to you" from *The Maximus Poems* by Charles Olson, copyright © 1960 Charles Olson, Corinth Books/Jargon Books. For prose statements by Paul Blackburn, Denise Levertov, Kenneth Rexroth, and Gilbert Sorrentino from *The Sullen Art,* edited by David Ossman, copyright © 1961 by David Ossman. Reprinted by permission of the publisher.

CURTIS BROWN LTD., LONDON for "January 1940" from *The Middle of the War* and "Spring 1942," "Spring 1943," "The Tribes" and "Versions of Love" from *Collected Poems: 1936–1961* by Roy Fuller.

CURTIS BROWN LTD., NEW YORK for "The Farm," © 1959 and "An Airstrip in Essex," © 1960 by Donald Hall. Reprinted by permission of Curtis Brown Ltd.

THE JOHN DAY COMPANY, INC. for "Fife Tune," "The Sirens," and "Nightpiece," copyright © 1946 by The John Day Co., Inc. Reprinted from *Selected Verse* by John Manifold by permission of the publisher.

J. M. DENT & SONS LTD. and the TRUSTEES FOR THE COPYRIGHTS OF THE LATE DYLAN THOMAS for eight poems by Dylan Thomas from *Collected Poems.*

DODD, MEAD & COMPANY for "The Hound of Heaven" by Francis Thompson.

DOUBLEDAY & COMPANY, INC. for "I Knew a Woman," copyright © 1955 by Theodore Roethke; "Elegy for Jane," copyright 1950 by Theodore Roethke; "Dolor," copyright 1943 by Modern Poetry Association, Inc.; "The Waking," copyright 1953 by Theodore Roethke; "A Field of Light," copyright 1948 by Tiger's Eye; "The Lost Son," copyright 1947 by Theodore Roethke; "My Papa's Waltz," copyright 1942 by Hearst Magazines, Inc. All from *The Collected Poems of Theodore Roethke.* For "The Sequel," copyright © 1958 by Delmore Schwartz, from *Summer Knowledge* by Delmore Schwartz. All reprinted by permission of the publisher.

JOHN DRINKWATER for "Sunrise at Rydal Water," copyright 1919 by John Drinkwater.

ALAN DUGAN for "The Mirror Perilous" from *Poems,* copyright © 1961. Reprinted by permission of Alan Dugan and Yale University Press.

E. P. DUTTON & CO., INC. for four poems from *Collected Poems* by Lawrence Durrell, copyright © 1956, 1960 by Lawrence Durrell. Reprinted by permission of the publisher.

NORMA MILLAY ELLIS for four poems by Edna St. Vincent Millay from *Collected Poems,* Harper & Row, copyright 1921, 1922, 1928, 1931, 1948, 1950, 1955, 1958 by Edna St. Vincent Millay and Norma Millay Ellis.

FABER & FABER LTD. for seven poems from *Collected Poems* by Stephen Spender. For "Innocence," "Considering the Snail," and "My Sad Captains" from *My Sad Captains,* "A Mirror for Poets" from *Fighting Terms,* and "On the Move" from *The Sense of Movement* by Thom Gunn. For nine poems from *Collected Poems* by Edwin Muir. For ten poems from *Collected Poems of Louis MacNeice.* For four poems from *Collected Poems* by Lawrence Durrell. For seven poems from *Collected Poems 1909–1962* by T. S. Eliot. For "Listen. Put on Morning" from *The White Threshold* by W. S. Graham. For "Hawk Roosting," "View of a Pig," and "Pike" from *Lupercal* by Ted Hughes. For nine poems from *Collected Shorter Poems 1927–1957* and *Collected Poetry of W. H. Auden.* For "Missing Dates," "Ignorance of Death," and "Just a Smack at Auden" from *Collected Poems by William Empson.* For "Summer Rain" and "To a Conscript of 1940" from *Collected Poems* by Herbert Read. For "A Child Expected" from *The Nine Bright Shiners* by Anne Ridler. For "St. Ursanne" from *Orion's Marches* by Michael Roberts. For five poems from *Selected Poems* and *The Lady with the Unicorn* by Vernon Watkins. For prose statements from *On Poetry and Poets* by T. S. Eliot. Reprinted by permission of the publisher.

FARRAR, STRAUS & GIROUX, INC. for four poems from *For the Union Dead* by Robert Lowell, copyright © 1960 by Robert Lowell; from *Life Studies* by Robert Lowell, copyright © 1959 by Robert Lowell; from *Near the Ocean* by Robert Lowell, copyright © 1965 by Robert Lowell. For four poems from *Collected Poems* by Louise Bogan, copyright 1937 by *The New Yorker,* copyright 1954 by Louise Bogan. For "Neither Here Nor There" from *Europa and the Bull* by W. R. Rodgers, copyright 1952 by W. R.

Rodgers. For six poems from *The Dispossessed* by John Berryman, copyright 1940 by New Directions, copyright 1948 by John Berryman and *77 Dream Songs* by John Berryman, copyright © 1959, 1962, 1963, 1964 by John Berryman. For six poems from *Collected Poems* by Elizabeth Bishop, copyright 1940, 1946, 1947, 1948, 1949, 1951, 1952, 1955 by Elizabeth Bishop. For "The Conspirators" from *The Assassins* by Frederic Prokosch, reprinted with the permission of Farrar, Straus & Giroux and Mr. Prokosch, copyright 1936 by Frederic Prokosch. For prose statements from *On Poetry and Poets* by T. S. Eliot, copyright © 1956, 1957 by T. S. Eliot. Reprinted by permission of the publisher.

FUNK & WAGNALLS for three poems from *Poems: A Selection* by Léonie Adams, copyright 1954. Reprinted by permission of the publisher.

ALLEN GINSBERG for prose statements from *The New American Poetry*, edited by Donald M. Allen, copyright 1960.

GROVE PRESS, INC. for "Orchard," "Helen," and "Lethe," from *Selected Poems* by H. D. (Hilda Doolittle), copyright © 1957 by Norman Holmes Pearson. For "Song" from *Collected Poems of H. D.*, copyright © 1925, 1953 by Norman Holmes Pearson. Reprinted by permission of the publisher.

HARCOURT, BRACE & WORLD, INC. for eight poems from *Collected Poems of William Empson*, copyright 1949 by William Empson. For six poems from *Lord Weary's Castle*, copyright 1946 by Robert Lowell. For "In the Smoking Car" from *Advice to a Prophet and Other Poems*, copyright © 1960 by Richard Wilbur. This poem was first published in *The New Yorker*. For six poems from *Ceremony and Other Poems*, copyright 1948, 1949, 1950 by Richard Wilbur. For "As Freedom Is a Breakfast Food" and "Anyone Lived in a Pretty How Town," copyright 1940 by E. E. Cummings; "What If a Much of a Which of a Wind," "Pity This Busy Monster Manunkind," and "It Was a Goodly Co," copyright 1944 by E. E. Cummings; "My Love" and "All in Green Went My Love Riding," copyright 1923, 1951 by E. E. Cummings; "A Man Who Had Fallen among Thieves," "Nobody Loses All the Time," and "Next to of Course God," copyright 1926 by Horace Liveright, copyright 1954 by E. E. Cummings; "Somewhere I Have Never Travelled" and "I Sing of Olaf," copyright 1931, 1959 by E. E. Cummings; all reprinted from his volume *Poems 1923–1954*. For two poems from *A Map of Verona* by Henry Reed. For "Confession Overheard in a Subway" from *Afternoon of a Pawnbroker* by Kenneth Fearing. For seven poems from *Collected Poems 1909–1962* by T. S. Eliot, copyright 1936 by Harcourt, Brace & World, Inc., copyright © 1962, 1963 by T. S. Eliot. All reprinted by permission of the publisher.

ESTATE OF THOMAS HARDY, MACMILLAN & CO. LTD., LONDON, and THE MACMILLAN COMPANY OF CANADA LIMITED for thirteen poems from *Collected Poems* by Thomas Hardy.

HARPER & ROW for "The Chicago Picasso" and "The Sermon on the Warpland," copyright © 1968 by Gwendolyn Brooks Blakely from *In the Mecca* by Gwendolyn Brooks. For "Saturday's Child," copyright 1925 by Harper & Brothers, renewed 1953 by Ida M. Cullen; for "From the Dark Tower," copyright 1927 by Harper & Brothers, renewed 1955 by Ida M. Cullen; both poems from *On These I Stand* by Countee Cullen. For "The Jaguar" and "Famous Poet," copyright © 1957, from *The Hawk in the Rain*, by Ted Hughes; "Hawk Roosting," copyright © 1959, "View of a Pig," copyright © 1960, "Pike," copyright © 1959, from *Lupercal*, by Ted Hughes. For "Daddy" from *Ariel* by Sylvia Plath, copyright © 1963 by Ted Hughes. For "The King of Ai" from *Aspects of Proteus*, copyright 1949 by Hyam Plutzik. For "A Flat One" from *After Experience*, copyright © 1960 by W. D. Snodgrass. For "Traveling through the Dark" and "At Cove on the

Crooked River" from *Traveling through the Dark*, copyright © 1960 by William Stafford; "At the Bomb Testing Site" from *The Rescued Year*, copyright © 1960 by William E. Stafford.

RUPERT HART-DAVIS LIMITED for "Soldiers Bathing" and "To a Friend on His Marriage" from *The Doors of Stone* by F. T. Prince.

HARVARD UNIVERSITY PRESS and the TRUSTEES OF AMHERST COLLEGE for twenty-one poems from *The Poems of Emily Dickinson*, Thomas H. Johnson, Editor, Cambridge, Mass.: The Belknap Press of Harvard University Press, copyright 1951, 1955 by The President and Fellows of Harvard College. Harvard University Press, for prose statements by E. E. Cummings from *i: Six Nonlectures* and Edwin Muir from *The Estate of Poetry* and *Essays on Literature and Society*.

DAVID HIGHAM ASSOCIATES, LTD. for "Still Falls the Rain" and "Lullaby" from *The Collected Poems of Edith Sitwell*. For three poems from *A Drunk in the Furnace* by W. S. Merwin. For two poems by Charles Causley from *Union Street*.

HILL AND WANG, INC. for "The Distant Runners" from *Collected and New Poems: 1924–1963* by Mark Van Doren, copyright © 1963 by Mark Van Doren. Reprinted by permission of the publisher.

MRS. RALPH HODGSON, MACMILLAN & CO. LTD., LONDON, and THE MAC-MILLAN COMPANY OF CANADA LIMITED for five poems from *Collected Poems* by Ralph Hodgson.

HOLT, RINEHART AND WINSTON, INC. for "Come In," "Once by the Pacific," "Bereft," "Acquainted with the Night," "The Impulse" from "The Hill Wife," "A Semi-Revolution," "Mending Wall," "Stopping by Woods on a Snowy Evening," "The Road Not Taken," "Fire and Ice," "Two Tramps in Mud Time," "The Gift Outright," "Birches" from *Complete Poems of Robert Frost*, copyright 1916, 1923, 1928, 1930, 1939 by Holt, Rinehart and Winston, Inc., copyright 1936, 1942, 1944, 1951, © 1956, 1958 by Robert Frost, copyright © 1964, 1967 by Lesley Frost Ballantine. For "The Witch of Coos," "The Lesson for Today," "Directive," "The Span of Life" from *Complete Poems of Robert Frost*, copyright 1923, 1947 by Holt, Rinehart and Winston, Inc., copyright 1936, 1942, 1951 by Robert Frost, copyright © 1964 by Lesley Frost Ballantine. For "Pod of the Milkweed," "Forgive, O Lord" from *In the Clearing* by Robert Frost, copyright 1954, © 1962 by Robert Frost. For "Is My Team Ploughing," "To an Athlete Dying Young," "I Hoed and Trenched and Weeded," "Reveille," " 'Terence, This Is Stupid Stuff' " from "A Shropshire Lad"—Authorised Edition—from *The Collected Poems of A. E. Housman*, copyright 1939, 1940, © 1959 by Holt, Rinehart and Winston, Inc. Copyright © 1967, 1968 by Robert E. Symons. For "I Did Not Lose My Heart In Summer's Even" from *More Poems* by A. E. Housman, copyright 1936 by Barclays Bank Ltd., copyright © 1964 by Robert E. Symons. For "Into My Heart an Air That Kills," "With Rue My Heart Is Laden," "When I Was One-and-Twenty," "Loveli-est of Trees, the Cherry Now" from "A Shropshire Lad"—Authorised Edition—from *The Collected Poems of A. E. Housman*, copyright 1939, 1940, © 1959 by Holt, Rinehart and Winston, Inc., copyright © 1967, 1968 by Robert E. Symons. For "Tell Me Not Here, It Needs Not Saying," "Could Man Be Drunk For Ever," "The Night Is Freezing Fast" from *The Collected Poems of A. E. Housman*, copyright 1922 by Holt, Rinehart and Winston, Inc., copyright 1950 by Barclays Bank Ltd. For "Chicago" from *Chicago Poems* by Carl Sandburg, copyright 1916 by Holt, Rinehart and Winston, Inc., copyright 1944 by Carl Sandburg. For prose selections from "The Figure a Poem Makes" from *Complete Poems of Robert Frost*, copy-right 1939, © 1967 by Holt, Rinehart and Winston, Inc. For "The Constant

Symbol" and "Education by Poetry" from *Selected Prose of Robert Frost,* edited by Hyde Cox and Edward Connery Lathem, copyright 1946 by Robert Frost, copyright © 1966 by Holt, Rinehart and Winston, Inc. All reprinted by permission of the publisher.

HORIZON PRESS for two poems from *Collected Poems* by Herbert Read, copyright 1966. Reprinted by permission of the U.S. publisher.

HOUGHTON MIFFLIN COMPANY for "Ars Poetica," "The Too-Late Born," "L'An Trentiesme de Mon Eage," "You, Andrew Marvell," "Invocation to the Social Muse," "The End of the World" from *The Collected Poems of Archibald MacLeish,* copyright © 1962 by Archibald MacLeish. For "First Song" and "The Avenue Bearing the Initial of Christ into the New World" (parts 1, 2) from *What a Kingdom It Was,* copyright © 1960 by Galway Kinnell. For "Her Kind" and "The Farmer's Wife" from *To Bedlam and Part Way Back,* copyright © 1960 by Anne Sexton. For "The Fortress" from *All My Pretty Ones,* copyright © 1961, 1962 by Anne Sexton. Reprinted by permission of the publisher.

TED HUGHES for "The Colossus," "Black Rook in Rainy Weather" from *The Colossus* and "Daddy" from *Ariel* by Sylvia Plath.

INDIANA UNIVERSITY PRESS for "Monkey," "The Savages," and "Voyage" from *Poems 1930–1960* by Josephine Miles.

MRS. RANDALL JARRELL for "The State," "Second Air Force," "The Death of the Ball Turret Gunner," "Losses," and "The Snow Leopard," copyright 1967.

DONNAN AND GARTH JEFFERS for "Black-Out" by Robinson Jeffers. This poem originally appeared in *New Poems 1940, 1944,* edited by Oscar Williams, copyright 1941, 1944 by Yardstick Press and Oscar Williams.

LE ROI JONES for prose statements from *The New American Poetry,* edited by Donald M. Allen, copyright 1960.

ALFRED A. KNOPF, INC. for "The Elephant Is Slow to Mate," "How Beastly the Bourgeois Is," and "Don'ts" by D. H. Lawrence from *Pansies,* copyright 1929. For "Little Boy Blue" from *Two Gentlemen in Bonds,* copyright 1927; for "Captain Carpenter," "The Equilibrists," "Here Lies a Lady," "Judith of Bethulia," "Bells for John Whiteside's Daughter," "Her Eyes," "Painted Head," "Man without Sense of Direction," and "Address to the Scholars of New England" from *Selected Poems* by John Crowe Ransom, copyright 1963. For "Wild Peaches," copyright 1921, 1932; "Hymn to Earth," copyright 1929; "The Eagle and the Mole," copyright 1921; "Address to My Soul," copyright 1928; "Let No Charitable Hope," copyright 1923 from *Collected Poems of Elinor Wylie.* For "Sunday Morning," "Thirteen Ways of Looking at a Blackbird," "Peter Quince at the Clavier," "Le Monocle de Mon Oncle," "An Extract," "Sense of the Sleight of Hand Man," "Conoisseur of Chaos," "The Prejudice against the Past," "Soldier, There Is a War," "Bethou Me, Said the Sparrow," "Continual Conversations with a Silent Man," "Crude Foyer," and "Esthetique du Mal" from *Collected Poems of Wallace Stevens,* copyright 1967; for "So-and-So Reclining on Her Couch," copyright 1942, 1947 from *The Collected Poems of Wallace Stevens.* For "The Colossus" from *The Colossus,* copyright 1961 by Sylvia Plath. For "April Inventory," copyright 1957 and "The Campus on the Hill," copyright 1958 from *Heart's Needle* by W. D. Snodgrass. For "The Heart," "War Is Kind," "A Man Said to the Universe," "I Saw a Man Pursuing the Horizon," "A Slant of Sun," "In the Desert," and "The Trees in the Garden" from *The Collected Poems of Stephen Crane,* published 1930, reprinted courtesy of the publisher. For "Cross," copyright 1926, renewed 1954 by Langston Hughes from *Selected Poems* by Langston

Hughes; "Harlem Sweeties," copyright 1942 by Langston Hughes from *Shakespeare in Harlem* by Langston Hughes; "Dream Deferred" and "American Heartbreak," copyright 1951 by Langston Hughes; "Slave," "Undertow," "Impasse," and "Go Slow," copyright © by Arna Bontemps and George Houston Bass from *The Panther and the Lash* by Langston Hughes. Reprinted by permission of the publisher.

LAURIE LEE for "Field of Autumn" from *The Bloom of Candles* by Laurie Lee.

LITTLE, BROWN AND CO. for "The First Day's Night Had Come" from *The Complete Poems of Emily Dickinson,* edited by Thomas H. Johnson, copyright 1935 by Martha Dickinson Bianchi, © renewed by Mary L. Hampson. For "Reflections on Ice-Breaking," copyright 1930 by Ogden Nash; originally appeared in *The New Yorker;* for "Portrait of the Artist as a Prematurely Old Man," copyright 1934 by The Curtis Publishing Company, both poems from *The Face Is Familiar* by Ogden Nash. Reprinted by permission of the publisher.

LIVERIGHT PUBLISHING CORPORATION for twelve poems from *The Complete Poems and Selected Letters and Prose of Hart Crane,* copyright 1933, 1958, 1966 by Liveright Publishing Corporation. Reprinted by permission of the publisher.

THE STERLING LORD AGENCY for "An Agony As Now" and "The Invention of Comics" by LeRoi Jones from *The Dead Lecturer,* copyright © 1964 by LeRoi Jones.

ARCHIBALD MACLEISH and HOUGHTON MIFFLIN COMPANY for prose statements from *Poetry and Opinion* by Archibald MacLeish.

MACMILLAN & CO. LTD., LONDON, and THE MACMILLAN COMPANY OF CANADA LIMITED for "This Above All" and "Brooklyn Heights" from *Weep before God* by John Wain, copyright © 1961.

THE MACMILLAN COMPANY, NEW YORK for thirteen poems from *Collected Poems* by Thomas Hardy, copyright 1925 by The Macmillan Company. For "The Lake Isle of Innisfree" and "When You Are Old," copyright 1906 by The Macmillan Company, renewed 1934 by William Butler Yeats; "Crazy Jane Talks with the Bishop," "For Anne Gregory," "After Long Silence," and "A Dialogue of Self and Soul," copyright 1933 by The Macmillan Company, renewed 1961 by Bertha Georgie Yeats; "An Irish Airman Foresees His Death," copyright 1919 by The Macmillan Company, renewed 1946 by Bertha Georgie Yeats; "Cuchulain Comforted," "The Apparitions," "Under Ben Bulben," "John Kinsella's Lament for Mrs. Mary Moore," "Lapis Lazuli," "Long-Legged Fly," and "News for the Delphic Oracle," copyright 1940 by Georgie Yeats; "A Prayer for My Daughter," "The Second Coming," "Easter 1916," copyright 1924 by The Macmillan Company, renewed 1952 by Bertha Georgie Yeats; "To a Friend Whose Work Has Come to Nothing," and "A Coat," copyright 1916 by The Macmillan Company, renewed 1944 by Bertha Georgie Yeats; "The Tower," copyright 1928 by The Macmillan Company, renewed 1956 by Georgie Yeats; "Among School Children," "Sailing to Byzantium," and "Leda and the Swan," copyright 1928 by The Macmillan Company, renewed 1956 by Georgie Yeats; "Byzantium," copyright 1935 by The Macmillan Company, renewed 1961 by Bertha Georgie Yeats; all from *Collected Poems* by William Butler Yeats. For "Flammonde," "Cassandra," and "Eros Turannos," copyright 1916 by Edwin Arlington Robinson, renewed 1944 by Ruth Nivison; "Mr. Flood's Party," copyright 1921 by Edwin Arlington Robinson, renewed 1949 by Ruth Nivison; "The Dark Hills," copyright 1920 by Edwin Arlington Robinson, renewed 1948 by Ruth Nivison; all from *Collected Poems* by Edwin Arlington Robinson. For "On Growing Old," copyright 1920 by

John Masefield, renewed 1948 by John Masefield; "The West Wind," "Cargoes," and "C.L.M.," copyright 1912 by The Macmillan Company, renewed 1940 by John Masefield; "I Could Not Sleep for Thinking of the Sky," "Night Is on the Downland," copyright 1917, 1945 by John Masefield; "In the Great Green Commonwealth of Thought," "Flesh, I Have Knocked at Many a Dusty Door," copyright 1916, 1944 by John Masefield, all from *Poems* by John Masefield. For "The Bull," "Time, You Old Gypsy Man," "Stupidity Street," "The Bells of Heaven," and "Eve," copyright 1917, by The Macmillan Company, renewed 1945 by Ralph Hodgson, from *Collected Poems* by Ralph Hodgson. For "Poetry" and "Roses Only," copyright 1935 by Marianne Moore, renewed 1963 by Marianne Moore and T. S. Eliot; "His Shield," copyright 1951 by The Macmillan Company; "In Distrust of Merits," "A Carriage from Sweden," "Spenser's Ireland," copyright 1944 by Marianne Moore, all from *Collected Poems*, by Marianne Moore. For "General Booth Enters into Heaven," copyright 1913 by The Macmillan Company from *Collected Poems* by Vachel Lindsay. For "O Wha's the Bride," and "With the Herring Fishers" from *Collected Poems* by Hugh MacDiarmid, copyright 1948, 1962 by Christopher Murray Grieve. For "Swedish Angel," copyright 1941 by Winfield Townley Scott; "Annual Legend," "The U.S. Sailor with the Japanese Skull," copyright 1945 by Winfield Townley Scott from *Collected Poems* by Winfield Townley Scott. For "The Stranger," "Forest," and "False Country of the Zoo" from *New and Selected Poetry* by Jean Garrigue, copyright © 1947, 1953, 1959, 1960, 1962, 1964, 1966, 1967 by Jean Garrigue. For prose statements by W. B. Yeats from *Essays and Introductions* copyright © 1961 by Mrs. W. B. Yeats. All reprinted by permission of the publisher.

THE MARVELL PRESS for "Church Going" and "If, My Darling" by Philip Larkin from *The Less Deceived*, copyright © 1955, 1960 by The Marvell Press, Hessle, Yorkshire, England.

ELLEN C. MASTERS for "The Hill," "Lucinda Matlock," "Henry C. Calhoun," "Carl Hamblin," "Davis Matlock," and "Anne Rutledge" from *The Spoon River Anthology* by Edgar Lee Masters, copyright 1914, 1942 by The Macmillan Co.

HAROLD MATSON COMPANY, INC. for "November Twenty-Six Nineteen Hundred Sixty-Three," copyright 1963 by Wendell Berry. For five poems from *The Collected Poems of C. Day-Lewis*, copyright 1959. Reprinted by permission of the Harold Matson Co., Inc.

MC CLELLAND & STEWART LTD. for "The Permanent Tourists" from *Cry Ararat!* and "The Stenographers" from *As Ten, As Twenty*, both by P. K. Page. Reprinted by permission of the publisher.

ROBERT MEZEY for "Street Scene" and "The Funeral Home" from *The Lovemaker* by Robert Mezey.

WILLIAM MORROW AND COMPANY, INC. for "Sunken Evening" from *My Many-Coated Man* by Laurie Lee, copyright 1961. Reprinted by permission of William Morrow and Company, Inc. All rights reserved.

HOWARD MOSS for "The Lie" and "Elegy for My Father" from *The Toy Fair* by Howard Moss.

HOWARD NEMEROV for "Truth," "Redeployment," "The Phoenix," "Boom!" and "The Goose Fish" from *New and Selected Poetry*, copyright 1960 by Howard Nemerov and the University of Chicago Press; "Spell before Winter" from *The Next Room of the Dream*, copyright 1962 by Howard Nemerov.

NEW DIRECTIONS for "Marriage" by Gregory Corso from *The Happy Birthday of Death*, copyright © 1960 by New Directions Publishing Corporation.

by Arna Bontemps. Reprinted by permission of Harold Ober Associates, Incorporated.

OCTOBER HOUSE INC. for "Resolution of Dependence," "News of the World: Part III," "And Now There Is Nothing Left," "To Any Member of My Generation," "O Golden Fleece," "To My Mother," "The Crystal," "Dog, Dog in My Manger," "Memorial for Two Young Seamen" from *Collected Poems 1930–1965* by George Barker, copyright © 1957, 1962, 1965 by George Barker. Reprinted by permission of the publisher.

OXFORD UNIVERSITY PRESS, LONDON for "A War Time Dawn," "Ecce Homo" and "A Tough Generation" from *Collected Poems* by David Gascoyne. For seventeen poems by Gerard Manley Hopkins from *Poems of Gerard Manley Hopkins*. For prose statements from *The Fire and the Fountain* by John Press. Reprinted by permission of the publisher.

OXFORD UNIVERSITY PRESS, NEW YORK for "Tetelestai," "Morning Song of Senlin," "Sea Holly," "Preludes for Memnon" Parts I, LII, LVI, "Music I Heard," and "The Room" from *Collected Poems* by Conrad Aiken, copyright 1953 by Conrad Aiken. For "On Shooting Particles Beyond the World," "The Groundhog," "In a Hard Intellectual Light," Rumination," "Seals, Terns, Time," "On a Squirrel Crossing a Road," "For a Lamb," "The Cancer Cells," "If I Could Only Live at the Pitch," "Fury of Aerial Bombardment," "New Hampshire, February" and "The Horse Chestnut Tree" from *Collected Poems 1930–1960* by Richard Eberhart, copyright © 1960 by Richard Eberhart; "Marrakech" from *Shifts of Being* by Richard Eberhart, copyright © 1968 by Richard Eberhart. For "The Kingdom" Parts I and II, "Perseus," "Alcohol," "The British Museum Reading Room," "Among These Turf-Stacks," "Snow," "August," "Jehu," and "Bagpipe Music" from *The Collected Poems of Louis MacNeice*, edited by E. R. Dodds, copyright © 1966 by the Estate of Louis MacNeice. For "The Voyage," "The Human Fold," "The Window," "The Gate," "The Grove," "In Love for Long," "The Road," "The Rider Victory," and "The Trophy" from *Collected Poems* by Edwin Muir, copyright © 1960 by Willa Muir. All reprinted by permission of the publisher.

PARTISAN REVIEW for prose statements by Karl Shapiro from "The Question of the Pound Award," copyright © 1949 by *Partisan Review*.

A. D. PETERS & COMPANY for "The Pike" by Edmund Blunden. For prose statements from *The Making of a Poem* by Stephen Spender. Reprinted by permission of A. D. Peters & Company.

LAURENCE POLLINGER LIMITED for "Field of Autumn" from *The Bloom of Candles* published by John Lehman, Ltd. and "Sunken Evening" from *My Many-Coated Man* published by Andre Deutsch, Ltd., both poems by Laurie Lee.

RANDOM HOUSE, INC. for "Musée des Beaux Arts," "In Memory of W. B. Yeats," "Voltaire at Ferney," "Refugee Blues," "As I Walked Out One Evening," and "The Unknown Citizen," copyright 1940, renewed 1968 by W. H. Auden; "O Where Are You Going," copyright 1934, renewed 1962 by W. H. Auden; "Mundus et Infans," copyright 1942 by W. H. Auden, all from *Collected Shorter Poems 1927–1957* by W. H. Auden; for "Fugal Chorus" from "For the Time Being," copyright 1944 by W. H. Auden from *The Collected Poetry of W. H. Auden*. For "Ultima Ratio Regum" and "The Double Shame," copyright 1942 by Stephen Spender; "Not Palaces, an Era's Crown," "I Think Continually of Those Who Were Truly Great," "The Landscape Near an Aerodrome" and "The Express," copyright 1934, renewed 1962 by Stephen Spender from *Selected Poems* by Stephen Spender; "After They Have Tired," copyright 1934, renewed

1962 by Stephen Spender from *Collected Poems 1928–1953* by Stephen Spender. For "Colder Fire," copyright © 1955 by Robert Penn Warren from *Promises: Poems 1954–1956;* "Original Sin: A Short Story" and "Bearded Oaks," copyright 1942 by Robert Penn Warren; "Country Burying," copyright © 1957 by Robert Penn Warren from *Selected Poems: New and Old 1923–1966,* all by Robert Penn Warren. For "Auto Wreck," "A Dome of Sunday," and "Hollywood," copyright 1941 by Karl Shapiro; "Scyros," "The Fly," and "Poet," copyright 1942 by Karl Shapiro; "Elegy for a Dead Soldier," copyright 1944 by Karl Shapiro, all from *Selected Poems* by Karl Shapiro. For "The Stars Go Over the Lonely Ocean" and "Battle (May 28, 1940)," copyright 1920, renewed 1968 by Donnan and Garth Jeffers and "I Shall Laugh Purely," copyright 1941 by Robinson Jeffers, all from *Be Angry at the Sun and Other Poems* by Robinson Jeffers; "Hurt Hawks," copyright 1928, renewed 1956 by Robinson Jeffers; "Shine, Perishing Republic," copyright 1925, renewed 1953 by Robinson Jeffers from *Selected Poetry of Robinson Jeffers;* "The Eye" and Cassandra," copyright 1941 by Yardstick Press, 1944 by Oscar Williams and "The Bloody Sire," copyright 1940, renewed 1968 by Donnan and Garth Jeffers from *Selected Poems;* "Promise of Peace," copyright 1925, renewed 1953 by Robinson Jeffers from *Roan Stallion, Tamar and Other Poems,* all by Robinson Jeffers. For prose statements by W. H. Auden from *The Dyer's Hand,* copyright © 1962 by W. H. Auden; for prose statements by Karl Shapiro from *In Defense of Ignorance,* copyright © 1960 by Karl Shapiro. All reprinted by permission of the publisher.

PAUL REYNOLDS, INC. for "Between the World and Me" by Richard Wright, copyright © 1935 by Richard Wright. Reprinted by permission of Paul Reynolds, Inc.

ALAN ROSS LTD. for "Part of Plenty" by Bernard Spencer. Reprinted by permission of the publisher.

ROUTLEDGE & KEGAN PAUL LTD. for "The Wind at Penistone" and "Gardens No Emblems" from *A Winter Talent* by Donald Davie. Reprinted by permission of the publisher.

MURIEL RUKEYSER for "Ajanta" and "Boy with His Hair Cut Short" from *Waterlily Fire: Poems 1935–1962* by Muriel Rukeyser.

RYERSON PRESS for "Indian Reservation: Caughnawaga" from *The Rocking Chair and Other Poems* by A. M. Klein. Reprinted by permission of the publisher.

ST. MARTIN'S PRESS, INC. for "This Above All Is Precious and Remarkable" and "Brooklyn Heights" by John Wain from *Weep before God,* copyright © 1961 by John Wain. Reprinted by permission of the publisher.

G. T. SASSOON for "The General" and "The Death-Bed" by Siegfried Sassoon, from *Collected Poems 1908–1956* by Siegfried Sassoon.

SATURDAY REVIEW ASSOCIATES, INC. for "Praying Mantis Visits a Penthouse" by Oscar Williams from *Saturday Review of Literature,* copyright 1945 by the Saturday Review Associates, Inc.

SCHOCKEN BOOKS, INC. for "Dead Man's Dump" from *Collected Poems* by Isaac Rosenberg. Reprinted by permission of the publisher.

CHARLES SCRIBNER'S SONS for "A Marriage," copyright © 1962 by Robert Creeley; "The Immoral Proposition," copyright © 1962 by Robert Creeley, and "The Way," copyright © 1962 by Robert Creeley from *For Love* by Robert Creeley; "The Rhythm," copyright © 1962 by Robert Creeley from *Words* by Robert Creeley. For "Lion" copyright © 1951 by May Swenson and "Question," copyright © 1963 by May Swenson from *To Mix With Time* by May Swenson. For "A Sea Change: for Harold," © 1955 by Joseph Langland and "Hunters in the Snow: Brueghel," copyright © 1956 by Joseph Langland from *The Green Town: Poems* by Joseph Langland. For "Earth," copyright © 1960 by John Hall Wheelock from *The Gardner* by John Hall Wheelock; "Slow Summer Twilight," copyright © 1964 by John Hall Wheelock from *Dear Men and Women* by John Hall Wheelock; "Silence" and "The Black Panther" from *The Black Panther* by John Hall Wheelock, copyright © 1922 by Charles Scribner's Sons, renewed 1950 by John Hall Wheelock. For "Ode" and "This Dim and Ptolemaic Man" from *Now with His Love,* by John Peale Bishop, copyright © 1933 by Charles Scribner's Sons, renewed © 1961 by Margaret G. H. Bronson; "The Dream" from *The Collected Poems of John Peale Bishop,* edited by Allen Tate, copyright © 1948 by Charles Scribner's Sons. For "Richard Cory," "George Crabbe," "Luke Havergal," and "Credo" from *The Children of the Night,* by Edwin Arlington Robinson, copyright © 1897 by Charles Scribner's Sons; "For a Dead Lady" and "Miniver Cheevy," copyright © 1907, renewed 1935; and "The Master" copyright © 1910 by Charles Scribner's Sons, renewed 1938 by Ruth Nivison from *The Town Down the River* by Edwin Arlington Robinson. For "Ode to the Confederate Dead," "The Traveler," "The Mediterranean," "The Wolves," "A Pauper," "Sonnets at Christmas," "More Sonnets at Christmas," and "The Oath" from *Poems* by Allen Tate. Reprinted by permission of the publisher.

SECKER & WARBURG LIMITED for "Neither Here nor There" from *Europa and the Bull;* "White Christmas," "Awake," "Snow," and "Directions to a Rebel" from *Awake! and Other Poems,* all by W. R. Rodgers. Reprinted by permission of the publisher.

SOCIETY OF AUTHORS for thirteen poems by A. E. Housman from *Collected Poems* by A. E. Housman. Reprinted by permission of The Society of Authors as the literary representative of the Estate of A. E. Housman, and Messrs. Jonathan Cape Ltd., publishers. For six poems by Walter de la Mare from *Collected Poems* and *The Burning Glass* by Walter de la Mare reprinted by permission of The Society of Authors as representative for the Literary Trustees of Walter de la Mare.

WILLIAM STAFFORD for "West of Your City" from *West of Your City,* by William Stafford. Reprinted by permission of the author.

THE SWALLOW PRESS, INC. for prose statements by Allen Tate from *Essays of Four Decades,* copyright 1968. Reprinted by permission of the publisher.

TWAYNE PUBLISHERS, INC. for "Not to Forget Miss Dickinson" by Marshall Schacht. Reprinted by permission of the publisher.

UNIVERSITY OF CALIFORNIA PRESS for prose statements by Stephen Spender from *The Struggle of the Modern* by Stephen Spender, copyright 1963. Reprinted by permission of The Regents of the University of California.

THE UNIVERSITY OF CHICAGO PRESS for "Innocence," "Considering the Snail," and "My Sad Captains" from *My Sad Captains* by Thom Gunn, copyright © 1961 by Thom Gunn. All rights reserved.

UNIVERSITY OF MINNESOTA PRESS for "A Day with the Foreign Legion" from *Poems New and Selected* by Reed Whittemore, copyright © 1956 by Reed Whittemore. For prose statements from *Poetry and Journalism,* by Archibald MacLeish, copyright 1958. Reprinted by permission of the publisher.

UNIVERSITY OF NEBRASKA PRESS for prose statements from *A Primer for Poets,* by Karl Shapiro copyright © 1953 by University of Nebraska Press. All rights reserved.

THE UNIVERSITY PRESS OF WASHINGTON, D.C. for prose statements from *Dream and Responsibility*, by Peter Viereck, copyright 1953. Reprinted by permission of the publisher.

UNIVERSITY OF TORONTO PRESS for "Butterfly Bones; or, Sonnet against Sonnets" and "New Year's Poem" from *The Winter Sun* by Margaret Avison. Reprinted by permission of the publisher.

UNIVERSITY OF WASHINGTON PRESS for prose statements by Theodore Roethke from *On the Poet and His Craft*, edited by R. J. Mills, Jr., copyright 1965. Reprinted by permission of the publisher.

VANGUARD PRESS, INC. for "Still Falls the Rain," copyright 1948, 1949, 1954 by Edith Sitwell and "Lullaby," copyright 1949, 1954 by Edith Sitwell from *The Collected Poems of Edith Sitwell*. Reprinted by permission of the publisher.

THE VIKING PRESS, INC. for "Moonrise," "The Song of a Man Who Has Come Through," "Tortoise Shout," "Humming Bird," and "Snake" from *The Complete Poems of D. H. Lawrence*, Volume I, edited by Vivian de Sola Pinto and F. Warren Roberts, copyright 1923, 1951 by Frieda Lawrence. All rights reserved. For "The Atoll in the Mind," "Hoc Est Corpus," and "Notes for My Son" from *The Song of Lazarus* by Alex Comfort, copyright 1945 by Alex Comfort. For "I Hear an Army Charging upon the Land" from *Collected Poems* by James Joyce, copyright 1918 by B. W. Huebsch, Inc., 1946 by Nora Joyce. For "Tell Me, Tell Me" and "The Mind, Intractable Thing" from the *Complete Poems of Marianne Moore*, copyright © 1960, 1965 by Marianne Moore. Both poems originally appeared in *The New Yorker*. For prose statements by Lawrence Durrell, T. S. Eliot, Robert Lowell, Marianne Moore and Ezra Pound from *Writers at Work*: The Paris Review Interviews, Second Series, copyright © 1963 by The Paris Review, Inc. For two excerpts from *The Liberal Imagination* by Lionel Trilling, copyright 1945, 1949 by Lionel Trilling. All reprinted by permission of The Viking Press, Inc.

A. P. WATT & SON for twenty-four poems by William Butler Yeats from *Collected Poems* by William Butler Yeats. For three poems by Robert Graves from *Collected Poems 1955* by Robert Graves. Reprinted by permission.

WESLEYAN UNIVERSITY PRESS for "The Heaven of Animals" from *Drowning with Others*, copyright © 1961 by James Dickey; "The Dusk of Horses" from *Helmets*, copyright © 1962 by James Dickey (These two poems originally appeared in *The New Yorker*.); "The Performance" from *Poems 1957–1967*, copyright © 1960 by James Dickey. For "The Final Hunger" and "Bout with Burning" from *Wage War on Silence* by Vassar Miller, copyright © 1960 by Vassar Miller. For "The Mythos of Samuel Huntsman" from *Apples from Shinar* by Hyam Plutzik, copyright © 1959 by Hyam Plutzik. For "To the Western World" from *A Dream of Governors*, copyright © 1957 by Louis Simpson; "Walt Whitman at Bear Mountain" from *At the End of the Open Road*, copyright © 1960 by Louis Simpson. For "Leisure" and "Sheep" from *The Complete Poems by W. H. Davies*. All reprinted by permission of the publisher.

THE EXECUTORS OF THE ESTATE OF OSCAR WILLIAMS (TURK, MARSH, KELLY & HOARE) for eight poems by Oscar Williams. For four poems by Gene Derwood.

YALE UNIVERSITY PRESS for "Plague of Dead Sharks" from *Poems 2* by Alan Dugan, copyright © 1963 by Yale University. For "The Lady's-Maid Song" and "The Great Bear" from *A Crackling of Thorns* by John Hollander, copyright © 1958 by Yale University Press, Inc. For "On the Skeleton of a Hound" and "A Gesture by a Lady with an Assumed Name" from *The Green Wall* by James Wright, copyright © 1957 by Yale University Press, Inc. All reprinted by permission of the publisher.

MICHAEL YEATS and MACMILLAN & CO. LTD., LONDON for prose statements from *The Symbolism of Poetry* by William Butler Yeats.

PICTURE CREDITS

CONRAD AIKEN: Photograph by Ann Marshall, courtesy of Oxford University Press

W. H. AUDEN: Photograph by Jerry Bauer, courtesy of Faber & Faber Ltd.

GWENDOLYN BROOKS: Photograph by Myles De Russy, courtesy of Harper & Row, Publishers

CHARLES CAUSLEY: Photograph by Parkers, courtesy of David Higham Associates, Ltd.

GREGORY CORSO: Photograph by Howard Smith, courtesy of New Directions Publishing Corporation

ROBERT CREELEY: Photograph by Harry Redl, courtesy of Charles Scribner's Sons

COUNTEE CULLEN: Courtesy of Harper & Row, publishers

WALTER DE LA MARE: Photograph by Mark Gerson, courtesy of Faber & Faber Ltd.

JAMES DICKEY: Courtesy of Wesleyan University Press

EMILY DICKINSON: Courtesy of the Houghton Library, Harvard University

H. D. (HILDA DOOLITTLE): Courtesy of Norman Holmes Pearson

LAWRENCE DURRELL: Photograph by Mark Gerson, courtesy of E. P. Dutton & Co., Inc.

RICHARD EBERHART: Photograph by Mary Randlett, courtesy of Oxford University Press, N.Y.

T. S. ELIOT: Photograph by Angus McBean, courtesy of Faber & Faber Ltd.

LAWRENCE FERLINGHETTI: Photograph by Annette Lena, courtesy of New Directions Publishing Corporation

ROBERT GRAVES: Photograph by Marion Morehouse, courtesy of Collins-Knowlton-Wing, Inc.

THOM GUNN: Photograph by Ander Gunn, courtesy of The University of Chicago Press

DONALD HALL: Courtesy of Jim Galbraith, Livingston County Press

GERARD MANLEY HOPKINS: Courtesy of Oxford University Press, London

A. E. HOUSMAN: Drawing by Francis Dodd, courtesy of Jonathan Cape, Ltd.

TED HUGHES: Photograph by Ander Gunn, courtesy of Harper & Row, Publishers

LE ROI JONES: Photograph by Leroy McLucas, courtesy of Grove Press, Inc.

JAMES JOYCE: Photograph by Ruth Asch, courtesy of The Viking Press, Inc.

GALWAY KINNELL: Courtesy of Houghton Mifflin Company

STANLEY KUNITZ: Photograph by Clarence E. Preme, courtesy of Little, Brown and Company

D. H. LAWRENCE: Courtesy of The Viking Press, Inc.

LAURIE LEE: Photograph by Douglas Glass, courtesy of William Morrow & Co., Inc.

DENISE LEVERTOV: Photograph by The Luce Studio, courtesy of New Directions Publishing Corporation

ARCHIBALD MAC LEISH: Courtesy of Houghton Mifflin Company

LOUIS MAC NEICE: Photograph by Fine Art Engravers Ltd., London, courtesy of Oxford University Press, London

ROBERT MEZEY: Photograph by Douglas Hall, courtesy of The Bobbs-Merrill Co., Inc.

VASSAR MILLER: Courtesy of Wesleyan University Press

MARIANNE MOORE: Courtesy of The Viking Press, Inc.

HOWARD MOSS: Photograph by Mark Pagano, courtesy of Charles Scribner's Sons

EDWIN MUIR: Photograph by Mark Gerson, courtesy of Oxford University Press, London

OGDEN NASH: Photograph by Frederick Eberstadt, courtesy of Little, Brown and Company

HOWARD NEMEROV: Photograph by Lloyd Studio, courtesy of Margot Johnson Agency

CHARLES OLSON: Photograph by Jonathan Williams, courtesy of New Directions Publishing Corporation

WILFRED OWEN: Photograph © Copyright Harold Owen, courtesy of New Directions Publishing Corporation

P. K. PAGE: Photograph by Wheler-Scott Ltd., courtesy of McClelland & Stewart, Ltd.

KENNETH PATCHEN: Courtesy of New Directions Publishing Corporation

EZRA POUND: Photograph by Boris De Rachewiltz, courtesy of New Directions Publishing Corporation

SIR HERBERT READ: Courtesy of Horizon Press Publishers, New York

KENNETH REXROTH: Courtesy of New Directions Publishing Corporation

ADRIENNE RICH: Photograph by Jill Krementz, courtesy of W. W. Norton & Company, Inc.

THEODORE ROETHKE: Courtesy of Doubleday & Company, Inc.

DELMORE SCHWARTZ: Courtesy of New Directions Publishing Corporation

ANNE SEXTON: Photograph by T. Polumbaum, courtesy of Houghton Mifflin Company

KARL SHAPIRO: Photograph by Ron Warfield, courtesy of Random House, Inc.

LOUIS SIMPSON: Courtesy of Wesleyan University Press

EDITH SITWELL: Photograph by Rollie McKenna

W. D. SNODGRASS: Courtesy of Harper & Row, Publishers

STEPHEN SPENDER: Photograph by Jerry Bauer, courtesy of Faber & Faber Ltd.

MAY SWENSON: Courtesy of Charles Scribner's Sons

DYLAN THOMAS: Photograph by Marion Morehouse, courtesy of New Directions Publishing Corporation

CHARLES TOMLINSON: Photograph by Cedric Barker, courtesy of Oxford University Press, London

MARK VAN DOREN: Photograph by Arthur W. Wang, courtesy of Hill & Wang, Inc.

PETER VIERECK: Courtesy of The Bobbs-Merrill Co., Inc.

JOHN WAIN: Courtesy of Macmillan & Co. Ltd., London

ROBERT PENN WARREN: Photograph by Peter Fink, courtesy of Random House, Inc.

VERNON WATKINS: Portrait of Alfred Jones, photographed by Tai Jones, courtesy of New Directions Publishing Corporation

JOHN HALL WHEELOCK: Photograph by Lida Moser, courtesy of Charles Scribner's Sons

WILLIAM CARLOS WILLIAMS: Photograph by Charles Sheeler, courtesy of New Directions Publishing Corporation

JAMES WRIGHT: Courtesy of Wesleyan University Press

Publisher's Preface
to the Third Edition

Twenty years have passed since this book was last revised, and the state of poetry reflected in earlier editions has changed considerably. Today both student and general reader share a new awareness of poets and poetry: poets are honored participants at Presidential inaugurations, they demonstrate against Presidential policies; they lecture on college campuses in some countries, they are declared *persona non grata* in others; they read poetry at the Guggenheim Museum, they go naked in Greenwich Village. Entire generations of new poets have established themselves in the literature of both England and America; a few of the poets included in the "Major Poets" section of this book in the last edition no longer seem so important, while poets who were only beginning to write twenty years ago have since been hailed as the dominant voices of our time.

In the Third Edition of *A Little Treasury of Modern Poetry* every effort has been made to reflect this new state of poetry in England and America today while preserving the scope, character and comprehensiveness of the earlier editions. Based upon a plan submitted by Oscar Williams before his death in 1964, this edition follows the pattern of organization familiar to readers of previous editions, but with one notable exception: the poetry previously included in Part V, "A Little Treasury of Modern Light Verse," has been collected with the poets' other works as they appear elsewhere in the anthology.

Part I, "The Chief Modern Poets of England and America,"

has been extensively revised; such poets as John Berryman, Elizabeth Bishop, Walter de la Mare, Robert Lowell, Karl Shapiro, Richard Wilbur and William Carlos Williams have been moved to "The Chief Modern Poets" section with properly amplified representation. Such poets as Stephen Crane, Langston Hughes, Randall Jarrell, Howard Nemerov and Theodore Roethke have been added to this section, and the representation of many of the "Chief Poets" has been slightly augmented or revised to include more recent poems.

Part II, "A Little Treasury of Modern Lyrics," has been revised, and although reduced in size new poets have been added and representation has been augmented. This section contains a group of fine lyrics which could neither be included in the main section, "The Chief Poets," nor, because of earlier dates of composition or disparity of viewpoint, in Part III, "Poetry in Progress." Many poets who do not have a large body of work nevertheless write individual poems of importance and it is from these that the group was selected. Each of the poems contributes substantially to the richness of modern poetry. The sequence is by alphabetical order of authors' names.

Part III has been retitled "A Little Treasury of Poetry in Progress," and features the new and younger poets of the forties, fifties and sixties. With a few exceptions—Gene Derwood, Kenneth Fearing, Alun Lewis, Sylvia Plath, Hyam Plutzik, W. T. Scott—all of the poets represented in this section are writing now, forming the poetry of today and influencing the shape of tomorrow and tomorrow's poetry.

Part IV, "Appendix," has been revised to better serve the interests of today's reader. "On Poets and Poetry: Prose Statements by Modern Poets" offers statements by such poets as T. S. Eliot, Robert Frost, Ezra Pound and W. B. Yeats while featuring the statements of new and younger poets such as James Dickey, Robert Lowell, Charles Olson, and Theodore Roethke. "On Society and Poetry" features statements on the role of poets and poetry in society, and on the influences of society on poets and poetry. "A Bibliography of Modern Poetic Criticism" has been revised and enlarged to include not only the most recent but some of the best of modern poetic criticism. "Photographs of the Poets," always a trademark of an Oscar Williams anthology, has been completely revised with many new photographs added.

The publisher is grateful for the special contributions of the following persons: Professor Herbert Rosengarten, The University of British Columbia; Professor William Pratt, Miami University of Ohio; Professor Chad Walsh, Beloit College; and Professor Eva T. Walsh, Rockford College.

Introduction to the First Edition

I

*I think England has had more good poets from 1900
to the present day than during any period of the
same length since the early seventeenth century.*

W. B. YEATS

If we include in the list of good poets both the American
and the English, the modern period shows itself resplendent
in its wealth of poetry. So I have decided to call this collection of modern poetry a *treasury*, although that word con-
notes such riches that it has been applied before only to
anthologies that draw their selections from centuries. I have
taken the poems here included mostly from the time between
1896, the year of the publication of A. E. Housman's *Shropshire Lad*, and the present, a period of not much more than
fifty years, yet so abundant, not only in the number of its
good poets and good poems, but also in its variety of poetic
techniques and subject matters, that it rivals any preceding
century.

Perhaps variety is exactly its chief characteristic. Former
periods have had a discernible prevailing poetic attitude
and a permissible kind of poetic subject matter. We have
achieved limitless freedom of choice as to subject matter:
anything that can be thought or talked about is acceptable
as material for poems. And the range of what educated and
sensitive persons do think and talk about would not too long
ago have seemed incredible. Awareness has been sharpened
by knowledge of all geographical *loci*, has been broadened
by the study of the literatures and customs of all nations,
has been intensified by knowledge of depth psychology and
kept sensitized by the incessant impact of those emotions

inevitable when life is uncertain and tragic through war and the nature-disturbing activities of the scientists. We have not only been taught by the cultures of all past societies, in which sense we are great inheritors, but we have also had forced upon our vision innumerable vistas of possible new environments, choosing among which coerces us into being the arbiters of the future. Certainly this extension of influences, material, and conflicts, has been a stimulus to the development of good poets.

Also, the desuetude of nineteenth century materialism, with its obverse of belief in "progress," a philosophy so narrow that it imposed a mental stricture upon imagination which even poets could not escape, has brought about a freer and more truthful manipulation of ideas. The central attitude of science has, ever since its rise to power, positively affected all contemporary attitudes, even of those who deny scientific values. So that, when science itself swung round to at least an oblique recognition of the non-material mysteries of life, the essentially spiritual art of poetry could flourish less self-consciously. It is now possible for a truth-respecting poet to admit the validity of much scientific discovery without denying the mysterious realities.

In fact, certain scientific data have become material which the poet can comfortably use. Devices which have evolved from an understanding of the new psychology are part of modern poetic equipment, and may, in some measure, add to the effectiveness of a poem which, if written by a poet of like calibre in the nineteenth century, would have been of little interest. And, whatever we may think of the end results of science, we must admit that scientific method, both logical and empirical, has contributed to literary craftsmanship by way of its influence upon recent literary criticism. Extraordinary advances in critical method make the inspection of a poem today by a first-class critic as close and careful as a chemical analysis. Poets read, practice, and write in the light of this severe and agile examination, with the result that contemporary minor poetry, at least, has reached an unprecedented high of quality.

Of course this observation upon the general production of verse does not hold for the work of major poets. In any age the major poet acts as though by revelation, in strict conformance to the truth of life, which is his base, no matter how his form may depend upon tradition. He does not have to wait for any formulation of the fundamentals of depth psychology in order to use its reality in his work. It is not by accident that the Œdipus Complex derives its name from the work of an ancient poet. The vital perception of a major poet makes all his discoveries of the future with an urgent immediacy and contrives from them the theme of his poems, which he produces as by an act of nature. An insight which the poet considers only structural material incidental to the integral whole of his poem is, for the scientist, a discovery upon the exposition of which he may expend the energies of a lifetime.

In our time, all that is extrovert is worshipped; therefore the scientist has a numerous following; the poet is revealed to a diminishing few. Nevertheless, though the audience diminishes, this century has had, and now has living, an astonishing number of good poets. Of major poets it may have produced no more than has any other like number of years. But all good poetry is not the work of major poets alone. A fair percentage of the finest English poetry has sprung from minor poets. When I say "minor" I mean neither impostors nor poetasters; I mean good poets who have either not managed to produce in quantity or who have not had great individual influence upon the main stream of English literature.

The major poet is almost always a technical innovator, the minor poet utilizes devices already evolved but, in their use, creates poems distinctly his own and thus distinctly valuable. I have included many such poems by minor poets because they seem to me to represent their period, as well as being in themselves, as poems, effective.

II

. . . people are exasperated by poetry which they
do not understand, and contemptuous of poetry
which they understand without effort . . .

T. S. ELIOT

Readers' objections to verse are various. Not long ago the use of "unpoetic" subject matter was decried; I doubt if many people are left who raise this particular objection. But there is still a rather considerable, and especially vociferous, group who are angered by texturally loaded and technically or semantically complex poetry. They impugn it on the ground of obscurity, *i.e.,* their own inability to understand it. It would not be important to take notice of these objectors were it not that they have, firstly, gotten the bulk of the attention which the popular press gives to poetry, and secondly, that many of them, if they could be persuaded to do some attentive reading of good verse and good criticism, would quickly lose their hasty prejudice and discover the exhilaration that competently read complex poetry might give them.

Poetry is an art that yields its effects to those who are educated in reading it. Skill is almost as essential in reading as in writing. I have often noticed that the loudest in declaiming against the best of our contemporary poets are those who have, in the main, confined their reading of Shakespeare to the Sonnets, of the great English lyric poetry to *The Golden Treasury* and the Victorians, while their inspection of American poetry has been limited to Whitman (and his many imitators) and the Imagists (minus Pound). As to any kind of analysis of poems, they are ignorant. They have never heard of the excellent criticism available which might make them aware of what values to look for in a poem. I have included in this collection several poems sure to irritate this group, but I can assure them that their irritation will give way to pleasure if they will gather up their tolerance and courage and undergo a course of reading of the best poets, old and new, and of the modern critics. They will discover, for instance, that a poet such as Dylan Thomas is not writing obscure private nonsense any more than did John Donne.

Readers who have already made the initial discoveries and are alert to the subtleties and bits of puzzle that a good poem has to offer, will, I am sure, find much in this *Little Treasury* to please them. Nevertheless, I have some fears that readers most eager to play the kind of game that Empson has to offer will not take kindly to certain of my choices. For I have also included poems very simple in meaning and treatment. Much as I respect the admirable jugglery of several components spun into perfect integration by a poem-

maker alive at all points of the intellect as well as of the
senses, my principal criterion for the choice of individual
poems was such as admitted many different kinds of verse,
whether from the point of view of content or form.

III

And I think that to transfuse emotion—not to transmit
thought but to set up in the reader's sense a vibration
corresponding to what was felt by the writer—is the
peculiar function of poetry.

A. E. HOUSMAN

Whatever the magic of poetry, it exists in the realm of feeling. In that realm each poem has its own organic unity,
obeying the laws of its own nature. The natural laws of one
poem may vary a good deal from those of another, just as
the natural laws of the bee's organism are quite different from
those of the cat's. Yet both move about in the same universe,
each admirable and complete in its own way. One poem may
have a higher kind of being than another, it may have more
organs and thus function through a larger body of sensations. But, simple or complex, so long as it is not maimed by
the lack of its own peculiar emotional unity, it is a poem.

So I made my basic rule for the choice of poems very
simple: if a poem gave me that experience which I have
learned comes as a reaction to reading a true poem, I included it, provided it conformed to my space limitations.
In other words, I *felt* the poem.

I am sorry that I cannot be explicit in expository terms
as to what I mean when I say that I felt or experienced a
certain work as a poem. In so far as I know, though many
definitions have been offered, no one has ever made a
definition of a poem that has been satisfactory to all of the
best poets and critics. Some have spoken of their physiological
reactions, such as a chill, a sensation in the chest or the pit
of the stomach, *etc.*, others have used the term "aesthetic
emotion" which, to my mind, is just calling the reaction by
another name, others have gone very thoroughly into every
detail of the poem's construction. But the mystery remains.
Something beyond superior craftsmanship enters into the
structure of a good poem, and in that something the magic is
contained.

Also, opinions differ as to the meaning of "pure" poetry, or as to whether such an expression should be used at all. T. S. Eliot has written, ". . . indeed it might be said in our time that the man who cannot enjoy Pope as poetry probably understands no poetry." On the other hand, Housman, while a great admirer of Pope, would not concede Pope's work or most of the work written in the eighteenth century to be "pure" poetry in the sense that Blake's is.

No two persons are likely to be equally stirred by all of any one list of poems. Every human being has a different complex of associations and will react more or less strongly to the vocabulary or imagery of a particular poet, in accordance with his own psychological nature. If he has critical acumen, he is likely to come pretty close to choosing, as genuine poetry, a majority of the poems that would be chosen by someone else of like acumen, but his rating of individual poems would be different. Some poems are more richly embellished as to vocabulary, images, phonetic cadences, and the like, while others may be salted with ideas, or ironical, or witty, undecorated and even "dry." One reader may prefer those poems which are romantic and rich in texture, another may look especially for excellences of form. The value of one poem may be predominantly that of its content, that of another of its form or its embellishment. The best poems are those in which form, texture and theme are all in perfect harmony. It is from these last that the reader is most likely to receive the emotional experience closest to that of the poet, or to what the poet intended.

IV

When we read Kipling we can usually say, "That is just how I feel." Of course there is nothing "wrong" with that, but, when we read a great poet, we say, "I never realized before what I felt. From now on, thanks to this poem, I shall feel differently."

W. H. AUDEN

Most of us are not given to accuracy when we formulate our thoughts about what we perceive or feel, and we perceive only a small fraction of the world about us, so intent are we upon the business of existence. But the poet is, by the peculiar usefulness of his nature, under a compulsion to be fully accurate in his medium of words when he puts into form his response to a concept or percept. This drive to accuracy causes him to explore the details of his theme and to feel it completely as a whole. In the process, if he is a good poet, he clarifies in his poem something that has not been fully expressed before. This compelling need for precision also causes a condensation of thought and feeling which loads the poem with its emotional charge. The irrelevant and the expository are not to be found in poetry. The display of the poet is not an explanation or a description of a thing, it is the thing itself. He exhibits the tiger or the dove; he does not tell its habitat, its usefulness or its history, he allows the reader to see for himself what it is.

A poem which shows us a feeling that we have had before may be valuable in that it keeps the emotional faculty alive. As we learn to look for something better, we may outgrow poems like this, but they are a necessary state in our growth and their value for others is not impaired as we pass on to other poetic experiences. There are a few poems of this kind in this book. Since they at one time gave me enjoyment and enlightenment, and as I still realize them as emotional wholes, I have included them.

But the majority of the poems herein present their themes in such fashion as to show fresh ways of feeling or knowing, so they function as nourishment for the *growth* of emotional, or perceptual capacity. Some of them as, for example, *The Waste Land*, have had this effect not only upon readers as individuals, but upon our literary generation as a whole, thus affecting, and developing, the tradition of English poetry itself.

A poem of such magnitude is not quite the result of "inspiration," which is considered by some to be the only authentic source of poetry. Without the "divine fire" no man would be a poet; but without intellect no man would be a great poet. Nor can such a poem be read without the use of an intelligence to some degree comparable with that of the author. Some people object to the notion that the intellect should be called into operation at all during the reading of a poem. They have somehow acquired the idea that feeling and intellect are opposites. A little reflection will show that, on the contrary, emotion deepens when the intellect is aroused to action simultaneously with the feeling. You cannot feel anything unless your mind is brought to attention upon the idea of it, and the more definitely you think about it, the stronger your emotion is likely to be. For instance, if you hear of the death of a friend, you think of him; the clearer your concept of him, the more strongly you are likely to feel. If you at the same time begin to ask "Why did he die?" "How did he die?" "What did his life signify?" *etc.*, this very use of analytical thought will deepen your emotion. Thus it is with poetry. It has many devices for producing a clear emotional experience and those of the intellect are not the least significant.

V

The pleasure is the pleasure of powers that create a
truth that cannot be arrived at by the reason alone,
a truth that the poet recognizes by sensation. The morality
of the poet's radiant and productive atmosphere is
the morality of the right sensation.

WALLACE STEVENS

Most of what we may call "educated" humanity, while imbued with respect for science, neglects poetry, considering it not compatible with, or, at least, not directed by reality. Now reason is worthy of all respect, and is nowhere more respected than among poets. But any one avenue of reason may well become a rut. No one is more reasonable than the scientist, yet is he not a man who travels an undeviating road with such intentness on his direction that he loses the faculty of turning his head about to see the countryside? The poet knows that life is a whole commingled of reason, instinct and the objective world of *all* phenomena. He keeps it knit together by a spiritual understanding which is above reason, which it supervises through virtue of its ability to comprehend all, rather than one segment or function of life. Reason is a tool and not an accomplishment, a tool that the poet can on occasion use as well as the scientist. Because he is aware of life as a totality, the poet is closer to truth than the scientist and, above all, does surely the right thing at the right time.

The scientist discovers, reveals, invents, but is his invention ever produced at the right time in so far as humanity is concerned? If so, it is only by accident and not by insight of the scientist. Did radio appear at the exact moment when it would answer a need in the enrichment of the human mind? Or did atomic power? The one came before public taste was educated in the values of music, or was so trained in psychology that it could resist advertising, the other just in time to improve killing instead of leisure. No poet would so mistake his timing. The poet perceives, he has the right sensation for his hour and he articulates this sensation. Moreover, it is only when he is right for his time and communicates the essentials of his time that he is a true poet who will communicate to the ages.

Occasionally a poet seems to come too early; he represents not his own time but a later one. This might be said of Gerard Manley Hopkins, who is included in this anthology because he was first published in 1918, and has had a profound influence upon poets since that year. Hopkins was born in 1844, as was Robert Bridges, who outlived him by more than forty years. It is to the latter that we owe the miraculous fortune of Hopkins' publication.

From Hopkins' concentrated style we receive a terrific charge of emotion fused with a religious content which had long been lacking in poetry. The advent of this major poetry has, in its effect upon younger poets, extended the resources of poetic technique. But its impetus to new directions in English poetry has been greater than that: the younger poets have learned a lesson in the admixture of intelligence with fully expressed emotion, a lesson badly needed. And no less was Hopkins' kind of feeling needed by mankind at that time, and all through the twentieth century. The pity is that mankind rarely has an appetite for what it needs. I doubt if Hopkins really wrote ahead of his time. It was at the precise moment when he was writing his poetry that, had it been accepted by its proper audience, it would have produced the fullest effect. The almost blank period between 1900 and 1910 would have been a little fuller, and the stance of the Georgians would have been less tit-willowy.

There is a relation between the state of society and the poet's poem, there is a relationship between the contemporary poet and the contemporary reader, which is exactly right. If people had learned earlier to expose themselves to poetry undoubtedly we should not now be accustomed to contemplating the end of the world as imminent. (Thanks to the atomic bomb today's poets may end the tradition, so they had better be read now.) For the poet is always on the side of life; consistent readers of poetry are also on the side of life. When a poet promulgates the sensuous pleasures he is no less moral than when he paints the hope of heaven, or reveals the truth of tragedy. To be on the side of life is to be moral.

VI

Poetry . . . is the supreme form of EMOTIVE *language.*
                                        I. A. RICHARDS

The direct intensity of Hopkins' passion was set into verse before most of the other poems in this anthology were written. Such utterance as his was impossible to poets who wrote between his time and the nineteen-thirties. Feeling was not rushed forth in such a way as to take us by storm. Hardy's realism, Bridges' deliberation (in America, Marianne Moore's syllabic patterns and Wallace Stevens' colorful irony) had not this kind of direct expression. Both the Georgians with their claim of writing from pure feeling and the Imagists with theirs of recording pure percepts, seem to us now not to have expressed emotion at all. The poetry of Wilfred Owen, another innovator of major importance, releases the impact of its feeling with a kind of delayed action. It is not until the advent in the middle 'thirties of such poets as George Barker and Dylan Thomas that we find emotion again released immediately and directly. In Hart Crane there is, however, a rising curve of such release.

We can now clearly see the mounting graph of intensity as it passed through the poetry of the first half of the twentieth century, nourished by increments of the intelligence, which presents the issues of reality, and of the creative imagination, which expands the sensibility. This increase and this clarification are exemplified in the work of a single poet, W. B. Yeats, who was born in 1865 and lived to 1939. Yeats' verse began with the weakly esotericism of the 'nineties and developed to a full expression of the poetic strength of his period, a period when poetry took cognizance, for the first time in the history of that period, of the whole situation of mankind as well as of individual experience.

Oddly enough the round outflow of direct passion seems to have become again possible to poets in general only after the development of the other, and greater, new impetus given to poetry in our time. This new direction was, of course, that given by T. S. Eliot, to whom twentieth-century literature is so greatly indebted, not only for poetry of the very first order, but also for criticism without which we cannot help feeling we should be as though blind. Mr. Eliot made poets and readers alike aware of the fundamental importance of intelligence in both the making and appraisal of poems. Ezra Pound helped to sharpen the wits and scholarship of talented poets. But, except upon the highly gifted few, the knowledge of Eliot's and Pound's complexity might well have had the stultifying effect of drying up the juices of feeling by an overdose of erudition. Hopkins' influence has balanced this tendency without reducing respect for intelligence. It would be almost impossible for minor verse so devoid of real values as that of the Georgians to "get by" today.

VII

The rhetorician would deceive his neighbors,
The sentimentalist himself; while art
Is but a vision of reality.

                              W. B. YEATS

Without doubt some readers will miss some poems which they like, or have been taught to admire, and object to their omission. I may say bluntly that there are some poets whom I consider spurious in spite of their having achieved a full measure of popularity or of acceptance by the schools. Sham poems do not deserve to lie alongside the pages graced by the real thing. If any such have slipped past my guard I do not know it.

The poetasters and the sentimentalists are always with us; serious readers are not likely to be deceived by them. But even competent critics are occasionally taken in by the skillful rhetorician. The term "academic" is generally applied to work easy to spot from its very dullness. However, the true academic is that literary figure who confuses his contemporaries by displaying a mock talent wrapped in the cellophane of rhetoric that obeys all the rules, even to the simulation of the faults of the best poets. But a watchful eye

can spy the academic no matter how quick his leap into
the devices of the great. Even if he is as fast as Superman
there are a few simple characteristics of the careerist that cannot be hidden. He absorbs the most talked about traits of a
model. Then he adds characteristics from this great poet and
that (provided always that the poets he imitates are those
most recently lauded), patches out a style for himself and
achieves a career by the same strategy that men in other
fields achieve careers by. This academic is the most subtle
and dangerous of the enemies of art. He penetrates everywhere, since he is an accomplished salesman of his personality; his line is almost erudite and his morals lacking in the
one essential morality of the real poet: the kind of honesty
that can understand its own heart. The academic is likely to
know everything there is to know about poetry except its
essence; his critical acumen consists in waiting until he hears
another voice recommending.

Good poets have their influences and models, true, but
of these they make a distinctive integer; the academic bor-
rows without respecting. Appropriating someone else's possession is not the same thing as endeavoring to model oneself
after another man's admired character. Nor does the rhetorician present us with simple pastiche; he flourishes something slicker than that: it shines but has no heat, the dress
is stolen but worn with such effrontery you might think
it his own. I have done my best to keep this impostor out of
good company.

Other omissions I have made upon the ground that certain writings look like poetry, have passed as poetry, but
are demonstrably not so; among their authors are certain
members of past "schools," the Imagists, *etc*. A few poets,
whom I willingly concede to be genuine since they have
had the right effect upon people whose sensitivity I respect, I myself have been unable to "feel" and nevertheless have persuaded myself to include.

This revised edition remedies a fault of the first by including many long poems which were previously omitted.
While no anthology can fully represent a major *poet* (only
his complete works can do *that*) yet the inclusion of longer
poems makes *The Little Treasury* as a whole more representative of the poetic *period* by suggesting the relative im-

portance and the individual significance of it major figures. The collection unavoidably makes an evaluation of rank among the poets, but it is the evaluation of only one man's taste. No reader can be either a perfect, or even an un-prejudiced, critic. Nor can he have a foreknowledge of the standards of posterity. And I am only one reader among many; my judgments are always arrived at through the medium of my own taste, *i.e.*, what I am activated into liking.

VIII

It is a fact that both an epic and a limerick
are poems. . . . You can only distinguish in
them differences of effect and quality.
            GEOFFREY GRIGSON

Now I like high and serious poetry to such a degree that I cannot imagine life worth living without it, but for that very reason I like light verse also: it is poetry at play. It is significant that so important a poet as Auden should have found it well within his concept of poetry to write light verse. Indeed, a considerable body of his writing has been in this category. No one can completely understand the character of poetry unless he sees it in all its aspects, just as he cannot understand a friend unless he sees him having fun as often as he sees him serious. Our century has not been an easy one and its hard circumstances are reflected in the fact that the percentage of light verse of quality which it has produced is small, and the percentage of serious verse, large. Yet we have had enough of it, I believe, to warrant my inclusion of a section of this poetry at play.

Exactly what makes a poem "light" is hard to define, but I shall give some of my own thoughts about the matter. Light verse might be defined quite as, in drama, comedy is defined, as a form which takes the accepted social *mores* for granted, a means of expression that gives a sense of security because it never lets in the notion of that outer chaos and question-ability of fundamental axioms which tragedy presents.

Light verse is not necessarily funny or entertaining; it can have a serious content and purpose. It is play partly because it is very consciously constructed, but play is not always laughter-provoking, witness the football game. But it can be very funny indeed. It utilizes, to produce its effects, pun and satire, meter and nonsense, and other effective devices. Some light verse is farce and we enjoy it as such.

It is interesting to try and trace the methods which recur as a kind of principle in the making of such poetry. Light verse is written in a familiar, everyday kind of speech. It often makes outrageous statements in the offhand tone of a housewife discussing the most commonplace details of daily life. For instance,

> Billy, in one of his nice new sashes,
>   Fell in the fire and was burned to ashes;
> Now, although the room grows chilly,
>   I haven't the heart to poke poor Billy.

In "Billy," the announcement is made that the child met a horrible death and the poet goes on with the most matter-of-fact, everyday air to comment on this tragedy as if not poking Billy's ashes were on the same level as giving him a piece of candy. "I haven't the heart to refuse him." But this quatrain is "light" also because it shows, by the very point it makes in showing that it is nonsense, complete agreement with our social *mores*, in this instance that it is so bad a crime to kill or be callous to children that even to think of such a thing is funny. The ancients who exposed unwanted babies to die would not have considered this thought nonsense.

The same principle is behind the funniness of Miss Twye. If our women were accustomed to taking their baths in mixed company, which they say is a Japanese custom, the point of the situation would not exist, even if the matter-of-fact tone were present.

We are also amused by over-emphasis of the trivial or by under-emphasis of the large. I have included curses, tirades, satires and other poems that illustrate this principle. When we hear Pound curse out the rain, we enjoy having the weather get the attention that it wouldn't get if we really were the noble creatures we sometimes like to think ourselves. So much rage at a little discomfort makes us smile over the fallibility of humans. When we hear ANON. discuss the merits of being either a rooster or a crow with the absolute assumption that he might become either with the seriousness of a man choosing a career, it is the attitude more than the homely speech that furnishes the fun.

IX

To maintain gaiety at a definite level of taste is as difficult and requires as much composed unity of approach and as mature an attitude towards the material as is required to maintain fury or disgust. . . . Gaiety, and especially gaiety in finished form, is the last thing to be caught in a formula of facility . . .

R. P. BLACKMUR

But, even in light verse, not every attempt that follows the rules is poetry. Light verse may be written more by wit and cynicism than by inspiration, yet the point it makes and the style it dons must be in agreement, the joke or flavor sharp enough to retain its freshness and please a quick mind. Children are fond of puns, no matter what, but adults will not tolerate bad ones.

There is a certain kind of ostensibly funny rhyming which is generally referred to as "society" verse. It is favored by newspapers and the lay public that likes to try its hand at stanzaic humor. Some of its prototypes have been good, Gilbert is an example. I have avoided most of this material because it exercises neither the mind nor the funny bone. One imperative of humor is to engage the mind. In Ogden Nash's

> *Candy*
> *Is dandy*
> *But liquor*
> *Is quicker*

the reader must complete the thought for himself. So too in *Head and Heart* by C. D. B. Ellis. It is not enough for the rhymes themselves to be funny. Neither does the use of dialect or slang constitute genuinely humorous poetry.

A few readers may object to my placing certain poems in the light, instead of the serious, verse section. But a little thought about each will give them the clue as to why I did so. The poems which comment upon the social scene may especially seem to them not of proper content for this classification. But it is the poet's rôle to speak for the issues of the day in whatever tone he finds fitting; the greater the range of tones, the more fully will poetry perform this one of its functions.

X

> . . . *no one comes so near the invisible world as the sage and the poet, unless it be the saint—who is but one spirit with God, and so infinitely closer to Him than anyone. I also point out the benefits men receive from poetry. Though in themselves of no help to the attainment of eternal life, art and poetry are more necessary than bread to the human race. They fit it for the life of the spirit.*
>
> JACQUES MARITAIN

The majority of mankind today knows nothing of poetry, the name for them means hifalutin doggerel. The educated minority is, during school days, exposed to poetry instead of being inoculated with it. For this art is neither an extraneous growth upon the pragmatic activity which has become so universally synonymous with existence, nor an obsolete organ like the appendix. On the contrary, it is the ichor which man's spiritual nature secretes for the purpose of healing the kind of wounds from which we today suffer. Just as medical science used to make the mistake of draining off the very blood needed to restore health, modern society is ever busy trying to dry up the real essence of the arts, because their usefulness has been forgotten and not rediscovered.

The poet has a high and responsible position to fill in the complex of society. Humanity's ignorance of this necessity, and some others, has directly led to the terrible distortion of the whole social mechanism, which is so misdirected that its energies rush to the end of universal murder instead of maintaining the precise balance of natural and enjoyable living for all. Almost perfunctory statements of alarm over the use of the atomic bomb barely conceal a fundamental indifference to its threat, or what must follow from the fulfillment of that threat. All the elaborate inventiveness of man has been turned to manipulation of the inanimate; human emotions would have responded as miraculously to a like well-developed technique of expansion and control.

Poetry explores the possibilities of emotion, couples its niceties with thought, and thereby creates a kind of discipline for the whole man, not neglecting his physical nature. And poetry is made by the poet, much more definitively made by an individual man than any other product, except those of the other arts, Presidents and scientists are honored although they function only as part of a group, and their product is ephemeral in that it is sure to be quickly replaced by a better. This is probably because the apparent benefits received from politicians and scientists need only be accepted, the salutary delights of poetry must be worked for if the reader is to have them. The poet is doing enough to prepare the way for the millennium. He mitigates none of his own suffering, as he refuses no labor, to bring up, from what today is an abyss not pleasant to enter, the poems that would nourish man back to fullness of health.

XI

The world grown wiser is its wisdom gone. The machines are working but we have lost the arts. Our degradation spreads along the winds. There is no corner of the world that is not sullied with our news.

SACHEVERELL SITWELL

But, unless the human heart can cleanse itself faster than the laboratory can manufacture its hell-fire, it is now too late. Eyes trained to mere spectacle are not attracted by the sunny landscape of the spirit but find the sun more dazzling in the absolute of an atomic explosion. Almost no rôles except those of Jeremiah and Cassandra are left to saint and poet, and even they must be played in the wings. The audience insists upon chief actors who are senseless enough to perform a cataclysm.

However we must continue to set life into form. Readers of poetry, no less than its makers, have an urgent task: to create a focus of understanding. Since with God all things are possible, poets and readers in unison may still work their own miracle by which the human heart may yet so enlarge that it outweighs the atomic bomb.

OSCAR WILLIAMS

New York City,
January 2, 1946.

Contents

PART I

A Little Treasury of the Chief
Modern Poets of England and America

EMILY DICKINSON / 1830–1886
Success Is Counted Sweetest, 3
I Taste a Liquor Never Brewed, 3
There's a Certain Slant of Light, 4
Before I Got My Eye Put Out, 5
A Bird Came Down the Walk, 5
The First Day's Night Had Come, 6
'Twas Like a Maelstrom, with a Notch, 7
Much Madness Is Divinest Sense, 8
Undue Significance a Starving Man Attaches, 8
I Died for Beauty—But Was Scarce, 9
I Heard a Fly Buzz—When I Died, 9
I Started Early—Took My Dog, 10
I Had Been Hungry, All the Years, 11

I Like to See It Lap the Miles, 11
Our Journey Had Advanced, 12
Pain—Has an Element of Blank, 12
Because I Could Not Stop for Death, 13
A Narrow Fellow in the Grass, 14
I Never Saw a Moor, 14
Tell All the Truth but Tell It Slant, 15
As Imperceptibly As Grief, 15
My Life Closed Twice Before Its Close, 16

THOMAS HARDY / 1840–1928
In Tenebris II, 16
The Darkling Thrush, 17
The Man He Killed, 18
The Convergence of the Twain, 19
The Blinded Bird, 20
The Oxen, 21
For Life I Had Never Cared Greatly, 22

THOMAS HARDY (*cont.*)
The Pity of It, 23
In Time of "The Breaking of
    Nations," 23
Afterwards, 24
The Contretemps, 25
And There Was a Great Calm,
    26
An Ancient to Ancients, 28

GERARD MANLEY HOPKINS /
    1844–1889
The Wreck of the Deutschland,
    30
God's Grandeur, 40
The Starlight Night, 40
Spring, 41
The Windhover, 41
Pied Beauty, 42
The Caged Skylark, 42
The Candle Indoors, 43
Felix Randal, 43
Spring and Fall, 44
Inversnaid, 45
As Kingfishers Catch Fire,
    Dragonflies Dráw Fláme,
    45
The Leaden Echo and the
    Golden Echo, 46
Spelt from Sibyl's Leaves, 48
No Worst, There Is None.
    Pitched Past Pitch of Grief,
    49
My Own Heart Let Me More
    Have Pity On, 49
Thou Art Indeed Just, Lord,
    if I Contend, 50

ROBERT BRIDGES / 1844–1930
I Heard a Linnet Courting, 51
A Passer-by, 52
London Snow, 52
On a Dead Child, 54
The Philosopher to His Mis-
    tress, 55
The Idle Life I Lead, 56

The Storm Is Over, the Land
    Hushes to Rest, 56
Nightingales, 57

A. E. HOUSMAN / 1859–1936
Loveliest of Trees, the Cherry
    Now, 58
Reveille, 59
When I Was One-and-Twenty,
    59
To an Athlete Dying Young,
    60
Is My Team Ploughing, 61
Into My Heart an Air That
    Kills, 62
With Rue My Heart Is Laden,
    62
Terence, This Is Stupid Stuff,
    63
I Hoed and Trenched and
    Weeded, 65
Could Man Be Drunk for Ever,
    65
The Night Is Freezing Fast,
    66
Tell Me Not Here, It Needs
    Not Saying, 66
I Did Not Lose My Heart in
    Summer's Even, 67

WILLIAM BUTLER YEATS /
    1865–1939
The Lake Isle of Innisfree, 68
When You Are Old, 68
To a Friend Whose Work Has
    Come to Nothing, 69
A Coat, 69
An Irish Airman Forsees His
    Death, 70
Easter 1916, 70
The Second Coming, 72
A Prayer for My Daughter, 73
Sailing to Byzantium, 75
The Tower, 76
Leda and the Swan, 82
Among School Children, 82

A Dialogue of Self and Soul, 84
For Anne Gregory, 86
Byzantium, 87
Crazy Jane and the Bishop, 88
After Long Silence, 89
Lapis Lazuli, 89
News for the Delphic Oracle, 91
Long-Legged Fly, 92
John Kinsella's Lament for Mrs. Mary Moore, 93
The Apparitions, 94
Cuchulain Comforted, 95
Under Ben Bulben, 96

EDWIN ARLINGTON ROBINSON / 1869–1935
Luke Havergal, 99
Richard Cory, 100
George Crabbe, 100
Credo, 101
The Master, 101
Miniver Cheevy, 103
For a Dead Lady, 104
Flammonde, 105
Cassandra, 108
Eros Turannos, 109
The Dark Hills, 111
Mr. Flood's Party, 111

EDGAR LEE MASTERS / 1869–1950
The Hill, 113
Carl Hamblin, 114
Henry C. Calhoun, 115
Anne Rutledge, 116
Lucinda Matlock, 116
Davis Matlock, 117

STEPHEN CRANE / 1871–1900
In the Desert, 117
I Saw a Man Pursuing the Horizon, 118
War Is Kind, 118
On the Desert, 119

A Slant of Sun on Dull Brown Walls, 120
A Man Said to the Universe, 120
The Trees in the Garden Rained Flowers, 121

RALPH HODGSON / 1871–1962
Time, You Old Gipsy Man, 122
Eve, 123
Stupidity Street, 125
The Bells of Heaven, 125
The Bull, 125

WALTER DE LA MARE / 1873–1956
The Listeners, 131
An Epitaph, 132
The Ghost, 132
In the Dock, 133
Sunk Lyonesse, 133
Nostalgia, 134

WALLACE STEVENS / 1875–1955
Le Monocle de Mon Oncle, 135
Sunday Morning, 139
Peter Quince at the Clavier, 142
Thirteen Ways of Looking at a Blackbird, 144
Connoisseur of Chaos, 146
The Sense of the Sleight-of-Hand Man, 147
From Extracts from Addresses to the Academy of Fine Ideas, 148
So-and-So Reclining on Her Couch, 149
Crude Foyer, 150
Esthétique du Mal, 151
Continual Conversation with a Silent Man, 160
The Prejudice against the Past, 161

WALLACE STEVENS (*cont.*)
From Notes toward a Supreme
    Fiction—It Must Change,
    162
Soldier, There Is a War be-
    tween the Mind, *163*

ROBERT FROST / 1875–1963
Mending Wall, *164*
The Road Not Taken, *165*
Birches, *166*
The Hill Wife, *167*
The Witch of Coös, *170*
Fire and Ice, *174*
Stopping by Woods on a
    Snowy Evening, *174*
Once by the Pacific, *175*
Bereft, *175*
Acquainted with the Night,
    176
Two Tramps in Mud Time,
    177
The Span of Life, *179*
Come In, *179*
The Gift Outright, *179*
The Lesson for Today, *180*
A Semi-Revolution, *184*
Directive, *185*
Pod of the Milkweed, *186*
Forgive, O Lord, My Little
    Jokes on Thee, *188*

JOHN MASEFIELD / 1878–1967
The West Wind, *188*
Cargoes, *189*
C. L. M., *190*
Flesh, I Have Knocked at
    Many a Dusty Door, *191*
Is There a Great Green Com-
    monwealth of Thought,
    191
I Could Not Sleep for Think-
    ing of the Sky, *192*
Night Is on the Downland, on
    the Lonely Moorland, *192*
On Growing Old, *193*

WILLIAM CARLOS WILLIAMS /
                1883–1963
The Yachts, *194*
Tract, *195*
The Widow's Lament in
    Springtime, *197*
Spring and All, *198*
The Red Wheelbarrow, *199*
The Bull, *199*
The Dance, *200*
Burning the Christmas Greens,
    200
To a Dog Injured in the Street,
    203

ELINOR WYLIE / 1885–1928
The Eagle and the Mole, *205*
Wild Peaches, *206*
Let No Charitable Hope, *207*
Address to My Soul, *208*
Hymn to Earth, *209*

D. H. LAWRENCE / 1885–1930
Moonrise, *211*
The Song of a Man Who Has
    Come Through, *212*
Snake, *212*
Tortoise Shout, *215*
Humming-Bird, *218*
How Beastly the Bourgeois Is,
    219
Don'ts, *220*
The Elephant Is Slow to Mate,
    221

EZRA POUND / 1885–
Ballad for Gloom, *222*
Ballad of the Goodly Fere, *223*
An Immorality, *225*
Ancient Music, *226*
Near Perigord, *226*
Hugh Selwyn Mauberley, *232*
Canto XLV, *244*

EDWIN MUIR / 1887–1959
The Road, *246*
The Human Fold, *247*

The Grove, 249
The Gate, 250
The Trophy, 251
The Voyage, 251
The Rider Victory, 254
The Window, 255
In Love for Long, 256

ROBINSON JEFFERS / 1887–1962
Shine, Perishing Republic, 257
Promise of Peace, 258
Hurt Hawks, 258
The Stars Go over the Lonely
    Ocean, 259
Battle, 260
The Bloody Sire, 261
Black-Out, 262
I Shall Laugh Purely, 263
The Eye, 266
Cassandra, 266

MARIANNE MOORE / 1887–
Poetry, 267
Roses Only, 268
Spenser's Ireland, 269
A Carriage from Sweden, 271
In Distrust of Merits, 272
His Shield, 275
Tell Me, Tell Me, 276
The Mind, Intractable Thing,
    277

T. S. ELIOT / 1888–1965
The Love Song of J. Alfred
    Prufrock, 278
Gerontion, 282
Sweeney among the Nightin-
    gales, 285
The Waste Land, 286
The Hollow Men, 302
Journey of the Magi, 305
Burnt Norton, 306

JOHN CROWE RANSOM / 1888–
Bells for John Whiteside's
    Daughter, 311
Here Lies a Lady, 312

Judith of Bethulia, 313
Captain Carpenter, 314
Her Eyes, 316
Man without Sense of Direc-
    tion, 317
The Equilibrists, 319
Little Boy Blue, 321
Painted Head, 321
Address to the Scholars of New
    England, 323

CONRAD AIKEN / 1889–
From Discordants, 325
From Senlin: A Biography, 325
Tetélestai, 327
Sea Holly, 331
The Room, 332
Preludes for Memnon, 333
    I
    LII
    LVI

EDNA ST. VINCENT MILLAY /
                    1892–1950
Recuerdo, 337
Elegy Before Death, 338
On Hearing a Symphony of
    Beethoven, 339
Oh, Sleep Forever in the Lat-
    mian Cave, 339

ARCHIBALD MAC LEISH / 1892–
The Silent Slain, 340
L'an Trentiesme de Mon Eage,
    340
The End of the World, 341
Ars Poetica, 341
You, Andrew Marvell, 342
Invocation to the Social Muse,
    344

WILFRED OWEN / 1893–1918
Insensibility, 345
Apologia Pro Poemate Meo,
    347
Greater Love, 348
Arms and the Boy, 349

WILFRED OWEN (*cont.*)
Anthem for Doomed Youth, 350
The Show, 350
Dulce et Decorum Est, 351
A Terre, 352
Disabled, 354
From My Diary, July 1914, 356

E. E. CUMMINGS / 1894–1962
All in green went my love riding, 357
my love, 358
nobody loses all the time, 359
a man who had fallen among thieves, 360
"next to of course god america i, 361
i sing of Olaf glad and big, 362
somewhere i have never travelled,gladly beyond, 363
as freedom is a breakfastfood, 364
anyone lived in a pretty how town, 365
it was a goodly co, 366
pity this busy monster,manunkind, 367
what if a much of a which of a wind, 368

ROBERT GRAVES / 1895–
The Bards, 368
Traveller's Curse after Misdirection, 369
The Legs, 369
Flying Crooked, 371
The Devil's Advice to Story-Tellers, 371
Interruption, 372
Recalling War, 373
Down, Wanton, Down!, 374
Time, 375
Ogres and Pygmies, 376
The Thieves, 377

To Juan at the Winter Solstice, 377
The Persian Version, 379

LOUISE BOGAN / 1897–
Men Loved Wholly Beyond Wisdom, 379
The Sleeping Fury, 380
Putting to Sea, 381
The Dream, 382

HART CRANE / 1899–1932
To Brooklyn Bridge, 383
The Dance, 385
National Winter Garden, 388
Quaker Hill, 389
Atlantis, 391
Emblems of Conduct, 394
Praise for an Urn, 394
Chaplinesque, 395
Repose of Rivers, 396
From For the Marriage of Faustus and Helen, 397
From Voyages, 398
The Broken Tower, 399

ALLEN TATE / 1899–
The Mediterranean, 401
Ode to the Confederate Dead, 402
Sonnets at Christmas, 405
More Sonnets at Christmas, 406
The Traveller, 407
The Oath, 408
The Wolves, 409
A Pauper, 410

OSCAR WILLIAMS / 1900–1964
The Last Supper, 411
I Sing an Old Song, 412
The Mirage, 413
By Fiat of Adoration, 414
Dwarf of Disintegration, 415
The Praying Mantis Visits a Penthouse, 417

The Leg in the Subway, *418*
Shopping for Meat in Winter, *420*

LANGSTON HUGHES / 1902–1967
Harlem Sweeties, *420*
Cross, *421*
Dream Deferred, *422*
American Heartbreak, *422*
Slave, *423*
Undertow, *423*
Impasse, *424*
Go Slow, *424*

C. DAY-LEWIS / 1904–
It Is Becoming Now to Declare
    My Allegiance, *425*
As One Who Wanders into Old
    Workings, *426*
Do Not expect Again a Phoenix
    Hour, *427*
Consider These, for We Have
    Condemned Them, *428*
The Conflict, *429*

RICHARD EBERHART / 1904–
For a Lamb, *430*
The Groundhog, *430*
'In a Hard Intellectual Light,'
    432
Rumination, *433*
'If I Could Only Live at the
    Pitch That Is Near Mad-
    ness,' *433*
On Shooting Particles Beyond
    the World, *434*
The Cancer Cells, *435*
Seals, Terns, Time, *436*
The Horse Chestnut Tree, *437*
The Fury of Aerial Bombard-
    ment, *438*
New Hampshire, February,
    438
On a Squirrel Crossing the
    Road in Autumn, in New
    England, *439*
Marrakech, *440*

WILLIAM EMPSON / 1906–
The Scales, *441*
Legal Fiction, *442*
This Last Pain, *442*
Homage to the British Mu-
    seum, *444*
Ignorance of Death, *444*
Missing Dates, *445*
Just a Smack at Auden, *446*
Sonnet, *447*

VERNON WATKINS / 1906–
The Dead Words, *448*
Discoveries, *448*
The Song of the Good Samari-
    tan, *450*
Music of Colours—White Blos-
    som . . . , *453*
The Fire in the Snow, *454*

LOUIS MAC NEICE / 1907–1963
Turf-Stacks, *455*
August, *456*
Perseus, *457*
Snow, *458*
Bagpipe Music, *458*
The British Museum Reading
    Room, *460*
Jehu, *460*
Alcohol, *462*
From The Kingdom, *463*
    I
    II

W. H. AUDEN / 1907–
From Five Songs, *465*
As I Walked Out One Evening,
    465
Musée des Beaux Arts, *467*
In Memory of W. B. Yeats,
    468
Voltaire at Ferney, *470*
The Unknown Citizen, *471*
From Twelve Songs, *472*
Mundus et Infans, *474*
From "For the Time Being,"
    476

THEODORE ROETHKE / 1908–1963
My Papa's Waltz, 478
Dolor, 478
The Lost Son, 479
A Field of Light, 484
Elegy for Jane, 486
The Waking, 487
I Knew a Woman, 487

W. R. RODGERS / 1909–
Directions to a Rebel, 488
Snow, 491
White Christmas, 492
Awake!, 493
Neither Here nor There, 495

STEPHEN SPENDER / 1909–
I Think Continually of Those
    Who Were Truly Great,
    496
After They Have Tired of the
    Brilliance of Cities, 497
The Express, 498
The Landscape Near an Aero-
    drome, 499
Not Palaces, an Era's Crown,
    500
Ultima Ratio Regum, 501
The Double Shame, 502

ELIZABETH BISHOP / 1911–
The Imaginary Iceberg, 503
The Man-Moth, 504
Roosters, 506
The Fish, 510
At the Fishhouses, 512
The Prodigal, 514

DELMORE SCHWARTZ /
        1913–1966
In the Naked Bed, in Plato's
    Cave, 515
Tired and Unhappy, You Think
    of Houses, 516
For the One Who Would Take
    Man's Life in His Hands,
    517

Socrates' Ghost Must Haunt
    Me Now, 518
Calmly We Walk Through
    This April's Day, 519
The Heavy Bear Who Goes
    with Me, 520
A Dog Named Ego, the
    Snowflakes as Kisses, 521
The Sequel, 522
I Did Not Know the Truth of
    Growing Trees, 522

GEORGE BARKER / 1913–
The Crystal, 523
Resolution of Dependence, 524
From Pacific Sonnets, 526
    V
    VI
    VII
    XII
From Secular Elegies, 527
    V
To My Mother, 528
To Any Member of My Gen-
    eration, 529
News of the World III, 529
Dog, Dog in My Manger, 531

KARL SHAPIRO / 1913–
The Dome of Sunday, 532
The Fly, 533
Auto Wreck, 535
Scyros, 536
Hollywood, 537
Poet, 539
Elegy for a Dead Soldier, 541

DYLAN THOMAS / 1914–1953
The Force That Through the
    Green Fuse Drives the
    Flower, 545
And Death Shall Have No
    Dominion, 546
Altarwise by Owl-Light, 546
A Refusal to Mourn the Death,
    by Fire, of a Child in
    London, 550

Do Not Go Gentle into That
    Good Night, *551*
In My Craft or Sullen Art, *552*
Vision and Prayer, *553*
Fern Hill, *559*

RANDALL JARRELL /
                    1914–1965
The Snow-Leopard, *560*
The Death of the Ball Turret
    Gunner, *561*
Losses, *562*
Second Air Force, *563*
The State, *564*
The Woman at the Washing-
    ton Zoo, *565*

JOHN BERRYMAN / 1914–
Winter Landscape, *566*
Desires of Men and Women,
    567
Conversation, *567*
Whether There Is Sorrow in
    the Demons, *568*
New Year's Eve, *570*
Dream Song 14, *571*

ROBERT LOWELL / 1917–
New Year's Day, *572*

The Quaker Graveyard in Nan-
    tucket, *573*
The Drunken Fisherman, *577*
As a Plane Tree by the Water,
    578
Mr. Edwards and the Spider,
    579
The Dead in Europe, *581*
Soft Wood, *581*
For the Union Dead, *583*
Grandparents, *585*
Central Park, *586*

HOWARD NEMEROV / 1920–
Truth, *588*
Boom!, *589*
The Goose Fish, *590*
Redeployment, *591*
The Phoenix, *592*
A Spell before Winter, *593*

RICHARD WILBUR / 1921–
Tywater, *593*
"A World without Objects Is a
    Sensible Emptiness," *594*
Juggler, *595*
Years-End, *596*
Still, Citizen Sparrow, *597*
The Death of a Toad, *598*
In the Smoking-Car, *599*

PART II

A Little Treasury of Modern Lyrics

LÉONIE ADAMS / 1899–
Caryatid, *603*
Early Waking, *603*
Country Summer, *604*

JOHN PEALE BISHOP /
                    1892–1944
Ode, *606*

This Dim and Ptolemaic Man,
    607
The Dream, *608*

EDMUND BLUNDEN /
                    1896–
The Pike, *609*

ARNA BONTEMPS / 1902–
Southern Mansion, *611*
Length of Moon, *611*

RUPERT BROOKE / 1887–1915
The Soldier, *612*
The Great Lover, *613*
Heaven, *615*

COUNTEE CULLEN / 1903–1946
Saturday's Child, *616*
From the Dark Tower, *616*

W. H. DAVIES / 1871–1940
Leisure, *617*
Sheep, *618*

H. D. (HILDA DOOLITTLE) /
1886–1961
Song, *618*
Orchard, *619*
Helen, *620*
Lethe, *621*

JOHN DRINKWATER /
1882–1937
Sunrise on Rydal Water, *621*

JAMES JOYCE / 1882–1941
I Hear an Army Charging upon
the Land, *623*

VACHEL LINDSAY / 1879–1931
General William Booth Enters
into Heaven, *624*

HUGH MAC DIARMID / 1892–
O Wha's the Bride?, *626*
With the Herring Fishers, *627*

OGDEN NASH / 1902–
Portrait of the Artist as a Prematurely Old Man, *628*
Reflections on Ice-Breaking,
629

FREDERIC PROKOSCH / 1908–
The Conspirators, *629*

PETER QUENNELL / 1905–
The Flight into Egypt, *630*
Procne, *632*

HERBERT READ / 1889–
Summer Rain, *632*
To a Conscript of 1940, *633*

MICHAEL ROBERTS / 1902–1948
St. Ursanne, *635*

ISAAC ROSENBERG / 1890–1918
Dead Man's Dump, *636*

CARL SANDBURG / 1878–1967
Chicago, *638*

SIEGFRIED SASSOON /
1887–1967
The Death-Bed, *640*
The General, *641*

MARSHALL SCHACHT / 1905–
Not to Forget Miss Dickinson,
642

EDITH SITWELL / 1887–1964
Still Falls the Rain, *642*
Lullaby, *644*

BERNARD SPENCER / 1909–1963
Part of Plenty, *645*

EDWARD THOMAS / 1878–1917
Old Man, *646*
Out in the Dark, *647*

FRANCIS THOMPSON /
1859–1907
The Hound of Heaven, *648*

MARK VAN DOREN / 1894–
The Distant Runners, *653*

JOHN HALL WHEELOCK /
1886–
The Black Panther, *654*
Silence, *655*
Earth, *655*
Slow Summer Twilight, *655*

YVOR WINTERS / 1900–1967
A Summer Commentary, *656*

RICHARD WRIGHT / 1908–1960
Between the World and Me,
657

PART III

A Little Treasury of Poetry in Progress

MARGARET AVISON / 1918–
Butterfly Bones; or Sonnet
    Against Sonnets, *661*
New Year's Poem, *661*

WENDELL BERRY / 1934–
November Twenty-Sixth Nine-
    teen Hundred and Sixty-
    Three, *662*

GWENDOLYN BROOKS / 1917–
The Chicago Picasso, *665*
The Sermon on the Warpland,
    666

CHARLES CAUSLEY / 1917–
On Seeing a Poet of the First
    World War on the Station
    at Abbeville, *667*
Autobiography, *668*

JOHN CIARDI / 1916–
Ode for the Burial of a Citizen,
    668
To Judith Asleep, *669*
The Gift, *670*

ALEX COMFORT / 1920–
The Atoll in the Mind, *671*
Hoc Est Corpus, *672*
Notes for My Son, *672*

GREGORY CORSO / 1930–
Marriage, *673*

ROBERT CREELEY / 1926–
The Immoral Proposition, *677*
The Rhythm, *678*
The Way, *679*
A Marriage, *679*

DONALD DAVIE / 1922–
The Wind at Penistone, *680*
Gardens no Emblems, *681*

GENE DERWOOD / 1900–1954
With God Conversing, *682*
Elegy, *683*
After Reading St. John the Di-
    vine, *685*
Rides, *686*

JAMES DICKEY / 1923–
The Heaven of Animals, *687*
The Performance, *688*
The Dusk of Horses, *689*

ALAN DUGAN / 1923–
The Mirror Perilous, *691*
Plague of Dead Sharks, *692*

LAWRENCE DURRELL / 1912–
In Crisis, *692*
On Seeming to Presume, *693*

LAWRENCE DURRELL (*cont.*)
On First Looking into Loeb's Horace, *695*
A Ballad of the Good Lord Nelson, *697*

KENNETH FEARING / 1902–1961
Confession Overheard in a Subway, *699*

LAWRENCE FERLINGHETTI / 1919–
From A Coney Island of the Mind, *701*
    1
    3
    15

ROY FULLER / 1912–
January 1940, *704*
Spring 1942, *705*
Spring 1943, *705*
The Tribes, *706*
Versions of Love, *708*

JEAN GARRIGUE / 1914–
The Stranger, *709*
Forest, *710*
False Country of the Zoo, *711*

DAVID GASCOYNE / 1916–
A Wartime Dawn, *713*
Ecce Homo, *715*
A Tough Generation, *717*

ALLEN GINSBERG / 1926–
A Supermarket in California, *718*
To Aunt Rose, *719*

W. S. GRAHAM / 1917–
Listen. Put on Morning, *720*

THOM GUNN / 1929–
A Mirror for Poets, *722*
On the Move, *723*
Innocence, *724*
Considering the Snail, *725*
My Sad Captains, *726*

DONALD HALL / 1928–
An Airstrip in Essex, 1960, *727*
The Farm, *727*

ANTHONY HECHT / 1923–
Japan, *728*
Samuel Sewall, *730*
The End of the Weekend, *731*

JOHN HOLLANDER / 1929–
The Lady's-Maid's Song, *732*
The Great Bear, *733*

TED HUGHES / 1930–
Hawk Roosting, *735*
The Jaguar, *736*
Famous Poet, *737*
View of a Pig, *738*
Pike, *739*

ELIZABETH JENNINGS / 1926–
The Counterpart, *741*
Not in the Guide-Books, *742*

LE ROI JONES / 1934–
An Agony. As Now., *743*
The Invention of Comics, *744*

GALWAY KINNELL / 1927–
First Song, *745*
The Avenue Bearing the Initial of Christ into the New World, *746*

ABRAHAM KLEIN / 1909–
Indian Reservation: Caughnawaga, *748*

STANLEY KUNITZ / 1905–
A Choice of Weapons, *749*
Foreign Affairs, *750*

JOSEPH LANGLAND / 1917–
A Sea-Change: For Harold, *752*
Hunters in the Snow: Brueghel, *753*

PHILIP LARKIN / 1922–
Church Going, 754
If, My Darling, 756

LAURIE LEE / 1914–
Field of Autumn, 757
Sunken Evening, 758

DENISE LEVERTOV / 1923–
The Goddess, 759
Obsessions, 760
To the Snake, 760
Scenes from the Life of the
    Peppertrees, 761

ALUN LEWIS / 1915–1944
Song, 763
The Peasants, 764

JOHN MANIFOLD / 1915–
Fife Tune, 765
The Sirens, 766
Night Piece, 766

W. S. MERWIN / 1927–
The Bones, 767
Grandfather in the Old Men's
    Home, 768
The Drunk in the Furnace,
    769

ROBERT MEZEY / 1935–
Street Scene, 770
The Funeral Home, 771

JOSEPHINE MILES / 1911–
Monkey, 772
The Savages, 772
Voyage, 774

VASSAR MILLER / 1924–
The Final Hunger, 775
Bout with Burning, 776

HOWARD MOSS / 1922–
The Lie, 776
Elegy for My Father, 777

CHARLES OLSON / 1910–
I, Maximus of Gloucester, to
    You, 778

P. K. PAGE / 1916–
The Stenographers, 782
The Permanent Tourists, 783

KENNETH PATCHEN / 1911–
At the New Year, 784
The Constant Bridegrooms,
    785
Where?, 786
All the Roary Night, 786

SYLVIA PLATH / 1932–1963
The Colossus, 787
Black Rook in Rainy Weather,
    788
Daddy, 789

HYAM PLUTZIK / 1911–1962
The Mythos of Samuel Hunts-
    man, 791
The King of Ai, 792

F. T. PRINCE / 1912–
Soldiers Bathing, 793
To a Friend on His Marriage,
    795

HENRY REED / 1914–
Naming of Parts, 796
Chard Whitlow, 797

KENNETH REXROTH / 1905–
A Living Pearl, 798

ADRIENNE RICH / 1929–
After Dark, 801
Face to Face, 803

ANNE RIDLER / 1912–
For a Child Expected, 804

MURIEL RUKEYSER / 1913–
Boy with His Hair Cut Short,
    805
Ajanta, 806

W. T. SCOTT / 1910–1968
Swedish Angel, *810*
Annual Legend, *811*
The U.S. Sailor with the Japanese Skull, *812*

ANNE SEXTON / 1928–
Her Kind, *813*
The Fortress, *814*
The Farmer's Wife, *816*

LOUIS SIMPSON / 1923–
To the Western World, *817*
Walt Whitman at Bear Mountain, *817*

W. D. SNODGRASS / 1926–
April Inventory, *819*
The Campus on the Hill, *821*
A Flat One, *822*

WILLIAM STAFFORD / 1914–
At Cove on the Crooked River, *825*
West of Your City, *825*
Traveling Through the Dark, *826*
At the Bomb Testing Site, *827*

MAY SWENSON / 1919–
Lion, *827*
Question, *829*

CHARLES TOMLINSON / 1927–
Winter Encounters, *829*
How Still the Hawk, *830*

PETER VIERECK / 1916–
Blindman's Buff, *831*
Vale from Carthage, *832*

JOHN WAIN / 1925–
This Above All Is Precious and Remakable, *833*
Brooklyn Heights, *834*

ROBERT PENN WARREN / 1905–
Colder Fire, *835*
Country Burying (1919), *837*
Original Sin: A Short Story, *839*
Bearded Oaks, *840*

REED WHITTEMORE / 1919–
A Day with the Foreign Legion, *842*

JAMES WRIGHT / 1927–
On the Skeleton of a Hound, *844*
A Gesture by a Lady with an Assumed Name, *846*

PART IV

Appendix

I ON POETS AND POETRY
 Prose Statements by Modern Poets

II ON SOCIETY AND POETRY
 Ezra Pound and the Bollingen Prize
 Poets on Society and Poetry

III A BIBLIOGRAPHY OF MODERN POETIC CRITICISM

IV PHOTOGRAPHS OF THE POETS

INDEX OF AUTHORS AND TITLES

PART I

A Little Treasury of
the Chief Modern Poets
of England and America

Emily Dickinson / 1830–1886

SUCCESS IS COUNTED SWEETEST

Success is counted sweetest
By those who ne'er succeed.
To comprehend a nectar
Requires sorest need.

Not one of all the purple Host
Who took the Flag today
Can tell the definition
So clear of Victory

As he defeated – dying –
On whose forbidden ear
The distant strains of triumph
Burst agonized and clear!

I TASTE A LIQUOR NEVER BREWED

I taste a liquor never brewed –
From Tankards scooped in Pearl –
Not all the Vats upon the Rhine
Yield such an Alcohol!

Inebriate of Air – am I –
And Debauchee of Dew –

Reeling – thro endless summer days –
From inns of Molten Blue –

When "Landlords" turn the drunken Bee
Out of the Foxglove's door –
When Butterflies – renounce their "drams" –
I shall but drink the more!

Till Seraphs swing their snowy Hats –
And Saints – to windows run –
To see the little Tippler
Leaning against the – Sun –

THERE'S A CERTAIN SLANT
OF LIGHT

There's a certain Slant of light,
Winter Afternoons –
That oppresses, like the Heft
Of Cathedral Tunes –

Heavenly Hurt, it gives us –
We can find no scar,
But internal difference,
Where the Meanings, are –

None may teach it – Any –
'Tis the Seal Despair –
An imperial affliction
Sent us of the Air –

When it comes, the Landscape listens –
Shadows – hold their breath –
When it goes, 'tis like the Distance
On the look of Death –

BEFORE I GOT MY EYE PUT OUT

Before I got my eye put out
I liked as well to see –
As other Creatures, that have Eyes
And know no other way –

But were it told to me – Today –
That I might have the sky
For mine – I tell you that my Heart
Would split, for size of me –

The Meadows – mine –
The Mountains – mine –
All Forests – Stintless Stars –
As much of Noon as I could take
Between my finite eyes –

The Motions of the Dipping Birds –
The Morning's Amber Road –
For mine – to look at when I liked –
The News would strike me dead –

So safer – guess – with just my soul
Upon the Window pane –
Where other Creatures put their eyes –
Incautious – of the Sun –

A BIRD CAME DOWN THE WALK

A Bird came down the Walk –
He did not know I saw –
He bit an Angleworm in halves
And ate the fellow, raw,

And then he drank a Dew
From a convenient Grass —
And then hopped sidewise to the Wall
To let a Beetle pass —

He glanced with rapid eyes
That hurried all around —
They looked like frightened Beads, I thought —
He stirred his Velvet Head

Like one in danger, Cautious,
I offered him a Crumb
And he unrolled his feathers
And rowed him softer home —

Than Oars divide the Ocean,
Too silver for a seam —
Or Butterflies, off Banks of Noon
Leap, plashless as they swim.

THE FIRST DAY'S NIGHT
HAD COME

The first Day's Night had come —
And grateful that a thing
So terrible — had been endured —
I told my Soul to sing —

She said her Strings were snapt —
Her Bow — to Atoms blown —
And so to mend her — gave me work
Until another Morn —

And then — a Day as huge
As Yesterdays in pairs,
Unrolled its horror in my face —
Until it blocked my eyes —

My Brain – begun to laugh –
I mumbled – like a fool –
And tho' 'tis Years ago – that Day –
My Brain keeps giggling – still.

And Something's odd – within –
That person that I was –
And this One – do not feel the same –
Could it be Madness – this?

'TWAS LIKE A MAELSTROM, WITH A NOTCH

'Twas like a Maelstrom, with a notch,
That nearer, every Day,
Kept narrowing its boiling Wheel
Until the Agony

Toyed coolly with the final inch
Of your delirious Hem –
And you dropt, lost,
When something broke –
And let you from a Dream –

As if a Goblin with a Gauge –
Kept measuring the Hours –
Until you felt your Second
Weigh, helpless, in his Paws –

And not a Sinew – stirred – could help,
And sense was setting numb –
When God – remembered – and the Fiend
Let go, then, Overcome –

As if your Sentence stood – pronounced –
And you were frozen led
From Dungeon's luxury of Doubt
To Gibbets, and the Dead –

And when the Film had stitched your eyes
A Creature gasped "Reprieve"!
Which Anguish was the utterest – then –
To perish, or to live?

MUCH MADNESS IS DIVINEST SENSE

Much Madness is divinest Sense –
To a discerning Eye –
Much Sense – the starkest Madness –
'Tis the Majority
In this, as All, prevail –
Assent – and you are sane –
Demur – you're straightway dangerous –
And handled with a Chain –

UNDUE SIGNIFICANCE A STARVING MAN ATTACHES

Undue Significance a starving man attaches
To Food –
Far off – He sighs – and therefore – Hopeless –
And therefore – Good –

Partaken – it relieves – indeed –
But proves us
That Spices fly
In the Receipt – It was the Distance –
Was Savory –

I DIED FOR BEAUTY—BUT WAS SCARCE

I died for Beauty – but was scarce
Adjusted in the Tomb
When One who died for Truth, was lain
In an adjoining Room –

He questioned softly "Why I failed"?
"For Beauty", I replied –
"And I – for Truth – Themself are One –
We Brethren, are", He said –

And so, as Kinsmen, met a Night –
We talked between the Rooms –
Until the Moss had reached our lips –
And covered up – our names –

I HEARD A FLY BUZZ—WHEN I DIED

I heard a Fly buzz – when I died –
The Stillness in the Room
Was like the Stillness in the Air –
Between the Heaves of Storm –

The Eyes around – had wrung them dry –
And Breaths were gathering firm
For that last Onset – when the King
Be witnessed – in the Room –

I willed my Keepsakes – Signed away
What portion of me be
Assignable – and then it was
There interposed a Fly –

With Blue – uncertain stumbling Buzz –
Between the light – and me –
And then the Windows failed – and then
I could not see to see –

I STARTED EARLY—TOOK MY DOG

I started Early – Took my Dog –
And visited the Sea –
The Mermaids in the Basement
Came out to look at me –

And Frigates – in the Upper Floor
Extended Hempen Hands –
Presuming Me to be a Mouse –
Aground – upon the Sands –

But no Man moved Me – till the Tide
Went past my simple Shoe –
And past my Apron – and my Belt
And past my Bodice – too –

And made as He would eat me up –
As wholly as a Dew
Upon a Dandelion's Sleeve –
And then – I started – too –

And He – He followed – close behind –
I felt His Silver Heel
Upon my Ankle – Then my Shoes
Would overflow with Pearl –

Until We met the Solid Town –
No One He seemed to know –
And bowing – with a Mighty look –
At me – The Sea withdrew –

I HAD BEEN HUNGRY,
ALL THE YEARS

I had been hungry, all the Years –
My Noon had Come – to dine –
I trembling drew the Table near –
And touched the Curious Wine –

'Twas this on Tables I had seen –
When turning, hungry, Home
I looked in Windows, for the Wealth
I could not hope – for Mine –

I did not know the ample Bread –
'Twas so unlike the Crumb
The Birds and I, had often shared
In Nature's – Dining Room –

The Plenty hurt me – 'twas so new –
Myself felt ill – and odd –
As Berry – of a Mountain Bush –
Transplanted – to the Road –

Nor was I hungry – so I found
That Hunger – was a way
Of Persons outside Windows –
The Entering – takes away –

I LIKE TO SEE IT LAP THE MILES

I like to see it lap the Miles –
And lick the Valleys up –
And stop to feed itself at Tanks –
And then – prodigious step

Around a Pile of Mountains –
And supercilious peer

In Shanties – by the sides of Roads –
And then a Quarry pare

To fit its Ribs
And crawl between
Complaining all the while
In horrid – hooting stanza –
Then chase itself down Hill –

And neigh like Boanerges –
Then – punctual as a Star
Stop – docile and omnipotent
At its own stable door –

OUR   JOURNEY   HAD   ADVANCED

Our journey had advanced –
Our feet were almost come
To that odd Fork in Being's Road –
Eternity – by Term –

Our pace took sudden awe –
Our feet – reluctant – led –
Before – were Cities – but Between –
The Forest of the Dead –

Retreat – was out of Hope –
Behind – a Sealed Route –
Eternity's White Flag – Before –
And God – at every Gate –

PAIN—HAS   AN   ELEMENT   OF   BLANK

Pain – has an Element of Blank –
It cannot recollect
When it begun – or if there were
A time when it was not –

It has no Future – but itself –
Its Infinite contain
Its Past – enlightened to perceive
New Periods – of Pain.

BECAUSE I COULD NOT STOP FOR DEATH

Because I could not stop for Death –
He kindly stopped for me –
The Carriage held but just Ourselves –
And Immortality.

We slowly drove – He knew no haste
And I had put away
My labor and my leisure too,
For His Civility –

We passed the School, where Children strove
At Recess – in the Ring –
We passed the Fields of Gazing Grain –
We passed the Setting Sun –

Or rather – He passed Us –
The Dews drew quivering and chill –
For only Gossamer, my Gown –
My Tippet – only Tulle –

We paused before a House that seemed
A Swelling of the Ground –
The Roof was scarcely visible –
The Cornice – in the Ground –

Since then – 'tis Centuries – and yet
Feels shorter than the Day
I first surmised the Horses' Heads
Were toward Eternity –

A NARROW FELLOW IN THE GRASS

A narrow Fellow in the Grass
Occasionally rides –
You may have met Him – did you not
His notice sudden is –

The Grass divides as with a Comb –
A spotted shaft is seen –
And then it closes at your feet
And opens further on –

He likes a Boggy Acre
A Floor too cool for Corn –
Yet when a Boy, and Barefoot –
I more than once at Noon
Have passed, I thought, a Whip lash
Unbraiding in the Sun
When stooping to secure it
It wrinkled, and was gone –

Several of Nature's People
I know, and they know me –
I feel for them a transport
Of cordiality –

But never met this Fellow
Attended, or alone
Without a tighter breathing
And Zero at the Bone –

I NEVER SAW A MOOR

I never saw a Moor –
I never saw the Sea –
Yet know I how the Heather looks
And what a Billow be.

I never spoke with God
Nor visited in Heaven –
Yet certain am I of the spot
As if the Checks were given –

TELL ALL THE TRUTH BUT TELL IT SLANT

Tell all the Truth but tell it slant –
Success in Circuit lies
Too bright for our infirm Delight
The Truth's superb surprise

As Lightning to the Children eased
With explanation kind
The Truth must dazzle gradually
Or every man be blind –

AS IMPERCEPTIBLY AS GRIEF

As imperceptibly as Grief
The Summer lapsed away –
Too imperceptible at last
To seem like Perfidy –
A Quietness distilled
As Twilight long begun,
Or Nature spending with herself
Sequestered Afternoon –
The Dusk drew earlier in –
The Morning foreign shone –
A courteous, yet harrowing Grace,
As Guest, that would be gone –
And thus, without a Wing
Or service of a Keel
Our Summer made her light escape
Into the Beautiful.

MY LIFE CLOSED TWICE
BEFORE ITS CLOSE

My life closed twice before its close –
It yet remains to see
If Immortality unveil
A third event to me

So huge, so hopeless to conceive
As these that twice befell.
Parting is all we know of heaven,
And all we need of hell.

Thomas Hardy / 1840–1928

IN TENEBRIS

II

*"Considerabam ad dexteram, et videbam; et non erat qui
cognosceret me. . . . Non est qui requirat animam meam."*
PSALM *cxli.*

When the clouds' swoln bosoms echo back the shouts of the
     many and strong
That things are all as they best may be, save a few to be
     right ere long,
And my eyes have not the vision in them to discern what
     to these is so clear,
The blot seems straightway in me alone; one better he were
     not here.

The stout upstanders say, All's well with us: ruers have
     nought to rue!
And what the potent say so oft, can it fail to be somewhat
     true?

Breezily go they, breezily come; their dust smokes around
    their career,
Till I think I am one born out of due time, who has no
    calling here.

Their dawns bring lusty joys, it seems; their evenings all
    that is sweet;
Our times are blessed times, they cry: Life shapes it as is
    most meet,
And nothing is much the matter; there are many smiles to
    a tear;
Then what is the matter is I, I say. Why should such an one
    be here? . . .

Let him in whose ears the low-voiced Best is killed by the
    clash of the First,
Who holds that if way to the Better there be, it exacts a
    full look at the Worst,
Who feels that delight is a delicate growth cramped by
    crookedness, custom, and fear,
Get him up and be gone as one shaped awry; he disturbs
    the order here.

THE DARKLING THRUSH

I leant upon a coppice gate
    When Frost was spectre-gray,
And Winter's dregs made desolate
    The weakening eye of day.
The tangled bine-stems scored the sky
    Like strings of broken lyres,
And all mankind that haunted nigh
    Had sought their household fires.

The land's sharp features seemed to be
    The Century's corpse outleant,
His crypt the cloudy canopy,
    The wind his death-lament.

The ancient pulse of germ and birth
    Was shrunken hard and dry,
And every spirit upon earth
    Seemed fervourless as I.

At once a voice arose among
    The bleak twigs overhead
In a full-hearted evensong
    Of joy illimited;
An aged thrush, frail, gaunt, and small,
    In blast-beruffled plume,
Had chosen thus to fling his soul
    Upon the growing gloom.

So little cause for carolings
    Of such ecstatic sound
Was written on terrestrial things
    Afar or nigh around,
That I could think there trembled through
    His happy good-night air
Some blessed Hope, whereof he knew
    And I was unaware.

THE MAN HE KILLED

    "Had he and I but met
      By some old ancient inn,
We should have sat us down to wet
      Right many a nipperkin!

    "But ranged as infantry,
      And staring face to face,
I shot at him as he at me,
      And killed him in his place.

    "I shot him dead because—
      Because he was my foe,
Just so: my foe of course he was;
      That's clear enough; although

"He thought he'd 'list, perhaps,
Off-hand like—just as I—
Was out of work—had sold his traps—
No other reason why.

"Yes; quaint and curious war is!
You shoot a fellow down
You'd treat if met where any bar is,
Or help to half-a-crown."

THE CONVERGENCE OF THE TWAIN

Lines on the loss of the "Titanic"

I

In a solitude of the sea
Deep from human vanity,
And the Pride of Life that planned her, stilly couches she.

II

Steel chambers, late the pyres
Of her salamandrine fires,
Cold currents thrid, and turn to rhythmic tidal lyres.

III

Over the mirrors meant
To glass the opulent
The sea-worm crawls—grotesque, slimed, dumb, indifferent.

IV

Jewels in joy designed
To ravish the sensuous mind
Lie lightless, all their sparkles bleared and black and blind.

V

Dim moon-eyed fishes near
Gaze at the gilded gear
And query: "What does this vaingloriousness down
here?" . . .

VI

> Well: while was fashioning
> This creature of cleaving wing,
> The Immanent Will that stirs and urges everything

VII

> Prepared a sinister mate
> For her—so gaily great—
> A Shape of Ice, for the time far and dissociate.

VIII

> And as the smart ship grew
> In stature, grace, and hue,
> In shadowy silent distance grew the Iceberg too.

IX

> Alien they seemed to be:
> No mortal eye could see
> The intimate welding of their later history.

X

> Or sign that they were bent
> By paths coincident
> On being anon twin halves of one august event,

XI

> Till the Spinner of the Years
> Said "Now!" And each one hears,
> And consummation comes, and jars two hemispheres.

THE BLINDED BIRD

So zestfully canst thou sing?
And all this indignity,
With God's consent, on thee!
Blinded ere yet a-wing
By the red-hot needle thou,
I stand and wonder how
So zestfully thou canst sing!

Resenting not such wrong,
Thy grievous pain forgot,
Eternal dark thy lot,
Groping thy whole life long,
After that stab of fire;
Enjailed in pitiless wire;
Resenting not such wrong!

Who hath charity? This bird.
Who suffereth long and is kind,
Is not provoked, though blind
And alive ensepulchred?
Who hopeth, endureth all things?
Who thinketh no evil, but sings?
Who is divine? This bird.

THE   OXEN

Christmas Eve, and twelve of the clock.
  "Now they are all on their knees,"
An elder said as we sat in a flock
  By the embers in hearthside ease.

We pictured the meek mild creatures where
  They dwelt in their strawy pen,
Nor did it occur to one of us there
  To doubt they were kneeling then.

So fair a fancy few would weave
  In these years! Yet, I feel,
If someone said on Christmas Eve,
  "Come; see the oxen kneel,

"In the lonely barton by yonder coomb
  Our childhood used to know,"
I should go with him in the gloom,
  Hoping it might be so.

FOR LIFE I HAD NEVER CARED GREATLY

For Life I had never cared greatly,
        As worth a man's while;
        Peradventures unsought,
    Peradventures that finished in nought,
Had kept me from youth and through manhood till lately
        Unwon by its style.

In earliest years—why I know not—
        I viewed it askance;
        Conditions of doubt,
    Conditions that leaked slowly out,
May haply have bent me to stand and to show not
        Much zest for its dance.

With symphonies soft and sweet colour
        It courted me then,
        Till evasions seemed wrong,
    Till evasions gave in to its song,
And I warmed, until living aloofly loomed duller
        Than life among men.

Anew I found nought to set eyes on,
        When, lifting its hand,
        It uncloaked a star,
    Uncloaked it from fog-damps afar,
And showed its beams burning from pole to horizon
        As bright as a brand.

And so, the rough highway forgetting,
        I pace hill and dale
        Regarding the sky,
    Regarding the vision on high,
And thus re-illumed have no humour for letting
        My pilgrimage fail.

THE PITY OF IT

I walked in loamy Wessex lanes, afar
From rail-track and from highway, and I heard
In field and farmstead many an ancient word
Of local lineage like "Thu bist," "Er war,"

"Ich woll," "Er sholl," and by-talk similar,
Nigh as they speak who in this month's moon gird
At England's very loins, thereunto spurred
By gangs whose glory threats and slaughters are.

Then seemed a Heart crying: "Whosoever they be
At root and bottom of this, who flung this flame
Between kin folk kin tongued even as are we,

"Sinister, ugly, lurid, be their fame;
May their familiars grow to shun their name,
And their brood perish everlastingly."

IN TIME OF "THE BREAKING OF NATIONS"

I

Only a man harrowing clods
    In a slow silent walk
With an old horse that stumbles and nods
    Half asleep as they stalk.

II

Only thin smoke without flame
    From the heaps of couch-grass;
Yet this will go onward the same
    Though Dynasties pass.

III

Yonder a maid and her wight
   Come whispering by:
War's annals will fade into night
   Ere their story die.

AFTERWARDS

When the Present has latched its postern behind my
      tremulous stay,
   And the May month flaps its glad green leaves like wings,
Delicate-filmed as new-spun silk, will the neighbours say,
   "He was a man who used to notice such things"?

If it be in the dusk when, like an eyelid's soundless blink,
   The dewfall-hawk comes crossing the shades to alight
Upon the wind-warped upland thorn, a gazer may think,
   "To him this must have been a familiar sight."

If I pass during some nocturnal blackness, mothy and warm,
   When the hedgehog travels furtively over the lawn,
One may say, "He strove that such innocent creatures
      should come to no harm,
   But he could do little for them; and now he is gone."

If, when hearing that I have been stilled at last, they stand
      at the door,
   Watching the full-starred heavens that winter sees,
Will this thought rise on those who will meet my face no
      more,
   "He was one who had an eye for such mysteries"?

And will any say when my bell of quittance is heard in the
      gloom,
   And a crossing breeze cuts a pause in its outrollings,
Till they rise again, as they were a new bell's boom,
   "He hears it not now, but used to notice such things?"

THE CONTRETEMPS

A forward rush by the lamp in the gloom,
    And we clasped, and almost kissed;
    But she was not the woman whom
    I had promised to meet in the thawing brume
On that harbour-bridge; nor was I he of her tryst.

So loosening from me swift she said:
    "O why, why feign to be
    The one I had meant!—to whom I have sped
    To fly with, being so sorrily wed!"
—'Twas thus and thus that she upbraided me.

My assignation had struck upon
    Some others' like it, I found.
    And her lover rose on the night anon;
    And then her husband entered on
The lamplit, snowflaked, sloppiness around.

"Take her and welcome, man!" he cried:
    "I wash my hands of her.
    I'll find me twice as good a bride!"
    —All this to me, whom he had eyed,
Plainly, as his wife's planned deliverer.

And next the lover: "Little I knew,
    Madam, you had a third!
    Kissing here in my very view!"
    —Husband and lover then withdrew.
I let them; and I told them not they erred.

Why not? Well, there faced she and I—
    Two strangers who'd kissed, or near,
    Chancewise. To see stand weeping by
    A woman once embraced, will try
The tension of a man the most austere.

So it began; and I was young,
    She pretty, by the lamp,

As flakes came waltzing down among
        The waves of her clinging hair, that hung
Heavily on her temples, dark and damp.

And there alone still stood we two;
        She one cast off for me,
        Or so it seemed: while night ondrew,
        Forcing a parley what should do
We twain hearts caught in one catastrophe.

In stranded souls a common strait
        Wakes latencies unknown,
        Whose impulse may precipitate
        A life-long leap. The hour was late,
And there was the Jersey boat with its funnel agroan.

"Is wary walking worth much pother?"
        It grunted, as still it stayed.
        "One pairing is as good as another
        Where all is venture! Take each other,
And scrap the oaths that you have aforetime made." . . .

—Of the four involved there walks but one
        On earth at this late day.
        And what of the chapter so begun?
        In that odd complex what was done?
        Well; happiness comes in full to none:
Let peace lie on lulled lips: ·I will not say.

AND THERE WAS A GREAT CALM

On the Signing of the Armistice, Nov. 11, 1918

I

There had been years of Passion—scorching, cold,
And much Despair, and Anger heaving high,
Care whitely watching, Sorrows manifold,
Among the young, among the weak and old,
And the pensive Spirit of Pity whispered, "Why?"

II

Men had not paused to answer. Foes distraught
Pierced the thinned peoples in a brute-like blindness,
Philosophies that sages long had taught,
And Selflessness, were as an unknown thought,
And "Hell!" and "Shell!" were yapped at Lovingkindness.

III

The feeble folk at home had grown full-used
To "dug-outs," "snipers," "Huns," from the war-adept
In the mornings heard, and at evetides perused;
To day-dreamt men in millions, when they mused—
To nightmare-men in millions when they slept.

IV

Waking to wish existence timeless, null,
Sirius they watched above where armies fell;
He seemed to check his flapping when, in the lull
Of night a boom came thencewise, like the dull
Plunge of a stone dropped into some deep well.

V

So, when old hopes that earth was bettering slowly
Were dead and damned, there sounded "War is done!"
One morrow. Said the bereft, and meek, and lowly,
"Will men some day be given to grace? yea, wholly,
And in good sooth, as our dreams used to run?"

VI

Breathless they paused. Out there men raised their glance
To where had stood those poplars lank and lopped,
As they had raised it through the four years' dance
Of Death in the now familiar flats of France;
And murmured, "Strange, this! How? All firing stopped?"

VII

Aye; all was hushed. The about-to-fire fired not,
The aimed-at moved away in trance-lipped song.
One checkless regiment slung a clinching shot
And turned. The Spirit of Irony smirked out, "What?
Spoil peradventures woven of Rage and Wrong?"

VIII

Thenceforth no flying fires inflamed the gray,
No hurtlings shook the dewdrop from the thorn,
No moan perplexed the mute bird on the spray;
Worn horses mused: "We are not whipped to-day";
No weft-winged engines blurred the moon's thin horn.

IX

Calm fell. From Heaven distilled a clemency;
There was peace on earth, and silence in the sky;
Some could, some could not, shake off misery:
The Sinister Spirit sneered: "It had to be!"
And again the Spirit of Pity whispered, "Why?"

AN ANCIENT TO ANCIENTS

Where once we danced, where once we sang,
          Gentlemen,
The floors are sunken, cobwebs hang,
And cracks creep; worms have fed upon
The doors. Yea, sprightlier times were then
Than now, with harps and tabrets gone,
          Gentlemen!

Where once we rowed, where once we sailed,
          Gentlemen,
And damsels took the tiller, veiled
Against too strong a stare (God wot
Their fancy, then or anywhen!)
Upon that shore we are clean forgot,
          Gentlemen!

We have lost somewhat, afar and near.
          Gentlemen,
The thinning of our ranks each year
Affords a hint we are nigh undone,
That we shall not be ever again
The marked of many, loved of one,
          Gentlemen.

In dance the polka hit our wish,
           Gentlemen,
The paced quadrille, the spry schottische,
"Sir Roger."—And in opera spheres
The "Girl" (the famed "Bohemian"),
And "Trovatore," held the ears,
           Gentlemen.

This season's paintings do not please,
           Gentlemen,
Like Etty, Mulready, Maclise;
Throbbing romance has waned and wanned,
No wizard wields the witching pen
Of Bulwer, Scott, Dumas, and Sand,
           Gentlemen.

The bower we shrined to Tennyson,
           Gentlemen,
Is roof-wrecked; damps there drip upon
Sagged seats, the creeper-nails are rust,
The spider is sole denizen;
Even she who voiced those rhymes is dust,
           Gentlemen!

We who met sunrise sanguine-souled,
           Gentlemen,
Are wearing weary. We are old;
These younger press; we feel our rout
Is imminent to Aïdes' den,—
That evening shades are stretching out,
           Gentlemen!

And yet, though ours be failing frames,
           Gentlemen,
So were some others' history names,
Who trode their track light-limbed and fast
As these youth, and not alien
From enterprise, to their long last,
           Gentlemen.

Sophocles, Plato, Socrates,
           Gentlemen,

Pythagoras, Thucydides,
Herodotus, and Homer,—yea,
Clement, Augustin, Origen,
Burnt brightlier towards their setting-day,
        Gentlemen.

And ye, red-lipped and smooth-browed; list,
        Gentlemen;
Much is there waits you we have missed;
Much lore we leave you worth the knowing,
Much, much has lain outside our ken:
Nay, rush not: time serves: we are going,
        Gentlemen.

Gerard Manley Hopkins / 1844–1889

THE WRECK OF THE DEUTSCHLAND

*To the happy memory of five Franciscan Nuns
exiles by the Falk Laws drowned between
midnight and morning of Dec. 7th, 1875*

PART THE FIRST

I

        Thou mastering me
      God! giver of breath and bread;
    World's strand, sway of the sea;
      Lord of living and dead;
Thou hast bound, bones and veins in me, fastened me
        flesh,
And after it almost unmade, what with dread,
    Thy doing: and dost thou touch me afresh?
Over again I feel thy finger and find thee.

II

        I did say yes
      O at lightning and lashed rod;
    Thou heardst me truer than tongue confess
      Thy terror, O Christ, O God;
  Thou knowest the walls, altar and hour and night:
  The swoon of a heart that the sweep and the hurl of thee
        trod
    Hard down with a horror of height:
And the midriff astrain with leaning of, laced with fire of
        stress.

III

      The frown of his face
     Before me, the hurtle of hell
   Behind, where, where was a, where was a place?
     I whirled out wings that spell
 And fled with a fling of the heart to the heart of the Host.
 My heart, but you were dovewinged, I can tell,
    Carrier-witted, I am bold to boast,
To flash from the flame to the flame then, tower from the
        grace to the grace.

IV

       I am soft sift
     In an hourglass—at the wall
   Fast, but mined with a motion, a drift,
     And it crowds and it combs to the fall;
 I steady as a water in a well, to a poise, to a pane,
  But roped with, always, all the way down from the tall
    Fells or flanks of the voel, a vein
Of the gospel proffer, a pressure, a principle, Christ's gift.

V

       I kiss my hand
     To the stars, lovely-asunder
   Starlight, wafting him out of it; and
     Glow, glory in thunder;
 Kiss my hand to the dappled-with-damson west:
 Since, tho' he is under the world's splendour and wonder,
    His mystery must be instressed, stressed;

For I greet him the days I meet him, and bless when I
        understand.

VI

            Not out of his bliss
          Springs the stress felt
      Nor first from heaven (and few know this)
          Swings the stroke dealt—
    Stroke and a stress that stars and storms deliver,
      That guilt is hushed by, hearts are flushed by and melt—
        But it rides time like riding a river
(And here the faithful waver, the faithless fable and miss).

VII

            It dates from day
          Of his going in Galilee;
      Warm-laid grave of a womb-life grey;
          Manger, maiden's knee;
    The dense and the driven Passion, and frightful sweat;
      Thence the discharge of it, there its swelling to be,
        Though felt before, though in high flood yet—
What none would have known of it, only the heart, being
        hard at bay,

VIII

            Is out with it! Oh,
          We lash with the best or worst
      Word last! How a lush-kept plush-capped sloe
          Will, mouthed to flesh-burst,
    Gush!—flush the man, the being with it, sour or sweet,
      Brim, in a flash, full!—Hither then, last or first,
        To hero of Calvary, Christ's feet—
Never ask if meaning it, wanting it, warned of it—men go.

IX

            Be adored among men,
          God, three-numberèd form;
      Wring thy rebel, dogged in den,
          Man's malice, with wrecking and storm.
    Beyond saying sweet, past telling of tongue,
      Thou art lightning and love, I found it, a winter and
        warm;

Father and fondler of heart thou has wrung:
Hast thy dark descending and most art merciful then.

X

          With an anvil-ding
       And with fire in him forge thy will
   Or rather, rather then, stealing as Spring
       Through him, melt him but master him still:
  Whether at once, as once at a crash Paul,
  Or as Austin, a lingering-out swéet skíll,
    Make mercy in all of us, out of us all
Mastery, but be adored, but be adored King.

PART THE SECOND

XI

        'Some find me a sword; some
       The flange and the rail: flame,
  Fang, or flood' goes Death on drum,
     And storms bugle his fame.
  But wé dream we are rooted in earth—Dust!
  Flesh falls within sight of us, we, though our flower the
        same,
    Wave with the meadow, forget that there must
The sour scythe cringe, and the blear share come.

XII

       On Saturday sailed from Bremen,
       American-outward-bound,
   Take settler and seamen, tell men with women,
     Two hundred souls in the round—
  O Father, not under thy feathers nor ever as guessing
  The goal was a shoal, of a fourth the doom to be
        drowned;
    Yet did the dark side of the bay of thy blessing
Not vault them, the millions of rounds of thy mercy not
       reeve even them in?

XIII

       Into the snows she sweeps,
       Hurling the haven behind,

The Deutschland, on Sunday; and so the sky keeps,
    For the infinite air is unkind,
And the sea flint-flake, black-backed in the regular blow,
Sitting Eastnortheast, in cursed quarter, the wind;
    Wiry and white-fiery and whirlwind-swivellèd snow
Spins to the widow-making unchilding unfathering deeps.

XIV

    She drove in the dark to leeward,
        She struck—not a reef or a rock
    But the combs of a smother of sand: night drew her
        Dead to the Kentish Knock;
    And she beat the bank down with her bows and the ride
        of her keel:
    The breakers rolled on her beam with ruinous shock;
        And canvas and compass, the whorl and the wheel
Idle for ever to waft her or wind her with, these she
        endured.

XV

    Hope had grown grey hairs,
        Hope had mourning on,
    Trenched with tears, carved with cares,
        Hope was twelve hours gone;
    And frightful a nightfall folded rueful a day
    Nor rescue, only rocket and lightship, shone,
        And lives at last were washing away:
To the shrouds they took,—they shook in the hurling and
        horrible airs.

XVI

    One stirred from the rigging to save
        The wild woman-kind below,
    With a rope's end round the man, handy and brave—
        He was pitched to his death at a blow,
    For all his dreadnought breast and braids of thew:
    They could tell him for hours, dandled the to and fro
        Through the cobbled foam-fleece, what could he do
With the burl of the fountains of air, buck and the flood of
        the wave?

XVII

> They fought with God's cold—
> And they could not and fell to the deck
> (Crushed them) or water (and drowned them) or
> rolled
> With the sea-romp over the wreck.
> Night roared, with the heart-break hearing a heart-broke
> rabble,
> The woman's wailing, the crying of child without check—
> Till a lioness arose breasting the babble,
> A prophetess towered in the tumult, a virginal tongue told.

XVIII

> Ah, touched in your bower of bone
> Are you! turned for an exquisite smart,
> Have you! make words break from me here all alone,
> Do you!—mother of being in me, heart.
> O unteachably after evil, but uttering truth,
> Why, tears! is it? tears; such a melting, a madrigal start!
> Never-eldering revel and river of youth,
> What can it be, this glee? the good you have there of your
> own?

XIX

> Sister, a sister calling
> A master, her master and mine!—
> And the inboard seas run swirling and hawling;
> The rash smart sloggering brine
> Blinds her; but she that weather sees one thing, one;
> Has one fetch in her: she rears herself to divine
> Ears, and the call of the tall nun
> To the men in the tops and the tackle rode over the storm's
> brawling.

XX

> She was first of a five and came
> Of a coifèd sisterhood.
> (O Deutschland, double a desperate name!
> O world wide of its good!
> But Gertrude, lily, and Luther, are two of a town,

Christ's lily and beast of the waste wood:
  From life's dawn it is drawn down,
Abel is Cain's brother and breasts they have sucked the
      same.)

XXI

      Loathed for a love men knew in them,
        Banned by the land of their birth,
      Rhine refused them. Thames would ruin them;
        Surf, snow, river and earth
    Gnashed: but thou art above, thou Orion of light;
    Thy unchancelling poising palms were weighing the
        worth,
      Thou martyr-master: in thy sight
Storm flakes were scroll-leaved flowers, lily showers—
      sweet heaven was astrew in them.

XXII

      Five! the finding and sake
        And cipher of suffering Christ.
      Mark, the mark is of man's make
        And the word of it Sacrificed.
    But he scores it in scarlet himself on his own bespoken,
    Before-time-taken, dearest prizèd and priced—
      Stigma, signal, cinquefoil token
For lettering of the lamb's fleece, ruddying of the rose-flake.

XXIII

      Joy fall to thee, father Francis,
        Drawn to the Life that died;
      With the gnarls of the nails in thee, niche of the lance,
        his
        Lovescape crucified
    And seal of his seraph-arrival! and these thy daughters
    And five-livèd and leavèd favour and pride,
      Are sisterly sealed in wild waters,
To bathe in his fall-gold mercies, to breathe in his all-
      fire glances.

XXIV

      Away in the loveable west,
        On a pastoral forehead of Wales,

I was under a roof here, I was at rest,
  And they the prey of the gales;
She to the black-about air, to the breaker, the thickly
  Falling flakes, to the throng that catches and quails
   Was calling 'O Christ, Christ, come quickly':
The cross to her she calls Christ to her, christens her wild-
    worst Best.

XXV

   The majesty! what did she mean?
   Breathe, arch and original Breath.
  Is it love in her of the being as her lover had been?
   Breathe, body of lovely Death.
  They were else-minded then, altogether, the men
  Woke thee with a *we are perishing* in the weather of
    Gennesareth.
   Or is it that she cried for the crown then,
The keener to come at the comfort for feeling the
    combating keen?

XXVI

   For how to the heart's cheering
   The down-dugged ground-hugged grey
  Hovers off, the jay-blue heavens appearing
   Of pied and peeled May!
  Blue-beating and hoary-glow height; or night, still higher,
  With belled fire and the moth-soft Milky Way,
   What by your measure is the heaven of desire,
The treasure never eyesight got, nor was ever guessed what
    for the hearing?

XXVII

   No, but it was not these.
   The jading and jar of the cart,
  Time's tasking, it is fathers that asking for ease
   Of the sodden-with-its-sorrowing heart,
  Not danger, electrical horror; then further it finds
  The appealing of the Passion is tenderer in prayer apart:
   Other, I gather, in measure her mind's
Burden, in wind's burly and beat of endragonèd seas.

XXVIII
>   But how shall I . . . make me room there:
>   Reach me a . . . Fancy, come faster—
>   Strike you the sight of it? look at it loom there,
>   Thing that she . . . there then! the Master,
> *Ipse*, the only one, Christ, King, Head:
> He was to cure the extremity where he had cast her;
>   Do, deal, lord it with living and dead;
> Let him ride, her pride, in his triumph, despatch and have
>   done with his doom there.

XXIX
>   Ah! there was a heart right
>   There was single eye!
>   Read the unshapeable shock night
>   And knew the who and the why;
> Wording it how but by him that present and past,
> Heaven and earth are word of, worded by?—
>   The Simon Peter of a soul! to the blast
> Tarpeian-fast, but a blown beacon of light.

XXX
>   Jesu, heart's light,
>   Jesu, maid's son,
>   What was the feast followed the night
>   Thou hadst glory of this nun?—
> Feast of the one woman without stain.
> For so conceivèd, so to conceive thee is done;
>   But here was heart-throe, birth of a brain,
> Word, that heard and kept thee and uttered thee outright.

XXXI
>   Well, she has thee for the pain, for the
>   Patience; but pity of the rest of them!
>   Heart, go and bleed at a bitterer vein for the
>   Comfortless unconfessed of them—
> No not uncomforted: lovely-felicitous Providence
> Finger of a tender of, O of a feathery delicacy, the breast
>   of the
>   Maiden could obey so, be a bell to, ring of it, and
> Startle the poor sheep back! is the shipwrack then a harvest,
>   does tempest carry the grain for thee?

XXXII

       I admire thee, master of the tides,
         Of the Yore-flood, of the year's fall;
    The recurb and the recovery of the gulf's sides,
      The girth of it and the wharf of it and the wall;
Stanching, quenching ocean of a motionable mind;
Ground of being, and granite of it: past all
      Grasp God, throned behind
Death with a sovereignty that heeds but hides, bodes but
        abides;

XXXIII

       With a mercy that outrides
         The all of water, an ark
    For the listener; for the lingerer with a love glides
      Lower than death and the dark;
A vein for the visiting of the past-prayer, pent in prison,
The-last-breath penitent spirits—the uttermost mark
      Our passion-plungèd giant risen,
The Christ of the Father compassionate, fetched in the
        storm of his strides.

XXXIV

       Now burn, new born to the world,
         Doubled-naturèd name,
    The heaven-flung, heart-fleshed, maiden-furled
      Miracle-in-Mary-of-flame,
Mid-numbered He in three of the thunder-throne!
Not a dooms-day dazzle in his coming nor dark as he
        came;
      Kind, but royally reclaiming his own;
A released shower, let flash to the shire, not a lightning of
        fire hard-hurled.

XXXV

       Dame, at our door
         Drowned, and among our shoals,
    Remember us in the roads, the heaven-haven of the
      Reward:
      Our King back, oh, upon English souls!
Let him easter in us, be a dayspring to the dimness of us,
        be a crimson-cresseted east,

More brightening her, rare-dear Britain, as his reign rolls,
    Pride, rose, prince, hero of us, high-priest,
Our hearts' charity's hearth's fire, our thoughts' chivalry's
    throng's Lord.

GOD'S GRANDEUR

The world is charged with the grandeur of God.
    It will flame out, like shining from shook foil;
    It gathers to a greatness, like the ooze of oil
Crushed. Why do men then now not reck his rod?
Generations have trod, have trod, have trod;
    And all is seared with trade; bleared, smeared with toil;
    And wears man's smudge and shares man's smell: the soil
Is bare now, nor can foot feel, being shod.

And for all this, nature is never spent;
    There lives the dearest freshness deep down things;
And though the last lights off the black West went
    Oh, morning, at the brown brink eastward, springs—
Because the Holy Ghost over the bent
    World broods with warm breast and with ah! bright wings.

THE STARLIGHT NIGHT

Look at the stars! look, look up at the skies!
    O look at all the fire-folk sitting in the air!
    The bright boroughs, the circle-citadels there!
Down in dim woods the diamond delves! the elves'-eyes!
The grey lawns cold where gold, where quickgold lies!
    Wind-beat whitebeam! airy abeles set on a flare!
    Flake-doves sent floating forth at a farmyard scare!—
Ah well! it is all a purchase, all is a prize.

Buy then! bid then!—What?—Prayer, patience, alms, vows.
Look, look: a May-mess, like on orchard boughs!
   Look! March-bloom, like on mealed-with-yellow sallows!
These are indeed the barn; withindoors house
The shocks. This piece-bright paling shuts the spouse
   Christ home, Christ and his mother and all his hallows.

SPRING

Nothing is so beautiful as spring—
   When weeds, in wheels, shoot long and lovely and lush;
   Thrush's eggs look little low heavens, and thrush
Through the echoing timber does so rinse and wring
The ear, it strikes like lightnings to hear him sing;
   The glassy peartree leaves and blooms, they brush
   The descending blue; that blue is all in a rush
With richness; the racing lambs too have fair their fling.

What is all this juice and all this joy?
   A strain of the earth's sweet being in the beginning
In Eden garden.—Have, get, before it cloy,
   Before it cloud, Christ, lord, and sour with sinning,
Innocent mind and Mayday in girl and boy,
   Most, O maid's child, thy choice and worthy the winning.

THE WINDHOVER:

To Christ our Lord

I caught this morning morning's minion, king-
   dom of daylight's dauphin, dapple-dawn-drawn Falcon,
     in his riding
Of the rolling level underneath him steady air, and striding
High there, how he rung upon the rein of a wimpling wing
In his ecstasy! then off, off forth on swing,

As a skate's heel sweeps smooth on a bow-bend: the hurl
    and gliding
Rebuffed the big wind. My heart in hiding
Stirred for a bird:—the achieve of, the mastery of the thing!

Brute beauty and valour and act, oh, air, pride, plume, here
    Buckle! AND the fire that breaks from thee then, a billion
Times told lovelier, more dangerous, O my chevalier!

No wonder of it: shéer plód makes plough down sillion
Shine, and blue-bleak embers, ah my dear,
    Fall, gall themselves, and gash gold-vermillion.

PIED BEAUTY

Glory be to God for dappled things—
    For skies of couple-colour as a brinded cow;
        For rose-moles all in stipple upon trout that swim;
Fresh-firecoal chestnut-falls; finches' wings;
    Landscape plotted and pieced—fold, fallow, and plough;
        And áll trádes, their gear and tackle and trim.

All things counter, original, spare, strange;
    Whatever is fickle, freckled (who knows how?)
        With swift, slow; sweet, sour; adazzle, dim;
He fathers-forth whose beauty is past change:
           Praise him.

THE CAGED SKYLARK

As a dare-gale skylark scanted in a dull cage
    Man's mounting spirit in his bone-house, mean house,
        dwells—
    That bird beyond the remembering his free fells;
This in drudgery, day-labouring-out life's age.

Though aloft on turf or perch or poor low stage,
  Both sing sometímes the sweetest, sweetest spells
  Yet both droop deadly sómetimes in their cells
Or wring their barriers in bursts of fear or rage.

Not that the sweet-fowl, song-fowl, needs no rest—
Why, hear him, hear him babble and drop down to his nest,
  But his own nest, wild nest, no prison.

Man's spirit will be flesh-bound when found at best,
But uncumbered: meadow-down is not distressed
  For a rainbow footing it nor he for his bónes rísen.

THE CANDLE INDOORS

Some candle clear burns somewhere I come by.
I muse at how its being puts blissful back
With yellowy moisture mild night's blear-all black,
Or to-fro tender trambeams truckle at the eye.
By that window what task what fingers ply,
I plod wondering, a-wanting, just for lack
Of answer the eagerer a-wanting Jessy or Jack
There God to aggrándise, God to glorify.—

Come you indoors, come home; your fading fire
Mend first and vital candle in close heart's vault:
You there are master, do your own desire;
What hinders? Are you beam-blind, yet to a fault
In a neighbour deft-handed? are you that liar
And, cast by conscience out, spendsavour salt?

FELIX RANDAL

Felix Randal the farrier, O he is dead then? my duty all
    ended,

Who have watched his mould of man, big-boned and
    hardy-handsome
Pining, pining, till time when reason rambled in it and some
Fatal four disorders, fleshed there, all contended?

Sickness broke him. Impatient he cursed at first, but
    mended
Being anointed and all; though a heavenlier heart began
    some
Months earlier, since I had our sweet reprieve and ransom
Tendered to him. Ah well, God rest him all road ever he
    offended!

This seeing the sick endears them to us, us too it endears.
My tongue had taught thee comfort, touch had quenched
    thy tears,
Thy tears that touched my heart, child, Felix, poor Felix
    Randal;

How far from then forethought of, all thy more boisterous
    years,
When thou at the random grim forge, powerful amidst
    peers,
Didst fettle for the great grey dray horse his bright and
    battering sandal!

SPRING AND FALL:

To a Young Child

Márgarét, are you gríeving
Over Goldengrove unleaving?
Leáves, líke the things of man, you
With your fresh thoughts care for, can you?
Áh! ás the heart grows older
It will come to such sights colder
By and by, nor spare a sigh
Though worlds of wanwood leafmeal lie;
And yet you wíll weep and know why.

Now no matter, child, the name:
Sórrow's springs áre the same.
Nor mouth had, no nor mind, expressed
What heart heard of, ghost guessed:
It ís the blight man was born for,
It is Margaret you mourn for.

INVERSNAID

This darksome burn, horseback brown,
His rollrock highroad roaring down,
In coop and in comb the fleece of his foam
Flutes and low to the lake falls home.

A windpuff-bonnet of fáwn-fróth
Turns and twindles over the broth
Of a pool so pitchblack, féll-frówning,
It rounds and rounds Despair to drowning.

Degged with dew, dappled with dew
Are the groins of the braes that the brook treads through,
Wiry heathpacks, flitches of fern,
And the beadbonny ash that sits over the burn.

What would the world be, once bereft
Of wet and of wildness? Let them be left,
O let them be left, wildness and wet;
Long live the weeds and the wilderness yet.

AS KINGFISHERS CATCH FIRE,
DRAGONFLIES DRÁW FLÁME

As kingfishers catch fire, dragonflies dráw fláme;
As tumbled over rim in roundy wells
Stones ring; like each tucked string tells, each hung bell's
Bow swung finds tongue to fling out broad its name;

Each mortal thing does one thing and the same:
Deals out that being indoors each one dwells;
Selves—goes itself; *myself* it speaks and spells;
Crying *Whát I dó is me: for that I came.*

Í say móre: the just man justices;
Kéeps gráce: thát keeps all his goings graces;
Acts in God's eye what in God's eye he is—
Chríst—for Christ plays in ten thousand places,
Lovely in limbs, and lovely in eyes not his
To the Father through the features of men's faces.

THE LEADEN ECHO AND
THE GOLDEN ECHO

Maiden's song from St. Winefred's Well

THE LEADEN ECHO

How to kéep—is there ány any, is there none such, nowhere
      known some, bow or brooch or braid or brace, láce, latch
      or catch or key to keep
Back beauty, keep it, beauty, beauty, beauty, . . . from
      vanishing away?
Ó is there no frowning of these wrinkles, rankèd wrinkles
      deep,
Dówn? no waving off of these most mournful messengers,
      still messengers, sad and stealing messengers of grey?
No there's none, there's none, O no there's none,
Nor can you long be, what you now are, called fair,
Do what you may do, what, do what you may,
And wisdom is early to despair:
Be beginning; since, no, nothing can be done
To keep at bay
Age and age's evils, hoar hair,
Ruck and wrinkle, drooping, dying, death's worst, winding
      sheets, tombs and worms and tumbling to decay;
So be beginning, be beginning to despair.

O there's none; no no no there's none:
Be beginning to despair, to despair,
Despair, despair, despair, despair.

THE GOLDEN ECHO

     Spare!
There ís one, yes I have one (Hush there!);
Only not within seeing of the sun,
Not within the singeing of the strong sun,
Tall sun's tingeing, or treacherous the tainting of the earth's
    air,
Somewhere elsewhere there is ah well where! one,
Óne. Yes I cán tell such a key, I dó know such a place,
Where whatever's prized and passes of us, everything that's
    fresh and fast flying of us, seems to us sweet of us and
    swiftly away with, done away with, undone,
Undone, done with, soon done with, and yet dearly and
    dangerously sweet
Of us, the wimpled-water-dimpled, not-by-morning-matchèd
    face,
The flower of beauty, fleece of beauty, too too apt to, ah! to
    fleet,
Never fleets móre, fastened with the tenderest truth
To its own best being and its loveliness of youth: it is an
    everlastingness of, O it is an all youth!
Come then, your ways and airs and looks, locks, maiden gear,
    gallantry and gaiety and grace,
Winning ways, airs innocent, maiden manners, sweet looks,
    loose locks, long locks, lovelocks, gaygear, going gallant,
    girlgrace—
Resign them, sign them, seal them, send them, motion them
    with breath,
And with sighs soaring, soaring, síghs deliver
Them; beauty-in-the-ghost, deliver it, early now, long before
    death
Give beauty back, beauty, beauty, beauty, back to God,
    beauty's self and beauty's giver.
See; not a hair is, not an eyelash, not the least lash lost; every
    hair
Is, hair of the head, numbered.
Nay, what we had lighthanded left in surly the mere mould

Will have waked and have waxed and have walked with the
    wind what while we slept,
This side, that side hurling a heavyheaded hundredfold
What while we, while we slumbered.
O then, weary then whý should we tread? O why are we so
    haggard at the heart, so care-coiled, care-killed, so
    fagged, so fashed, so cogged, so cumbered,
When the thing we freely fórfeit is kept with fonder a care,
Fonder a care kept than we could have kept it, kept
Far with fonder a care (and we, we should have lost it) finer,
    fonder
A care kept.—Where kept? Do but tell us where kept,
    where.—
Yonder.—What high as that! We follow, now we follow.—
    Yonder, yes yonder, yonder,
Yonder.

SPELT FROM SIBYL'S LEAVES

Earnest, earthless, equal, attuneable, vaulty, voluminous, . . .
    stupendous
Evening strains to be tíme's vást, womb-of-all, home-of-all,
    hearse-of-all night.
Her fond yellow hornlight wound to the west, her wild hollow
    hoarlight hung to the height
Waste; her earliest stars, earl-stars, stárs principal, overbend
    us,
Fíre-féaturing heaven. For earth her being has unbound, her
    dapple is at an end, as-
tray or aswarm, all throughther, in throngs; self ín self steepèd
    and páshed—qúite
Disremembering, dísmémbering áll now. Heart, you round me
    right
With: Óur évening is over us; óur night whélms, whélms, ánd
    will end us.
Only the beak-leaved boughs dragonish damask the tool-
    smooth bleak light; black,
Ever so black on it. Óur tale, O óur oracle; Lét life, wáned,
    ah lét life wind

Off hér once skéined stained véined varíety upon, áll on twó
    spools; párt, pen, páck
Now her áll in twó flocks, twó folds—black, white; right,
    wrong; reckon but, reck but, mind
But thése two; wáre of a wórld where bút these twó tell, each
    off the óther; of a rack
Where, selfwrung, selfstrung, sheathe-and shelterless, thóughts
    agaínst thoughts ín groans grínd.

NO WORST, THERE IS NONE.
PITCHED PAST PITCH OF GRIEF

No worst, there is none. Pitched past pitch of grief,
More pangs will, schooled at forepangs, wilder wring.
Comforter, where, where is your comforting?
Mary, mother of us, where is your relief?
My cries heave, herds-long; huddle in a main, a chief
Woe, world-sorrow; on an age-old anvil wince and sing—
Then lull, then leave off. Fury had shrieked 'No lingering!
Let me be fell: force I must be brief'.

   O the mind, mind has mountains; cliffs of fall
Frightful, sheer, no-man-fathomed. Hold them cheap
May who ne'er hung there. Nor does long our small
Durance deal with that steep or deep. Here! creep,
Wretch, under a comfort serves in a whirlwind: all
Life death does end and each day dies with sleep.

MY OWN HEART LET ME
MORE HAVE PITY ON

My own heart let me more have pity on; let
Me live to my sad self hereafter kind,
Charitable; not live this tormented mind
With this tormented mind tormenting yet.
   I cast for comfort I can no more get

By groping round my comfortless, than blind
Eyes in their dark can day or thirst can find
Thirst's all-in-all in all a world of wet.

Soul, self; come, poor Jackself, I do advise
You, jaded, let be; call off thoughts awhile
Elsewhere; leave comfort root-room; let joy size
At God knows when to God knows what; whose smile
's not wrung, see you; unforeseen times rather—as skies
Betweenpie mountains—lights a lovely mile.

THOU ART INDEED JUST, LORD, IF I CONTEND

*Justus quidem tu es, Domine, si disputem tecum: verumtamen
justa loquar ad te: Quare via impiorum prosperatur? &c.*

Thou art indeed just, Lord, if I contend
With thee; but, sir, so what I plead is just.
Why do sinners' ways prosper? and why must
Disappointment all I endeavour end?
    Wert thou my enemy, O thou my friend,
How wouldst thou worse, I wonder, than thou dost
Defeat, thwart me? Oh, the sots and thralls of lust
Do in spare hours more thrive than I that spend,
Sir, life upon thy cause. See, banks and brakes
Now, leavèd how thick! lacèd they are again
With fretty chervil, look, and fresh wind shakes
Them; birds build—but not I build; no, but strain,
Time's eunuch, and not breed one work that wakes.
Mine, O thou lord of life, send my roots rain.

Robert Bridges / 1844–1930

I HEARD A LINNET COURTING

I heard a linnet courting
   His lady in the spring:
His mates were idly sporting,
   Nor stayed to hear him sing
      His song of love.—
I fear my speech distorting
      His tender love.

The phrases of his pleading
   Were full of young delight;
And she that gave him heeding
   Interpreted aright
      His gay, sweet notes,—
So sadly marred in the reading,—
      His tender notes.

And when he ceased, the hearer
   Awaited the refrain,
Till swiftly perching nearer
   He sang his song again,
      His pretty song:—
Would that my verse spake clearer
      His tender song!

Ye happy, airy creatures!
   That in the merry spring
Think not of what misfeatures
   Or cares the year may bring;
      But unto love
Resign your simple natures,
      To tender love.

A PASSER-BY

Whither, O splendid ship, thy white sails crowding,
    Leaning across the bosom of the urgent West,
That fearest nor sea rising, nor sky clouding,
    Whither away, fair rover, and what thy quest?
    Ah! soon, when Winter has all our vales opprest,
When skies are cold and misty, and hail is hurling,
    Wilt thóu glíde on the blue Pacific, or rest
In a summer haven asleep, thy white sails furling.

I there before thee, in the country that well thou knowest,
    Already arrived am inhaling the odorous air:
I watch thee enter unerringly where thou goest,
    And anchor queen of the strange shipping there,
    Thy sails for awnings spread, thy masts bare:
Nor is aught from the foaming reef to the snowcapped,
        grandest
    Peak, that is over the feathery palms more fair
Than thou, so upright, so stately, and still thou standest.

And yet, O splendid ship, unhailed and nameless,
    I know not if, aiming a fancy, I rightly divine
That thou hast a purpose joyful, a courage blameless,
    Thy port assured in a happier land than mine.
    But for all I have given thee, beauty enough is thine,
As thou, aslant with trim tackle and shrouding,
    From the proud nostril curve of a prow's line
In the offing scatterest foam, thy white sails crowding.

LONDON SNOW

When men were all asleep the snow came flying,
In large white flakes falling on the city brown,
Stealthily and perpetually settling and loosely lying,
    Hushing the latest traffic of the drowsy town;

Deadening, muffling, stifling its murmurs failing;
Lazily and incessantly floating down and down:
   Silently sifting and veiling road, roof and railing;
Hiding difference, making unevenness even,
Into angles and crevices softly drifting and sailing.
   All night it fell, and when full inches seven
It lay in the depth of its uncompacted lightness,
The clouds blew off from a high and frosty heaven;
   And all woke earlier for the unaccustomed brightness
Of the winter dawning, the strange unheavenly glare:
The eye marvelled—marvelled at the dazzling whiteness;
   The ear hearkened to the stillness of the solemn air;
No sound of wheel rumbling nor of foot falling,
And the busy morning cries came thin and spare.
   Then boys I heard, as they went to school, calling,
They gathered up the crystal manna to freeze
Their tongues with tasting, their hands with snowballing;
   Or rioted in a drift, plunging up to the knees;
Or peering up from under the white-mossed wonder,
'O look at the trees!' they cried, 'O look at the trees!'
   With lessened load a few carts creak and blunder,
Following along the white deserted way,
A country company long dispersed asunder:
   When now already the sun, in pale display
Standing by Paul's high dome, spread forth below
His sparkling beams, and awoke the stir of the day.
   For now doors open, and war is waged with the snow;
And trains of sombre men, past tale of number,
Tread long brown paths, as toward their toil they go:
   But even for them awhile no cares encumber
Their minds diverted; the daily word is unspoken,
The daily thoughts of labour and sorrow slumber
At the sight of the beauty that greets them, for the charm
     they have broken.

ON A DEAD CHILD

Perfect little body, without fault or stain on thee,
    With promise of strength and manhood full and fair!
        Though cold and stark and bare,
The bloom and the charm of life doth awhile remain on
    thee.

Thy mother's treasure wert thou;—alas! no longer
    To visit her heart with wondrous joy; to be
        Thy father's pride;—ah, he
Must gather his faith together, and his strength make
    stronger.

To me, as I move thee now in the last duty,
    Dost thou with a turn or gesture anon respond;
        Startling my fancy fond
With a chance attitude of the head, a freak of beauty.

Thy hand clasps, as 'twas wont, my finger, and holds it:
    But the grasp is the clasp of Death, heartbreaking and
        stiff;
        Yet feels to my hand as if
'Twas still thy will, thy pleasure and trust that enfolds it.

So I lay thee there, thy sunken eyelids closing,—
    Go lie thou there in thy coffin, thy last little bed!—
        Propping thy wise, sad head,
Thy firm, pale hands across thy chest disposing.

So quiet! doth the change content thee?—Death, whither
    hath he taken thee?
    To a world, do I think, that rights the disaster of this?
        The vision of which I miss,
Who weep for the body, and wish but to warm thee and
    awaken thee?

Ah! little at best can all our hopes avail us
    To lift this sorrow, or cheer us, when in the dark.
        Unwilling, alone we embark,

And the things we have seen and have known and have
    heard of, fail us.

THE PHILOSOPHER TO
HIS MISTRESS

Because thou canst not see,
Because thou canst not know
The black and hopeless woe
That hath encompassed me:
Because, should I confess
The thought of my despair
My words would wound thee less
Than swords can hurt the air:

Because with thee I seem
As one invited near
To taste the faery cheer
Of spirits in a dream;
Of whom he knoweth nought
Save that they vie to make
All motion, voice and thought
A pleasure for his sake:

Therefore more sweet and strange
Has been the mystery
Of thy long love to me,
That doth not quit, nor change,
Nor tax my solemn heart,
That kisseth in a gloom,
Knowing not who thou art
That givest, nor to whom.

Therefore the tender touch
Is more; more dear the smile:
And thy light words beguile
My wisdom overmuch:
And O with swiftness fly

The fancies of my song
To happy worlds, where I
Still in thy love belong.

THE IDLE LIFE I LEAD

The idle life I lead
Is like a pleasant sleep,
Wherein I rest and heed
The dreams that by me sweep.

And still of all my dreams
In turn so swiftly past,
Each in its fancy seems
A nobler than the last.

And every eve I say,
Noting my step in bliss,
That I have known no day
In all my life like this.

THE STORM IS OVER, THE LAND HUSHES TO REST

The storm is over, the land hushes to rest:
The tyrannous wind, its strength fordone,
Is fallen back in the west
To couch with the sinking sun.
The last clouds fare
With fainting speed, and their thin streamers fly
In melting drifts of the sky.
Already the birds in the air
Appear again; the rooks return to their haunt,
And one by one,
Proclaiming aloud their care,
Renew their peaceful chant.

Torn and shattered the trees their branches again reset,
They trim afresh the fair
Few green and golden leaves withheld from the storm,
And awhile will be handsome yet.
To-morrow's sun shall caress
Their remnant of loveliness:
In quiet days for a time
Sad Autumn lingering warm
Shall humour their faded prime.

But ah! the leaves of summer that lie on the ground!
What havoc! The laughing timbrels of June,
That curtained the birds' cradles, and screened their song.
That sheltered the cooing doves at noon,
Of airy fans the delicate throng,—
Torn and scattered around:
Far out afield they lie,
In the watery furrows die,
In grassy pools of the flood they sink and drown,
Green-golden, orange, vermilion, golden and brown,
The high year's flaunting crown
Shattered and trampled down.

The day is done: the tired land looks for night:
She prays to the night to keep
In peace her nerves of delight:
While silver mist upstealeth silently,
And the broad cloud-driving moon in the clear sky
Lifts o'er the firs her shining shield,
And in her tranquil light
Sleep falls on forest and field.
Sée! sléep hath fallen: the trees are asleep:
The night is come. The land is wrapt in sleep.

NIGHTINGALES

Beautiful must be the mountains whence ye come,
And bright in the fruitful valleys the streams, wherefrom
Ye learn your song:

Where are those starry woods? O might I wander there,
  Among the flowers, which in that heavenly air
      Bloom the year long!

  Nay, barren are those mountains and spent the streams:
  Our song is the voice of desire, that haunts our dreams,
      A throe of the heart,
Whose pining visions dim, forbidden hopes profound,
  No dying cadence nor long sigh can sound,
      For all our art.

  Alone, aloud in the raptured ear of men
  We pour our dark nocturnal secret; and then,
      As night is withdrawn
From these sweet-springing meads and bursting boughs of
      May,
  Dream, while the innumerable choir of day
      Welcome the dawn.

A. E. Housman / 1859–1936

LOVELIEST OF TREES, THE CHERRY NOW

Loveliest of trees, the cherry now
Is hung with bloom along the bough,
And stands about the woodland ride
Wearing white for Eastertide.

Now, of my threescore years and ten,
Twenty will not come again,
And take from seventy springs a score,
It only leaves me fifty more.

And since to look at things in bloom
Fifty springs are little room,
About the woodlands I will go
To see the cherry hung with snow.

REVEILLE

Wake: the silver dusk returning
  Up the beach of darkness brims,
And the ship of sunrise burning
  Strands upon the eastern rims.

Wake: the vaulted shadow shatters,
  Trampled to the floor it spanned,
And the tent of night in tatters
  Straws the sky-pavilioned land.

Up, lad, up, 'tis late for lying:
  Hear the drums of morning play;
Hark, the empty highways crying
  'Who'll beyond the hills away?'

Towns and countries woo together,
  Forelands beacon, belfries call;
Never lad that trod on leather
  Lived to feast his heart with all.

Up, lad: thews that lie and cumber
  Sunlit pallets never thrive;
Morns abed and daylight slumber
  Were not meant for man alive.

Clay lies still, but blood's a rover;
  Breath's a ware that will not keep.
Up, lad: when the journey's over
  There'll be time enough to sleep.

WHEN I WAS ONE-AND-TWENTY

When I was one-and-twenty
  I heard a wise man say,
'Give crowns and pounds and guineas
  But not your heart away;

Give pearls away and rubies
   But keep your fancy free.'
But I was one-and-twenty,
   No use to talk to me.

When I was one-and-twenty
   I heard him say again,
'The heart out of the bosom
   Was never given in vain;
'Tis paid with sighs a plenty
   And sold for endless rue.'
And I am two-and-twenty,
   And oh, 'tis true, 'tis true.

TO AN ATHLETE DYING YOUNG

The time you won your town the race
We chaired you through the market-place;
Man and boy stood cheering by,
And home we brought you shoulder-high.

To-day, the road all runners come,
Shoulder-high we bring you home,
And set you at your threshold down,
Townsman of a stiller town.

Smart lad, to slip betimes away
From fields where glory does not stay
And early though the laurel grows
It withers quicker than the rose.

Eyes the shady night has shut
Cannot see the record cut,
And silence sounds no worse than cheers
After earth has stopped the ears:

Now you will not swell the rout
Of lads that wore their honours out,

Runners whom renown outran
And the name died before the man.

So set, before its echoes fade,
The fleet foot on the sill of shade,
And hold to the low lintel up
The still-defended challenge-cup.

And round that early-laurelled head
Will flock to gaze the strengthless dead
And find unwithered on its curls
The garland briefer than a girl's.

IS MY TEAM PLOUGHING

'Is my team ploughing,
    That I was used to drive
And hear the harness jingle
    When I was man alive?'

Ay, the horses trample,
    The harness jingles now;
No change though you lie under
    The land you used to plough.

'Is football playing
    Along the river shore,
With lads to chase the leather,
    Now I stand up no more?'

Ay, the ball is flying,
    The lads play heart and soul;
The goal stands up, the keeper
    Stands up to keep the goal.

'Is my girl happy,
    That I thought hard to leave,
And has she tired of weeping
    As she lies down at eve?'

Ay, she lies down lightly,
    She lies not down to weep:
Your girl is well contented.
    Be still, my lad, and sleep.

'Is my friend hearty,
    Now I am thin and pine,
And has he found to sleep in
    A better bed than mine?'

Yes, lad, I lie easy,
    I lie as lads would choose;
I cheer a dead man's sweetheart,
    Never ask me whose.

INTO MY HEART AN AIR
THAT KILLS

Into my heart an air that kills
    From yon far country blows:
What are those blue remembered hills,
    What spires, what farms are those?

That is the land of lost content,
    I see it shining plain,
The happy highways where I went
    And cannot come again.

WITH RUE MY HEART IS LADEN

With rue my heart is laden
    For golden friends I had,
For many a rose-lipt maiden
    And many a lightfoot lad.

By brooks too broad for leaping
   The lightfoot boys are laid;
The rose-lipt girls are sleeping
   In fields where roses fade.

TERENCE, THIS IS STUPID STUFF

'Terence, this is stupid stuff:
You eat your victuals fast enough;
There can't be much amiss, 'tis clear,
To see the rate you drink your beer.
But oh, good Lord, the verse you make,
It gives a chap the belly-ache.
The cow, the old cow, she is dead;
It sleeps well, the horned head:
We poor lads, 'tis our turn now
To hear such tunes as killed the cow.
Pretty friendship 'tis to rhyme
Your friends to death before their time
Moping melancholy mad:
Come, pipe a tune to dance to, lad.'

   Why, if 'tis dancing you would be,
There's brisker pipes than poetry.
Say, for what were hop-yards meant,
Or why was Burton built on Trent?
Oh many a peer of England brews
Livelier liquor than the Muse,
And malt does more than Milton can
To justify God's ways to man.
Ale, man, ale's the stuff to drink
For fellows whom it hurts to think:
Look into the pewter pot
To see the world as the world's not.
And faith, 'tis pleasant till 'tis past:
The mischief is that 'twill not last.
Oh I have been to Ludlow fair
And left my necktie God knows where,

And carried half-way home, or near,
Pints and quarts of Ludlow beer:
Then the world seemed none so bad,
And I myself a sterling lad;
And down in lovely muck I've lain,
Happy till I woke again.
Then I saw the morning sky:
Heigho, the tale was all a lie;
The world, it was the old world yet,
I was I, my things were wet,
And nothing now remained to do
But begin the game anew.

Therefore, since the world has still
Much good, but much less good than ill,
And while the sun and moon endure
Luck's a chance, but trouble's sure,
I'd face it as a wise man would,
And train for ill and not for good.
'Tis true, the stuff I bring for sale
Is not so brisk a brew as ale:
Out of a stem that scored the hand
I wrung it in a weary land.
But take it: if the smack is sour,
The better for the embittered hour;
It should do good to heart and head
When your soul is in my soul's stead;
And I will friend you, if I may,
In the dark and cloudy day.

There was a king reigned in the East:
There, when kings will sit to feast,
They get their fill before they think
With poisoned meat and poisoned drink.
He gathered all that springs to birth
From the many-venomed earth;
First a little, thence to more,
He sampled all her killing store;
And easy, smiling, seasoned sound,
Sate the king when healths went round.
They put arsenic in his meat
And stared aghast to watch him eat;

They poured strychnine in his cup
And shook to see him drink it up:
They shook, they stared as white's their shirt:
Them it was their poison hurt.
—I tell the tale that I heard told.
Mithridates, he died old.

I HOED AND TRENCHED
AND WEEDED

I hoed and trenched and weeded,
    And took the flowers to fair:
I brought them home unheeded;
    The hue was not the wear.

So up and down I sow them
    For lads like me to find,
When I shall lie below them,
    A dead man out of mind.

Some seed the birds devour,
    And some the season mars,
But here and there will flower
    The solitary stars,

And fields will yearly bear them
    As light-leaved spring comes on,
And luckless lads will wear them
    When I am dead and gone.

COULD MAN BE DRUNK FOR EVER

Could man be drunk for ever
    With liquor, love, or fights,
Lief should I rouse at morning
    And lief lie down of nights.

But men at whiles are sober
   And think by fits and starts,
And if they think, they fasten
   Their hands upon their hearts.

THE NIGHT IS FREEZING FAST

The night is freezing fast,
   To-morrow comes December;
      And winterfalls of old
Are with me from the past;
   And chiefly I remember
      How Dick would hate the cold.

Fall, winter, fall; for he,
   Prompt hand and headpiece clever,
      Has woven a winter robe,
And made of earth and sea
   His overcoat for ever,
      And wears the turning globe.

TELL ME NOT HERE, IT NEEDS NOT SAYING

Tell me not here, it needs not saying,
   What tune the enchantress plays
In aftermaths of soft September
   Or under blanching mays,
For she and I were long acquainted
   And I knew all her ways.

On russet floors, by waters idle,
   The pine lets fall its cone;
The cuckoo shouts all day at nothing
   In leafy dells alone;

And traveller's joy beguiles in autumn
    Hearts that have lost their own.

On acres of the seeded grasses
    The changing burnish heaves;
Or marshalled under moons of harvest
    Stand still all night the sheaves;
Or beeches strip in storms for winter
    And stain the wind with leaves.

Possess, as I possessed a season,
    The countries I resign,
Where over elmy plains the highway
    Would mount the hills and shine,
And full of shade the pillared forest
    Would murmur and be mine.

For nature, heartless, witless nature,
    Will neither care nor know
What stranger's feet may find the meadow
    And trespass there and go,
Nor ask amid the dews of morning
    If they are mine or no.

I DID NOT LOSE MY HEART IN SUMMER'S EVEN

I did not lose my heart in summer's even,
    When roses to the moonrise burst apart:
When plumes were under heel and lead was flying,
    In blood and smoke and flame I lost my heart.

I lost it to a soldier and a foeman,
    A chap that did not kill me, but he tried;
That took the sabre straight and took it striking,
    And laughed and kissed his hand to me and died.

William Butler Yeats / 1865–1939

THE LAKE ISLE OF INNISFREE

I will arise and go now, and go to Innisfree,
And a small cabin build there, of clay and wattles made:
Nine bean rows will I have there, a hive for the honey-bee,
And live alone in the bee-loud glade.

And I shall have some peace there, for peace comes dropping
    slow,
Dropping from the veils of the morning to where the cricket
    sings;
There midnight's all a glimmer, and noon a purple glow,
And evening full of the linnet's wings.

I will arise and go now, for always night and day
I hear lake water lapping with low sounds by the shore;
While I stand on the roadway, or on the pavements grey,
I hear it in the deep heart's core.

WHEN YOU ARE OLD

When you are old and grey and full of sleep,
And nodding by the fire, take down this book,
And slowly read, and dream of the soft look
Your eyes had once, and of their shadows deep;

How many loved your moments of glad grace,
And loved your beauty with love false or true,
But one man loved the pilgrim soul in you,
And loved the sorrows of your changing face;

And bending down beside the glowing bars,
Murmur, a little sadly, how Love fled
And paced upon the mountains overhead
And hid his face amid a crowd of stars.

TO A FRIEND WHOSE WORK
HAS COME TO NOTHING

Now all the truth is out,
Be secret and take defeat
From any brazen throat,
For how can you compete,
Being honour bred, with one
Who, were it proved he lies,
Were neither shamed in his own
Nor in his neighbours' eyes?
Bred to a harder thing
Than Triumph, turn away
And like a laughing string
Whereon mad fingers play
Amid a place of stone,
Be secret and exult,
Because of all things known
That is most difficult.

A COAT

I made my song a coat
Covered with embroideries
Out of old mythologies
From heel to throat;
But the fools caught it,
Wore it in the world's eyes
As though they'd wrought it.

Song, let them take it,
For there's more enterprise
In walking naked.

AN IRISH AIRMAN FORESEES
HIS DEATH

I know that I shall meet my fate
Somewhere among the clouds above;
Those that I fight I do not hate,
Those that I guard I do not love;
My country is Kiltartan Cross,
My countrymen Kiltartan's poor,
No likely end could bring them loss
Or leave them happier than before.
Nor law, nor duty bade me fight,
Nor public men, nor cheering crowds,
A lonely impulse of delight
Drove to this tumult in the clouds;
I balanced all, brought all to mind,
The years to come seemed waste of breath,
A waste of breath the years behind
In balance with this life, this death.

EASTER 1916

I have met them at close of day
Coming with vivid faces
From counter or desk among grey
Eighteenth-century houses.
I have passed with a nod of the head
Or polite meaningless words,
Or have lingered awhile and said
Polite meaningless words,
And thought before I had done

Of a mocking tale or a gibe
To please a companion
Around the fire at the club,
Being certain that they and I
But lived where motley is worn:
All changed, changed utterly:
A terrible beauty is born.

That woman's days were spent
In ignorant good-will,
Her nights in argument
Until her voice grew shrill.
What voice more sweet than hers
When, young and beautiful,
She rode to harriers?
This man had kept a school
And rode our wingèd horse;
This other his helper and friend
Was coming into his force;
He might have won fame in the end,
So sensitive his nature seemed,
So daring and sweet his thought.
This other man I had dreamed
A drunken, vainglorious lout.
He had done most bitter wrong
To some who are near my heart,
Yet I number him in the song;
He, too, has resigned his part
In the casual comedy;
He, too, has been changed in his turn,
Transformed utterly:
A terrible beauty is born.

Hearts with one purpose alone
Through summer and winter seem
Enchanted to a stone
To trouble the living stream.
The horse that comes from the road,
The rider, the birds that range
From cloud to tumbling cloud,
Minute by minute they change;

A shadow of cloud on the stream
Changes minute by minute;
A horse-hoof slides on the brim,
And a horse plashes within it;
The long-legged moor-hens dive,
And hens to moor-cocks call;
Minute by minute they live:
The stone's in the midst of all.

Too long a sacrifice
Can make a stone of the heart.
O when may it suffice?
That is Heaven's part, our part
To murmur name upon name,
As a mother names her child
When sleep at last has come
On limbs that had run wild.
What is it but nightfall?
No, no, not night but death;
Was it needless death after all?
For England may keep faith
For all that is done and said.
We know their dream; enough
To know they dreamed and are dead;
And what if excess of love
Bewildered them till they died?
I write it out in a verse—
MacDonagh and MacBride
And Connolly and Pearse
Now and in time to be,
Wherever green is worn,
Are changed, changed utterly:
A terrible beauty is born.

THE SECOND COMING

Turning and turning in the widening gyre
The falcon cannot hear the falconer;

Things fall apart; the centre cannot hold;
Mere anarchy is loosed upon the world,
The blood-dimmed tide is loosed, and everywhere
The ceremony of innocence is drowned;
The best lack all conviction, while the worst
Are full of passionate intensity.

Surely some revelation is at hand;
Surely the Second Coming is at hand.
The Second Coming! Hardly are those words out
When a vast image out of *Spiritus Mundi*
Troubles my sight: somewhere in sands of the desert
A shape with lion body and the head of a man,
A gaze blank and pitiless as the sun,
Is moving its slow thighs, while all about it
Reel shadows of the indignant desert birds.
The darkness drops again; but now I know
That twenty centuries of stony sleep
Were vexed to nightmare by a rocking cradle,
And what rough beast, its hour come round at last,
Slouches towards Bethlehem to be born?

A PRAYER FOR MY DAUGHTER

Once more the storm is howling, and half hid
Under this cradle-hood and coverlid
My child sleeps on. There is no obstacle
But Gregory's wood and one bare hill
Whereby the haystack- and roof-levelling wind,
Bred on the Atlantic, can be stayed;
And for an hour I have walked and prayed
Because of the great gloom that is in my mind.

I have walked and prayed for this young child an hour
And heard the sea-wind scream upon the tower,
And under the arches of the bridge, and scream
In the elms above the flooded stream;
Imagining in excited reverie

That the future years had come,
Dancing to a frenzied drum,
Out of the murderous innocence of the sea.

May she be granted beauty and yet not
Beauty to make a stranger's eye distraught,
Or hers before a looking-glass, for such,
Being made beautiful overmuch,
Consider beauty a sufficient end,
Lose natural kindness and maybe
The heart-revealing intimacy
That chooses right, and never find a friend.

Helen being chosen found life flat and dull
And later had much trouble from a fool,
While that great Queen, that rose out of the spray,
Being fatherless could have her way
Yet chose a bandy-leggèd smith for man.
It's certain that fine women eat
A crazy salad with their meat
Whereby the Horn of Plenty is undone.

In courtesy I'd have her chiefly learned;
Hearts are not had as a gift but hearts are earned
By those that are not entirely beautiful;
Yet many, that have played the fool
For beauty's very self, has charm made wise,
And many a poor man that has roved,
Loved and thought himself beloved,
From a glad kindness cannot take his eyes.

May she become a flourishing hidden tree
That all her thoughts may like the linnet be,
And have no business but dispensing round
Their magnanimities of sound,
Nor but in merriment begin a chase,
Nor but in merriment a quarrel.
O may she live like some green laurel
Rooted in one dear perpetual place.

My mind, because the minds that I have loved,
The sort of beauty that I have approved,

Prosper but little, has dried up of late,
Yet knows that to be choked with hate
May well be of all evil chances chief.
If there's no hatred in a mind
Assault and battery of the wind
Can never tear the linnet from the leaf.

An intellectual hatred is the worst,
So let her think opinions are accursed.
Have I not seen the loveliest woman born
Out of the mouth of Plenty's horn,
Because of her opinionated mind
Barter that horn and every good
By quiet natures understood
For an old bellows full of angry wind?

Considering that, all hatred driven hence,
The soul recovers radical innocence
And learns at last that it is self-delighting,
Self-appeasing, self-affrighting,
And that its own sweet will is Heaven's will;
She can, though every face should scowl
And every windy quarter howl
Or every bellows burst, be happy still.

And may her bridegroom bring her to a house
Where all's accustomed, ceremonious;
For arrogance and hatred are the wares
Peddled in the thoroughfares.
How but in custom and in ceremony
Are innocence and beauty born?
Ceremony's a name for the rich horn,
And custom for the spreading laurel tree.

SAILING TO BYZANTIUM

I

That is no country for old men. The young
In one another's arms, birds in the trees
—Those dying generations—at their song,
The salmon-falls, the mackerel-crowded seas,

Fish, flesh, or fowl, commend all summer long
Whatever is begotten, born, and dies.
Caught in that sensual music all neglect
Monuments of unageing intellect.

II

An aged man is but a paltry thing,
A tattered coat upon a stick, unless
Soul clap its hands and sing, and louder sing
For every tatter in its mortal dress,
Nor is there singing school but studying
Monuments of its own magnificence;
And therefore I have sailed the seas and come
To the holy city of Byzantium.

III

O sages standing in God's holy fire
As in the gold mosaic of a wall,
Come from the holy fire, perne in a gyre,
And be the singing-masters of my soul.
Consume my heart away; sick with desire
And fastened to a dying animal
It knows not what it is; and gather me
Into the artifice of eternity.

IV

Once out of nature I shall never take
My bodily form from any natural thing,
But such a form as Grecian goldsmiths make
Of hammered gold and gold enamelling
To keep a drowsy Emperor awake;
Or set upon a golden bough to sing
To lords and ladies of Byzantium
Of what is past, or passing, or to come.

THE TOWER

I

What shall I do with this absurdity—
O heart, O troubled heart—this caricature,

Decrepit age that has been tied to me
As to a dog's tail?
                    Never had I more
Excited, passionate, fantastical
Imagination, nor an ear and eye
That more expected the impossible—
No, not in boyhood when with rod and fly,
Or the humbler worm, I climbed Ben Bulben's back
And had the livelong summer day to spend.
It seems that I must bid the Muse go pack,
Choose Plato and Plotinus for a friend
Until imagination, ear and eye,
Can be content with argument and deal
In abstract things; or be derided by
A sort of battered kettle at the heel.

II

I pace upon the battlements and stare
On the foundations of a house, or where
Tree, like a sooty finger, starts from the earth;
And send imagination forth
Under the day's declining beam, and call
Images and memories
From ruin or from ancient trees,
For I would ask a question of them all.

Beyond that ridge lived Mrs. French, and once
When every silver candlestick or sconce
Lit up the dark mahogany and the wine,
A serving-man, that could divine
That most respected lady's every wish,
Ran and with the garden shears
Clipped an insolent farmer's ears
And brought them in a little covered dish.

Some few remembered still when I was young
A peasant girl commended by a song,
Who'd lived somewhere upon that rocky place,
And praised the colour of her face,
And had the greater joy in praising her,
Remembering that, if walked she there,

Farmers jostled at the fair
So great a glory did the song confer.

And certain men, being maddened by those rhymes,
Or else by toasting her a score of times,
Rose from the table and declared it right
To test their fancy by their sight;
But they mistook the brightness of the moon
For the prosaic light of day—
Music had driven their wits astray—
And one was drowned in the great bog of Cloone.

Strange, but the man who made the song was blind;
Yet, now I have considered it, I find
That nothing strange; the tragedy began
With Homer that was a blind man,
And Helen has all living hearts betrayed.
O may the moon and sunlight seem
One inextricable beam.
For if I triumph I must make men mad.

And I myself created Hanrahan
And drove him drunk or sober through the dawn
From somewhere in the neighbouring cottages.
Caught by an old man's juggleries
He stumbled, tumbled, fumbled to and fro
And had but broken knees for hire
And horrible splendour of desire;
I thought it all out twenty years ago:

Good fellows shuffled cards in an old bawn;
And when that ancient ruffian's turn was on
He so bewitched the cards under his thumb
That all but the one card became
A pack of hounds and not a pack of cards,
And that he changed into a hare.
Hanrahan rose in frenzy there
And followed up those baying creatures towards—

O towards I have forgotten what—enough!
I must recall a man that neither love

Nor music nor an enemy's clipped ear
Could, he was so harried, cheer;
A figure that has grown so fabulous
There's not a neighbour left to say
When he finished his dog's day:
An ancient bankrupt master of this house.
Before that ruin came, for centuries,
Rough men-at-arms, cross-gartered to the knees
Or shod in iron, climbed the narrow stairs,
And certain men-at-arms there were
Whose images, in the Great Memory stored,
Come with loud cry and panting breast
To break upon a sleeper's rest
While their great wooden dice beat on the board.

As I would question all, come all who can;
Come old, necessitous, half-mounted man;
And bring beauty's blind rambling celebrant;
The red man the juggler sent
Through God-forsaken meadows; Mrs. French,
Gifted with so fine an ear;
The man drowned in a bog's mire,
When mocking Muses chose the country wench.

Did all old men and women, rich and poor,
Who trod upon these rocks or passed this door,
Whether in public or in secret rage
As I do now against old age?
But I have found an answer in those eyes
That are impatient to be gone;
Go therefore; but leave Hanrahan,
For I need all his mighty memories.

Old lecher with a love on every wind,
Bring up out of that deep considering mind
All that you have discovered in the grave,
For it is certain that you have
Reckoned up every unforeknown, unseeing
Plunge, lured by a softening eye,
Or by a touch or a sigh,
Into the labyrinth of another's being;

Does the imagination dwell the most
Upon a woman won or a woman lost?
If on the lost, admit you turned aside
From a great labyrinth out of pride,
Cowardice, some silly over-subtle thought
Or anything called conscience once;
And that if memory recur, the sun's
Under eclipse and the day blotted out.

III

It is time that I wrote my will;
I choose upstanding men
That climb the streams until
The fountain leap, and at dawn
Drop their cast at the side
Of dripping stone; I declare
They shall inherit my pride,
The pride of people that were
Bound neither to Cause nor to State,
Neither to slaves that were spat on,
Nor to the tyrants that spat,
The people of Burke and of Grattan
That gave, though free to refuse—
Pride, like that of the morn,
When the headlong light is loose,
Or that of the fabulous horn,
Or that of the sudden shower
When all streams are dry,
Or that of the hour
When the swan must fix his eye
Upon a fading gleam,
Float out upon a long
Last reach of glittering stream
And there sing his last song.
And I declare my faith:
I mock Plotinus' thought
And cry in Plato's teeth,
Death and life were not
Till man made up the whole,
Made lock, stock and barrel
Out of his bitter soul,

Aye, sun and moon and star, all,
And further add to that
That, being dead, we rise,
Dream and so create
Translunar Paradise.
I have prepared my peace
With learned Italian things
And the proud stones of Greece,
Poet's imaginings
And memories of love,
Memories of the words of women,
All those things whereof
Man makes a superhuman
Mirror-resembling dream.

As at the loophole there
The daws chatter and scream,
And drop twigs layer upon layer.
When they have mounted up,
The mother bird will rest
On their hollow top,
And so warm her wild nest.

I leave both faith and pride
To young upstanding men
Climbing the mountain-side,
That under bursting dawn
They may drop a fly;
Being of that metal made
Till it was broken by
This sedentary trade.

Now shall I make my soul,
Compelling it to study
In a learned school
Till the wreck of body,
Slow decay of blood,
Testy delirium
Or dull decrepitude,
Or what worse evil come—
The death of friends, or death

Of every brilliant eye
That made a catch in the breath—
Seem but the clouds of the sky
When the horizon fades,
Or a bird's sleepy cry
Among the deepening shades.

LEDA AND THE SWAN

A sudden blow: the great wings beating still
Above the staggering girl, her thighs caressed
By the dark webs, her nape caught in his bill,
He holds her helpless breast upon his breast.

How can those terrified vague fingers push
The feathered glory from her loosening thighs?
And how can body, laid in that white rush,
But feel the strange heart beating where it lies?

A shudder in the loins engenders there
The broken wall, the burning roof and tower
And Agamemnon dead.
                              Being so caught up,
So mastered by the brute blood of the air,
Did she put on his knowledge with his power
Before the indifferent beak could let her drop?

AMONG SCHOOL CHILDREN

I

I walk through the long schoolroom questioning;
A kind old nun in a white hood replies;
The children learn to cipher and to sing,
To study reading-books and history,
To cut and sew, be neat in everything
In the best modern way—the children's eyes

In momentary wonder stare upon
A sixty-year-old smiling public man.

II

I dream of a Ledaean body, bent
Above a sinking fire, a tale that she
Told of a harsh reproof, or trivial event
That changed some childish day to tragedy—
Told, and it seemed that our two natures blent
Into a sphere from youthful sympathy,
Or else, to alter Plato's parable,
Into the yolk and white of the one shell.

III

And thinking of that fit of grief or rage
I look upon one child or t'other there
And wonder if she stood so at that age—
For even daughters of the swan can share
Something of every paddler's heritage—
And had that colour upon cheek or hair,
And thereupon my heart is driven wild:
She stands before me as a living child.

IV

Her present image floats into the mind—
Did Quattrocento finger fashion it
Hollow of cheek as though it drank the wind
And took a mess of shadows for its meat?
And I though never of Ledaean kind
Had pretty plumage once—enough of that,
Better to smile on all that smile, and show
There is a comfortable kind of old scarecrow.

V

What youthful mother, a shape upon her lap
Honey of generation had betrayed,
And that must sleep, shriek, struggle to escape
As recollection or the drug decide,
Would think her son, did she but see that shape
With sixty or more winters on its head,
A compensation for the pang of his birth,
Or the uncertainty of his setting forth?

VI

Plato thought nature but a spume that plays
Upon a ghostly paradigm of things;
Solider Aristotle played the taws
Upon the bottom of a king of kings;
World-famous golden-thighed Pythagoras
Fingered upon a fiddle-stick or strings
What a star sang and careless Muses heard:
Old clothes upon old sticks to scare a bird.

VII

Both nuns and mothers worship images,
But those the candles light are not as those
That animate a mother's reveries,
But keep a marble or a bronze repose.
And yet they too break hearts—O Presences
That passion, piety or affection knows,
And that all heavenly glory symbolise—
O self-born mockers of man's enterprise;

VIII

Labour is blossoming or dancing where
The body is not bruised to pleasure soul,
Nor beauty born out of its own despair,
Nor blear-eyed wisdom out of midnight oil.
O chestnut-tree, great-rooted blossomer,
Are you the leaf, the blossom or the bole?
O body swayed to music, O brightening glance,
How can we know the dancer from the dance?

A DIALOGUE OF SELF AND SOUL

I

My Soul. I summon to the winding ancient stair;
    Set all your mind upon the steep ascent,
    Upon the broken, crumbling battlement,
    Upon the breathless starlit air,
    Upon the star that marks the hidden pole;
    Fix every wandering thought upon

That quarter where all thought is done:
Who can distinguish darkness from the soul?

My Self. The consecrated blade upon my knees
Is Sato's ancient blade, still as it was,
Still razor-keen, still like a looking-glass
Unspotted by the centuries;
That flowering, silken, old embroidery, torn
From some court-lady's dress and round
The wooden scabbard bound and wound,
Can, tattered, still protect, faded adorn.

My Soul. Why should the imagination of a man
Long past his prime remember things that are
Emblematical of love and war?
Think of ancestral night that can,
If but imagination scorn the earth
And intellect its wandering
To this and that and t'other thing,
Deliver from the crime of death and birth.

My Self. Montashigi, third of his family, fashioned it
Five hundred years ago, about it lie
Flowers from I know not what embroidery—
Heart's purple—and all these I set
For emblems of the day against the tower
Emblematical of the night,
And claim as by a soldier's right
A charter to commit the crime once more.

My Soul. Such fullness in that quarter overflows
And falls into the basin of the mind
That man is stricken deaf and dumb and blind,
For intellect no longer knows
Is from the *Ought*, or *Knower* from the *Known*—
That is to say, ascends to Heaven;
Only the dead can be forgiven;
But when I think of that my tongue's a stone.

II

My Self. A living man is blind and drinks his drop.
What matter if the ditches are impure?

What matter if I live it all once more?
Endure that toil of growing up;
The ignominy of boyhood; the distress
Of boyhood changing into man;
The unfinished man and his pain
Brought face to face with his own clumsiness;

The finished man among his enemies?—
How in the name of Heaven can he escape
That defiling and disfigured shape
The mirror of malicious eyes
Casts upon his eyes until at last
He thinks that shape must be his shape?
And what's the good of an escape
If honour find him in the wintry blast?

I am content to live it all again
And yet again, if it be life to pitch
Into the frog-spawn of a blind man's ditch,
A blind man battering blind men;
Or into that most fecund ditch of all,
The folly that man does
Or must suffer, if he woos
A proud woman not kindred of his soul.

I am content to follow to its source
Every event in action or in thought;
Measure the lot; forgive myself the lot!
When such as I cast out remorse
So great a sweetness flows into the breast
We must laugh and we must sing,
We are blest by everything,
Everything we look upon is blest.

FOR ANNE GREGORY

'Never shall a young man,
Thrown into despair

By those great honey-coloured
Ramparts at your ear,
Love you for yourself alone
And not your yellow hair.'

'But I can get a hair-dye
And set such colour there,
Brown, or black, or carrot,
That young men in despair
May love me for myself alone
And not my yellow hair.'

'I heard an old religious man
But yesternight declare
That he had found a text to prove
That only God, my dear,
Could love you for yourself alone
And not your yellow hair.'

BYZANTIUM

The unpurged images of day recede;
The Emperor's drunken soldiery are abed;
Night resonance recedes, night-walkers' song
After great cathedral gong;
A starlit or a moonlit dome disdains
All that man is,
All mere complexities,
The fury and the mire of human veins.

Before me floats an image, man or shade,
Shade more than man, more image than a shade;
For Hades' bobbin bound in mummy-cloth
May unwind the winding path;
A mouth that has no moisture and no breath
Breathless mouths may summon;
I hail the superhuman;
I call it death-in-life and life-in-death.

Miracle, bird or golden handiwork,
More miracle than bird or handiwork,
Planted on the star-lit golden bough,
Can like the cocks of Hades crow,
Or, by the moon embittered, scorn aloud
In glory of changeless metal
Common bird or petal
And all complexities of mire or blood.

At midnight on the Emperor's pavement flit
Flames that no faggot feeds, nor steel has lit,
Nor storm disturbs, flames begotten of flame,
Where blood-begotten spirits come
And all complexities of fury leave,
Dying into a dance,
An agony of trance,
An agony of flame that cannot singe a sleeve.

Astraddle on the dolphin's mire and blood,
Spirit after spirit! The smithies break the flood,
The golden smithies of the Emperor!
Marbles of the dancing floor
Break bitter furies of complexity,
Those images that yet
Fresh images beget,
That dolphin-torn, that gong-tormented sea.

CRAZY JANE AND THE BISHOP

Bring me to the blasted oak
That I, midnight upon the stroke,
(*All find safety in the tomb.*)
May call down curses on his head
Because of my dear Jack that's dead.
Coxcomb was the least he said:
The solid man and the coxcomb.

Nor was he Bishop when his ban
Banished Jack the Journeyman,
(*All find safety in the tomb.*)

Nor so much as parish priest,
Yet he, an old book in his fist,
Cried that we lived like beast and beast:
The solid man and the coxcomb.

The Bishop has a skin, God knows,
Wrinkled like the foot of a goose,
(*All find safety in the tomb.*)
Nor can he hide in holy black
The heron's hunch upon his back,
But a birch-tree stood my Jack:
The solid man and the coxcomb.

Jack had my virginity,
And bids me to the oak, for he
(*All find safety in the tomb.*)
Wanders out into the night
And there is shelter under it,
But should that other come, I spit:
The solid man and the coxcomb.

AFTER LONG SILENCE

Speech after long silence; it is right,
All other lovers being estranged or dead,
Unfriendly lamplight hid under its shade,
The curtains drawn upon unfriendly night,
That we descant and yet again descant
Upon the supreme theme of Art and Song:
Bodily decrepitude is wisdom; young
We loved each other and were ignorant.

LAPIS LAZULI

for Harry Clifton

I have heard that hysterical women say
They are sick of the palette and fiddle-bow,

Of poets that are always gay,
For everybody knows or else should know
That if nothing drastic is done
Aeroplane and Zeppelin will come out,
Pitch like King Billy bomb-balls in
Until the town lie beaten flat.

All perform their tragic play,
There struts Hamlet, there is Lear,
That's Ophelia, that Cordelia;
Yet they, should the last scene be there,
The great stage curtain about to drop,
If worthy their prominent part in the play,
Do not break up their lines to weep.
They know that Hamlet and Lear are gay;
Gaiety transfiguring all that dread.
All men have aimed at, found and lost;
Black out; Heaven blazing into the head:
Tragedy wrought to its uttermost.
Though Hamlet rambles and Lear rages,
And all the drop-scenes drop at once
Upon a hundred thousand stages,
It cannot grow by an inch or an ounce.

On their own feet they came, or on shipboard,
Camel-back, horse-back, ass-back, mule-back,
Old civilisations put to the sword.
Then they and their wisdom went to rack:
No handiwork of Callimachus,
Who handled marble as if it were bronze,
Made draperies that seemed to rise
When sea-wind swept the corner, stands;
His long lamp-chimney shaped like the stem
Of a slender palm, stood but a day;
All things fall and are built again,
And those that build them again are gay.

Two Chinamen, behind them a third,
Are carved in lapis lazuli,
Over them flies a long-legged bird,
A symbol of longevity;

The third, doubtless a serving-man,
Carries a musical instrument.

Every discoloration of the stone,
Every accidental crack or dent,
Seems a water-course or an avalanche,
Or lofty slope where it still snows
Though doubtless plum or cherry-branch
Sweetens the little half-way house
Those Chinamen climb towards, and I
Delight to imagine them seated there;
There, on the mountain and the sky,
On all the tragic scene they stare.
One asks for mournful melodies;
Accomplished fingers begin to play.
Their eyes mid many wrinkles, their eyes,
Their ancient, glittering eyes, are gay.

NEWS FOR THE DELPHIC ORACLE

I

There all the golden codgers lay,
There the silver dew,
And the great water sighed for love,
And the wind sighed too.
Man-picker Niamh leant and sighed
By Oisin on the grass;
There sighed amid his choir of love
Tall Pythagoras.
Plotinus came and looked about,
The salt-flakes on his breast,
And having stretched and yawned awhile
Lay sighing like the rest.

II

Straddling each a dolphin's back
And steadied by a fin,
Those Innocents re-live their death,
Their wounds open again.

The ecstatic waters laugh because
Their cries are sweet and strange,
Through their ancestral patterns dance,
And the brute dolphins plunge
Until, in some cliff-sheltered bay
Where wades the choir of love
Proffering its sacred laurel crowns,
They pitch their burdens off.

III

Slim adolescence that a nymph has stripped,
Peleus on Thetis stares.
Her limbs are delicate as an eyelid,
Love has blinded him with tears;
But Thetis' belly listens.
Down the mountain walls
From where Pan's cavern is
Intolerable music falls.
Foul goat-head, brutal arm appear,
Belly, shoulder, bum,
Flash fishlike; nymphs and satyrs
Copulate in the foam.

LONG-LEGGED FLY

That civilisation may not sink,
Its great battle lost,
Quiet the dog, tether the pony
To a distant post;
Our master Caesar is in the tent
Where the maps are spread,
His eyes fixed upon nothing,
A hand under his head.
Like a long-legged fly upon the stream
His mind moves upon silence.

That the topless towers be burnt
And men recall that face,

Move most gently if move you must
In this lonely place.
She thinks, part woman, three parts a child,
That nobody looks; her feet
Practise a tinker shuffle
Picked up on a street.
Like a long-legged fly upon the stream
Her mind moves upon silence.

That girls at puberty may find
The first Adam in their thought,
Shut the door of the Pope's chapel,
Keep those children out.
There on that scaffolding reclines
Michael Angelo.
With no more sound than the mice make
His hand moves to and fro.
Like a long-legged fly upon the stream
His mind moves upon silence.

JOHN KINSELLA'S LAMENT FOR
MRS. MARY MOORE

A bloody and a sudden end,
    Gunshot or a noose,
For Death who takes what man would keep,
    Leaves what man would lose.
He might have had my sister,
    My cousins by the score,
But nothing satisfied the fool
    But my dear Mary Moore,
None other knows what pleasures man
    At table or in bed.
What shall I do for pretty girls
    Now my old bawd is dead?

Though stiff to strike a bargain,
    Like an old Jew man,

Her bargain struck we laughed and talked
    And emptied many a can;
And O! but she had stories,
    Though not for the priest's ear,
To keep the soul of man alive,
    Banish age and care,
And being old she put a skin
    On everything she said.
What shall I do for pretty girls
    Now my old bawd is dead?

The priests have got a book that says
    But for Adam's sin
Eden's Garden would be there
    And I there within.
No expectation fails there,
    No pleasing habit ends,
No man grows old, no girl grows cold,
    But friends walk by friends.
Who quarrels over halfpennies
    That plucks the trees for bread?
What shall I do for pretty girls
    Now my old bawd is dead?

THE APPARITIONS

Because there is safety in derision
I talked about an apparition,
I took no trouble to convince,
Or seem plausible to a man of sense,
Distrustful of that popular eye
Whether it be bold or sly.
Fifteen apparitions have I seen;
The worst a coat upon a coat-hanger.

I have found nothing half so good
As my long-planned half solitude,
Where I can sit up half the night
With some friend that has the wit

Not to allow his looks to tell
When I am unintelligible.
Fifteen apparitions have I seen;
The worst a coat upon a coat-hanger.

When a man grows old his joy
Grows more deep day after day,
His empty heart is full at length,
But he has need of all that strength
Because of the increasing Night
That opens her mystery and fright.
Fifteen apparitions have I seen;
The worst a coat upon a coat-hanger.

CUCHULAIN COMFORTED

A man that had six mortal wounds, a man
Violent and famous, strode among the dead;
Eyes stared out of the branches and were gone.

Then certain Shrouds that muttered head to head
Came and were gone. He leant upon a tree
As though to meditate on wounds and blood.

A Shroud that seemed to have authority
Among those bird-like things came, and let fall
A bundle of linen. Shrouds by two and three

Came creeping up because the man was still.
And thereupon that linen-carrier said:
'Your life can grow much sweeter if you will

'Obey our ancient rule and make a shroud;
Mainly because of what we only know
The rattle of those arms makes us afraid.

'We thread the needles' eyes, and all we do
All must together do.' That done, the man
Took up the nearest and began to sew.

'Now must we sing and sing the best we can,
But first you must be told our character:
Convicted cowards all, by kindred slain

'Or driven from home and left to die in fear.'
They sang, but had nor human tunes nor words,
Though all was done in common as before;

They had changed their throats and had the throats of birds.

UNDER BEN BULBEN

I

Swear by what the sages spoke
Round the Mareotic Lake
That the Witch of Atlas knew,
Spoke and set the cocks a-crow.

Swear by those horsemen, by those women
Complexion and form prove superhuman,
That pale, long-visaged company
That air in immortality
Completeness of their passions won;
Now they ride the wintry dawn
Where Ben Bulben sets the scene.

Here's the gist of what they mean.

II

Many times man lives and dies
Between his two eternities,
That of race and that of soul,
And ancient Ireland knew it all.
Whether man die in his bed
Or the rifle knocks him dead,
A brief parting from those dear
Is the worst man has to fear.
Though grave-diggers' toil is long,
Sharp their spades, their muscles strong,

They but thrust their buried men
Back in the human mind again.

III

You that Mitchel's prayer have heard,
'Send war in our time, O Lord!'
Know that when all words are said
And a man is fighting mad,
Something drops from eyes long blind,
He completes his partial mind,
For an instant stands at ease,
Laughs aloud, his heart at peace.
Even the wisest man grows tense
With some sort of violence
Before he can accomplish fate,
Know his work or choose his mate.

IV

Poet and sculptor, do the work,
Nor let the modish painter shirk
What his great forefathers did,
Bring the soul of man to God.
Make him fill the cradles right.

Measurement began our might:
Forms a stark Egyptian thought,
Forms that gentler Phidias wrought.
Michael Angelo left a proof
On the Sistine Chapel roof,
Where but half-awakened Adam
Can disturb globe-trotting Madam
Till her bowels are in heat,
Proof that there's a purpose set
Before the secret working mind:
Profane perfection of mankind.

Quattrocento put in paint
On backgrounds for a God or Saint
Gardens where a soul's at ease;
Where everything that meets the eye,
Flowers and grass and cloudless sky,

Resemble forms that are or seem
When sleepers wake and yet still dream,
And when it's vanished still declare,
With only bed and bedstead there,
That heavens had opened.

                              Gyres run on;
When that greater dream had gone
Calvert and Wilson, Blake and Claude,
Prepared a rest for the people of God,
Palmer's phrase, but after that
Confusion fell upon our thought.

v

Irish poets, learn your trade,
Sing whatever is well made,
Scorn the sort now growing up
All out of shape from toe to top,
Their unremembering hearts and heads
Base-born products of base beds.
Sing the peasantry, and then
Hard-riding country gentlemen,
The holiness of monks, and after
Porter-drinkers' randy laughter;
Sing the lords and ladies gay
That were beaten into the clay
Through seven heroic centuries;
Cast your mind on other days
That we in coming days may be
Still the indomitable Irishry.

vi

Under bare Ben Bulben's head
In Drumcliff churchyard Yeats is laid.
An ancestor was rector there
Long years ago, a church stands near,
By the road an ancient cross.
No marble, no conventional phrase;
On limestone quarried near the spot
By his command these words are cut:

> *Cast a cold eye*
> *On life, on death.*
> *Horseman, pass by!*

Edwin Arlington Robinson / 1869–1935

LUKE HAVERGAL

Go to the western gate, Luke Havergal,
There where the vines cling crimson on the wall,
And in the twilight wait for what will come.
The leaves will whisper there of her, and some,
Like flying words, will strike you as they fall;
But go, and if you listen she will call.
Go to the western gate, Luke Havergal—
Luke Havergal.

No, there is not a dawn in eastern skies
To rift the fiery night that's in your eyes;
But there, where western glooms are gathering,
The dark will end the dark, if anything:
God slays Himself with every leaf that flies,
And hell is more than half of paradise.
No, there is not a dawn in eastern skies—
In eastern skies.

Out of a grave I come to tell you this.
Out of a grave I come to quench the kiss
That flames upon your forehead with a glow
That blinds you to the way that you must go.
Yes, there is yet one way to where she is,
Bitter, but one that faith may never miss.
Out of a grave I come to tell you this—
To tell you this.

There is the western gate, Luke Havergal,
There are the crimson leaves upon the wall.
Go, for the winds are tearing them away,—
Nor think to riddle the dead words they say,
Nor any more to feel them as they fall;

But go, and if you trust her she will call.
There is the western gate, Luke Havergal—
Luke Havergal.

RICHARD CORY

Whenever Richard Cory went down town,
We people on the pavement looked at him:
He was a gentleman from sole to crown,
Clean favored, and imperially slim.

And he was always quietly arrayed,
And he was always human when he talked;
But still he fluttered pulses when he said,
"Good-morning," and he glittered when he walked.

And he was rich—yes, richer than a king—
And admirably schooled in every grace:
In fine, we thought that he was everything
To make us wish that we were in his place.

So on we worked, and waited for the light,
And went without the meat, and cursed the bread;
And Richard Cory, one calm summer night,
Went home and put a bullet through his head.

GEORGE CRABBE

Give him the darkest inch your shelf allows,
Hide him in lonely garrets, if you will,—
But his hard, human pulse is throbbing still
With the sure strength that fearless truth endows.
In spite of all fine science disavows,
Of his plain excellence and stubborn skill
There yet remains what fashion cannot kill,
Though years have thinned the laurel from his brows.

Whether or not we read him, we can feel
From time to time the vigor of his name
Against us like a finger for the shame
And emptiness of what our souls reveal
In books that are as altars where we kneel
To consecrate the flicker, not the flame.

CREDO

I cannot find my way: there is no star
In all the shrouded heavens anywhere;
And there is not a whisper in the air
Of any living voice but one so far
That I can hear it only as a bar
Of lost, imperial music, played when fair
And angel fingers wove, and unaware,
Dead leaves to garlands where no roses are.

No, there is not a glimmer, nor a call,
For one that welcomes, welcomes when he fears,
The black and awful chaos of the night;
For through it all—above, beyond it all—
I know the far-sent message of the years,
I feel the coming glory of the Light.

THE   MASTER *

Lincoln

A flying word from here and there
Had sown the name at which we sneered,
But soon the name was everywhere,
To be reviled and then revered:
A presence to be loved and feared,
We cannot hide it, or deny

* Supposed to have been written not long after the Civil War.

That we, the gentlemen who jeered,
May be forgotten by and by.

He came when days were perilous
And hearts of men were sore beguiled;
And having made his note of us,
He pondered and was reconciled.
Was ever master yet so mild
As he, and so untamable?
We doubted, even when he smiled,
Not knowing what he knew so well.

He knew that undeceiving fate
Would shame us whom he served unsought;
He knew that he must wince and wait—
The jest of those for whom he fought;
He knew devoutly what he thought
Of us and of our ridicule;
He knew that we must all be taught
Like little children in a school.

We gave a glamour to the task
That he encountered and saw through,
But little of us did he ask,
And little did we ever do.
And what appears if we review
The season when we railed and chaffed?
It is the face of one who knew
That we were learning while we laughed.

The face that in our vision feels
Again the venom that we flung,
Transfigured to the world reveals
The vigilance to which we clung.
Shrewd, hallowed, harassed, and among
The mysteries that are untold,
The face we see was never young
Nor could it wholly have been old.

For he, to whom we had applied
Our shopman's test of age and worth,

Was elemental when he died,
As he was ancient at his birth:
The saddest among kings of earth,
Bowed with a galling crown, this man
Met rancor with a cryptic mirth,
Laconic—and Olympian.

The love, the grandeur, and the fame
Are bounded by the world alone;
The calm, the smouldering, and the flame
Of awful patience were his own:
With him they are forever flown
Past all our fond self-shadowings,
Wherewith we cumber the Unknown
As with inept, Icarian wings.

For we were not as other men:
'Twas ours to soar and his to see;
But we are coming down again,
And we shall come down pleasantly;
Nor shall we longer disagree
On what it is to be sublime,
But flourish in our perigee
And have one Titan at a time.

MINIVER CHEEVY

Miniver Cheevy, child of scorn,
   Grew lean while he assailed the seasons;
He wept that he was ever born,
   And he had reasons.

Miniver loved the days of old
   When swords were bright and steeds were prancing;
The vision of a warrior bold
   Would set him dancing.

Miniver sighed for what was not,
   And dreamed, and rested from his labors;

He dreamed of Thebes and Camelot,
  And Priam's neighbors.

Miniver mourned the ripe renown
  That made so many a name so fragrant;
He mourned Romance, now on the town,
  And Art, a vagrant.

Miniver loved the Medici,
  Albeit he had never seen one;
He would have sinned incessantly
  Could he have been one.

Miniver cursed the commonplace
  And eyed a khaki suit with loathing;
He missed the mediæval grace
  Of iron clothing.

Miniver scorned the gold he sought,
  But sore annoyed was he without it;
Miniver thought, and thought, and thought,
  And thought about it.

Miniver Cheevy, born too late,
  Scratched his head and kept on thinking;
Miniver coughed, and called it fate,
  And kept on drinking.

FOR A DEAD LADY

No more with overflowing light
Shall fill the eyes that now are faded,
Nor shall another's fringe with night
Their woman-hidden world as they did.
No more shall quiver down the days
The flowing wonder of her ways,
Whereof no language may requite
The shifting and the many-shaded.

The grace, divine, definitive,
Clings only as a faint forestalling;
The laugh that love could not forgive
Is hushed, and answers to no calling;
The forehead and the little ears
Have gone where Saturn keeps the years;
The breast where roses could not live
Has done with rising and with falling.

The beauty, shattered by the laws
That have creation in their keeping,
No longer trembles at applause,
Or over children that are sleeping;
And we who delve in beauty's lore
Know all that we have known before
Of what inexorable cause
Makes Time so vicious in his reaping.

FLAMMONDE

The man Flammonde, from God knows where,
With firm address and foreign air,
With news of nations in his talk
And something royal in his walk,
With glint of iron in his eyes,
But never doubt, nor yet surprise,
Appeared, and stayed, and held his head
As one by kings accredited.

Erect, with his alert repose
About him, and about his clothes,
He pictured all tradition hears
Of what we owe to fifty years.
His cleansing heritage of taste
Paraded neither want nor waste;
And what he needed for his fee
To live, he borrowed graciously.

He never told us what he was,
Or what mischance, or other cause,
Had banished him from better days
To play the Prince of Castaways.
Meanwhile he played surpassing well
A part, for most, unplayable;
In fine, one pauses, half afraid
To say for certain that he played.

For that, one may as well forego
Conviction as to yes or no;
Nor can I say just how intense
Would then have been the difference
To several, who, having striven
In vain to get what he was given,
Would see the stranger taken on
By friends not easy to be won.

Moreover, many a malcontent
He soothed and found munificent;
His courtesy beguiled and foiled
Suspicion that his years were soiled;
His mien distinguished any crowd,
His credit strengthened when he bowed;
And women, young and old, were fond
Of looking at the man Flammonde.

There was a woman in our town
On whom the fashion was to frown;
But while our talk renewed the tinge
Of a long-faded scarlet fringe,
The man Flammonde saw none of that,
And what he saw we wondered at—
That none of us, in her distress,
Could hide or find our littleness.

There was a boy that all agreed
Had shut within him the rare seed
Of learning. We could understand,
But none of us could lift a hand.
The man Flammonde appraised the youth,
And told a few of us the truth;

And thereby, for a little gold,
A flowered future was unrolled.

There were two citizens who fought
For years and years, and over nought;
They made life awkward for their friends,
And shortened their own dividends.
The man Flammonde said what was wrong
Should be made right; nor was it long
Before they were again in line,
And had each other in to dine.

And these I mention are but four
Of many out of many more.
So much for them. But what of him—
So firm in every look and limb?
What small satanic sort of kink
Was in his brain? What broken link
Withheld him from the destinies
That came so near to being his?

What was he, when we came to sift
His meaning, and to note the drift
Of incommunicable ways
That make us ponder while we praise?
Why was it that his charm revealed
Somehow the surface of a shield?
What was it that we never caught?
What was he, and what was he not?

How much it was of him we met
We cannot ever know; nor yet
Shall all he gave us quite atone
For what was his, and his alone;
Nor need we now, since he knew best,
Nourish an ethical unrest:
Rarely at once will nature give
The power to be Flammonde and live.

We cannot know how much we learn
From those who never will return,
Until a flash of unforeseen

Remembrance falls on what has been.
We've each a darkening hill to climb;
And this is why, from time to time
In Tilbury Town, we look beyond
Horizons for the man Flammonde.

CASSANDRA

I heard one who said: "Verily,
    What word have I for children here?
Your Dollar is your only Word,
    The wrath of it your only fear.

"You build it altars tall enough
    To make you see, but you are blind;
You cannot leave it long enough
    To look before you or behind.

"When Reason beckons you to pause,
    You laugh and say that you know best;
But what it is you know, you keep
    As dark as ingots in a chest.

"You laugh and answer, 'We are young;
    O leave us now, and let us grow.'—
Not asking how much more of this
    Will Time endure or Fate bestow.

"Because a few complacent years
    Have made your peril of your pride,
Think you that you are to go on
    Forever pampered and untried?

"What lost eclipse of history,
    What bivouac of the marching stars,
Has given the sign for you to see
    Millenniums and last great wars?

"What unrecorded overthrow
  Of all the world has ever known,
Or ever been, has made itself
  So plain to you, and you alone?

"Your Dollar, Dove and Eagle make
  A Trinity that even you
Rate higher than you rate yourselves;
  It pays, it flatters, and it's new.

"And though your very flesh and blood
  Be what your Eagle eats and drinks,
You'll praise him for the best of birds,
  Not knowing what the Eagle thinks.

"The power is yours, but not the sight;
  You see not upon what you tread;
You have the ages for your guide,
  But not the wisdom to be led.

"Think you to tread forever down
  The merciless old verities?
And are you never to have eyes
  To see the world for what it is?

"Are you to pay for what you have
  With all you are?"—No other word
We caught, but with a laughing crowd
  Moved on. None heeded, and few heard.

EROS   TURANNOS

She fears him, and will always ask
  What fated her to choose him;
She meets in his engaging mask
  All reasons to refuse him;
But what she meets and what she fears
Are less than are the downward years,

Drawn slowly to the foamless weirs
  Of age, were she to lose him.

Between a blurred sagacity
  That once had power to sound him,
And Love, that will not let him be
  The Judas that she found him,
Her pride assuages her almost,
As if it were alone the cost.—
He sees that he will not be lost,
  And waits and looks around him.

A sense of ocean and old trees
  Envelops and allures him;
Tradition, touching all he sees,
  Beguiles and reassures him;
And all her doubts of what he says
Are dimmed with what she knows of days—
Till even prejudice delays
  And fades, and she secures him.

The falling leaf inaugurates
  The reign of her confusion:
The pounding wave reverberates
  The dirge of her illusion;
And home, where passion lived and died,
Becomes a place where she can hide,
While all the town and harbor side
  Vibrate with her seclusion.

We tell you, tapping on our brows,
  The story as it should be,—
As if the story of a house
  Were told, or ever could be;
We'll have no kindly veil between
Her visions and those we have seen,—
As if we guessed what hers have been,
  Or what they are or would be.

Meanwhile we do no harm; for they
  That with a god have striven,

Not hearing much of what we say,
   Take what the god has given;
Though like waves breaking it may be
Or like a changed familiar tree,
Or like a stairway to the sea
   Where down the blind are driven.

THE DARK HILLS

Dark hills at evening in the west,
Where sunset hovers like a sound
Of golden horns that sang to rest
Old bones of warriors under ground,
Far now from all the bannered ways
Where flash the legions of the sun,
You fade—as if the last of days
Were fading, and all wars were done.

MR. FLOOD'S PARTY

Old Eben Flood, climbing alone one night
Over the hill between the town below
And the forsaken upland hermitage
That held as much as he should ever know
On earth again of home, paused warily.
The road was his with not a native near;
And Eben, having leisure, said aloud,
For no man else in Tilbury Town to hear:

"Well, Mr. Flood, we have the harvest moon
Again, and we may not have many more;
The bird is on the wing, the poet says,
And you and I have said it here before.
Drink to the bird." He raised up to the light
The jug that he had gone so far to fill,

And answered huskily: "Well, Mr. Flood,
Since you propose it, I believe I will."

Alone, as if enduring to the end
A valiant armor of scarred hopes outworn,
He stood there in the middle of the road
Like Roland's ghost winding a silent horn.
Below him, in the town among the trees,
Where friends of other days had honored him,
A phantom salutation of the dead
Rang thinly till old Eben's eyes were dim.

Then, as a mother lays her sleeping child
Down tenderly, fearing it may awake,
He set the jug down slowly at his feet
With trembling care, knowing that most things break;
And only when assured that on firm earth
It stood, as the uncertain lives of men
Assuredly did not, he paced away,
And with his hand extended paused again:

"Well, Mr. Flood, we have not met like this
In a long time; and many a change has come
To both of us, I fear, since last it was
We had a drop together. Welcome home!"
Convivially returning with himself,
Again he raised the jug up to the light;
And with an acquiescent quaver said:
"Well, Mr. Flood, if you insist, I might."

"Only a very little, Mr. Flood—
For auld lang syne. No more, sir; that will do."
So, for the time, apparently it did,
And Eben evidently thought so too;
For soon amid the silver loneliness
Of night he lifted up his voice and sang,
Secure, with only two moons listening,
Until the whole harmonious landscape rang—

"For auld lang syne." The weary throat gave out,
The last word wavered, and the song was done.

He raised again the jug regretfully
And shook his head, and was again alone.
There was not much that was ahead of him,
And there was nothing in the town below—
Where strangers would have shut the many doors
That many friends had opened long ago.

Edgar Lee Masters / 1869–1950

THE HILL

Where are Elmer, Herman, Bert, Tom and Charley,
The weak of will, the strong of arm, the clown, the boozer,
      the fighter?
All, all, are sleeping on the hill.

One passed in a fever,
One was burned in a mine,
One was killed in a brawl,
One died in a jail,
One fell from a bridge toiling for children and wife—
All, all are sleeping, sleeping, sleeping on the hill.

Where are Ella, Kate, Mag, Lizzie and Edith,
The tender heart, the simple soul, the loud, the proud, the
      happy one?—
All, all, are sleeping on the hill.

One died in shameful child-birth,
One of a thwarted love,
One at the hands of a brute in a brothel,
One of a broken pride, in the search for heart's desire,
One after life in far-away London and Paris
Was brought to her little space by Ella and Kate and Mag—
All, all are sleeping, sleeping, sleeping on the hill.

Where are Uncle Isaac and Aunt Emily,
And old Towny Kincaid and Sevigne Houghton,
And Major Walker who had talked
With venerable men of the revolution?—
All, all, are sleeping on the hill.

They brought them dead sons from the war,
And daughters whom life had crushed,
And their children fatherless, crying—
All, all are sleeping, sleeping, sleeping on the hill.

Where is Old Fiddler Jones
Who played with life all his ninety years,
Braving the sleet with bared breast,
Drinking, rioting, thinking neither of wife nor kin,
Nor gold, nor love, nor heaven?
Lo! he babbles of the fish-frys of long ago,
Of the horse-races of long ago at Clary's Grove,
Of what Abe Lincoln said
One time at Springfield.

CARL   HAMBLIN

The press of the Spoon River *Clarion* was wrecked,
And I was tarred and feathered,
For publishing this on the day the Anarchists were hanged
    in Chicago:
"I saw a beautiful woman with bandaged eyes
Standing on the steps of a marble temple.
Great multitudes passed in front of her,
Lifting their faces to her imploringly.
In her left hand she held a sword.
She was brandishing the sword,
Sometimes striking a child, again a laborer,
Again a slinking woman, again a lunatic.
In her right hand she held a scale;
Into the scale pieces of gold were tossed

By those who dodged the strokes of the sword.
A man in a black gown read from a manuscript:
'She is no respecter of persons.'
Then a youth wearing a red cap
Leaped to her side and snatched away the bandage.
And lo, the lashes had been eaten away
From the oozy eye-lids;
The eye-balls were seared with a milky mucus;
The madness of a dying soul
Was written on her face—
But the multitude saw why she wore the bandage."

HENRY C. CALHOUN

I reached the highest place in Spoon River,
But through what bitterness of spirit!
The face of my father, sitting speechless,
Child-like, watching his canaries,
And looking at the court-house window
Of the county judge's room,
And his admonitions to me to seek
My own in life, and punish Spoon River
To avenge the wrong the people did him,
Filled me with furious energy
To seek for wealth and seek for power.
But what did he do but send me along
The path that leads to the grove of the Furies?
I followed the path and I tell you this:
On the way to the grove you'll pass the Fates,
Shadow-eyed, bent over their weaving.
Stop for a moment, and if you see
The thread of revenge leap out of the shuttle
Then quickly snatch from Atropos
The shears and cut it, lest your sons,
And the children of them and their children
Wear the envenomed robe.

ANNE RUTLEDGE

Out of me unworthy and unknown
The vibrations of deathless music;
"With malice toward none, with charity for all."
Out of me the forgiveness of millions toward millions,
And the beneficent face of a nation
Shining with justice and truth.
I am Anne Rutledge who sleep beneath these weeds,
Beloved in life of Abraham Lincoln,
Wedded to him, not through union,
But through separation.
Bloom forever, O Republic,
From the dust of my bosom!

LUCINDA MATLOCK

I went to the dances at Chandlerville,
And played snap-out at Winchester.
One time we changed partners,
Driving home in the moonlight of middle June,
And then I found Davis.
We were married and lived together for seventy years,
Enjoying, working, raising the twelve children,
Eight of whom we lost
Ere I had reached the age of sixty.
I spun, I wove, I kept the house, I nursed the sick,
I made the garden, and for holiday
Rambled over the fields where sang the larks,
And by Spoon River gathering many a shell,
And many a flower and medicinal weed—
Shouting to the wooded hills, singing to the green valleys.
At ninety-six I had lived enough, that is all,
And passed to a sweet repose.
What is this I hear of sorrow and weariness,
Anger, discontent and drooping hopes?
Degenerate sons and daughters,

Life is too strong for you—
It takes life to love Life.

DAVIS MATLOCK

Suppose it is nothing but the hive:
That there are drones and workers
And queens, and nothing but storing honey—
(Material things as well as culture and wisdom)—
For the next generation, this generation never living,
Except as it swarms in the sun-light of youth,
Strengthening its wings on what has been gathered,
And tasting, on the way to the hive
From the clover field, the delicate spoil.
Suppose all this, and suppose the truth:
That the nature of man is greater
Than nature's need in the hive;
And you must bear the burden of life,
As well as the urge from your spirit's excess—
Well, I say to live it out like a god
Sure of immortal life, though you are in doubt,
Is the way to live it.
If that doesn't make God proud of you
Then God is nothing but gravitation,
Or sleep is the golden goal.

Stephen Crane / 1871–1900

IN THE DESERT

In the desert
I saw a creature, naked, bestial,
Who, squatting upon the ground,

Held his heart in his hands,
And ate of it.
I said, "Is it good, friend?"
"It is bitter—bitter," he answered;
"But I like it
Because it is bitter,
And because it is my heart."

I SAW A MAN PURSUING

THE HORIZON

I saw a man pursuing the horizon;
Round and round they sped.
I was disturbed at this;
I accosted the man.
"It is futile," I said,
"You can never——"

"You lie," he cried,
And ran on.

WAR IS KIND

Do not weep, maiden, for war is kind.
Because your lover threw wild hands toward the sky
And the affrighted steed ran on alone,
Do not weep.
War is kind.

    Hoarse, booming drums of the regiment,
    Little souls who thirst for fight,
    These men were born to drill and die.
    The unexplained glory flies above them,
    Great is the battle-god, great, and his kingdom—
    A field where a thousand corpses lie.

Do not weep, babe, for war is kind.
Because your father tumbled in the yellow trenches,
Raged at his breast, gulped and died,
Do not weep.
War is kind.

> Swift blazing flag of the regiment,
> Eagle with crest of red and gold,
> These men were born to drill and die.
> Point for them the virtue of slaughter,
> Make plain to them the excellence of killing
> And a field where a thousand corpses lie.

Mother whose heart hung humble as a button
On the bright splendid shroud of your son,
Do not weep.
War is kind.

ON THE DESERT

On the desert
A silence from the moon's deepest valley.
Fire rays fall athwart the robes
Of hooded men, squat and dumb.
Before them, a woman
Moves to the blowing of shrill whistles
And distant thunder of drums,
While mystic things, sinuous, dull with terrible colour,
Sleepily fondle her body
Or move at her will, swishing stealthily over the sand.
The snakes whisper softly;
The whispering, whispering snakes,
Dreaming and swaying and staring,
But always whispering, softly whispering.
The wind streams from the lone reaches
Of Arabia, solemn with night,
And the wild fire makes shimmer of blood
Over the robes of the hooded men
Squat and dumb.

Bands of moving bronze, emerald, yellow,
Circle the throat and the arms of her,
And over the sands serpents move warily
Slow, menacing and submissive,
Swinging to the whistles and drums,
The whispering, whispering snakes,
Dreaming and swaying and staring,
But always whispering, softly whispering.
The dignity of the accursèd;
The glory of slavery, despair, death,
Is in the dance of the whispering snakes.

A SLANT OF SUN ON DULL
BROWN WALLS

A slant of sun on dull brown walls,
A forgotten sky of bashful blue.

Toward God a mighty hymn,
A song of collisions and cries,
Rumbling wheels, hoof-beats, bells,
Welcomes, farewells, love-calls, final moans,
Voices of joy, idiocy, warning, despair,
The unknown appeals of brutes,
The chanting of flowers,
The screams of cut trees,
The senseless babble of hens and wise men—
A cluttered incoherency that says at the stars:
"O God, save us!"

A MAN SAID TO THE UNIVERSE

A man said to the universe:
"Sir, I exist!"
"However," replied the universe,

"The fact has not created in me
A sense of obligation."

THE TREES IN THE GARDEN
RAINED FLOWERS

The trees in the garden rained flowers.
Children ran there joyously.
They gathered the flowers
Each to himself.
Now there were some
Who gathered great heaps—
Having opportunity and skill—
Until, behold, only chance blossoms
Remained for the feeble.
Then a little spindling tutor
Ran importantly to the father, crying:
"Pray, come hither!
See this unjust thing in your garden!"
But when the father had surveyed,
He admonished the tutor:
"Not so, small sage!
This thing is just.
For, look you,
Are not they who possess the flowers
Stronger, bolder, shrewder
Than they who have none?
Why should the strong—
The beautiful strong—
Why should they not have the flowers?"
Upon reflection, the tutor bowed to the ground,
"My lord," he said,
"The stars are displaced
By this towering wisdom."

Ralph Hodgson / 1871–1962

TIME, YOU OLD GIPSY MAN

Time, you old gipsy man,
    Will you not stay,
Put up your caravan
    Just for one day?

All things I'll give you
Will you be my guest,
Bells for your jennet
Of silver the best,
Goldsmiths shall beat you
A great golden ring,
Peacocks shall bow to you,
Little boys sing,
Oh, and sweet girls will
Festoon you with may,
Time, you old gipsy,
Why hasten away?

Last week in Babylon,
Last night in Rome,
Morning, and in the crush
Under Paul's dome;
Under Paul's dial
You tighten your rein—
Only a moment,
And off once again;
Off to some city
Now blind in the womb,
Off to another
Ere that's in the tomb.

Time, you old gipsy man,
   Will you not stay,
Put up your caravan
   Just for one day?

EVE

Eve, with her basket, was
Deep in the bells and grass,
Wading in bells and grass
Up to her knees,
Picking a dish of sweet
Berries and plums to eat,
Down in the bells and grass
Under the trees.

Mute as a mouse in a
Corner the cobra lay,
Curled round a bough of the
Cinnamon tall. . . .
Now to get even and
Humble proud Heaven and
Now was the moment or
Never at all.

'Eva!' Each syllable
Light as a flower fell,
'Eva!' he whispered the
Wondering maid,
Soft as a bubble sung
Out of a linnet's lung,
Soft and most silverly
'Eva!' he said.

Picture that orchard sprite,
Eve, with her body white,
Supple and smooth to her
Slim finger tips,

Wondering, listening,
Listening, wondering,
Eve with a berry
Half-way to her lips.

Oh had our simple Eve
Seen through the make-believe!
Had she but known the
Pretender he was!
Out of the boughs he came,
Whispering still her name,
Tumbling in twenty rings
Into the grass.

Here was the strangest pair
In the world anywhere,
Eve in the bells and grass
Kneeling, and he
Telling his story low. . . .
Singing birds saw them go
Down the dark path to
The Blasphemous Tree.

Oh what a clatter when
Titmouse and Jenny Wren
Saw him successful and
Taking his leave!
How the birds rated him,
How they all hated him!
How they all pitied
Poor motherless Eve!

Picture her crying
Outside in the lane,
Eve, with no dish of sweet
Berries and plums to eat,
Haunting the gate of the
Orchard in vain. . . .
Picture the lewd delight
Under the hill to-night—
'Eva!' the toast goes round,
'Eva!' again.

STUPIDITY STREET

I saw with open eyes
Singing birds sweet
Sold in the shops
For the people to eat,
Sold in the shops of
Stupidity Street.

I saw in vision
The worm in the wheat,
And in the shops nothing
For people to eat;
Nothing for sale in
Stupidity Street.

THE BELLS OF HEAVEN

'Twould ring the bells of Heaven
The wildest peal for years,
If Parson lost his senses
And people came to theirs,
And he and they together
Knelt down with angry prayers
For tamed and shabby tigers
And dancing dogs and bears,
And wretched, blind pit ponies,
And little hunted hares.

THE BULL

See an old unhappy bull,
Sick in soul and body both,
Slouching in the undergrowth

Of the forest beautiful,
Banished from the herd he led,
Bulls and cows a thousand head.

Cranes and gaudy parrots go
Up and down the burning sky;
Tree-top cats purr drowsily
In the dim-day green below;
And troops of monkeys, nutting, some,
All disputing, go and come;

And things abominable sit
Picking offal buck or swine,
On the mess and over it
Burnished flies and beetles shine,
And spiders big as bladders lie
Under hemlocks ten foot high;

And a dotted serpent curled
Round and round and round a tree,
Yellowing its greenery,
Keeps a watch on all the world,
All the world and this old bull
In the forest beautiful.

Bravely by his fall he came:
One he led, a bull of blood
Newly come to lustihood,
Fought and put his prince to shame,
Snuffed and pawed the prostrate head
Tameless even while it bled.

There they left him, every one,
Left him there without a lick,
Left him for the birds to pick,
Left him there for carrion,
Vilely from their bosom cast
Wisdom, worth and love at last.

When the lion left his lair
And roared his beauty through the hills,

And the vultures pecked their quills
And flew into the middle air,
Then this prince no more to reign
Came to life and lived again.

He snuffed the herd in far retreat,
He saw the blood upon the ground,
And snuffed the burning airs around
Still with beevish odours sweet,
While the blood ran down his head
And his mouth ran slaver red.

Pity him, this fallen chief,
All his splendour, all his strength,
All his body's breadth and length
Dwindled down with shame and grief,
Half the bull he was before,
Bones and leather, nothing more.

See him standing dewlap-deep
In the rushes at the lake,
Surly, stupid, half asleep,
Waiting for his heart to break
And the birds to join the flies
Feasting at his bloodshot eyes;

Standing with his head hung down
In a stupor, dreaming things:
Green savannas, jungles brown,
Battlefields and bellowings,
Bulls undone and lions dead
And vultures flapping overhead.

Dreaming things: of days he spent
With his mother gaunt and lean
In the valley warm and green,
Full of baby wonderment,
Blinking out of silly eyes
At a hundred mysteries;

Dreaming over once again
How he wandered with a throng
Of bulls and cows a thousand strong,
Wandered on from plain to plain,
Up the hill and down the dale,
Always at his mother's tail;

How he lagged behind the herd,
Lagged and tottered, weak of limb,
And she turned and ran to him
Blaring at the loathly bird
Stationed always in the skies,
Waiting for the flesh that dies.

Dreaming maybe of a day
When her drained and drying paps
Turned him to the sweets and saps,
Richer fountains by the way,
And she left the bull she bore
And he looked to her no more;

And his little frame grew stout,
And his little legs grew strong,
And the way was not so long;
And his little horns came out,
And he played at butting trees
And boulder-stones and tortoises,

Joined a game of knobby skulls
With the youngsters of his year,
All the other little bulls,
Learning both to bruise and bear,
Learning how to stand a shock
Like a little bull of rock.

Dreaming of a day less dim,
Dreaming of a time less far,
When the faint but certain star
Of destiny burned clear for him,
And a fierce and wild unrest
Broke the quiet of his breast,

And the gristles of his youth
Hardened in his comely pow,
And he came to fighting growth,
Beat his bull and won his cow,
And flew his tail and trampled off
Past the tallest, vain enough,

And curved about in splendour full
And curved again and snuffed the airs
As who should say Come out who dares!
And all beheld a bull, a Bull,
And knew that here was surely one
That backed for no bull, fearing none.

And the leader of the herd
Looked and saw, and beat the ground,
And shook the forest with his sound,
Bellowed at the loathly bird
Stationed always in the skies,
Waiting for the flesh that dies.

Dreaming, this old bull forlorn,
Surely dreaming of the hour
When he came to sultan power,
And they owned him master-horn,
Chiefest bull of all among
Bulls and cows a thousand strong;

And in all the tramping herd
Not a bull that barred his way,
Not a cow that said him nay,
Not a bull or cow that erred
In the furnace of his look
Dared a second, worse rebuke;

Not in all the forest wide,
Jungle, thicket, pasture, fen,
Not another dared him then,
Dared him and again defied;
Not a sovereign buck or boar
Came a second time for more;

Not a serpent that survived
Once the terrors of his hoof
Risked a second time reproof,
Came a second time and lived,
Not a serpent in its skin
Came again for discipline;

Not a leopard bright as flame,
Flashing fingerhooks of steel
That a wooden tree might feel,
Met his fury once and came
For a second reprimand,
Not a leopard in the land;

Not a lion of them all,
Not a lion of the hills,
Hero of a thousand kills,
Dared a second fight and fall,
Dared that ram terrific twice,
Paid a second time the price. . . .

Pity him, this dupe of dream,
Leader of the herd again
Only in his daft old brain,
Once again the bull supreme
And bull enough to bear the part
Only in his tameless heart.

Pity him that he must wake;
Even now the swarm of flies
Blackening his bloodshot eyes
Bursts and blusters round the lake,
Scattered from the feast half-fed,
By great shadows overhead.

And the dreamer turns away
From his visionary herds
And his splendid yesterday,
Turns to meet the loathly birds
Flocking round him from the skies,
Waiting for the flesh that dies.

Walter de la Mare / 1873–1956

THE LISTENERS

"Is there anybody there?" said the Traveller,
 Knocking on the moonlit door;
And his horse in the silence champed the grasses
 Of the forest's ferny floor:
And a bird flew up out of the turret,
 Above the Traveller's head:
And he smote upon the door again a second time;
 "Is there anybody there?" he said.
But no one descended to the Traveller;
 No head from the leaf-fringed sill
Leaned over and looked into his grey eyes,
 Where he stood perplexed and still.
But only a host of phantom listeners
 That dwelt in the lone house then
Stood listening in the quiet of the moonlight
 To that voice from the world of men:
Stood thronging the faint moonbeams on the dark stair,
 That goes down to the empty hall,
Hearkening in an air stirred and shaken
 By the lonely Traveller's call.
And he felt in his heart their strangeness,
 Their stillness answering his cry,
While his horse moved, cropping the dark turf,
 'Neath the starred and leafy sky;
For he suddenly smote on the door, even
 Louder, and lifted his head:—
"Tell them I came, and no one answered,
 That I kept my word," he said.
Never the least stir made the listeners,
 Though every word he spake
Fell echoing through the shadowiness of the still house
 From the one man left awake:

Ay, they heard his foot upon the stirrup,
   And the sound of iron on stone,
And how the silence surged softly backward,
   When the plunging hoofs were gone.

AN EPITAPH

Here lies a most beautiful lady,
Light of step and heart was she;
I think she was the most beautiful lady
That ever was in the West Country.
But beauty vanishes; beauty passes;
However rare—rare it be;
And when I crumble, who will remember
This lady of the West Country?

THE GHOST

"Who knocks?" "I who was beautiful,
   Beyond all dreams to restore,
I, from the roots of the dark thorn am hither.
   And knock on the door."

"Who speaks?" "I—once was my speech
   Sweet as the bird's on the air,
When echo lurks by the waters to heed;
   'Tis I speak thee fair."

"Dark is the hour!" "Ay, and cold."
   "Lone is my house." "Ah, but mine?"
"Sight, touch, lips, eyes yearned in vain."
   "Long dead these to thine . . ."

Silence. Still faint on the porch
   Brake the flames of the stars.

In gloom groped a hope-wearied hand
   Over keys, bolts, and bars.

A face peered. All the grey night
   In chaos of vacancy shone;
Nought but vast sorrow was there—
   The sweet cheat gone.

IN THE DOCK

Pallid, mis-shapen he stands. The world's grimed thumb,
Now hooked securely in his matted hair,
Has haled him struggling from his poisonous slum
And flung him mute as fish close-netted there.
His bloodless hands entalon that iron rail.
He gloats in beastlike trance. His settling eyes
From staring face to face rove on—and quail.
Justice for carrion pants; and these the flies.
Voice after voice in smooth impartial drone
Erects horrific in his darkening brain
A timber framework, where agape, alone
Bright life will kiss good-bye the cheek of Cain.
Sudden like wolf he cries; and sweats to see
When howls man's soul, it howls inaudibly.

SUNK LYONESSE

In sea-cold Lyonesse,
When the Sabbath eve shafts down
On the roofs, walls, belfries
Of the foundered town,
The Nereids pluck their lyres
Where the green translucency beats,
And with motionless eyes at gaze
Make minstrelsy in the streets.

And the ocean water stirs
In salt-worn casemate and porch.
Plies the blunt-snouted fish
With fire in his skull for torch.
And the ringing wires resound;
And the unearthly lovely weep,
In lament of the music they make
In the sullen courts of sleep:
Whose marble flowers bloom for aye:
And—lapped by the moon-guiled tide—
Mock their carver with heart of stone,
Caged in his stone-ribbed side.

NOSTALGIA

In the strange city of life
A house I know full well—
That wherein Silence a refuge has,
Where Dark doth dwell.

Gable and roof it stands,
Fronting the dizzied street,
Where Vanity flaunts her gilded booths
In the noontide glare and heat.

Green-graped upon its walls
Earth's ancient hoary vine
Clusters the carven lichenous stone
With tendril serpentine.

Deafened, incensed, dismayed,
Dazed in the clamorous throng,
I thirst for the soundless fount that rills
As if from my inmost heart, and fills
The stillness with its song.

As yet I knock in vain:
Nor yet what is hidden can tell;
Where Silence perpetual vigil keeps,
    Where Dark doth dwell.

Wallace Stevens / 1875–1955

LE MONOCLE DE MON ONCLE

"Mother of heaven, regina of the clouds,
O sceptre of the sun, crown of the moon,
There is not nothing, no, no, never nothing,
Like the clashed edges of two words that kill."
And so I mocked her in magnificent measure.
Or was it that I mocked myself alone?
I wish that I might be a thinking stone.
The sea of spuming thought foists up again
The radiant bubble that she was. And then
A deep up-pouring from some saltier well
Within me, bursts its watery syllable.

II

A red bird flies across the golden floor.
It is a red bird that seeks out his choir
Among the choirs of wind and wet and wing.
A torrent will fall from him when he finds.
Shall I uncrumple this much-crumpled thing?
I am a man of fortune greeting heirs;
For it has come that thus I greet the spring.
These choirs of welcome choir for me farewell.
No spring can follow past meridian.
Yet you persist with anecdotal bliss
To make believe a starry *connaissance*.

III

Is it for nothing, then, that old Chinese
Sat tittivating by their mountain pools
Or in the Yangtse studied out their beards?
I shall not play the flat historic scale.
You know how Utamaro's beauties sought
The end of love in their all-speaking braids.

You know the mountainous coiffures of Bath.
Alas! Have all the barbers lived in vain
That not one curl in nature has survived?
Why, without pity on these studious ghosts,
Do you come dripping in your hair from sleep?

IV

This luscious and impeccable fruit of life
Falls, it appears, of its own weight to earth.
When you were Eve, its acrid juice was sweet,
Untasted, in its heavenly, orchard air.
An apple serves as well as any skull
To be the book in which to read a round,
And is as excellent, in that it is composed
Of what, like skulls, comes rotting back to ground
But it excels in this, that as the fruit
Of love, it is a book too mad to read
Before one merely reads to pass the time.

V

In the high west there burns a furious star.
It is for fiery boys that star was set
And for sweet-smelling virgins close to them.
The measure of the intensity of love
Is measure, also, of the verve of earth.
For me, the firefly's quick, electric stroke
Ticks tediously the time of one more year.
And you? Remember how the crickets came
Out of their mother grass, like little kin,
In the pale nights, when your first imagery
Found inklings of your bond to all that dust.

VI

If men at forty will be painting lakes
The ephemeral blues must merge for them in one,
The basic slate, the universal hue.
There is a substance in us that prevails.
But in our amours amorists discern
Such fluctuations that their scrivening
Is breathless to attend each quirky turn.
When amorists grow bald, then amours shrink

Into the compass and curriculum
Of introspective exiles, lecturing.
It is a theme for Hyacinth alone.

VII

The mules that angels ride come slowly down
The blazing passes, from beyond the sun.
Descensions of their tinkling bells arrive.
These muleteers are dainty of their way.
Meantime, centurions guffaw and beat
Their shrilling tankards on the table-boards.
This parable, in sense, amounts to this:
The honey of heaven may or may not come,
But that of earth both comes and goes at once.
Suppose these couriers brought amid their train
A damsel heightened by eternal bloom.

VIII

Like a dull scholar, I behold, in love,
An ancient aspect touching a new mind.
It comes, it blooms, it bears its fruit and dies.
This trivial trope reveals a way of truth.
Our bloom is gone. We are the fruit thereof.
Two golden gourds distended on our vines,
Into the autumn weather, splashed with frost,
Distorted by hale fatness, turned grotesque.
We hang like warty squashes, streaked and rayed,
The laughing sky will see the two of us
Washed into rinds by rotting winter rains.

IX

In verses wild with motion, full of din,
Loudened by cries, by clashes, quick and sure
As the deadly thought of men accomplishing
Their curious fates in war, come, celebrate
The faith of forty, ward of Cupido.
Most venerable heart, the lustiest conceit
Is not too lusty for your broadening.
I quiz all sounds, all thoughts, all everything
For the music and manner of the paladins

To make oblation fit. Where shall I find
Bravura adequate to this great hymn?

X

The fops of fancy in their poems leave
Memorabilia of the mystic spouts,
Spontaneously watering their gritty soils.
I am a yeoman, as such fellows go.
I know no magic trees, no balmy boughs,
No silver-ruddy, gold-vermilion fruits.
But, after all, I know a tree that bears
A semblance to the thing I have in mind.
It stands gigantic, with a certain tip
To which all birds come sometime in their time.
But when they go that tip still tips the tree.

XI

If sex were all, then every trembling hand
Could make us squeak, like dolls, the wished-for words.
But note the unconscionable treachery of fate,
That makes us weep, laugh, grunt and groan, and shout
Doleful heroics, pinching gestures forth
From madness or delight, without regard
To that first, foremost law. Anguishing hour!
Last night, we sat beside a pool of pink,
Clippered with lilies scudding the bright chromes,
Keen to the point of starlight, while a frog
Boomed from his very belly odious chords.

XII

A blue pigeon it is, that circles the blue sky,
On sidelong wing, around and round and round.
A white pigeon it is, that flutters to the ground,
Grown tired of flight. Like a dark rabbi, I
Observed, when young, the nature of mankind,
In lordly study. Every day, I found
Man proved a gobbet in my mincing world.
Like a rose rabbi, later, I pursued,
And still pursue, the origin and course
Of love, but until now I never knew
That fluttering things have so distinct a shade.

SUNDAY MORNING

I

Complacencies of the peignoir, and late
Coffee and oranges in a sunny chair,
And the green freedom of a cockatoo
Upon a rug mingle to dissipate
The holy hush of ancient sacrifice.
She dreams a little, and she feels the dark
Encroachment of that old catastrophe,
As a calm darkens among water-lights.
The pungent oranges and bright, green wings
Seem things in some procession of the dead,
Winding across wide water, without sound.
The day is like wide water, without sound,
Stilled for the passing of her dreaming feet
Over the seas, to silent Palestine,
Dominion of the blood and sepulchre.

II

Why should she give her bounty to the dead?
What is divinity if it can come
Only in silent shadows and in dreams?
Shall she not find in comforts of the sun,
In pungent fruit and bright, green wings, or else
In any balm or beauty of the earth,
Things to be cherished like the thought of heaven?
Divinity must live within herself:
Passions of rain, or moods in falling snow;
Grievings in loneliness, or unsubdued
Elations when the forest blooms; gusty
Emotions on wet roads on autumn nights;
All pleasures and all pains, remembering
The bough of summer and the winter branch.
These are the measures destined for her soul.

III

Jove in the clouds had his inhuman birth.
No mother suckled him, no sweet land gave
Large-mannered motions to his mythy mind

He moved among us, as a muttering king,
Magnificent, would move among his hinds,
Until our blood, commingling, virginal,
With heaven, brought such requital to desire
The very hinds discerned it, in a star.
Shall our blood fail? Or shall it come to be
The blood of paradise? And shall the earth
Seem all of paradise that we shall know?
The sky will be much friendlier then than now,
A part of labor and a part of pain,
And next in glory to enduring love,
Not this dividing and indifferent blue.

IV

She says, "I am content when wakened birds,
Before they fly, test the reality
Of misty fields, by their sweet questionings;
But when the birds are gone, and their warm fields
Return no more, where, then, is paradise?"
There is not any haunt of prophecy,
Nor any old chimera of the grave,
Neither the golden underground, nor isle
Melodious, where spirits gat them home,
Nor visionary south, nor cloudy palm
Remote on heaven's hill, that has endured
As April's green endures; or will endure
Like her remembrance of awakened birds,
Or her desire for June and evening, tipped
By the consummation of the swallow's wings.

V

She says, "But in contentment I still feel
The need of some imperishable bliss."
Death is the mother of beauty; hence from her,
Alone, shall come fulfilment to our dreams
And our desires. Although she strews the leaves
Of sure obliteration on our paths,
The path sick sorrow took, the many paths
Where triumph rang its brassy phrase, or love
Whispered a little out of tenderness,
She makes the willow shiver in the sun
For maidens who were wont to sit and gaze

Upon the grass, relinquished to their feet.
She causes boys to pile new plums and pears
On disregarded plate. The maidens taste
And stray impassioned in the littering leaves.

VI

Is there no change of death in paradise?
Does ripe fruit never fall? Or do the boughs
Hang always heavy in that perfect sky,
Unchanging, yet so like our perishing earth,
With rivers like our own that seek for seas
They never find, the same receding shores
That never touch with inarticulate pang?
Why set the pear upon those river-banks
Or spice the shores with odors of the plum?
Alas, that they should wear our colors there,
The silken weavings of our afternoons,
And pick the strings of our insipid lutes!
Death is the mother of beauty, mystical,
Within whose burning bosom we devise
Our earthly mothers waiting, sleeplessly.

VII

Supple and turbulent, a ring of men
Shall chant in orgy on a summer morn
Their boisterous devotion to the sun,
Not as a god, but as a god might be,
Naked among them, like a savage source.
Their chant shall be a chant of paradise,
Out of their blood, returning to the sky;
And in their chant shall enter, voice by voice,
The windy lake wherein their lord delights,
The trees, like serafin, and echoing hills,
That choir among themselves long afterward.
They shall know well the heavenly fellowship
Of men that perish and of summer morn.
And whence they came and whither they shall go
The dew upon their feet shall manifest.

VIII

She hears, upon that water without sound,
A voice that cries, "The tomb in Palestine

Is not the porch of spirits lingering.
It is the grave of Jesus, where he lay."
We live in an old chaos of the sun,
Or old dependency of day and night,
Or island solitude, unsponsored, free,
Of that wide water, inescapable.
Deer walk upon our mountains, and the quail
Whistle about us their spontaneous cries;
Sweet berries ripen in the wilderness;
And, in the isolation of the sky,
At evening, casual flocks of pigeons make
Ambiguous undulations as they sink,
Downward to darkness, on extended wings.

PETER QUINCE AT THE CLAVIER

I

Just as my fingers on these keys
Make music, so the selfsame sounds
On my spirit make a music, too.

Music is feeling, then, not sound;
And thus it is that what I feel,
Here in this room, desiring you,

Thinking of your blue-shadowed silk,
Is music. It is like the strain
Waked in the elders by Susanna.

Of a green evening, clear and warm,
She bathed in her still garden, while
The red-eyed elders watching, felt

The basses of their beings throb
In witching chords, and their thin blood
Pulse pizzicati of Hosanna.

II

In the green water, clear and warm,
Susanna lay.

She searched
The touch of springs,
And found
Concealed imaginings.
She sighed,
For so much melody.

Upon the bank, she stood
In the cool
Of spent emotions.
She felt, among the leaves,
The dew
Of old devotions.

She walked upon the grass,
Still quavering.
The winds were like her maids,
On timid feet,
Fetching her woven scarves,
Yet wavering.

A breath upon her hand
Muted the night.
She turned—
A cymbal crashed,
And roaring horns.

III

Soon, with a noise like tambourines,
Came her attendant Byzantines.

They wondered why Susanna cried
Against the elders by her side;

And as they whispered, the refrain
Was like a willow swept by rain.

Anon, their lamps' uplifted flame
Revealed Susanna and her shame.

And then, the simpering Byzantines
Fled, with a noise like tambourines.

IV

Beauty is momentary in the mind—
The fitful tracing of a portal;
But in the flesh it is immortal.

The body dies; the body's beauty lives.
So evenings die, in their green going,
A wave, interminably flowing.
So gardens die, their meek breath scenting
The cowl of winter, done repenting.
So maidens die, to the auroral
Celebration of a maiden's choral.
Susanna's music touched the bawdy strings
Of those white elders; but, escaping,
Left only Death's ironic scraping.
Now, in its immortality, it plays
On the clear viol of her memory,
And makes a constant sacrament of praise.

THIRTEEN WAYS OF LOOKING
AT A BLACKBIRD

I

Among twenty snowy mountains,
The only moving thing
Was the eye of the blackbird.

II

I was of three minds,
Like a tree
In which there are three blackbirds.

III

The blackbird whirled in the autumn winds.
It was a small part of the pantomime.

IV

A man and a woman
Are one.

A man and a woman and a blackbird
Are one.

V

I do not know which to prefer,
The beauty of inflections
Or the beauty of innuendoes,
The blackbird whistling
Or just after.

VI

Icicles filled the long window
With barbaric glass.
The shadow of the blackbird
Crossed it, to and fro.
The mood
Traced in the shadow
An indecipherable cause.

VII

O thin men of Haddam,
Why do you imagine golden birds?
Do you not see how the blackbird
Walks around the feet
Of the women about you?

VIII

I know noble accents
And lucid, inescapable rhythms;
But I know, too,
That the blackbird is involved
In what I know.

IX

When the blackbird flew out of sight,
It marked the edge
Of one of many circles.

X

At the sight of blackbirds
Flying in a green light,

Even the bawds of euphony
Would cry out sharply.

XI

He rode over Connecticut
In a glass coach.
Once, a fear pierced him,
In that he mistook
The shadow of his equipage
For blackbirds.

XII

The river is moving.
The blackbird must be flying.

XIII

It was evening all afternoon.
It was snowing
And it was going to snow.
The blackbird sat
In the cedar-limbs.

CONNOISSEUR OF CHAOS

I

A.   A violent order is disorder; and
B.   A great disorder is an order. These
Two things are one. (Pages of illustrations.)

II

If all the green of spring was blue, and it is;
If the flowers of South Africa were bright
On the tables of Connecticut, and they are;
If Englishmen lived without tea in Ceylon, and they do;
And if it all went on in an orderly way,
And it does; a law of inherent opposites,
Of essential unity, is as pleasant as port,
As pleasant as the brush-strokes of a bough,
An upper, particular bough in, say, Marchand.

III

After all the pretty contrast of life and death
Proves that these opposite things partake of one,
At least that was the theory, when bishops' books
Resolved the world. We cannot go back to that.
The squirming facts exceed the squamous mind,
If one may say so. And yet relation appears,
A small relation expanding like the shade
Of a cloud on sand, a shape on the side of a hill.

IV

A.   Well, an old order is a violent one.
This proves nothing. Just one more truth, one more
Element in the immense disorder of truths.
B.   It is April as I write. The wind
Is blowing after days of constant rain.
All this, of course, will come to summer soon.
But suppose the disorder of truths should ever come
To an order, most Plantagenet, most fixed . . .
A great disorder is an order. Now, A
And B are not like statuary, posed
For a vista in the Louvre. They are things chalked
On the sidewalk so that the pensive man may see.

V

The pensive man . . . He sees that eagle float
For which the intricate Alps are a single nest.

THE SENSE OF THE SLEIGHT-OF-HAND MAN

One's grand flights, one's Sunday baths,
One's tootings at the weddings of the soul
Occur as they occur. So bluish clouds
Occurred above the empty house and the leaves
Of the rhododendrons rattled their gold,

As if someone lived there. Such floods of white
Came bursting from the clouds. So the wind
Threw its contorted strength around the sky.

Could you have said the bluejay suddenly
Would swoop to earth? It is a wheel, the rays
Around the sun. The wheel survives the myths.
The fire eye in the clouds survives the gods.
To think of a dove with an eye of grenadine
And pines that are cornets, so it occurs,
And a little island full of geese and stars:
It may be that the ignorant man, alone,
Has any chance to mate his life with life
That is the sensual, pearly spouse, the life
That is fluent in even the wintriest bronze.

from EXTRACTS FROM ADDRESSES
TO THE ACADEMY OF FINE IDEAS

IV

On an early Sunday in April, a feeble day,
He felt curious about the winter hills
And wondered about the water in the lake.
It had been cold since December. Snow fell, first,
At New Year and, from then until April, lay
On everything. Now it had melted, leaving
The gray grass like a pallet, closely pressed;
And dirt. The wind blew in the empty place.
The winter wind blew in an empty place—
There was that difference between the and an,
The difference between himself and no man,
No man that heard a wind in an empty place.
It was time to be himself again, to see
If the place, in spite of its witheredness, was still
Within the difference. He felt curious
Whether the water was black and lashed about
Or whether the ice still covered the lake. There was still

Snow under the trees and on the northern rocks,
The dead rocks not the green rocks, the live rocks. If,
When he looked, the water ran up the air or grew white
Against the edge of the ice, the abstraction would
Be broken and winter would be broken and done,
And being would be being himself again,
Being, becoming seeing and feeling and self,
Black water breaking into reality.

SO-AND-SO RECLINING ON HER COUCH

On her side, reclining on her elbow.
This mechanism, this apparition,
Suppose we call it Projection A.

She floats in air at the level of
The eye, completely anonymous,
Born, as she was, at twenty-one,

Without lineage or language, only
The curving of her hip, as motionless gesture,
Eyes dripping blue, so much to learn.

If just above her head there hung,
Suspended in air, the slightest crown
Of Gothic prong and practick bright,

The suspension, as in solid space,
The suspending hand withdrawn, would be
An invisible gesture. Let this be called

Projection B. To get at the thing
Without gestures is to get at it as
Idea. She floats in the contention, the flux

Between the thing as idea and
The idea as thing. She is half who made her.
This is the final Projection, C.

The arrangement contains the desire of
The artist. But one confides in what has no
Concealed creator. One walks easily

The unpainted shore, accepts the world
As anything but sculpture. Good-bye,
Mrs. Pappadopoulos, and thanks.

CRUDE   FOYER

Thought is false happiness: the idea
That merely by thinking one can,
Or may, penetrate, not may,
But can, that one is sure to be able—

That there lies at the end of thought
A foyer of the spirit in a landscape
Of the mind, in which we sit
And wear humanity's bleak crown;

In which we read the critique of paradise
And say it is the work
Of a comedian, this critique;
In which we sit and breathe

An innocence of an absolute,
False happiness, since we know that we use
Only the eye as faculty, that the mind
Is the eye, and that this landscape of the mind

Is a landscape only of the eye; and that
We are ignorant men incapable
Of the least, minor, vital metaphor, content,
At last, there, when it turns out to be here.

ESTHÉTIQUE DU MAL

I

He was at Naples writing letters home
And, between his letters, reading paragraphs
On the sublime. Vesuvius had groaned
For a month. It was pleasant to be sitting there,
While the sultriest fulgurations, flickering,
Cast corners in the glass. He could describe
The terror of the sound because the sound
Was ancient. He tried to remember the phrases: pain
Audible at noon, pain torturing itself,
Pain killing pain on the very point of pain.
The volcano trembled in another ether,
As the body trembles at the end of life.

It was almost time for lunch. Pain is human.
There were roses in the cool café. His book
Made sure of the most correct catastrophe.
Except for us, Vesuvius might consume
In solid fire the utmost earth and know
No pain (ignoring the cocks that crow us up
To die). This is a part of the sublime
From which we shrink. And yet, except for us,
The total past felt nothing when destroyed.

II

At a town in which acacias grew, he lay
On his balcony at night. Warblings became
Too dark, too far, too much the accents of
Afflicted sleep, too much the syllables
That would form themselves, in time, and communicate
The intelligence of his despair, express
What meditation never quite achieved.

The moon rose up as if it had escaped
His meditation. It evaded his mind.
It was part of a supremacy always
Above him. The moon was always free from him,
As night was free from him. The shadow touched

Or merely seemed to touch him as he spoke
A kind of elegy he found in space:

It is pain that is indifferent to the sky
In spite of the yellow of the acacias, the scent
Of them in the air still hanging heavily
In the hoary-hanging night. It does not regard
This freedom, this supremacy, and in
Its own hallucination never sees
How that which rejects it saves it in the end.

III

His firm stanzas hang like hives in hell
Or what hell was, since now both heaven and hell
Are one, and here, O terra infidel.

The fault lies with an over-human god,
Who by sympathy has made himself a man
And is not to be distinguished, when we cry

Because we suffer, our oldest parent, peer
Of the populace of the heart, the reddest lord,
Who has gone before us in experience.

If only he would not pity us so much,
Weaken our fate, relieve us of woe both great
And small, a constant fellow of destiny,

A too, too human god, self-pity's kin
And uncourageous genesis . . . It seems
As if the health of the world might be enough.

It seems as if the honey of common summer
Might be enough, as if the golden combs
Were part of a sustenance itself enough,

As if hell, so modified, had disappeared,
As if pain, no longer satanic mimicry,
Could be borne, as if we were sure to find our way.

IV

Livre de Toutes Sortes de Fleurs d'après Nature.
All sorts of flowers. That's the sentimentalist.
When B. sat down at the piano and made
A transparence in which we heard music, made music,
In which we heard transparent sounds, did he play
All sorts of notes? Or did he play only one
In an ecstasy of its associates,
Variations in the tones of a single sound,
The last, or sounds so single they seemed one?

And then that Spaniard of the rose, itself
Hot-hooded and dark-blooded, rescued the rose
From nature, each time he saw it, making it,
As he saw it, exist in his own especial eye.
Can we conceive of him as rescuing less,
As muffing the mistress for her several maids,
As foregoing the nakedest passion for barefoot
Philandering? . . . The genius of misfortune
Is not a sentimentalist. He is
That evil, that evil in the self, from which
In desperate hallow, rugged gesture, fault
Falls out on everything: the genius of
The mind, which is our being, wrong and wrong,
The genius of the body, which is our world,
Spent in the false engagements of the mind.

V

Softly let all true sympathizers come,
Without the inventions of sorrow or the sob
Beyond invention. Within what we permit,
Within the actual, the warm, the near,
So great a unity, that it is bliss,
Ties us to those we love. For this familiar,
This brother even in the father's eye,
This brother half-spoken in the mother's throat
And these regalia, these things disclosed,
These nebulous brilliancies in the smallest look
Of the being's deepest darling, we forego
Lament, willingly forfeit the ai-ai

Of parades in the obscurer selvages.
Be near me, come closer, touch my hand, phrases
Compounded of dear relation, spoken twice,
Once by the lips, once by the services
Of central sense, these minutiae mean more
Than clouds, benevolences, distant heads.
These are within what we permit, in-bar
Exquisite in poverty against the suns
Of ex-bar, in-bar retaining attributes
With which we vested, once, the golden forms
And the damasked memory of the golden forms
And ex-bar's flower and fire of the festivals
Of the damasked memory of the golden forms,
Before we were wholly human and knew ourselves.

VI

The sun, in clownish yellow, but not a clown,
Brings the day to perfection and then fails. He dwells
In a consummate prime, yet still desires
A further consummation. For the lunar month
He makes the tenderest research, intent
On a transmutation which, when seen, appears
To be askew. And space is filled with his
Rejected years. A big bird pecks at him
For food. The big bird's bony appetite
Is as insatiable as the sun's. The bird
Rose from an imperfection of its own
To feed on the yellow bloom of the yellow fruit
Dropped down from turquoise leaves. In the landscape of
The sun, its grossest appetite becomes less gross,
Yet, when corrected, has its curious lapses,
Its glitters, its divinations of serene
Indulgence out of all celestial sight.

The sun is the country wherever he is. The bird
In the brightest landscape downwardly revolves
Disdaining each astringent ripening,
Evading the point of redness, not content
To repose in an hour or season or long era
Of the country colors crowding against it, since
The yellow grassman's mind is still immense,
Still promises perfections cast away.

VII

How red the rose that is the soldier's wound,
The wounds of many soldiers, the wounds of all
The soldiers that have fallen, red in blood,
The soldier of time grown deathless in great size.

A mountain in which no ease is ever found,
Unless indifference to deeper death
Is ease, stands in the dark, a shadows' hill,
And there the soldier of time has deathless rest.

Concentric circles of shadows, motionless
Of their own part, yet moving on the wind,
Form mystical convolutions in the sleep
Of time's red soldier deathless on his bed.

The shadows of his fellows ring him round
In the high night, the summer breathes for them
Its fragrance, a heavy somnolence, and for him,
For the soldier of time, it breathes a summer sleep,

In which his wound is good because life was.
No part of him was ever part of death.
A woman smoothes her forehead with her hand
And the soldier of time lies calm beneath that stroke.

VIII

The death of Satan was a tragedy
For the imagination. A capital
Negation destroyed him in his tenement
And, with him, many blue phenomena.
It was not the end he had foreseen. He knew
That his revenge created filial
Revenges. And negation was eccentric.
It had nothing of the Julian thunder-cloud:
The assassin flash and rumble . . . He was denied.
Phantoms, what have you left? What underground?
What place in which to be is not enough
To be? You go, poor phantoms, without place
Like silver in the sheathing of the sight,
As the eye closes . . . How cold the vacancy

When the phantoms are gone and the shaken realist
First sees reality. The mortal no
Has its emptiness and tragic expirations.
The tragedy, however, may have begun,
Again, in the imagination's new beginning,
In the yes of the realist spoken because he must
Say yes, spoken because under every no
Lay a passion for yes that had never been broken.

IX

Panic in the face of the moon—round effendi
Or the phosphored sleep in which he walks abroad
Or the majolica dish heaped up with phosphored fruit
That he sends ahead, out of the goodness of his heart,
To anyone that comes—panic, because
The moon is no longer these nor anything
And nothing is left but comic ugliness
Or a lustred nothingness. Effendi, he
That has lost the folly of the moon becomes
The prince of the proverbs of pure poverty.
To lose sensibility, to see what one sees,
As if sight had not its own miraculous thrift,
To hear only what one hears, one meaning alone,
As if the paradise of meaning ceased
To be paradise, it is this to be destitute.
This is the sky divested of its fountains.
Here in the west indifferent crickets chant
Through our indifferent crises. Yet we require
Another chant, an incantation, as in
Another and later genesis, music
That buffets the shapes of its possible halcyon
Against the haggardie . . . A loud, large water
Bubbles up in the night and drowns the crickets' sound.
It is a declaration, a primitive ecstasy,
Truth's favors sonorously exhibited.

X

He had studied the nostalgias. In these
He sought the most grossly maternal, the creature
Who most fecundly assuaged him, the softest
Woman with a vague moustache and not the mauve

Maman. His anima liked its animal
And liked it unsubjugated, so that home
Was a return to birth, a being born
Again in the savagest severity,
Desiring fiercely, the child of a mother fierce
In his body, fiercer in his mind, merciless
To accomplish the truth in his intelligence.
It is true there were other mothers, singular
In form, lovers of heaven and earth, she-wolves
And forest tigresses and women mixed
With the sea. These were fantastic. There were homes
Like things submerged with their englutted sounds,
That were never wholly still. The softest woman,
Because she is as she was, reality,
The gross, the fecund, proved him against the touch
Of impersonal pain. Reality explained.
It was the last nostalgia: that he
Should understand. That he might suffer or that
He might die was the innocence of living, if life
Itself was innocent. To say that it was
Disentangled him from sleek ensolacings.

XI

Life is a bitter aspic. We are not
At the centre of a diamond. At dawn,
The paratroopers fall and as they fall
They mow the lawn. A vessel sinks in waves
Of people, as big bell-billows from its bell
Bell-bellow in the village steeple. Violets,
Great tufts, spring up from buried houses
Of poor, dishonest people, for whom the steeple,
Long since, rang out farewell, farewell, farewell.

Natives of poverty, children of malheur,
The gaiety of language is our seigneur.

A man of bitter appetite despises
A well-made scene in which paratroopers
Select adieux; and he despises this:
A ship that rolls on a confected ocean,
The weather pink, the wind in motion; and this:

A steeple that tip-tops the classic sun's
Arrangements; and the violets' exhumo.
The tongue caresses these exacerbations.
They press it as epicure, distinguishing
Themselves from its essential savor,
Like hunger that feeds on its own hungriness.

XII

He disposes the world in categories, thus:
The peopled and the unpeopled. In both, he is
Alone. But in the peopled world, there is,
Besides the people, his knowledge of them. In
The unpeopled, there is his knowledge of himself.
Which is more desperate in the moments when
The will demands that what he thinks be true?

Is it himself in them that he knows or they
In him? If it is himself in them, they have
No secret from him. If it is they in him,
He has no secret from them. This knowledge
Of them and of himself destroys both worlds,
Except when he escapes from it. To be
Alone is not to know them or himself.

This creates a third world without knowledge,
In which no one peers, in which the will makes no
Demands. It accepts whatever is as true,
Including pain, which, otherwise, is false.
In the third world, then, there is no pain. Yes, but
What lover has one in such rocks, what woman,
However known, at the centre of the heart?

XIII

It may be that one life is a punishment
For another, as the son's life for the father's.
But that concerns the secondary characters.
It is a fragmentary tragedy
Within the universal whole. The son
And the father alike and equally are spent,
Each one, by the necessity of being
Himself, the unalterable necessity

Of being this unalterable animal.
This force of nature in action is the major
Tragedy. This is destiny unperplexed,
The happiest enemy. And it may be
That in his Mediterranean cloister a man,
Reclining, eased of desire, establishes
The visible, a zone of blue and orange
Versicolorings, establishes a time
To watch the fire-feinting sea and calls it good,
The ultimate good, sure of a reality
Of the longest meditation, the maximum,
The assassin's scene. Evil in evil is
Comparative. The assassin discloses himself,
The force that destroys us is disclosed, within
This maximum, an adventure to be endured
With the politest helplessness. Ay-mi!
One feels its action moving in the blood.

XIV

Victor Serge said, "I followed his argument
With the blank uneasiness which one might feel
In the presence of a logical lunatic."
He said it of Konstantinov. Revolution
Is the affair of logical lunatics.
The politics of emotion must appear
To be an intellectual structure. The cause
Creates a logic not to be distinguished
From lunacy . . . One wants to be able to walk
By the lake at Geneva and consider logic:
To think of the logicians in their graves
And of the worlds of logic in their great tombs.
Lakes are more reasonable than oceans. Hence,
A promenade amid the grandeurs of the mind,
By a lake, with clouds like lights among great tombs,
Gives one a blank uneasiness, as if
One might meet Konstantinov, who would interrupt
With his lunacy. He would not be aware of the lake.
He would be the lunatic of one idea
In a world of ideas, who would have all the people
Live, work, suffer and die in that idea
In a world of ideas. He would not be aware of the clouds,

Lighting the martyrs of logic with white fire.
His extreme of logic would be illogical.

xv

The greatest poverty is not to live
In a physical world, to feel that one's desire
Is too difficult to tell from despair. Perhaps,
After death, the non-physical people, in paradise,
Itself non-physical, may, by chance, observe
The green corn gleaming and experience
The minor of what we feel. The adventurer
In humanity has not conceived of a race
Completely physical in a physical world.
The green corn gleams and the metaphysicals
Lie sprawling in majors of the August heat,
The rotund emotions, paradise unknown.
This is the thesis scrivened in delight,
The reverberating psalm, the right chorale.

One might have thought of sight, but who could think
Of what it sees, for all the ill it sees?
Speech found the ear, for all the evil sound,
But the dark italics it could not propound.
And out of what one sees and hears and out
Of what one feels, who could have thought to make
So many selves, so many sensuous worlds,
As if the air, the mid-day air, was swarming
With the metaphysical changes that occur,
Merely in living as and where we live.

CONTINUAL   CONVERSATION

WITH   A   SILENT   MAN

The old brown hen and the old blue sky,
Between the two we live and die—
The broken cartwheel on the hill.

As if, in the presence of the sea,
We dried our nets and mended sail
And talked of never-ending things,

Of the never-ending storm of will,
One will and many wills, and the wind,
Of many meanings in the leaves,

Brought down to one below the eaves,
Link, of that tempest, to the farm,
The chain of the turquoise hen and sky

And the wheel that broke as the cart went by.
It is not a voice that is under the eaves.
It is not speech, the sound we hear

In this conversation, but the sound
Of things and their motion: the other man,
A turquoise monster moving round.

THE PREJUDICE AGAINST
THE PAST

Day is the children's friend.
It is Marianna's Swedish cart.
It is that and a very big hat.

Confined by what they see,
Aquiline pedants treat the cart,
As one of the relics of the heart.

They treat the philosopher's hat,
Left thoughtlessly behind,
As one of the relics of the mind . . .

Of day, then, children make
What aquiline pedants take
For souvenirs of time, lost time,

Adieux, shapes, images—
No, not of day, but of themselves,
Not of perpetual time.

And, therefore, aquiline pedants find
The philosopher's hat to be part of the mind,
The Swedish cart to be part of the heart.

from NOTES TOWARD A SUPREME
FICTION——IT MUST CHANGE

VI

Bethou me, said sparrow, to the crackled blade,
And you, and you, bethou me as you blow,
When in my coppice you behold me be.

Ah, ké! the bloody wren, the felon jay,
Ké-ké, the jug-throated robin pouring out,
Bethou, bethou, bethou me in my glade.

There was such idiot minstrelsy in rain,
So many clappers going without bells,
That these bethous compose a heavenly gong.

One voice repeating, one tireless chorister,
The phrases of a single phrase, ké-ké,
A single text, granite monotony,

One sole face, like a photograph of fate,
Glass-blower's destiny, bloodless episcopus,
Eye without lid, mind without any dream—

These are of minstrels lacking minstrelsy,
Of an earth in which the first leaf is the tale
Of leaves, in which the sparrow is a bird

Of stone, that never changes. Bethou him, you
And you, bethou him and bethou. It is
A sound like any other. It will end.

SOLDIER, THERE IS A WAR
BETWEEN THE MIND

Soldier, there is a war between the mind
And sky, between thought and day and night. It is
For that the poet is always in the sun,

Patches the moon together in his room
To his Virgilian cadences, up down,
Up down. It is a war that never ends.

Yet it depends on yours. The two are one.
They are a plural, a right and left, a pair,
Two parallels that meet if only in

The meeting of their shadows or that meet
In a book in a barrack, a letter from Malay.
But your war ends. And after it you return

With six meats and twelve wines or else without
To walk another room . . . Monsieur and comrade,
The soldier is poor without the poet's lines,

His petty syllabi, the sounds that stick,
Inevitably modulating, in the blood.
And war for war, each has its gallant kind.

How simply the fictive hero becomes the real;
How gladly with proper words the soldier dies,
If he must or lives on the bread of faithful speech.

Robert Frost / 1875–1963

MENDING WALL

Something there is that doesn't love a wall,
That sends the frozen-ground-swell under it,
And spills the upper boulders in the sun;
And makes gaps even two can pass abreast.
The work of hunters is another thing:
I have come after them and made repair
Where they have left not one stone on a stone,
But they would have the rabbit out of hiding,
To please the yelping dogs. The gaps I mean,
No one has seen them made or heard them made,
But at spring mending-time we find them there.
I let my neighbor know beyond the hill;
And on a day we meet to walk the line
And set the wall between us once again.
We keep the wall between us as we go.
To each the boulders that have fallen to each.
And some are loaves and some so nearly balls
We have to use a spell to make them balance:
'Stay where you are until our backs are turned!'
We wear our fingers rough with handling them.
Oh, just another kind of outdoor game,
One on a side. It comes to little more:
There where it is we do not need the wall:
He is all pine and I am apple orchard.
My apple trees will never get across
And eat the cones under his pines, I tell him
He only says, 'Good fences make good neighbors.'
Spring is the mischief in me, and I wonder
If I could put a notion in his head:
'*Why* do they make good neighbors? Isn't it
Where there are cows? But here there are no cows.

Before I built a wall I'd ask to know
What I was walling in or walling out,
And to whom I was like to give offense.
Something there is that doesn't love a wall,
That wants it down.' I could say 'Elves' to him,
But it's not elves exactly, and I'd rather
He said it for himself. I see him there
Bringing a stone grasped firmly by the top
In each hand, like an old-stone savage armed.
He moves in darkness as it seems to me,
Not of woods only and the shade of trees
He will not go behind his father's saying,
And he likes having thought of it so well
He says again, 'Good fences make good neighbors.'

THE ROAD NOT TAKEN

Two roads diverged in a yellow wood,
And sorry I could not travel both
And be one traveler, long I stood
And looked down one as far as I could
To where it bent in the undergrowth;

Then took the other, as just as fair,
And having perhaps the better claim,
Because it was grassy and wanted wear;
Though as for that the passing there
Had worn them really about the same,

And both that morning equally lay
In leaves no step had trodden black.
Oh, I kept the first for another day!
Yet knowing how way leads on to way,
I doubted if I should ever come back.

I shall be telling this with a sigh
Somewhere ages and ages hence:
Two roads diverged in a wood, and I—

I took the one less traveled by,
And that has made all the difference.

BIRCHES

When I see birches bend to left and right
Across the lines of straighter darker trees,
I like to think some boy's been swinging them.
But swinging doesn't bend them down to stay
As ice-storms do. Often you must have seen them
Loaded with ice a sunny winter morning
After a rain. They click upon themselves
As the breeze rises, and turn many-colored
As the stir cracks and crazes their enamel.
Soon the sun's warmth makes them shed crystal shells
Shattering and avalanching on the snow-crust—
Such heaps of broken glass to sweep away
You'd think the inner dome of heaven had fallen.
They are dragged to the withered bracken by the load,
And they seem not to break; though once they are bowed
So low for long, they never right themselves:
You may see their trunks arching in the woods
Years afterwards, trailing their leaves on the ground
Like girls on hands and knees that throw their hair
Before them over their heads to dry in the sun.
But I was going to say when Truth broke in
With all her matter-of-fact about the ice-storm
I should prefer to have some boy bend them
As he went out and in to fetch the cows—
Some boy too far from town to learn baseball,
Whose only play was what he found himself,
Summer or winter, and could play alone.
One by one he subdued his father's trees
By riding them down over and over again
Until he took the stiffness out of them,
And not one but hung limp, not one was left
For him to conquer. He learned all there was
To learn about not launching out too soon
And so not carrying the tree away

Clear to the ground. He always kept his poise
To the top branches, climbing carefully
With the same pains you use to fill a cup
Up to the brim, and even above the brim.
Then he flung outward, feet first, with a swish,
Kicking his way down through the air to the ground.
So was I once myself a swinger of birches.
And so I dream of going back to be.
It's when I'm weary of considerations,
And life is too much like a pathless wood
Where your face burns and tickles with the cobwebs
Broken across it, and one eye is weeping
From a twig's having lashed across it open.
I'd like to get away from earth awhile
And then come back to it and begin over.
May no fate willfully misunderstand me
And half grant what I wish and snatch me away
Not to return. Earth's the right place for love:
I don't know where it's likely to go better.
I'd like to go by climbing a birch tree,
And climb black branches up a snow-white trunk
Toward heaven, till the tree could bear no more,
But dipped its top and set me down again.
That would be good both going and coming back.
One could do worse than be a swinger of birches.

THE HILL WIFE

LONELINESS

Her Word

One ought not to have to care
    So much as you and I
Care when the birds come round the house
    To seem to say good-by;

Or care so much when they come back
    With whatever it is they sing;

The truth being we are as much
  Too glad for the one thing

As we are too sad for the other here—
  With birds that fill their breasts
But with each other and themselves
  And their built or driven nests.

HOUSE FEAR

Always—I tell you this they learned—
Always at night when they returned
To the lonely house from far away
To lamps unlighted and fire gone gray,
They learned to rattle the lock and key
To give whatever might chance to be
Warning and time to be off in flight:
And preferring the out- to the in-door night,
They learned to leave the house-door wide
Until they had lit the lamp inside.

THE SMILE

Her Word

I didn't like the way he went away.
That smile! It never came of being gay.
Still he smiled—did you see him?—I was sure!
Perhaps because we gave him only bread
And the wretch knew from that that we were poor.
Perhaps because he let us give instead
Of seizing from us as he might have seized.
Perhaps he mocked at us for being wed,
Or being very young (and he was pleased
To have a vision of us old and dead).
I wonder how far down the road he's got.
He's watching from the woods as like as not.

THE OFT-REPEATED DREAM

She had no saying dark enough
  For the dark pine that kept
Forever trying the window-latch
  Of the room where they slept.

The tireless but ineffectual hands
  That with every futile pass
Made the great tree seem as a little bird
  Before the mystery of glass!

It never had been inside the room,
  And only one of the two
Was afraid in an oft-repeated dream
  Of what the tree might do.

THE IMPULSE

It was too lonely for her there,
  And too wild,
And since there were but two of them,
  And no child,

And work was little in the house,
  She was free,
And followed where he furrowed field,
  Or felled tree.

She rested on a log and tossed
  The fresh chips,
With a song only to herself
  On her lips.

And once she went to break a bough
  Of black alder.
She strayed so far she scarcely heard
  When he called her—

And didn't answer—didn't speak—
  Or return.
She stood, and then she ran and hid
  In the fern.

He never found her, though he looked
  Everywhere,
And he asked at her mother's house
  Was she there.

Sudden and swift and light as that
   The ties gave,
And he learned of finalities
   Besides the grave.

from TWO WITCHES

THE WITCH OF COÖS

I stayed the night for shelter at a farm
Behind the mountain, with a mother and son,
Two old-believers. They did all the talking.

MOTHER. Folks think a witch who has familiar spirits
She could call up to pass a winter evening,
But won't, should be burned at the stake or something.
Summoning spirits isn't 'Button, button,
Who's got the button,' I would have them know.

SON. Mother can make a common table rear
And kick with two legs like an army mule.

MOTHER. And when I've done it, what good have I done?
Rather than tip a table for you, let me
Tell you what Ralle the Sioux Control once told me.
He said the dead had souls, but when I asked him
How could that be—I thought the dead were souls,
He broke my trance. Don't that make you suspicious
That there's something the dead are keeping back?
Yes, there's something the dead are keeping back.

SON. You wouldn't want to tell him what we have
Up attic, mother?

MOTHER. Bones—a skeleton.

SON. But the headboard of mother's bed is pushed
Against the attic door: the door is nailed.

It's harmless. Mother hears it in the night
Halting perplexed behind the barrier
Of door and headboard. Where it wants to get
Is back into the cellar where it came from.

MOTHER. We'll never let them, will we, son! We'll never!

SON. It left the cellar forty years ago
And carried itself like a pile of dishes
Up one flight from the cellar to the kitchen,
Another from the kitchen to the bedroom,
Another from the bedroom to the attic,
Right past both father and mother, and neither stopped it.
Father had gone upstairs; mother was downstairs.
I was a baby: I don't know where I was.

MOTHER. The only fault my husband found with me—
I went to sleep before I went to bed,
Especially in winter when the bed
Might just as well be ice and the clothes snow.
The night the bones came up the cellar-stairs
Toffile had gone to bed alone and left me,
But left an open door to cool the room off
So as to sort of turn me out of it.
I was just coming to myself enough
To wonder where the cold was coming from,
When I heard Toffile upstairs in the bedroom
And thought I heard him downstairs in the cellar.
The board we had laid down to walk dry-shod on
When there was water in the cellar in spring
Struck the hard cellar bottom. And then someone
Began the stairs, two footsteps for each step,
The way a man with one leg and a crutch,
Or a little child, comes up. It wasn't Toffile:
It wasn't anyone who could be there.
The bulkhead double-doors were double-locked
And swollen tight and buried under snow.
The cellar windows were banked up with sawdust
And swollen tight and buried under snow.
It was the bones. I knew them—and good reason.
My first impulse was to get to the knob

And hold the door. But the bones didn't try
The door; they halted helpless on the landing,
Waiting for things to happen in their favor.
The faintest restless rustling ran all through them.
I never could have done the thing I did
If the wish hadn't been too strong in me
To see how they were mounted for this walk.
I had a vision of them put together
Not like a man, but like a chandelier.
So suddenly I flung the door wide on him.
A moment he stood balancing with emotion,
And all but lost himself. (A tongue of fire
Flashed out and licked along his upper teeth.
Smoke rolled inside the sockets of his eyes.)
Then he came at me with one hand outstretched,
The way he did in life once; but this time
I struck the hand off brittle on the floor,
And fell back from him on the floor myself.
The finger-pieces slid in all directions.
(Where did I see one of those pieces lately?
Hand me my button-box—it must be there.)
I sat up on the floor and shouted, 'Toffile,
It's coming up to you.' It had its choice
Of the door to the cellar or the hall.
It took the hall door for the novelty,
And set off briskly for so slow a thing,
Still going every which way in the joints, though,
So that it looked like lightning or a scribble,
From the slap I had just now given its hand.
I listened till it almost climbed the stairs
From the hall to the only finished bedroom,
Before I got up to do anything;
Then ran and shouted, 'Shut the bedroom door,
Toffile, for my sake!' 'Company?' he said,
'Don't make me get up; I'm too warm in bed.'
So lying forward weakly on the handrail
I pushed myself upstairs, and in the light
(The kitchen had been dark) I had to own
I could see nothing. 'Toffile, I don't see it.
It's with us in the room though. It's the bones.'
'What bones?' 'The cellar bones—out of the grave.'
That made him throw his bare legs out of bed

And sit up by me and take hold of me.
I wanted to put out the light and see
If I could see it, or else mow the room,
With our arms at the level of our knees,
And bring the chalk-pile down. 'I'll tell you what—
It's looking for another door to try.
The uncommonly deep snow has made him think
Of his old song, *The Wild Colonial Boy*,
He always used to sing along the tote road.
He's after an open door to get outdoors.
Let's trap him with an open door up attic.'
Toffile agreed to that, and sure enough,
Almost the moment he was given an opening,
The steps began to climb the attic stairs.
I heard them. Toffile didn't seem to hear them.
'Quick!' I slammed to the door and held the knob.
'Toffile, get nails.' I made him nail the door shut
And push the headboard of the bed against it.
Then we asked was there anything
Up attic that we'd ever want again.
The attic was less to us than the cellar.
If the bones liked the attic, let them have it.
Let them stay in the attic. When they sometimes
Come down the stairs at night and stand perplexed
Behind the door and headboard of the bed,
Brushing their chalky skull with chalky fingers,
With sounds like the dry rattling of a shutter,
That's what I sit up in the dark to say—
To no one any more since Toffile died.
Let them stay in the attic since they went there.
I promised Toffile to be cruel to them
For helping them be cruel once to him.

SON. We think they had a grave down in the cellar.

MOTHER. We know they had a grave down in the cellar.

SON. We never could find out whose bones they were.

MOTHER. Yes, we could too, son. Tell the truth for once.
They were a man's his father killed for me.
I mean a man he killed instead of me.

The least I could do was to help dig their grave.
We were about it one night in the cellar.
Son knows the story: but 'twas not for him
To tell the truth, suppose the time had come.
Son looks surprised to see me end a lie
We'd kept all these years between ourselves
So as to have it ready for outsiders.
But tonight I don't care enough to lie—
I don't remember why I ever cared.
Toffile, if he were here, I don't believe
Could tell you why he ever cared himself. . . .

She hadn't found the finger-bone she wanted
Among the buttons poured out in her lap.
I verified the name next morning: Toffile.
The rural letter box said Toffile Lajway.

FIRE AND ICE

Some say the world will end in fire,
Some say in ice.
From what I've tasted of desire
I hold with those who favor fire.
But if it had to perish twice,
I think I know enough of hate
To say that for destruction ice
Is also great
And would suffice.

STOPPING BY WOODS ON
A SNOWY EVENING

Whose woods these are I think I know.
His house is in the village though;
He will not see me stopping here
To watch his woods fill up with snow.

My little horse must think it queer
To stop without a farmhouse near
Between the woods and frozen lake
The darkest evening of the year.

He gives his harness bells a shake
To ask if there is some mistake.
The only other sound's the sweep
Of easy wind and downy flake.

The woods are lovely, dark and deep,
But I have promises to keep,
And miles to go before I sleep,
And miles to go before I sleep.

ONCE BY THE PACIFIC

The shattered water made a misty din.
Great waves looked over others coming in,
And thought of doing something to the shore
That water never did to land before.
The clouds were low and hairy in the skies,
Like locks blown forward in the gleam of eyes.
You could not tell, and yet it looked as if
The shore was lucky in being backed by cliff,
The cliff in being backed by continent;
It looked as if a night of dark intent
Was coming, and not only a night, an age.
Someone had better be prepared for rage.
There would be more than ocean-water broken
Before God's last *Put out the Light* was spoken.

BEREFT

Where had I heard this wind before
Change like this to a deeper roar?

What would it take my standing there for,
Holding open a restive door,
Looking down hill to a frothy shore?
Summer was past and day was past.
Somber clouds in the west were massed.
Out in the porch's sagging floor,
Leaves got up in a coil and hissed,
Blindly struck at my knee and missed.
Something sinister in the tone
Told me my secret must be known:
Word I was in the house alone
Somehow must have gotten abroad,
Word I was in my life alone,
Word I had no one left but God.

ACQUAINTED WITH THE NIGHT

I have been one acquainted with the night.
I have walked out in rain—and back in rain.
I have outwalked the furthest city light.

I have looked down the saddest city lane.
I have passed by the watchman on his beat
And dropped my eyes, unwilling to explain.

I have stood still and stopped the sound of feet
When far away an interrupted cry
Came over houses from another street,

But not to call me back or say good-by;
And further still at an unearthly height,
One luminary clock against the sky

Proclaimed the time was neither wrong nor right.
I have been one acquainted with the night.

TWO TRAMPS IN MUD TIME

Out of the mud two strangers came
And caught me splitting wood in the yard.
And one of them put me off my aim
By hailing cheerily 'Hit them hard!'
I knew pretty well why he dropped behind
And let the other go on a way.
I knew pretty well what he had in mind:
He wanted to take my job for pay.

Good blocks of oak it was I split,
As large around as the chopping block;
And every piece I squarely hit
Fell splinterless as a cloven rock.
The blows that a life of self-control
Spares to strike for the common good
That day, giving a loose to my soul,
I spent on the unimportant wood.

The sun was warm but the wind was chill.
You know how it is with an April day
When the sun is out and the wind is still,
You're one month on in the middle of May.
But if you so much as dare to speak,
A cloud comes over the sunlit arch,
A wind comes off a frozen peak,
And you're two months back in the middle of March.

A bluebird comes tenderly up to alight
And turns to the wind to unruffle a plume
His song so pitched as not to excite
A single flower as yet to bloom.
It is snowing a flake: and he half knew
Winter was only playing possum.
Except in color he isn't blue,
But he wouldn't advise a thing to blossom.

The water for which we may have to look
In summertime with a witching-wand,

In every wheelrut's now a brook,
In every print of a hoof a pond.
Be glad of water, but don't forget
The lurking frost in the earth beneath
That will steal forth after the sun is set
And show on the water its crystal teeth.

The time when most I loved my task
These two must make me love it more
By coming with what they came to ask.
You'd think I never had felt before
The weight of an ax-head poised aloft,
The grip on earth of outspread feet.
The life of muscles rocking soft
And smooth and moist in vernal heat.

Out of the woods two hulking tramps
(From sleeping God knows where last night,
But not long since in the lumber camps).
They thought all chopping was theirs of right
Men of the woods and lumberjacks,
They judged me by their appropriate tool.
Except as a fellow handled an ax,
They had no way of knowing a fool.

Nothing on either side was said.
They knew they had but to stay their stay
And all their logic would fill my head:
As that I had no right to play
With what was another man's work for gain.
My right might be love but theirs was need.
And where the two exist in twain
Theirs was the better right—agreed.

But yield who will to their separation,
My object in living is to unite
My avocation and my vocation
As my two eyes make one in sight.
Only where love and need are one,
And the work is play for mortal stakes,
Is the deed ever really done
For Heaven and the future's sakes.

THE SPAN OF LIFE

The old dog barks backward without getting up.
I can remember when he was a pup.

COME IN

As I came to the edge of the woods,
Thrush music—hark!
Now if it was dusk outside,
Inside it was dark.

Too dark in the woods for a bird
By sleight of wing
To better its perch for the night,
Though it still could sing.

The last of the light of the sun
That had died in the west
Still lived for one song more
In a thrush's breast.

Far in the pillared dark
Thrush music went—
Almost like a call to come in
To the dark and lament.

But no, I was out for stars:
I would not come in.
I meant not even if asked,
And I hadn't been.

THE GIFT OUTRIGHT

The land was ours before we were the land's.
She was our land more than a hundred years

Before we were her people. She was ours
In Massachusetts, in Virginia,
But we were England's, still colonials,
Possessing what we still were unpossessed by,
Possessed by what we now no more possessed.
Something we were withholding made us weak
Until we found out that it was ourselves
We were withholding from our land of living,
And forthwith found salvation in surrender.
Such as we were we gave ourselves outright
(The deed of gift was many deeds of war)
To the land vaguely realizing westward,
But still unstoried, artless, unenhanced,
Such as she was, such as she would become.

THE LESSON FOR TODAY

If this uncertain age in which we dwell
Were really as dark as I hear sages tell,
And I convinced that they were really sages,
I should not curse myself with it to hell,
But leaving not the chair I long have sat in,
I should betake me back ten thousand pages
To the world's undebatably dark ages,
And getting up my medieval Latin,
Seek converse common cause and brotherhood
(By all that's liberal—I should, I should)
With poets who could calmly take the fate
Of being born at once too early and late,
And for these reasons kept from being great.
Yet singing but Dione in the wood
And *ver aspergit terram floribus*
They slowly led old Latin verse to rhyme
And to forget the ancient lengths of time,
And so began the modern world for us.

   I'd say, O Master of the Palace School,
You were not Charles' nor anybody's fool:

Tell me as pedagogue to pedagogue,
You did not know that since King Charles did rule
You had no chance but to be minor, did you?
Your light was spent perhaps as in a fog
That at once kept you burning low and hid you.
The age may very well have been to blame
For your not having won to Virgil's fame.
But no one ever heard you make the claim.
You would not think you knew enough to judge
The age when full upon you. That's my point.
We have today and I could call their name
Who know exactly what is out of joint
To make their verse and their excuses lame.
They've tried to grasp with too much social fact
Too large a situation. You and I
Would be afraid if we should comprehend
And get outside of too much bad statistics
Our muscles never could again contract:
We never could recover human shape,
But must live lives out mentally agape,
Or die of philosophical distention.
That's how we feel—and we're no special mystics.

We can't appraise the time in which we act.
But for the folly of it, let's pretend
We know enough to know it for adverse.
One more millennium's about to end.
Let's celebrate the event, my distant friend,
In publicly disputing which is worse,
The present age or your age. You and I
As schoolmen of repute should qualify
To wage a fine scholastical contention
As to whose age deserves the lower mark,
Or should I say the higher one, for dark.
I can just hear the way you make it go:
There's always something to be sorry for,
A sordid peace or an outrageous war.
Yes, yes, of course. We have the same convention.
The groundwork of all faith is human woe.
It was well worth preliminary mention.
There's nothing but injustice to be had,

No choice is left a poet, you might add,
But how to take the curse, tragic or comic.
It was well worth preliminary mention.
But let's go on to where our cases part,
If part they do. Let me propose a start.
(We're rivals in the badness of our case,
Remember, and must keep a solemn face.)
Space ails us moderns: we are sick with space.
Its contemplation makes us out as small
As a brief epidemic of microbes
That in a good glass may be seen to crawl
The patina of this the least of globes.
But have we there the advantage after all?
You were belittled into vilest worms
God hardly tolerated with his feet;
Which comes to the same thing in different terms.
We both are the belittled human race,
One as compared with God and one with space.
I had thought ours the more profound disgrace;
But doubtless this was only my conceit.
The cloister and the observatory saint
Take comfort in about the same complaint.
So science and religion really meet.

I can just hear you call your Palace class:
Come learn the Latin Eheu for alas.
You may not want to use it and you may.
O paladins, the lesson for today
Is how to be unhappy yet polite.
And at the summons Roland, Olivier,
And every sheepish paladin and peer,
Being already more than proved in fight,
Sits down in school to try if he can write
Like Horace in the true Horatian vein,
Yet like a Christian discipline to bend
His mind to thinking always of the end.
Memento mori and obey the Lord.
Art and religion love the somber chord.
Earth's a hard place in which to save the soul,
And could it be brought under state control,
So automatically we all were saved,

Its separateness from Heaven could be waived;
It might as well at once be kingdom-come.
(Perhaps it will be next millennium.)

But these are universals, not confined
To any one time, place, or human kind.
We're either nothing or a God's regret.
As ever when philosophers are met,
No matter where they stoutly mean to get,
Nor what particulars they reason from,
They are philosophers, and from old habit
They end up in the universal Whole
As unoriginal as any rabbit.

One age is like another for the soul.
I'm telling you. You haven't said a thing,
Unless I put it in your mouth to say.
I'm having the whole argument my way.—
But in your favor—please to tell your King—
In having granted you all ages shine
With equal darkness, yours as dark as mine.
I'm liberal. You, you aristocrat,
Won't know exactly what I mean by that.
I mean so altruistically moral
I never take my own side in a quarrel.
I'd lay my hand on his hand on his staff,
Lean back and have my confidential laugh,
And tell him I had read his Epitaph.

It sent me to the graves the other day.
The only other there was far away
Across the landscape with a watering pot
At his devotions in a special plot.
And he was there resuscitating flowers
(Make no mistake about its being bones);
But I was only there to read the stones
To see what on the whole they had to say
About how long a man may think to live,
Which is becoming my concern of late.
And very wide the choice they seemed to give;

The ages ranging all the way from hours
To months and years and many many years.
One man had lived one hundred years and eight.
But though we all may be inclined to wait
And follow some development of state,
Or see what comes of science and invention,
There is a limit to our time extension.
We all are doomed to broken-off careers,
And so's the nation, so's the total race.
The earth itself is liable to the fate
Of meaninglessly being broken off.
(And hence so many literary tears
At which my inclination is to scoff.)
I may have wept that any should have died
Or missed their chance, or not have been their best,
Or been their riches, fame, or love denied;
On me as much as any is the jest.
I take my incompleteness with the rest.
God bless himself can no one else be blessed.

    I hold your doctrine of Memento Mori.
And were an epitaph to be my story
I'd have a short one ready for my own.
I would have written of me on my stone:
I had a lover's quarrel with the world.

A SEMI-REVOLUTION

I advocate a semi-revolution.
The trouble with a total revolution
(Ask any reputable Rosicrucian)
Is that it brings the same class up on top.
Executives of skillful execution
Will therefore plan to go halfway and stop.
Yes, revolutions are the only salves,
But they're one thing that should be done by halves.

DIRECTIVE

Back out of all this now too much for us,
Back in a time made simple by the loss
Of detail, burned, dissolved, and broken off
Like graveyard marble sculpture in the weather,
There is a house that is no more a house
Upon a farm that is no more a farm
And in a town that is no more a town.
The road there, if you'll let a guide direct you
Who only has at heart your getting lost,
May seem as if it should have been a quarry—
Great monolithic knees the former town
Long since gave up pretense of keeping covered.
And there's a story in a book about it:
Besides the wear of iron wagon wheels
The ledges show lines ruled southeast northwest,
The chisel work of an enormous Glacier
That braced his feet against the Arctic Pole.
You must not mind a certain coolness from him
Still said to haunt this side of Panther Mountain.
Nor need you mind the serial ordeal
Of being watched from forty cellar holes
As if by eye pairs out of forty firkins.
As for the woods' excitement over you
That sends light rustle rushes to their leaves,
Charge that to upstart inexperience.
Where were they all not twenty years ago?
They think too much of having shaded out
A few old pecker-fretted apple trees.
Make yourself up a cheering song of how
Someone's road home from work this once was,
Who may be just ahead of you on foot
Or creaking with a buggy load of grain.
The height of the adventure is the height
Of country where two village cultures faded
Into each other. Both of them are lost.
And if you're lost enough to find yourself
By now, pull in your ladder road behind you

And put a sign up CLOSED to all but me.
Then make yourself at home. The only field
Now left's no bigger than a harness gall.
First there's the children's house of make believe,
Some shattered dishes underneath a pine,
The playthings in the playhouse of the children.
Weep for what little things could make them glad.
Then for the house that is no more a house,
But only a belilaced cellar hole,
Now slowly closing like a dent in dough.
This was no playhouse but a house in earnest.
Your destination and your destiny's
A brook that was the water of the house,
Cold as a spring as yet so near its source,
Too lofty and original to rage.
(We know the valley streams that when aroused
Will leave their tatters hung on barb and thorn.)
I have kept hidden in the instep arch
Of an old cedar at the waterside
A broken drinking goblet like the Grail
Under a spell so the wrong ones can't find it,
So can't get saved, as Saint Mark says they mustn't.
(I stole the goblet from the children's playhouse.)
Here are your waters and your watering place.
Drink and be whole again beyond confusion.

POD   OF   THE   MILKWEED

Calling all butterflies of every race
From source unknown but from no special place
They ever will return to all their lives,
Because unlike the bees they have no hives,
The milkweed brings up to my very door
The theme of wanton waste in peace and war
As it has never been to me before.
And so it seems a flower's coming out
That should if not be talked then sung about.
The countless wings that from the infinite

Make such a noiseless tumult over it
Do no doubt with their color compensate
For what the drab weed lacks of the ornate.
For drab it is its fondest must admit.
And yes, although it is a flower that flows
With milk and honey, it is bitter milk,
As anyone who ever broke its stem
And dared to taste the wound a little knows.
It tastes as if it might be opiate.
But whatsoever else it may secrete,
Its flowers' distilled honey is so sweet
It makes the butterflies intemperate.
There is no slumber in its juice for them.
One knocks another off from where he clings.
They knock the dyestuff off each other's wings—
With thirst on hunger to the point of lust.
They raise in their intemperance a cloud
Of mingled butterfly and flower dust
That hangs perceptibly above the scene.
In being sweet to these ephemerals
The sober weed has managed to contrive
In our three hundred days and sixty five
One day too sweet for beings to survive.
Many shall come away as struggle worn
And spent and dusted off of their regalia
To which at daybreak they were freshly born
As after one-of-them's proverbial failure
From having beaten all day long in vain
Against the wrong side of a window pane.

But waste was of the essence of the scheme.
And all the good they did for man or god
To all those flowers they passionately trod
Was leave as their posterity one pod
With an inheritance of restless dream.
He hangs on upside down with talon feet
In an inquisitive position odd
As any Guatemalan parakeet.
Something eludes him. Is it food to eat?
Or some dim secret of the good of waste?
He almost has it in his talon clutch.

Where have those flowers and butterflies all gone
That science may have staked the future on?
He seems to say the reason why so much
Should come to nothing must be fairly faced.*

FORGIVE, O LORD, MY LITTLE JOKES ON THEE

Forgive, O Lord, my little jokes on Thee
And I'll forgive Thy great big one on me.

John Masefield / 1878–1967

THE WEST WIND

It's a warm wind, the west wind, full of birds' cries;
I never hear the west wind but tears are in my eyes.
For it comes from the west lands, the old brown hills,
And April's in the west wind, and daffodils.

It's a fine land, the west land, for hearts as tired as mine,
Apple orchards blossom there, and the air's like wine.
There is cool green grass there, where men may lie at rest,
And the thrushes are in song there, fluting from the nest.

"Will you not come home, brother? you have been long
        away,
It's April, and blossom time, and white is the spray,
And bright is the sun, brother, and warm is the rain,—
Will you not come home, brother, home to us again?

* And shall be in due course.

The young corn is green, brother, where the rabbits run,
It's blue sky, and white clouds, and warm rain and sun.
It's song to a man's soul, brother, fire to a man's brain,
To hear the wild bees and see the merry spring again.

Larks are singing in the west, brother, above the green
    wheat,
So will ye not come home, brother, and rest your tired
    feet?
I've a balm for bruised hearts, brother, sleep for aching
    eyes,"
Says the warm wind, the west wind, full of birds' cries.

It's the white road westwards is the road I must tread
To the green grass, the cool grass, and rest for heart and
    head,
To the violets and the brown brooks and the thrushes' song,
In the fine land, the west land, the land where I belong.

CARGOES

Quinquireme of Nineveh from distant Ophir,
Rowing home to haven in sunny Palestine,
With a cargo of ivory,
And apes and peacocks,
Sandalwood, cedarwood, and sweet white wine.

Stately Spanish galleon coming from the Isthmus,
Dipping through the Tropics by the palm-green shores,
With a cargo of diamonds,
Emeralds, amethysts,
Topazes, and cinnamon, and gold moidores.

Dirty British coaster with a salt-caked smoke stack,
Butting through the Channel in the mad March days,
With a cargo of Tyne coal,
Road-rails, pig-lead,
Firewood, iron-ware, and cheap tin trays.

C. L. M.

In the dark womb where I began
My mother's life made me a man.
Through all the months of human birth
Her beauty fed my common earth.
I cannot see, nor breathe, nor stir,
But through the death of some of her.

Down in the darkness of the grave
She cannot see the life she gave.
For all her love, she cannot tell
Whether I use it ill or well,
Nor knock at dusty doors to find
Her beauty dusty in the mind.

If the grave's gates could be undone,
She would not know her little son,
I am so grown. If we should meet
She would pass by me in the street,
Unless my soul's face let her see
My sense of what she did for me.

What have I done to keep in mind
My debt to her and womankind?
What woman's happier life repays
Her for those months of wretched days?
For all my mouthless body leeched
Ere Birth's releasing hell was reached?

What have I done, or tried, or said
In thanks to that dear woman dead?
Men triumph over women still,
Men trample women's rights at will,
And man's lust roves the world untamed.

.   .   .

O grave, keep shut lest I be shamed.

FLESH, I HAVE KNOCKED
AT MANY A DUSTY DOOR

Flesh, I have knocked at many a dusty door,
Gone down full many a windy midnight lane,
Probed in old walls and felt along the floor,
Pressed in blind hope that lighted window-pane.
But useless all, though sometimes, when the moon
Was full in heaven and the sea was full,
Along my body's alleys came a tune
Played in the tavern by the Beautiful.
Then for an instant I have felt at point
To find and seize her, whosoe'er she be,
Whether some saint whose glory doth anoint
Those whom she loves, or but a part of me,
Or something that the things not understood
Make for their uses out of flesh and blood.

IS THERE A GREAT GREEN
COMMONWEALTH OF THOUGHT

Is there a great green commonwealth of Thought
Which ranks the yearly pageant, and decides
How Summer's royal progress shall be wrought,
By secret stir which in each plant abides?
Does rocking daffodil consent that she,
The snowdrop of wet winters, shall be first?
Does spotted cowslip with the grass agree
To hold her pride before the rattle burst?
And in the hedge what quick agreement goes,
When hawthorn blossoms redden to decay,
That Summer's pride shall come, the Summer's rose,
Before the flower be on the bramble spray?
Or is it, as with us, unresting strife,
And each consent a lucky gasp for life?

I COULD NOT SLEEP FOR
THINKING OF THE SKY

I could not sleep for thinking of the sky,
The unending sky, with all its million suns
Which turn their planets everlastingly
In nothing, where the fire-haired comet runs.
If I could sail that nothing, I should cross
Silence and emptiness with dark stars passing;
Then, in the darkness, see a point of gloss
Burn to a glow, and glare, and keep amassing,
And rage into a sun with wandering planets,
And drop behind; and then, as I proceed,
See his last light upon his last moon's granites
Die to a dark that would be night indeed:
Night where my soul might sail a million years
In nothing, not even Death, not even tears.

NIGHT IS ON THE DOWNLAND,
ON THE LONELY MOORLAND

Night is on the downland, on the lonely moorland,
On the hills where the wind goes over sheep-bitten turf,
Where the bent grass beats upon the unploughed poorland
And the pine-woods roar like the surf.

Here the Roman lived on the wind-barren lonely,
Dark now and haunted by the moorland fowl;
None comes here now but the peewit only,
And moth-like death in the owl.

Beauty was here, on this beetle-droning downland;
The thought of a Caesar in the purple came
From the palace by the Tiber in the Roman townland
To this wind-swept hill with no name.

Lonely Beauty came here and was here in sadness,
Brave as a thought on the frontier of the mind,

In the camp of the wild upon the march of madness,
The bright-eyed Queen of the Blind.

Now where Beauty was are the wind-withered gorses,
Moaning like old men in the hill-wind's blast;
The flying sky is dark with running horses,
And the night is full of the past.

ON GROWING OLD

Be with me, Beauty, for the fire is dying,
My dog and I are old, too old for roving.
Man, whose young passion sets the spindrift flying,
Is soon too lame to march, too cold for loving.
I take the book and gather to the fire,
Turning old yellow leaves; minute by minute,
The clock ticks to my heart; a withered wire
Moves a thin ghost of music in the spinet.
I cannot sail your seas, I cannot wander,
Your cornland, nor your hill-land nor your valleys,
Ever again, nor share the battle yonder
Where the young knight the broken squadron rallies.
Only stay quiet while my mind remembers
The beauty of fire from the beauty of embers.

Beauty, have pity, for the strong have power,
The rich their wealth, the beautiful their grace,
Summer of man its sunlight and its flower,
Spring-time of man all April in a face.
Only, as in the jostling in the Strand,
Where the mob thrusts or loiters or is loud,
The beggar with the saucer in his hand
Asks only a penny from the passing crowd,
So, from this glittering world with all its fashion,
Its fire and play of men, its stir, its march,
Let me have wisdom, Beauty, wisdom and passion,
Bread to the soul, rain where the summers parch.
Give me but these, and though the darkness close
Even the night will blossom as the rose.

William Carlos Williams / 1883–1963

THE YACHTS

contend in a sea which the land partly encloses
shielding them from the too-heavy blows
of an ungoverned ocean which when it chooses

tortures the biggest hulls, the best man knows
to pit against its beatings, and sinks them pitilessly.
Mothlike in mists, scintillant in the minute

brilliance of cloudless days, with broad bellying sails
they glide to the wind tossing green water
from their sharp prows while over them the crew crawls

ant-like, solicitously grooming them, releasing,
making fast as they turn, lean far over and having
caught the wind again, side by side, head for the mark.

In a well guarded arena of open water surrounded by
lesser and greater craft which, sycophant, lumbering
and flittering follow them, they appear youthful, rare

as the light of a happy eye, live with the grace
of all that in the mind is fleckless, free and
naturally to be desired. Now the sea which holds them

is moody, lapping their glossy sides, as if feeling
for some slightest flaw but fails completely.
Today no race. Then the wind comes again. The yachts

move, jockeying for a start, the signal is set and they
are off. Now the waves strike at them but they are too
well made, they slip through, though they take in canvas.

Arms with hands grasping seek to clutch at the prows.
Bodies thrown recklessly in the way are cut aside.
It is a sea of faces about them in agony, in despair

until the horror of the race dawns staggering the mind,
the whole sea become an entanglement of watery bodies
lost to the world bearing what they cannot hold. Broken,

beaten, desolate, reaching from the dead to be taken up
they cry out, failing, failing! their cries rising
in waves still as the skillful yachts pass over.

TRACT

I will teach you my townspeople
how to perform a funeral
for you have it over a troop
of artists—
unless one should scour the world—
you have the ground sense necessary.

See! the hearse leads.
I begin with a design for a hearse.
For Christ's sake not black—
nor white either—and not polished!
Let it be weathered—like a farm wagon—
with gilt wheels (this could be
applied fresh at small expense)
or no wheels at all:
a rough dray to drag over the ground.

Knock the glass out!
My God—glass, my townspeople!
For what purpose? Is it for the dead
to look out or for us to see
how well he is housed or to see
the flowers or the lack of them—
or what?

To keep the rain and snow from him?
He will have a heavier rain soon:
pebbles and dirt and what not.
Let there be no glass—
and no upholstery, phew!
and no little brass rollers
and small easy wheels on the bottom—
my townspeople what are you thinking of?

A rough plain hearse then
with gilt wheels and no top at all.
On this the coffin lies
by its own weight.

                    No wreaths please—
especially no hot house flowers.
Some common memento is better,
something he prized and is known by:
his old clothes—a few books perhaps—
God knows what! You realize
how we are about these things
my townspeople—
something will be found—anything
even flowers if he had come to that.
So much for the hearse.

For heaven's sake though see to the driver!
Take off the silk hat! In fact
that's no place at all for him—
up there unceremoniously
dragging our friend out to his own dignity!
Bring him down—bring him down!
Low and inconspicuous! I'd not have him ride
on the wagon at all—damn him—
the undertaker's understrapper!
Let him hold the reins
and walk at the side
and inconspicuously too!

Then briefly as to yourselves:
Walk behind—as they do in France,

seventh class, or if you ride
Hell take curtains! Go with some show
of inconvenience; sit openly—
to the weather as to grief.
Or do you think you can shut grief in?
What—from us? We who have perhaps
nothing to lose? Share with us
share with us—it will be money
in your pockets.

                    Go now
I think you are ready.

THE WIDOW'S LAMENT
IN SPRINGTIME

Sorrow is my own yard
where the new grass
flames as it has flamed
often before but not
with the cold fire
that closes round me this year.
Thirtyfive years
I lived with my husband.
The plumtree is white today
with masses of flowers.
Masses of flowers
load the cherry branches
and color some bushes
yellow and some red
but the grief in my heart
is stronger than they
for though they were my joy
formerly, today I notice them
and turned away forgetting.
Today my son told me
that in the meadows,
at the edge of the heavy woods

in the distance, he saw
trees of white flowers.
I feel that I would like
to go there
and fall into those flowers
and sink into the marsh near them.

SPRING AND ALL

By the road to the contagious hospital
under the surge of the blue
mottled clouds driven from the
northeast—a cold wind. Beyond, the
waste of broad, muddy fields
brown with dried weeds, standing and fallen

patches of standing water
the scattering of tall trees

All along the road the reddish
purplish, forked, upstanding, twiggy
stuff of bushes and small trees
with dead, brown leaves under them
leafless vines—

Lifeless in appearance, sluggish
dazed spring approaches—

They enter the new world naked,
cold, uncertain of all
save that they enter. All about them
the cold, familiar wind—

Now the grass, tomorrow
the stiff curl of wildcarrot leaf
One by one objects are defined—
It quickens: clarity, outline of leaf

But now the stark dignity of
entrance—Still, the profound change

has come upon them: rooted, they
grip down and begin to awaken

THE RED WHEELBARROW

so much depends
upon

a red wheel
barrow

glazed with rain
water

beside the white
chickens.

THE BULL

It is in captivity—
ringed, haltered, chained
to a drag
the bull is godlike

Unlike the cows
he lives alone, nozzles
the sweet grass gingerly
to pass the time away

He kneels, lies down
and stretching out
a foreleg licks himself
about the hoof

then stays
with half-closed eyes,
Olympian commentary on
the bright passage of days.

—The round sun
smooth his lacquer
through
the glossy pinetrees

his substance hard
as ivory or glass—
through which the wind
yet plays—
                milkless
he nods
the hair between his horns
and eyes matted
with hyacinthine curls

THE DANCE

In Breughel's great picture, The Kermess,
the dancers go round, they go round and
around, the squeal and the blare and the
tweedle of bagpipes, a bugle and fiddles
tipping their bellies (round as the thick-
sided glasses whose wash they impound)
their hips and their bellies off balance
to turn them. Kicking and rolling about
the Fair Grounds, swinging their butts, those
shanks must be sound to bear up under such
rollicking measures, prance as they dance
in Breughel's great picture, The Kermess.

BURNING THE CHRISTMAS GREENS

Their time past, pulled down
cracked and flung to the fire
—go up in a roar

All recognition lost, burnt clean
clean in the flame, the green
dispersed, a living red,
flame red, red as blood wakes
on the ash—

and ebbs to a steady burning
the rekindled bed become
a landscape of flame

At the winter's midnight
we went to the trees, the coarse
holly, the balsam and
the hemlock for their green

At the thick of the dark
the moment of the cold's
deepest plunge we brought branches
cut from the green trees

to fill our need, and over
doorways, about paper Christmas
bells covered with tinfoil
and fastened by red ribbons

we stuck the green prongs
in the windows hung
woven wreaths and above pictures
the living green. On the

mantle we built a green forest
and among those hemlock
sprays put a herd of small
white deer as if they

were walking there. All this!
and it seemed gentle and good
to us. Their time past,
relief! The room bare. We

stuffed the dead grate
with them upon the half burnt out

log's smoldering eye, opening
red and closing under them

and we stood there looking down.
Green is a solace
a promise of peace, a fort
against the cold (though we

did not say so) a challenge
above the snow's
hard shell. Green (we might
have said) that, where

small birds hide and dodge
and lift their plaintive
rallying cries, blocks for them
and knocks down

the unseeing bullets of
the storm. Green spruce boughs
pulled down by a weight of
snow—Transformed!

Violence leaped and appeared.
Recreant! roared to life
as the flame rose through and
our eyes recoiled from it.

In the jagged flames green
to red, instant and alive. Green!
those sure abutments . . . Gone!
lost to mind

and quick in the contracting
tunnel of the grate
appeared a world! Black
mountains, black and red—as

yet uncolored—and ash white,
an infant landscape of shimmering
ash and flame and we, in
that instant, lost,

breathless to be witnesses,
as if we stood
ourselves refreshed among
the shining fauna of that fire.

TO A DOG INJURED IN THE STREET

It is myself,
          not the poor beast lying there
                    yelping with pain
that brings me to myself with a start—
          as at the explosion
                    of a bomb, a bomb that has laid
all the world waste.
          I can do nothing
                    but sing about it
and so I am assuaged
          from my pain.

A drowsy numbness drowns my sense
          as if of hemlock
                    I had drunk. I think
of the poetry
          of René Char
                    and all he must have seen
and suffered
          that has brought him
                    to speak only of
sedgy rivers,
          of daffodils and tulips
                    whose roots they water,
even to the free-flowing river
          that laves the rootlets
                    of those sweet-scented flowers
that people the
          milky
                    way

I remember Norma
        our English setter of my childhood
                her silky ears
and expressive eyes.
        She had a litter
              of pups one night
in our pantry and I kicked
        one of them
              thinking, in my alarm,
that they
        were biting her breasts
           to destroy her.

I remember also
        a dead rabbit
           lying harmlessly
on the outspread palm
        of a hunter's hand.
           As I stood by
watching
        he took a hunting knife
           and with a laugh
thrust it
        up into the animal's private parts.
        I almost fainted.

Why should I think of that now?
        The cries of a dying dog
           are to be blotted out
as best I can.
        René Char
           you are a poet who believes
in the power of beauty
        to right all wrongs.
        I believe it also.
With invention and courage
        we shall surpass
           the pitiful dumb beasts,
let all men believe it,
        as you have taught me also
           to believe it.

Elinor Wylie / 1885–1928

THE EAGLE AND THE MOLE

Avoid the reeking herd,
Shun the polluted flock,
Live like that stoic bird,
The eagle of the rock.

The huddled warmth of crowds
Begets and fosters hate;
He keeps, above the clouds,
His cliff inviolate.

When flocks are folded warm,
And herds to shelter run,
He sails above the storm,
He stares into the sun.

If in the eagle's track
Your sinews cannot leap,
Avoid the lathered pack,
Turn from the steaming sheep.

If you would keep your soul
From spotted sight or sound,
Live like the velvet mole;
Go burrow underground.

And there hold intercourse
With roots of trees and stones,
With rivers at their source,
And disembodied bones.

WILD PEACHES

I

When the world turns completely upside down
You say we'll emigrate to the Eastern Shore
Aboard a river-boat from Baltimore;
We'll live among wild peach trees, miles from town,
You'll wear a coonskin cap, and I a gown
Homespun, dyed butternut's dark gold colour.
Lost, like your lotus-eating ancestor,
We'll swim in milk and honey till we drown.

The winter will be short, the summer long,
The autumn amber-hued, sunny and hot,
Tasting of cider and of scuppernong;
All seasons sweet, but autumn best of all.
The squirrels in their silver fur will fall
Like falling leaves, like fruit, before your shot.

II

The autumn frosts will lie upon the grass
Like bloom on grapes of purple-brown and gold.
The misted early mornings will be cold;
The little puddles will be roofed with glass.
The sun, which burns from copper into brass,
Melts these at noon, and makes the boys unfold
Their knitted mufflers; full as they can hold,
Fat pockets dribble chestnuts as they pass.

Peaches grow wild, and pigs can live in clover;
A barrel of salted herrings lasts a year;
The spring begins before the winter's over.
By February you may find the skins
Of garter snakes and water moccasins
Dwindled and harsh, dead-white and cloudy-clear.

III

When April pours the colours of a shell
Upon the hills, when every little creek
Is shot with silver from the Chesapeake

In shoals new-minted by the ocean swell,
When strawberries go begging, and the sleek
Blue plums lie open to the blackbird's beak,
We shall live well—we shall live very well.

The months between the cherries and the peaches
Are brimming cornucopias which spill
Fruits red and purple, sombre-bloomed and black;
Then, down rich fields and frosty river beaches
We'll trample bright persimmons, while you kill
Bronze partridge, speckled quail, and canvasback.

IV

Down to the Puritan marrow of my bones
There's something in this richness that I hate.
I love the look, austere, immaculate,
Of landscapes drawn in pearly monotones.
There's something in my very blood that owns
Bare hills, cold silver on a sky of slate,
A thread of water, churned to milky spate
Streaming through slanted pastures fenced with stones.

I love those skies, thin blue or snowy gray,
Those fields sparse-planted, rendering meagre sheaves;
That spring, briefer than apple-blossom's breath,
Summer, so much too beautiful to stay,
Swift autumn, like a bonfire of leaves,
And sleepy winter, like the sleep of death.

LET NO CHARITABLE HOPE

Now let no charitable hope
Confuse my mind with images
Of eagle and of antelope:
I am in nature none of these.

I was, being human, born alone;
I am, being woman, hard beset;

I live by squeezing from a stone
The little nourishment I get.

In masks outrageous and austere
The years go by in single file;
But none has merited my fear,
And none has quite escaped my smile.

ADDRESS TO MY SOUL

My soul, be not disturbed
By planetary war;
Remain securely orbed
In this contracted star.

Fear not, pathetic flame;
Your sustenance is doubt:
Glassed in translucent dream
They cannot snuff you out.

Wear water, or a mask
Of unapparent cloud;
Be brave and never ask
A more defunctive shroud.

The universal points
Are shrunk into a flower;
Between its delicate joints
Chaos keeps no power.

The pure integral form,
Austere and silver-dark,
Is balanced on the storm
In its predestined arc.

Small as a sphere of rain
It slides along the groove
Whose path is furrowed plain
Among the suns that move.

The shapes of April buds
Outlive the phantom year:
Upon the void at odds
The dewdrop falls severe.

Five-petalled flame, be cold:
Be firm, dissolving star:
Accept the stricter mould
That makes you singular.

HYMN TO EARTH

Farewell, incomparable element,
Whence man arose, where he shall not return;
And hail, imperfect urn
Of his last ashes, and his firstborn fruit;
Farewell, the long pursuit,
And all the adventures of his discontent;
The voyages which sent
His heart averse from home:
Metal of clay, permit him that he come
To thy slow-burning fire as to a hearth;
Accept him as a particle of earth.

Fire, being divided from the other three,
It lives removed, or secret at the core;
Most subtle of the four,
When air flies not, nor water flows,
It disembodied goes,
Being light, elixir of the first decree,
More volatile than he;
With strength and power to pass
Through space, where never his least atom was:
He has no part in it, save as his eyes
Have drawn its emanation from the skies.

A wingless creature heavier than air,
He is rejected of its quintessence;
Coming and going hence,

In the twin minutes of his birth and death,
He may inhale as breath,
As breath relinquish heaven's atmosphere,
Yet in it have no share,
Nor can survive therein
Where its outer edge is filtered pure and thin:
It doth but lend its crystal to his lungs
For his early crying, and his final songs.

The element of water has denied
Its child; it is no more his element;
It never will relent;
Its silver harvests are more sparsely given
Than the rewards of heaven,
And he shall drink cold comfort at its side:
The water is too wide:
The seamew and the gull
Feather a nest made soft and pitiful
Upon its foam; he has not any part
In the long swell of sorrow at its heart.

Hail and farewell, beloved element,
Whence he departed, and his parent once;
See where thy spirit runs
Which for so long hath had the moon to wife;
Shall this support his life
Until the arches of the waves be bent
And grow shallow and spent?
Wisely it cast him forth
With his dead weight of burdens nothing worth,
Leaving him, for the universal years,
A little seawater to make his tears.

Hail, element of earth, receive thy own,
And cherish, at thy charitable breast,
This man, this mongrel beast:
He ploughs the sand, and, at his hardest need,
He sows himself for seed;
He ploughs the furrow, and in this lies down
Before the corn is grown;
Between the apple bloom

And the ripe apple is sufficient room
In time, and matter, to consume his love
And make him parcel of a cypress grove.

Receive him as thy lover for an hour
Who will not weary, by a longer stay,
The kind embrace of clay;
Even within thine arms he is dispersed
To nothing, as at first;
The air flings downward from its four-quartered tower
Him whom the flames devour;
At the full tide, at the flood,
The sea is mingled with his salty blood:
The traveller dust, although the dust be vile,
Sleeps as thy lover for a little while.

D. H. Lawrence / 1885–1930

MOONRISE

And who has seen the moon, who has not seen
Her rise from out of the chamber of the deep,
Flushed and grand and naked, as from the chamber
Of finished bridegroom, seen her rise and throw
Confession of delight upon the wave,
Littering the waves with her own superscription
Of bliss, till all her lambent beauty shakes towards us
Spread out and known at last, and we are sure
That beauty is a thing beyond the grave,
That perfect, bright experience never falls
To nothingness, and time will dim the moon
Sooner than our full consummation here
In this odd life will tarnish or pass away.

THE SONG OF A MAN WHO HAS COME THROUGH

Not I, not I, but the wind that blows through me!
A fine wind is blowing the new direction of Time.
If only I let it bear me, carry me, if only it carry me!
If only I am sensitive, subtle, oh, delicate, a winged gift!
If only, most lovely of all, I yield myself and am borrowed
By the fine, fine wind that takes its course through the
    chaos of the world
Like a fine, an exquisite chisel, a wedge-blade inserted;
If only I am keen and hard like the sheer tip of a wedge
Driven by invisible blows,
The rock will split, we shall come at the wonder, we shall
    find the Hesperides.

Oh, for the wonder that bubbles into my soul,
I would be a good fountain, a good well-head,
Would blur no whisper, spoil no expression.

What is the knocking?
What is the knocking at the door in the night?
It is somebody wants to do us harm.

No, no, it is the three strange angels.
Admit them, admit them.

SNAKE

A snake came to my water-trough
On a hot, hot day, and I in pyjamas for the heat,
To drink there.

In the deep, strange-scented shade of the great dark carobtree
I came down the steps with my pitcher
And must wait, must stand and wait, for there he was at
    the trough before me.

He reached down from a fissure in the earth-wall in the
     gloom
And trailed his yellow-brown slackness soft-bellied down,
     over the edge of the stone trough
And rested his throat upon the stone bottom,
And where the water had dripped from the tap, in a small
     clearness,
He sipped with his straight mouth,
Softly drank through his straight gums, into his slack long
     body,
Silently.

Someone was before me at my water-trough,
And I, like a second comer, waiting.

He lifted his head from his drinking, as cattle do,
And looked at me vaguely, as drinking cattle do,
And flickered his two-forked tongue from his lips, and
     mused a moment,
And stooped and drank a little more,
Being earth-brown, earth-golden from the burning bowels
     of the earth
On the day of Sicilian July, with Etna smoking.

The voice of my education said to me
He must be killed,
For in Sicily the black, black snakes are innocent, the gold
     are venomous.

And voices in me said, If you were a man
You would take a stick and break him now, and finish him
     off.

But must I confess how I liked him,
How glad I was he had come like a guest in quiet, to drink
     at my water-trough
And depart peaceful, pacified, and thankless,
Into the burning bowels of this earth?

Was it cowardice, that I dared not kill him?
Was it perversity, that I longed to talk to him?
Was it humility, to feel so honoured?
I felt so honoured.

And yet those voices:
If you were not afraid, you would kill him!

And truly I was afraid, I was most afraid,
But even so, honoured still more
That he should seek my hospitality
From out the dark door of the secret earth.

He drank enough
And lifted his head, dreamily, as one who has drunken,
And flickered his tongue like a forked night on the air, so
        black;
Seeming to lick his lips,
And looked around like a god, unseeing, into the air,
And slowly turned his head,
And slowly, very slowly, as if thrice adream,
Proceeded to draw his slow length curving round
And climb again the broken bank of my wall-face.

And as he put his head into that dreadful hole,
And as he slowly drew up, snake-easing his shoulders, and
        entered farther,
A sort of horror, a sort of protest against his withdrawing
        into that horrid black hole,
Deliberately going into the blackness, and slowly drawing
        himself after,
Overcame me now his back was turned.

I looked round, I put down my pitcher,
I picked up a clumsy log
And threw it at the water-trough with a clatter.

I think it did not hit him,
But suddenly that part of him that was left behind convulsed
        in undignified haste,
Writhed like lightning, and was gone
Into the black hole, the earth-lipped fissure in the wall-
        front,
At which, in the intense still noon, I stared with fascination.

And immediately I regretted it.
I thought how paltry, how vulgar, what a mean act!

I despised myself and the voices of my accursed human
    education.

And I thought of the albatross,
And I wished he would come back, my snake.

For he seemed to me again like a king,
Like a king in exile, uncrowned in the underworld,
Now due to be crowned again.

And so, I missed my chance with one of the lords
Of life.
And I have something to expiate;
A pettiness.

Taormina.

TORTOISE SHOUT

I thought he was dumb,
I said he was dumb,
Yet I've heard him cry.

First faint scream,
Out of life's unfathomable dawn,
Far off, so far, like a madness, under the horizon's dawning
    rim,
Far, far off, far scream.

Tortoise *in extremis.*

Why were we crucified into sex?
Why were we not left rounded off, and finished in
    ourselves,
As we began,
As he certainly began, so perfectly alone?

A far, was-it-audible scream,
Or did it sound on the plasm direct?

Worse than the cry of the new-born,
A scream,
A yell,
A shout,
A pæan,
A death-agony,
A birth-cry,
A submission,
All, tiny, far away, reptile under the first dawn.

War-cry, triumph, acute-delight, death-scream reptilian,
Why was the veil torn?
The silken shriek of the soul's torn membrane?
The male soul's membrane
Torn with a shriek half music, half horror.

Crucifixion.
Male tortoise, cleaving behind the hovel-wall of that dense
    female,
Mounted and tense, spread-eagle, out-reaching out of the
    shell
In tortoise-nakedness,
Long neck, and long vulnerable limbs extruded, spread-eagle
    over her house-roof,
And the deep, secret, all-penetrating tail curved beneath
    her walls,
Reaching and gripping tense, more reaching anguish in
    uttermost tension
Till suddenly, in the spasm of coition, tupping like a jerking
    leap, and oh!
Opening its clenched face from his outstretched neck
And giving that fragile yell, that scream,
Super-audible,
From his pink, cleft, old-man's mouth,
Giving up the ghost,
Or screaming in Pentecost, receiving the ghost.

His scream, and his moment's subsidence,
The moment of eternal silence,
Yet unreleased, and after the moment, the sudden, startling
    jerk of coition, and at once

The inexpressible faint yell—
And so on, till the last plasm of my body was melted back
To the primeval rudiments of life, and the secret.

So he tups, and screams
Time after time that frail, torn scream
After each jerk, the longish interval,
The tortoise eternity,
Age-long, reptilian persistence,
Hart-throb, slow heart-throb, persistent for the next spasm.

I remember, when I was a boy,
I heard the scream of a frog, which was caught with his
        foot in the mouth of an up-starting snake;
I remember when I first heard bull-frogs break into sound
        in the spring;
I remember hearing a wild goose out of the throat of night
Cry loudly, beyond the lake of waters;
I remember the first time, out of a bush in the darkness, a
        nightingale's piercing cries and gurgles startled the
        depths of my soul;
I remember the scream of a rabbit as I went through a
        wood at midnight;
I remember the heifer in her heat, blorting and blorting
        through the hours, persistent and irrepressible;
I remember my first terror hearing the howl of weird,
        amorous cats;
I remember the scream of a terrified, injured horse, the
        sheet-lightning,
And running away from the sound of a woman in labour,
        something like an owl whooing,
And listening inwardly to the first bleat of a lamb,
The first wail of an infant,
And my mother singing to herself,
And the first tenor singing of the passionate throat of a
        young collier, who has long since drunk himself to
        death,
The first elements of foreign speech
On wild dark lips.

And more than all these,
And less than all these,

This last,
Strange, faint coition yell
Of the male tortoise at extremity,
Tiny from under the very edge of the farthest far-off
    horizon of life.

The cross,
The wheel on which our silence first is broken,
Sex, which breaks up our integrity, our single inviolability,
    our deep silence,
Tearing a cry from us.

Sex, which breaks us into voice, sets us calling across the
    deeps, calling, calling for the complement,
Singing, and calling, and singing again, being answered,
    having found.
Torn, to become whole again, after long seeking for what
    is lost,
The same cry from the tortoise as from Christ, the Osiris-cry
    of abandonment,
That which is whole, torn asunder,
That which is in part, finding its whole again throughout
    the universe.

HUMMING-BIRD

I can imagine, in some otherworld
Primeval-dumb, far back
In that most awful stillness, that only gasped and hummed,
Humming-birds raced down the avenues.

Before anything had a soul,
While life was a heave of Matter, half inanimate,
This little bit chipped off in brilliance
And went whizzing through the slow, vast, succulent
    stems.

I believe there were no flowers then,
In the world where the humming-bird flashed ahead of
    creation.

I believe he pierced the slow vegetable veins with his long
    beak.

Probably he was big
As mosses, and little lizards, they say, were once big.
Probably he was a jabbing, terrifying monster.

We look at him through the wrong end of the long
    telescope of Time,
Luckily for us.

Española.

HOW BEASTLY THE
BOURGEOIS IS—

How beastly the bourgeois is
especially the male of the species—

Presentable eminently presentable—
shall I make you a present of him?

Isn't he handsome? isn't he healthy? Isn't he a fine
    specimen?
doesn't he look the fresh clean englishman, outside?
Isn't it god's own image? tramping his thirty miles a day
after partridges, or a little rubber ball?
wouldn't you like to be like that, well off, and quite the
    thing?

Oh, but wait!
Let him meet a new emotion, let him be faced with another
    man's need,
let him come home to a bit of moral difficulty, let life face
    him with a new demand on his understanding
and then watch him go soggy, like a wet meringue.
Watch him turn into a mess, either a fool or a bully.
Just watch the display of him, confronted with a new
    demand on his intelligence,
a new life-demand.

How beastly the bourgeois is
especially the male of the species—

Nicely groomed, like a mushroom
standing there so sleek and erect and eyeable—
and like a fungus, living on the remains of bygone life
sucking his life out of the dead leaves of greater life than
   his own.

And even so, he's stale, he's been there too long.
Touch him, and you'll find he's all gone inside
just like an old mushroom, all wormy inside, and hollow
under a smooth skin and an upright appearance.

Full of seething, wormy, hollow feelings
rather nasty—
How beastly the bourgeois is!

Standing in their thousands, these appearances, in damp
   England
what a pity they can't all be kicked over
like sickening toadstools, and left to melt back, swiftly
into the soil of England.

DON'TS

Fight your little fight, my boy,
fight and be a man.
Don't be a good little, good little boy
being as good as you can
and agreeing with all the mealy-mouthed, mealy-mouthed
truths that the sly trot out
to protect themselves and their greedy-mouthed,
   greedy-mouthed
cowardice, every old lout.

Don't live up to the dear little girl who costs
you your manhood, and makes you pay.

Nor the dear old mater who so proudly boasts
that you'll make your way.

Don't earn golden opinions, opinions golden,
or at least worth Treasury notes,
from all sorts of men; don't be beholden
to the herd inside the pen.

Don't long to have dear little, dear little boys
whom you'll have to educate
to earn their livings; nor yet girls, sweet joys
who will find it so hard to mate.

Nor a dear little home, with its cost, its cost
that you have to pay,
earning your living while your life is lost
and dull death comes in a day.

Don't be sucked in by the su-superior,
don't swallow the culture bait,
don't drink, don't drink and get beerier and beerier,
do learn to discriminate.

Do hold yourself together, and fight
with a hit-hit here and a hit-hit there,
and a comfortable feeling at night
that you've let in a little air.

A little fresh air in the money sty,
knocked a little hole in the holy prison,
done your own little bit, made your own little try
that the risen Christ should *be* risen.

THE ELEPHANT IS SLOW
TO MATE—

The elephant, the huge old beast,
        is slow to mate;

he finds a female, they show no haste
        they wait

for the sympathy in their vast shy hearts
        slowly, slowly to rouse
as they loiter along the river-beds
        and drink and browse

and dash in panic through the brake
        of forest with the herd,
and sleep in massive silence, and wake
        together, without a word.

So slowly the great hot elephant hearts
        grow full of desire,
and the great beasts mate in secret at last,
        hiding their fire.

Oldest they are and the wisest of beasts
        so they know at last
how to wait for the loneliest of feasts
        for the full repast.

They do not snatch, they do not tear;
        their massive blood
moves as the moon-tides, near, more near,
        till they touch in flood.

Ezra Pound / 1885–

BALLAD FOR GLOOM

For God, our God, is a gallant foe
That playeth behind the veil.

I have loved my God as a child at heart
That seeketh deep bosoms for rest,
I have loved my God as maid to man
But lo, this thing is best:

To love your God as a gallant foe
        that plays behind the veil,
To meet your God as the night winds meet
        beyond Arcturus' pale.

I have played with God for a woman,
I have staked with my God for truth,
I have lost to my God as a man, clear-eyed,
    His dice be not of ruth,

For I am made as a naked blade,
    But hear ye this thing in sooth:

Who loseth to God as a man to man
    Shall win at the turn of the game.
I have drawn my blade where the lightnings meet
    But the ending is the same:
Who loseth to God as the sword blades lose
    Shall win at the end of the game.

For God, our God, is a gallant foe
        that playeth behind the veil;
Whom God deigns not to overthrow
    Hath need of triple mail.

BALLAD OF THE GOODLY FERE

Simon Zelotes speaketh it somewhile after the Crucifixion
Fere = Mate, Companion.

Ha' we lost the goodliest fere o' all
For the priests and the gallows tree?
Aye lover he was of brawny men,
O' ships and the open sea.

When they came wi' a host to take Our Man
His smile was good to see,
"First let these go!" quo' our Goodly Fere,
"Or I'll see ye damned," says he.

Aye he sent us out through the crossed high spears
And the scorn of his laugh rang free,
"Why took ye not me when I walked about
Alone in the town?" says he.

Oh we drunk his "Hale" in the good red wine
When we last made company,
No capon priest was the Goodly Fere
But a man o' men was he.

I ha' seen him drive a hundred men
Wi' a bundle o' cords swung free,
That they took the high and holy house
For their pawn and treasury.

They'll no' get him a' in a book I think
Though they write it cunningly;
No mouse of the scrolls was the Goodly Fere
But aye loved the open sea.

If they think they ha' snared our Goodly Fere
They are fools to the last degree.
"I'll go to the feast," quo' our Goodly Fere,
"Though I go to the gallows tree."

"Ye ha' seen me heal the lame and blind,
And wake the dead," says he,
"Ye shall see one thing to master all:
'Tis how a brave man dies on the tree."

A son of God was the Goodly Fere
That bade us his brothers be.
I ha' seen him cow a thousand men.
I have seen him upon the tree.

He cried no cry when they drave the nails
And the blood gushed hot and free,
The hounds of the crimson sky gave tongue
But never a cry cried he.

I ha' seen him cow a thousand men
On the hills o' Galilee,
They whined as he walked out calm between,
Wi' his eyes like the grey o' the sea,

Like the sea that brooks no voyaging
With the winds unleashed and free,
Like the sea that he cowed at Genseret
Wi' twey words spoke' suddently.

A master of men was the Goodly Fere,
A mate of the wind and sea,
If they think they ha' slain our Goodly Fere
They are fools eternally.

I ha' seen him eat o' the honey-comb
Sin' they nailed him to the tree.

AN IMMORALITY

Sing we for love and idleness,
Naught else is worth the having.

Though I have been in many a land,
There is naught else in living.

And I would rather have my sweet,
Though rose-leaves die of grieving,

Than do high deeds in Hungary
To pass all men's believing.

ANCIENT MUSIC

Winter is icummen in,
Lhude sing Goddamm,
Raineth drop and staineth slop,
And how the wind doth ramm!
                Sing: Goddamm.
Skiddeth bus and sloppeth us,
An ague hath my ham.
Freezeth river, turneth liver,
                  Damn you, sing: Goddamm.
Goddamm, Goddamm, 'tis why I am, Goddamm,
                  So 'gainst the winter's balm.
Sing goddamm, damm, sing Goddamm,
Sing goddamm, sing goddamm, DAMM.

NOTE. This is not folk music, but Dr. Ker writes that the tune is to be found under the Latin words of a very ancient canon.

NEAR PERIGORD

A Perigord, pres del muralh
  Tan que i puosch' om gitar ab malh.

You'd have men's hearts up from the dust
And tell their secrets, Messire Cino,
Right enough? Then read between the lines of Uc St. Circ,
Solve me the riddle, for you know the tale.

Bertrans, En Bertrans, left a fine canzone:
"Maent, I love you, you have turned me out.
The voice at Montfort, Lady Agnes' hair,
Bel Miral's stature, the viscountess' throat,
Set all together, are not worthy of you. . . ."
And all the while you sing out that canzone,
Think you that Maent lived at Montaignac,
One at Chalais, another at Malemort

Hard over Brive—for every lady a castle,
Each place strong.

      Oh, *is* it easy enough?
Tairiran held hall in Montaignac,
His brother-in-law was all there was of power
In Perigord, and this good union
Gobbled all the land, and held it later for some hundred
    years.
And our En Bertrans was in Altafort,
Hub of the wheel, the stirrer-up of strife,
As caught by Dante in the last wallow of hell—
The headless trunk "that made its head a lamp,"
For separation wrought out separation,
And he who set the strife between brother and brother
And had his way with the old English king,
Vice in such torture for the "counterpass."
How would you live, with neighbours set about you—
Poictiers and Brive, untaken Rochecouart,
Spread like the finger-tips of one frail hand;
And you on that great mountain of a palm—
Not a neat ledge, not Foix between its streams,
But one huge back half-covered up with pine,
Worked for and snatched from the string-purse of Born—
The four round towers, four brothers—mostly fools:
What could he do but play the desperate chess,
And stir old grudges?
      "Pawn your castles, lords!
Let the Jews pay."
      And the great scene—
(That, maybe, never happened!)
      Beaten at last,
Before the hard old king:
      "Your son, ah, since he died
"My wit and worth are cobwebs brushed aside
"In the full flare of grief. Do what you will."

    Take the whole man, and ravel out the story.
He loved this lady in castle Montaignac?
The castle flanked him—he had need of it.
You read to-day, how long the overlords of Perigord,

The Talleyrands, have held the place; it was no transient
     fiction.
And Maent failed him? Or saw through the scheme?

     And all his net-like thought of new alliance?
Chalais is high, a-level with the poplars.
Its lowest stones just meet the valley tips
Where the low Dronne is filled with water-lilies.
And Rochecouart can match it, stronger yet,
The very spur's end, built on sheerest cliff,
And Malemort keeps its close hold on Brive,
While Born, his own close purse, his rabbit warren,
His subterranean chamber with a dozen doors,
A-bristle with antennæ to feel roads,
To sniff the traffic into Perigord.
And that hard phalanx, that unbroken line,
The ten good miles from there to Maent's castle,
All of his flank—how could he do without her?
And all the road to Cahors, to Toulouse?
What would he do without her?

     "Papiol,
Go forthright singing—Anhes, Cembelins.
There is a throat; ah, there are two white hands;
There is a trellis full of early roses,
And all my heart is bound about with love.
Where am I come with compound flatteries—
What doors are open to fine compliment?"
And every one half jealous of Maent?
He wrote the catch to pit their jealousies
Against her; give her pride in them?

Take his own speech, make what you will of it—
And still the knot, the first knot, of Maent?

     Is it a love poem? Did he sing of war?
Is it an intrigue to run subtly out,
Born of a jongleur's tongue, freely to pass
Up and about and in and out the land,
Mark him a craftsman and a strategist?
(St. Leider had done as much as Polhonac,
Singing a different stave, as closely hidden.)

Oh, there is precedent, legal tradition,
To sing one thing when your song means another,
"Et albirar ab lor bordon—"
Foix' count knew that. What is Sir Bertrans' singing?
Maent, Maent, and yet again Maent,
Or war and broken heaumes and politics?

II

    End fact. Try fiction. Let us say we see
En Bertrans, a tower-room at Hautefort,
Sunset, the ribbon-like road lies, in red cross-light,
Southward toward Montaignac, and he bends at a table
Scribbling, swearing between his teeth; by his left hand
Lie little strips of parchment covered over,
Scratched and erased with *al* and *ochaisos*.
Testing his list of rhymes, a lean man? Bilious?
With a red straggling beard?
And the green cat's-eye lifts toward Montaignac.

    Or take his "magnet" singer setting out,
Dodging his way past Aubeterre, singing at Chalais
    In the vaulted hall,
Or, by a lichened tree at Rochecouart
Aimlessly watching a hawk above the valleys,
Waiting his turn in the mid-summer evening,
Thinking of Aelis, whom he loved heart and soul . . .
To find her half alone, Montfort away,
And a brown, placid, hated woman visiting her,
Spoiling his visit, with a year before the next one.
Little enough?
Or carry him forward. "Go through all the courts,
My Magnet," Bertrans had said.

    We came to Ventadour
In the mid love court, he sings out the canzon,
No one hears save Arrimon Luc D'Esparo—
No one hears aught save the gracious sound of compliments.
Sir Arrimon counts on his fingers, Montfort,
Rochecouart, Chalais, the rest, the tactic,
Malemort, guesses beneath, sends word to Cœur-de-Lion:
The compact, de Born smoked out, trees felled

About his castle, cattle driven out!
Or no one sees it, and En Bertrans prospered?

    And ten years after, or twenty, as you will,
Arnaut and Richard lodge beneath Chalus:
The dull round towers encroaching on the field,
The tents tight drawn, horses at tether
Further and out of reach, the purple night,
The crackling of small fires, the bannerets,
The lazy leopards on the largest banner,
Stray gleams on hanging mail, an armourer's torch-flare
Melting on steel.

    And in the quietest space
They probe old scandals, say de Born is dead;
And we've the gossip (skipped six hundred years).
Richard shall die to-morrow—leave him there
Talking of *trobar clus* with Daniel.
And the "best craftsman" sings out his friend's song,
Envies its vigour . . . and deplores the technique,
Dispraises his own skill?—That's as you will.
And they discuss the dead man,
Plantagenet puts the riddle: "Did he love her?"
And Arnaut parries: "Did he love your sister?
True, he has praised her, but in some opinion
He wrote that praise only to show he had
The favour of your party; had been well received."

"You knew the man."
        "*You* knew the man."
"I am an artist, you have tried both métiers."
"You were born near him."
        "Do we know our friends?"
"Say that he saw the castles, say that he loved Maent!"
"Say that he loved her, does it solve the riddle?"
    End the discussion, Richard goes out next day
And gets a quarrel-bolt shot through his vizard,
Pardons the bowman, dies,

        Ends our discussion. Arnaut ends
"In sacred odour"—(that's apocryphal!)

And we can leave the talk till Dante writes:
Surely I saw, and still before my eyes
Goes on that headless trunk, that bears for light
Its own head swinging, gripped by the dead hair,
And like a swinging lamp that says, "Ah me!
I severed men, my head and heart
Ye see here severed, my life's counterpart."

Or take En Bertrans?

III

Ed eran due in uno, ed uno in due;
                    INFERNO, XXVIII, 125.

Bewildering spring, and by the Auvezere
Poppies and day's eyes in the green émail
Rose over us; and we knew all that stream,
And our two horses had traced out the valleys;
Knew the low flooded lands squared out with poplars,
In the young days when the deep sky befriended.
            And great wings beat above us in the twilight,
And the great wheels in heaven
Bore us together . . . surging . . . and apart . . .
Believing we should meet with lips and hands,

    High, high and sure . . . and then the counterthrust:
'Why do you love me? Will you always love me?
But I am like the grass, I can not love you.'
Or, 'Love, and I love and love you,
And hate your mind, not *you*, your soul, your hands.'

        So to this last estrangement, Tairiran!

        There shut up in his castle, Tairiran's,
She who had nor ears nor tongue save in her hands,
Gone—ah, gone—untouched, unreachable!
She who could never live save through one person,
She who could never speak save to one person,
And all the rest of her a shifting change,
A broken bundle of mirrors . . . !

HUGH SELWYN MAUBERLEY

Life and Contacts

"*Vocat Aestus in Umbram*,"
                        Nemesianus, ec. iv.

I

E. P. ODE POUR L'ELECTION DE SON SEPULCHRE

For three years, out of key with his time,
He strove to resuscitate the dead art
Of poetry; to maintain "the sublime"
In the old sense. Wrong from the start—

No, hardly, but seeing he had been born
In a half savage country, out of date;
Bent resolutely on wringing lilies from the acorn;
Capaneus; trout for factitious bait;

Ἴδμεν γάρ τοι πάνθ', ὅσ' ἐνὶ Τροίη
Caught in the unstopped ear;
Giving the rocks small lee-way
The chopped seas held him, therefore, that year.

His true Penelope was Flaubert,
He fished by obstinate isles;
Observed the elegance of Circe's hair
Rather than the mottoes on sun-dials.

Unaffected by "the march of events,"
He passed from men's memory in *l'an trentiesme
De son eage*; the case presents
No adjunct to the Muses' diadem.

II

The age demanded an image
Of its accelerated grimace,
Something for the modern stage,
Not, at any rate, an Attic grace;

Not, not certainly, the obscure reveries
Of the inward gaze;
Better mendacities
Than the classics in paraphrase!

The "age demanded" chiefly a mould in plaster,
Made with no loss of time,
A prose kinema, not, not assuredly, alabaster
Or the "sculpture" of rhyme.

III

The tea-rose tea-gown, etc.
Supplants the mousseline of Cos,
The pianola "replaces"
Sappho's barbitos.

Christ follows Dionysus,
Phallic and ambrosial
Made way for macerations;
Caliban casts out Ariel.

All things are a flowing,
Sage Heracleitus says;
But a tawdry cheapness
Shall outlast our days.

Even the Christian beauty
Defects—after Samothrace;
We see τὸ καλὸν
Decreed in the market place.

Faun's flesh is not to us,
Nor the saint's vision.
We have the press for wafer;
Franchise for circumcision.

All men, in law, are equals.
Free of Pisistratus,
We choose a knave or an eunuch
To rule over us.

O bright Apollo,
τίν' ἄνδρα, τίν' ἥρωα, τίνα θεὸν,
What god, man, or hero
Shall I place a tin wreath upon!

IV

These fought in any case,
and some believing,

            pro domo, in any case . . .

Some quick to arm,
some for adventure,
some from fear of weakness,
some from fear of censure,
some for love of slaughter, in imagination,
learning later . . .
some in fear, learning love of slaughter;

Died some, pro patria,

            non "dulce" non "et decor" . . .

walked eye-deep in hell
believing in old men's lies, then unbelieving
came home, home to a lie,
home to many deceits,
home to old lies and new infamy;
usury age-old and age-thick
and liars in public places.

Daring as never before, wastage as never before.
Young blood and high blood,
fair cheeks, and fine bodies;

fortitude as never before

frankness as never before,
disillusions as never told in the old days,
hysterias, trench confessions,
laughter out of dead bellies.

V

There died a myriad,
And of the best, among them,

For an old bitch gone in the teeth,
For a botched civilization,

Charm, smiling at the good mouth,
Quick eyes gone under earth's lid,

For two gross of broken statues,
For a few thousand battered books.

YEUX GLAUQUES

Gladstone was still respected,
When John Ruskin produced
"King's Treasuries"; Swinburne
And Rossetti still abused.

Fœtid Buchanan lifted up his voice
When that faun's head of hers
Became a pastime for
Painters and adulterers.

The Burne-Jones cartons
Have preserved her eyes;
Still, at the Tate, they teach
Cophetua to rhapsodize;

Thin like brook-water,
With a vacant gaze.
The English Rubaiyat was still-born
In those days.

The thin, clear gaze, the same
Still darts out faun-like from the half-ruin'd face,
Questing and passive. . . .
"Ah, poor Jenny's case" . . .

Bewildered that a world
Shows no surprise
At her last maquero's
Adulteries.

"SIENA MI FE'; DISFECEMI MAREMMA"

Among the pickled fœtuses and bottled bones,
Engaged in perfecting the catalogue,

I found the last scion of the
Senatorial families of Strasbourg, Monseiur Verog.

For two hours he talked of Gallifet;
Of Dowson; of the Rhymers' Club;
Told me how Johnson (Lionel) died
By falling from a high stool in a pub . . .

But showed no trace of alcohol
At the autopsy, privately performed—
Tissue preserved—the pure mind
Arose toward Newman as the whiskey warmed.

Dowson found harlots cheaper than hotels;
Headlam for uplift; Image impartially imbued
With raptures for Bacchus, Terpsichore and the Church.
So spoke the author of "The Dorian Mood,"

M. Verog, out of step with the decade,
Detached from his contemporaries,
Neglected by the young,
Because of these reveries.

BRENNBAUM

The sky-like limpid eyes,
The circular infant's face,
The stiffness from spats to collar
Never relaxing into grace;

The heavy memories of Horeb, Sinai and the forty years,
Showed only when the daylight fell
Level across the face
Of Brennbaum "The Impeccable."

MR. NIXON

In the cream gilded cabin of his steam yacht
Mr. Nixon advised me kindly, to advance with fewer
Dangers of delay. "Consider

"Carefully the reviewer.

"I was as poor as you are;
"When I began I got, of course,

"Advance on royalties, fifty at first," said Mr. Nixon,
"Follow me, and take a column,
"Even if you have to work free.

"Butter reviewers. From fifty to three hundred
"I rose in eighteen months;
"The hardest nut I had to crack
"Was Dr. Dundas.

"I never mentioned a man but with the view
"Of selling my own works.
"The tip's a good one, as for literature
"It gives no man a sinecure.

"And no one knows, at sight, a masterpiece.
"And give up verse, my boy,
"There's nothing in it."

. . .

Likewise a friend of Bloughram's once advised me:
Don't kick against the pricks,
Accept opinion. The "Nineties" tried your game
And died, there's nothing in it.

X

Beneath the sagging roof
The stylist has taken shelter,
Unpaid, uncelebrated,
At last from the world's welter

Nature receives him;
With a placid and uneducated mistress
He exercises his talents
And the soil meets his distress.

The haven from sophistications and contentions
Leaks through its thatch;
He offers succulent cooking;
The door has a creaking latch.

XI

"Conservatrix of Milésien"
Habits of mind and feeling,

Possibly. But in Ealing
With the most bank-clerkly of Englishmen?

No, "Milésian" is an exaggeration.
No instinct has survived in her
Older than those her grandmother
Told her would fit her station.

XII

"Daphne with her thighs in bark
Stretches toward me her leafy hands,"—
Subjectively. In the stuffed-satin drawing-room
I await The Lady Valentine's commands,

Knowing my coat has never been
Of precisely the fashion
To stimulate, in her,
A durable passion;

Doubtful, somewhat, of the value
Of well-gowned approbation
Of literary effort,
But never of The Lady Valentine's vocation:

Poetry, her border of ideas,
The edge, uncertain, but a means of blending
With other strata
Where the lower and higher have ending;

A hook to catch the Lady Jane's attention,
A modulation toward the theatre,
Also, in the case of revolution,
A possible friend and comforter.

.   .   .

Conduct, on the other hand, the soul
"Which the highest cultures have nourished"
To Fleet St. where
Dr. Johnson flourished;

Beside this thoroughfare
The sale of half-hose has

Long since superseded the cultivation
Of Pierian roses.

ENVOI (1919)

Go, dumb-born book,
Tell her that sang me once that song of Lawes:
Hadst thou but song
As thou hast subjects known,
Then were there cause in thee that should condone
Even my faults that heavy upon me lie,
And build her glories their longevity.

Tell her that sheds
Such treasure in the air,
Recking naught else but that her graces give
Life to the moment,
I would bid them live
As roses might, in magic amber laid,
Red overwrought with orange and all made
One substance and one colour
Braving time.

Tell her that goes
With song upon her lips
But sings not out the song, nor knows
The maker of it, some other mouth,
May be as fair as hers,
Might, in new ages, gain her worshippers,
When our two dusts with Waller's shall be laid,
Siftings on siftings in oblivion,
Till change hath broken down
All things save Beauty alone.

MAUBERLEY (1920)

"Vacuos exercet aera morsus."

I

Turned from the "eau-forte
Par Jaquemart"
To the strait head
Of Messalina:

"His true Penelope
Was Flaubert,"
And his tool
The engraver's.

Firmness,
Not the full smile,
His art, but an art
In profile;

Colourless
Pier Francesca,
Pisanello lacking the skill
To forge Achaia.

II

*"Qu'est ce qu'ils savent de l'amour, et qu'est ce qu'ils
peuvent comprendre?*
   *S'ils ne comprennent pas la poésie, s'ils ne sentent pas
la musique, qu'est ce qu'ils peuvent comprendre de cette
passion en comparaison avec laquelle la rose est grossière
et le parfum des violettes un tonnerre?"*   CAID ALI

For three years, diabolus in the scale,
He drank ambrosia,
All passes, ANANGKE prevails,
Came end, at last, to that Arcadia.

He had moved amid her phantasmagoria,
Amid her galaxies,
NUKTIS 'AGALMA

. . .

Drifted . . . drifted precipitate,
Asking time to be rid of . . .
Of his bewilderment; to designate
His new found orchid. . . .

To be certain . . . certain . . .
(Amid ærial flowers) . . . time for arrangements—
Drifted on
To the final estrangement;

Unable in the supervening blankness
To sift TO AGATHON from the chaff
Until he found his sieve . . .
Ultimately, his seismograph:

—Given that is his "fundamental passion,"
This urge to convey the relation
Of eye-lid and cheek-bone
By verbal manifestations;

To present the series
Of curious heads in medallion—

He had passed, inconscient, full gaze,
The wide-banded irides
And botticellian sprays implied
In their diastasis;

Which anæthesis, noted a year late,
And weighed, revealed his great affect,
(Orchid), mandate
Of Eros, a retrospect.

.   .   .

Mouths biting empty air,
The still stone dogs,
Caught in metamorphosis, were
Left him as epilogues.

"THE AGE DEMANDED"

Vide Poem II. Page 232

For this agility chance found
Him of all men, unfit
As the red-beaked steeds of
The Cytheræan for a chain bit.

The glow of porcelain
Brought no reforming sense
To his perception
Of the social inconsequence.

Thus, if her colour
Came against his gaze,
Tempered as if
It were through a perfect glaze

He made no immediate application
Of this to relation of the state
To the individual, the month was more temperate
Because this beauty had been.

        The coral isle, the lion-coloured sand
        Burst in upon the porcelain revery:
        Impetuous troubling
        Of his imagery.

Mildness, amid the neo-Nietzschean clatter,
His sense of graduations,
Quite out of place amid
Resistance to current exacerbations,

Invitation, mere invitation to perceptivity
Gradually led him to the isolation
Which these presents place
Under a more tolerant, perhaps, examination.

By constant elimination
The manifest universe
Yielded an armour
Against utter consternation,

A Minoan undulation,
Seen, we admit, amid ambrosial circumstances
Strengthened him against
The discouraging doctrine of chances,

And his desire for survival,
Faint in the most strenuous moods,
Became an Olympian *apathein*
In the presence of selected perceptions.

A pale gold, in the aforesaid pattern,
The unexpected palms

Destroying, certainly, the artist's urge,
Left him delighted with the imaginary
Audition of the phantasmal sea-surge,

Incapable of the last utterance or composition,
Emendation, conservation of the "better tradition,"
Refinement of medium, elimination of superfluities,
August attraction or concentration.

Nothing, in brief, but maudlin confession,
Irresponse to human aggression,
Amid the precipitation, down-float
Of insubstantial manna,
Lifting the faint susurrus
Of his subjective hosannah.

Ultimate affronts to
Human redundancies;

Non-esteem of self-styled "his betters"
Leading, as he well knew,
To his final
Exclusion from the world of letters.

IV

Scattered Moluccas
Not knowing, day to day,
The first day's end, in the next noon;
The placid water
Unbroken by the Simoon;

Thick foliage
Placid beneath warm suns,
Tawn fore-shores
Washed in the cobalt of oblivions;

Or through dawn-mist
The grey and rose
Of the juridical
Flamingoes;

A consciousness disjunct,
Being but this overblotted

Series
Of intermittences;

Coracle of Pacific voyages,
The unforecasted beach;
Then on an oar
Read this:

"I was
And I no more exist;
Here drifted
An hedonist."

MEDALLION

Luini in porcelain!
The grand piano
Utters a profane
Protest with her clear soprano.

The sleek head emerges
From the gold-yellow frock
As Anadyomene in the opening
Pages of Reinach.

Honey-red, closing the face-oval,
A basket-work of braids which seem as if they were
Spun in King Minos' hall
From metal, or intractable amber;

The face-oval beneath the glaze,
Bright in its suave bounding-line, as,
Beneath half-watt rays,
The eyes turn topaz.

CANTO   XLV

With *Usura*
With usura hath no man a house of good stone

each block cut smooth and well fitting
that design might cover their face,
with usura
hath no man a painted paradise on his church wall
harpes et luthes
or where virgin receiveth message
and halo projects from incision,
with usura
seeth no man Gonzaga his heirs and his concubines
no picture is made to endure nor to live with
but it is made to sell and sell quickly
with usura, sin against nature,
is thy bread ever more of stale rags
is thy bread dry as paper,
with no mountain wheat, no strong flour
with usura the line grows thick
with usura is no clear demarcation
and no man can find site for his dwelling.
Stone cutter is kept from his stone
weaver is kept from his loom
WITH USURA
wool comes not to market
sheep bringeth no gain with usura
Usura is a murrain, usura
blunteth the needle in the maid's hand
and stoppeth the spinner's cunning. Pietro Lombardo
came not by usura
Duccio came not by usura
nor Pier della Francesca; Zuan Bellin' not by usura
nor was 'La Calunnia' painted.
Came not by usura Angelico; came not Ambrogio Praedis,
Came no church of cut stone signed: *Adamo me fecit.*
Not by usura St Trophime
Not by usura Saint Hilaire,
Usura rusteth the chisel
It rusteth the craft and the craftsman
It gnaweth the thread in the loom
None learneth to weave gold in her pattern;
Azure hath a canker by usura; cramoisi is unbroidered
Emerald findeth no Memling
Usura slayeth the child in the womb
It stayeth the young man's courting

It hath brought palsey to bed, lyeth
between the young bride and her bridegroom
                    CONTRA NATURAM
They have brought whores for Eleusis
Corpses are set to banquet
at behest of usura.

Edwin Muir / 1887–1959

THE ROAD

There is a road that turning always
    Cuts off the country of Again.
Archers stand there on every side
    And as it runs time's deer is slain,
    And lies where it has lain.

That busy clock shows never an hour.
    All flies and all in flight must tarry.
The hunter shoots the empty air
    Far on before the quarry,
    Which falls though nothing's there to parry.

The lion crouching in the centre
    With mountain head and sunset brow
Rolls down the everlasting slope
    Bones picked an age ago,
    And the bones rise up and go.

There the beginning finds the end
    Before beginning ever can be,
And the great runner never leaves
    The starting and the finishing tree,
    The budding and the fading tree.

There the ship sailing safe in harbour
    Long since in many a sea was drowned.

The treasure burning in her hold
   So near will never be found,
     Sunk past all sound.

There a man on a summer evening
   Reclines at ease upon his tomb
And is his mortal effigy.
   And there within the womb,
     The cell of doom,

The ancestral deed is thought and done,
   And in a million Edens fall
A million Adams drowned in darkness,
   For small is great and great is small,
     And a blind seed all.

THE HUMAN FOLD

Here penned within the human fold
No longer now we shake the bars,
Although the ever-moving stars
Night after night in order rolled
Rebuke this stationary farce.
There's no alternative here but love,
So far as genuine love can be
Where there's no genuine liberty
To give or take, to lose or have,
And having rots with wrong, and loss
Itself has no security
Except in the well-managed grave,
And all we do is done to prove
Content and discontent both are gross.
Yet sometimes here we still can see
The dragon with his tears of gold,
The bat-browed sphinx
Shake loose her wings
That have no hold and fan no air,
All struck dead by her stare.

Hell shoots its avalanche at our feet,
In heaven the souls go up and down,
And we can see from this our seat
The heavenly and the hellish town,
The green cross growing in a wood
Close by old Eden's crumbling wall,
And God Himself in full manhood
Riding against the Fall.
All this; but here our sight is bound
By ten dull faces in a round,
Each with a made-to-measure glance
That is in misery till it's found.
Yet looking at each countenance
I read this burden in them all:
'I lean my cheek from eternity
For time to slap, for time to slap.
I gather my bones from the bottomless clay
To lay my head in the light's lap.'

By what long way, by what dark way,
From what unpredetermined place,
Did we creep severally to this hole
And bring no memory and no grace
To furnish evidence of the soul,
Though come of an ancient race?
All gone, where now we cannot say,
Altar and shrine and boundary stone,
And of the legends of our day
This one remains alone:
'They loved and might have loved for ever,
But public trouble and private care
Faith and hope and love can sever
And strip the bed and the altar bare'.
Forward our towering shadows fall
Upon the naked nicheless wall,
And all we see is that shadow-dance.
Yet looking at each countenance
I read this burden in them all:
'I lean my cheek from eternity
For time to slap, for time to slap.
I gather my bones from the bottomless clay
To lay my head in the light's lap'.

THE GROVE

There was no road at all to that high place
But through the smothering grove,
Where as we went the shadows wove
Adulterous shapes of animal hate and love,
The idol-crowded nightmare Space,
Wood beyond wood, tree behind tree,
And every tree an empty face
Gashed by the casual lightning mark
The first great Luciferian animal
Scored on leaf and bark.
This was, we knew, the heraldic ground,
And therefore now we heard our footsteps fall
With the true legendary sound,
Like secret trampling behind a wall,
As if they were saying: To be: to be.

And oh the silence, the drugged thicket dozing
Deep in its dream of fear,
The ring closing
And coming near,
The well-bred self-sufficient animals
With clean rank pelts and proud and fetid breath,
Screaming their arrogant calls,
Their moonstone eyes set straight at life and death.
Did we see or dream it? And the jungle cities—
For there were cities there and civilizations
Deep in the forest; powers and dominations
Like shapes begotten by dreaming animals,
Proud animal dreams uplifted high,
Booted and saddled on the animal's back
And staring with the arrogant animal's eye:
The golden dukes, the silver earls, and gleaming black
The curvetting knights sitting their curvetting steeds,
The sweet silk-tunicked eunuchs singing ditties,
Swaying like wandering weeds,
The scarlet cardinals,
And lions high in the air on the banner's field,
Crowns, sceptres, spears and stars and moons of blood,

And sylvan wars in bronze within the shield,
All quartered in the wide world's wood,
The smothering grove where there was place for pities.

We trod the maze like horses in a mill,
And then passed through it
As in a dream of the will.
How could it be? There was the stifling grove,
Yet here was light; what wonder led us to it?
How could the blind path go
To climb the crag and top the towering hill,
And all that splendour spread? We know
There was no road except the smothering grove.

THE GATE

We sat, two children, warm against the wall
Outside the towering stronghold of our fathers
That frowned its stern security down upon us.
We could not enter there. That fortress life,
Our safe protection, was too gross and strong
For our unpractised palates. Yet our guardians
Cherished our innocence with gentle hands,
(They, who had long since lost their innocence,)
And in grave play put on a childish mask
Over their tell-tale faces, as in shame
For the rich food that plumped their lusty bodies
And made them strange as gods. We sat that day
With that great parapet behind us, safe
As every day, yet outcast, safe and outcast
As castaways thrown upon an empty shore.
Before us lay the well-worn scene, a hillock
So small and smooth and green, it seemed intended
For us alone and childhood, a still pond
That opened upon no sight a quiet eye,
A little stream that tinkled down the slope.
But suddenly all seemed old
And dull and shrunken, shut within itself

In a sullen dream. We were outside, alone.
And then behind us the huge gate swung open.

THE TROPHY

The wise king dowered with blessings on his throne,
The rebel raising the flag in the market place,
Haunt me like figures on an ancient stone
The ponderous light of history beats upon,
Or the enigma of a single face
Handed unguessed, unread from father to son,
As if it dreamed within itself alone.

Regent and rebel clash in horror and blood
Here on the blindfold battlefield. But there,
Motionless in the grove in evil and good
They grow together and their roots are twined
In deep confederacy far from the air,
Sharing the secret trophy each with other;
And king and rebel are like brother and brother,
Or father and son, co-princes of one mind,
Irreconcilables, their treaty signed.

THE VOYAGE

for Eric Linklater

That sea was greater than we knew.
Week after week the empty round
Went with us; the Unchanging grew,
And we were headed for that bound.

How we came there we could not tell.
Seven storms had piled us in that peace,
Put us in check and barred us well
With seven walls of seven seas.

As one may vanish in a day
In some untravelled fold of space
And there pursue his patient way
Yet never come to any place

Though following still by star and sun,
For every chart is rased and furled,
And he out of this world has run
And wanders now another world,

So we by line and compass steered
And conned the book of sun and star,
Yet where it should no sign appeared
To tell us, You are there or there,

Familiar landfall, slender mast:
We on the ocean were alone.
The busy lanes where fleets had passed
Showed us no sail except our own.

Still south we steered day after day
And only water lay around
As if the land had stolen away
Or sprawled upon the ocean ground.

The sun by day, the stars by night
Had only us to look upon,
Bent on us their collected light,
And followed on as we went on.

Sometimes in utter wonder lost
That loneliness like this could be
We stood and stared until almost
We saw no longer sky or sea,

But only the frame of time and space,
An empty floor, a vacant wall,
And on that blank no line to trace
Movement, if we moved at all.

What thoughts came then! Sometimes it seemed
We long had passed the living by

On other seas and only dreamed
This sea, this journey and this sky,

Or traced a ghostly parallel
That limned the land but could not merge,
And haven and home and harbour bell
Were just behind the horizon verge,

Or the world itself had ended so
Without a cry, and we should sail
To and fro, to and fro,
Long past the lightning and the gale.

O then what crowding fantasies
Poured in from empty sea and sky!
At night we heard the whispering quays,
Line after line, slide softly by.

Delusions in the silent noon;
Fields in the hollows of the waves;
Or spread beneath the yellow moon,
A land of harvests and of graves.

The soft sea-sounds beguiled our ear.
We thought we walked by mountain rills
Or listened half a night to hear
The spring wind hunting on the hills.

And faces, faces, faces came
Across the salt sea-desert air,
And rooms in which a candle flame
Made everything renowned and rare.

The words we knew like our right hand,
Mountain and valley, meadow and grove,
Composed a legendary land
Rich with the broken tombs of love.

Delusion or truth? We were content
Thenceforth to sail the harmless seas
Safe past the Fate and the Accident,
And called a blessing on that peace.

And blessing, we ourselves were blest,
Lauded the loss that brought our gain,
Sang the tumultuous world to rest,
And wishless called it back again.

For loss was then our only joy,
Privation of all, fulfilled desire,
The world our treasure and our toy
In destitution clean as fire.

Our days were then—I cannot tell
How we were then fulfilled and crowned
With life as in a parable,
And sweetly as gods together bound.

Delusion and dream! Our captain knew
Compass and clock had never yet
Failed him; the sun and stars were true.
The mark was there that we should hit.

And it rose up, a sullen stain
Flawing the crystal firmament.
A wound! We felt the familiar pain
And knew the place to which we were sent.

THE RIDER VICTORY

The rider Victory reins his horse
Midway across the empty bridge
As if head-tall he had met a wall.
Yet there was nothing there at all,
No bodiless barrier, ghostly ridge
To check the charger in his course
So suddenly, you'd think he'd fall.

Suspended, horse and rider stare
Leaping on air and legendary.

In front the waiting kingdom lies,
The bridge and all the roads are free;
But halted in implacable air
Rider and horse with stony eyes
Uprear their motionless statuary.

THE WINDOW

Within the great wall's perfect round
Bird, beast and child serenely grew
In endless change on changeless ground
That in a single pattern bound
The old perfection and the new.

There was a tower set in the wall
And a great window in the tower,
And if one looked, beyond recall
The twisting glass kept him in thrall
With changing marvels hour by hour.
And there one day we looked and saw
Marsh, mere and mount in anger shaken,
The world's great side, the giant flaw,
And watched the stately forests fall,
The white ships sinking in the sea,
The tower run toppling in the field,
The last left stronghold sacked and taken,
And earth and heaven in jeopardy.
Then turning towards you I beheld
The wrinkle writhe across your brow,
And felt time's cap clapped on my head,
And all within the enclosure now,
Light leaf and smiling flower, was false,
The great wall breached, the garden dead.

Across the towering window fled
Disasters, victories, festivals.

IN LOVE FOR LONG

I've been in love for long
With what I cannot tell
And will contrive a song
For the intangible
That has no mould or shape,
From which there's no escape.

It is not even a name,
Yet is all constancy;
Tried or untried, the same,
It cannot part from me;
A breath, yet as still
As the established hill.

It is not any thing,
And yet all being is;
Being, being, being,
Its burden and its bliss.
How can I ever prove
What it is I love?

This happy happy love
Is sieged with crying sorrows,
Crushed beneath and above
Between to-days and morrows;
A little paradise
Held in the world's vice.

And there it is content
And careless as a child,
And in imprisonment
Flourishes sweet and wild;
In wrong, beyond wrong,
All the world's day long.

This love a moment known
For what I do not know

And in a moment gone
Is like the happy doe
That keeps its perfect laws
Between the tiger's paws
And vindicates its cause.

Robinson Jeffers / 1887–1962

SHINE, PERISHING REPUBLIC

While this America settles in the mould of its vulgarity,
    heavily thickening to empire,
And protest, only a bubble in the molten mass, pops and
    sighs out, and the mass hardens,

I sadly smiling remember that the flower fades to make
    fruit, the fruit rots to make earth.
Out of the mother; and through the spring exultances,
    ripeness and decadence; and home to the mother.

You making haste haste on decay: not blameworthy, life is
    good, be it stubbornly long or suddenly
A mortal splendor: meteors are not needed less than
    mountains: shine, perishing republic.

But for my children, I would have them keep their distance
    from the thickening center; corruption
Never has been compulsory, when the cities lie at the
    monster's feet there are left the mountains.

And boys, be in nothing so moderate as in love of man, a
    clever servant, insufferable master.
There is the trap that catches noblest spirits, that caught—
    they say—God, when he walked on earth.

PROMISE OF PEACE

The heads of strong old age are beautiful
Beyond all grace of youth. They have strange quiet,
Integrity, health, soundness, to the full
They've dealt with life and been atempered by it.
A young man must not sleep, his years are war
Civil and foreign but the former's worse;
But the old can breathe in safety now they are
Forgetting what youth meant, the being perverse,
Running the fool's gauntlet and getting cut
By the whips of the five senses. As for me,
If I should wish to live long it were but
To trade those fevers for tranquillity,
Thinking though that's entire and sweet in the grave
How shall the dead taste the deep treasure they have?

HURT HAWKS

I

The broken pillar of the wing jags from the clotted
    shoulder,
The wing trails like a banner in defeat,
No more to use the sky forever but live with famine
And pain a few days: cat nor coyote
Will shorten the week of waiting for death, there is game
    without talons.
He stands under the oak-bush and waits
The lame feet of salvation; at night he remembers freedom
And flies in a dream, the dawns ruin it.
He is strong and pain is worse to the strong, incapacity is
    worse.
The curs of the day come and torment him
At distance, no one but death the redeemer will humble
    that head,
The intrepid readiness, the terrible eyes.
The wild God of the world is sometimes merciful to those

That ask mercy, not often to the arrogant.
You do not know him, you communal people, or you have
    forgotten him;
Intemperate and savage, the hawk remembers him;
Beautiful and wild, the hawks, and men that are dying,
    remember him.

II

I'd sooner, except the penalties, kill a man than a hawk;
    but the great redtail
Had nothing left but unable misery
From the bone too shattered for mending, the wing that
    trailed under his talons when he moved.
We had fed him six weeks, I gave him freedom,
He wandered over the foreland hill and returned in the
    evening, asking for death,
Not like a beggar, still eyed with the old
Implacable arrogance. I gave him the lead gift in the
    twilight. What fell was relaxed,
Owl-downy, soft feminine feathers; but what
Soared: the fierce rush: the night-herons by the flooded
    river cried fear at its rising
Before it was quite unsheathed from reality.

THE STARS GO OVER
THE LONELY OCEAN

Unhappy about some far off things
That are not my affair, wandering
Along the coast and up the lean ridges,
I saw in the evening
The stars go over the lonely ocean,
And a black-maned wild boar
Plowing with his snout on Mal Paso Mountain.

The old monster snuffled, "Here are sweet roots,
Fat grubs, slick beetles and sprouted acorns.

The best nation in Europe has fallen,
And that is Finland,
But the stars go over the lonely ocean,"
The old black-bristled boar,
Tearing the sod on Mal Paso Mountain.

"The world's in a bad way, my man,
And bound to be worse before it mends;
Better lie up in the mountain here
Four or five centuries,
While the stars go over the lonely ocean,"
Said the old father of wild pigs,
Plowing the fallow on Mal Paso Mountain.

"Keep clear of the dupes that talk democracy
And the dogs that talk revolution,
Drunk with talk, liars and believers.
I believe in my tusks.
Long live freedom and damn the ideologies,"
Said the gamey black-maned wild boar
Tusking the turf on Mal Paso Mountain.

BATTLE

May 28, 1940

Forseen for so many years: these evils, this monstrous
        violence, these massive agonies: no easier to bear.
We saw them with slow stone strides approach, everyone
        saw them; we closed our eyes against them, we
        looked
And they had come nearer. We ate and drank and slept,
        they came nearer. Sometimes we laughed, they
        were nearer. Now
They are here. And now a blind man foresees what follows
        them: degradation, famine, despair and so forth,
        and the
Epidemic manias: but not enough death to serve us, not
        enough death. It would be better for men

To be few and live far apart, where none could infect
        another; then slowly the sanity of field and
        mountain
And the cold ocean and glittering stars might enter their
        minds.
        Another dream, another dream.
We shall have to accept certain limitations
In future, and abandon some humane dreams; only
        hard-minded, sleepless and realist can ride this
        rockslide
To new fields down the dark mountain; and we shall have
        to perceive that these insanities are normal;
We shall have to perceive that battle is a burning flower or
        like a huge music, and the dive-bomber's screaming
        orgasm
As beautiful as other passions; and that death and life are
        not serious alternatives. One has known all these
        things
For many years: there is greater and darker to know
In the next hundred.
And why do you cry, my dear, why do you cry?
It is all in the whirling circles of time.
If millions are born millions will die;
In bed or in battle is no great matter
In the long orbits of time.
If England goes down and Germany up
The stronger dog will still be on top,
All in the turning of time.
If civilization goes down—that
Would be an event to contemplate.
It will not be in our time, alas, my dear,
It will not be in our time.

THE BLOODY SIRE

It is not bad. Let them play.
Let the guns bark and the bombing-plane
Speak his prodigious blasphemies.

It is not bad, it is high time,
Stark violence is still the sire of all the world's values.

What but the wolf's tooth whittled so fine
The fleet limbs of the antelope?
What but fear winged the birds, and hunger
Jeweled with such eyes that great goshawk's head?
Violence has been the sire of all the world's values.

Who would remember Helen's face
Lacking the terrible halo of spears?
Who formed Christ but Herod and Caesar,
The cruel and bloody victories of Caesar?
Violence, the bloody sire of all the world's values.

Never weep, let them play,
Old violence is not too old to beget new values.

BLACK-OUT

The war that we have carefully for years provoked
Comes on us unprepared, amazed and indignant. Our
        warships are shot
Like sitting ducks and our planes like nest-birds, both our
        coasts ridiculously panicked,
And our leaders make orations. This is the people
That hopes to impose on the whole planetary world
An American peace.
        (Oh, we'll win our war. My money on amazed Gulliver
And his horse-pistols.)
                Meanwhile our prudent officers
Have cleared the coast-long ocean of ships and fishing
        craft, the sky of planes, the windows of light: these
        clearings
Make a strange beauty. Watch the wide sea, there is
        nothing human, the gulls have it. Watch the wide
        sky,

All day clean of machines, only at dawn and dusk a
          military hawk passes
High on patrol. Walk at night on the shore,
The pretty firefly spangle that used to line it
Perfectly silent, shut are the shops, mouse-dark the houses.
      Here the prehuman dignity of night
Stands, as it was and will be again. Oh beautiful
Darkness and silence, the two eyes that see God. Great
          staring eyes.

I SHALL LAUGH PURELY

I

Turn from that girl
Your fixed blue eyes.
Boy-slender she is,
And a face as beautiful as a hawk's face.
History passes like falling rocks.

I am old as a stone,
But she is beautiful.
War is coming.
All the fine boys will go off to war.
History passes like falling rocks.

Oh, that one's to marry
Another old man;
You won't be helped
When your tall sons go away to war.
History falls on your head like rocks.

Keep a straight mind
In the evil time.
In the mad-dog time
Why may not an old man run mad?
History falls like rocks in the dark,
All will be worse confounded soon.

II

Count the glories of this time,
Count that girl's beauty, then count England,
Bleeding, at bay, magnificent,
At last a lion,
For all will be worse confounded soon.

Count that girl's beauty, count the coast-range,
The steep rock that stops the Pacific,
Count the surf on its precipice,
The hawks in its air,
For all will be worse confounded soon.

Count its eagles and wild boars,
Count the great blue-black winter storms,
Heavy rain and the hurricane,
Get them by heart,
For all will be worse confounded soon.

Count no human thing but only
England's great fight and that girl's beauty,
History passes like falling
Rocks in the dark,
And all will be worse confounded soon.

III

But this, I steadily assure you, is not the world's end,
Nor even the end of a civilization. It is not so late as you
     think: give nature time.
These wars will end, and I shall lead a troupe of shaky old
     men through Europe and America,
Old drunkards, worn-out lechers; fallen dictators, cast
     kings, a disgraced president; some cashiered generals
And collapsed millionaires: we shall enact a play, I shall
     announce to the audience:
"All will be worse confounded soon."

We shall beware of wild dogs in Europe, and of the police
     in armed imperial America:—

For all that pain was mainly a shift of power:—we shall
     enact our play: "Oh Christian era,
Make a good end," but first I announce to our audiences:
     "This play is prophetic, it will be centuries.
This play does not represent the world's end,
But only the fall of a civilization. It is not so late as you
     think: give nature time."

In Europe we shall beware of starving dogs and political
     commissars, and of the police in America.
We shall rant on our makeshift stages in our cracked
     voices: "Oh Christian era,
Era of chivalry and the barbarians and the machines, era
     of science and the saints,
When you go down make a good sunset.
Never linger superfluous, old and holy and paralytic like
     India,
Go down in conclusive war and a great red sunset, great
     age go down,
For all will be worse confounded soon."
We shall tour to the last verge and the open Pacific, we
     shall sit on the yellow cliffs at Hurricane Point
And watch the centaurs come from the sea; their splayed
     hooves plunge and stutter on the tide-rocks,
The hairy and foamy flanks, the naked destructive
     shoulders, the brutal faces and the bent bows,
Horde after horde under the screaming gulls: my old men
     will cough in the fog and baa like sheep,
"Here comes the end of a civilization. Give nature time,"
And spit, and make lewd jokes. But I shall laugh purely,
Remembering what old enthusiast named a girl's beauty
     and England's battle
Among the lights of his time: she being by then a dyed
     hag, or more likely
One of those embalmer-fingered smiles in the subsoil; and
     England will be
Not admirable. I shall laugh purely, knowing the next age
Lives on not-human beauty, waiting on circumstance and
     its April, weaving its winter chrysalis;
Thin snow falls on historical rocks.

THE EYE

The Atlantic is a stormy moat; and the Mediterranean,
The blue pool in the old garden,
More than five thousand years has drunk sacrifice
Of ships and blood, and shines in the sun; but here the
    Pacific—
Our ships, planes, wars are perfectly irrelevant.
Neither our present blood-feud with the brave dwarfs
Nor any future world-quarrel of westering
And eastering man, the bloody migrations, greed of power,
    clash of faiths—
Is a speck of dust on the great scale-pan.
Here from this mountain shore, headland beyond stormy
    headland plunging like dolphins through the blue
    sea-smoke
Into pale sea—look west at the hill of water: it is half the
    planet: this dome, this half-globe, this bulging
Eyeball of water, arched over to Asia,
Australia and white Antarctica: those are the eyelids that
    never close; this is the staring unsleeping
Eye of the earth; and what it watches is not our wars.

CASSANDRA

The mad girl with the staring eyes and long white fingers
Hooked in the stones of the wall,
The storm-wrack hair and the screeching mouth: does it
    matter, Cassandra,
Whether the people believe
Your bitter fountain? Truly men hate the truth; they'd
    liefer
Meet a tiger on the road.
Therefore the poets honey their truth with lying; but
    religion-
Venders and political men

Pour from the barrel, new lies on the old, and are praised
    for kindly
Wisdom. Poor bitch, be wise.
No: you'll still mumble in a corner a crust of truth, to men
And gods disgusting.—You and I, Cassandra.

Marianne Moore / 1887–

POETRY

I, too, dislike it: there are things that are important be-
            yond all this fiddle.
Reading it, however, with a perfect contempt for it, one
            discovers in
it after all, a place for the genuine.
    Hands that can grasp, eyes
    that can dilate, hair that can rise
        if it must, these things are important not because a

high-sounding interpretation can be put upon them but
            because they are
    useful. When they become so derivative as to become
            unintelligible,
    the same thing may be said for all of us, that we
        do not admire what
        we cannot understand: the bat
            holding on upside down or in quest of something
                to

eat, elephants pushing, a wild horse taking a roll, a tireless
            wolf under
    a tree, the immovable critic twitching his skin like a
            horse that feels a flea, the base-
        ball fan, the statistician—
            nor is it valid
                to discriminate against 'business documents and

school-books'; all these phenomena are important. One
    must make a distinction
  however: when dragged into prominence by half poets,
    the result is not poetry,
  nor till the poets among us can be
      'literalists of
        the imagination'—above
          insolence and triviality and can present

for inspection, imaginary gardens with real toads in them,
    shall we have
  it. In the meantime, if you demand on the one hand,
    the raw material of poetry in
      all its rawness and
        that which is on the other hand
          genuine, then you are interested in poetry.

ROSES   ONLY

You do not seem to realize that beauty is a liability rather
    than
  an asset—that in view of the fact that spirit creates form
    we are justified in supposing
      that you must have brains. For you, a symbol of the
        unit, stiff and sharp,
  conscious of surpassing by dint of native superiority and
    liking for everything
self-dependent, anything an

ambitious civilization might produce: for you, unaided, to
    attempt through sheer
  reserve,   to   confuse   presumptions   resulting   from
    observation, is idle. You cannot make us
      think you a delightful happen-so. But rose, if you are
        brilliant, it
  is not because your petals are the without-which-nothing
    of pre-eminence. Would you not, minus
thorns, be a what-is-this, a mere

peculiarity? They are not proof against a worm, the
    elements, or mildew;
  but what about the predatory hand? What is brilliance
    without co-ordination? Guarding the
infinitesimal pieces of your mind, compelling audience to
the remark that it is better to be forgotten than to be re-
    membered too violently,
your thorns are the best part of you.

SPENSER'S IRELAND

has not altered;—
  a place as kind as it is green,
    the greenest place I've never seen.
Every name is a tune.
Denunciations do not affect
    the culprit; nor blows, but it
is torture to him to not be spoken to.
They're natural—
    the coat, like Venus'
mantle lined with stars,
buttoned close at the neck—the sleeves new from disuse.

If in Ireland
  they play the harp backward at need,
    and gather at midday the seed
of the fern, eluding
their "giants all covered with iron," might
    there be fern seed for unlearn-
ing obduracy and for reinstating
the enchantment?
    Hindered characters
seldom have mothers
in Irish stories, but they all have grandmothers.

It was Irish;
  a match not a marriage was made
    when my great great grandmother'd said

with native genius for
disunion, "Although your suitor be
      perfection, one objection
is enough; he is not
Irish." Outwitting
          the fairies, befriending the furies,
whoever again
and again says, "I'll never give in," never sees

that you're not free
    until you've been made captive by
    supreme belief—credulity
you say? When large dainty
fingers tremblingly divide the wings
      of the fly for mid-July
with a needle and wrap it with peacock tail,
or tie wool and
          buzzard's wing, their pride,
like the enchanter's
is in care, not madness. Concurring hands divide

flax for damask
    that when bleached by Irish weather
    has the silvered chamois-leather
water-tightness of a
skin. Twisted torcs and gold new-moon-shaped
      lunulae aren't jewelry
like the purple-coral fuchsia-tree's. Eire—
the guillemot
          so neat and the hen
of the heath and the
linnet spinet-sweet—bespeak relentnessness? Then

they are to me
    like enchanted Earl Gerald who
    changed himself into a stag, to
a great green-eyed cat of
the mountain. Discommodity makes
      them invisible; they've dis-
appeared. The Irish say your trouble is their
trouble and your
          joy their joy? I wish

I could believe it;
I am troubled, I'm dissatisfied, I'm Irish.

A CARRIAGE FROM SWEDEN

They say there is a sweeter air
        where it was made, than we have here;
        a Hamlet's castle atmosphere.
At all events there is in Brooklyn
something that makes me feel at home.

No one may see this put-away
        museum-piece, this country cart
        that inner happiness made art;
and yet, in this city of freckled
integrity it is a vein

of resined straightness from north-wind
        hardened Sweden's once-opposed-to-
        compromise archipelago
of rocks. Washington and Gustavus
Adolphus, forgive our decay.

Seats, dashboard and sides of smooth gourd-
        rind texture, a flowered step, swan-
        dart brake, and swirling crustacean-
tailed equine amphibious creatures
that garnish the axletree! What

a fine thing! What unannoying
        romance! And how beautiful, she
        with the natural stoop of the
snowy egret, gray-eyed and straight-haired,
for whom it should come to the door—

of whom it reminds me. The split
        pine fair hair, steady gannet-clear
        eyes and the pine-needled-path deer-
swift step; that is Sweden, land of the
free and the soil for a spruce tree—

vertical though a seedling—all
    needles: from a green trunk, green shelf
    on shelf fanning out by itself.
The deft white-stockinged dance in thick-soled
shoes! Denmark's sanctuaried Jews!

The puzzle-jugs and hand-spun rugs,
    the root-legged kracken shaped like dogs,
    the hanging buttons and the frogs
that edge the Sunday jackets! Sweden,
you have a runner called the Deer, who

when he's won a race, likes to run
    more; you have the sun-right gable-
    ends due east and west, the table
spread as for a banquet; and the put-
in twin vest-pleats with a fish-fin

effect when you need none. Sweden,
    what makes the people dress that way
    and those who see you wish to stay?
The runner, not too tired to run more
at the end of the race? And that

cart, dolphin-graceful? A Dalen
    lighthouse, self-lit?—responsive and
    responsible. I understand;
it's not pine-needle-paths that give spring
when they're run on, it's a Sweden

of moated white castles—the bed
    of white flowers densely grown in an S
    meaning Sweden and stalwartness,
skill, and a surface that says
Made in Sweden: carts are my trade.

IN DISTRUST OF MERITS

Strengthened to live, strengthened to die for
    medals and positioned victories?

They're fighting, fighting, fighting the blind
    man who thinks he sees—
who cannot see that the enslaver is
enslaved; the hater, harmed. O shining O
        firm star, O tumultuous
            ocean lashed till small things go
      as they will, the mountainous
        wave makes us who look, know

depth. Lost at sea before they fought! O
    star of David, star of Bethlehem,
O black imperial lion
    of the Lord—emblem
of a risen world—be joined at last, be
joined. There is hate's crown beneath which all is
        death; there's love's without which none
            is king; the blessed deeds bless
      the halo. As contagion
        of sickness makes sickness,

contagion of trust can make trust. They're
    fighting in deserts and caves, one by
one, in battalions and squadrons;
    they're fighting that I
may yet recover from the disease, My
Self; some have it lightly; some will die. "Man's
        wolf to man" and we devour
            ourselves. The enemy could not
      have made a greater breach in our
        defenses. One pilot-

ing a blind man can escape him, but
    Job disheartened by false comfort knew
that nothing can be so defeating
    as a blind man who
can see. O alive who are dead, who are
proud not to see, O small dust of the earth
        that walks so arrogantly,
            trust begets power and faith is
      an affectionate thing. We
        vow, we make this promise

to the fighting—it's a promise—"We'll
    never hate black, white, red, yellow, Jew,
Gentile, Untouchable." We are
    not competent to
make our vows. With set jaw they are fighting,
fighting, fighting—some we love whom we know,
        some we love but know not—that
            hearts may feel and not be numb.
        It cures me; or am I what
            I can't believe in? Some

in snow, some on crags, some in quicksands,
    little by little, much by much, they
are fighting fighting fighting that where
    there was death there may
be life. "When a man is prey to anger,
he is moved by outside things; when he holds
        his ground in patience patience
            patience, that is action or
        beauty," the soldier's defense
        and hardest armor for

the fight. The world's an orphans' home. Shall
    we never have peace without sorrow?
without pleas of the dying for
    help that won't come? O
quiet form upon the dust, I cannot
look and yet I must. If these great patient
        dyings—all these agonies
            and wound-bearings and bloodshed—
        can teach us how to live, these
        dyings were not wasted.

Hate-hardened heart, O heart of iron,
    iron is iron till it is rust.
There never was a war that was
    not inward; I must
fight till I have conquered in myself what
causes war, but I would not believe it.
        I inwardly did nothing.
            O Iscariot-like crime!

Beauty is everlasting
    and dust is for a time.

HIS SHIELD

The pin-swin or spine-swine
      (the edgehog miscalled hedgehog) with all his edges
      out,
   echidna and echinoderm in distressed-
pin-cushion thorn-fur coats, the spiny pig or porcupine,
      the rhino with horned snout—
   everything is battle-dressed.

Pig-fur won't do, I'll wrap
      myself in salamander-skin like Presbyter John.
   A lizard in the midst of flames, a firebrand
that is life, asbestos-eyed asbestos-eared, with tattooed nap
      and permanent pig on
   the instep; he can withstand

fire and won't drown. In his
      unconquerable country of unpompous gusto,
   gold was so common none considered it; greed
and flattery were unknown. Though rubies large as tennis
      balls conjoined in streams so
   that the mountain seemed to bleed,

the inextinguishable
      salamander styled himself but presbyter. His shield
   was his humility. In Carpasian
linen coat, flanked by his household lion cubs and sable
      retinue, he revealed
   a formula safer than

an armorer's: the power of relinquishing
      what one would keep; that is freedom. Become
      dinosaur-
   skulled, quilled or salamander-wooled, more ironshod

and javelin-dressed than a hedgehog battalion of steel,
        but be
    dull. Don't be envied or
armed with a measuring-rod.

TELL ME, TELL ME

    where might there be a refuge for me
        from egocentricity
and its propensity to bisect,
mis-state, misunderstand
        and obliterate continuity?
            Why, oh why, one ventures to ask, set
flatness on some cindery pinnacle
as if on Lord Nelson's revolving diamond rosette?

    It appeared: gem, burnished rarity
        and peak of delicacy—
in contrast with grievance touched off on
any ground—the absorbing
        geometry of a fantasy:
            a James, Miss Potter, Chinese
"passion for the particular," of a
tired man who yet, at dusk,
            cut a masterpiece of cerise—

    for no tailor-and-cutter jury—
        only a few mice to see,
who "breathed inconsistency and drank
contradiction," dazzled
        not by the sun but by "shadowy
            possibility." (I'm referring
to Henry James and Beatrix Potter's Tailor.)
I vow, rescued tailor
        of Gloucester, I am going

    to flee; by engineering strategy—
        the viper's traffic-knot—flee

to metaphysical newmown hay,
honeysuckle, or woods fragrance.
     Might one say or imply T.S.V.P.—
          Taisez-vous? "Please" does not make sense
to a refugee from verbal ferocity; I am
perplexed. Even so, "deference";
          yes, deference may be my defense.

A *précis?*
     In this told-backward biography
     of how the cat's mice when set free
by the tailor of Gloucester, finished
the Lord Mayor's cerise coat—
     the tailor's tale ended captivity
          in two senses. Besides having told
of a coat which made the tailor's fortune,
it rescued a reader
          from being driven mad by a scold.

THE MIND, INTRACTABLE THING

     even with its own ax to grind, sometimes
          helps others. Why can't it help me?

          O imagnifico,
wizard in words—poet, was it, as
Alfredo Panzini defined you?
Weren't you refracting just now
on my eye's half-closed triptych
          the image, enhanced, of a glen—
"the foxgrape festoon as sere leaves fell"
on the sand-pale dark byroad, one leaf adrift
          from the thin-twigged persimmon; again,

          a bird—Arizona
caught-up-with, uncatchable cuckoo
after two hours' pursuit, zigzagging
road-runner, stenciled in black

stripes all over, the tail
    windmilling up to defy me?
You understand terror, know how to deal
with pent-up emotion, a ballad, witchcraft.
    I don't. O Zeus and O Destiny!

Unafraid of what's done,
undeterred by apparent defeat,
you, imagnifico, unafraid
of disparagers, death, dejection,
have out-wiled the Mermaid of Zennor,
    made wordcraft irresistible:
reef, wreck, lost lad, and "sea-foundered bell"—
as near a thing as we have to a king—
    craft with which I don't know how to deal.

T. S. Eliot / 1888–1965

THE LOVE SONG OF
J. ALFRED PRUFROCK

S'io credesse che mia risposta fosse
A persona che mai tornasse al mondo,
Questa fiamma staria senza piu scosse.
Ma perciocche giammai di questo fondo
Non torno vivo alcun, s'i'odo il vero,
Senza tema d'infamia ti rispondo

Let us go then, you and I,
When the evening is spread out against the sky
Like a patient etherised upon a table;
Let us go, through certain half-deserted streets,
The muttering retreats
Of restless nights in one-night cheap hotels

And sawdust restaurants with oyster-shells:
Streets that follow like a tedious argument
Of insidious intent
To lead you to an overwhelming question . . .
Oh, do not ask, "What is it?"
Let us go and make our visit.

In the room the women come and go
Talking of Michelangelo.

The yellow fog that rubs its back upon the window-panes,
The yellow smoke that rubs its muzzle on the window-panes
Licked its tongue into the corners of the evening,
Lingered upon the pools that stand in drains,
Let fall upon its back the soot that falls from chimneys,
Slipped by the terrace, made a sudden leap,
And seeing that it was a soft October night,
Curled once about the house, and fell asleep.

And indeed there will be time
For the yellow smoke that slides along the street,
Rubbing its back upon the window-panes;
There will be time, there will be time
To prepare a face to meet the faces that you meet;
There will be time to murder and create,
And time for all the works and days of hands
That lift and drop a question on your plate;
Time for you and time for me,
And time yet for a hundred indecisions,
And for a hundred visions and revisions,
Before the taking of a toast and tea.

In the room the women come and go
Talking of Michelangelo.

And indeed there will be time
To wonder, "Do I dare?" and, "Do I dare?"
Time to turn back and descend the stair,
With a bald spot in the middle of my hair—
[They will say: "How his hair is growing thin!"]
My morning coat, my collar mounting firmly to the chin,

My necktie rich and modest, but asserted by a simple pin—
[They will say: "But how his arms and legs are thin!"]
Do I dare
Disturb the universe?
In a minute there is time
For decisions and revisions which a minute will reverse.

For I have known them all already, known them all:—
Have known the evenings, mornings, afternoons,
I have measured out my life with coffee spoons;
I know the voices dying with a dying fall
Beneath the music from a farther room.
  So how should I presume?

And I have known the eyes already, known them all—
The eyes that fix you in a formulated phrase,
And when I am formulated, sprawling on a pin,
When I am pinned and wriggling on the wall,
Then how should I begin
To spit out all the butt-ends of my days and ways?
  And how should I presume?

And I have known the arms already, known them all—
Arms that are braceleted and white and bare
[But in the lamplight, downed with light brown hair!]
Is it perfume from a dress
That makes me so digress?
Arms that lie along a table, or wrap about a shawl.
  And should I then presume?
  And how should I begin?

  . . .

Shall I say, I have gone at dusk through narrow streets
And watched the smoke that rises from the pipes
Of lonely men in shirt-sleeves, leaning out of windows? . . .

  I should have been a pair of ragged claws
Scuttling across the floors of silent seas.

  . . .

And the afternoon, the evening, sleeps so peacefully!
Smoothed by long fingers,

Asleep . . . tired . . . or it malingers,
Stretched on the floor, here beside you and me.
Should I, after tea and cakes and ices,
Have the strength to force the moment to its crisis?
But though I have wept and fasted, wept and prayed,
Though I have seen my head [grown slightly bald] brought
    in upon a platter,
I am no prophet—and here's no great matter;
I have seen the moment of my greatness flicker,
And I have seen the eternal Footman hold my coat, and
    snicker,
And in short, I was afraid.

   And would it have been worth it, after all,
After the cups, the marmalade, the tea,
Among the porcelain, among some talk of you and me,
Would it have been worth while,
To have bitten off the matter with a smile,
To have squeezed the universe into a ball
To roll it toward some overwhelming question,
To say: "I am Lazarus, come from the dead,
Come back to tell you all, I shall tell you all"—
If one, settling a pillow by her head,
    Should say: "That is not what I meant at all.
    That is not it, at all."

   And would it have been worth it, after all,
Would it have been worth while,
After the sunsets and the dooryards and the sprinkled
    streets,
After the novels, after the teacups, after the skirts that trail
    along the floor—
And this, and so much more?—
It is impossible to say just what I mean!
But as if a magic lantern threw the nerves in patterns on a
    screen:
Would it have been worth while
If one, settling a pillow or throwing off a shawl,
And turning toward the window, should say:
    "That is not it at all,
    That is not what I meant, at all."

. . .

No! I am not Prince Hamlet, nor was meant to be;
Am an attendant lord, one that will do
To swell a progress, start a scene or two,
Advise the prince; no doubt, an easy tool,
Deferential, glad to be of use,
Politic, cautious, and meticulous;
Full of high sentence, but a bit obtuse;
At times, indeed, almost ridiculous—
Almost, at times, the Fool.

I grow old . . . I grow old . . .
I shall wear the bottoms of my trousers rolled.

Shall I part my hair behind? Do I dare to eat a peach?
I shall wear white flannel trousers, and walk upon the
      beach.
I have heard the mermaids singing, each to each.

I do not think that they will sing to me.

I have seen them riding seaward on the waves
Combing the white hair of the waves blown back
When the wind blows the water white and black.

We have lingered in the chambers of the sea
By sea-girls wreathed with seaweed red and brown
Till human voices wake us, and we drown.

GERONTION

Thou hast nor youth nor age
But as it were an after dinner sleep
Dreaming of both.

Here I am, an old man in a dry month,
Being read to by a boy, waiting for rain.
I was neither at the hot gates
Nor fought in the warm rain

Nor knee deep in the salt marsh, heaving a cutlass,
Bitten by flies, fought.
My house is a decayed house,
And the jew squats on the window sill, the owner,
Spawned in some estaminet of Antwerp,
Blistered in Brussels, patched and peeled in London.
The goat coughs at night in the field overhead;
Rocks, moss, stonecrop, iron, merds.
The woman keeps the kitchen, makes tea,
Sneezes at evening, poking the peevish gutter.
                              I an old man,
A dull head among windy spaces.

Signs are taken for wonders. "We would see a sign!"
The word within a word, unable to speak a word,
Swaddled with darkness. In the juvescence of the year
Came Christ the tiger

In depraved May, dogwood and chestnut, flowering
        judas,
To be eaten, to be divided, to be drunk
Among whispers; by Mr. Silvero
With caressing hands, at Limoges
Who walked all night in the next room;

By Hakagawa, bowing among the Titians;
By Madame de Tornquist, in the dark room
Shifting the candles; Fräulein von Kulp
Who turned in the hall, one hand on the door.
    Vacant shuttles
Weave the wind. I have no ghosts,
An old man in a draughty house
Under a windy knob.

After such knowledge, what forgiveness? Think now
History has many cunning passages, contrived corridors
And issues, deceives with whispering ambitions,
Guides us by vanites. Think now
She gives when our attention is distracted
And what she gives, gives with such supple confusions
That the giving famishes the craving. Gives too late

What's not believed in, or if still believed,
In memory only, reconsidered passion. Gives too soon
Into weak hands, what's thought can be dispensed with
Till the refusal propagates a fear. Think
Neither fear nor courage saves us. Unnatural vices
Are fathered by our heroism. Virtues
Are forced upon us by our impudent crimes.
These tears are shaken from the wrath-bearing tree.

    The tiger springs in the new year. Us he devours. Think
        at last
We have not reached conclusion, when I
Stiffen in a rented house. Think at last
I have not made this show purposelessly
And it is not by any concitation
Of the backward devils.
I would meet you upon this honestly.
I that was near your heart was removed therefrom
To lose beauty in terror, terror in inquisition.
I have lost my passion: why should I need to keep it
Since what is kept must be adulterated?
I have lost my sight, smell, hearing, taste and touch:
How should I use them for your closer contact?

    These with a thousand small deliberations
Protract the profit of their chilled delirium,
Excite the membrane, when the sense has cooled,
With pungent sauces, multiply variety
In a wilderness of mirrors. What will the spider do,
Suspend its operations, will the weevil
Delay? De Bailhache, Fresca, Mrs. Cammel, whirled
Beyond the circuit of the shuddering Bear
In fractured atoms. Gull against the wind, in the windy
        straits
Of Belle Isle, or running on the Horn,
White feathers in the snow, the Gulf claims,
And an old man driven by the Trades
To a sleepy corner.

                  Tenants of the house,
Thoughts of a dry brain in a dry season.

SWEENEY AMONG THE NIGHTINGALES

ὤμοι, πέπληγμαι καιρίαν πληγὴν ἔσω.

Apeneck Sweeney spreads his knees
Letting his arms hang down to laugh,
The zebra stripes along his jaw
Swelling to maculate giraffe.

The circles of the stormy moon
Slide westward toward the River Plate,
Death and the Raven drift above
And Sweeney guards the hornèd gate.

Gloomy Orion and the Dog
Are veiled; and hushed the shrunken seas;
The person in the Spanish cape
Tries to sit on Sweeney's knees

Slips and pulls the table cloth
Overturns a coffee-cup,
Reorganized upon the floor
She yawns and draws a stocking up;

The silent man in mocha brown
Sprawls at the window-sill and gapes;
The waiter brings in oranges
Bananas figs and hothouse grapes;

The silent vertebrate in brown
Contracts and concentrates, withdraws;
Rachel *née* Rabinovitch
Tears at the grapes with murderous paws;

She and the lady in the cape
Are suspect, thought to be in league;
Therefore the man with heavy eyes
Declines the gambit, shows fatigue,

Leaves the room and reappears
Outside the window, leaning in,
Branches of wistaria
Circumscribe a golden grin;

The host with someone indistinct
Converses at the door apart,
The nightingales are singing near
The Convent of the Sacred Heart,

And sang within the bloody wood
When Agamemnon cried aloud,
And let their liquid siftings fall
To stain the stiff dishonoured shroud.

THE WASTE LAND *

"Nam Sibyllam quidem Cumis ego ipse oculis meis vidi in ampulla pendere, et cum illi pueri dicerent: Σίβυλλα τί θέλεις; *respondebat illa:* ἀποθανεῖν θέλω."

For Ezra Pound
il miglior fabbro.

I. THE BURIAL OF THE DEAD

April is the cruellest month, breeding
Lilacs out of the dead land, mixing
Memory and desire, stirring
Dull roots with spring rain.
Winter kept us warm, covering
Earth in forgetful snow, feeding
A little life with dried tubers.
Summer surprised us, coming over the Starnbergersee
With a shower of rain; we stopped in the colonnade,
And went on in sunlight, into the Hofgarten,
And drank coffee, and talked for an hour.
Bin gar keine Russin, stamm' aus Litauen, echt deutsch.

* For T. S. Eliot's notes on "The Waste Land" see page 298.

And when we were children, staying at the archduke's,
My cousin's, he took me out on a sled,
And I was frightened. He said, Marie,
Marie, hold on tight. And down we went.
In the mountains, there you feel free.
I read, much of the night, and go south in the winter.

What are the roots that clutch, what branches grow
Out of this stony rubbish? Son of man,
You cannot say, or guess, for you know only
A heap of broken images, where the sun beats,
And the dead tree gives no shelter, the cricket no relief,
And the dry stone no sound of water. Only
There is shadow under this red rock,
(Come in under the shadow of this red rock),
And I will show you something different from either
Your shadow at morning striding behind you
Or your shadow at evening rising to meet you;
I will show you fear in a handful of dust.
            Frisch weht der Wind
            Der Heimat zu
            Mein Irisch Kind,
            Wo weilest du?
"You gave me hyacinths first a year ago;
"They called me the hyacinth girl."
—Yet when we came back, late, from the Hyacinth garden,
Your arms full, and your hair wet, I could not
Speak, and my eyes failed, I was neither
Living nor dead, and I knew nothing,
Looking into the heart of light, the silence.
Oed' und leer das Meer.

Madame Sosostris, famous clairvoyante,
Had a bad cold, nevertheless
Is known to be the wisest woman in Europe,
With a wicked pack of cards. Here, said she,
Is your card, the drowned Phoenician Sailor,
(Those are pearls that were his eyes. Look!)
Here is Belladonna, the Lady of the Rocks,
The lady of situations.
Here is the man with three staves, and here the Wheel,
And here is the one-eyed merchant, and this card,

Which is blank, is something he carries on his back,
Which I am forbidden to see. I do not find
The Hanged Man. Fear death by water.
I see crowds of people, walking round in a ring.
Thank you. If you see dear Mrs. Equitone,
Tell her I bring the horoscope myself:
One must be so careful these days.

    Unreal City,
Under the brown fog of a winter dawn,
A crowd flowed over London Bridge, so many,
I had not thought death had undone so many.
Sighs, short and infrequent, were exhaled,
And each man fixed his eyes before his feet.
Flowed up the hill and down King William Street,
To where Saint Mary Woolnoth kept the hours
With a dead sound on the final stroke of nine.
There I saw one I knew, and stopped him, crying: "Stetson!
"You who were with me in the ships at Mylae!
"That corpse you planted last year in your garden,
"Has it begun to sprout? Will it bloom this year?
"Or has the sudden frost disturbed its bed?
"Oh keep the Dog far hence, that's friend to men,
"Or with his nails he'll dig it up again!
"You! hypocrite lecteur!—mon semblable,—mon frère!"

II. A GAME OF CHESS

The Chair she sat in, like a burnished throne,
Glowed on the marble, where the glass
Held up by standards wrought with fruited vines
From which a golden Cupidon peeped out
(Another hid his eyes behind his wing)
Doubled the flames of sevenbranched candelabra
Reflecting light upon the table as
The glitter of her jewels rose to meet it,
From satin cases poured in rich profusion;
In vials of ivory and coloured glass
Unstoppered, lurked her strange synthetic perfumes,
Unguent, powdered, or liquid—troubled, confused
And drowned the sense in odours; stirred by the air
That freshened from the window, these ascended
In fattening the prolonged candle-flames,

Flung their smoke into the laquearia,
Stirring the pattern on the coffered ceiling.
Huge sea-wood fed with copper
Burned green and orange, framed by the coloured stone,
In which sad light a carvèd dolphin swam.
Above the antique mantel was displayed
As though a window gave upon the sylvan scene
The change of Philomel, by the barbarous king
So rudely forced; yet there the nightingale
Filled all the desert with inviolable voice
And still she cried, and still the world pursues,
"Jug Jug" to dirty ears.
And other withered stumps of time
Were told upon the walls; staring forms
Leaned out, leaning, hushing the room enclosed.
Footsteps shuffled on the stair.
Under the firelight, under the brush, her hair
Spread out in fiery points
Glowed into words, then would be savagely still.

"My nerves are bad to-night. Yes, bad. Stay with me.
"Speak to me. Why do you never speak. Speak.
   "What are you thinking of? What thinking? What?
"I never know what you are thinking. Think."

   I think we are in rats' alley
Where the dead men lost their bones.

   "What is that noise?"
                    The wind under the door.
"What is that noise now? What is the wind doing?"
                    Nothing again nothing.
                                        "Do
"You know nothing? Do you see nothing? Do you remember
"Nothing?"

      I remember
Those are pearls that were his eyes.
"Are you alive, or not? Is there nothing in your head?"
                                                    But

O O O O that Shakespeherian Rag—
It's so elegant

So intelligent
"What shall I do now? What shall I do?"
"I shall rush out as I am, and walk the street
"With my hair down, so. What shall we do to-morrow?
"What shall we ever do?"
                              The hot water at ten.
And if it rains, a closed car at four.
And we shall play a game of chess,
Pressing lidless eyes and waiting for a knock upon the door.

    When Lil's husband got demobbed, I said—
I didn't mince my words, I said to her myself,
HURRY UP PLEASE ITS TIME
Now Albert's coming back, make yourself a bit smart.
He'll want to know what you done with that money he
        gave you
To get yourself some teeth. He did, I was there.
You have them all out, Lil, and get a nice set,
He said, I swear, I can't bear to look at you.
And no more can't I, I said, and think of poor Albert,
He's been in the army four years, he wants a good time,
And if you don't give it him, there's others will, I said.
Oh is there, she said. Something o' that, I said.
Then I'll know who to thank, she said, and give me a
        straight look.
HURRY UP PLEASE ITS TIME
If you don't like it you can get on with it, I said.
Others can pick and choose if you can't.
But if Albert makes off, it won't be for lack of telling.
You ought to be ashamed, I said, to look so antique.
(And her only thirty-one.)
I can't help it, she said, pulling a long face,
It's them pills I took, to bring it off, she said.
(She's had five already, and nearly died of young George.)
The chemist said it would be all right, but I've never been
        the same.
You are a proper fool, I said.
Well, if Albert won't leave you alone, there it is, I said,
What you get married for if you don't want children?
HURRY UP PLEASE ITS TIME
Well, that Sunday Albert was home, they had a hot
        gammon,

And they asked me in to dinner, to get the beauty of it
      hot—
HURRY UP PLEASE ITS TIME
HURRY UP PLEASE ITS TIME
Goonight Bill. Goonight Lou. Goonight May. Goonight.
Ta ta. Goonight. Goonight.
Good night, ladies, good night, sweet ladies, good night,
      good night.

III. THE FIRE SERMON

The river's tent is broken: the last fingers of leaf
Clutch and sink into the wet bank. The wind
Crosses the brown land, unheard. The nymphs are
      departed.
Sweet Thames, run softly, till I end my song.
The river bears no empty bottles, sandwich papers,
Silk handkerchiefs, cardboard boxes, cigarette ends
Or other testimony of summer nights. The nymphs are
      departed.
And their friends, the loitering heirs of city directors;
Departed, have left no addresses.
By the waters of Leman I sat down and wept . . .
Sweet Thames, run softly till I end my song,
Sweet Thames, run softly, for I speak not loud or long.
But at my back in a cold blast I hear
The rattle of the bones, and chuckle spread from ear to ear.
A rat crept softly through the vegetation
Dragging its slimy belly on the bank
While I was fishing in the dull canal
On a winter evening round behind the gashouse
Musing upon the king my brother's wreck
And on the king my father's death before him.
White bodies naked on the low damp ground
And bones cast in a little low dry garret,
Rattled by the rat's foot only, year to year.
But at my back from time to time I hear
The sound of horns and motors, which shall bring
Sweeney to Mrs. Porter in the spring.
O the moon shone bright on Mrs. Porter
And on her daughter
They wash their feet in soda water
Et O ces voix d'enfants, chantant dans la coupole!

Twit twit twit
Jug jug jug jug jug jug
So rudely forc'd.
Tereu

Unreal City
Under the brown fog of a winter noon
Mr. Eugenides, the Smyrna merchant
Unshaven, with a pocket full of currants
C.i.f. London: documents at sight,
Asked me in demotic French
To luncheon at the Cannon Street Hotel
Followed by a weekend at the Metropole.

At the violet hour, when the eyes and back
Turn upward from the desk, when the human engine waits
Like a taxi throbbing waiting,
I Tiresias, though blind, throbbing between two lives,
Old man with wrinkled female breasts, can see
At the violet hour, the evening hour that strives
Homeward, and brings the sailor home from sea,
The typist home at teatime, clears her breakfast, lights
Her stove, and lays out food in tins.
Out of the window perilously spread
Her drying combinations touched by the sun's last rays,
On the divan are piled (at night her bed)
Stockings, slippers, camisoles, and stays.
I Tiresias, old man with wrinkled dugs
Perceived the scene, and foretold the rest—
I too awaited the expected guest.
He, the young man carbuncular, arrives,
A small house agent's clerk, with one bold stare,
One of the low on whom assurance sits
As a silk hat on a Bradford millionaire.
The time is now propitious, as he guesses,
The meal is ended, she is bored and tired,
Endeavours to engage her in caresses
Which still are unreproved, if undesired.
Flushed and decided, he assaults at once;
Exploring hands encounter no defence;
His vanity requires no response,
And makes a welcome of indifference.

(And I Tiresias have foresuffered all
Enacted on this same divan or bed;
I who have sat by Thebes below the wall
And walked among the lowest of the dead.)
Bestows one final patronising kiss,
And gropes his way, finding the stairs unlit . . .

   She turns and looks a moment in the glass,
Hardly aware of her departed lover;
Her brain allows one half-formed thought to pass:
"Well now that's done: and I'm glad it's over."
When lovely woman stoops to folly and
Paces about her room again, alone,
She smoothes her hair with automatic hand,
And puts a record on the gramophone.

   "This music crept by me upon the waters"
And along the Strand, up Queen Victoria Street.
O City city, I can sometimes hear
Beside a public bar in Lower Thames Street,
The pleasant whining of a mandoline
And a clatter and a chatter from within
Where fishermen lounge at noon: where the walls
Of Magnus Martyr hold
Inexplicable splendour of Ionian white and gold.

      The river sweats
      Oil and tar
      The barges drift
      With the turning tide
      Red sails
      Wide
      To leeward, swing on the heavy spar.
      The barges wash
      Drifting logs
      Down Greenwich reach
      Past the Isle of Dogs.
              Weialala leia
              Wallala leialala

    Elizabeth and Leicester
    Beating oars

The stern was formed
A gilded shell
Red and gold
The brisk swell
Rippled both shores
Southwest wind
Carried down stream
The peal of bells
White towers
                    Weialala leia
                    Wallala leialala

"Trams and dusty trees.
Highbury bore me. Richmond and Kew
Undid me. By Richmond I raised my knees
Supine on the floor of a narrow canoe."

"My feet are at Moorgate, and my heart
Under my feet. After the event
He wept. He promised 'a new start.'
I made no comment. What should I resent?"

"On Margate Sands.
I can connect
Nothing with nothing.
The broken fingernails of dirty hands.
My people humble people who expect
Nothing."
                    la la

To Carthage then I came

Burning burning burning burning
O Lord Thou pluckest me out
O Lord Thou pluckest

burning

IV. DEATH BY WATER

Phlebas the Phoenician, a fortnight dead,
Forgot the cry of gulls, and the deep sea swell
And the profit and loss.

A current under sea
Picked his bones in whispers. As he rose and fell
He passed the stages of his age and youth
Entering the whirlpool.
                    Gentile or Jew
O you who turn the wheel and look to windward,
Consider Phlebas, who was once handsome and tall as you.

V. WHAT THE THUNDER SAID

After the torchlight red on sweaty faces
After the frosty silence in the gardens
After the agony in stony places
The shouting and the crying
Prison and palace and reverberation
Of thunder of spring over distant mountains
He who was living is now dead
We who were living are now dying
With a little patience

   Here is no water but only rock
Rock and no water and the sandy road
The road winding above among the mountains
Which are mountains of rock without water
If there were water we should stop and drink
Amongst the rock one cannot stop or think
Sweat is dry and feet are in the sand
If there were only water amongst the rock
Dead mountain mouth of carious teeth that cannot spit
Here one can neither stand nor lie nor sit
There is not even silence in the mountains
But dry sterile thunder without rain
There is not even solitude in the mountains
But red sullen faces sneer and snarl
From doors of mudcracked houses
                         If there were water

   And no rock
   If there were rock
   And also water
   And water
   A spring
   A pool among the rock

If there were the sound of water only
Not the cicada
And dry grass singing
But sound of water over a rock
Where the hermit-thrush sings in the pine trees
Drip drop drip drop drop drop drop
But there is no water

Who is the third who walks always beside you?
When I count, there are only you and I together
But when I look ahead up the white road
There is always another one walking beside you
Gliding wrapt in a brown mantle, hooded
I do not know whether a man or a woman
—But who is that on the other side of you?

What is that sound high in the air
Murmur of maternal lamentation
Who are those hooded hordes swarming
Over endless plains, stumbling in cracked earth
Ringed by the flat horizon only
What is the city over the mountains
Cracks and reforms and bursts in the violet air
Falling towers
Jerusalem Athens Alexandria
Vienna London
Unreal

A woman drew her long black hair out tight
And fiddled whisper music on those strings
And bats with baby faces in the violet light
Whistled, and beat their wings
And crawled head downward down a blackened wall
And upside down in air were towers
Tolling reminiscent bells, that kept the hours
And voices singing out of empty cisterns and exhausted
     wells.

In this decayed hole among the mountains
In the faint moonlight, the grass is singing
Over the tumbled graves, about the chapel

There is the empty chapel, only the wind's home.
It has no windows, and the door swings,
Dry bones can harm no one.
Only a cock stood on the rooftree
Co co rico co co rico
In a flash of lightning. Then a damp gust
Bringing rain

Ganga was sunken, and the limp leaves
Waited for rain, while the black clouds
Gathered far distant, over Himavant.
The jungle crouched, humped in silence.
Then spoke the thunder
DA
Datta: what have we given?
My friend, blood shaking my heart
The awful daring of a moment's surrender
Which an age of prudence can never retract
By this, and this only, we have existed
Which is not to be found in our obituaries
Or in memories draped by the beneficent spider
Or under seals broken by the lean solicitor
In our empty rooms
DA
Dayadhvam: I have heard the key
Turn in the door once and turn once only
We think of the key, each in his prison
Thinking of the key, each confirms a prison
Only at nightfall, aethereal rumours
Revive for a moment a broken Coriolanus
DA
Damyata: The boat responded
Gaily, to the hand expert with sail and oar
The sea was calm, your heart would have responded
Gaily, when invited, beating obedient
To controlling hands

                        I sat upon the shore
Fishing, with the arid plain behind me
Shall I at least set my lands in order?
London Bridge is falling down falling down falling down

Poi s'ascose nel foco che gli affina
Quando fiam uti chelidon—O swallow swallow
Le Prince d'Aquitaine à la tour abolie
These fragments I have shored against my ruins
Why then Ile fit you. Hieronymo's mad againe.
Datta. Dayadhvam. Damyata.
            Shantih   shantih   shantih

NOTES ON "THE WASTE LAND"

Not only the title, but the plan and a good deal of the incidental symbolism of the poem were suggested by Miss Jessie L. Weston's book on the Grail legend: *From Ritual to Romance* (Cambridge). Indeed, so deeply am I indebted, Miss Weston's book will elucidate the difficulties of the poem much better than my notes can do; and I recommend it (apart from the great interest of the book itself) to any who think such elucidation of the poem worth the trouble. To another work of anthropology I am indebted in general, one which has influenced our generation profoundly; I mean *The Golden Bough;* I have used especially the two volumes *Adonis, Attis, Osiris.* Anyone who is acquainted with these works will immediately recognise in the poem certain references to vegetation ceremonies.

I. *The Burial of the Dead*

Line 20. Cf. Ezekiel II, i.
23. Cf. Ecclesiastes XII, v.
31. V. Tristan und Isolde, I, verses 5–8.
42. Id. III, verse 24.
46. I am not familiar with the exact constitution of the Tarot pack of cards, from which I have obviously departed to suit my own convenience. The Hanged Man, a member of the traditional pack, fits my purpose in two ways: because he is associated in my mind with the Hanged God of Frazer, and because I associate him with the hooded figure in the passage of the disciples to Emmaus in Part V. The Phoenician Sailor and the Merchant appear later; also the "crowds of people," and Death by Water is executed in Part IV. The Man with Three Staves (an authentic member of the Tarot pack) I associate, quite arbitrarily, with the Fisher King himself.
60. Cf. Baudelaire:
        "Fourmillante cité, cité pleine de rêves,
        "Où le spectre en plein jour raccroche le passant."

63. Cf. Inferno III, 55–57:

> "si lunga tratta
> di gente, ch'io non avrei mai creduto
> che morte tanta n'avesse disfatta."

64. Cf. Inferno IV, 25–27:

> "Quivi, secondo che per ascoltare,
> "non avea pianto, ma' che di sospiri,
> "che l'aura eterna facevan tremare."

68. A phenomenon which I have often noticed.

74. Cf. the Dirge in Webster's *White Devil*.

76. V. Baudelaire, Preface to *Fleurs du Mal*.

III. *The Fire Sermon*

176. V. Spenser, *Prothalamion*.

192. Cf. *The Tempest*, I, ii.

196. Cf. Marvell, *To His Coy Mistress*.

197. Cf. Day, *Parliament of Bees*:

> "When of the sudden, listening, you shall hear,
> "A noise of horns and hunting, which shall bring
> "Actaeon to Diana in the spring,
> "Where all shall see her naked skin . . ."

199. I do not know the origin of the ballad from which these lines are taken: it was reported to me from Sydney, Australia.

202. V. Verlaine, *Parsifal*.

210. The currants were quoted at a price "carriage and insurance free to London"; and the Bill of Lading etc. were to be handed to the buyer upon payment of the sight draft.

218. Tiresias, although a mere spectator and not indeed a "character," is yet the most important personage in the poem, uniting all the rest. Just as the one-eyed merchant, seller of currants, melts into the Phoenician Sailor, and the latter is not wholly distinct from Ferdinand Prince of Naples, so all the women are one woman, and the two sexes meet in Tiresias. What Tiresias *sees*, in fact, is the substance of the poem. The whole passage from Ovid is of great anthropological interest:

> '. . . Cum Iunone iocos et maior vestra profecto est
> Quam, quae contingit maribus,' dixisse, 'voluptas.'
> Illa negat; placuit quae sit sententia docti
> Quaerere Tiresiae: venus huic erat utraque nota.
> Nam duo magnorum viridi coeuntia silva
> Corpora serpentum baculi violaverat ictu
> Deque viro factus, mirabile, femina septem
> Egerat autumnos; octavo rursus eosdem
> Vidit et 'est vestrae si tanta potentia plagae,'
> Dixit 'ut auctoris sortem in contraria mutet,

Nunc quoque vos feriam!' percussis anguibus isdem
Forma prior rediit genetivaque venit imago.
Arbiter hic igitur sumptus de lite iocosa
Dicta Iovis firmat; gravius Saturnia iusto
Nec pro materia fertur doluisse suique
Iudicis aeterna damnavit lumina nocte,
At pater omnipotens (neque enim licet inrita cuiquam
Facta dei fecisse deo) pro lumine adempto
Scire futura dedit poenamque levavit honore.

221. This may not appear as exact as Sappho's lines, but I had in mind the "longshore" or "dory" fisherman, who returns at nightfall.

253. V. Goldsmith, the song in *The Vicar of Wakefield*.

257. V. *The Tempest*, as above.

264. The interior of St. Magnus Martyr is to my mind one of the finest among Wren's interiors. See *The Proposed Demolition of Nineteen City Churches*: (P. S. King & Son, Ltd.).

266. The Song of the (three) Thames-daughters begins here. From line 292 to 306 inclusive they speak in turn. V. *Götterdämmerung*, III, i: the Rhine-daughters.

279. V. Froude, *Elizabeth*, Vol. I, ch. iv, letter of De Quadra to Philip of Spain:
"In the afternoon we were in a barge, watching the games on the river. (The queen) was alone with Lord Robert and myself on the poop, when they began to talk nonsense, and went so far that Lord Robert at last said, as I was on the spot there was no reason why they should not be married if the queen pleased."

293. Cf. *Purgatorio*, V, 133:
    "Ricorditi di me, che son la Pia;
    "Siena mi fe', disfecemi Maremma."

307. V. St. Augustine's *Confessions*: "to Carthage then I came, where a cauldron of unholy loves sang all about mine ears."

308. The complete text of the Buddha's Fire Sermon (which corresponds in importance to the Sermon on the Mount) from which these words are taken, will be found translated in the late Henry Clarke Warren's *Buddism in Translation* (Harvard Oriental Series). Mr. Warren was one of the great pioneers of Buddhist studies in the Occident.

309. From St. Augustine's *Confessions* again. The collocation of these two representatives of eastern and western asceticism, as the culmination of this part of the poem, is not an accident.

V. *What the Thunder Said*

In the first part of Part V three themes are employed: the journey to Emmaus, the approach to the Chapel Perilous (see Miss Weston's book) and the present decay of eastern Europe.

357. This is *Turdus aonalaschkae pallasii*, the hermit-thrush which I have heard in Quebec Province. Chapman says (*Handbook of Birds of Eastern North America*) "it is most at home in secluded woodland and thickety retreats. . . . Its notes are not remarkable for variety or volume, but in purity and sweetness of tone and exquisite modulation they are unequalled." Its "water-dripping song" is justly celebrated.

360. The following lines were stimulated by the account of one of the Antarctic expeditions (I forget which, but I think one of Shackleton's): it was related that the party of explorers, at the extremity of their strength, had the constant delusion that there was *one more member* than could actually be counted.

367-77. Cf. Hermann Hesse, *Blick ins Chaos:* "Schon ist halb Europa, schon ist zumindest der halbe Osten Europas auf dem Wege zum Chaos, fährt betrunken im heiligem Wahn am Abgrund entlang und singt dazu, singt betrunken und hymnisch wie Dmitri Karamasoff sang. Ueber diese Lieder lacht der Bürger beleidigt, der Heilige und Seher hört sie mit Tränen."

402. "Datta, dayadhvam, damyata" (Give, sympathise, control). The fable of the meaning of the Thunder is found in the *Brihadaranyaka—Upanishad*, 5, 1. A translation is found in Deussen's *Sechzig Upanishads des Veda*, p. 489.

408. Cf. Webster, *The White Devil*, V, vi:
> ". . . they'll remarry
> Ere the worm pierce your winding-sheet, ere the spider
> Make a thin curtain for your epitaphs."

412. Cf. *Inferno*, XXXIII, 46:
> "ed io sentii chiavar l'uscio di sotto
> all'orribile torre."

Also F. H. Bradley, *Appearance and Reality*, p. 346.
"My external sensations are no less private to myself than are my thoughts or my feelings. In either case my experience falls within my own circle, a circle closed on the outside; and, with all its elements alike, every sphere is opaque to the others which surround it. . . . In brief, regarded as an existence which appears in a soul, the whole world for each is peculiar and private to that soul."

425. V. Weston: *From Ritual to Romance*; chapter on the Fisher King.

428. V. *Purgatorio*, XXVI, 148.
> " 'Ara vos prec per aquella valor
> 'que vos guida al som de l'escalina,
> 'sovegna vos a temps de ma dolor.'
> Poi s'ascose nel foco che gli affina."

429. V. *Pervigilium Veneris*. Cf. Philomela in Parts II and III.

430. V. Gerard de Nerval, Sonnet *El Desdichado*.
432. V. Kyd's *Spanish Tragedy*.
434. Shantih. Repeated as here, a formal ending to an Upanishad. "The Peace which passeth understanding" is our equivalent to this word.

THE HOLLOW MEN

Mistah Kurtz—he dead.
> *A penny for the Old Guy*

I

We are the hollow men
We are the stuffed men
Leaning together
Headpiece filled with straw. Alas!
Our dried voices, when
We whisper together
Are quiet and meaningless
As wind in dry grass
Or rats' feet over broken glass
In our dry cellar

Shape without form, shade without colour,
Paralysed force, gesture without motion;

Those who have crossed
With direct eyes, to death's other Kingdom
Remember us—if at all—not as lost
Violent souls, but only
As the hollow men
The stuffed men.

II

Eyes I dare not meet in dreams
In death's dream kingdom
These do not appear:

There, the eyes are
Sunlight on a broken column
There, is a tree swinging
And voices are
In the wind's singing
More distant and more solemn
Than a fading star.

   Let me be no nearer
In death's dream kingdom
Let me also wear
Such deliberate disguises
Rat's coat, crowskin, crossed staves
In a field
Behaving as the wind behaves
No nearer—

   Not that final meeting
In the twilight kingdom

III

This is the dead land
This is cactus land
Here the stone images
Are raised, here they receive
The supplication of a dead man's hand
Under the twinkle of a fading star.

   Is it like this
In death's other kingdom
Waking alone
At the hour when we are
Trembling with tenderness
Lips that would kiss
Form prayers to broken stone.

IV

The eyes are not here
There are no eyes here
In this valley of dying stars

In this hollow valley
This broken jaw of our lost kingdoms

   In this last of meeting places
We grope together
And avoid speech
Gathered on this beach of the tumid river

   Sightless, unless
The eyes reappear
As the perpetual star
Multifoliate rose
Of death's twilight kingdom
The hope only
Of empty men.

v

Here we go round the prickly pear
Prickly pear prickly pear
Here we go round the prickly pear
At five o'clock in the morning.

   Between the idea
And the reality
Between the motion
And the act
Falls the Shadow
        For Thine is the Kingdom

   Between the conception
And the creation
Between the emotion
And the response
Falls the Shadow
        Life is very long

   Between the desire
And the spasm
Between the potency
And the existence
Between the essence

And the descent
Falls the Shadow
            For Thine is the Kingdom

    For Thine is
Life is
For Thine is the

    This is the way the world ends
This is the way the world ends
This is the way the world ends
Not with a bang but a whimper.

JOURNEY OF THE MAGI

'A cold coming we had of it,
Just the worst time of the year
For a journey, and such a long journey:
The ways deep and the weather sharp,
The very dead of winter.'
And the camels galled, sore-footed, refractory,
Lying down in the melting snow.
There were times we regretted
The summer palaces on slopes, the terraces,
And the silken girls bringing sherbet.
Then the camel men cursing and grumbling
And running away, and wanting their liquor and women,
And the night-fires going out, and the lack of shelters,
And the cities hostile and the towns unfriendly
And the villages dirty and charging high prices:
A hard time we had of it.
At the end we preferred to travel all night,
Sleeping in snatches,
With the voices singing in our ears, saying
That this was all folly.

    Then at dawn we came down to a temperate valley,
Wet, below the snow line, smelling of vegetation;

With a running stream and a water-mill beating the
    darkness,
And three trees on the low sky,
And an old white horse galloped away in the meadow.
Then we came to a tavern with vine-leaves over the lintel,
Six hands at an open door dicing for pieces of silver,
And feet kicking the empty wine-skins.
But there was no information, and so we continued
And arrived at evening, not a moment too soon
Finding the place; it was (you may say) satisfactory.

    All this was a long time ago, I remember,
And I would do it again, but set down
This set down
This: were we led all that way for
Birth or Death? There was a Birth, certainly,
We had evidence and no doubt. I had seen birth and death,
But had thought they were different; this Birth was
Hard and bitter agony for us, like Death, our death.
We returned to our places, these Kingdoms,
But no longer at ease here, in the old dispensation,
With an alien people clutching their gods.
I should be glad of another death.

BURNT NORTON

τοῦ λόγου δ' ἐόντος ξυνοῦ ζώουσιν οἱ πολλοί
ὡς ἰδίαν ἔχοντες φρόνησιν.
                     I. p. 77. Fr. 2.

ὁδὸς ἄνω κάτω μία καὶ ὡυτή.
                     I. p. 89. Fr. 60.

Diels: *Die Fragmente der Vorsokratiker* (Herakleitos).

I

Time present and time past
Are both perhaps present in time future,

And time future contained in time past.
If all time is eternally present
All time is unredeemable.
What might have been is an abstraction
Remaining a perpetual possibility
Only in a world of speculation.
What might have been and what has been
Point to one end, which is always present.
Footfalls echo in the memory
Down the passage which we did not take
Towards the door we never opened
Into the rose-garden. My words echo
Thus, in your mind.
                    But to what purpose
Disturbing the dust on a bowl of rose-leaves
I do not know.
                    Other echoes
Inhabit the garden. Shall we follow?
Quick, said the bird, find them, find them,
Round the corner. Through the first gate,
Into our first world, shall we follow
The deception of the thrush? Into our first world.
There they were, dignified, invisible,
Moving without pressure, over the dead leaves,
In the autumn heat, through the vibrant air,
And the bird called, in response to
The unheard music hidden in the shrubbery,
And the unseen eyebeam crossed, for the roses
Had the look of flowers that are looked at.
There they were as our guests, accepted and accepting.
So we moved, and they, in a formal pattern,
Along the empty alley, into the box circle,
To look down into the drained pool.
Dry the pool, dry concrete, brown edged,
And the pool was filled with water out of sunlight,
And the lotos rose, quietly, quietly,
The surface glittered out of heart of light,
And they were behind us, reflected in the pool.
Then a cloud passed, and the pool was empty.
Go, said the bird, for the leaves were full of children,

Hidden excitedly, containing laughter.
Go, go, go, said the bird: human kind
Cannot bear very much reality.
Time past and time future
What might have been and what has been
Point to one end, which is always present.

II

Garlic and sapphires in the mud
Clot the bedded axle-tree.
The trilling wire in the blood
Sings below inveterate scars
And reconciles forgotten wars.
The dance along the artery
The circulation of the lymph
Are figured in the drift of stars
Ascend to summer in the tree
We move above the moving tree
In light upon the figured leaf
And hear upon the sodden floor
Below, the boarhound and the boar
Pursue their pattern as before
But reconciled among the stars.

　　At the still point of the turning world. Neither flesh nor
　　　　fleshless;
Neither from nor towards; at the still point, there the dance is,
But neither arrest nor movement. And do not call it fixity,
Where past and future are gathered. Neither movement from
　　　　nor towards,
Neither ascent nor decline. Except for the point, the still point,
There would be no dance, and there is only the dance.
I can only say, *there* we have been: but I cannot say where.
And I cannot say, how long, for that is to place it in time.

　　The inner freedom from the practical desire,
The release from action and suffering, release from the inner
And the outer compulsion, yet surrounded
By a grace of sense, a white light still and moving,
Erhebung without motion, concentration
Without elimination, both a new world

And the old made explicit, understood
In the completion of its partial ecstasy,
The resolution of its partial horror.
Yet the enchainment of past and future
Woven in the weakness of the changing body,
Protects mankind from heaven and damnation
Which flesh cannot endure.

                      Time past and time future
Allow but a little consciousness.
To be conscious is not to be in time
But only in time can the moment in the rose-garden,
The moment in the arbour where the rain beat,
The moment in the draughty church at smokefall
Be remembered; involved with past and future.
Only through time time is conquered.

III

Here is a place of disaffection
Time before and time after
In a dim light: neither daylight
Investing form with lucid stillness
Turning shadow into transient beauty
With slow rotation suggesting permanence
Nor darkness to purify the soul
Emptying the sensual with deprivation
Cleansing affection from the temporal.
Neither plentitude nor vacancy. Only a flicker
Over the strained time-ridden faces
Distracted from distraction by distraction
Filled with fancies and empty of meaning
Tumid apathy with no concentration
Men and bits of paper, whirled by the cold wind
That blows before and after time,
Wind in and out of unwholesome lungs
Time before and time after.
Eructation of unhealthy souls
Into the faded air, the torpid
Driven on the wind that sweeps the gloomy hills of London,
Hampstead and Clerkenwell, Campden and Putney,
Highgate, Primrose and Ludgate. Not here
Not here the darkness, in this twittering world.

Descend lower, descend only
Into the world of perpetual solitude,
World not world, but that which is not world,
Internal darkness, deprivation
And destitution of all property,
Desiccation of the world of sense,
Evacuation of the world of fancy,
Inoperancy of the world of spirit;
This is the one way, and the other
Is the same, not in movement
But abstention from movement; while the world moves
In appetency, on its metalled ways
Of time past and time future.

IV

Time and the bell have buried the day,
The black cloud carries the sun away.
Will the sunflower turn to us, will the clematis
Stray down, bend to us; tendril and spray
Clutch and cling?
Chill
Fingers of yew be curled
Down on us? After the kingfisher's wing
Has answered light to light, and is silent, the light is still
At the still point of the turning world.

V

Words move, music moves
Only in time; but that which is only living
Can only die. Words, after speech, reach
Into the silence. Only by the form, the pattern,
Can words or music reach
The stillness, as a Chinese jar still
Moves perpetually in its stillness.
Not the stillness of the violin, while the note lasts,
Not that only, but the co-existence,
Or say that the end precedes the beginning,
And the end and the beginning were always there
Before the beginning and after the end.
And all is always now. Words strain,
Crack and sometimes break, under the burden,

Under the tension, slip, slide, perish,
Decay with imprecision, will not stay in place,
Will not stay still. Shrieking voices
Scolding, mocking, or merely chattering,
Always assail them. The Word in the desert
Is most attacked by voices of temptation,
The crying shadow in the funeral dance,
The loud lament of the disconsolate chimera.

    The detail of the pattern is movement,
As in the figure of the ten stairs.
Desire itself is movement
Not in itself desirable;
Love is itself unmoving,
Only the cause and end of movement,
Timeless, and undesiring
Except in the aspect of time
Caught in the form of limitation
Between un-being and being.
Sudden in a shaft of sunlight
Even while the dust moves
There rises the hidden laughter
Of children in the foliage
Quick now, here, now, always—
Ridiculous the waste sad time
Stretching before and after.

John Crowe Ransom / 1888–

BELLS FOR JOHN WHITESIDE'S
DAUGHTER

There was such speed in her little body,
And such lightness in her footfall,

It is no wonder her brown study
Astonishes us all.

Her wars were bruited in our high window.
We looked among orchard trees and beyond
Where she took arms against her shadow,
Or harried unto the pond

The lazy geese, like a snow cloud
Dripping their snow on the green grass,
Tricking and stopping, sleepy and proud,
Who cried in goose, Alas,

For the tireless heart within the little
Lady with rod that made them rise
From their noon apple-dreams and scuttle
Goose-fashion under the skies!

But now go the bells, and we are ready,
In one house we are sternly stopped
To say we are vexed at her brown study,
Lying so primly propped.

HERE   LIES   A   LADY

Here lies a lady of beauty and high degree.
Of chills and fever she died, of fever and chills,
The delight of her husband, her aunt, an infant of three,
And of medicos marveling sweetly on her ills.

For either she burned, and her confident eyes would blaze,
And her fingers fly in a manner to puzzle their heads—
What was she making? Why, nothing; she sat in a maze
Of old scraps of laces, snipped into curious shreds—

Or this would pass, and the light of her fire decline
Till she lay discouraged and cold, like a thin stalk white
    and blown,

And would not open her eyes, to kisses, to wine;
The sixth of these states was her last; the cold settled down.

Sweet ladies, long may ye bloom, and toughly I hope ye
        may thole,
But was she not lucky? In flowers and lace and mourning,
In love and great honor we bade God rest her soul
After six little spaces of chill, and six of burning.

JUDITH OF BETHULIA

Beautiful as the flying legend of some leopard
She had not yet chosen her great captain or prince
Depositary to her flesh, and our defense;
And a wandering beauty is a blade out of its scabbard.
You know how dangerous, gentlemen of threescore?
May you know it yet ten more.

Nor by process of veiling she grew the less fabulous.
Grey or blue veils, we were desperate to study
The invincible emanations of her white body,
And the winds at her ordered raiment were ominous.
Might she walk in the market, sit in the council of soldiers?
Only of the extreme elders.

But a rare chance was the girl's then, when the Invader
Trumpeted from the south, and rumbled from the north,
Beleaguered the city from four quarters of the earth,
Our soldiery too craven and sick to aid her—
Where were the arms could countervail this horde?
Her beauty was the sword.

She sat with the elders, and proved on their blear visage
How bright was the weapon unrusted in her keeping,
While he lay surfeiting on their harvest heaping,
Wasting the husbandry of their rarest vintage—
And dreaming of the broad-breasted dames for concubine?
These floated on his wine.

He was lapped with bay-leaves, and grass and fumiter
        weed,
And from under the wine-film encountered his mortal
        vision,
For even within his tent she accomplished his derision;
She loosed one veil and another, standing unafraid;
And he perished. Nor brushed her with even so much as a
        daisy?
She found his destruction easy.

The heathen are all perished. The victory was furnished,
We smote them hiding in our vineyards, barns, annexes,
And now their white bones clutter the holes of foxes,
And the chieftain's head, with grinning sockets, and
        varnished—
Is it hung on the sky with a hideous epitaphy?
No, the woman keeps the trophy.

May God send unto our virtuous lady her prince.
It is stated she went reluctant to that orgy,
Yet a madness fevers our young men, and not the clergy
Nor the elders have turned them unto modesty since.
Inflamed by the thought of her naked beauty with desire?
Yes, and chilled with fear and despair.

CAPTAIN CARPENTER

Captain Carpenter rose up in his prime
Put on his pistols and went riding out
But had got wellnigh nowhere at that time
Till he fell in with ladies in a rout.

It was a pretty lady and all her train
That played with him so sweetly but before
An hour she'd taken a sword with all her main
And twined him of his nose for evermore.

Captain Carpenter mounted up one day
And rode straight way into a stranger rogue

That looked unchristian but be that as may
The Captain did not wait upon prologue.

But drew upon him out of his great heart
The other swung against him with a club
And cracked his two legs at the shinny part
And let him roll and stick like any tub.

Captain Carpenter rode many a time
From male and female took he sundry harms
He met the wife of Satan crying "I'm
The she-wolf bids you shall bear no more arms."

Their strokes and counters whistled in the wind
I wish he had delivered half his blows
But where she should have made off like a hind
The bitch bit off his arms at the elbows.

And Captain Carpenter parted with his ears
To a black devil that used him in this wise
O Jesus ere his threescore and ten years
Another had plucked out his sweet blue eyes.

Captain Carpenter got up on his roan
And sallied from the gate in hell's despite
I heard him asking in the grimmest tone
If any enemy yet there was to fight?

"To any adversary it is fame
If he risk to be wounded by my tongue
Or burnt in two beneath my red heart's flame
Such are the perils he is cast among.

"But if he can he has a pretty choice
From an anatomy with little to lose
Whether he cut my tongue and take my voice
Or whether it be my round red heart he choose."

It was the neatest knave that ever was seen
Stepping in perfume from his lady's bower
Who at this word put in his merry mien
And fell on Captain Carpenter like a tower.

I would not knock old fellows in the dust
But there lay Captain Carpenter on his back
His weapons were the old heart in his bust
And a blade shook between rotten teeth alack.

The rogue in scarlet and grey soon knew his mind
He wished to get his trophy and depart
With gentle apology and touch refined
He pierced him and produced the Captain's heart.

God's mercy rest on Captain Carpenter now
I thought him Sirs an honest gentleman
Citizen husband soldier and scholar enow
Let jangling kites eat of him if they can.

But God's deep curses follow after those
That shore him of his goodly nose and ears
His legs and strong arms at the two elbows
And eyes that had not watered seventy years.

The curse of hell upon the sleek upstart
That got the Captain finally on his back
And took the red red vitals of his heart
And made the kites to whet their beaks clack clack.

HER EYES

To a woman that I knew
Were eyes of an extravagant hue:
Viz., china blue.

Those I wear upon my head
Are sometimes green and sometimes red,
I said.

My mother's eyes are wet and blear,
My little sister's are not clear,
Poor silly dear.

It must be given to but few,
A pair of eyes so utter blue
And new;

Where does she keep them from this glare
Of the monstrous sun and the wind's flare
Without any wear;

And were they never in the night
Poisoned by artificial light
Much too bright;

And had the splendid beast no heart
That boiled with tears and baked with smart
The ocular part?

I'll have no business with those eyes,
They are not kind, they are not wise,
They are two great lies.

A woman shooting such blue flame
I apprehend will get some blame
On her good name.

MAN WITHOUT SENSE
OF DIRECTION

Tell this to ladies: how a hero man
Assail a thick and scandalous giant
Who casts true shadow in the sun,
And die, but play no truant.

This is more horrible: that the darling egg
Of the chosen people hatch a creature
Of noblest mind and powerful leg
Who cannot fathom nor perform his nature.

The larks' tongues are never stilled
Where the pale spread straw of sunlight lies
Then what invidious gods have willed
Him to be seized so otherwise?

Birds of the field and beasts of the stable
Are swollen with rapture and make uncouth
Demonstration of joy, which is a babble
Offending the ear of the fervorless youth.

Love—is it the cause? the proud shamed spirit?
Love has slain some whom it possessed,
But his was requited beyond his merit
And won him in bridal the loveliest.

Yet scarcely he issues from the warm chamber,
Flushed with her passion, when cold as dead
Once more he walks where waves past number
Of sorrow buffet his curse-hung head.

Whether by street, or in field full of honey,
Attended by clouds of the creatures of air
Or shouldering the city's companioning many,
His doom is on him; and how can he care

For the shapes that would fiddle upon his senses,
Wings and faces and mists that move,
Words, sunlight, the blue air which rinses
The pure pale head which he must love?

And he writhes like an antique man of bronze
That is beaten by furies visible,
Yet he is punished not knowing his sins
And for his innocence walks in hell.

He flails his arms, he moves his lips:
"Rage have I none, cause, time, nor country—
Yet I have traveled land and ships
And knelt my seasons in the chantry."

So he stands muttering; and rushes
Back to the tender thing in his charge

With clamoring tongue and taste of ashes
And a small passion to feign large.

But let his cold lips be her omen,
She shall not kiss that harried one
To peace, as men are served by women
Who comfort them in darkness and in sun.

THE EQUILIBRISTS

Full of her long white arms and milky skin
He had a thousand times remembered sin.
Alone in the press of people traveled he,
Minding her jacinth, and myrrh, and ivory.

Mouth he remembered: the quaint orifice
From which came heat that flamed upon the kiss,
Till cold words came down spiral from the head.
Grey doves from the officious tower illsped.

Body: it was a white field ready for love,
On her body's field, with the gaunt tower above,
The lilies grew, beseeching him to take,
If he would pluck and wear them, bruise and break.

Eyes talking: Never mind the cruel words,
Embrace my flowers, but not embrace the swords.
But what they said, the doves came straightway flying
And unsaid: Honor, Honor, they came crying.

Importunate her doves. Too pure, too wise,
Clambering on his shoulder, saying, Arise,
Leave me now, and never let us meet,
Eternal distance now command thy feet.

Predicament indeed, which thus discovers
Honor among thieves, Honor between lovers.
O such a little word is Honor, they feel!
But the grey word is between them cold as steel.

At length I saw these lovers fully were come
Into their torture of equilibrium;
Dreadfully had forsworn each other, and yet
They were bound each to each, and they did not forget.

And rigid as two painful stars, and twirled
About the clustered night their prison world,
They burned with fierce love always to come near,
But honor beat them back and kept them clear.

Ah, the strict lovers, they are ruined now!
I cried in anger. But with puddled brow
Devising for those gibbeted and brave
Came I descanting: Man, what would you have?

For spin your period out, and draw your breath,
A kinder saeculum begins with Death.
Would you ascend to Heaven and bodiless dwell?
Or take your bodies honorless to Hell?

In Heaven you have heard no marriage is,
No white flesh tinder to your lecheries,
Your male and female tissue sweetly shaped
Sublimed away, and furious blood escaped.

Great lovers lie in Hell, the stubborn ones
Infatuate of the flesh upon the bones;
Stuprate, they rend each other when they kiss,
The pieces kiss again, no end to this.

But still I watched them spinning, orbited nice.
Their flames were not more radiant than their ice.
I dug in the quiet earth and wrought the tomb
And made these lines to memorize their doom:—

EPITAPH

Equilibrists lie here; stranger, tread light;
Close, but untouching in each other's sight;
Mouldered the lips and ashy the tall skull.
Let them lie perilous and beautiful.

LITTLE BOY BLUE

He rubbed his eyes and wound the silver horn.
Then the continuum was cracked and torn
With tumbling imps of music being born.

The blowzy sheep lethargic on the ground
Suddenly burned where no fire could be found
And straight up stood their fleeces every pound.

The old bellwether rose and rang his bell,
The seven-days' lambs went skipping and skipped well,
And Baa Baa Baa, the flock careered pellmell.

The yellow cows that milked the savoury cud
Propped on the green grass or the yellow mud
Felt such a tingle in their lady blood,

They ran and tossed their hooves and horns of blue
And jumped the fence and gambolled kangaroo,
Divinely singing as they wandered Moo.

A plague on such a shepherd of the sheep
That careless boy with pretty cows to keep!
With such a burden I should never sleep.

But when his notes had run around the sky,
When they proceeded to grow faint and die,
He stuffed his horn with straw and put it by.

And when the legs were tired beneath the sheep
And there were spent and sleepy cows to keep,
He rubbed his eyes again and went to sleep.

PAINTED HEAD

By dark severance the apparition head
Smiles from the air a capital on no

Column or a Platonic perhaps head
On a canvas sky depending from nothing;

Stirs up an old illusion of grandeur
By tickling the instinct of heads to be
Absolute and to try decapitation
And to play truant from the body bush;

But too happy and beautiful for those sorts
Of head (homekeeping heads are happiest)
Discovers maybe thirty unwidowed years
Of not dishonoring the faithful stem;

Is nameless and has authored for the evil
Historian headhunters neither book
Nor state and is therefore distinct from tart
Heads with crowns and guilty gallery heads;

Wherefore the extravagant device of art
Unhousing by abstraction this once head
Was capital irony by a loving hand
That knew the no treason of a head like this;

Makes repentance in an unlovely head
For having vinegarly traduced the flesh
Till, the hurt flesh recusing, the hard egg
Is shrunken to its own deathlike surface;

And an image thus. The body bears the head
(So hardly one they terribly are two)
Feeds and obeys and unto please what end?
Not to the glory of tyrant head but to

The being of body. Beauty is of body.
The flesh contouring shallowly on a head
Is a rock-garden needing body's love
And best bodiness to colorify

The big blue birds sitting and sea-shell flats
And caves, and on the iron acropolis
To spread the hyacinthine hair and rear
The olive garden for the nightingales.

ADDRESS TO THE SCHOLARS OF
NEW ENGLAND

Harvard Phi Beta Kappa Poem, June 23, 1939

When Sarah Pierrepont let her spirit rage
Her love and scorn refused the bauble earth
(Which took bloom even here, under the Bear)
And groped for the Essence sitting in himself,
Subtle, I think, for a girl's unseasoned rage.

The late and sudden extravagance of soul
By which they all were swollen exalted her
At seventeen years to Edwards' canopy,
A match pleasing to any Heaven, had not
The twelve mortal labors harassed her soul.

Thrifty and too proud were the sea-borne fathers
Who fetched the Pure Idea in a bound box
And fastened him in a steeple, to have his court
Shabby with an unkingly establishment
And Sabbath levees for the minion fathers.

The majesty of Heaven has a great house,
And even if the Indian kingdom or the fox
Ran barking mad in a wide forest place,
They had his threshold, and you had the dream
Of property in him by a steepled house.

If once the entail shall come on raffish sons,
Knife-wit scholar and merchant sharp in thumb,
With positive steel they'll pry into the steeple,
And blinking through the cracked ribs at the void
A judgment laughter rakes the cynic sons.

But like prevailing wind New England's honor
Carried, and teased small Southern boys in school,
Whose heads the temperate birds fleeing your winter
Construed for, but the stiff heroes abashed
With their frozen fingers and unearthly honor.

Scared by the holy megrims of those Pilgrims,
I thought the unhumbled and outcast and cold
Were the rich Heirs traveling incognito,
Bred too fine for the country's sweet produce
And but affecting that dog's life of pilgrims.

There used to be debate of soul and body,
The soul storming incontinent with shrew's tongue
Against what natural brilliance body had loved,
Even the green phases though deciduous
Of earth's zodiac homage to the body.

Plato, before Plotinus gentled him,
Spoke the soul's part, and though its vice is known
We're in his shadow still, and it appears
Your founders most of all the nations held
By his scandal-mongering, and established him.

Perfect was the witch foundering in water,
The blasphemer that spraddled in the stocks,
The woman branded with her sin, the whales
Of ocean taken with a psalmer's sword,
The British tea infusing the bay's water.

But they reared heads into the always clouds
And stooped to the event of war or bread,
The secular perforces and short speech
Being labors surlily done with the left hand,
The chief strength giddying with transcendent clouds.

The tangent Heavens mocked the fathers' strength,
And how the young sons know it, and study now
To take fresh conquest of the conquered earth,
But they're too strong for that, you've seen them whip
The laggard will to deeds of lunatic strength.

To incline the powerful living unto peace
With Heaven is easier now, with Earth is hard,
Yet a rare metaphysic makes them one,
A gentle Majesty, whose myrtle and rain
Enforce the fathers' gravestones unto peace.

I saw the youngling bachelors of Harvard
Lit like torches, and scrambling to disperse
Like aimless firebrands pitiful to slake,
And if there's passion enough for half their flame,
Your wisdom has done this, sages of Harvard.

Conrad Aiken / 1889-

DISCORDANTS

I

Music I heard with you was more than music,
And bread I broke with you was more than bread;
Now that I am without you, all is desolate;
All that was once so beautiful is dead.

Your hands once touched this table and this silver,
And I have seen your fingers hold this glass.
These things do not remember you, belovèd,—
And yet your touch upon them will not pass.

For it was in my heart you moved among them,
And blessed them with your hands and with your eyes;
And in my heart they will remember always,—
They knew you once, O beautiful and wise.

SENLIN: A BIOGRAPHY

from II. HIS FUTILE PREOCCUPATIONS

2

It is morning, Senlin says, and in the morning
When the light drips through the shutters like the dew,
I arise, I face the sunrise,

And do the things my fathers learned to do.
Stars in the purple dusk above the rooftops
Pale in a saffron mist and seem to die,
And I myself on a swiftly tilting planet
Stand before a glass and tie my tie.

Vine leaves tap my window,
Dew-drops sing to the garden stones,
The robin chirps in the chinaberry tree
Repeating three clear tones.

It is morning. I stand by the mirror
And tie my tie once more.
While waves far off in a pale rose twilight
Crash on a coral shore.
I stand by a mirror and comb my hair:
How small and white my face!—
The green earth tilts through a sphere of air
And bathes in a flame of space.

There are houses hanging above the stars
And stars hung under a sea.
And a sun far off in a shell of silence
Dapples my walls for me.

It is morning, Senlin says, and in the morning
Should I not pause in the light to remember god?
Upright and firm I stand on a star unstable,
He is immense and lonely as a cloud.
I will dedicate this moment before my mirror
To him alone, for him I will comb my hair.
Accept these humble offerings, cloud of silence!
I will think of you as I descend the stair.

Vine leaves tap my window,
The snail-track shines on the stones,
Dew-drops flash from the chinaberry tree
Repeating two clear tones.

It is morning, I awake from a bed of silence,
Shining I rise from the starless waters of sleep.

The walls are about me still as in the evening,
I am the same, and the same name still I keep.
The earth revolves with me, yet makes no motion,
The stars pale silently in a coral sky.
In a whistling void I stand before my mirror,
Unconcerned, and tie my tie.

There are horses neighing on far-off hills
Tossing their long white manes,
And mountains flash in the rose-white dusk,
Their shoulders black with rains.
It is morning. I stand by the mirror
And surprise my soul once more;
The blue air rushes above my ceiling,
There are suns beneath my floor.

. . . It is morning, Senlin says, I ascend from darkness
And depart on the winds of space for I know not where,
My watch is wound, a key is in my pocket,
And the sky is darkened as I descend the stair.
There are shadows across the windows, clouds in heaven,
And a god among the stars; and I will go
Thinking of him as I might think of daybreak
And humming a tune I know.

Vine leaves tap at the window,
Dew-drops sing to the garden stones,
The robin chirps in the chinaberry tree
Repeating three clear tones.

TETÉLESTAI

I

How shall we praise the magnificence of the dead,
The great man humbled, the haughty brought to dust?
Is there a horn we should not blow as proudly
For the meanest of us all, who creeps his days,
Guarding his heart from blows, to die obscurely?
I am no king, have laid no kingdoms waste,

Taken no princes captive, led no triumphs
Of weeping women through long walls of trumpets;
Say rather, I am no one, or an atom;
Say rather, two great gods, in a vault of starlight,
Play ponderingly at chess, and at the game's end
One of the pieces, shaken, falls to the floor
And runs to the darkest corner; and that piece
Forgotten there, left motionless, is I . . .
Say that I have no name, no gifts, no power,
Am only one of millions, mostly silent;
One who came with eyes and hands and a heart,
Looked on beauty, and loved it, and then left it.
Say that the fates of time and space obscured me,
Led me a thousand ways to pain, bemused me,
Wrapped me in ugliness; and like great spiders
Dispatched me at their leisure . . . Well, what then?
Should I not hear, as I lie down in dust,
The horns of glory blowing above my burial?

II

Morning and evening opened and closed above me:
Houses were built above me; trees let fall
Yellowing leaves upon me, hands of ghosts;
Rain has showered its arrows of silver upon me
Seeking my heart; winds have roared and tossed me;
Music in long blue waves of sound has borne me
A helpless weed to shores of unthought silence;
Time, above me, within me, crashed its gongs
Of terrible warning, sifting the dust of death;
And here I lie. Blow now your horns of glory
Harshly over my flesh, you trees, you waters!
You stars and suns, Canopus, Deneb, Rigel,
Let me, as I lie down, here in this dust,
Hear, far off, your whispered salutation!
Roar now above my decaying flesh, you winds,
Whirl out your earth-scents over this body, tell me
Of ferns and stagnant pools, wild roses, hillsides!
Anoint me, rain, let crash your silver arrows
On this hard flesh! I am the one who named you,
I lived in you, and now I die in you.
I your son, your daughter, treader of music,
Lie broken, conquered . . . Let me not fall in silence.

III

I, the restless one; the circler of circles;
Herdsman and roper of stars, who could not capture
The secret of self; I who was tyrant to weaklings,
Striker of children; destroyer of women; corrupter
Of innocent dreamers, and laugher at beauty; I,
Too easily brought to tears and weakness by music,
Baffled and broken by love, the helpless beholder
Of the war in my heart of desire with desire, the struggle
Of hatred with love, terror with hunger; I
Who laughed without knowing the cause of my laughter, who grew
Without wishing to grow, a servant to my own body;
Loved without reason the laughter and flesh of a woman,
Enduring such torments to find her! I who at last
Grow weaker, struggle more feebly, relent in my purpose,
Choose for my triumph an easier end, look backward
At earlier conquests; or, caught in the web, cry out
In a sudden and empty despair, 'Tetélestai!'
Pity me, now! I, who was arrogant, beg you!
Tell me, as I lie down, that I was courageous.
Blow horns of victory now, as I reel and am vanquished.
Shatter the sky with trumpets above my grave.

IV

. . . Look! this flesh how it crumbles to dust and is blown!
These bones, how they grind in the granite of frost and are
    nothing!
This skull, how it yawns for a flicker of time in the darkness,
Yet laughs not and sees not! It is crushed by a hammer of
    sunlight,
And the hands are destroyed . . . Press down through the
    leaves of the jasmine,
Dig through the interlaced roots—nevermore will you find
    me;
I was no better than dust, yet you cannot replace me . . .
Take the soft dust in your hand—does it stir: does it sing?
Has it lips and a heart? Does it open its eyes to the sun?
Does it run, does it dream, does it burn with a secret, or
    tremble
In terror of death? Or ache with tremendous decisions? . . .

330 A *Little Treasury of Modern Poetry*

Listen! . . . It says: 'I lean by the river. The willows
Are yellowed with bud. White clouds roar up from the
    south
And darken the ripples; but they cannot darken my heart,
Nor the face like a star in my heart! . . . Rain falls on the
    water
And pelts it, and rings it with silver. The willow trees
    glisten,
The sparrows chirp under the eaves; but the face in my
    heart
Is a secret of music . . . I wait in the rain and am silent.'
Listen again! . . . It says 'I have worked, I am tired,
The pencil dulls in my hand: I see through the window
Walls upon walls of windows with faces behind them,
Smoke floating up to the sky, an ascension of sea-gulls.
I am tired. I have struggled in vain, my decision was
    fruitless,
Why then do I wait? with darkness, so easy, at hand! . . .
But tomorrow, perhaps . . . I will wait and endure till
    tomorrow!' . . .
Or again: 'It is dark. The decision is made. I am vanquished
By terror of life. The walls mount slowly about me
In coldness. I had not the courage. I was forsaken
I cried out, was answered by silence . . . Tetélestai! . . .'

v

Hear how it babbles!—Blow the dust out of your hand,
With its voices and visions, tread on it, forget it, turn
    homeward
With dreams in your brain . . . This, then, is the humble,
    the nameless,—
The lover, the husband and father, the struggler with
    shadows,
The one who went down under shoutings of chaos, the
    weakling
Who cried his 'forsaken!' like Christ on the darkening
    hilltop! . . .
This, then, is the one who implores, as he dwindles to
    silence,
A fanfare of glory . . . And which of us dares to deny him?

SEA HOLLY

Begotten by the meeting of rock with rock,
The mating of rock and rock, rocks gnashing together;
Created so, and yet forgetful, walks
The seaward path, puts up her left hand, shades
Blue eyes, the eyes of rock, to see better
In slanting light the ancient sheep (which kneels
Biting the grass) the while her other hand,
Hooking the wicker handle, turns the basket
Of eggs. The sea is high to-day. The eggs
Are cheaper. The sea is blown from the southwest,
Confused, taking up sand and mud in waves,
The waves break, sluggish, in brown foam, the wind
Disperses (on the sheep and hawthorn) spray,—
And on her cheeks, the cheeks engendered of rock,
And eyes, the colour of rock. The left hand
Falls from the eyes, and undecided slides
Over the left breast on which muslin lightly
Rests, touching the nipple, and then down
The hollow side, virgin as rock, and bitterly
Caresses the blue hip.

                    It was for this,
This obtuse taking of the seaward path,
This stupid hearing of larks, this hooking
Of wicker, this absent observation of sheep
Kneeling in harsh sea-grass, the cool hand shading
The spray-stung eyes—it was for this the rock
Smote itself. The sea is higher to-day,
And eggs are cheaper. The eyes of rock take in
The seaward path that winds toward the sea,
The thistle-prodder, old woman under a bonnet,
Forking the thistles, her back against the sea,
Pausing, with hard hands on the handle, peering
With rock eyes from her bonnet.

                    It was for this,
This rock-lipped facing of brown waves, half sand
And half water, this tentative hand that slides

Over the breast of rock, and into the hollow
Soft side of muslin rock, and then fiercely
Almost as rock against the hip of rock—
It was for this in midnight the rocks met,
And dithered together, cracking and smoking.

It was for this
Barren beauty, barrenness of rock that aches
On the seaward path, seeing the fruitful sea,
Hearing the lark of rock that sings, smelling
The rock-flower of hawthorn, sweetness of rock—
It was for this, stone pain in the stony heart,
The rock loved and laboured; and all is lost.

THE ROOM

Through that window—all else being extinct
Except itself and me—I saw the struggle
Of darkness against darkness. Within the room
It turned and turned, dived downward. Then I saw
How order might—if chaos wished—become:
And saw the darkness crush upon itself,
Contracting powerfully; it was as if
It killed itself: slowly: and with much pain.
Pain. The scene was pain, and nothing but pain.
What else, when chaos draws all forces inward
To shape a single leaf? . . .

For the leaf came,
Alone and shining in the empty room;
After a while the twig shot downward from it;
And from the twig a bough; and then the trunk,
Massive and coarse; and last the one black root.
The black root cracked the walls. Boughs burst the window:
The great tree took possession.

Tree of trees!
Remember (when time comes) how chaos died
To shape the shining leaf. Then turn, have courage,

Wrap arms and roots together, be convulsed
With grief, and bring back chaos out of shape.
I will be watching then as I watch now.
I will praise darkness now, but then the leaf.

PRELUDES FOR MEMNON

or

PRELUDES TO ATTITUDE

I

Winter for a moment takes the mind; the snow
Falls past the arclight; icicles guard a wall;
The wind moans through a crack in the window;
A keen sparkle of frost is on the sill.
Only for a moment; as spring too might engage it,
With a single crocus in the loam, or a pair of birds;
Or summer with hot grass; or autumn with a yellow leaf.
Winter is there, outside, is here in me:
Drapes the planets with snow, deepens the ice on the moon,
Darkens the darkness that was already darkness.
The mind too has its snows, its slippery paths,
Walls bayonetted with ice, leaves ice-encased.
Here is the in-drawn room, to which you return
When the wind blows from Arcturus: here is the fire
At which you warm your hands and glaze your eyes;
The piano, on which you touch the cold treble;
Five notes like breaking icicles; and then silence.

The alarm-clock ticks, the pulse keeps time with it,
Night and the mind are full of sounds. I walk
From the fire-place, with its imaginary fire,
To the window, with its imaginary view.
Darkness, and snow ticking the window: silence,
And the knocking of chains on a motor-car, the tolling
Of a bronze bell, dedicated to Christ.
And then the uprush of angelic wings, the beating
Of wings demonic, from the abyss of the mind:
The darkness filled with a feathery whistling, wings
Numberless as the flakes of angelic snow,

The deep void swarming with wings and sound of wings,
The winnowing of chaos, the aliveness
Of depth and depth and depth dedicated to death.

Here are the bickerings of the inconsequential,
The chatterings of the ridiculous, the iterations
Of the meaningless. Memory, like a juggler,
Tosses its colored balls into the light, and again
Receives them into darkness. Here is the absurd,
Grinning like an idiot, and the omnivorous quotidian,
Which will have its day. A handful of coins,
Tickets, items from the news, a soiled handkerchief,
A letter to be answered, notice of a telephone call,
The petal of a flower in a volume of Shakspere,
The program of a concert. The photograph, too,
Propped on the mantel, and beneath it a dry rosebud;
The laundry bill, matches, an ash-tray, Utamaro's
Pearl-fishers. And the rug, on which are still the crumbs
Of yesterday's feast. These are the void, the night,
And the angelic wings that make it sound.

What is the flower? It is not a sigh of color,
Suspiration of purple, sibilation of saffron,
Nor aureate exhalation from the tomb.
Yet it is these because you think of these,
An emanation of emanations, fragile
As light, or glisten, or gleam, or coruscation,
Creature of brightness, and as brightness brief.
What is the frost? It is not the sparkle of death,
The flash of time's wing, seeds of eternity;
Yet it is these because you think of these.
And you, because you think of these, are both
Frost and flower, the bright ambiguous syllable
Of which the meaning is both no and yes.

Here is the tragic, the distorting mirror
In which your gesture becomes grandiose;
Tears form and fall from your magnificent eyes,
The brow is noble, and the mouth is God's.
Here is the God who seeks his mother, Chaos,—
Confusion seeking solution, and life seeking death.

Here is the rose that woos the icicle; the icicle
That woos the rose. Here is the silence of silences
Which dreams of becoming a sound, and the sound
Which will perfect itself in silence. And all
These things are only the uprush from the void,
The wings angelic and demonic, the sound of the abyss
Dedicated to death. And this is you.

LII

Stood, at the closed door, and remembered—
Hand on the doorpost faltered, and remembered—
The long ago, the far away, the near
With its absurdities—the calendar,
The one-eyed calendar upon the wall,
And time dispersed, and in a thousand ways,
Calendars torn, appointments made and kept,
Or made and broken, and the shoes worn out
Going and coming, street and stair and street,
Lamplight and starlight, fog and northeast wind,
St. Mary's ringing the angelus at six—

And it was there, at eight o'clock, I saw
Vivien and the infinite, together,
And it was here I signed my name in pencil
Against the doorpost, and later saw the snow
Left by the messenger, and here were voices—
Come back later, do come back later, if you can,
And tell us what it was, tell us what you saw,
Put your heart on the table with your hand
And tell us all those secrets that are known
In the profound interstices of time—
The glee, the wickedness, the smirk, the sudden
Divine delight—do come back and tell us,
The clock has stopped, sunset is on the snow,
Midnight is far away, and morning farther—

And then the trains that cried at night, the ships
That mourned in fog, the days whose gift was rain,
June's daisy, and she loved me not, the skull
Brought from the tomb—and I was there, and saw
The bright spade break the bone, the trumpet-vine

Bugled with bees, and on my knees I picked
One small white clover in the cactus shade,
Put it in water and took it to that room
Where blinds were drawn and all was still—

                    Neighbors, I have come
From a vast everything whose sum is nothing,
From a complexity whose speech is simple,
Here are my hands and heart, and I have brought
Nothing you do not know, and do not fear.
Here is the evening paper at your door—
Here are your letters, I have brought the tickets,
The hour is early, and the speech is late.
Come, we are gods,—let us discourse as gods;
And weigh the grain of sand with Socrates;
Before we fall to kissing, and to bed.

LVI

Rimbaud and Verlaine, precious pair of poets,
Genius in both (but what is genius?) playing
Chess on a marble table at an inn
With chestnut blossom falling in blond beer
And on their hair and between knight and bishop—
Sunlight squared between them on the chess-board
Cirrus in heaven, and a squeal of music
Blown from the leathern door of Ste. Sulpice—

Discussing, between moves, iamb and spondee
Anacoluthon and the open vowel
God the great peacock with his angel peacocks
And his dependent peacocks the bright stars:
Disputing too of fate as Plato loved it,
Or Sophocles, who hated and admired,
Or Socrates, who loved and was amused:

Verlaine puts down his pawn upon a leaf
And closes his long eyes, which are dishonest,
And says 'Rimbaud, there is one thing to do:
We must take rhetoric, and wring its neck! . . .'
Rimbaud considers gravely, moves his Queen;
And then removes himself to Timbuctoo.

And Verlaine dead,—with all his jades and mauves;
And Rimbaud dead in Marseilles with a vision,
His leg cut off, as once before his heart;
And all reported by a later lackey,
Whose virtue is his tardiness in time.

Let us describe the evening as it is:—
The stars disposed in heaven as they are:
Verlaine and Shakspere rotting, where they rot,
Rimbaud remembered, and too soon forgot;

Order in all things, logic in the dark;
Arrangement in the atom and the spark;
Time in the heart and sequence in the brain—

Such as destroyed Rimbaud and fooled Verlaine.
And let us then take godhead by the neck—

And strangle it, and with it, rhetoric.

Edna St. Vincent Millay / 1892–1950

RECUERDO

We were very tired, we were very merry—
We had gone back and forth all night on the ferry.
It was bare and bright, and smelled like a stable—
But we looked into a fire, we leaned across a table,
We lay on a hill-top underneath the moon;
And the whistles kept blowing, and the dawn came soon.

We were very tired, we were very merry—
We had gone back and forth all night on the ferry.
And you ate an apple, and I ate a pear,

From a dozen of each we had bought somewhere;
And the sky went wan, and the wind came cold,
And the sun rose dripping, a bucketful of gold.

We were very tired, we were very merry,—
We had gone back and forth all night on the ferry.
We hailed, "Good morrow, mother!" to a shawl-covered
    head
And bought a morning paper, which neither of us read;
And she wept, "God bless you!" for the apples and pears,
And we gave her all our money but our subway fares.

ELEGY BEFORE DEATH

There will be rose and rhododendron
    When you are dead and under ground;
Still will be heard from white syringas
    Heavy with bees, a sunny sound;

Still will the tamaracks be raining
    After the rain has ceased, and still
Will there be robins in the stubble,
    Grey sheep upon the warm green hill.

Spring will not ail nor autumn falter;
    Nothing will know that you are gone,—
Saving alone some sullen plough-land
    None but yourself sets foot upon;

Saving the may-weed and the pig-weed
    Nothing will know that you are dead,—
These, and perhaps a useless wagon
    Standing beside some tumbled shed.

Oh, there will pass with your great passing
    Little of beauty not your own,—
Only the light from common water,
    Only the grace from simple stone!

ON HEARING A SYMPHONY OF BEETHOVEN

Sweet sounds, oh, beautiful music, do not cease!
Reject me not into the world again.
With you alone is excellence and peace,
Mankind made plausible, his purpose plain.
Enchanted in your air benign and shrewd,
With limbs a-sprawl and empty faces pale,
The spiteful and the stingy and the rude
Sleep like the scullions in the fairy-tale.
This moment is the best the world can give:
The tranquil blossom on the tortured stem.
Reject me not, sweet sounds! oh, let me live,
Till Doom espy my towers and scatter them.
A city spell-bound under the aging sun,
Music my rampart, and my only one.

OH, SLEEP FOREVER IN THE LATMIAN CAVE

Oh, sleep forever in the Latmian cave,
Mortal Endymion, darling of the Moon!
Her silver garments by the senseless wave
Shouldered and dropped and on the shingle strewn,
Her fluttering hand against her forehead pressed,
Her scattered looks that trouble all the sky,
Her rapid footsteps running down the west—
Of all her altered state, oblivious lie!
Whom earthen you, by deathless lips adored,
Wild-eyed and stammering to the grasses thrust,
And deep into her crystal body poured
The hot and sorrowful sweetness of the dust:
Whereof she wanders mad, being all unfit
For mortal love, that might not die of it.

Archibald MacLeish / 1892–

THE SILENT SLAIN

for Kenneth MacLeish, 1894–1918

We too, we too, descending once again
The hills of our own land, we too have heard
Far off—Ah, que ce cor a longue haleine—
The horn of Roland in the passages of Spain,
The first, the second blast, the failing third,
And with the third turned back and climbed once more
The steep road southward, and heard faint the sound
Of swords, of horses, the disastrous war,
And crossed the dark defile at last, and found
At Roncevaux upon the darkening plain
The dead against the dead and on the silent ground
The silent slain—

L'AN TRENTIESME DE MON EAGE

And I have come upon this place
By lost ways, by a nod, by words,
By faces, by an old man's face
At Morlaix lifted to the birds,

By hands upon the tablecloth
At Aldebori's, by the thin
Child's hands that opened to the moth
And let the flutter of the moonlight in,

By hands, by voices, by the voice
Of Mrs. Whitman on the stair,

By Margaret's "If we had the choice
To choose or not—" through her thick hair,

By voices, by the creak and fall
Of footsteps on the upper floor,
By silence waiting in the hall
Between the doorbell and the door,

By words, by voices, a lost way—
And here above the chimney stack
The unknown constellations sway—
And by what way shall I go back?

THE END OF THE WORLD

Quite unexpectedly as Vasserot
The armless ambidextrian was lighting
A match between his great and second toe
And Ralph the lion was engaged in biting
The neck of Madame Sossman while the drum
Pointed, and Teeny was about to cough
In waltz-time swinging Jocko by the thumb—
Quite unexpectedly the top blew off:

And there, there overhead, there, there, hung over
Those thousands of white faces, those dazed eyes,
There in the starless dark the poise, the hover,
There with vast wings across the canceled skies,
There in the sudden blackness the black pall
Of nothing, nothing, nothing—nothing at all.

ARS POETICA

A poem should be palpable and mute
As a globed fruit,

Dumb
As old medallions to the thumb,

Silent as the sleeve-worn stone
Of casement ledges where the moss has grown—

A poem should be wordless
As the flight of birds.

.   .   .

A poem should be motionless in time
As the moon climbs,

Leaving, as the moon releases
Twig by twig the night-entangled trees,

Leaving, as the moon behind the winter leaves,
Memory by memory the mind—

A poem should be motionless in time
As the moon climbs.

.   .   .

A poem should be equal to:
Not true.

For all the history of grief
An empty doorway and a maple leaf.

For love
The leaning grasses and two lights above the sea—

A poem should not mean
But be.

YOU,   ANDREW   MARVELL

And here face down beneath the sun
And here upon earth's noonward height

To feel the always coming on
The always rising of the night:

To feel creep up the curving east
The earthy chill of dusk and slow
Upon those under lands the vast
And ever climbing shadow grow

And strange at Ecbatan the trees
Take leaf by leaf the evening strange
The flooding dark about their knees
The mountains over Persia change

And now at Kermanshah the gate
Dark empty and the withered grass
And through the twilight now the late
Few travelers in the westward pass

And Baghdad darken and the bridge
Across the silent river gone
And through Arabia the edge
Of evening widen and steal on

And deepen on Palmyra's street
The wheel rut in the ruined stone
And Lebanon fade out and Crete
High through the clouds and overblown

And over Sicily the air
Still flashing with the landward gulls
And loom and slowly disappear
The sails above the shadowy hulls

And Spain go under and the shore
Of Africa the gilded sand
And evening vanish and no more
The low pale light across that land

Nor now the long light on the sea:

And here face downward in the sun
To feel how swift how secretly
The shadow of the night comes on . . .

INVOCATION TO THE SOCIAL MUSE

Señora, it is true the Greeks are dead.

It is true also that we here are Americans:
That we use the machines: that a sight of the god is
        unusual:
That more people have more thoughts: that there are

Progress and science and tractors and revolutions and
Marx and the wars more antiseptic and murderous
And music in every home: there is also Hoover.

Does the lady suggest we should write it out in The Word?
Does Madame recall our responsibilities? We are
Whores, Fräulein: poets, Fräulein, are persons of

Known vocation following troops: they must sleep with
Stragglers from either prince and of both views.
The rules permit them to further the business of neither.

It is also strictly forbidden to mix in maneuvers.
Those that infringe are inflated with praise on the plazas—
Their bones are resultantly afterwards found under
        newspapers.

Preferring life with the sons to death with the fathers,
We also doubt on the record whether the sons
Will still be shouting around with the same huzzas—

For we hope Lady to live to lie with the youngest.
There are only a handful of things a man likes,
Generation to generation, hungry or

Well fed: the earth's one: life's
One: Mister Morgan is not one.

There is nothing worse for our trade than to be in style.

He that goes naked goes further at last than another.
Wrap the bard in a flag or a school and they'll jimmy his
Door down and be thick in his bed—for a month:

(Who recalls the address now of the Imagists?)
But the naked man has always his own nakedness.
People remember forever his live limbs.

They may drive him out of the camps but one will take him.
They may stop his tongue on his teeth with a rope's
        argument—
He will lie in a house and be warm when they are shaking.

Besides, Tovarishch, how to embrace an army?
How to take to one's chamber a million souls?
How to conceive in the name of a column of marchers?

The things of the poet are done to a man alone
As the things of love are done—or of death when he hears
        the
Step withdraw on the stair and the clock tick only.

Neither his class nor his kind nor his trade may come
        near him
There where he lies on his left arm and will die,
Nor his class nor his kind nor his trade when the blood is
        jeering

And his knee's in the soft of the bed where his love lies.

I remind you, Barinya, the life of the poet is hard—
A hardy life with a boot as quick as a fiver:

Is it just to demand of us also to bear arms?

Wilfred Owen / 1893–1918

INSENSIBILITY

I

Happy are men who yet before they are killed
Can let their veins run cold

Whom no compassion fleers
Or makes their feet
Sore on the alleys cobbled with their brothers.
The front line withers,
But they are troops who fade, not flowers
For poets' tearful fooling:
Men, gaps for filling:
Losses, who might have fought
Longer; but no one bothers.

II

And some cease feeling
Even themselves or for themselves.
Dullness best solves
The tease and doubt of shelling,
And Chance's strange arithmetic
Comes simpler than the reckoning of their shilling.
They keep no check on armies' decimation.

III

Happy are these who lose imagination:
They have enough to carry with ammunition.
Their spirit drags no pack,
Their old wounds, save with cold, can not more ache.
Having seen all things red,
Their eyes are rid
Of the hurt of the colour of blood for ever.
And terror's first constriction over,
Their hearts remain small-drawn.
Their senses in some scorching cautery of battle
Now long since ironed,
Can laugh among the dying, unconcerned.

IV

Happy the soldier home, with not a notion
How somewhere, every dawn, some men attack,
And many sighs are drained.
Happy the lad whose mind was never trained:
His days are worth forgetting more than not.
He sings along the march
Which we march taciturn, because of dusk,

The long, forlorn, relentless trend
From larger day to huger night.

v

We wise, who with a thought besmirch
Blood over all our soul,
How should we see our task
But through his blunt and lashless eyes?
Alive, he is not vital overmuch;
Dying, not mortal overmuch;
Nor sad, nor proud,
Nor curious at all.
He cannot tell
Old men's placidity from his.

vi

But cursed are dullards whom no cannon stuns,
That they should be as stones;
Wretched are they, and mean
With paucity that never was simplicity.
By choice they made themselves immune
To pity and whatever mourns in man
Before the last sea and the hapless stars;
Whatever mourns when many leave these shores;
Whatever shares
The eternal reciprocity of tears.

APOLOGIA PRO POEMATE MEO

I, too, saw God through mud,—
    The mud that cracked on cheeks when wretches smiled.
    War brought more glory to their eyes than blood,
    And gave their laughs more glee than shakes a child.

Merry it was to laugh there—
    Where death becomes absurd and life absurder.
    For power was on us as we slashed bones bare
    Not to feel sickness or remorse of murder.

I, too, have dropped off fear—
    Behind the barrage, dead as my platoon,
    And sailed my spirit surging light and clear
    Past the entanglement where hopes lay strewn;

And witnessed exultation—
    Faces that used to curse me, scowl for scowl,
    Shine and lift up with passion of oblation,
    Seraphic for an hour; though they were foul.

I have made fellowships—
    Untold of happy lovers in old song.
    For love is not the binding of fair lips
    With the soft silk of eyes that look and long,

By Joy, whose ribbon slips,—
    But wound with war's hard wire whose stakes are strong;
    Bound with the bandage of the arm that drips;
    Knit in the webbing of the rifle-thong.

I have perceived much beauty
    In the hoarse oaths that kept our courage straight;
    Heard music in the silentness of duty;
    Found peace where shell-storms spouted reddest spate.

Nevertheless, except you share
    With them in hell the sorrowful dark of hell,
    Whose world is but the trembling of a flare,
    And heaven but as the highway for a shell,

You shall not hear their mirth:
    You shall not come to think them well content
    By any jest of mine. These men are worth
    Your tears. You are not worth their merriment.

November 1917.

GREATER LOVE

Red lips are not so red
    As the stained stones kissed by the English dead.

Kindness of wooed and wooer
Seems shame to their love pure.
O Love, your eyes lose lure
    When I behold eyes blinded in my stead!

Your slender attitude
    Trembles not exquisite like limbs knife-skewed,
Rolling and rolling there
Where God seems not to care;
Till the fierce love they bear
    Cramps them in death's extreme decrepitude.

Your voice sings not so soft,—
    Though even as wind murmuring through raftered loft,—
Your dear voice is not dear,
Gentle, and evening clear,
As theirs whom none now hear,
    Now earth has stopped their piteous mouths that
        coughed.

Heart, you were never hot
    Nor large, nor full like hearts made great with shot;
And though your hand be pale,
Paler are all which trail
Your cross through flame and hail:
    Weep, you may weep, for you may touch them not.

ARMS AND THE BOY

Let the boy try along this bayonet-blade
How cold steel is, and keen with hunger of blood;
Blue with all malice, like a madman's flash;
And thinly drawn with famishing for flesh.

Lend him to stroke these blind, blunt bullet-leads
Which long to nuzzle in the hearts of lads,
Or give him cartridges of fine zinc teeth,
Sharp with the sharpness of grief and death.

For his teeth seem for laughing round an apple.
There lurk no claws behind his fingers supple;
And God will grow no talons at his heels,
Nor antlers through the thickness of his curls.

ANTHEM FOR DOOMED YOUTH

What passing-bells for these who die as cattle?
    Only the monstrous anger of the guns.
    Only the stuttering rifles' rapid rattle
Can patter out their hasty orisons.
No mockeries now for them; no prayers nor bells,
    Nor any voice of mourning save the choirs,—
The shrill, demented choirs of wailing shells;
    And bugles calling for them from sad shires.

What candles may be held to speed them all?
    Not in the hands of boys, but in their eyes
Shall shine the holy glimmers of good-byes.
    The pallor of girls' brows shall be their pall;
Their flowers the tenderness of patient minds,
And each slow dusk a drawing-down of blinds.

THE SHOW

We have fallen in the dreams the ever-living
Breathe on the tarnished mirror of the world,
And then smooth out with ivory hands and sigh.
           W. B. YEATS

My soul looked down from a vague height, with Death,
As unremembering how I rose or why,
And saw a sad land, weak with sweats of dearth,
Gray, cratered like the moon with hollow woe,
And pitted with great pocks and scabs of plagues.

Across its beard, that horror of harsh wire,
There moved thin caterpillars, slowly uncoiled.
It seemed they pushed themselves to be as plugs
Of ditches, where they writhed and shrivelled, killed.

By them had slimy paths been trailed and scraped
Round myriad warts that might be little hills.

From gloom's last dregs these long-strung creatures crept,
And vanished out of dawn down hidden holes.

(And smell came up from those foul openings
As out of mouths, or deep wounds deepening.)

On dithering feet upgathered, more and more,
Brown strings, towards strings of gray, with bristling spines,
All migrants from green fields, intent on mire.

Those that were gray, of more abundant spawns,
Ramped on the rest and ate them and were eaten.

I saw their bitten backs curve, loop, and straighten,
I watched those agonies curl, lift, and flatten.
Whereat, in terror what that sight might mean,
I reeled and shivered earthward like a feather.

And Death fell with me, like a deepening moan.
And He, picking a manner of worm, which half had hid
Its bruises in the earth, but crawled no further,
Showed me its feet, the feet of many men,
And the fresh-severed head of it, my head.

DULCE ET DECORUM EST

Bent double, like old beggars under sacks,
Knock-kneed, coughing like hags, we cursed through
    sludge,
Till on the haunting flares we turned our backs

And towards our distant rest began to trudge.
Men marched asleep. Many had lost their boots
But limped on, blood-shod. All went lame; all blind;
Drunk with fatigue; deaf even to the hoots
Of tired, outstripped Five-Nines that dropped behind.

Gas! Gas! Quick, boys!—An ecstasy of fumbling,
Fitting the clumsy helmets just in time;
But someone still was yelling out and stumbling
And flound'ring like a man in fire or lime . . .
Dim, through the misty panes and thick green light,
As under a green sea, I saw him drowning.

In all my dreams, before my helpless sight,
He plunges at me, guttering, choking, drowning.

If in some smothering dreams you too could pace
Behind the wagon that we flung him in,
And watch the white eyes writhing in his face,
His hanging face, like a devil's sick of sin;
If you could hear, at every jolt, the blood
Come gargling from the froth-corrupted lungs,
Obscene as cancer, bitter as the cud
Of vile, incurable sores on innocent tongues,—
My friend, you would not tell with such high zest
To children ardent for some desperate glory,
The old Lie: Dulce et decorum est
Pro patria mori.

A TERRE

Being the Philosophy of Many Soldiers

Sit on the bed. I'm blind, and three parts shell.
Be careful; can't shake hands now; never shall.
Both arms have mutinied against me,—brutes.
My fingers fidget like ten idle brats.

I tried to peg out soldierly,—no use!
One dies of war like any old disease.

This bandage feels like pennies on my eyes.
I have my medals?—Discs to make eyes close.
My glorious ribbons?—Ripped from my own back
In scarlet shreds. (That's for your poetry book.)

A short life and a merry one, my buck!
We used to say we'd hate to live dead-old,—
Yet now . . . I'd willingly be puffy, bald,
And patriotic. Buffers catch from boys
At least the jokes hurled at them. I suppose
Little I'd ever teach a son, but hitting,
Shooting, war, hunting, all the arts of hurting.
Well, that's what I learnt,—that, and making money.

Your fifty years ahead seem none too many?
Tell me how long I've got? God! For one year
To help myself to nothing more than air!
One Spring! Is one too good to spare, too long?
Spring wind would work its own way to my lung,
And grow me legs as quick as lilac-shoots.

My servant's lamed, but listen how he shouts!
When I'm lugged out, he'll still be good for that.
Here in this mummy-case, you know, I've thought
How well I might have swept his floors for ever.
I'd ask no nights off when the bustle's over,
Enjoying so the dirt. Who's prejudiced
Against a grimed hand when his own's quite dust,
Less live than specks that in the sun-shafts turn,
Less warm than dust that mixes with arms' tan?
I'd love to be a sweep, now, black as Town,
Yes, or a muckman. Must I be his load?

O Life, Life, let me breathe,—a dug-out rat!
Not worse than ours the existences rats lead—
Nosing along at night down some safe rut,
They find a shell-proof home before they rot.
Dead men may envy living mites in cheese,
Or good germs even. Microbes have their joys,
And subdivide, and never come to death.
Certainly flowers have the easiest time on earth.
"I shall be one with nature, herb, and stone",

Shelley would tell me. Shelley would be stunned:
The dullest Tommy hugs that fancy now.
"Pushing up daisies" is their creed, you know.
To grain, then, go my fat, to buds my sap,
For all the usefulness there is in soap.
D'you think the Boche will ever stew man-soup?
Some day, no doubt, if . . .

                Friend, be very sure
I shall be better off with plants that share
More peaceably the meadow and the shower.
Soft rains will touch me,—as they could touch once,
And nothing but the sun shall make me ware.
Your guns may crash around me. I'll not hear;
Or, if I wince, I shall not know I wince.
Don't take my soul's poor comfort for your jest.
Soldiers may grow a soul when turned to fronds,
But here the thing's best left at home with friends.

My soul's a little grief, grappling your chest,
To climb your throat on sobs; easily chased
On other sighs and wiped by fresher winds.

Carry my crying spirit till it's weaned
To do without what blood remained these wounds.

DISABLED

He sat in a wheeled chair, waiting for dark,
And shivered in his ghastly suit of grey,
Legless, sewn short at elbow. Through the park
Voices of boys rang saddening like a hymn,
Voices of play and pleasure after day,
Till gathering sleep had mothered them from him.

  . . .

About this time Town used to swing so gay
When glow-lamps budded in the light blue trees,
And girls glanced lovelier as the air grew dim,—

In the old times, before he threw away his knees.
Now he will never feel again how slim
Girls' waists are, or how warm their subtle hands;
All of them touch him like some queer disease.

.   .   .

There was an artist silly for his face,
For it was younger than his youth, last year.
Now, he is old; his back will never brace;
He's lost his colour very far from here,
Poured it down shell-holes till the veins ran dry,
And half his lifetime lapsed in the hot race,
And leap of purple spurted from his thigh.

.   .   .

One time he liked a blood-smear down his leg,
After the matches, carried shoulder-high.
It was after football, when he'd drunk a peg,
He thought he'd better join.—He wonders why.
Someone had said he'd look a god in kilts,
That's why; and may be, too, to please his Meg;
Aye, that was it, to please the giddy jilts
He asked to join. He didn't have to beg;
Smiling they wrote his lie; aged nineteen years.
Germans he scarcely thought of; all their guilt,
And Austria's, did not move him. And no fears
Of Fear came yet. He thought of jewelled hilts
For daggers in plaid socks; of smart salutes;
And care of arms; and leave; and pay arrears;
Esprit de corps; and hints for young recruits.
And soon, he was drafted out with drums and cheers.

.   .   .

Some cheered him home, but not as crowds cheer Goal.
Only a solemn man who brought him fruits
Thanked him; and then inquired about his soul.

.   .   .

Now, he will spend a few sick years in Institutes,
And do what things the rules consider wise,
And take whatever pity they may dole.
To-night he noticed how the women's eyes

Passed from him to the strong men that were whole.
How cold and late it is! Why don't they come
And put him into bed? Why don't they come?

FROM MY DIARY, JULY 1914

Leaves
    Murmuring by myriads in the shimmering trees.
Lives
    Wakening with wonder in the Pyrenees.
Birds
    Cheerily chirping in the early day.
Bards
    Singing of summer, scything thro' the hay.
Bees
    Shaking the heavy dews from bloom and frond.
Boys
    Bursting the surface of the ebony pond.
Flashes
    Of swimmers carving thro' the sparkling cold.
Fleshes
    Gleaming with wetness to the morning gold.
A mead
    Bordered about with warbling water brooks.
A maid
    Laughing the love-laugh with me; proud of looks.
The heat
    Throbbing between the upland and the peak.
Her heart
    Quivering with passion to my pressèd cheek.
Braiding
    Of floating flames across the mountain brow.
Brooding
    Of stillness; and a sighing of the bough.
Stirs
    Of leaflets in the gloom; soft petal-showers;
Stars
    Expanding with the starr'd nocturnal flowers.

E. E. Cummings / 1894–1962

ALL IN GREEN WENT
MY LOVE RIDING

All in green went my love riding
on a great horse of gold
into the silver dawn.

four lean hounds crouched low and smiling
the merry deer ran before.

Fleeter be they than dappled dreams
the swift sweet deer
the red rare deer.

Four red roebuck at a white water
the cruel bugle sang before.

Horn at hip went my love riding
riding the echo down
into the silver dawn.

four lean hounds crouched low and smiling
the level meadows ran before.

Softer be they than slippered sleep
the lean lithe deer
the fleet flown deer.

Four fleet does at a gold valley
the famished arrow sang before.

Bow at belt went my love riding
riding the mountain down
into the silver dawn.

four lean hounds crouched low and smiling
the sheer peaks ran before.

Paler be they than daunting death
the sleek slim deer
the tall tense deer.

Four tall stags at a green mountain
the lucky hunter sang before.

All in green went my love riding
on a great horse of gold
into the silver dawn.

four lean hounds crouched low and smiling
my heart fell dead before.

M Y   L O V E

my love
thy hair is one kingdom
    the king whereof is darkness
thy forehead is a flight of flowers

thy head is a quick forest
    filled with sleeping birds
thy breasts are swarms of white bees
    upon the bough of thy body
thy body to me is April
in whose armpits is the approach of spring

thy thighs are white horses yoked to a chariot
    of kings
they are the striking of a good minstrel
between them is always a pleasant song

my love
thy head is a casket

of the cool jewel of thy mind
the hair of thy head is one warrior
   innocent of defeat
thy hair upon thy shoulders is an army
   with victory and with trumpets

thy legs are the trees of dreaming
whose fruit is the very eatage of forgetfulness

thy lips are satraps in scarlet
   in whose kiss is the combining of kings
thy wrists
are holy
   which are the keepers of the keys of thy blood
thy feet upon thy ankles are flowers in vases
   of silver

in thy beauty is the dilemma of flutes

   thy eyes are the betrayal
of bells comprehended through incense

NOBODY LOSES ALL THE TIME

nobody loses all the time

i had an uncle named
Sol who was a born failure and
nearly everybody said he should have gone
into vaudeville perhaps because my Uncle Sol could
sing McCann He Was A Diver on Xmas Eve like Hell Itself
   which
may or may not account for the fact that my Uncle

Sol indulged in that possibly most inexcusable
of all to use a highfalootin phrase
luxuries that is or to
wit farming and be

it needlessly
added

my Uncle Sol's farm
failed because the chickens
ate the vegetables so
my Uncle Sol had a
chicken farm till the
skunks ate the chickens when

my Uncle Sol
had a skunk farm but
the skunks caught cold and
died and so
my Uncle Sol imitated the
skunks in a subtle manner

or by drowning himself in the watertank
but somebody who'd given my Uncle Sol a Victor
Victrola and records while he lived presented to
him upon the auspicious occasion of his decease a
scrumptious not to mention splendiferous funeral with
tall boys in black gloves and flowers and everything and

i remember we all cried like the Missouri
when my Uncle Sol's coffin lurched because
somebody pressed a button
(and down went
my Uncle
Sol

and started a worm farm)

A MAN WHO HAD FALLEN
AMONG THIEVES

a man who had fallen among thieves
lay by the roadside on his back

dressed in fifteenthrate ideas
wearing a round jeer for a hat

fate per a somewhat more than less
emancipated evening
had in return for consciousness
endowed him with a changeless grin

whereon a dozen staunch and leal
citizens did graze at pause
then fired by hypercivic zeal
sought newer pastures or because

swaddled with a frozen brook
of pinkest vomit out of eyes
which noticed nobody he looked
as if he did not care to rise

one hand did nothing on the vest
its wideflung friend clenched weakly dirt
while the mute trouserfly confessed
a button solemnly inert.

Brushing from whom the stiffened puke
i put him all into my arms
and staggered banged with terror through
a million billion trillion stars

NEXT TO OF COURSE GOD
AMERICA I

"next to of course god america i
love you land of the pilgrims' and so forth oh
say can you see by the dawn's early my
country 'tis of centuries come and go
and are no more what of it we should worry
in every language even deafanddumb
thy sons acclaim your glorious name by gorry

by jingo by gee by gosh by gum
why talk of beauty what could be more beautiful than these heroic happy dead
who rushed like lions to the roaring slaughter
they did not stop to think they died instead
then shall the voices of liberty be mute?"

He spoke. And drank rapidly a glass of water

I SING OF OLAF GLAD AND BIG

i sing of Olaf glad and big
whose warmest heart recoiled at war:
a conscientious object-or

his wellbelovéd colonel(trig
westpointer most succinctly bred)
took erring Olaf soon in hand;
but—though an host of overjoyed
noncoms(first knocking on the head
him)do through icy waters roll
that helplessness which others stroke
with brushes recently employed
anent this muddy toiletbowl,
while kindred intellects evoke
allegiance per blunt instruments—
Olaf(being to all intents
a corpse and wanting any rag
upon what God unto him gave)
responds, without getting annoyed
"I will not kiss your f.ing flag"

straightway the silver bird looked grave
(departing hurriedly to shave)

but—though all kinds of officers
(a yearning nation's blueeyed pride)
their passive prey did kick and curse
until for wear their clarion

voices and boots were much the worse,
and egged the firstclassprivates on
his rectum wickedly to tease
by means of skilfully applied
bayonets roasted hot with heat—
Olaf(upon what were once knees)
does almost ceaselessly repeat
"there is some s. I will not eat"

our president,being of which
assertions duly notified
threw the yellowsonofabitch
into a dungeon,where he died

Christ(of His mercy infinite)
i pray to see;and Olaf, too

preponderatingly because
unless statistics lie he was
more brave than me:more blond than you.

SOMEWHERE I HAVE NEVER
TRAVELLED, GLADLY BEYOND

somewhere i have never travelled,gladly beyond
any experience,your eyes have their silence:
in your most frail gesture are things which enclose me,
or which i cannot touch because they are too near

your slightest look easily will unclose me
though i have closed myself as fingers,
you open always petal by petal myself as Spring opens
(touching skilfully,mysteriously)her first rose

or if your wish be to close me,i and
my life will shut very beautifully,suddenly,
as when the heart of this flower imagines
the snow carefully everywhere descending;

nothing which we are to perceive in this world equals
the power of your intense fragility:whose texture
compels me with the colour of its countries,
rendering death and forever with each breathing

(i do not know what it is about you that closes
and opens;only something in me understands
the voice of your eyes is deeper than all roses)
nobody,not even the rain,has such small hands

AS FREEDOM IS A BREAKFASTFOOD

as freedom is a breakfastfood
or truth can live with right and wrong
or molehills are from mountains made
—long enough and just so long
will being pay the rent of seem
and genius please the talentgang
and water most encourage flame

as hatracks into peachtrees grow
or hopes dance best on bald men's hair
and every finger is a toe
and any courage is a fear
—long enough and just so long
will the impure think all things pure
and hornets wail by children stung

or as the seeing are the blind
and robins never welcome spring
nor flatfolk prove their world is round
nor dingsters die at break of dong
and common's rare and millstones float
—long enough and just so long
tomorrow will not be too late

worms are the words but joy's the voice
down shall go which and up come who

breasts will be breasts thighs will be thighs
deeds cannot dream what dreams can do
—time is a tree(this life one leaf)
but love is the sky and i am for you
just so long and long enough

ANYONE LIVED IN A PRETTY
HOW TOWN

anyone lived in a pretty how town
(with up so floating many bells down)
spring summer autumn winter
he sang his didn't he danced his did.

Women and men(both little and small)
cared for anyone not at all
they sowed their isn't they reaped their same
sun moon stars rain

children guessed(but only a few
and down they forgot as up they grew
autumn winter spring summer)
that noone loved him more by more

when by now and tree by leaf
she laughed his joy she cried his grief
bird by snow and stir by still
anyone's any was all to her

someones married their everyones
laughed their cryings and did their dance
(sleep wake hope and then)they
said their nevers they slept their dream

stars rain sun moon
(and only the snow can begin to explain
how children are apt to forget to remember
with up so floating many bells down)

one day anyone died i guess
(and noone stooped to kiss his face)
busy folk buried them side by side
little by little and was by was

all by all and deep by deep
and more by more they dream their sleep
noone and anyone earth by april
wish by spirit and if by yes.

Women and men(both dong and ding)
summer autumn winter spring
reaped their sowing and went their came
sun moon stars rain

IT WAS A GOODLY CO

it was a goodly co
which paid to make man free
(for man is enslaved by a dread dizziz
and the sooner it's over the sooner to biz
don't ask me what it's pliz)

then up rose bishop budge from kew
a anglican was who
(with a rag and a bone and a hank of hair)'d
he picked up a thousand pounds or two
and he smote the monster merde

then up rose pride and up rose pelf
and ghibelline and guelph
and ladios and laddios
(on radios and raddios)
did save man from himself

ye duskiest despot's goldenest gal
did wring that dragon's tail
(for men must loaf and women must lay)

and she gave him a desdemonial
that took his breath away

all history oped her teeming womb
said demon for to doom
yea(fresh complexions being oke
with him)one william shakespeare broke
the silence of the tomb

then up rose mr lipshits pres
(who always nothing says)
and he kisséd the general menedjerr
and they smokéd a robert burns cigerr
to the god of things like they err

PITY THIS BUSY MONSTER,
MANUNKIND

pity this busy monster,manunkind,

not.   Progress is a comfortable disease:
your victim(death and life safely beyond)

plays with the bigness of his littleness
—electrons deify one razorblade
into a mountainrange;lenses extend

unwish through curving wherewhen till unwish
returns on its unself.
                        A world of made
is not a world of born—pity poor flesh

and trees,poor stars and stones,but never this
fine specimen of hypermagical

ultraomnipotence.   We doctors know

a hopeless case if—listen:there's a hell
of a good universe next door;let's go

WHAT IF A MUCH OF A WHICH
OF A WIND

what if a much of a which of a wind
gives the truth to summer's lie;
bloodies with dizzying leaves the sun
and yanks immortal stars awry?
Blow king to beggar and queen to seem
(blow friend to fiend:blow space to time)
—when skies are hanged and oceans drowned,
the single secret will still be man

what if a keen of a lean wind flays
screaming hills with sleet and snow:
strangles valleys by ropes of thing
and stifles forests in white ago?
Blow hope to terror;blow seeing to blind
(blow pity to envy and soul to mind)
—whose hearts are mountains,roots are trees,
it's they shall cry hello to the spring

what if a dawn of a doom of a dream
bites this universe in two,
peels forever out of his grave
and sprinkles nowhere with me and you?
Blow soon to never and never to twice
(blow life to isn't:blow death to was)
—all nothing's only our hugest home;
the most who die,the more we live

Robert Graves / 1895–

THE BARDS

The bards falter in shame, their running verse
Stumbles, with marrow-bones the drunken diners

Pelt them for their delay.
It is a something fearful in the song
Plagues them—an unknown grief that like a churl
Goes commonplace in cowskin
And bursts unheralded, crowing and coughing,
An unpilled holly-club twirled in his hand,
Into their many-shielded, samite-curtained,
Jewel-bright hall where twelve kings sit at chess
Over the white-bronze pieces and the gold;
And by a gross enchantment
Flails down the rafters and leads off the queens—
The wild-swan-breasted, the rose-ruddy-cheeked
Raven-haired daughters of their admiration—
To stir his black pots and to bed on straw.

TRAVELLER'S CURSE AFTER MISDIRECTION

from the Welsh

May they stumble, stage by stage
On an endless pilgrimage,
Dawn and dusk, mile after mile,
At each and every step, a stile;
At each and every step withal
May they catch their feet and fall;
At each and every fall they take
May a bone within them break;
And may the bone that breaks within
Not be, for variation's sake,
Now rib, now thigh, now arm, now shin,
But always, without fail, THE NECK.

THE LEGS

There was this road,
And it led up-hill,

And it led down-hill,
And round and in and out.

And the traffic was legs,
Legs from the knees down,
Coming and going,
Never pausing.

And the gutters gurgled
With the rain's overflow,
And the sticks on the pavement
Blindly tapped and tapped.

What drew the legs along
Was the never-stopping,
And the senseless, frightening
Fate of being legs.

Legs for the road,
The road for legs,
Resolutely nowhere
In both directions.

My legs at least
Were not in that rout:
On grass by the roadside
Entire I stood,

Watching the unstoppable
Legs go by
With never a stumble
Between step and step.

Though my smile was broad
The legs could not see,
Though my laugh was loud
The legs could not hear.

My head dizzied, then:
I wondered suddenly,
Might I too be a walker
From the knees down?

Gently I touched my shins.
The doubt unchained them:
They had run in twenty puddles
Before I regained them.

FLYING CROOKED

The butterfly, a cabbage-white,
(His honest idiocy of flight)
Will never now, it is too late,
Master the art of flying straight,
Yet has—who knows so well as I?—
A just sense of how not to fly:
He lurches here and here by guess
And God and hope and hopelessness.
Even the aerobatic swift
Has not his flying-crooked gift.

THE DEVIL'S ADVICE TO STORY-TELLERS

Lest men suspect your tale to be untrue,
Keep probability—some say—in view.
But my advice to story-tellers is:
Weigh out no gross of probabilities,
Nor yet make diligent transcriptions of
Known instances of virtue, crime or love.
To forge a picture that will pass for true,
Do conscientiously what liars do—
Born liars, not the lesser sort that raid
The mouths of others for their stock-in-trade:
Assemble, first, all casual bits and scraps
That may shake down into a world perhaps;
People this world, by chance created so,
With random persons whom you do not know—

The teashop sort, or travellers in a train
Seen once, guessed idly at, not seen again;
Let the erratic course they steer surprise
Their own and your own and your readers' eyes;
Sigh then, or frown, but leave (as in dispair)
Motive and end and moral in the air;
Nice contradiction between fact and fact
Will make the whole read human and exact.

INTERRUPTION

If ever against this easy blue and silver
Hazed-over countryside of thoughtfulness,
Far behind in the mind and above,
Boots from before and below approach tramping,
Watch how their premonition will display
A forward countryside, low in the distance—
A picture-postcard square of June grass;
Will warm a summer season, trim the hedges,
Cast the river about on either flank,
Start the late cuckoo emptily calling,
Invent a rambling tale of moles and voles,
Furnish a path with stiles.
Watch how the field will broaden, the feet nearing,
Sprout with great dandelions and buttercups,
Widen and heighten. The blue and silver
Fogs at the border of this all-grass.
Interruption looms gigantified,
Lurches against, treads thundering through,
Blots the landscape, scatters all,
Roars and rumbles like a dark tunnel,
Is gone.

The picture-postcard grass and trees
Swim back to central: it is a large patch,
It is a modest, failing patch of green,
The postage-stamp of its departure,
Clouded with blue and silver, closing in now

To a plain countryside of less and less,
Unpeopled and unfeatured blue and silver,
Before, behind, above.

RECALLING WAR

Entrance and exit wounds are silvered clean,
The track aches only when the rain reminds.
The one-legged man forgets his leg of wood,
The one-armed man his jointed wooden arm.
The blinded man sees with his ears and hands
As much or more than once with both his eyes.
Their war was fought these twenty years ago
And now assumes the nature-look of time,
As when the morning traveller turns and views
His wild night-stumbling carved into a hill.

What, then, was war? No mere discord of flags
But an infection of the common sky
That sagged ominously upon the earth
Even when the season was the airiest May.
Down pressed the sky, and we, oppressed, thrust out
Boastful tongue, clenched fist and valiant yard.
Natural infirmities were out of mode,
For Death was young again: patron alone
Of healthy dying, premature fate-spasm.

Fear made fine bed-fellows. Sick with delight
At life's discovered transitoriness,
Our youth became all-flesh and waived the mind.
Never was such antiqueness of romance,
Such tasty honey oozing from the heart.
And old importances came swimming back—
Wine, meat, log-fires, a roof over the head,
A weapon at the thigh, surgeons at call.
Even there was a use again for God—
A word of rage in lack of meat, wine, fire,
In ache of wounds beyond all surgeoning.

War was return of earth to ugly earth,
War was foundering of sublimities,
Extinction of each happy art and faith
By which the world had still kept head in air,
Protesting logic or protesting love,
Until the unendurable moment struck—
The inward scream, the duty to run mad.

And we recall the merry ways of guns—
Nibbling the walls of factory and church
Like a child, piecrust; felling groves of trees
Like a child, dandelions with a switch.
Machine-guns rattle toy-like from a hill,
Down in a row the brave tin-soldiers fall:
A sight to be recalled in elder days
When learnedly the future we devote
To yet more boastful visions of despair.

DOWN, WANTON, DOWN!

Down, wanton, down! Have you no shame
That at the whisper of Love's name,
Or Beauty's, presto! up you raise
Your angry head and stand at gaze?

Poor bombard-captain, sworn to reach
The ravelin and effect a breach—
Indifferent what you storm or why,
So be that in the breach you die!

Love may be blind, but Love at least
Knows what is man and what mere beast;
Or Beauty wayward, but requires
More delicacy from her squires.

Tell me, my witless, whose one boast
Could be your staunchness at the post,

When were you made a man of parts
To think fine and profess the arts?

Will many-gifted Beauty come
Bowing to your bald rule of thumb,
Or Love swear loyalty to your crown?
Be gone, have done! Down, wanton, down!

TIME

The vague sea thuds against the marble cliffs
And from their fragments age-long grinds
Pebbles like flowers.

Or the vague weather wanders in the fields,
And up spring flowers with coloured buds
Like marble pebbles.

The beauty of the flowers is Time, death-grieved;
The pebbles' beauty too is Time,
Life-wearied.

It is easy to admire a blowing flower
Or a smooth pebble flower-like freaked
By Time and vagueness.

Time is Time's lapse, the emulsive element coaxing
All obstinate locks and rusty hinges
To loving-kindness.

And am I proof against that lovesome pair,
Old age and childhood, twins in Time,
In sorrowful vagueness?

And will I not pretend the accustomed thanks:
Humouring age with filial flowers,
Childhood with pebbles?

OGRES AND PYGMIES

Those famous men of old, the Ogres—
They had long beards and stinking arm-pits,
They were wide-mouthed, long-yarded and great-bellied
Yet not of taller stature, Sirs, than you.
They lived on Ogre-Strand, which was no place
But the churl's terror of their vast extent,
Where every foot was three-and-thirty inches
And every penny bought a whole hog.
Now of their company none survive, not one,
The times being, thank God, unfavourable
To all but nightmare shadows of their fame;
Their images stand howling on the hill
(The winds enforced against those wide mouths),
Whose granite haunches country-folk salute
With May Day kisses, and whose knobbed knees.

So many feats they did to admiration:
With their enormous throats they sang louder
Than ten cathedral choirs, with their grand yards
Stormed the most rare and obstinate maidenheads,
With their strong-gutted and capacious bellies
Digested stones and glass like ostriches.
They dug great pits and heaped huge mounds,
Deflected rivers, wrestled with the bear
And hammered judgements for posterity—
For the sweet-cupid-lipped and tassel-yarded
Delicate-stomached dwellers
In Pygmy Alley, where with brooding on them
A foot is shrunk to seven inches
And twelve-pence will not buy a spare rib.
And who would judge between Ogres and Pygmies—
The thundering text, the snivelling commentary—
Reading between such covers he will marvel
How his own members bloat and shrink again.

THE THIEVES

Lovers in the act dispense
With such meum-tuum sense
As might warningly reveal
What they must not pick or steal,
And their nostrum is to say:
'I and you are both away.'

After, when they disentwine
You from me and yours from mine,
Neither can be certain who
Was that I whose mine was you.
To the act again they go
More completely not to know.

Theft is theft and raid is raid
Though reciprocally made.
Lovers, the conclusion is
Doubled sighs and jealousies
In a single heart that grieves
For lost honour among thieves.

TO JUAN AT THE WINTER SOLSTICE

There is one story and one story only
That will prove worth your telling,
Whether as learned bard or gifted child;
To it all lines or lesser gauds belong
That startle with their shining
Such common stories as they stray into.

Is it of trees you tell, their months and virtues,
Or strange beasts that beset you,

Of birds that croak at you the Triple will?
Or of the Zodiac and how slow it turns
Below the Boreal Crown,
Prison of all true kings that ever reigned?

Water to water, ark again to ark,
From woman back to woman:
So each new victim treads unfalteringly
The never altered circuit of his fate,
Bringing twelve peers as witness
Both to his starry rise and starry fall.

Or is it of the Virgin's silver beauty,
All fish below the thighs?
She in her left hand bears a leafy quince;
When with her right she crooks a finger, smiling,
How may the King hold back?
Royally then he barters life for love.

Or of the undying snake from chaos hatched,
Whose coils contain the ocean,
Into whose chops with naked sword he springs,
Then in black water, tangled by the reeds,
Battles three days and nights,
To be spewed up beside her scalloped shore?

Much snow is falling, winds roar hollowly,
The owl hoots from the elder,
Fear in your heart cries to the loving-cup:
Sorrow to sorrow as the sparks fly upward.
The log groans and confesses:
There is one story and one story only.

Dwell on her graciousness, dwell on her smiling,
Do not forget what flowers
The great boar trampled down in ivy time.
Her brow was creamy as the crested wave,
Her sea-blue eyes were wild
But nothing promised that is not performed.

THE PERSIAN VERSION

Truth-loving Persians do not dwell upon
The trivial skirmish fought near Marathon.
As for the Greek theatrical tradition
Which represents that summer's expedition
Not as a mere reconnaissance in force
By three brigades of foot and one of horse
(Their left flank covered by some obsolete
Light craft detached from the main Persian fleet)
But as a grandiose, ill-starred attempt
To conquer Greece—they treat it with contempt;
And only incidentally refute
Major Greek claims, by stressing what repute
The Persian monarch and the Persian nation
Won by this salutary demonstration:
Despite a strong defence and adverse weather
All arms combined magnificently together.

Louise Bogan / 1897–

MEN LOVED WHOLLY
BEYOND WISDOM

Men loved wholly beyond wisdom
Have the staff without the banner.
Like a fire in a dry thicket
Rising within women's eyes
Is the love men must return.
Heart, so subtle now, and trembling,
What a marvel to be wise,
To love never in this manner!

To be quiet in the fern
Like a thing gone dead and still,
Listening to the prisoned cricket
Shake its terrible, dissembling
Music in the granite hill.

THE SLEEPING FURY

You are here now,
Who were so loud and feared, in a symbol before me,
Alone and asleep, and I at last look long upon you.

Your hair fallen on your cheek, no longer in the semblance
  of serpents,
Lifted in the gale; your mouth, that shrieked so, silent.
You, my scourge, my sister, lie asleep, like a child,
Who, after rage, for an hour quiet, sleeps out its tears.

The days close to winter
Rough with strong sound. We hear the sea and the forest,
And the flames of your torches fly, lit by others,
Ripped by the wind, in the night. The black sheep for
  sacrifice
Huddle together. The milk is cold in the jars.

All to no purpose, as before, the knife whetted and plunged,
The shout raised, to match the clamor you have given them.
You alone turn away, not appeased; unaltered, avenger.

Hands full of scourges, wreathed with your flames and
  adders,
You alone turned away, but did not move from my side,
Under the broken light, when the soft nights took the
  torches.

At thin morning you showed, thick and wrong in that calm,
The ignoble dream and the mask, sly, with slits at the eyes,
Pretence and half-sorrow, beneath which a coward's hope
  trembled.

You uncovered at night, in the locked stillness of houses,
False love due the child's heart, the kissed-out lie, the
    embraces,
Made by the two who for peace tenderly turned to each
    other.

You who know what we love, but drive us to know it;
You with your whips and shrieks, bearer of truth and of
    solitude;
You who give, unlike men, to expiation your mercy.

Dropping the scourge when at last the scourged advances
    to meet it,
You, when the hunted turns, no longer remain the hunter
But stand silent and wait, at last returning his gaze.

Beautiful now as a child whose hair, wet with rage and tears
Clings to its face. And now I may look upon you,
Having once met your eyes. You lie in sleep and forget me.
Alone and strong in my peace, I look upon you in yours.

PUTTING TO SEA

Who, in the dark, has cast the harbor-chain?
This is no journey to a land we know.
The autumn night receives us, hoarse with rain;
Storm flakes with roaring foam the way we go.

Sodden with summer, stupid with its loves,
The country which we leave, and now this bare
Circle of ocean which the heaven proves
Deep as its height, and barren with despair.

Now this whole silence, through which nothing breaks,
Now this whole sea, which we possess alone,
Flung out from shore with speed a missile takes
When some hard hand, in hatred, flings a stone.

The Way should mark our course within the night,
The streaming System, turned without a sound.

What choice is this—profundity and flight—
Great sea? Our lives through we have trod the ground.

Motion beneath us, fixity above.

"O, but you should rejoice! The course we steer
Points to a beach bright to the rocks with love,
Where, in hot calms, blades clatter on the ear;

And spiny fruits up through the earth are fed
With fire; the palm trees clatter; the wave leaps.
Fleeing a shore where heart-loathed love lies dead
We point lands where love fountains from its deeps.

Through every season the coarse fruits are set
In earth not fed by streams." Soft into time
Once broke the flower: pear and violet,
The cinquefoil. The tall elm tree and the lime

Once held out fruitless boughs, and fluid green
Once rained about us, pulse of earth indeed.
There, out of metal, and to light obscene,
The flamy blooms burn backward to their seed.

With so much hated still so close behind
The sterile shores before us must be faced;
Again, against the body and the mind,
The hate that bruises, though the heart is braced.

Bend to the chart, in the extinguished night
Mariners! Make way slowly; stay from sleep;
That we may have short respite from such light.

And learn, with joy, the gulf, the vast, the deep.

THE DREAM

O God, in the dream the terrible horse began
To paw at the air, and make for me with his blows.

Fear kept for thirty-five years poured through his mane,
And retribution equally old, or nearly, breathed through
    his nose.

Coward complete, I lay and wept on the ground
When some strong creature appeared, and leapt for the
    rein.
Another woman, as I lay half in a swound,
Leapt in the air, and clutched at the leather and chain.

Give him, she said, something of yours as a charm.
Throw him, she said, some poor thing you alone claim.
No, no, I cried, he hates me; he's out for harm,
And whether I yield or not, it is all the same.

But, like a lion in a legend, when I flung the glove
Pulled from my sweating, my cold right hand,
The terrible beast, that no one may understand,
Came to my side, and put down his head in love.

Hart Crane / 1899–1932

TO BROOKLYN BRIDGE

How many dawns, chill from his rippling rest
The seagull's wings shall dip and pivot him,
Shedding white rings of tumult, building high
Over the chained bay waters Liberty—

Then, with inviolate curve, forsake our eyes
As apparitional as sails that cross
Some page of figures to be filed away;
—Till elevators drop us from our day . . .

I think of cinemas, panoramic sleights
With multitudes bent toward some flashing scene

Never disclosed, but hastened to again,
Foretold to other eyes on the same screen;

And Thee, across the harbor, silver-paced
As though the sun took step of thee, yet left
Some motion ever unspent in thy stride,—
Implicitly thy freedom staying thee!

Out of some subway scuttle, cell or loft
A bedlamite speeds to thy parapets,
Tilting there momently, shrill shirt ballooning,
A jest falls from the speechless caravan.

Down Wall, from girder into street noon leaks,
A rip-tooth of the sky's acetylene;
All afternoon the cloud-flown derricks turn . . .
Thy cables breathe the North Atlantic still.

And obscure as that heaven of the Jews,
Thy guerdon . . . Accolade thou dost bestow
Of anonymity time cannot raise:
Vibrant reprieve and pardon thou dost show.

O harp and altar, of the fury fused,
(How could mere toil align thy choiring strings!)
Terrific threshold of the prophet's pledge,
Prayer of pariah, and the lover's cry,—

Again the traffic lights that skim thy swift
Unfractioned idiom, immaculate sigh of stars,
Beading thy path—condense eternity:
And we have seen night lifted in thine arms.

Under thy shadow by the piers I waited;
Only in darkness is thy shadow clear.
The City's fiery parcels all undone,
Already snow submerges an iron year . . .

O Sleepless as the river under thee,
Vaulting the sea, the prairies' dreaming sod,
Unto us lowliest sometime sweep, descend
And of the curveship lend a myth to God.

THE DANCE

The swift red flesh, a winter king—
Who squired the glacier woman down the sky?
She ran the neighing canyons all the spring;
She spouted arms; she rose with maize—to die.

And in the autumn drouth, whose burnished hands
With mineral wariness found out the stone
Where prayers, forgotten, streamed the mesa sands?
He holds the twilight's dim, perpetual throne.

Mythical brows we saw retiring—loth,
Disturbed and destined, into denser green.
Greeting they sped us, on the arrow's oath:
Now lie incorrigibly what years between . . .

There was a bed of leaves, and broken play;
There was a veil upon you, Pocahontas, bride—
O Princess whose brown lap was virgin May;
And bridal flanks and eyes hid tawny pride.

I left the village for dogwood. By the canoe
Tugging below the mill-race, I could see
Your hair's keen crescent running, and the blue
First moth of evening take wing stealthily.

What laughing chains the water wove and threw!
I learned to catch the trout's moon whisper; I
Drifted how many hours I never knew,
But, watching, saw that fleet young crescent die,—

And one star, swinging, take its place, alone,
Cupped in the larches of the mountain pass—
Until, immortally, it bled into the dawn.
I left my sleek boat nibbling margin grass . . .

I took the portage climb, then chose
A further valley-shed; I could not stop.

Then you
shall see her
truly — your
blood
remembering
its first
invasion of
her secrecy,
its first
encounters
with her kin,
her chieftain
lover . . . his
shade that
haunts the
lakes and
hills

Feet nozzled wat'ry webs of upper flows;
One white veil gusted from the very top.

O Appalachian Spring! I gained the ledge;
Steep, inaccessible smile that eastward bends
And northward reaches in that violet wedge
Of Adirondacks!—wisped of azure wands,

Over how many bluffs, tarns, streams I sped!
—And knew myself within some boding shade:—
Grey tepees tufting the blue knolls ahead,
Smoke swirling through the yellow chestnut glade . . .

A distant cloud, a thunder-bud—it grew,
That blanket of the skies: the padded foot
Within,—I heard it; 'til its rhythm drew,
—Siphoned the black pool from the heart's hot root!

A cyclone threshes in the turbine crest,
Swooping in eagle feathers down your back;
Know, Maquokeeta, greeting; know death's best;
—Fall, Sachem, strictly as the tamarack!

A birch kneels. All her whistling fingers fly.
The oak grove circles in a crash of leaves;
The long moan of a dance is in the sky.
Dance, Maquokeeta: Pocahontas grieves . . .

And every tendon scurries toward the twangs
Of lightning deltaed down your saber hair.
Now snaps the flint in every tooth; red fangs
And splay tongues thinly busy the blue air . . .

Dance, Maquokeeta! snake that lives before,
That casts his pelt, and lives beyond! Sprout, horn!
Spark, tooth! Medicine-man, relent, restore—
Lie to us,—dance us back the tribal morn!

Spears and assemblies: black drums thrusting on—
O yelling battlements,—I, too, was liege
To rainbows currying each pulsant bone:
Surpassed the circumstance, danced out the siege!

And buzzard-circleted, screamed from the stake;
I could not pick the arrows from my side.
Wrapped in that fire, I saw more escorts wake—
Flickering, sprint up the hill groins like a tide.

I heard the hush of lava wrestling your arms,
And stag teeth foam about the raven throat;
Flame cataracts of heaven in seething swarms
Fed down your anklets to the sunset's moat.

O, like the lizard in the furious noon,
That drops his legs and colors in the sun,
—And laughs, pure serpent, Time itself, and moon
Of his own fate, I saw thy change begun!

And saw thee dive to kiss that destiny
Like one white meteor, sacrosanct and blent
At last with all that's consummate and free
There, where the first and last gods keep thy tent.

.   .   .

Thewed of the levin, thunder-shod and lean,
Lo, through what infinite seasons dost thou gaze—
Across what bivouacs of thin angered slain,
And see'st thy bride immortal in the maize!

Totem and fire-gall, slumbering pyramid—
Though other calendars now stack the sky,
Thy freedom is her largesse, Prince, and hid
On paths thou knewest best to claim her by.

High unto Labrador the sun strikes free
Her speechless dream of snow, and stirred again,
She is the torrent and the singing tree;
And she is virgin to the last of men . . .

West, west and south! winds over Cumberland
And winds across the llano grass resume
Her hair's warm sibilance. Her breasts are fanned
O stream by slope and vineyard—into bloom!

And when the caribou slant down for salt
Do arrows thirst and leap? Do antlers shine

Alert, star-triggered in the listening vault
Of dusk?—And are her perfect brows to thine?

We danced, O Brave, we danced beyond their farms,
In cobalt desert closures made our vows . . .
Now is the strong prayer folded in thine arms,
The serpent with the eagle in the boughs.

NATIONAL WINTER GARDEN

Outspoken buttocks in pink beads
Invite the necessary cloudy clinch
Of bandy eyes. . . . No extra mufflings here:
The world's one flagrant, sweating cinch.

And while legs waken salads in the brain
You pick your blonde out neatly through the smoke.
Always you wait for someone else though, always—
(Then rush the nearest exit through the smoke).

Always and last, before the final ring
When all the fireworks blare, begins
A tom-tom scrimmage with a somewhere violin,
Some cheapest echo of them all—begins.

And shall we call her whiter than the snow?
Sprayed first with ruby, then with emerald sheen—
Least tearful and least glad (who knows her smile?)
A caught slide shows her sandstone grey between.

Her eyes exist in swivellings of her teats,
Pearls whip her hips, a drench of whirling strands.
Her silly snake rings begin to mount, surmount
Each other—turquoise fakes on tinselled hands.

We wait that writhing pool, her pearls collapsed,
—All but her belly buried in the floor;
And the lewd trounce of a final muted beat!
We flee her spasm through a fleshless door. . . .

Yet, to the empty trapeze of your flesh,
O Magdalene, each comes back to die alone.
Then you, the burlesque of our lust—and faith,
Lug us back lifeward—bone by infant bone.

QUAKER HILL

*I see only the ideal. But no ideals have
ever been fully successful on this earth.*
                    ISADORA DUNCAN

*The gentian weaves her fringes,
The maple's loom is red.*
                    EMILY DICKINSON

Perspective never withers from their eyes;
They keep that docile edict of the Spring
That blends March with August Antarctic skies:
These are but cows that see no other thing
Than grass and snow, and their own inner being
Through the rich halo that they do not trouble
Even to cast upon the seasons fleeting
Though they should thin and die on last year's stubble.

And they are awkward, ponderous and uncoy . . .
While we who press the cider mill, regarding them—
We, who with pledges taste the bright annoy
Of friendship's acid wine, retarding phlegm,
Shifting reprisals ('til who shall tell us when
The jest is too sharp to be kindly?) boast
Much of our store of faith in other men
Who would, ourselves, stalk down the merriest ghost.

Above them old Mizzentop, palatial white
Hostelry—floor by floor to cinquefoil dormer
Portholes the ceilings stack their stoic height.
Long tiers of windows staring out toward former
Faces—loose panes crown the hill and gleam
At sunset with a silent, cobwebbed patience . . .
See them, like eyes that still uphold some dream
Through mapled vistas, cancelled reservations!

High from the central cupola, they say
One's glance could cross the borders of three states;
But I have seen death's stare in slow survey
From four horizons that no one relates . . .
Weekenders avid of their turf-won scores,
Here three hours from the semaphores, the Czars
Of golf, by twos and threes in plaid plusfours
Alight with sticks abristle and cigars.

This was the Promised Land, and still it is
To the persuasive suburban land agent
In bootleg roadhouses where the gin fizz
Bubbles in time to Hollywood's new love-nest pageant.
Fresh from the radio in the old Meeting House
(Now the New Avalon Hotel) volcanoes roar
A welcome to highsteppers that no mouse
Who saw the Friends there ever heard before.

What cunning neighbors history has in fine!
The woodlouse mortgages the ancient deal
Table that Powitzky buys for only nine-
Ty-five at Adams' auction,—eats the seal,
The spinster polish of antiquity . . .
Who holds the lease on time and on disgrace?
What eats the pattern with ubiquity?
Where are my kinsmen and the patriarch race?

The resigned factions of the dead preside.
Dead rangers bled their comfort on the snow;
But I must ask slain Iroquois to guide
Me farther than scalped Yankees knew to go:
Shoulder the curse of sundered parentage,
Wait for the postman driving from Birch Hill
With birthright by blackmail, the arrant page
That unfolds a new distiny to fill. . . .

So, must we from the hawk's far stemming view,
Must we descend as worm's eye to construe
Our love of all we touch, and take it to the Gate
As humbly as a guest who knows himself too late,
His news already told? Yes, while the heart is wrung,

Arise—yes, take this sheaf of dust upon your tongue!
In one last angelus lift throbbing throat—
Listen, transmuting silence with that stilly note

Of pain that Emily, that Isadora knew!
While high from dim elm-chancels hung with dew,
That triple-noted clause of moonlight—
Yes, whip-poor-will, unhusks the heart of fright,
Breaks us and saves, yes, breaks the heart, yet yields
That patience that is armour and that shields
Love from despair—when love foresees the end—
Leaf after autumnal leaf
                    break off,
                              descend—
                                        descend—

ATLANTIS

*Music is then the knowledge of that which
relates to love in harmony and system.*
                                   PLATO

Through the bound cable strands, the arching path
Upward, veering with light, the flight of strings,—
Taut miles of shuttling moonlight syncopate
The whispered rush, telepathy of wires.
Up the index of night, granite and steel—
Transparent meshes—fleckless the gleaming staves—
Sibylline voices flicker, waveringly stream
As though a god were issue of the strings. . . .

And through that cordage, threading with its call
One arc synoptic of all tides below—
Their labyrinthine mouths of history
Pouring reply as though all ships at sea
Complighted in one vibrant breath made cry,—
"Make thy love sure—to weave whose song we ply!"
—From black embankments, moveless soundings hailed,
So seven oceans answer from their dream.

And on, obliquely up bright carrier bars
New octaves trestle the twin monoliths
Beyond whose frosted capes the moon bequeaths
Two worlds of sleep (O arching strands of song!)—
Onward and up the crystal-flooded aisle
White tempest nets file upward, upward ring
With silver terraces the humming spars,
The loft of vision, palladium helm of stars.

Sheerly the eyes, like seagulls stung with rime—
Slit and propelled by glistening fins of light—
Pick biting way up towering looms that press
Sidelong with flight of blade on tendon blade
—Tomorrows into yesteryear—and link
What cipher-script of time no traveller reads
But who, through smoking pyres of love and death,
searches the timeless laugh of mythic spears.

Like hails, farewells—up planet-sequined heights
Some trillion whispering hammers glimmer Tyre:
Serenely, sharply up the long anvil cry
Of inchling æons silence rivets Troy.
And you, aloft there—Jason! hesting Shout!
Still wrapping harness to the swarming air!
Silvery the rushing wake, surpassing call,
Beams yelling Æolus! splintered in the straits!

From gulfs unfolding, terrible of drums,
Tall Vision-of-the-Voyage, tensely spare—
Bridge, lifting night to cycloramic crest
Of deepest day—O Choir, translating time
Into what multitudinous Verb the suns
And synergy of waters ever fuse, recast
In myriad syllables,—Psalm of Cathay!
O Love, thy white, pervasive Paradigm . . . !

We left the haven hanging in the night—
Sheened harbor lanterns backward fled the keel.
Pacific here at time's end, bearing corn,—
Eyes stammer through the pangs of dust and steel.
And still the circular, indubitable frieze
Of heaven's meditation, yoking wave

To kneeling wave, one song devoutly binds—
The vernal strophe chimes from deathless strings!

O Thou steeled Cognizance whose leap commits
The agile precincts of the lark's return;
Within whose lariat sweep encinctured sing
In single chrysalis the many twain,—
Of stars Thou art the stitch and stallion glow
And like an organ, Thou, with sound of doom—
Sight, sound and flesh Thou leadest from time's realm
As love strikes clear direction for the helm.

Swift peal of secular light, intrinsic Myth
Whose fell unshadow is death's utter wound,—
O River-throated—iridescently upborne
Through the bright drench and fabric of our veins;
With white escarpments swinging into light,
Sustained in tears the cities are endowed
And justified conclamant with ripe fields
Revolving through their harvests in sweet torment.

Forever Deity's glittering Pledge, O Thou
Whose canticle fresh chemistry assigns
To rapt inception and beatitude,—
Always through blinding cables, to our joy,
Of thy white seizure springs the prophecy:
Always through spiring cordage, pyramids
Of silver sequel, Deity's young name
Kinetic of white choiring wings . . . ascends.

Migrations that must needs void memory,
Inventions that cobblestone the heart,—
Unspeakable Thou Bridge to Thee, O Love.
Thy pardon for this history, whitest Flower,
O Answerer of all,—Anemone,—
Now while thy petals spend the suns about us, hold—
(O Thou whose radiance doth inherit me)
Atlantis,—hold thy floating singer late!

So to thine Everpresence, beyond time,
Like spears ensanguined of one tolling star
That bleeds infinity—the orphic strings,

Sidereal phalanxes, leap and converge:
—One Song, one Bridge of Fire! Is it Cathay,
Now pity steeps the grass and rainbows ring
The serpent with the eagle in the leaves . . . ?
Whispers antiphonal in azure swing.

EMBLEMS OF CONDUCT

By a peninsula the wanderer sat and sketched
The uneven valley graves. While the apostle gave
Alms to the meek the volcano burst
With sulphur and aureate rocks . . .
For joy rides in stupendous coverings
Luring the living into spiritual gates.

Orators follow the universe
And radio the complete laws to the people.
The apostle conveys thought through discipline.
Bowls and cups fill historians with adorations,—
Dull lips commemorating spiritual gates.

The wanderer later chose this spot of rest
Where marble clouds support the sea
And where was finally borne a chosen hero.
By that time summer and smoke were past.
Dolphins still played, arching the horizons,
But only to build memories of spiritual gates.

PRAISE FOR AN URN

In Memoriam: Ernest Nelson

It was a kind and northern face
That mingled in such exile guise
The everlasting eyes of Pierrot
And, of Gargantua, the laughter.

His thoughts, delivered to me
From the white coverlet and pillow,
I see now, were inheritances—
Delicate riders of the storm.

The slant moon on the slanting hill
Once moved us toward presentiments
Of what the dead keep, living still,
And such assessments of the soul

As, perched in the crematory lobby,
The insistent clock commented on,
Touching as well upon our praise
Of glories proper to the time.

Still, having in mind gold hair,
I cannot see that broken brow
And miss the dry sound of bees
Stretching across a lucid space.

Scatter these well-meant idioms
Into the smoky spring that fills
The suburbs, where they will be lost.
They are no trophies of the sun.

CHAPLINESQUE

We make our meek adjustments,
Contented with such random consolations
As the wind deposits
In slithered and too ample pockets.

For we can still love the world, who find
A famished kitten on the step, and know
Recesses for it from the fury of the street,
Or warm torn elbow coverts.

We will sidestep and to the final smirk
Dally the doom of that inevitable thumb

That slowly chafes its puckered index toward us,
Facing the dull squint with what innocence
And what surprise!

And yet these fine collapses are not lies
More than the pirouettes of any pliant cane;
Our obsequies are, in a way, no enterprise.
We can evade you, and all else but the heart:
What blame to us if the heart live on.

The game enforces smirks; but we have seen
The moon in lonely alleys make
A grail of laughter of an empty ash can,
And through all sound of gaiety and quest
Have heard a kitten in the wilderness.

REPOSE OF RIVERS

The willows carried a slow sound,
A sarabande the wind mowed on the mead.
I could never remember
That seething, steady leveling of the marshes
Till age had brought me to the sea.

Flags, weeds. And remembrance of steep alcoves
Where cypresses shared the noon's
Tyranny; they drew me into hades almost.
And mammoth turtles climbing sulphur dreams
Yielded, while sun-silt rippled them
Asunder . . .

How much I would have bartered! the black gorge
And all the singular nestings in the hills
Where beavers learn stitch and tooth.
The pond I entered once and quickly fled—
I remember now its singing willow rim.

And finally, in that memory all things nurse;
After the city that I finally passed

With scalding unguents spread and smoking darts
The monsoon cut across the delta
At gulf gates . . . There, beyond the dykes

I heard wind flaking sapphire, like this summer,
And willows could not hold more steady sound.

FOR THE MARRIAGE OF
FAUSTUS AND HELEN

III

Capped arbiter of beauty in this street
That narrows darkly into motor dawn,—
You, here beside me, delicate ambassador
Of intricate slain numbers that arise
In whispers, naked of steel;
                  religious gunman!
Who faithfully, yourself, will fall too soon,
And in other ways than as the wind settles
On the sixteen thrifty bridges of the city:
Let us unbind our throats of fear and pity.

                  We even,
Who drove speediest destruction
In corymbulous formations of mechanics,—
Who hurried the hill breezes, spouting malice
Plangent over meadows, and looked down
On rifts of torn and empty houses
Like old women with teeth unjubilant
That waited faintly, briefly and in vain:

We know, eternal gunman, our flesh remembers
The tensile boughs, the nimble blue plateaus,
The mounted, yielding cities of the air!
That saddled sky that shook down vertical
Repeated play of fire—no hypogeum
Of wave or rock was good against one hour.

We did not ask for that, but have survived,
And will persist to speak again before
All stubble streets that have not curved
To memory, or known the ominous lifted arm
That lowers down the arc of Helen's brow
To saturate with blessing and dismay.

A goose, tobacco and cologne—
Three-winged and gold-shod prophecies of heaven,
The lavish heart shall always have to leaven
And spread with bells and voices, and atone
The abating shadows of our conscript dust.

Anchises' navel, dripping of the sea,—
The hands Erasmus dipped in gleaming tides,
Gathered the voltage of blown blood and vine;
Delve upward for the new and scattered wine,
O brother-thief of time, that we recall.
Laugh out the meager penance of their days
Who dare not share with us the breath released,
The substance drilled and spent beyond repair
For golden, or the shadow of gold hair.

Distinctly praise the years, whose volatile
Blamed bleeding hands extend and thresh the height
The imagination spans beyond despair,
Outpacing bargain, vocable and prayer.

VOYAGES

II

And yet this great wink of eternity,
Of rimless floods, unfettered leewardings,
Samite sheeted and processioned where
Her undinal vast belly moonward bends,
Laughing the wrapt inflections of our love;

Take this Sea, whose diapason knells
On scrolls of silver snowy sentences,

The sceptred terror of whose sessions rends
As her demeanors motion well or ill,
All but the pieties of lovers' hands.

And onward, as bells off San Salvador
Salute the crocus lustres of the stars,
In these poinsettia meadows of her tides,—
Adagios of islands, O my Prodigal,
Complete the dark confessions her veins spell.

Mark how her turning shoulders wind the hours,
And hasten while her penniless rich palms
Pass superscription of bent foam and wave,—
Hasten, while they are true,—sleep, death, desire,
Close round one instant in one floating flower.

Bind us in time, O Seasons clear, and awe.
O minstrel galleons of Carib fire,
Bequeath us to no earthly shore until
Is answered in the vortex of our grave
The seal's wide spindrift gaze toward paradise.

THE BROKEN TOWER

The bell-rope that gathers God at dawn
Dispatches me as though I dropped down the knell
Of a spent day—to wander the cathedral lawn
From pit to crucifix, feet chill on steps from hell.

Have you not heard, have you not seen that corps
Of shadows in the tower, whose shoulders sway
Antiphonal carillons launched before
The stars are caught and hived in the sun's ray?

The bells, I say, the bells break down their tower;
And swing I know not where. Their tongues engrave
Membrane through marrow, my long-scattered score
Of broken intervals. . . . And I, their sexton slave!

Oval encyclicals in canyons heaping
The impasse high with choir. Banked voices slain!
Pagodas, campaniles with reveilles outleaping—
O terraced echoes prostrate on the plain! . . .

And so it was I entered the broken world
To trace the visionary company of love, its voice
An instant in the wind (I know not whither hurled)
But not for long to hold each desperate choice.

My word I poured. But was it cognate, scored
Of that tribunal monarch of the air
Whose thigh embronzes earth, strikes crystal Word
In wounds pledged once to hope—cleft to despair?

The steep encroachments of my blood left me
No answer (could blood hold such a lofty tower
As flings the question true?)—or is it she
Whose sweet mortality stirs latent power?—

And through whose pulse I hear, counting the strokes
My veins recall and add, revived and sure
The angelus of wars my chest evokes:
What I hold healed, original now, and pure . . .

And builds, within, a tower that is not stone
(Not stone can jacket heaven)—but slip
Of pebbles—visible wings of silence sown
In azure circles, widening as they dip

The matrix of the heart, lift down the eye
That shrines the quiet lake and swells a tower . . .
The commodious, tall decorum of that sky
Unseals her earth, and lifts love in its shower.

Allen Tate / 1899–

THE MEDITERRANEAN

Quem das finem, rex magne, dolorum?

Where we went in the boat was a long bay
A slingshot wide, walled in by towering stone—
Peaked margin of antiquity's delay,
And we went there out of time's monotone:

Where we went in the black hull no light moved
But a gull white-winged along the feckless wave,
The breeze, unseen but fierce as a body loved,
That boat drove onward like a willing slave:

Where we went in the small ship the seaweed
Parted and gave to us the murmuring shore,
And we made feast and in our secret need
Devoured the very plates Aeneas bore:

Where derelict you see through the low twilight
The green coast that you, thunder-tossed, would win,
Drop sail, and hastening to drink all night
Eat dish and bowl to take that sweet land in!

Where we feasted and caroused on the sandless
Pebbles, affecting our day of piracy,
What prophecy of eaten plates could landless
Wanderers fulfil by the ancient sea?

We for that time might taste the famous age
Eternal here yet hidden from our eyes
When lust of power undid its stuffless rage;
They, in a wineskin, bore earth's paradise.

Let us lie down once more by the breathing side
Of Ocean, where our live forefathers sleep
As if the Known Sea still were a month wide—
Atlantis howls but is no longer steep!

What country shall we conquer, what fair land
Unman our conquest and locate our blood?
We've cracked the hemispheres with careless hand!
Now, from the Gates of Hercules we flood

Westward, westward till the barbarous brine
Whelms us to the tired land where tasseling corn,
Fat beans, grapes sweeter than muscadine
Rot on the vine: in that land were we born.

ODE TO THE CONFEDERATE DEAD

Row after row with strict impunity
The headstones yield their names to the element,
The wind whirrs without recollection;
In the riven troughs the splayed leaves
Pile up, of nature the casual sacrament
To the seasonal eternity of death;
Then driven by the fierce scrutiny
Of heaven to their election in the vast breath,
They sough the rumour of mortality.

Autumn is desolation in the plot
Of a thousand acres where these memories grow
From the inexhaustible bodies that are not
Dead, but feed the grass row after rich row.
Think of the autumns that have come and gone!—
Ambitious November with the humors of the year,
With a particular zeal for every slab,
Staining the uncomfortable angels that rot
On the slabs, a wing chipped here, an arm there:
The brute curiosity of an angel's stare
Turns you, like them, to stone,

Transforms the heaving air
Till plunged to a heavier world below
You shift your sea-space blindly
Heaving, turning like the blind crab.

    Dazed by the wind, only the wind
    The leaves flying, plunge

You know who have waited by the wall
The twilight certainty of an animal,
Those midnight restitutions of the blood
You know—the immitigable pines, the smoky frieze
Of the sky, the sudden call: you know the rage,
The cold pool left by the mounting flood,
Of muted Zeno and Parmenides.
You who have waited for the angry resolution
Of those desires that should be yours tomorrow,
You know the unimportant shrift of death
And praise the vision
And praise the arrogant circumstance
Of those who fall
Rank upon rank, hurried beyond decision—
Here by the sagging gate, stopped by the wall.

    Seeing, seeing only the leaves
    Flying, plunge and expire

Turn your eyes to the immoderate past,
Turn to the inscrutable infantry rising
Demons out of the earth—they will not last.
Stonewall, Stonewall, and the sunken fields of hemp,
Shiloh, Antietam, Malvern Hill, Bull Run.
Lost in that orient of the thick-and-fast
You will curse the setting sun.

    Cursing only the leaves crying
    Like an old man in a storm

You hear the shout, the crazy hemlocks point
With troubled fingers to the silence which
Smothers you, a mummy, in time.

                                    The hound bitch
Toothless and dying, in a musty cellar
Hears the wind only.

                        Now that the salt of their blood
Stiffens the saltier oblivion of the sea,
Seals the malignant purity of the flood,
What shall we who count our days and bow
Our heads with a commemorial woe
In the ribboned coats of grim felicity,
What shall we say of the bones, unclean,
Whose verdurous anonymity will grow?
The ragged arms, the ragged heads and eyes
Lost in these acres of the insane green?
The gray lean spiders come, they come and go;
In a tangle of willows without light
The singular screech-owl's tight
Invisible lyric seeds the mind
With the furious murmur of their chivalry.

    We shall say only the leaves
    Flying, plunge and expire

We shall say only the leaves whispering
In the improbable mist of nightfall
That flies on multiple wing;
Night is the beginning and the end
And in between the ends of distraction
Waits mute speculation, the patient curse
That stones the eyes, or like the jaguar leaps
For his own image in a jungle pool, his victim.

What shall we say, who have knowledge
Carried to the heart? Shall we take the act
To the grave? Shall we, more hopeful, set up the grave
In the house? The ravenous grave?
                                    Leave now
The shut gate and the decomposing wall:
The gentle serpent, green in the mulberry bush,

Riots with his tongue through the hush—
Sentinel of the grave who counts us all!

SONNETS AT CHRISTMAS

1934

I

This is the day His hour of life draws near,
Let me get ready from head to foot for it
Most handily with eyes to pick the year
For small feed to reward a feathered wit.
Some men would see it an epiphany
At ease, at food and drink, others at chase
Yet I, stung lassitude, with ecstasy
Unspent argue the season's difficult case
So: Man, dull critter of enormous head,
What would he look at in the coiling sky?
But I must kneel again unto the Dead
While Christmas bells of paper white and red,
Figured with boys and girls spilt from a sled,
Ring out the silence I am nourished by.

II

Ah, Christ, I love you rings to the wild sky
And I must think a little of the past:
When I was ten I told a stinking lie
That got a black boy whipped; but now at last
The going years, caught in an accurate glow,
Reverse like balls englished upon green baize—
Let them return, let the round trumpets blow
The ancient crackle of the Christ's deep gaze.
Deafened and blind, with senses yet unfound,
Am I, untutored to the after-wit
Of knowledge, knowing a nightmare has no sound;
Therefore with idle hands and head I sit
In late December before the fire's daze
Punished by crimes of which I would be quit.

MORE SONNETS AT CHRISTMAS

1942

To Denis Devlin

I

Again the native hour lets down the locks
Uncombed and black, but gray the bobbing beard;
Ten years ago His eyes, fierce shuttlecocks,
Pierced the close net of what I failed: I feared
The belly-cold, the grave-clout, that betrayed
Me dithering in the drift of cordial seas;
Ten years are time enough to be dismayed
By mummy Christ, head crammed between his knees.

Suppose I take an arrogant bomber, stroke
By stroke, up to the frazzled sun to hear
Sun-ghostlings whisper: Yes, the capital yoke—
Remove it and there's not a ghost to fear
This crucial day, whose decapitate joke
Languidly winds into the inner ear.

II

The day's at end and there's nowhere to go,
Draw to the fire, even this fire is dying;
Get up and once again politely lying
Invite the ladies toward the mistletoe
With greedy eyes that stare like an old crow.
How pleasantly the holly wreaths did hang
And how stuffed Santa did his reindeer clang
Above the golden oaken mantel, years ago!

Then hang this picture for a calendar,
As sheep for goat, and pray most fixedly
For the cold martial progress of your star,
With thoughts of commerce and society,
Well-milked Chinese, Negroes who cannot sing,
The Huns gelded and feeding in a ring.

III

Give me this day a faith not personal
As follows: The American people fully armed

With assurance policies, righteous and harmed,
Battle the world of which they're not at all.
That lying boy of ten who stood in the hall,
His hat in hand (thus by his father charmed:
"You may be President"), was not alarmed
Nor even left uneasy by his fall.

Nobody said that he could be a plumber,
Carpenter, clerk, bus-driver, bombardier;
Let little boys go into violent slumber,
Aegean squall and squalor where their fear
Is of an enemy in remote oceans
Unstalked by Christ: these are the better notions.

IV

Gay citizen, myself, and thoughtful friend,
Your ghosts are Plato's Christians in the cave.
Unfix your necks, turn to the door; the nave
Gives back the cheated and light dividend
So long sequestered; now, new-rich, you'll spend
Flesh for reality inside a stone
Whose light obstruction, like a gossamer bone,
Dead or still living, will not break or bend.

Thus light, your flesh made pale and sinister
And put off like a dog that's had his day,
You will be Plato's kept philosopher,
Albino man bleached from the mortal clay,
Mild-mannered, gifted in your master's ease
While the sun squats upon the waveless seas.

THE TRAVELLER

To Archibald MacLeish

The afternoon with heavy hours
Lies vacant on the wanderer's sight
And sunset waits whose cloudy towers
Expect the legions of the night

Till sullen thunder from the cave
Of twilight with deliberate swell
Whispers the air his darkening slave
To loose the nether bolts of hell

To crush the battlements of cloud
The wall of light around the West
So that the swarming dark will crowd
The traveller upon his quest

And all the air with heavy hours
Sinks on the wanderer's dull sight
And the thick dark whose hidden towers
Menace his travel to the night

Rolls forward, backward hill to hill
Until the seeker knows not where
Beyond the shade of Peachers' Mill
In the burnt meadow, with colourless hair

The secret ones around a stone
Their lips withdrawn in meet surprise
Lie still, being naught but bone
With naught but space within their eyes

Until bewildered by the road
And half-forgetful of his quest
The wanderer with such a load
Of breathing, being too late a guest

Turns back, so near the secret stone,
Falls down breathless at last and blind,
And a dark shift within the bone
Brings him the end he could not find.

THE OATH

In was near evening, the room was cold
Half dark; Uncle Ben's brass bullet-mould

And powder-horn and Major Bogan's face
Above the fire in the half-light plainly said:
There's naught to kill but the animated dead.
Horn nor mould nor major follows the chase.
Being cold I urged Lytle to the fire
In the blank twilight with not much left untold
By two old friends when neither's a great liar.
We sat down evenly in the smoky chill.
There's precious little to say between day and dark,
Perhaps a few words on the implacable will
Of time sailing like a magic barque
Or something as fine for the amenities,
Till dusk seals the window, the fire grows bright,
And the wind saws the hill with a swarm of bees.
Now meditating a little on the firelight
We heard the darkness grapple with the night
And give an old man's valedictory wheeze
From his westward breast between his polar jaws;
Then Lytle asked: Who are the dead?
Who are the living and the dead?
And nothing more was said.
So I, leaving Lytle to that dream,
Decided what it is in time that gnaws
The ageing fury of a mountain stream
When suddenly as an ignorant mind will do
I thought I heard the dark pounding its head
On a rock, crying: *Who are the dead?*
Then Lytle turned with an oath—By God it's true!

THE WOLVES

There are wolves in the next room waiting
With heads bent low, thrust out, breathing
At nothing in the dark; between them and me
A white door patched with light from the hall
Where it seems never (so still is the house)
A man has walked from the front door to the stair.
It has all been forever. Beasts claw the floor.
I have brooded on angels and archfiends

But no man has ever sat where the next room's
Crowded with wolves, and for the honor of man
I affirm that never have I before. Now while
I have looked for the evening star at a cold window
And whistled when Arcturus spilt his light,
I've heard the wolves scuffle, and said: So this
Is man; so—what better conclusion is there—
The day will not follow night, and the heart
Of man has a little dignity, but less patience
Than a wolf's, and a duller sense that cannot
Smell its own mortality. (This and other
Meditations will be suited to other times
After dog silence howls his epitaph.)
Now remember courage, go to the door,
Open it and see whether coiled on the bed
Or cringing by the wall, a savage beast
Maybe with golden hair, with deep eyes
Like a bearded spider on a sunlit floor
Will snarl—and man can never be alone.

A   P A U P E R

. . . and the children's teeth shall be set on edge.

I see him old, trapped in a burly house
Cold in the angry spitting of a rain
Come down these sixty years.

                              Why vehemently
Astride the threshold do I wait, marking
The ice softly pendent on his broken temple?
Upon the silence I cast the mesh of rancor
By which the gentler convergences of the flesh
Scatter untokened, mercilessly estopped.

Why so illegal these tears?

The years' incertitude and
The dirty white fates trickling

Blackly down the necessary years
Define no attitude to the present winter,
No mood to the cold matter.

(I remember my mother, my mother,
A stiff wind halted outside,
In the hard ear my country
Was a far shore crying
With invisible seas)

When tomorrow pleads the mortal decision
Sifting rankly out of time's sieve today,
No words differently will be uttered
Nor stuttered, like sheep astray.

A pauper in the swift denominating
Of a bald cliff with a proper name, having words
As strumpets only, I cannot beat off
Invincible modes of the sea, hearing:

Be a man my son by God.

He turned again
To the purring jet yellowing the murder story,
Deaf to the pathos circling in the air.

Oscar Williams / 1900–1964

THE LAST SUPPER

I

Apostles of the hidden sun
Are come unto the room of breath
Hung with the banging blinds of death,
The body twelve, the spirit one,
Far as the eye, in earth arrayed,
The night shining, the supper laid.

II

The wine shone on the table that evening of history
Like an enormous ruby in the bauble and mystery.

In the glowing walls of the flickering decanter
There moved His face as at the world's center.

The hands of Judas showed up red and hurried
And the light hit them so, like a cross carried.

The faces of the others were there and moving
In the crystal of the dome, swiftly hovering.

The saints, under a lens, shrunken to pigmies,
Gesticulated in birds or in colored enigmas.

Outside there was a storm, the sound of temblors,
The blood bubbled and sprang into the tumblers.

When the morning came like a white wall of stone,
The day lay in the glass and the blood was gone.

I SING AN OLD SONG

I sing an old song, bird on a charcoal bough,
Silver voice on the black black bough, singing,
Rolling heirloom eyes, burning holes in time,
Drenching the flank of nearness with drip-music:
The disturbed owner who hides everywhere
Lumbers through the miles of thick indignation:
The subconscious parts the nap-gold of afternoon.

I sing an old song, bird scything the silence,
Bundling sabres at the cornerstone of sense:
Bird, pulley on a hillheap of elves' eyelashes,
Silver piston sunk to a bud on the bough,
Sing, bird, sing, from the black black bough,
Shake the enormous atmosphere from your small fist

Of body, tear the colossal ear of the all around
Hanging loosely, like forest outside a window:
Open all the fluteholes of days until the world
Weeps music, and sweats light from every facet,
And tumbles to the smoking knees of its orbit.

I sing an old song, bead in the hair of the park,
Bird-knot in the weave of leaves, nugget in sieve
Straining gravel of Utopia to shining beginnings,
Deed, navel of matter, fleck of the future,
Knuckle knock on finality, sing, bird, sing:
Ride the groundswell of heartbreak, tap thick wrist
Of branch, lump of utterance in the cup of sunlight
Melt into the sweetness of reality, O:
Sprinkle effigies on the gauze of stillness,
Aim your gold beak from the nest, from the crook
Of the leafy black arm, toward the poised sun
Swing girders from your beak through tin pretense
Into the underground room of man, the pallid palace.

I sing an old song, bird, toe-hold of song on bough,
Bundle in the bush of radiance: birth-cry of poem!

THE MIRAGE

I lived a life without love, and saw the being
I loved on every branch; then that bare tree
Stood up with all its branches up, a great harp,
Growing straight out of the ground, and there I saw
A squadron of bright birds clothing the bare limbs;
The music notes sat on the harp; it was all love.

This was the heart inside the starved body;
Love grew images like cactus, and planted roses
On the walls of the mirage, and the garden grew
Shining with perfume and the senses dwindled to dew,
The century was rolled into one formation aloft,
A cloud, like St. Veronica's handkerchief of love.

There I saw the face of the one without whom
I lived, two soft jewels implanted in her face,
Her hair pouring around her face without sound,
And her love for me sprang on her skin like dew,
Pearl-grey as the flower of the brain she lay
Quivering on the soft cushion of the great day.

I heard a roar of buildings at my conscience,
I looked up and saw a wall of windows glowing,
And there my love leaned out of each window,
There she leaned out multiplied like heaven
In that vast wall of lights, every light her face,
Suns of a thousand mornings ranging on one day.

And all the machines were running, and yes, great
Was the sound of their running downward and down
Into the blind chutes of their rooted feet,
And all of the windows quivered with my many loves,
Like apples they fell off at one windfall, all,
And I awoke on the starved pavements of no love.

BY FIAT OF ADORATION

This is what we really want
Who drink the kingdom of the heart
A toast to the imagination

She is flowering in a doorway
Eyes cheeks haze of hair
Stepping out of time into here

This is what we really have
Who see the one we adore becoming
The two that she is in the light

Ah God bounces all the waters
From hand to jubilant hand
He cannot contain Himself

But comes over into being
With benediction of painted cloud
The being whom to look at is to become

By fiat of adoration do we reach
The very muscle of miracle
The ease with which beauty is beauty

DWARF OF DISINTEGRATION

I

Who is it runs through the many-storied mansion of myth
With the exaggerated child's-head among pillars and
        palings,
Holding in his grip the balloons of innumerable windows
And chased by the flowing malevolent army of the
        ceilings?

It is the dwarf, the yellow dwarf, with the minted cheeks,
With the roots of the fingers, with the wafer-thin cry,
In a maze of walls, lost in the nurseries of definition—
Shadows dance on shins of trumpets in a waning sky.

Voices are wired in the walls, rats are gnawing rumors,
The throat of music is bursting with the leadpipes of lust,
And the giant's face on the dwarf's shoulders is frightened
As the battle sounds strike the panes from the near-by
        past.

The pillars in the palace are reclining about like pistons:
The horses of parenthesis have run away into the woods:
The king is caught on the vast flypaper of the people:
There are holes as big as hovels in the wall of platitude.

The queen is ill from planting the garden with progeny
And her eyes are crossed off by vicious marks from her
        face:
She telephones the dwarf who puts his head in the
        instrument
To find his features come out in glacial coal bins of space.

The orgasms of distant guns attack at the lustful curtains
And soldiers are standing about in historical knots of lies
Warming frozen tag-ends of lives around the spontaneous
Combustion of bosses who are stoking hollows of hired
    eyes.

The swine bulge in the snake bellies of the telegraph
    wires
And bellow under flat clouds of ceilings in the interior;
Communication swallows the quicksilver swords of
    distance;
Headlines perform, in squadrons of plumes, on the
    warriors.

But the draughty palace of fable is full of feeble splendor:
The yellow dwarf now in possession of knowing documents
Runs after the newspapers cackling on the edge of
    freedom—
The golden cupboards tremble for the aging sentiments.

The music of battlefields exhilarates the hidden overhead
And injects into the air a breakdown sense of release,
And the numerals wriggle off the lock boxes of the world
Unloosing a swarm of the venomous vultures of the peace.

But the dwarf, the yellow dwarf, with sunspots for eyes
Is hunting in the archives in the moth holes in the palace,
And he tightens the torture boot around the spinal
    column,
The steel twilight gleaming with the sweat of his malice.

II

Now that the battle is on, keep off the palace grounds,
You can hear the dwarf rummaging in the elephant
    inside:
It's better to draw a curtain of birds around your eyes—
Fall into the picture book under the thumb of a landslide—

Than to come upon spiders eating the iris of the eyeball,
Glimpse the yellow dwarf digesting the members of
    princes,

Or see famous paintings loll, like tongues, from their
frames
Into a roomful of heroes pretending to harass pretenses.

The sagging structure propped between thought and
thinker,
The gilded lawns flow on under the smokescreen of the
laws:
The allover attack of a decaying body infiltrates to the
atom,
Even the beast in the violin hangs out with lopped-off
paws.

Run! run into the first thicket of verbs, the nest of deeds!
Place a skyline between yourself and the grandiose
emblem!
For the inquisition wears the hypocritical jowls of a
palace,
There's nothing here to salvage, and yours is another
problem.

THE PRAYING MANTIS VISITS
A PENTHOUSE

The praying Mantis with its length of straw
Out of the nowhere's forehead born full armed
Engages the century at my terrace door.
Focused at inches the dinosaur insect sends
Broadsides of epic stillness at my eye,
Above the deafening projects of the age.
My love, who fears the thunder of its poise,
Has seen it and cries out. The clouds like curls
Fall in my faith as I seize a stick to stop
This Martian raid distilled to a straw with legs,
To wisps of prowess. Bristling with motionlessness
The Mantis prays to the Stick twice armed with Man.

I strike, the stick whistles, shearing off two legs
Which run off by themselves beneath some boards.
The Mantis spreads out tints of batlike wing,
The many colored pennants of its blood,
And hugs my weapon; the frantic greens come out,
The reds and yellows blurt out from the straw,
All sinews doubtless screaming insect death.
Against the railing's edge I knock the stick
Sending that gay mad body into the gulf.
Such noisy trappings in defeat wake doubts.
I search my mind for possible wounds and feel
The victim's body heavy on the victor's heart.

THE LEG IN THE SUBWAY

When I saw the woman's leg on the floor of the subway train,
Protrude beyond the panel (while her body overflowed my
    mind's eye),
When I saw the pink stocking, black shoe, curve bulging with
    warmth,
The delicate etching of the hair behind the flesh-colored
    gauze,
When I saw the ankle of Mrs. Nobody going nowhere for a
    nickel,
When I saw this foot motionless on the moving motionless
    floor,
My mind caught on a nail of a distant star, I was wrenched
    out
Of the reality of the subway ride, I hung in a socket of
    distance: and this is what I saw:

The long tongue of the earth's speed was licking the leg,
Upward and under and around went the long tongue of speed:
It was made of a flesh invisible, it dripped the saliva of miles:
It drank moment, lit shivers of insecurity in niches between
    bones:
It was full of eyes, it stopped licking to look at the passengers:

It was as alive as a worm, and busier than anybody in the
    train:
It spoke saying: To whom does this leg belong? Is it a
    bonus leg
For the rush hour? Is it a forgotten leg? Among the many
Myriads of legs did an extra leg fall in from the Out There?

O woman, sliced off bodily by the line of the panel, shall I roll
Your leg into the abdominal nothing, among digestive teeth?
Or shall I fit it in with the pillars that hold up the headlines?
But nobody spoke, though all the faces were talking
    silently,
As the train zoomed, a zipper closing up swiftly the seam of
    time.

Alas, said the long tongue of the speed of the earth quite
    faintly,
What is one to do with an incorrigible leg that will not melt—
But everybody stopped to listen to the train vomiting
    cauldrons
Of silence, while somebody's jolted-out afterthought
    trickled down
The blazing shirt-front solid with light bulbs, and just then
The planetary approach of the next station exploded atoms of
    light,
And when the train stopped, the leg had grown a surprising
    mate,
And the long tongue had slipped hurriedly out through a
    window:

I perceived through the hole left by the nail of the star in my
    mind
How civilization was as dark as a wood and dimensional
    with things
And how birds dipped in chromium sang in the crevices
    of our deeds.

SHOPPING FOR MEAT IN WINTER

What lewd, naked and revolting shape is this?
A frozen oxtail in the butcher's shop
Long and lifeless upon the huge block of wood
On which the ogre's axe begins *chop chop.*

The sun like incense fumes on the smoky glass,
The street frets with people, the winter wind
Throws knives, prices dangle from shoppers' mouths
While the grim vegetables, on parade, bring to mind

The great countryside bathed in golden sleep,
The trees, the bees, the soft peace everywhere—
I think of the cow's tail, how all summer long
It beat the shapes of harps into the air.

Langston Hughes / 1902–1967

HARLEM SWEETIES

Have you dug the spill
Of Sugar Hill?
Cast your gims
On this sepia thrill:
Brown sugar lassie,
Caramel treat,
Honey-gold baby
Sweet enough to eat.
Peach-skinned girlie,
Coffee and cream,
Chocolate darling

Out of a dream.
Walnut tinted
Or cocoa brown,
Pomegranate-lipped
Pride of the town.
Rich cream-colored
To plum-tinted black,
Feminine sweetness
In Harlem's no lack.
Glow of the quince
To blush of the rose.
Persimmon bronze
To cinnamon toes.
Blackberry cordial,
Virginia Dare wine—
All those sweet colors
Flavor Harlem of mine!
Walnut or cocoa,
Let me repeat:
Caramel, brown sugar,
A chocolate treat.
Molasses taffy,
Coffee and cream,
Licorice, clove, cinnamon
To a honey-brown dream.
Ginger, wine-gold,
Persimmon, blackberry,
All through the spectrum
Harlem girls vary—
So if you want to know beauty's
Rainbow-sweet thrill,
Stroll down luscious,
Delicious, *fine* Sugar Hill.

CROSS

My old man's a white old man
And my old mother's black.

If ever I cursed my white old man
I take my curses back.

If ever I cursed my black old mother
And wished she were in hell,
I'm sorry for that evil wish
And now I wish her well.

My old man died in a fine big house,
My ma died in a shack.
I wonder where I'm gonna die,
Being neither white nor black?

DREAM DEFERRED

What happens to a dream deferred?

Does it dry up
like a raisin in the sun?
Or fester like a sore—
And then run?
Does it stink like rotten meat?
Or crust and sugar over—
like a syrupy sweet?

Maybe it just sags
like a heavy load.

Or does it explode?

AMERICAN HEARTBREAK

I am the American heartbreak—
The rock on which Freedom
Stumped its toe—
The great mistake

That Jamestown made
Long ago.

SLAVE

To ride piggy-back
to the market of death
there to purchase a slave,
a slave who died young,
having given up breath—
unwittingly,
of course—
a slave who died young,
perhaps from a fix
with a rusty needle
infected,
to purchase a slave
to the market of death
I ride protected.

UNDERTOW

The solid citizens
Of the country club set,
Caught between
Selma and Peking,
Feel the rug of dividends,
Bathmats of pride,
Even soggy country club
Pink paper towels
Dropped on the MEN'S ROOM floor
Slipping out from under them
Like waves of sea
Between Selma, Peking,
Westchester
And me.

IMPASSE

I could tell you,
If I wanted to,
What makes me
What I am.

But I don't
Really want to—
And you don't
Give a damn.

GO SLOW

Go slow, they say—
While the bite
Of the dog is fast.
Go slow, I hear—
While they tell me
You can't eat here!
You can't live here!
You can't work here!
Don't demonstrate! Wait!—
While they lock the gate.

Am I supposed to be God,
Or an angel with wings
And a halo on my head
While jobless I starve dead?
Am I supposed to forgive
And meekly live
Going slow, slow, slow,
Slow, slow, slow,
Slow, slow,
Slow,
Slow,

Slow?
????
???
??
?

C. Day-Lewis / 1904–

IT IS BECOMING NOW TO DECLARE MY ALLEGIANCE

It is becoming now to declare my allegiance,
To dig some reservoir for my springtime's pain,
Bewilderment and pride, before their insurgence
Is all sopped up in this dry regimen.

Laughable dwarfs, you may twirl and tweak my heart, –
Have I not fought with Anakim at the crossways?
Once I was Cicero, though pedant fate
Now bids me learn the grammar of my days.

These, then, have my allegiance; they whose shining
Convicted my false dawn of flagrant night,
Yet ushered up the sun, as poets leaning
Upon a straw surmise the infinite.

You, first, who ground my lust to love upon
Your gritty humorous virginity,
Then yielding to its temper suddenly
Proved what a Danube can be struck from stone:
With you I ran the gauntlet for my prime,
Then living in the moment lived for all time.

Next the hawk-faced man, who could praise an apple
In terms of peach and win the argument. Quick
Was he to trip the shambling rhetoric

Of laws and lions: yet abstract turned the tables
And his mind, almost, with a whiff of air
Clothed first in a woman and after in a nightmare.

She next, sorrow's familiar, who turned
Her darkness to our light; that 'brazen leech'
Alleviating the vain cosmic itch
With fact coated in formulæ lest it be burned
Our tongue. She who released my struggling days
Shall live in me, not memory, for always.

Last the tow-haired poet, never done
With cutting and planing some new gnomic prop
To jack his all too stable universe up: –
Conduct's Old Dobbin, thought's chameleon.
Single mind copes with split intelligence,
Breeding a piebald strain of truth and nonsense.

These have I loved and chosen, once being sure
Some spacious vision waved upon their eyes
That troubles not the common register;
And love them still, knowing it otherwise.

Knowing they held no mastership in wisdom
Or wit save by certificate of my love,
I have found out a better way to praise them –
Nestor shall die and let Patroclus live.

So I declare it. These are they who built
My house and never a stone of it laid agley.
So cheat I memory that works in gilt
And stucco to restore a fallen day.

AS ONE WHO WANDERS INTO OLD WORKINGS

As one who wanders into old workings
Dazed by the noonday, desiring coolness,

Has found retreat barred by fall of rockface;
Gropes through galleries where granite bruises
Taut palm and panic patters close at heel;
Must move forward as tide to the moon's nod,
As mouth to breast in blindness is beckoned.
Nightmare nags at his elbow and narrows
Horizon to pinpoint, hope to hand's breadth.
Slow drip the seconds, time is stalactite,
For nothing intrudes here to tell the time,
Sun marches not, nor moon with muffled step.
He wants an opening, — only to break out,
To see the dark glass cut by day's diamond,
To relax again in the lap of light.

But we seek a new world through old workings,
Whose hope lies like seed in the loins of earth,
Whose dawn draws gold from the roots of darkness.
Not shy of light nor shrinking from shadow
Like Jesuits in jungle we journey
Deliberately bearing to brutish tribes
Christ's assurance, arts of agriculture.
As a train that travels underground track
Feels current flashed from far-off dynamos,
Our wheels whirling with impetus elsewhere
Generated we run, are ruled by rails.
Train shall spring from tunnel to terminus,
Out on to plain shall the pioneer plunge,
Earth reveal what veins fed, what hill covered.
Lovely the leap, explosion into light.

DO NOT EXPECT AGAIN
A PHOENIX HOUR

Do not expect again a phœnix hour,
The triple-towered sky, the dove complaining,
Sudden the rain of gold and heart's first ease
Tranced under trees by the eldritch light of sundown.

By a blazed trail our joy will be returning:
One burning hour throws light a thousand ways,
And hot blood stays into familiar gestures.
The best years wait, the body's plenitude.

Consider then, my lover, this is the end
Of the lark's ascending, the hawk's unearthly hover:
Spring seaon is over soon and first heatwave;
Grave-browed with cloud ponders the huge horizon.

Draw up the dew. Swell with pacific violence.
Take shape in silence. Grow as the clouds grew.
Beautiful brood the cornlands, and you are heavy;
Leafy the boughs – they also hide big fruit.

CONSIDER THESE, FOR WE
HAVE CONDEMNED THEM

Consider these, for we have condemned them;
Leaders to no sure land, guides their bearings lost
Or in league with robbers have reversed the signposts,
Disrespectful to ancestors, irresponsible to heirs.
Born barren, a freak growth, root in rubble,
Fruitlessly blossoming, whose foliage suffocates,
Their sap is sluggish, they reject the sun.

The man with his tongue in his cheek, the woman
With her heart in the wrong place, unhandsome,
        unwholesome;
Have exposed the new-born to worse than weather,
Exiled the honest and sacked the seer.
These drowned the farms to form a pleasure-lake,
In time of drought they drain the reservoir
Through private pipes for baths and sprinklers.

Getters not begetters; gainers not beginners;
Whiners, no winners; no triers, betrayers;
Who steer by no star, whose moon means nothing.

Daily denying, unable to dig:
At bay in villas from blood relations,
Counters of spoons and content with cushions
They pray for peace, they hand down disaster.

They that take the bribe shall perish by the bribe,
Dying of dry rot, ending in asylums,
A curse to children, a charge on the state.
But still their fears and frenzies infect us;
Drug nor isolation will cure this cancer:
It is now or never, the hour of the knife,
The break with the past, the major operation.

THE CONFLICT

I sang as one
Who on a tilting deck sings
To keep men's courage up, though the wave hangs
That shall cut off their sun.

As storm-cocks sing,
Flinging their natural answer in the wind's teeth,
And care not if it is waste of breath
Or birth-carol of spring.

As ocean-flyer clings
To height, to the last drop of spirit driving on
While yet ahead is land to be won
And work for wings.

Singing I was at peace,
Above the clouds, outside the ring:
For sorrow finds a swift release in song
And pride its poise.

Yet living here,
As one between two massing powers I live
Whom neutrality cannot save
Nor occupation cheer.

None such shall be left alive:
The innocent wing is soon shot down,
And private stars fade in the blood-red dawn
Where two worlds strive.

The red advance of life
Contracts pride, calls out the common blood,
Beats song into a single blade,
Makes a depth-charge of grief.

Move then with new desires,
For where we used to build and love
Is no man's land, and only ghosts can live
Between two fires.

Richard Eberhart / 1904–

FOR A LAMB

I saw on the slant hill a putrid lamb,
Propped with daisies. The sleep looked deep,
The face nudged in the green pillow
But the guts were out for crows to eat.

Where's the lamb? whose tender plaint
Said all for the mute breezes.
Say he's in the wind somewhere,
Say, there's a lamb in the daisies.

THE GROUNDHOG

In June, amid the golden fields,
I saw a groundhog lying dead.

Dead lay he; my senses shook,
And mind outshot our naked frailty.
There lowly in the vigorous summer
His form began its senseless change,
And made my senses waver dim
Seeing nature ferocious in him.
Inspecting close his maggots' might
And seething cauldron of his being,
Half with loathing, half with a strange love,
I poked him with an angry stick.
The fever arose, became a flame
And Vigour circumscribed the skies,
Immense energy in the sun,
And through my frame a sunless trembling.
My stick had done nor good nor harm.
Then stood I silent in the day
Watching the object, as before;
And kept my reverence for knowledge
Trying for control, to be still,
To quell the passion of the blood;
Until I had bent down on my knees
Praying for joy in the sight of decay.
And so I left; and I returned
In Autumn strict of eye, to see
The sap gone out of the groundhog,
But the bony sodden hulk remained.
But the year had lost its meaning,
And in intellectual chains
I lost both love and loathing,
Mured up in the wall of wisdom.
Another summer took the fields again
Massive and burning, full of life,
But when I chanced upon the spot
There was only a little hair left,
And bones bleaching in the sunlight
Beautiful as architecture;
I watched them like a geometer,
And cut a walking stick from a birch.
It has been three years, now.
There is no sign of the groundhog.
I stood there in the whirling summer,

My hand capped a withered heart,
And thought of China and of Greece,
Of Alexander in his tent;
Of Montaigne in his tower,
Of Saint Theresa in her wild lament.

'IN A HARD INTELLECTUAL LIGHT'

In a hard intellectual light
I will kill all delight,
And I will build a citadel
Too beautiful to tell

O too austere to tell
And far too beautiful to see,
Whose evident distance
I will call the best of me.

And this light of intellect
Will shine on all my desires,
It will my flesh protect
And flare my bold constant fires,

For the hard intellectual light
Will lay the flesh with nails.
And it will keep the world bright
And closed the body's soft jails.

And from this fair edifice
I shall see, as my eyes blaze,
The moral grandeur of man
Animating all his days.

And peace will marry purpose,
And purity married to grace
Will make the human absolute
As sweet as the human face.

Until my hard vision blears,
And Poverty and Death return
In organ music like the years,
Making the spirit leap, and burn

For the hard intellectual light
That kills all delight
And brings the solemn, inward pain
Of truth into the heart again.

RUMINATION

When I can hold a stone within my hand
And feel time make it sand and soil, and see
The roots of living things grow in this land,
Pushing between my fingers flower and tree,
Then I shall be as wise as death,
For death has done this and he will
Do this to me, and blow his breath
To fire my clay, when I am still.

'IF I COULD ONLY LIVE AT THE PITCH THAT IS NEAR MADNESS'

If I could only live at the pitch that is near madness
When everything is as it was in my childhood
Violent, vivid, and of infinite possibility:
That the sun and the moon broke over my head.

Then I cast time out of the trees and fields,
Then I stood immaculate in the Ego;
Then I eyed the world with all delight,
Reality was the perfection of my sight.

And time has big handles on the hands,
Fields and trees a way of being themselves.
I saw battalions of the race of mankind
Standing stolid, demanding a moral answer.

I gave the moral answer and I died
And into a realm of complexity came
Where nothing is possible but necessity
And the truth wailing there like a red babe.

ON SHOOTING PARTICLES

BEYOND THE WORLD

*"White Sands, N.M. Dec. 18 (UP). 'We first throw a little
something into the skies,' Zwicky said. 'Then a little more,
then a shipload of instruments—then ourselves'."*

On this day man's disgust is known
Incipient before but now full blown
With minor wars of major consequence,
Duly building empirical delusions.

Now this little creature in a rage
Like new-born infant screaming compleat angler
Objects to the whole globe itself
And with a vicious lunge he throws

Metal particles beyond the orbit of mankind.
Beethoven shaking his fist at death,
A giant dignity in human terms,
Is nothing to this imbecile metal fury.

The world is too much for him. The green
Of earth is not enough, love's deities,
Peaceful intercourse, happiness of nations,
The wild animal dazzled on the desert.

If the maniac would only realize
The comforts of his padded cell

He would have penetrated the
Impenetrability of the spiritual.

It is not intelligent to go too far.
How he frets that he can't go too!
But his particles would maim a star,
His free-floating bombards rock the moon.

Good Boy! We pat the baby to eructate,
We pat him then for eructation.
Good Boy Man! Your innards are put out,
From now all space will be your vomitorium.

The atom bomb accepted this world,
Its hatred of man blew death in his face.
But not content, he'll send slugs beyond,
His particles of intellect will spit on the sun.

Not God he'll catch, in the mystery of space.
He flaunts his own out-cast state
As he throws his imperfections outward bound,
And his shout that gives a hissing sound.

THE CANCER CELLS

Today I saw a picture of the cancer cells,
Sinister shapes with menacing attitudes.
They had outgrown their test-tube and advanced,
Sinister shapes with menacing attitudes,
Into a world beyond, a virulent laughing gang.
They looked like art itself, like the artist's mind,
Powerful shaker, and the taker of new forms.
Some are revulsed to see these spiky shapes;
It is the world of the future too come to.
Nothing could be more vivid than their language,
Lethal, sparkling and irregular stars,
The murderous design of the universe,
The hectic dance of the passionate cancer cells.
O just phenomena to the calculating eye,

Originals of imagination. I flew
With them in a piled exuberance of time,
My own malignance in their racy, beautiful gestures
Quick and lean: and in their riot too
I saw the stance of the artist's make,
The fixed form in the massive fluxion.

I think Leonardo would have in his disinterest
Enjoyed them precisely with a sharp pencil.

SEALS, TERNS, TIME

The seals at play off Western Isle
In the loose flowing of the summer tide
And burden of our strange estate—

Resting on the oar and lolling on the sea,
I saw their curious images,
Hypnotic, sympathetic eyes

As the deep elapses of the soul.
O ancient blood, O blurred kind forms
That rise and peer from elemental water:

I loll upon the oar, I think upon the day,
Drawn by strong, by the animal soft bonds
Back to a dim pre-history;

While off the point of Jagged Light
In hundreds, gracefully, the fork-tailed terns
Draw swift esprits across the sky.

Their aspirations dip in mine,
The quick order of their changing spirit,
More freedom than the eye can see.

Resting lightly on the oarlocks,
Pondering, and balanced on the sea,
A gauze and spindrift of the world,

I am in compulsion hid and thwarted,
Pulled back in the mammal water,
Enticed to the release of the sky.

THE HORSE CHESTNUT TREE

Boys in sporadic but tenacious droves
Come with sticks, as certainly as Autumn,
To assault the great horse chestnut tree.

There is a law governs their lawlessness.
Desire is in them for a shining amulet
And the best are those that are highest up.

They will not pick them easily from the ground.
With shrill arms they fling to the higher branches,
To hurry the work of nature for their pleasure.

I have seen them trooping down the street
Their pockets stuffed with chestnuts shucked, unshucked.
It is only evening keeps them from their wish.

Sometimes I run out in a kind of rage
To chase the boys away: I catch an arm,
Maybe, and laugh to think of being the lawgiver.

I was once such a young sprout myself
And fingered in my pocket the prize and trophy.
But still I moralize upon the day

And see that we, outlaws on God's property,
Fling out imagination beyond the skies,
Wishing a tangible good from the unknown.

And likewise death will drive us from the scene
With the great flowering world unbroken yet,
Which we held in idea, a little handful.

THE FURY OF AERIAL BOMBARDMENT

You would think the fury of aerial bombardment
Would rouse God to relent; the infinite spaces
Are still silent. He looks on shock-pried faces.
History, even, does not know what is meant.

You would feel that after so many centuries
God would give man to repent; yet he can kill
As Cain could, but with multitudinous will,
No farther advanced than in his ancient furies.

Was man made stupid to see his own stupidity?
Is God by definition indifferent, beyond us all?
Is the eternal truth man's fighting soul
Wherein the Beast ravens in its own avidity?

Of Van Wettering I speak, and Averill,
Names on a list, whose faces I do not recall
But they are gone to early death, who late in school
Distinguished the belt feed lever from the belt holding
        pawl.

NEW HAMPSHIRE, FEBRUARY

Nature had made them hide in crevices,
Two wasps so cold they looked like bark.
Why I do not know, but I took them
And I put them
In a metal pan, both day and dark.

Like God touching his finger to Adam
I felt, and thought of Michaelangelo,
For whenever I breathed on them,
The slightest breath,
They leaped, and preened as if to go.

My breath controlled them always quite.
More sensitive than electric sparks
They came into life
Or they withdrew to ice,
While I watched, suspending remarks.

Then one in a blind career got out,
And fell to the kitchen floor. I
Crushed him with my cold ski boot,
By accident. The other
Had not the wit to try or die.

And so the other is still my pet.
The moral of this is plain.
But I will shirk it.
You will not like it. And
God does not live to explain.

ON A SQUIRREL CROSSING
THE ROAD IN AUTUMN,
IN NEW ENGLAND

It is what he does not know,
Crossing the road under the elm trees,
About the mechanism of my car,
About the Commonwealth of Massachusetts,
About Mozart, India, Arcturus,

That wins my praise. I engage
At once in whirling squirrel-praise.

He obeys the orders of nature
Without knowing them.
It is what he does not know
That makes him beautiful.
Such a knot of little purposeful nature!

I who can see him as he cannot see himself
Repose in the ignorance that is his blessing.

It is what man does not know of God
Composes the visible poem of the world.

        . . . Just missed him!

MARRAKECH

The dance begins with the sun descending
Beyond the Koutubia in Marrakech so ancient
And so fable present: the old tell fables
As the Moroccans listen in eyed attention
In the marketplace of vitality and veiled women.
But the dancers, O the dancers, priests of devotion
From the high Atlas mountains, perhaps twelve,
A boy of ten, shining men under thirty,
Their feet bare and hard on the bare, hard earth,
Begin to dance to two taut goatskin drums,
Beaten with hard crooked sticks, thin in the diameter,
The one fiercely antiphonal to the other,
Together beating compelling rhythm to action,
Action in the flow of the loose, ancient garments
Of the men as they strike in both hands
Double metal castanets in the dry, high air of late day.
One would come forth, loosening his devotion,
Gyrating and flashing in compelling immediacy,
Total in ecstasy, overwhelming the senses,
And fall back, and another would step forth lightly,
Deftly begin his interpretive energy, total
Devotion to sound, rhythm, style of the dance,
And fall back, and his fellow come out before
To outdo the predecessor, turn and leap and gyrate
In ochre ambience, and the drums' insistence
Proclaiming efficient animal action,
The passion of primitive man exultant,
And each came forward, each leaped taller,
Flashed lower, turned subtler, rose higher
Prolonging intensity of animal strategy,
A rapture of magnitude pervaded the air,
Sound and sense reached to magical ability,

One drummer on his knees, the drum head vertical,
Beat out the passion of ancient centuries,
Appeared the thronging nature of tribal power,
And the laughing gods fell to the earth, spent,
And the high heart bent down with them to the earth,
And the heart was raised up to the Atlas mountains,
In the superabundant, delirious air of sundown,
And the laughing gods fell to the earth, spent,
And the heart bent down with them to the earth,
Cleansed in the nature of rhythm and rite,
The dance was a thing in itself triumphant,
Music and dance the perfection of the free,
And before one could think of the meaning
The driven passion of the drums begins again,
O ancient Africa, O tribal ecstasy!
A dance of six hundred years on the same spot,
They come out again instantaneous and eternal,
And leap and turn, passionately leap and fall,
And all are made whole again under the red sky
And all is made whole in the heart and time.

William Empson / 1906–

THE SCALES

The proper scale would pat you on the head
But Alice showed her pup Ulysses' bough
Well from behind a thistle, wise with dread;

And though your gulf-sprung mountains I allow
(Snow-puppy curves, rose-solemn dado band)
Charming for nurse, I am not nurse just now.

Why pat or stride them, when the train will land
Me high, through climbing tunnels, at your side,
And careful fingers meet through castle sand.

Claim slyly rather that the tunnels hide
Solomon's gems, white vistas, preserved kings,
By jackal sandhole to your air flung wide.

Say (she suspects) to sea Nile only brings
Delta and indecision, who instead
Far back up country does enormous things.

LEGAL FICTION

Law makes long spokes of the short stakes of men.
Your well fenced out real estate of mind
No high flat of the nomad citizen
Looks over, or train leaves behind.

Your rights extend under and above your claim
Without bound; you own land in Heaven and Hell;
Your part of earth's surface and mass the same,
Of all cosmos' volume, and all stars as well.

Your rights reach down where all owners meet, in Hell's
Pointed exclusive conclave, at earth's centre
(Your spun farm's root still on that axis dwells);
And up, through galaxies, a growing sector.

You are nomad yet; the lighthouse beam you own
Flashes, like Lucifer, through the firmament.
Earth's axis varies; your dark central cone
Wavers, a candle's shadow, at the end.

THIS LAST PAIN

This last pain for the damned the Fathers found:
"they knew the bliss with which they were not crowned."
    Such, but on earth, let me foretell,
    Is all, of heaven or of hell.

Man, as the prying housemaid of the soul,
May know her happiness by eye to hole:
    He's safe; the key is lost; he knows
    Door will not open, nor hole close.

"What is conceivable can happen too,"
Said Wittgenstein, who had not dreamt of you;
    But wisely; if we worked it long
    We should forget where it was wrong.

Those thorns are crowns which, woven into knots,
Crackle under and soon boil fool's pots;
    And no man's watching, wise and long,
    Would ever stare them into song.

Thorns burn to a consistent ash, like man;
A splendid cleanser for the frying-pan:
    And those who leap from pan to fire
    Should this brave opposite admire.

All those large dreams by which men long live well
Are magic-lanterned on the smoke of hell;
    This then is real, I have implied,
    A painted, small, transparent slide.

These the inventive can hand-paint at leisure,
Or most emporia would stock our measure;
    And feasting in their dappled shade
    We should forget how they were made.

Feign then what's by a decent tact believed
And act that state is only so conceived,
    And build an edifice of form
    For house where phantoms may keep warm.

Imagine, then, by miracle, with me,
(Ambiguous gifts, as what gods give must be)
    What could not possibly be there,
    And learn a style from a despair.

HOMAGE TO THE BRITISH MUSEUM

There is a Supreme God in the ethnological section;
A hollow toad shape, faced with a blank shield.
He needs his belly to include the Pantheon,
Which is inserted through a hole behind.
At the navel, at the points formally stressed, at the organs
    of sense,
Lice glue themselves, dolls, local deities,
His smooth wood creeps with all the creeds of the world.

Attending there let us absorb the cultures of nations
And dissolve into our judgement all their codes.
Then, being clogged with a natural hesitation
(People are continually asking one the way out),
Let us stand here and admit that we have no road.
Being everything, let us admit that is to be something,
Or give ourselves the benefit of the doubt;
Let us offer our pinch of dust all to this God,
And grant his reign over the entire building.

IGNORANCE OF DEATH

Then there is this civilising love of death, by which
Even music and painting tell you what else to love.
Buddhists and Christians contrive to agree about death

Making death their ideal basis for different ideals.
The Communists however disapprove of death
Except when practical. The people who dig up

Corpses and rape them are I understand not reported.
The Freudians regard the death-wish as fundamental,
Though "the clamour of life" proceeds from its rival
    "Eros."

Whether you are to admire a given case for making less
    clamour
Is not their story. Liberal hopefulness
Regards death as a mere border to an improving picture.

Because we have neither hereditary nor direct knowledge
    of death
It is the trigger of the literary man's biggest gun
And we are happy to equate it to any conceived calm.

Heaven me, when a man is ready to die about something
Other than himself, and is in fact ready because of that,
Not because of himself, that is something clear about
    himself.

Otherwise I feel very blank upon this topic,
And think that though important, and proper for anyone
    to bring up,
It is one that most people should be prepared to be blank
    upon.

MISSING DATES

Slowly the poison the whole blood stream fills.
It is not the effort nor the failure tires.
The waste remains, the waste remains and kills.

It is not your system or clear sight that mills
Down small to the consequence a life requires;
Slowly the poison the whole blood stream fills.

They bled an old dog dry yet the exchange rills
Of young dog blood gave but a month's desires
The waste remains, the waste remains and kills.

It is the Chinese tombs and the slag hills
Usurp the soil, and not the soil retires.
Slowly the poison the whole blood stream fills.

Not to have fire is to be a skin that shrills.
The complete fire is death. From partial fires
The waste remains, the waste remains and kills.

It is the poems you have lost, the ills
From missing dates, at which the heart expires.
Slowly the poison the whole blood stream fills.
The waste remains, the waste remains and kills.

JUST A SMACK AT AUDEN

Waiting for the end, boys, waiting for the end.
What is there to be or do?
What's become of me or you?
Are we kind or are we true?
Sitting two and two, boys, waiting for the end.

Shall I build a tower, boys, knowing it will rend
Crack upon the hour, boys, waiting for the end?
Shall I pluck a flower, boys, shall I save or spend?
All turns sour, boys, waiting for the end.

Shall I send a wire, boys? Where is there to send?
All are under fire, boys, waiting for the end.
Shall I turn a sire, boys? Shall I choose a friend?
The fat is in the pyre, boys, waiting for the end.

Shall I make it clear, boys, for all to apprehend,
Those that will not hear, boys, waiting for the end,
Knowing it is near, boys, trying to pretend,
Sitting in cold fear, boys, waiting for the end?

Shall we send a cable, boys, accurately penned,
Knowing we are able, boys, waiting for the end,
Via the Tower of Babel, boys? Christ will not ascend.
He's hiding in his stable, boys, waiting for the end.

Shall we blow a bubble, boys, glittering to distend,
Hiding from our trouble, boys, waiting for the end?

When you build on rubble, boys, Nature will append
Double and re-double, boys, waiting for the end.

Shall we make a tale, boys, that things are sure to mend,
Playing bluff and hale, boys, waiting for the end?
It will be born stale, boys, stinking to offend,
Dying ere it fail, boys, waiting for the end.

Shall we go all wild, boys, waste and make them lend,
Playing at the child, boys, waiting for the end?
It has all been filed, boys, history has a trend,
Each of us enisled, boys, waiting for the end.

What was said by Marx, boys, what did he perpend?
No good being sparks, boys, waiting for the end.
Treason of the clerks, boys, curtains that descend,
Lights becoming darks, boys, waiting for the end.

Waiting for the end, boys, waiting for the end.
Not a chance of blend, boys, things have got to tend.
Think of those who vend, boys, think of how we wend,
Waiting for the end, boys, waiting for the end.

SONNET

Not wrongly moved by this dismaying scene
   The thinkers like the nations getting caught
   Joined in the organising that they fought
To scorch all earth of all but one machine.

It can be swung, is what these hopers mean,
   For all the loony hooters can be bought
   On the small ball. It can then all be taught
And reconverted to be kind and clean.

A more heartening fact about the cultures of man
   Is their appalling stubbornness. The sea
Is always calm ten fathoms down. The gigan-

tic anthropological circus riotously
Holds open all its booths. The pygmy plan
  Is one note each and the tune goes out free.

Vernon Watkins / 1906–

THE DEAD WORDS

So flies love's meteor to her shroud of winds.
The crisp words couch in their last battling-place
Where widowed silence, threaded like black lace,
Held a dumb minute, stabs the dark like pins.
It is so breathless. There the flower begins
To seed, we know not how. There blows the race
Of spirits, and they watch the stiff leaves brace
With last look backward to the town of sins.
There clenches the close fist through wreath and wraith
The sooted page where wrought like golden wire
The sly words glitter with an angel's breath;
Love's moistening seal is mastered there entire,
And the wind proves, where they are dressed for death,
Cinders are priestlike in their tale of fire.

DISCOVERIES

The poles are flying where the two eyes set:
America has not found Columbus yet.

Ptolemy's planets, playing fast and loose,
Foretell the wisdom of Copernicus.

Dante calls Primum Mobile, the First Cause:
'Love that moves the world and the other stars.'

Great Galileo, twisted by the rack,
Groans the bright sun from heaven, then breathes it back.

Blake, on the world alighting, holds the skies,
And all the stars shine down through human eyes.

Donne sees those stars, yet will not let them lie:
'We're tapers, too, and at our own cost die.'

The shroud-lamp catches. Lips are smiling there.
'Les flammes—déjà?'—The world dies, or Voltaire.

Swift, a cold mourner at his burial-rite,
Burns to the world's heart like a meteorite.

Beethoven deaf, in deafness hearing all,
Unwinds all music from sound's funeral.

Three prophets fall, the litter of one night:
Blind Milton gazes in fixed deeps of light.

Beggar of those Minute Particulars,
Yeats lights again the turmoil of the stars.

Motionless motion! Come, Tiresias,
The eternal flies, what's passing cannot pass.

'Solace in flight,' old Heraclitus cries;
Light changing to Von Hügel's butterflies.

Rilke bears all, thinks like a tree, believes,
Sinks in the hand that bears the falling leaves.

The stars! The signs! Great Angelo hurls them back.
His whirling ceiling draws the zodiac.

The pulse of Keats testing the axiom;
The second music when the sound is dumb.

The Christian Paradox, bringing its great reward
By loss; the moment known to Kierkegaard.

THE SONG OF THE
GOOD SAMARITAN

I sing of the Good Samaritan, of
Pity and the Fixed Stars. Him the Awakeners bless
Who heal the Earth with silent tumult of love.

There came the configuration of ages, less
Than his moment of deepest shadow. I sing of his
Leap into God, of the trial of gentleness.

Night. Death. And forever the distances
Woven by the pulse, that infinite loom of heaven;
Then out of the water a kiss, a leper's kiss,

Given through the dark. Look up! The moment is given
To the dog derided and scorned; and a look outpaces
The beautiful horses mythology thought to have driven.

Look. Look up! Frozen light! The Gorgon grimaces
Of the stone-blind heaven freeze blood in the marvelling
    child
Standing alone on the bed near the strange toy-faces.

Constellations! Look! The Fixed Stars! Blind meteors
    whirled!
Night's pattern, the clustered myths! On the Milky Road
Towards milk-white Jericho stumbles one from the world

Leading a mule, borne down with its dusty load,
To the shade of a tree, to a trough. The mythologies shrink,
And the nameless image is healed of its murderous goad.

Font of the fingers, water where asses drink,
Winged horses above you scattering, manes of the Norn,
And heroic Pegasus, leap into light from the brink.

Swallows quiver, rounding the magical horn
Of fullness, emptied for John's wild honey. They break
Light with their wings, and the era of love is born.

He broke the classical falsehood, summoned awake
A world from dust with the secret worlds of his tears.
Shut in those heavens he heard the mythologies shake.

Their violent haunches taut, their delicate ears
Coiled to a point, a horn growing out of each head,
They know they are crystal, their breath the smoke of the
        spheres.

Centaurs, unicorns, wondering, weaving a thread
From the loom of silence, coiling all ages at once
To a hero's masterful, measured, arrogant tread.

And music sprung from the rock, from the pagan dance
Of firelit bodies, heard in the cataract's head;
A prince of warriors, Venus guiding his lance.

Those heroes gather the spaces through which they have
        sped
To ivory silence or toil of intractable bronze,
Resurrecting the ravisher's cup, the wine of the dead.

Yet the buried see them as the unforgiving, spun
From cruelty's frenzy back through a minotaur maze,
A battle of Centaurs fled into the blaze of suns;

Fled, fled, in a furious pattern of praise
From the throat of light, a thunder of galloping feet
Riding the rim that acclaims their arrogant days.

What vision startled a prophet in that hard heat
Of the wayside's ultimate shadow? He bent to hear
The spheres from a donkey suffer their proud retreat.

Then, as he looked on those features, sphere upon sphere
Shone round the loom of the hand. No name had this
That buried and raised all time in the spring of a tear.

And he heard through heaven the retreating distances,
Timbrels, the long gold trumpet, the Pharaoh's car,
Heroic song, gold idols, the pagan dances.

Even as a child I began to say: How far?
Parting the curtain, the winding-sheet of the dead.
The loom of the hand has the pathway of every star.

Disappearance of the proud horses! Circling in dread,
Stampeding in light, he heard the mythologies shrink,
The rushing stars, their reverberant, thundering tread;

From a little worn-away trough where asses drink,
One by one, and above them, finding the sea,
Swallows pass, and their world ripples over the brink.

'O moment,' he breathed, 'frail as the branch of a tree,
This act is secret, eluding all fabulous joys.
The wound I suffer, the joy I am bearing, is he.

For they were movement itself, but mine was a choice
Between those visions acclaimed by pride overthrown,
And the downcast, intimate eyes, the source of the voice.

Dip, swallows. The Centaurs already are stone,
And the water listens, finding continually crooked
The path the asses have paced, the thread you have flown.

Now, if I speak, my words can belong to no book
For my fingers mingle the language of water and dove,
Ending, here at the source, the journey they took.

Out of the dust I raised this image of love.
Moment of darkness, moment, still you are mine,
Though the proud-winged, galloping horses disdainfully
            move

From the wounded god, the arena of dust and sand.

And only the tilted loom is lucky, divine,
Where the mocked, unpremeditated bowl of the hand
Makes the world nothing, pouring in oil and wine.'

MUSIC OF COLOURS—
WHITE BLOSSOM...

White blossom, white, white shell; the Nazarene
Walking in the ear; white touched by souls
Who know the music by which white is seen,
Blinding white, from strings and aureoles,
Until that is not white, seen at the two poles,
Nor white the Scythian hills, nor Marlowe's queen.

The spray looked white until this snowfall.
Now the foam is grey, the wave is dull.
Call nothing white again, we were deceived.
The flood of Noah dies, the rainbow is lived.
Yet from the deluge of illusions an unknown colour is saved.

White must die black, to be born white again
From the womb of sounds, the inscrutable grain,
From the crushed, dark fibre, breaking in pain.

The bud of the apple is already forming there.
The cherry-bud, too, is firm, and behind it the pear
Conspires with the racing cloud. I shall not look.
The rainbow is diving through the wide-open book
Past the rustling paper of birch, the sorceries of bark.

Buds in April, on the waiting branch,
Starrily opening, light raindrops drench,
Swinging from world to world when starlings sweep,
Where they alight in air, are white asleep.
They will not break, not break, until you say
White is not white again, nor may may.

White flowers die soonest, die into that chaste
Bride-bed of the moon, their lives laid waste.
Lilies of Solomon, taken by the gust,
Sigh, make way. And the dark forest
Haunts the lowly crib near Solomon's dust,
Rocked to the end of majesty, warmed by the low beast,
Locked in the liberty of his tremendous rest.

If there is white, or has been white, it must have been
When His eyes looked down and made the leper clean.
White will not be, apart, though the trees try
Spirals of blossom, their green conspiracy.
She who touched His garment saw no white tree.

Lovers speak of Venus, and the white doves,
Jubilant, the white girl, myth's whiteness, Jove's,
Of Leda, the swan, whitest of his loves.
Lust imagines him, web-footed Jupiter, great down
Of thundering light; love's yearning pulls him down
On the white swan-breast, the magical lawn,
Involved in plumage, mastered by the veins of dawn.

In the churchyard the yew is neither green nor black.
I know nothing of Earth or colour until I know I lack
Original white, by which the ravishing bird looks wan.
The mound of dust is nearer, white of mute dust that dies
In the soundfall's great light, the music in the eyes,
Transfiguring whiteness into shadows gone,
Utterly secret. I know you, black swan.

THE FIRE IN THE SNOW

White lambs leap. Through miles of snow
Across the muffled fields you go,
Frost-furled and gazing deep,
Lost in a world where white lambs leap.

Into a million eyes of light
You look, beneath that mask of white
Where lambs, wrinkled, without sound,
Bound in the air and print the ground.

You find through crystals white and wet
The buried breath of the violet,
And lost near sunken cairns of stone
Drone-suckled flowers that breed alone.

Your shadow, black on the white snow-field,
Covers the blades your mind revealed.
You linger where grey rocks are still
Covered by a drifted hill.

Your eyes, I know, now read the tract
Beneath snow, where the grain lies packed,
Nor can the Winter sun deceive:
Black shuttles give you their leaves to weave.

Crisp, where you touch the secret loom,
Snow, from the fire-blue sky and from
A black root where all leaves begin,
Flames with a white light on your skin.

Come in. The brilliant, beautiful
Sun has dropped, and the noon-cracked pool
Freezes back. Come, seek from night
Gloom's fire, where the unlit room is white.

I wait, intent, by the firelit stones
Strewn with chopped wood and fallen cones.
Come in, and watch with me in dark
The red spark eating the black bark.

Bright, from fields where the snow lies thick,
From sunk fields to the latch's click
You come; and your eyes, most watchful, glow,
Seeing in the firelight the brightness of snow.

Louis MacNeice / 1907–1963

TURF-STACKS

Among these turf-stacks graze no iron horses
Such as stalk, such as champ in towns and the soul of
        crowds,

Here is no mass-production of neat thoughts
No canvas shrouds for the mind nor any black hearses:
The peasant shambles on his boots like hooves
Without thinking at all or wanting to run in grooves.

But those who lack the peasant's conspirators,
The tawny mountain, the unregarded buttress,
Will feel the need of a fortress against ideas and against the
Shuddering insidious shock of the theory-vendors,
The little sardine men crammed in a monster toy
Who tilt their aggregate beast against our crumbling Troy.

For we are obsolete who like the lesser things
Who play in corners with looking-glasses and beads;
It is better we should go quickly, go into Asia
Or any other tunnel where the world recedes,
Or turn blind wantons like the gulls who scream
And rip the edge off any ideal or dream.

AUGUST

The shutter of time darkening ceaselessly
Has whisked away the foam of may and elder
And I realise how now, as every year before,
Once again the gay months have eluded me.

For the mind, by nature stagey, welds its frame
Tomb-like around each little world of a day;
We jump from picture to picture and cannot follow
The living curve that is breathlessly the same.

While the lawn-mower sings moving up and down
Spirting its little fountain of vivid green,
I, like Poussin, make a still-bound fête of us
Suspending every noise, of insect or machine.

Garlands at a set angle that do not slip,
Theatrically (and as if for ever) grace

You and me and the stone god in the garden
And Time who also is shown with a stone face.

But all this is a dilettante's lie,
Time's face is not stone nor still his wings;
Our mind, being dead, wishes to have time die
For we, being ghosts, cannot catch hold of things.

PERSEUS

Borrowed wings on his ankles,
Carrying a stone death,
The hero entered the hall,
All in the hall looked up,
Their breath frozen on them,
And there was no more shuffle or clatter in the hall at all.

So a friend of a man comes in
And leaves a book he is lending or flowers
And goes again, alive but as good as dead,
And you are left alive, no better than dead,
And you dare not turn the leaden pages of the book or
    touch the flowers, the hooded and arrested hours.

Close your eyes,
There are suns beneath your lids,
Or look in the looking-glass in the end room—
You will find it full of eyes,
The ancient smiles of men cut out with scissors and kept in
    mirrors.

Ever to meet me comes, in sun or dull,
The gay hero swinging the Gorgon's head
And I am left, with the dull drumming of the sun, suspended
    and dead,
Or the dumb grey-brown of the day is a leper's cloth,
And one feels the earth going round and round the globe of
    the blackening mantle, a mad moth.

SNOW

The room was suddenly rich and the great bay-window was
Spawning snow and pink roses against it
Soundlessly collateral and incompatible:
World is suddener than we fancy it.

World is crazier and more of it than we think,
Incorrigibly plural. I peel and portion
A tangerine and spit the pips and feel
The drunkenness of things being various.

And the fire flames with a bubbling sound for world
Is more spiteful and gay than one supposes—
On the tongue on the eyes on the ears in the palms of one's
   hands—
There is more than glass between the snow and the huge roses.

BAGPIPE MUSIC

It's no go the merrygoround, it's no go the rickshaw,
All we want is a limousine and a ticket for the peepshow.
Their knickers are made of crêpe-de-chine, their shoes
   are made of python,
Their halls are lined with tiger rugs and their walls with
   heads of bison.

John MacDonald found a corpse, put it under the sofa,
Waited till it came to life and hit it with a poker,
Sold its eyes for souvenirs, sold its blood for whisky,
Kept its bones for dumb-bells to use when he was fifty.

It's no go the Yogi-Man, it's no go Blavatsky,
All we want is a bank balance and a bit of skirt in a taxi.

Annie MacDougall went to milk, caught her foot in the
   heather,

Woke to hear a dance record playing of Old Vienna.
It's no go your maidenheads, it's no go your culture,
All we want is a Dunlop tyre and the devil mend the
          puncture.

The Laird o' Phelps spent Hogmanay declaring he was
          sober,
Counted his feet to prove the fact and found he had one
          foot over.
Mrs. Carmichael had her fifth, looked at the job with
          repulsion,
Said to the midwife 'Take it away; I'm through with
          over-production'.

It's no go the gossip column, it's no go the ceilidh,
All we want is a mother's help and a sugar-stick for the
          baby.

Willie Murray cut his thumb, couldn't count the damage,
Took the hide of an Ayrshire cow and used it for a
          bandage.
His brother caught three hundred cran when the seas
          were lavish,
Threw the bleeders back in the sea and went upon the
          parish.

It's no go the Herring Board, it's no go the Bible,
All we want is a packet of fags when our hands are idle.

It's no go the picture palace, it's no go the stadium,
It's no go the country cot with a pot of pink geraniums,
It's no go the Government grants, it's no go the elections,
Sit on your arse for fifty years and hang your hat on a
          pension.

It's no go my honey love, it's no go my poppet;
Work your hands from day to day, the winds will blow the
          profit.
The glass is falling hour by hour, the glass will fall for ever,
But if you break the bloody glass you won't hold up the
          weather.

THE BRITISH MUSEUM
READING ROOM

Under the hive-like dome the stooping haunted readers
Go up and down the alleys, tap the cells of knowledge—
   Honey and wax, the accumulation of years—
Some on commission, some for the love of learning,
Some because they have nothing better to do
Or because they hope these walls of books will deaden
   The drumming of the demon in their ears.

Cranks, hacks, poverty-stricken scholars,
In pince-nez, period hats or romantic beards
   And cherishing their hobby or their doom
Some are too much alive and some are asleep
Hanging like bats in a world of inverted values,
Folded up in themselves in a world which is safe and silent:
   This is the British Museum Reading Room.

Out on the steps in the sun the pigeons are courting,
Puffing their ruffs and sweeping their tails or taking
   A sun-bath at their ease
And under the totem poles—the ancient terror—
Between the enormous fluted Ionic columns
There seeps from heavily jowled or hawk-like foreign faces
   The guttural sorrow of the refugees.

JEHU

Peace on New England, on the shingled white houses, on
   golden
Rod and the red Turkey carpet spikes of sumach. The little
American flags are flapping in the graveyard. Continuous
   Chorus of grasshoppers. Fleece
Of quiet around the mind. Honey-suckle, phlox and
   smoke-bush,

Hollyhocks and nasturtium and corn on the cob. And the
  pine wood
  Smelling of outmoded peace.

A king sat over the gate looking to the desert. A spiral
Of dust came toward him, a special messenger asking
Anxiously 'Is it peace?' The heavy eyebrows lowered,
  He answered 'What have I
To do with peace?' and the messenger mopped the sweat
  and obedient
Took his place behind the king who still sat scanning
  Miles of desert and sky.

Negative prospect; sand in the lungs; blood in the sand;
  deceiving
Mirage of what were once ideals or even motives
And in this desert even a ghost can hardly
  Live—but in the long run what
Have I to do with life? He got up blandly, harnessed his
  horses
And furiously drove, his eyeballs burning and the chariot's
  Axles burning hot.

Someone sat in a window with a new coiffure, her raddled
Face, a Muse's possibly once but now a harlot's,
Smirked at the charioteer who, looking past her, signalled
  To the maids to throw her down
And they threw her down and the wheels went over her
  ribs and the carcase,
The one-time inspiration of artists, the toast of kings, was
  abandoned
  To the scavenger dogs of the town.

And now the sand blows over Kent and Wales where we
  may shortly
Learn the secret of the desert's purge, of the mad driving,
The cautery of the gangrened soul, though we are not
  certain
  Whether we shall stand beside
The charioteer, the surgeon, or shall be one with the
  pampered
Queen who tittered in the face of death, unable to imagine
  The meaning of the flood tide.

ALCOHOL

On golden seas of drink, so the Greek poet said,
Rich and poor are alike. Looking around in war
We watch the many who have returned to the dead
Ordering time-and-again the same-as-before:

Those Haves who cannot bear making a choice,
Those Have-nots who are bored with having nothing to
      choose,
Call for their drinks in the same tone of voice,
Find a factitious popular front in booze.

Another drink: Bacchylides was right
And self-deception golden—Serve him quick,
The siphon stutters in the archaic night,
The flesh is willing and the soul is sick.

Another drink: Adam is back in the Garden.
Another drink: the snake is back on the tree.
Let your brain go soft, your arteries will harden;
If God's a peeping tom he'll see what he shall see.

Another drink: Cain has slain his brother.
Another drink: Cain, they say, is cursed.
Another and another and another—
The beautiful ideologies have burst.

A bottle swings on a string. The matt-grey iron ship,
Which ought to have been the Future, sidles by
And with due auspices descends the slip
Into an ocean where no auspices apply.

Take away your slogans; give us something to swallow,
Give us beer or brandy or schnapps or gin;
This is the only road for the self-betrayed to follow—
The last way out that leads not out but in.

THE KINGDOM

I

Under the surface of flux and of fear there is an
      underground movement,
Under the crust of bureaucracy, quiet behind the posters,
Unconscious but palpably there—the Kingdom of
      individuals.

   And of these is the Kingdom—
Equal in difference, interchangeably sovereign—
The incorruptible souls who work without a commission,
The pairs of hands that are peers of hearts, the eyes that
      marry with eyes,
The candid scholar, the unselfish priest, the uncomplaining
      mothers of many,
The active men who are kind, the contemplative who give,
The happy-go-lucky saint and the peace-loving buccaneer.

These, as being themselves, are apart from not each other
But from such as being false are merely other,
So these are apart as parts within a pattern
Not merged nor yet excluded, members of a Kingdom
Which has no king except each subject, therefore
Apart from slaves and tyrants and from every
Community of mere convenience; these are
Apart from those who drift and those who force,
Apart from partisan order and egotistical anarchy,
Apart from the easy religion of him who would find in God
A boss, a ponce, an alibi, and apart from
The logic of him who arrogates to himself
The secret of the universe, the whole
Choreography of atoms; these are humble
And proud at once, working within their limits
And yet transcending them. These are the people
Who vindicate the species. And they are many. For go,
Go wherever you choose, among tidy villas or terrible
Docks, dumps and pitheads, or through the spangled
      moors
Or along the vibrant narrow intestines of great ships

Or into those countries of which we know very little—
Everywhere you will discover the men of the Kingdom
Loyal by intuition, born to attack, and innocent.

II

Take this old man with the soldierly straight back
Dressed in tweeds like a squire but he has not a squire's
    presumption,
His hands are gentle with wild flowers, his memory
Latticed with dialect and anecdotes
And wisps of nature poetry; he is of the Kingdom,
A country-lover and very English, the cadence
Of Christmas bells in his voice, his face like Cotswold stone
Severe but warm, a sureness in his walk
And his blood attuned to the seasons—whether it is the
    glyptic
Winter turning feathered twigs to stone
And making the Old Bill pollards monuments
Beside the dyke of Lethe—or if it is the frantic
Calf-love and early oratory of spring—
Or peony-time with the midges dancing—or later, sweeter,
That two-in-one of clarity and mist,
Of maidenlight and ripeness, which is autumn:
Every case is new and yet he knows the answers
For he is of the Kingdom. Through the serene and chequer
Fields that he knows he walks like a fallen angel
Whose fall has made him a man. Ladders of cirrhus cloud
Lead down as well as up, the ricochet of rain
Makes the clay smell sweet and snow in sunlight
Affirms the tussocks under it. Such changes—
The hedgerow stippled with hips or lathered with elder—
To him are his own rhythm like his breathing
And intimate as dreams. Hirsute or fluted earth,
Squares of plough and stubble, oatcake and corduroy,
Russet and emerald, and the shot-silk evening
And all the folk-song stars—these are his palette
And it is he who blends them with the brush-strokes
Of long experience and sudden insight,
Being mature and yet naïve, a lover
Of what is not himself—but it becomes himself
And he repays it interest, so has had

A happy life and will die happy; more—
Belongs, though he never knew it, to the Kingdom.

W. H. Auden / 1907–

from FIVE SONGS

v

'O where are you going?' said reader to rider,
'That valley is fatal when furnaces burn,
Yonder's the midden whose odours will madden,
That gap is the grave where the tall return.'

'O do you imagine,' said fearer to farer,
'That dusk will delay on your path to the pass,
Your diligent looking discover the lacking
Your footsteps feel from granite to grass?'

'O what was that bird,' said horror to hearer,
'Did you see that shape in the twisted trees?
Behind you swiftly the figure comes softly,
The spot on your skin is a shocking disease.'

'Out of this house'—said rider to reader,
'Yours never will'—said farer to fearer,
'They're looking for you'—said hearer to horror,
As he left them there, as he left them there.

AS I WALKED OUT ONE EVENING

As I walked out one evening,
    Walking down Bristol Street,

The crowds upon the pavement
    Were fields of harvest wheat.

And down by the brimming river
    I heard a lover sing
Under an arch of the railway:
    'Love has no ending.

'I'll love you, dear, I'll love you
    Till China and Africa meet,
And the river jumps over the mountain
    And the salmon sing in the street,

'I'll love you till the ocean
    Is folded and hung up to dry
And the seven stars go squawking
    Like geese about the sky.

The years shall run like rabbits,
    For in my arms I hold
The Flower of the Ages,
    And the first love of the world.'

But all the clocks in the city
    Began to whirr and chime:
'O let not Time deceive you,
    You cannot conquer Time.

'In the burrows of the Nightmare
    Where Justice naked is,
Time watches from the shadow
    And coughs when you would kiss.

'In headaches and in worry
    Vaguely life leaks away,
And Time will have his fancy
    To-morrow or to-day.

'Into many a green valley
    Drifts the appalling snow;
Time breaks the threaded dances
    And the diver's brilliant bow.

'O plunge your hands in water,
    Plunge them in up to the wrist;
Stare, stare in the basin
    And wonder what you've missed.

'The glacier knocks in the cupboard,
    The desert sighs in the bed,
And the crack in the tea-cup opens
    A lane to the land of the dead.

'Where the beggars raffle the banknotes
    And the Giant is enchanting to Jack,
And the Lily-white Boy is a Roarer,
    And Jill goes down on her back.

'O look, look in the mirror,
    O look in your distress;
Life remains a blessing
    Although you cannot bless.

'O stand, stand at the window
    As the tears scald and start;
You shall love your crooked neighbour
    With your crooked heart.'

It was late, late in the evening,
    The lovers they were gone;
The clocks had ceased their chiming,
    And the deep river ran on.

MUSÉE DES BEAUX ARTS

About suffering they were never wrong,
The Old Masters: how well they understood
Its human position; how it takes place
While someone else is eating or opening a window or just
        walking dully along;
How, when the aged are reverently, passionately waiting
For the miraculous birth, there always must be

Children who did not specially want it to happen, skating
On a pond at the edge of the wood:
They never forgot
That even the dreadful martyrdom must run its course
Anyhow in a corner, some untidy spot
Where the dogs go on with their doggy life and the
    torturer's horse
Scratches its innocent behind on a tree.

In Brueghel's *Icarus*, for instance: how everything turns
    away
Quite leisurely from the disaster; the ploughman may
Have heard the splash, the forsaken cry,
But for him it was not an important failure; the sun shone
As it had to on the white legs disappearing into the green
Water; and the expensive delicate ship that must have seen
Something amazing, a boy falling out of the sky,
Had somewhere to get to and sailed calmly on.

IN MEMORY OF W. B. YEATS

d. Jan. 1939

I

He disappeared in the dead of winter:
The brooks were frozen, the airports almost deserted,
And snow disfigured the public statues;
The mercury sank in the mouth of the dying day.
What instruments we have agree
The day of his death was a dark cold day.

Far from his illness
The wolves ran on through the evergreen forests,
The peasant river was untempted by the fashionable quays;
By mourning tongues
The death of the poet was kept from his poems.

But for him it was his last afternoon as himself,
An afternoon of nurses and rumours;
The provinces of his body revolted,

The squares of his mind were empty,
Silence invaded the suburbs,
The current of his feeling failed; he became his admirers.

Now he is scattered among a hundred cities
And wholly given over to unfamiliar affections,
To find his happiness in another kind of wood
And be punished under a foreign code of conscience.
The words of a dead man
Are modified in the guts of the living.

But in the importance and noise of to-morrow
When the brokers are roaring like beasts on the floor of the
        Bourse,
And the poor have the sufferings to which they are fairly
        accustomed,
And each in the cell of himself is almost convinced of his
        freedom,
A few thousand will think of this day
As one thinks of a day when one did something slightly
        unusual.
What instruments we have agree
The day of his death was a dark cold day.

II

You were silly like us; your gift survived it all:
The parish of rich women, physical decay,
Yourself. Mad Ireland hurt you into poetry.
Now Ireland has her madness and her weather still,
For poetry makes nothing happen: it survives
In the valley of its making where executives
Would never want to tamper, flows on south
From ranches of isolation and the busy griefs,
Raw towns that we believe and die in; it survives,
A way of happening, a mouth.

III

Earth, receive an honoured guest:
William Yeats is laid to rest.
Let the Irish vessel lie
Emptied of its poetry.

In the nightmare of the dark
All the dogs of Europe bark,
And the living nations wait,
Each sequestered in its hate;

Intellectual disgrace
Stares from every human face,
And the seas of pity lie
Locked and frozen in each eye.

Follow, poet, follow right
To the bottom of the night,
With your unconstraining voice
Still persuade us to rejoice;

With the farming of a verse
Make a vineyard of the curse,
Sing of human unsuccess
In a rapture of distress;

In the deserts of the heart
Let the healing fountain start,
In the prison of his days
Teach the free man how to praise.

VOLTAIRE AT FERNEY

Almost happy now, he looked at his estate.
An exile making watches glanced up as he passed,
And went on working; where a hospital was rising fast
A joiner touched his cap; an agent came to tell
Some of the trees he'd planted were progressing well.
The white alps glittered. It was summer. He was very great.

Far off in Paris, where his enemies
Whispered that he was wicked, in an upright chair
A blind old woman longed for death and letters. He would
      write

'Nothing is better than life'. But was it? Yes, the fight
Against the false and the unfair
Was always worth it. So was gardening. Civilize.

Cajoling, scolding, scheming, cleverest of them all,
He'd led the other children in a holy war
Against the infamous grown-ups, and, like a child, been sly
And humble when there was occasion for
The two-faced answer or the plain protective lie,
But, patient like a peasant, waited for their fall.

And never doubted, like D'Alembert, he would win:
Only Pascal was a great enemy, the rest
Were rats already poisoned; there was much, though, to be
    done,
And only himself to count upon.
Dear Diderot was dull but did his best;
Rousseau, he'd always known, would blubber and give in.

So, like a sentinel, he could not sleep. The night was full of
    wrong,
Earthquakes and executions. Soon he would be dead,
And still all over Europe stood the horrible nurses
Itching to boil their children. Only his verses
Perhaps could stop them: He must go on working.
    Overhead
The uncomplaining stars composed their lucid song.

THE UNKNOWN CITIZEN

To JS/07/M/378
This Marble Monument
Is Erected by the State

He was found by the Bureau of Statistics to be
One against whom there was no official complaint,
And all the reports on his conduct agree
That, in the modern sense of an old-fashioned word, he
    was a saint,

For in everything he did he served the Greater Community.
Except for the War till the day he retired
He worked in a factory and never got fired,
But satisfied his employers, Fudge Motors Inc.
Yet he wasn't a scab or odd in his views,
For his Union reports that he paid his dues,
(Our report on his Union shows it was sound)
And our Social Psychology workers found
That he was popular with his mates and liked a drink.
The Press are convinced that he bought a paper every day
And that his reactions to advertisements were normal in
      every way.
Policies taken out in his name prove that he was fully
      insured,
And his Health-card shows he was once in hospital but
      left it cured.
Both Producers Research and High-Grade Living declare
He was fully sensible to the advantages of the Instalment
      Plan
And had everything necessary to the Modern Man,
A phonograph, a radio, a car and a frigidaire.
Our researchers into Public Opinion are content
That he held the proper opinions for the time of year;
When there was peace, he was for peace; when there was
      war, he went.
He was married and added five children to the population,
Which our Eugenist says was the right number for a parent
      of his generation,
And our teachers report that he never interfered with their
      education.
Was he free? Was he happy? The question is absurd:
Had anything been wrong, we should certainly have heard.

from TWELVE SONGS

I

Say this city has ten million souls,
Some are living in mansions, some are living in holes:
Yet there's no place for us, my dear, yet there's no place
      for us.

Once we had a country and we thought it fair,
Look in the atlas and you'll find it there:
We cannot go there now, my dear, we cannot go there now.

In the village churchyard there grows an old yew,
Every spring it blossoms anew:
Old passports can't do that, my dear, old passports can't
    do that.

The consul banged the table and said:
'If you've got no passport you're officially dead':
But we are still alive, my dear, but we are still alive.

Went to a committee; they offered me a chair;
Asked me politely to return next year:
But where shall we go to-day, my dear, but where shall we
    go to-day?

Came to a public meeting; the speaker got up and said:
'If we let them in, they will steal our daily bread';
He was talking of you and me, my dear, he was talking of
    you and me.

Thought I heard the thunder rumbling in the sky;
It was Hitler over Europe, saying: 'They must die';
We were in his mind, my dear, we were in his mind.

Saw a poodle in a jacket fastened with a pin,
Saw a door opened and a cat let in:
But they weren't German Jews, my dear, but they weren't
    German Jews.

Went down the harbour and stood upon the quay,
Saw the fish swimming as if they were free:
Only ten feet away, my dear, only ten feet away.

Walked through a wood, saw the birds in the trees;
They had no politicians and sang at their ease:
They weren't the human race, my dear, they weren't the
    human race.

Dreamed I saw a building with a thousand floors,
A thousand windows and a thousand doors;

Not one of them was ours, my dear, not one of them was
  ours.

Stood on a great plain in the falling snow;
Ten thousand soldiers marched to and fro:
Looking for you and me, my dear, looking for you and me.

MUNDUS ET INFANS

for Albert and Angelyn Stevens

Kicking his mother until she let go of his soul
Has given him a healthy appetite: clearly, her rôle
  In the New Order must be
To supply and deliver his raw materials free;
  Should there be any shortage,
She will be held responsible; she also promises
To show him all such attentions as befit his age.
  Having dictated peace,

With one fist clenched behind his head, heel drawn up to
  thigh
The cocky little ogre dozes off, ready,
  Though, to take on the rest
Of the world at the drop of a hat or the mildest
  Nudge of the impossible,
Resolved, cost what it may, to seize supreme power and
Sworn to resist tyranny to the death with all
  Forces at his command.

A pantheist not a solipsist, he co-operates
With a universe of large and noisy feeling-states
  Without troubling to place
Them anywhere special, for, to his eyes, Funnyface
  Or Elephant as yet
Mean nothing. His distinction between Me and Us
Is a matter of taste; his seasons are Dry and Wet;
  He thinks as his mouth does.

Still, his loud iniquity is still what only the
Greatest of saints become—someone who does not lie:
    He because he cannot
Stop the vivid present to think, they by having got
    Past reflection into
A passionate obedience in time. We have our Boy-
Meets-Girl era of mirrors and muddle to work through,
    Without rest, without joy.

Therefore we love him because his judgments are so
Frankly subjective that his abuse carries no
    Personal sting. We should
Never dare offer our helplessness as a good
    Bargain, without at least
Promising to overcome a misfortune we blame
History or Banks or the Weather for: but this beast
    Dares to exist without shame.

Let him praise our Creator with the top of his voice,
Then, and the motions of his bowels; let us rejoice
    That he lets us hope, for
He may never become a fashionable or
    Important personage:
However bad he may be, he has not yet gone mad;
Whoever we are now, we were no worse at his age;
    So of course we ought to be glad

When he bawls the house down. Has he not a perfect right
To remind us at every moment how we quite
    Rightly expect each other
To go upstairs or for a walk, if we must cry over
    Spilt milk, such as our wish
That, since apparently we shall never be above
Either or both, we had never learned to distinguish
    Between hunger and love?

from "FOR THE TIME BEING"

III

FUGAL-CHORUS

Great is Caesar: He has conquered Seven Kingdoms.
The First was the Kingdom of Abstract Idea:
Last night it was Tom, Dick and Harry; tonight it is S's
    with P's;
Instead of inflexions and accents
There are prepositions and word-order;
Instead of aboriginal objects excluding each other
There are specimens reiterating a type;
Instead of wood-nymphs and river-demons,
There is one unconditioned ground of Being.
Great is Caesar: God must be with Him.

Great is Caesar: He has conquered Seven Kingdoms.
The Second was the Kingdom of Natural Cause:
Last night it was Sixes and Sevens; tonight it is One and
    Two;
Instead of saying, "Strange are the whims of the Strong,"
We say, "Harsh is the Law but it is certain";
Instead of building temples, we build laboratories;
Instead of offering sacrifices, we perform experiments;
Instead of reciting prayers, we note pointer-readings;
Our lives are no longer erratic but efficient.
Great is Caesar: God must be with Him.

Great is Caesar; He has conquered Seven Kingdoms.
The Third was the Kingdom of Infinite Number:
Last night it was Rule-of-Thumb, tonight it is To-a-T;
Instead of Quite-a-lot, there is Exactly-so-many;
Instead of Only-a-few, there is Just-these;
Instead of saying, "You must wait until I have counted,"
We say, "Here you are. You will find this answer correct";
Instead of a nodding acquaintance with a few integers
The Transcendentals are our personal friends.
Great is Caesar: God must be with Him.

Great is Caesar: He has conquered Seven Kingdoms.
The Fourth was the Kingdom of Credit Exchange:

Last night it was Tit-for-Tat, tonight it is C.O.D.;
When we have a surplus, we need not meet someone with
   a deficit;
When we have a deficit, we need not meet someone with
   a surplus;
Instead of heavy treasures, there are paper symbols of
   value;
Instead of Pay at Once, there is pay when you can;
Instead of My Neighbour, there is Our Customers;
Instead of Country Fair, there is World Market.
Great is Caesar: God must be with Him.

Great is Caesar; He has conquered Seven Kingdoms.
The Fifth was the Kingdom of Inorganic Giants:
Last night it was Heave-Ho, tonight it is Whee-Spree;
When we want anything, They make it;
When we dislike anything, They change it;
When we want to go anywhere, They carry us;
When the Barbarian invades us, They raise immovable
   shields,
When we invade the Barbarian, They brandish irresistible
   swords;
Fate is no longer a fiat of Matter, but a freedom of Mind.
Great is Caesar: God must be with Him.

Great is Caesar: He has conquered Seven Kingdoms.
The Sixth was the Kingdom of Organic Dwarfs:
Last night it was Ouch-Ouch, tonight it is Yum-Yum;
When diseases waylay us, They strike them dead;
When worries intrude on us, They throw them out;
When pain accosts us, They save us from embarrassment;
When we feel like sheep, They make us lions;
When we feel like geldings, They make us stallions;
Spirit is no longer under Flesh, but on top.
Great is Caesar: God must be with Him.

Great is Caesar: He has conquered Seven Kingdoms.
The Seventh was the Kingdom of Popular Soul:
Last night it was Order-Order, tonight it is Hear-Hear;
When he says, You are happy, we laugh;
When he says, You are wretched, we cry;
When he says, It is true, everyone believes it;

When he says, It is false, no one believes it;
When he says, This is good, this is loved;
When he says, That is bad, that is hated.
Great is Caesar: God must be with Him.

Theodore Roethke / 1908–1963

MY PAPA'S WALTZ

The whiskey on your breath
Could make a small boy dizzy;
But I hung on like death:
Such waltzing was not easy.

We romped until the pans
Slid from the kitchen shelf;
My mother's countenance
Could not unfrown itself.

The hand that held my wrist
Was battered on one knuckle;
At every step you missed
My right ear scraped a buckle.

You beat time on my head
With a palm caked hard by dirt,
Then waltzed me off to bed
Still clinging to your shirt.

DOLOR

I have known the inexorable sadness of pencils,
Neat in their boxes, dolor of pad and paper-weight,

All the misery of manilla folders and mucilage,
Desolation in immaculate public places,
Lonely reception room, lavatory, switchboard,
The unalterable pathos of basin and pitcher,
Ritual of multigraph, paper-clip, comma,
Endless duplication of lives and objects.
And I have seen dust from the walls of institutions,
Finer than flour, alive, more dangerous than silica,
Sift, almost invisible, though long afternoons of tedium,
Dropping a fine film on nails and delicate eyebrows,
Glazing the pale hair, the duplicate grey standard faces.

THE LOST SON

1. THE FLIGHT

At Woodlawn I heard the dead cry:
I was lulled by the slamming of iron,
A slow drip over stones,
Toads brooding wells.
All the leaves stuck out their tongues;
I shook the softening chalk of my bones,
Saying,
Snail, snail, glister me forward,
Bird, soft-sigh me home,
Worm, be with me.
This is my hard time.

Fished in an old wound,
The soft pond of repose;
Nothing nibbled my line,
Not even the minnows came.

Sat in an empty house
Watching shadows crawl,
Scratching.
There was one fly.

Voice, come out of the silence.
Say something.

Appear in the form of a spider
Or a moth beating the curtain.

Tell me:
Which is the way I take;
Out of what door do I go,
Where and to whom?

      Dark hollows said, lee to the wind,
      The moon said, back of an eel,
      The salt said, look by the sea,
      Your tears are not enough praise,
      You will find no comfort here,
      In the kingdom of bang and blab.

      Running lightly over spongy ground,
      Past the pasture of flat stones,
      The three elms,
      The sheep strewn on a field,
      Over a rickety bridge
      Toward the quick-water, wrinkling and rippling.

      Hunting along the river,
      Down among the rubbish, the bug-riddled foliage,
      By the muddy pond-edge, by the bog-holes,
      By the shrunken lake, hunting, in the heat of summer.

The shape of a rat?
        It's bigger than that.
        It's less than a leg
        And more than a nose,
        Just under the water
        It usually goes.

      Is it soft like a mouse?
      Can it wrinkle its nose?
      Could it come in the house
      On the tips of its toes?

        Take the skin of a cat
        And the back of an eel,

Then roll them in grease,—
That's the way it would feel.

It's sleek as an otter
With wide webby toes
Just under the water
It usually goes.

2. THE PIT

Where do the roots go?
    Look down under the leaves.
Who put the moss there?
    These stones have been here too long.
Who stunned the dirt into noise?
    Ask the mole, he knows.
I feel the slime of a wet nest.
    Beware Mother Mildew.
Nibble again, fish nerves.

3. THE GIBBER

At the wood's mouth,
By the cave's door,
I listened to something
I had heard before.

Dogs of the groin
Barked and howled,
The sun was against me,
The moon would not have me.

The weeds whined,
The snakes cried,
The cows and briars
Said to me: Die.

What a small song. What slow clouds. What dark water.
Hath the rain a father? All the caves are ice. Only the
    snow's here.
I'm cold. I'm cold all over. Rub me in father and mother.
Fear was my father, Father Fear.
His look drained the stones.

What gliding shape
Beckoning through halls,
Stood poised on the stair,
Fell dreamily down?

From the mouths of jugs
Perched on many shelves,
I saw substance flowing
That cold morning.

Like a slither of eels
That watery cheek
As my own tongue kissed
My lips awake.

Is this the storm's heart? The ground is unstilling itself.
My veins are running nowhere. Do the bones cast out their
    fire?
Is the seed leaving the old bed? These buds are live as birds.
Where, where are the tears of the world?
Let the kisses resound, flat like a butcher's palm;
Let the gestures freeze; our doom is already decided.
All the windows are burning! What's left of my life?
I want the old rage, the lash of primordial milk!
Goodbye, goodbye, old stones, the time-order is going,
I have married my hands to perpetual agitation,
I run, I run to the whistle of money.

Money money money
Water water water

How cool the grass is.
Has the bird left?
The stalk still sways.
Has the worm a shadow?
What do the clouds say?

These sweeps of light undo me.
Look, look, the ditch is running white!
I've more veins than a tree!
Kiss me, ashes, I'm falling through a dark swirl.

4. THE RETURN

The way to the boiler was dark,
Dark all the way,
Over slippery cinders
Through the long greenhouse.

The roses kept breathing in the dark.
They had many mouths to breathe with.
My knees made little winds underneath
Where the weeds slept.

There was always a single light
Swinging by the fire-pit,
Where the fireman pulled out roses,
The big roses, the big bloody clinkers.

Once I stayed all night.
The light in the morning come slowly over the white
Snow.
There were many kinds of cool
Air.
Then came steam.

Pipe-knock.

Scurry of warm over small plants.
Ordnung! ordnung!
Papa is coming!

A fine haze moved off the leaves;
Frost melted on far panes;
The rose, the chrysanthemum turned toward the light.
Even the hushed forms, the bent yellowy weeds
Moved in a slow up-sway.

5. "IT WAS BEGINNING WINTER"

It was beginning winter,
An in-between time,
The landscape still partly brown:
The bones of weeds kept swinging in the wind,
Above the blue snow.

It was beginning winter,
The light moved slowly over the frozen field,
Over the dry seed-crowns,
The beautiful surviving bones
Swinging in the wind.

Light traveled over the wide field;
Stayed.
The weeds stopped swinging.
The mind moved, not alone,
Through the clear air, in the silence.

> Was it light?
> Was it light within?
> Was it light within light?
> Stillness becoming alive,
> Yet still?

A lively understandable spirit
Once entertained you.
It will come again.
Be still.
Wait.

A FIELD OF LIGHT

1

Came to lakes; came to dead water,
Ponds with moss and leaves floating,
Planks sunk in the sand.

A log turned at the touch of a foot;
A long weed floated upward;
An eye tilted.

> Small winds made
> A chilly noise;
> The softest cove
> Cried for sound.

Reached for a grape
And the leaves changed;
A stone's shape
Became a clam.

A fine rain fell
On fat leaves;
I was there alone
In a watery drowse.

2

Angel within me, I asked,
Did I ever curse the sun?
Speak and abide.

Under, under the sheaves,
Under the blackened leaves,
Behind the green viscid trellis,
In the deep grass at the edge of field,
Along the low ground dry only in August,—

Was it dust I was kissing?
A sigh came far.
Alone, I kissed the skin of a stone;
Marrow-soft, danced in the sand.

3

The dirt left my hand, visitor.
I could feel the mare's nose.
A path went walking.
The sun glittered on a small rapids.
Some morning thing came, beating its wings.
The great elm filled with birds.

Listen, love,
The fat lark sang in the field;
I touched the ground, the ground warmed by the
    killdeer,
The salt laughed and the stones;
The ferns had their ways, and the pulsing lizards,
And the new plants, still awkward in their soil,

The lovely diminutives.
I could watch! I could watch!
I saw the separateness of all things!
My heart lifted up with the great grasses;
The weeds believed me, and the nesting birds.
There were clouds making a rout of shapes crossing a
    windbreak of cedars,
And a bee shaking drops from a rain-soaked honeysuckle.
The worms were delighted as wrens.
And I walked, I walked through the light air;
I moved with the morning.

ELEGY FOR JANE

My Student, Thrown by a Horse

I remember the neckcurls, limp and damp as tendrils;
And her quick look, a sidelong pickerel smile;
And how, once startled into talk, the light syllables leaped
    for her,
And she balanced in the delight of her thought,
A wren, happy, tail into the wind,
Her song trembling the twigs and small branches.
The shade sang with her;
The leaves, their whispers turned to kissing;
And the mold sang in the bleached valleys under the rose.

Oh, when she was sad, she cast herself down into such a
    pure depth,
Even a father could not find her:
Scraping her cheek against straw;
Stirring the clearest water.

My sparrow, you are not here,
Waiting like a fern, making a spiny shadow.
The sides of wet stones cannot console me,
Nor the moss, wound with the last light.

If only I could nudge you from this sleep,
My maimed darling, my skittery pigeon.

Over this damp grave I speak the words of my love:
I, with no rights in this matter,
Neither father nor lover.

THE WAKING

I wake to sleep, and take my waking slow.
I feel my fate in what I cannot fear.
I learn by going where I have to go.

We think by feeling. What is there to know?
I hear my being dance from ear to ear.
I wake to sleep, and take my waking slow.

Of those so close beside me, which are you?
God bless the Ground! I shall walk softly there,
And learn by going where I have to go.

Light takes the Tree; but who can tell us how?
The lowly worm climbs up a winding stair;
I wake to sleep, and take my waking slow.

Great Nature has another thing to do
To you and me; so take the lively air,
And, lovely, learn by going where to go.

This shaking keeps me steady. I should know.
What falls away is always. And is near.
I wake to sleep, and take my waking slow.
I learn by going where I have to go.

I KNEW A WOMAN

I knew a woman, lovely in her bones,
When small birds sighed, she would sigh back at them;
Ah, when she moved, she moved more ways than one:

The shapes a bright container can contain!
Of her choice virtues only gods should speak,
Or English poets who grew up on Greek
(I'd have them sing in chorus, cheek to cheek).

How well her wishes went! She stroked my chin,
She taught me Turn, and Counter-turn, and Stand;
She taught me Touch, that undulant white skin;
I nibbled meekly from her proffered hand;
She was the sickle; I, poor I, the rake,
Coming behind her for her pretty sake
(But what prodigious mowing we did make).

Love likes a gander, and adores a goose:
Her full lips pursed, the errant note to seize;
She played it quick, she played it light and loose;
My eyes, they dazzled at her flowing knees;
Her several parts could keep a pure repose,
Or one hip quiver with a mobile nose
(She moved in circles, and those circles moved).

Let seed be grass, and grass turn into hay:
I'm martyr to a motion not my own;
What's freedom for? To know eternity.
I swear she cast a shadow white as stone.
But who would count eternity in days?
These old bones live to learn her wanton ways:
(I measure time by how a body sways).

W. R. Rodgers / 1909–

DIRECTIONS TO A REBEL

Keep away from roads' webs, they always lead
To some spider-spot where, once spied, out speeds

The cop. Side-step the strict keepers of paths,
The pickets of prerogative; avoid
Conforming pass-word. But follow freely
The treeless plain of candour where shadows
Cannot hide or walk upright. Keep downwind;
Beware the water-hole of Want, for there
The hunter waits with widespread net of dole
And charity to take and tame you in;
(Observe his footmark firm in the meek muck
Of softness and servility). Do not
On the taut returning tether of self
Dally and circle, nor in pond explore
Your rare reflection, stopping and stooping.
Stride straight on, stay stretched out, anticipate
No respite. And let neither friend's defect
Nor foe's respect divert you. On your way
You will pass horrible warning corpses
Wrecked on the hairpin-bend of reaction:
Beyond the burning town of Sloth you'll see
The hopeless citizens look back in tears,
Salt pillars of self-pity, silhouettes
Of blank regret. But waste no word on them,
Go your way. Overhead, Fear and Favour,
The twin engines of Authority, will
Fill and fan your ears with their roaring. Scorn
Will curl suddenly round silent corners
Like bell-less bicycles: and Luxury
Draw up beside you, offering a seat
Moss-soft in idle limousine; foot-sore,
Refuse it. Marginal misgivings lie
In ambush. Crooked fingers will beckon,
Insistent strangers take you by the hand,
Dub you as friend, and plant their guilty coins
In unsuspecting pocket. So be you
Thorned and thicketed in reticence.
Make no loose friends: shun the too-nimble man
Who from being the heels of the hunted
Becomes the head of the hunter; be warned
Against the merchant who inflates and tags
His goods with flattery, or cellophanes
And surfaces his own self-interest

With saving and transparent honesty,
Who offers you his watertight word
Backed by his wickerwork act. Above all,
Beware the welcoming word on mat
Inviting the confiding footfall on;
Often it is stretched on slipperiness:
Avoid the hearty and enhancing handshake,
The prefatory fib that leads to worse
(Like gladiators' kisses, boxers' hugs,
The formal overtures to violence).
Accept no candid or contingent gift
From an ambiguous hand, or else like cog
You must have intercourse with ill, and will
Be geared to new and necessary wrong.
Rise from table! rush from hall! O do not
Acquiesce in their toadying truths, refuse
To sing their subsidised praises, or borrow
Their easy loans; those are the open traps
For apathy: boot and batter them. Be
Intolerant, not backward to applaud
But forward to condemn, giving no ease.
May no insolent stone turn back your step,
No sea-blow dent your boat, no landfall
End your voyage. Elbowed from port to port,
Signalled from point to point, drop no anchor;
Seek no safe caves or tied and tidy coves.
Let not lax beds or luxurious hugs hold
Or detain you. The harbour gapes, but not
For you; arms open, but they are not yours.
Along your road you will meet no great crowds
Going with gongs to greet you returning
With your gains to an ungrudged conclusion.
Only expulsion, obloquy, and shame
Watch for you. Welcome them. Welcome too
Smooth malice, smarmy enmity, these things
Will shape and sharp your purpose, stroke and strop
Your temper, point your passionate aim. So,
Gay in the midst of growling things, you'll go
Tip-toe, songs in your ears, sights in your eyes,
That blind and deafen you to compromise.

S N O W

Out of the grey air grew snow and more snow
Soundlessly in nonillions of flakes
Commingling and sinking negligently
To ground, soft as froth and easy as ashes
Alighting, closing the ring of sight. And,
Silting, it augmented everything,
Furring the bare leaf, blurring the thorn,
Fluffing, too, the telephone-wire, padding
All the paths and boosting boots, and puffing
Big over rims, like boiling milk, meekly
Indulging the bulging hill, and boldly
Bolstering the retiring hole, until
It owned and integrated all. And then
Snow stopped, disclosing anonymity
Imposed, the blank and blotless sea in which
Both dotted tree and dashing bird were sunk,
And anchored ground and rocking grass engrossed.

And soon the knock and hiss of cistern ceased as
Gradually with inklings and wrinkling strings
Of ice the thickening cold anchored the skin
And slow core of water, gluing and glossing
All leaks, niggling or great, naked or guarded.
Long snaughters of ice at the tap's snout hung
Jagged and stiff like straw-ends this hard morning.
At every vent things hesitated; here,
In conforming holes and huts, the shy creatures
Shrank from issuing, and, rooted together,
Stood arrested and irresolute at doors,
Peppering with peepings the surprising fields—
Fox in knoll, fowl in house, heifer in hovel.
Only the bull, dubious and delicate, stalked
In his paddock, distrust spiking his blind steps.
His spinning eye, his spoked glances, glinted and
Tilted. His horn gored and scorned the ground, and scored
The oak, and fans of vapour jetted and jumped
Stiffly from nostrils, incensing the loose snow

Like smoke, and powdering his knees. Noisily
On the sleeked lake onlookers lingered in ring
Round the single and deferent skater leaning over in flight,
    like grass slanted by wind,
Foot-engrossed, locked in his own looking-glass
Of conscious joy and evident finery
Of movement, forgetful of outer voices.
Forgetful of venom, of fame, of laughter,
Of flouting Evil and of touting Good that
Waited woodenly for him like tormentors
At the end and edge of his dream, to waken
And claim him. So he slid on, as we all do,
Forgetting the morrow, forgetting too
The marrow of water in the bone of ice
(Like the worm in the wood), the liquefaction
And friction in all fixed things, virtue in vice,
The bomb domanial in the dome of blue.

WHITE CHRISTMAS

Punctually at Christmas the soft plush
Of sentiment snows down, embosoms all
The sharp and pointed shapes of venom, shawls
The hills and hides the shocking holes of this
Uneven world of want and wealth, cushions
With cosy wish like cotton-wool the cool
Arm's-length interstices of caste and class,
And into obese folds subtracts from sight
All truculent acts, bleeding the world white.

Punctually that glib pair, Peace and Goodwill,
Emerge royally to take the air,
Collect the bows, assimilate the smiles,
Of waiting men. It is a genial time.
Angels, like stalactites, descend from heaven,
Bishops distribute their own weight in words,
Congratulate the poor on Christlike lack,
And the member for the constituency
Feeds the five thousand, and has plenty back.

Punctually to-night, in old stone circles
Of set reunion, families stiffly sit
And listen; this is the night, and this the happy time
When the tinned milk of human kindness is
Upheld and holed by radio-appeal.
Hushed are hurrying heels on hard roads,
And every parlour's a pink pond of light
To the cold and travelling man going by
In the dark, without a bark or a bite.

But punctually to-morrow you will see
All this silent and dissembling world
Of silted sentiment suddenly melt
Into mush and watery welter of words
Beneath the warm and moving traffic of
Feet and actual fact. Over the stark plain
The stilted mill-chimneys once again spread
Their sackcloth and ashes, a flowing mane
Of repentance for the false day that's fled.

A W A K E !

Wind that speeds the bee and plucks the bee-line
Into bows and bends, that clips the spoken word
From the open lips, that claps and batters
The bent-backed and running roaring waters,
That squats and squints and squeals evilly in trees,
That follows and faces the fleeing leaves,
That with hag hands hugs the hooked hawk down,
That hammers like rams' heads the humped body,
And that stamps flat like stallions the shaking
Flaking acres of grass—wind nine times named,
And by these wordy welts nine times inflamed
In mind—O mount now and mightily suck
Up all rooted breath out of the rooted mouth
Of man, collapse his plots and exploits, pluck
Every gut taut with terror, like weed
Tugged tight in withdrawing wave, and heedless
In high hangars hoard one blast, pack one breath.

Then fall, walled wind, all welded and one, clap
Wieldy water, scap, and valley gap
Together, and detach man from his map;
O wind, have no pity on the city
With buttery motto and lean dole-line
Like old tapeworm in its intestined street,
Or on the foreign laughter of those who boot
Through orchard pasted under foot with fruit,
Seek, suck, sack such, in each socket set tooth,
High over hoardings hurl, and all ways spill,
Hug the elbowing horde, hard under hill
Huddle hare and hound, let lion and lamb
Lump panic-struck, yoke in one choking hold
Victor and victim, rock trigger and target.
And O, halt our hates, file flat our flights,
With stiff pointed finger stuff and stifle
Every gaping gun and pouting rifle;
Pour over our floors and frontiers and leave
Pavement and field clean and ceiling clear,
And man, like Noah afloat in his ark
On a single sea, looking for landmark,
His heart's scope not yet shrunken into
Private and poisonous pools of feeling.

Alas! Æolus will not listen to
Our lot. No upright God angry and stiff
Will suddenly come turning somersaults
Of mercy and cartwheels of leniency
Toward us Noahs. Nor will words rock or wring,
Or invocation sting. At our appeal
No pulse will leap up like a bell-clapper
Proclaiming peace. To us no Nereus will
Rise from the ring of the sea like a rod,
His hair set and salty as dulse, bringing
Succour and promise. So spare your protests.
There are no interlopers in our fate.
Be sure of this, that in peace or war, we
Are where we are because of what we are:
No censor can excerpt, or scissor-snip
Excise this salient sentence from our lives.
O easy and peaceful were those days when
Our hopes bowled on before us like hoops,

And our biddable purposes pedalled
Slowly on rolling gradients of reason
And reform. Fools! in our stinking ditches
War was born, and grew gigantic legs that
Suddenly kicked the ground away like a frog
From under us all. For that is how
The world moves, not with meant and maintained pace
Toward some hill-horizon or held mood,
But in great jags and jerks, probed and prodded
From point to point of anger, exploded
By each new and opposed touch. So War came,
The late and urgent agent of Change, not
Of Chance. So will it always come to wake
The deep sleepers. See how its sudden hands
Now garter and grow round us like quicksands
Here in these islands. O awake! awake!
And let us like the trapped intrepid man
Who on prairie hears the holocaust roar
And sees his horizons running to meet him
In mutinous flames, while the still grasses fill
With rills of refugees, let us calmly
Stand now to windward, and here at our feet
Stooping, light fires of foresight that will clean
And clear the careless ground before us
Of all the dry and tindery increment
Of privilege. So will that other Fate
Arriving find no hold within our state,
And we on our ringed ground its roar will wait
Freely. Awake! before it is too late.

NEITHER   HERE   NOR   THERE

In that land all is, and nothing's ought;
No owners or notices, only birds;
No walls anywhere, only lean wire of words
Worming brokenly out from eaten thought;
No oats growing, only ankle-lace grass
Easing and not resenting the feet that pass;
No enormous beasts, only names of them;
No bones made, bans laid, or boons expected,

No contracts, entails, hereditaments,
Anything at all that might tie or hem.

In that land all's lackadaisical;
No lakes of coddled spawn, and no locked ponds
Of settled purpose, no netted fishes;
But only inkling streams and running fronds,
Fritillaried with dreams, weedy with wishes;
Nor arrogant talk is heard, haggling phrase,
But undertones, and hesitance, and haze;
On clear days mountains of meaning are seen
Humped high on the horizon; no one goes
To con their meaning, no one cares or knows.

In that land all's flat, indifferent; there
Is neither springing house or hanging tent,
No aims are entertained, and nothing is meant,
For there are no ends and no trends, no roads,
Only follow your nose to anywhere.
No one is born there, no one stays or dies,
For it is a timeless land, it lies
Between the act and the attrition, it
Marks off bound from rebound, make from break, tit
From tat, also today from tomorrow.
No Cause there comes to term, but each departs
Elsewhere to whelp its deeds, expel its darts;
There are no homecomings, of course, no good-byes
In that land, neither yearning nor scorning,
Though at night there is the smell of morning.

Stephen Spender / 1909–

I THINK CONTINUALLY OF THOSE
WHO WERE TRULY GREAT

I think continually of those who were truly great.
Who, from the womb, remembered the soul's history

Through corridors of light where the hours are suns,
Endless and singing. Whose lovely ambition
Was that their lips, still touched with fire,
Should tell of the Spirit, clothed from head to foot in song.
And who hoarded from the Spring branches
The desires falling across their bodies like blossoms.

What is precious, is never to forget
The essential delight of the blood drawn from ageless
    springs
Breaking through rocks in worlds before our earth.
Never to deny its pleasure in the morning simple light
Nor its grave evening demand for love.
Never to allow gradually the traffic to smother
With noise and fog, the flowering of the Spirit.

Near the snow, near the sun, in the highest fields,
See how these names are fêted by the waving grass
And by the streamers of white cloud
And whispers of wind in the listening sky.
The names of those who in their lives fought for life,
Who wore at their hearts the fire's centre.
Born of the sun, they travelled a short while toward the sun,
And left the vivid air signed with their honour.

AFTER THEY HAVE TIRED OF
THE BRILLIANCE OF CITIES

After they have tired of the brilliance of cities
And of striving for office where at last they may languish
Hung round with easy chains until
Death and Jerusalem glorify also the crossing sweeper:
Then those streets the rich built and their easy love
Fade like old cloths, and it is death stalks through life
Grinning white through all faces
Clean and equal like the shine from snow.

In this day when grief pours freezing over us,
When the hard light of pain gleams at every street corner,

When those who were pillars of yesterday's roof
Shrink in their clothes: then surely from hunger
We may strike fire, like fire from flint?
And our strength is now the strength of our bones
Clean and equal like the shine from snow
And the strength of famine and our enforced idleness,
And it is the strength of our love for one another.

Readers of this strange language,
We have come at last to a country
Where light equal, like the shine from snow, strikes all faces.
Here you may wonder
How it was that works, money, interest, building, could
ever hide
The palpable and obvious love of man for man.

Oh, comrades, let not those who follow after
—The beautiful generation that will spring from our sides—
Let them not wonder how after the failure of banks,
The failure of cathedrals and the declared insanity of our
rulers,
We lacked the Spring-like resources of the tiger
Or of plants which strike out new roots to urgent waters.
Through torn-down portions of fabric let their eyes
Witness the admiring dawn explode like a shell
Around us, dazing us with its light like snow.

THE EXPRESS

After the first powerful, plain manifesto
The black statement of pistons, without more fuss
But gliding like a queen, she leaves the station.
Without bowing and with restrained unconcern
She passes the houses which humbly crowd outside,
The gasworks, and at last the heavy page
Of death, printed by gravestones in the cemetery.
Beyond the town, there lies the open country
Where, gathering speed, she acquires mystery,

The luminous self-possession of ships on ocean.
It is now she begins to sing—at first quite low
Then loud, and at last with a jazzy madness—
The song of her whistle screaming at curves,
Of deafening tunnels, brakes, innumerable bolts.
And always light, aerial, underneath,
Retreats the elate metre of her wheels.
Steaming through metal landscape on her lines,
She plunges new eras of white happiness,
Where speed throws up strange shapes, broad curves
And parallels clean like trajectories from guns.
At last, further than Edinburgh or Rome,
Beyond the crest of the world, she reaches night
Where only a low stream-line brightness
Of phosphorus on the tossing hills is light.
Ah, like a comet through flame, she moves entranced,
Wrapt in her music no bird song, no, nor bough
Breaking with honey buds, shall ever equal.

THE LANDSCAPE NEAR
AN AERODROME

More beautiful and soft than any moth
With burring furred antennae feeling its huge path
Through dusk, the air liner with shut-off engines
Glides over suburbs and the sleeves set trailing tall
To point the wind. Gently, broadly, she falls,
Scarcely disturbing charted currents of air.

Lulled by descent, the travellers across sea
And across feminine land indulging its easy limbs
In miles of softness, now let their eyes trained by watching
Penetrate through dusk the outskirts of this town
Here where industry shows a fraying edge.
Here they may see what is being done.

Beyond the winking masthead light
And the landing ground, they observe the outposts

Of work: chimneys like lank black fingers
Or figures, frightening and mad: and squat buildings
With their strange air behind trees, like women's faces
Shattered by grief. Here where few houses
Moan with faint light behind their blinds,
They remark the unhomely sense of complaint, like a dog
Shut out, and shivering at the foreign moon.

In the last sweep of love, they pass over fields
Behind the aerodrome, where boys play all day
Hacking dead grass: whose cries, like wild birds,
Settle upon the nearest roofs
But soon are hid under the loud city.

Then, as they land, they hear the tolling bell
Reaching across the landscape of hysteria,
To where, louder than all those batteries
And charcoaled towers against that dying sky,
Religion stands, the Church blocking the sun.

NOT PALACES, AN ERA'S CROWN

Not palaces, an era's crown
Where the mind dwells, intrigues, rests;
Architectural gold-leaved flower
From people ordered like a single mind,
I build. This only what I tell:
It is too late for rare accumulation,
For family pride, for beauty's filtered dusts;
I say, stamping the words with emphasis,
Drink from here energy and only energy,
As from the electric charge of a battery,
To will this Time's change.
Eye, gazelle, delicate wanderer,
Drinker of horizon's fluid line;
Ear that suspends on a chord
The spirit drinking timelessness;
Touch, love, all senses;

Leave your gardens, your singing feasts,
Your dreams of suns circling before our sun,
Of heaven after our world.
Instead, watch images of flashing glass
That strike the outward sense, the polished will,
Flag of our purpose which the wind engraves.

No spirit seek here rest. But this: No one
Shall hunger: Man shall spend equally.
Our goal which we compel: Man shall be man.
          That programme of the antique Satan
Bristling with guns on the indented page,
With battleship towering from hilly waves:
For what? Drive of a ruining purpose
Destroying all but its age-long exploiters.
Our programme like this, but opposite,
Death to the killers, bringing light to life.

ULTIMA   RATIO   REGUM

The guns spell money's ultimate reason
In letters of lead on the Spring hillside.
But the boy lying dead under the olive trees
Was too young and too silly
To have been notable to their important eye.
He was a better target for a kiss.

When he lived, tall factory hooters never summoned him
Nor did restaurant plate-glass doors revolve to wave him in
His name never appeared in the papers.
The world maintained its traditional wall
Round the dead with their gold sunk deep as a well,
Whilst his life, intangible as a Stock Exchange rumour,
          drifted outside.

O too lightly he threw down his cap
One day when the breeze threw petals from the trees.
The unflowering wall sprouted with guns,

Machine-gun anger quickly scythed the grasses;
Flags and leaves fell from hands and branches;
The tweed cap rotted in the nettles.

Consider his life which was valueless
In terms of employment, hotel ledgers, news files.
Consider. One bullet in ten thousand kills a man.
Ask. Was so much expenditure justified
On the death of one so young, and so silly
Lying under the olive trees, O world, O death?

THE DOUBLE SHAME

You must live through the time when everything hurts
When the space of the ripe, loaded afternoon
Expands to a landscape of white heat frozen
And trees are weighed down with hearts of stone
And green stares back where you stare alone,
And the walking eyes throw flinty comments,
And the words which carry most knives are the blind
Phrases searching to be kind.

Solid and usual objects are ghosts
The furniture carries cargoes of memory,
The staircase has corners which remember
As fire blows reddest in gusty embers,
And each empty dress cuts out an image
In fur and evening and summer and spring
Of her who was different in each.

Pull down the blind and lie on the bed
And clasp the hour in the glass of one room
Against your mouth like a crystal doom.
Take up the book and stare at the letters
Hieroglyphs on sand and as meaningless—
Here birds crossed once and a foot once trod
In a mist where sight and sound are blurred.

The story of others who made their mistakes
And of one whose happiness pierced like a star
Eludes and evades between sentences
And the letters break into eyes which read
The story life writes now in your head
As though the characters sought for some clue
To their being transcendently living and dead
In your history, worse than theirs, but true.

Set in the mind of their poet, they compare
Their tragic sublime with your tawdry despair
And they have fingers which accuse
You of the double way of shame.
At first you did not love enough
And afterwards you loved too much
And you lacked the confidence to choose
And you have only yourself to blame.

Elizabeth Bishop / 1911–

THE IMAGINARY ICEBERG

We'd rather have the iceberg than the ship,
although it meant the end of travel.
Although it stood stock-still like cloudy rock
and all the sea were moving marble.
We'd rather have the iceberg than the ship;
we'd rather own this breathing plain of snow
though the ships' sails were laid upon the sea
as the snow lies undissolved upon the water.
O solemn, floating field,
are you aware an iceberg takes repose
with you, and when it wakes may pasture on your snows?

This is a scene a sailor'd give his eyes for.
The ship's ignored. The iceberg rises
and sinks again; its glassy pinnacles
correct elliptics in the sky.
This is a scene where he who treads the boards
is artlessly rhetorical. The curtain
is light enough to rise on finest ropes
that airy twists of snow provide.
The wits of these white peaks
spar with the sun. Its weight the iceberg dares
upon a shifting stage and stands and stares.

This iceberg cuts its facets from within.
Like jewelry from a grave
it saves itself perpetually and adorns
only itself, perhaps the snows
which so surprise us lying on the sea.
Good-bye, we say, good-bye, the ship steers off
where waves give in to one another's waves
and clouds run in a warmer sky.
Icebergs behoove the soul
(Both being self-made from elements least visible)
to see them so: fleshed, fair, erected indivisible.

THE MAN-MOTH *

                                    Here, above,
cracks in the buildings are filled with battered moonlight.
The whole shadow of Man is only as big as his hat.
It lies at his feet like a circle for a doll to stand on,
and he makes an inverted pin, the point magnetized to the
        moon.
He does not see the moon; he observes only her vast
        properties,
feeling the queer light on his hands, neither warm nor cold,
of a temperature impossible to record in thermometers.

* Newspaper misprint for "mammoth."

But when the Man-Moth
pays his rare, although occasional, visits to the surface,
the moon looks rather different to him. He emerges
from an opening under the edge of one of the sidewalks
and nervously begins to scale the faces of the buildings.
He thinks the moon is a small hole at the top of the sky,
proving the sky quite useless for protection.
He trembles, but must investigate as high as he can climb.

Up the façades,
his shadow dragging like a photographer's cloth behind him,
he climbs fearfully, thinking that this time he will manage
to push his small head through that round clean opening
and be forced through, as from a tube, in black scrolls on
    the light.
(Man, standing below him, has no such illusions.)
But what the Man-Moth fears most he must do, although
he fails, of course, and falls back scared but quite unhurt.

Then he returns
to the pale subways of cement he calls his home. He flits,
he flutters, and cannot get aboard the silent trains
fast enough to suit him. The doors close swiftly.
The Man-Moth always seats himself facing the wrong way
and the train starts at once at its full, terrible speed,
without a shift in gears or a gradation of any sort.
He cannot tell the rate at which he travels backwards.

Each night he must
be carried through artificial tunnels and dream recurrent
    dreams.
Just as the ties recur beneath his train, these underlie
his rushing brain. He does not dare look out the window,
for the third rail, the unbroken draught of poison,
runs there beside him. He regards it as a disease
he has inherited the susceptibility to. He has to keep
his hands in his pockets, as others must wear mufflers.

If you catch him,
hold up a flashlight to his eye. It's all dark pupil,
an entire night itself, whose haired horizon tightens

as he stares back, and closes up the eye. Then from the lids
one tear, his only possession, like the bee's sting, slips.
Slyly he palms it, and if you're not paying attention
he'll swallow it. However, if you watch, he'll hand it over,
cool as from underground springs and pure enough to drink.

ROOSTERS

At four o'clock
in the gun-metal blue dark
we hear the first crow of the first cock

just below
the gun-metal blue window
and immediately there is an echo

off in the distance,
then one from the back-yard fence,
then one, with horrible insistence,

grates like a wet match
from the broccoli patch,
flares, and all over town begins to catch.

Cries galore
come from the water-closet door,
from the dropping-plastered henhouse floor,

where in the blue blur
their rustling wives admire,
the roosters brace their cruel feet and glare

with stupid eyes
while from their beaks there rise
the uncontrolled, traditional cries.

Deep from protruding chests
in green-gold medals dressed,
planned to command and terrorize the rest,

the many wives
who lead hens' lives
of being courted and despised;

deep from raw throats
a senseless order floats
all over town. A rooster gloats

over our beds
from rusty iron sheds
and fences made from old bedsteads,

over our churches
where the tin rooster perches,
over our little wooden northern houses,

making sallies
from all the muddy alleys,
marking out maps like Rand McNally's:

glass headed pins,
oil-golds and copper greens,
anthracite blues, alizarins,

each one an active
displacement in perspective;
each screaming, "This is where I live!"

Each screaming
"Get up! Stop dreaming!"
Roosters, what are you projecting?

You, whom the Greeks elected
to shoot at on a post, who struggled
when sacrificed, you whom they labeled

"Very combative . . ."
what right have you to give
commands and tell us how to live,

cry "Here!" and "Here!"
and wake us here where are
unwanted love, conceit and war?

The crown of red
set on your little head
is charged with all your fighting blood.

Yes, that excrescence
makes a most virile presence,
plus all that vulgar beauty of iridescence.

Now in mid-air
by twos they fight each other.
Down comes a first flame-feather,

and one is flying,
with raging heroism defying
even the sensation of dying.

And one has fallen,
but still above the town
his torn-out, bloodied feathers drift down;

and what he sung
no matter. He is flung
on the gray ash-heap, lies in dung

with his dead wives
with open, bloody eyes,
while those metallic feathers oxidize.

St. Peter's sin
was worse than that of Magdalen
whose sin was of the flesh alone;

of spirit, Peter's,
falling, beneath the flares,
among the "servants and officers."

Old holy sculpture
could set it all together
in one small scene, past and future:

Christ stands amazed,
Peter, two fingers raised
to surprised lips, both as if dazed.

But in between
a little cock is seen
carved on a dim column in the travertine,

explained by *gallus canit*;
flet Petrus underneath it.
There is inescapable hope, the pivot;

yes, and there Peter's tears
run down our chanticleer's
sides and gem his spurs.

Tear-encrusted thick
as a medieval relic
he waits. Poor Peter, heart-sick,

still cannot guess
those cock-a-doodles yet might bless,
his dreadful rooster come to mean forgiveness,

a new weathervane
on basilica and barn,
and that outside the Lateran

there would always be
a bronze cock on a porphyry
pillar so the people and the Pope might see

that even the Prince
of the Apostles long since
had been forgiven, and to convince

all the assembly
that "Deny deny deny,"
is not all the roosters cry.

In the morning
a low light is floating
in the backyard, and gilding

from underneath
the broccoli, leaf by leaf;
how could the night have come to grief?

gilding the tiny
floating swallow's belly
and lines of pink cloud in the sky,

the day's preamble
like wandering lines in marble.
The cocks are now almost inaudible.

The sun climbs in,
following "to see the end,"
faithful as enemy, or friend.

THE FISH

I caught a tremendous fish
and held him beside the boat
half out of water, with my hook
fast in a corner of his mouth.
He didn't fight.
He hadn't fought at all.
He hung a grunting weight,
battered and venerable
and homely. Here and there
his brown skin hung in strips
like ancient wall-paper,
and its pattern of darker brown
was like wall-paper:
shapes like full-blown roses
stained and lost through age.
He was speckled with barnacles,

fine rosettes of lime,
and infested
with tiny white sea-lice,
and underneath two or three
rags of green weed hung down.
While his gills were breathing in
the terrible oxygen
—the frightening gills,
fresh and crisp with blood,
that can cut so badly—
I thought of the coarse white flesh
packed in like feathers,
the big bones and the little bones,
the dramatic reds and blacks
of his shiny entrails,
and the pink swim-bladder
like a big peony.
I looked into his eyes
which were far larger than mine
but shallower, and yellowed,
the irises backed and packed
with tarnished tinfoil
seen through the lenses
of old scratched isinglass.
They shifted a little, but not
to return my stare.
—It was more like the tipping
of an object toward the light.
I admired his sullen face,
the mechanism of his jaw,
and then I saw
that from his lower lip
—if you could call it a lip—
grim, wet, and weapon-like,
hung five old pieces of fish-line,
or four and a wire leader
with the swivel still attached,
with all their five big hooks
grown firmly in his mouth.
A green line, frayed at the end
where he broke it, two heavier lines,

and a fine black thread
still crimped from the strain and snap
when it broke and he got away.
Like medals with their ribbons
frayed and wavering,
a five-haired beard of wisdom
trailing from his aching jaw.
I stared and stared
and victory filled up
the little rented boat,
from the pool of bilge
where oil had spread a rainbow
around the rusted engine
to the bailer rusted orange,
the sun-cracked thwarts,
the oarlocks on their strings,
the gunnels—until everything
was rainbow, rainbow, rainbow!
And I let the fish go.

AT THE FISHHOUSES

Although it is a cold evening,
down by one of the fishhouses
an old man sits netting,
his net, in the gloaming almost invisible
a dark purple-brown,
and his shuttle worn and polished.
The air smells so strong of codfish
it makes one's nose run and one's eyes water.
The five fishhouses have steeply peaked roofs
and narrow, cleated gangplanks slant up
to storerooms in the gables
for the wheelbarrows to be pushed up and down on.
All is silver: the heavy surface of the sea,
swelling slowly as if considering spilling over,
is opaque, but the silver of the benches,
the lobster pots, and masts, scattered

among the wild jagged rocks,
is of an apparent translucence
like the small old buildings with an emerald moss
growing on their shoreward walls.
The big fish tubs are completely lined
with layers of beautiful herring scales
and the wheelbarrows are similarly plastered
with creamy iridescent coats of mail,
with small iridescent flies crawling on them.
Up on the little slope behind the houses,
set in the sparse bright sprinkle of grass,
is an ancient wooden capstan,
cracked, with two long bleached handles
and some melancholy stains, like dried blood,
where the ironwork has rusted.

The old man accepts a Lucky Strike.
He was a friend of my grandfather.
We talk of the decline in the population
and of codfish and herring
while he waits for a herring boat to come in.
There are sequins on his vest and on his thumb.
He has scraped the scales, the principal beauty,
from unnumbered fish with that black old knife,
the blade of which is almost worn away.

Down at the water's edge, at the place
where they haul up the boats, up the long ramp
descending into the water, thin silver
tree trunks are laid horizontally
across the gray stones, down and down
at intervals of four or five feet.

Cold dark deep and absolutely clear,
element bearable to no mortal,
to fish and to seals . . . One seal particularly
I have seen here evening after evening.
He was curious about me. He was interested in music;
like me a believer in total immersion,
so I used to sing him Baptist hymns.
I also sang "A Mighty Fortress Is Our God."

He stood up in the water and regarded me
steadily, moving his head a little.
Then he would disappear, then suddenly emerge
almost in the same spot, with a sort of shrug
as if it were against his better judgment.
Cold dark deep and absolutely clear,
the clear gray icy water . . . Back, behind us,
the dignified tall firs begin.
Bluish, associating with their shadows,
a million Christmas trees stand
waiting for Christmas. The water seems suspended
above the rounded gray and blue-gray stones.
I have seen it over and over, the same sea, the same,
slightly, indifferently swinging above the stones,
icily free above the stones,
above the stones and then the world.
If you should dip your hand in,
your wrist would ache immediately,
your bones would begin to ache and your hand would burn
as if the water were a transmutation of fire
that feeds on stones and burns with a dark gray flame.
If you tasted it, it would first taste bitter,
then briny, then surely burn your tongue.
It is like what we imagine knowledge to be:
dark, salt, clear, moving, utterly free,
drawn from the cold hard mouth
of the world, derived from the rocky breasts
forever, flowing and drawn, and since
our knowledge is historical, flowing, and flown.

THE PRODIGAL

The brown enormous odor he lived by
was too close, with its breathing and thick hair,
for him to judge. The floor was rotten; the sty
was plastered halfway up with glass-smooth dung.
Light-lashed, self-righteous, above moving snouts,
the pigs' eyes followed him, a cheerful stare—

even to the sow that always ate her young—
till, sickening, he leaned to scratch her head.
But sometimes mornings after drinking bouts
(he hid the pints behind a two-by-four),
the sunrise glazed the barnyard mud with red;
the burning puddles seemed to reassure.
And then he thought he almost might endure
his exile yet another year or more.

But evenings the first star came to warn.
The farmer whom he worked for came at dark
to shut the cows and horses in the barn
beneath their overhanging clouds of hay,
with pitchforks, faint forked lightnings, catching light,
safe and companionable as in the Ark.
The pigs stuck out their little feet and snored.
The lantern—like the sun, going away—
laid on the mud a pacing aureole.
Carrying a bucket along a slimy board,
he felt the bats' uncertain staggering flight,
his shuddering insights, beyond his control,
touching him. But it took him a long time
finally to make his mind up to go home.

Delmore Schwartz / 1913–1966

IN THE NAKED BED,
IN PLATO'S CAVE

In the naked bed, in Plato's cave,
Reflected headlights slowly slid the wall,
Carpenters hammered under the shaded window,
Wind troubled the window curtains all night long,
A fleet of trucks strained uphill, grinding,

Their freights covered, as usual.
The ceiling lightened again, the slanting diagram
Slid slowly forth.
                    Hearing the milkman's chop,
His striving up the stair, the bottle's chink,
I rose from bed, lit a cigarette,
And walked to the window. The stony street
Displayed the stillness in which buildings stand,
The streep-lamp's vigil and the horse's patience.
The winter sky's pure capital
Turned me back to bed with exhausted eyes.

Strangeness grew in the motionless air. The loose
Film grayed. Shaking wagons, hooves' waterfalls,
Sounded far off, increasing, louder and nearer.
A car coughed, starting. Morning, softly
Melting the air, lifted the half-covered chair
From underseas, kindled the looking-glass,
Distinguished the dresser and the white wall.
The bird called tentatively, whistled, called,
Bubbled and whistled, so! Perplexed, still wet
With sleep, affectionate, hungry and cold. So, so,
O son of man, the ignorant night, the travail
Of early morning, the mystery of beginning
Again and again,
                    while History is unforgiven.

TIRED AND UNHAPPY,
YOU THINK OF HOUSES

Tired and unhappy, you think of houses
Soft-carpeted and warm in the December evening,
While snow's white pieces fall past the window,
And the orange firelight leaps.

                    A young girl sings
That song of Gluck where Orpheus pleads with Death;

Her elders watch, nodding their happiness
To see time fresh again in her self-conscious eyes:
The servants bring the coffee, the children retire,
Elder and younger yawn and go to bed,
The coals fade and glow, rose and ashen,
It is time to shake yourself! and break this
Banal dream, and turn your head
Where the underground is charged, where the weight
Of the lean buildings is seen,
Where close in the subway rush, anonymous
In the audience, well-dressed or mean,
So many surround you, ringing your fate,
Caught in an anger exact as a machine!

FOR THE ONE WHO WOULD TAKE MAN'S LIFE IN HIS HANDS

Tiger Christ unsheathed his sword,
Threw it down, became a lamb.
Swift spat upon the species, but
Took two women to his heart.
Samson who was strong as death
Paid his strength to kiss a slut.
Othello that stiff warrior
Was broken by a woman's heart.
Troy burned for a sea-tax, also for
Possession of a charming whore.
What do all examples show?
What must the finished murderer know?

You cannot sit on bayonets,
Nor can you eat among the dead.
When all are killed, you are alone,
A vacuum comes where hate has fed.
Murder's fruit is silent stone,
The gun increases poverty.
With what do these examples shine?

The soldier turned to girls and wine.
Love is the tact of every good,
The only warmth, the only peace.

"What have I said?" asked Socrates,
"Affirmed extremes, cried yes and no,
Taken all parts, denied myself,
Praised the caress, extolled the blow,
Soldier and lover quite deranged
Until their motions are exchanged.
—What do all examples show?
What can any actor know?
The contradiction in every act,
The infinite task of the human heart."

SOCRATES' GHOST MUST
HAUNT ME NOW

Socrates' ghost must haunt me now,
Notorious death has let him go,
He comes to me with a clumsy bow,
Saying in his disused voice,
That I do not know I do not know,
The mechanical whims of appetite
Are all that I have of conscious choice,
The butterfly caged in electric light
Is my only day in the world's great night,
Love is not love, it is a child
Sucking his thumb and biting his lip,
But grasp it all, there may be more!
From the topless sky to the bottomless floor
With the heavy head and the fingertip:
All is not blind, obscene, and poor.
Socrates stands by me stockstill,
Teaching hope to my flickering will,
Pointing to the sky's inexorable blue
—Old Noumenon, come true, come true!

CALMLY WE WALK THROUGH
THIS APRIL'S DAY

Calmly we walk through this April's day,
Metropolitan poetry here and there,
In the park sit pauper and *rentier*,
The screaming children, the motor-car
Fugitive about us, running away,
Between the worker and the millionaire
Number provides all distances,
It is Nineteen Thirty-Seven now,
Many great dears are taken away,
What will become of you and me
(This is the school in which we learn . . .)
Besides the photo and the memory?
(. . . that time is the fire in which we burn.)

(This is the school in which we learn . . .)
What is the self amid this blaze?
What am I now that I was then
Which I shall suffer and act again,
The theodicy I wrote in my high school days
Restored all life from infancy,
The children shouting are bright as they run
(This is the school in which they learn . . .)
Ravished entirely in their passing play!
(. . . that time is the fire in which they burn.)

Avid its rush, that reeling blaze!
Where is my father and Eleanor?
Not where are they now, dead seven years,
But what they were then?
                              No more? No more?
From Nineteen-Fourteen to the present day,
Bert Spira and Rhoda consume, consume
Not where they are now (where are they now?)
But what they were then, both beautiful;
Each minute bursts in the burning room,
The great globe reels in the solar fire,

Spinning the trivial and unique away.
(How all things flash! How all things flare!)
What am I now that I was then?
May memory restore again and again
The smallest color of the smallest day:
Time is the school in which we learn,
Time is the fire in which we burn.

THE HEAVY BEAR WHO
GOES WITH ME

"the withness of the body"

The heavy bear who goes with me,
A manifold honey to smear his face,
Clumsy and lumbering here and there,
The central ton of every place,
The hungry beating brutish one
In love with candy, anger, and sleep,
Crazy factotum, dishevelling all,
Climbs the building, kicks the football,
Boxes his brother in the hate-ridden city.

Breathing at my side, that heavy animal,
That heavy bear who sleeps with me,
Howls in his sleep for a world of sugar,
A sweetness intimate as the water's clasp,
Howls in his sleep because the tight-rope
Trembles and shows the darkness beneath.
—The strutting show-off is terrified,
Dressed in his dress-suit, bulging his pants,
Trembles to think that his quivering meat
Must finally wince to nothing at all.

That inescapable animal walks with me,
Has followed me since the black womb held,
Moves where I move, distorting my gesture,

A caricature, a swollen shadow,
A stupid clown of the spirit's motive,
Perplexes and affronts with his own darkness,
The secret life of belly and bone,
Opaque, too near, my private, yet unknown,
Stretches to embrace the very dear
With whom I would walk without him near,
Touches her grossly, although a word
Would bare my heart and make me clear,
Stumbles, flounders, and strives to be fed
Dragging me with him in his mouthing care,
Amid the hundred million of his kind,
The scrimmage of appetite everywhere.

A DOG NAMED EGO,
THE SNOWFLAKES AS KISSES

A dog named Ego, the snowflakes as kisses
Fluttered, ran, came with me in December,
Snuffing the chill air, changing, and halting,
There where I walked toward seven o'clock,
Sniffed at some interests hidden and open,
Whirled, descending, and stood still, attentive
Seeking their peace, the stranger, unknown,
With me, near me, kissed me, touched my wound,
My simple face, obsessed and pleasure bound.

"Not free, no liberty, rock that you carry,"
So spoke Ego in his cracked and harsh voice,
While snowflakes kissed me and satisfied minutes,
Falling from some place half believed and unknown,
"You will not be free, nor ever alone,"
So spoke Ego, "Mine is the kingdom,
Dynasty's bone: you will not be free,
Go, choose, run, you will not be alone."

"Come, come, come," sang the whirling snowflakes,
Evading the dog who barked at their smallness,

"Come!" sang the snowflakes, "Come here! and here!"
How soon at the sidewalk, melted, and done,
One kissed me, two kissed me! So many died!
While Ego barked at them, swallowed their touch,
Ran this way! And that way! While they slipped to the
     ground,
Leading him further and farther away,
While night collapsed amid the falling,
And left me no recourse, far from my home,
And left me no recourse, far from my home.

THE SEQUEL

First love is first death. There is no other.
There is no death. But all men live forever
And die forever. If this were not true,
We would be more deceived, still more deceived
Than this belief deceives us, whether or not
We think that we believe or we think
Those who believe are deceived. But to believe
That death is the sweet asylum of nothingness:
Is the cruel sick dream of the criminal and the suicide:
Of those who deny reality, of those who steal from
     consciousness,
Of those who are often fugitive, of those who are afraid to
     live,
Of those who are terrified by love, and
          Those who try—before they
               Try to die—to disappear
                    And hide.

I DID NOT KNOW THE TRUTH
OF GROWING TREES

On the suburban street, guarded by patient trees
Two family houses huddled. As I passed the lamplight's
     teas,

In the mid-winter evening when the snow's light made
Of the glowing supper hour a blue lost shade:
A blond girl stood at the window and looked toward the
    snow:
Her glance hid hatred's hot-bed, which had sickened long
    ago,
And then our glances met: and I fell suddenly,
My eyes reached to touch the bark of the nearest tree,
My hands stretched to touch the rough and broken
Bark to feel, again and again, in instance and a token
Of reality's texture. The picture window showed
How often beauty conceals the heart's diseased death-
    ridden toad:
How often romance is a passing dance: but the tree is true:
And this is what I did not know, although I always thought
    I knew how a growing tree is true.

George Barker / 1913–

THE CRYSTAL

With burning fervour
I am forever
Turning in my hand
The crystal, this moment

Whose spatial glitter
Travelling erratically
Forward

Touches with permanent
Disturbance the pavements
The faked walls the crevices
Of futurity.

Sooner than darken
This crystal miracle

With a hand's
Vagary

One would dissever
This wrist this hand,
Or remove the eyelid
To see the end.

RESOLUTION OF DEPENDENCE

We poets in our youth begin in gladness
But thereof come in the end despondency and madness.
        WORDSWORTH: RESOLUTION AND INDEPENDENCE.

I encountered the crowd returning from amusements,
The Bournemouth Pavilion, or the marvellous gardens,
The Palace of Solace, the Empyrean Cinema: and saw
William Wordsworth was once, tawdrily conspicuous,
Obviously emulating the old man of the mountain-moor,
Traipsing along on the outskirts of the noisy crowd.

Remarkable I reflected that after all it is him.
The layers of time falling continually on Grasmere
        Churchyard,
The accumulation of year and year like calendar,
The acute superstition that Wordsworth is after all dead,
Should have succeeded in keeping him quiet and cold.
I resent the resurrection when I feel the updraft of fear.

But approaching me with a watch in his hand, he said:
'I fear you are early; I expected a man; I see
That already your private rebellion has been quelled.
Where are the violent gestures of the individualist?
I observe the absence of the erratic, the strange;
Where is the tulip, the rose, or the bird in hand?'

I had the heart to relate the loss of my charms,
The paradise pets I kept in my pocket, the bird,

The tulip trumpet, the penis water pistol;
I had the heart to have mourned them, but no word.
'I have done little reading,' I murmured, 'I have
Most of the time been trying to find an equation.'

He glanced over my shoulder at the evening promenade.
The passing people, like Saint Vitus, averted their eyes:
I saw his eyes like a bent pin searching for eyes
To grip and catch. 'It is a species,' he said,
'I feel I can hardly cope with—it is ghosts,
Trailing, like snails, an excrement of blood.

'I have passed my hand like a postman's into them;
The information I dropped in at once dropped out.'
'No,' I answered, 'they received your bouquet of daffodils,
They speak of your feeling for Nature even now.'
He glanced at his watch. I admired a face.
The town clock chimed like a cat in a well.

'Since the private rebellion, the personal turn,
Leads down to the river with the dead cat and dead dog,
Since the single act of protest like a foggy film
Looks like women bathing, the Irish Lakes, or Saint Vitus,
Susceptible of innumerable interpretations,
I can only advise a suicide or a resolution.'

'I can resolve,' I answered, 'if you can absolve.
Relieve me of my absurd and abysmal past.'
'I cannot relieve or absolve—the only absolution
Is final resolution to fix on the facts.
I mean more and less than Birth and Death; I also mean
The mechanical paraphernalia in between.

'Not you and not him, not me, but all of them.
It is the conspiracy of five hundred million
To keep alive and kick. This is the resolution,
To keep us alive and kicking with strength or joy.
The past's absolution is the present's resolution.
The equation is the interdependence of parts.'

from PACIFIC SONNETS

Three Memorial Sonnets for two young seamen lost overboard in a storm in Mid-Pacific, January, 1940.

v

The seagull, spreadeagled, splayed on the wind,
Span backwards shrieking, belly facing upward,
Fled backward with a gimlet in its heart
To see the two youths swimming hand in hand
Through green eternity. O swept overboard
Not could the thirty-foot jaws them part,
Or the flouncing skirts that swept them over
Separate what death pronounced was love.

I saw them, the hand flapping like a flag,
And another like a dolphin with a child
Supporting him. Was I the shape of Jesus
When to me hopeward their eyeballs swivelled,
Saw I was standing in the stance of vague
Horror; paralysed with mere pity's peace?

vi

From thorax of storms the voices of verbs
Shall call to me without sound, like the silence
Round which cyclones rage, to nurse my nerve
And hang my heart midway, where the balance
Meets. I taste sea swilling in my bowels
As I sit shivering in the swing of waves
Like a face in a bubble. As the hull heaves
I and my ghost tread water over hell.

The greedy bitch with sailors in her guts
Green as a dream and formidable as God,
Spitting at stars, gnawing at shores, mad randy,
Riots with us on her abdomen and puts
Eternity in our cabins, pitches our pod
To the mouth of the death for which no one is ready.

VII

At midday they looked up and saw their death
Standing up overhead as loud as thunder
As white as angels and as broad as God:
Then, then the shock, the last gasp of breath
As grazing the bulwark they swept over and under,
All the green arms around them that load
Their eyes their ears their stomachs with eternals,
Whirled away in a white pool to the stern.

But the most possible of all miracles
Is that the useless tear that did not fall
From the corner of their eyes, was the prize,
The flowers, the gifts, the crystal sepulchre,
The funeral contribution and memorial,
The perfect and nonexistent obsequies.

XII

And now there is nothing left to celebrate
But the individual death in a ditch or a plane
Like a cock o' the north in a hurricane.
Out of the bogus glory and the synthetic hate,
The welter of nations and the speeches, O step down
You corpse in the gold and blue, out of a cloud,
My dragonfly, step down into your own:
The ditch and the dislocated wings and the cold
Kiss of the not to be monumental stone.

This is the only dignity left, the single
Death without purpose and without understanding
Like birds boys drop with catapults. Not comprehending
Denudes us of the personal aim and angle,
And so we are perfect sacrifice to nothing.

from SECULAR ELEGIES

V

O Golden Fleece she is where she lies tonight
Trammelled in her sheets like midsummer on a bed,

Kisses like moths flitter over her bright
Mouth, and, as she turns her head,
All space moves over to give her beauty room.

Where her hand, like a bird on the branch of her arm,
Droops its wings over the bedside as she sleeps,
There the air perpetually stays warm
Since, nested, her hand rested there. And she keeps
Under her green thumb life like a growing poem.

My nine-tiered tigress in the cage of sex
I feed with meat that you tear from my side
Crowning your nine months with the paradox:
The love that kisses with a homicide
In robes of red generation resurrects.

The bride who rides the hymenæal waterfall
Spawning all possibles in her pools of surplus,
Whom the train rapes going into a tunnel,
The imperial multiplicator nothing can nonplus:
My mother Nature is the origin of it all.

At Pharaoh's Feast and in the family cupboard,
Gay corpse, bright skeleton, and the fly in amber,
She sits with her laws like antlers from her forehead
Enmeshing everyone, with flowers and thunder
Adorning the head that destiny never worried.

TO MY MOTHER

Most near, most dear, most loved and most far,
Under the window where I often found her
Sitting as huge as Asia, seismic with laughter,
Gin and chicken helpless in her Irish hand,
Irresistible as Rabelais, but most tender for
The lame dogs and hurt birds that surround her,—
She is a procession no one can follow after
But be like a little dog following a brass band.

She will not glance up at the bomber, or condescend
To drop her gin and scuttle to a cellar,
But lean on the mahogany table like a mountain
Whom only faith can move, and so I send
O all my faith, and all my love to tell her
That she will move from mourning into morning.

TO ANY MEMBER OF
MY GENERATION

What was it you remember—the summer mornings
Down by the river at Richmond with a girl,
And as you kissed, clumsy in bathing costumes,
History guffawed in a rosebush. O what a warning—
If only we had known, if only we had known!
And when you looked in mirrors was this meaning
Plain as the pain in the centre of a pearl?
Horrible tomorrow in Teutonic postures
Making absurd the past we cannot disown?

Whenever we kissed we cocked the future's rifles
And from our wild-oat words, like dragon's teeth,
Death underfoot now arises; when we were gay
Dancing together in what we hoped was life,
Who was it in our arms but the whores of death
Whom we have found in our beds today, today?

NEWS OF THE WORLD III

Let her lie naked here, my hand resting
Light on her broken breast, the sleeping world
Given into our far from careful keeping,
Terrestrial daughter of a disaster of waters
No master honours. Let her lie tonight

Attended by those visions of bright swords
That never defended but ended life.
My emerald trembler, my sky skipping scullion,
See, now, your sister, dipping into the horizon,
Leaves us in darkness; you, nude, and I
Seeking to loose what the day retrieves,
An immoderation of love. Bend your arm
Under my generation of heads. The seas enfold
My sleepless eye and save it weeping
For the dishonoured star. I hear your grave
Nocturnal lamentation, where, abandoned, far,
You, like Arabia in her tent, mourn through an evening
Of wildernesses. O what are you grieving for?
From the tiara'd palaces of the Andes
And the last Asiatic terraces, I see
The wringing of the hands of all of the world,
I hear your long lingering of disillusion.
Favour the viper, heaven, with one vision
That it may see what is lost. The crime is blended
With the time and the cause. But at your
Guilty and golden bosom, O daughter of laws,
I happy lie tonight, the fingering zephyr
Light and unlikely as a kiss. The shades creep
Out of their holes and graves for a last
Long look at your bare empire as it rolls
Its derelict glory away into darkness. Turn, liar,
Back. Our fate is in your face. Whom do you love
But those whom you doom to the happy disgrace
Of adoring you with degradations? I garb my wife,
The wide world of a bride, in devastations.
She has curled up in my hand, and, like a moth,
Died a legend of splendour along the line of my life.
But the congregation of clouds paces in dolour
Over my head and her never barren belly
Where we lie, summered, together, a world and I.
Her birdflecked hair, sunsetting the weather,
Feathers my eye, she shakes an ear-ring sky,
And her hand of a country trembles against me.
The glittering nightriders gambol through
A zodiac of symbols above our love
Promising, O my star-crossed, death and disasters.

But I want breath for nothing but your possession
Now, now, this summer midnight, before the dawn
Shakes its bright gun in the sky, before
The serried battalions of lies and organizations of hate
Entirely encompass us, buried; before the wolf and friend
Render us enemies. Before all this,
Lie one night in my arms and give me peace.

DOG, DOG IN MY MANGER

Dog, dog in my manger, drag at my heathen
Heart where the swearing smoke of Love
Goes up as I give everything to the blaze.
Drag at my fires, dog, drag at my altars
Where Aztec I over my tabernacle raise
The Absalom assassination I my murder.

Dog, drag off the gifts too much I load
My life as wishing tree too heavy with:
And, dog, guide you my stray down quiet roads
Where peace is—be my engine of myth
That, dog, so drags me down my time
Sooner I shall rest from my overload.

Dog, is my shake when I come from water,
The cataract of my days, as red as danger?
O my joy has jaws that seize in fangs
The gift and hand of love always I sought for.
They come to me with kingdoms for my paucity—
Dog, why is my tooth red with their charity?

Mourn, dog, mourn over me where I lie
Not dead but spinning on the pinpoint hazard,
The fiftieth angel. Bay, bay in the blizzard
That brings a tear to my snowman's eye
And buries us all in what we most treasured.
Dog, why do we die so often before we die?

Dog, good dog, trick do and make me take
Calmly the consciousness of the crime
Born in the blood simply because we are here.
Your father burns for his father's sake,
So will a son burn in a further time
Under the bush of joy you planted here.

Dog, dog, your bone I am, who tear my life
Tatterdemalion from me. From you I have no peace,
No life at all unless you break my bone,
No bed unless I sleep upon my grief
That without you we are too much alone,
No peace until no peace is a happy home:
O dog my god, how can I cease to praise!

Karl Shapiro / 1913–

THE DOME OF SUNDAY

With focus sharp as Flemish-painted face
In film of varnish brightly fixed
And through a polished hand-lens deeply seen,
Sunday at noon through hyaline thin air
Sees down the street,
And in the camera of my eye depicts
Row-houses and row-lives:
Glass after glass, door after door the same,
Face after face the same, the same,
The brutal visibility the same;

As if one life emerging from one house
Would pause, a single image caught between
Two facing mirrors where vision multiplies
Beyond perspective,
A silent clatter in the high-speed eye
Spinning out photo-circulars of sight.

I see slip to the curb the long machines
Out of whose warm and windowed rooms pirouette
Shellacked with silk and light
The hard legs of our women.
Our women are one woman, dressed in black.
The carmine printed mouth
And cheeks as soft as muslin-glass belong
Outright to one dark dressy man,
Merely a swagger at her curvy side.
This is their visit to themselves:
All day from porch to porch they weave
A nonsense pattern through the even glare,
Stealing in surfaces
Cold vulgar glances at themselves.

And high up in the heated room all day
I wait behind the plate glass pane for one,
Hot as a voyeur for a glimpse of one,
The vision to blot out this woman's sheen;
All day my sight records expensively
Row-houses and row-lives.

But nothing happens; no diagonal
With melting shadow falls across the curb:
Neither the blinded negress lurching through fatigue,
Nor exiles bleeding from their pores,
Nor that bright bomb slipped lightly from its rack
To splinter every silvered glass and crystal prism,
Witch-bowl and perfume bottle
And billion candle-power dressing-bulb,
No direct hit to smash the shatter-proof
And lodge at last the quivering needle
Clean in the eye of one who stands transfixed
In fascination of her brightness.

THE FLY

O hideous little bat, the size of snot,
With polyhedral eye and shabby clothes,

To populate the stinking cat you walk
The promontory of the dead man's nose,
Climb with the fine leg of a Duncan-Phyfe
    The smoking mountains of my food
        And in a comic mood
In mid-air take to bed a wife.

Riding and riding with your filth of hair
On gluey foot or wing, forever coy,
Hot from the compost and green sweet decay,
Sounding your buzzer like an urchin toy—
You dot all whiteness with diminutive stool,
    In the tight belly of the dead
        Burrow with hungry head
And inlay maggots like a jewel.

At your approach the great horse stomps and paws
Bringing the hurricane of his heavy tail;
Shod in disease you dare to kiss my hand
Which sweeps against you like an angry flail;
Still you return, return, trusting your wing
    To draw you from the hunter's reach
        That learns to kill to teach
Disorder to the tinier thing.

My peace is your disaster. For your death
Children like spiders cup their pretty hands
And wives resort to chemistry of war.
In fens of sticky paper and quicksands
You glue yourself to death. Where you are stuck
    You struggle hideously and beg,
        You amputate your leg
Imbedded in the amber muck.

But I, a man, must swat you with my hate,
Slap you across the air and crush your flight,
Must mangle with my shoe and smear your blood,
Expose your little guts pasty and white,
Knock your head sidewise like a drunkard's hat,
    Pin your wings under like a crow's,
        Tear off your flimsy clothes
And beat you as one beats a rat.

Then like Gargantua I stride among
The corpses strewn like raisins in the dust,
The broken bodies of the narrow dead
That catch the throat with fingers of disgust.
I sweep. One gyrates like a top and falls
   And stunned, stone blind, and deaf
     Buzzes its frightful F
   And dies between three cannibals.

AUTO WRECK

Its quick soft silver bell beating, beating,
And down the dark one ruby flare
Pulsing out red light like an artery,
The ambulance at top speed floating down
Past beacons and illuminated clocks
Wings in a heavy curve, dips down,
And brakes speed, entering the crowd.
The doors leap open, emptying light;
Stretchers are laid out, the mangled lifted
And stowed into the little hospital.
Then the bell, breaking the hush, tolls once,
And the ambulance with its terrible cargo
Rocking, slightly rocking, moves away,
As the doors, an afterthought, are closed.

We are deranged, walking among the cops
Who sweep glass and are large and composed.
One is still making notes under the light.
One with a bucket douches ponds of blood
Into the street and gutter.
One hangs lanterns on the wrecks that cling,
Empty husks of locusts, to iron poles.

Our throats were tight as tourniquets,
Our feet were bound with splints, but now,
Like convalescents intimate and gauche,
We speak through sickly smiles and warn

With the stubborn saw of common sense,
The grim joke and the banal resolution.
The traffic moves around with care,
But we remain, touching a wound
That opens to our richest horror.
Already old, the question Who shall die?
Becomes unspoken Who is innocent?
For death in war is done by hands;
Suicide has cause and stillbirth, logic;
And cancer, simple as a flower, blooms.
But this invites the occult mind,
Cancels our physics with a sneer,
And spatters all we knew of denouement
Across the expedient and wicked stones.

SCYROS

snuffle and sniff and handkerchief

    The doctor punched my vein
    The captain called me Cain
Upon my belly sat the sow of fear
    With coins on either eye
    The President came by
And whispered to the braid what none could hear

    High over where the storm
    Stood steadfast cruciform
The golden eagle sank in wounded wheels
    White Negroes laughing still
    Crept fiercely on Brazil
Turning the navies upward on their keels

    Now one by one the trees
    Stripped to their naked knees
To dance upon the heaps of shrunken dead

The roof of England fell
    Great Paris tolled her bell
And China staunched her milk and wept for bread

    No island singly lay
    But lost its name that day
The Ainu dived across the plunging sands
    From dawn to dawn to dawn
    King George's birds came on
Strafing the tulips from his children's hands

    Thus in the classic sea
    Southeast from Thessaly
The dynamited mermen washed ashore
    And tritons dressed in steel
    Trolled heads with rod and reel
And dredged potatoes from the Aegean floor

    Hot is the sky and green
    Where Germans have been seen
The moon leaks metal on the Atlantic fields
    Pink boys in birthday shrouds
    Loop lightly through the clouds
Or coast the peaks of Finland on their shields

    That prophet year by year
    Lay still but could not hear
Where scholars tapped to find his new remains
    Gog and Magog ate pork
    In vertical New York
And war began next Wednesday on the Danes

HOLLYWOOD

Farthest from any war, unique in time
Like Athens or Baghdad, this city lies
Between dry purple mountains and the sea.
The air is clear and famous, every day

Bright as a postcard, bringing bungalows
    And sights. The broad nights advertise
For love and music and astronomy.

Heart of a continent, the hearts converge
On open boulevards where palms are nursed
With flare-pots like a grove, on villa roads
Where castles cultivated like a style
Breed fabulous metaphors in foreign stone,
    And on enormous movie lots
Where history repeats its vivid blunders.

Alice and Cinderella are most real.
Here may the tourist, quite sincere at last,
Rest from his dream of travels. All is new,
No ruins claim his awe, and permanence,
Despised like customs, fails at every turn.
    Here where the eccentric thrives,
Laughter and love are leading industries.

Luck is another. Here the bodyguard,
The parasite, the scholar are well paid,
The quack erects his alabaster office,
The moron and the genius are enshrined,
And the mystic makes a fortune quietly;
    Here all superlatives come true
And beauty is marketed like a basic food.

O can we understand it? Is it ours,
A crude whim of a beginning people,
A private orgy in a secluded spot?
Or alien like the word *harem*, or true
Like hideous Pittsburgh or depraved Atlanta?
    Is adolescence just as vile
As this its architecture and its talk?

Or are they parvenus, like boys and girls?
Or ours and happy, cleverest of all?
Yes. Yes. Though glamorous to the ignorant
This is the simplest city, a new school.
What is more nearly ours? If soul can mean
    The civilization of the brain,
This is a soul, a possible proud Florence.

POET

Il arrive que l'esprit demande la poesie

Left leg flung out, head cocked to the right,
Tweed coat or army uniform, with book,
Beautiful eyes, who is this walking down?
Who, glancing at the pane of glass looks sharp
And thinks it is not he—as when a poet
Comes swiftly on some half-forgotten poem
And loosely holds the page, steady of mind,
           Thinking it is not his?

And when will *you* exist?—Oh, it is I,
Incredibly skinny, stooped, and neat as pie,
Ignorant as dirt, erotic as an ape,
Dreamy as puberty—with dirty hair!
Into the room like kangaroo he bounds,
Ears flopping like the most expensive hound's;
His chin receives all questions as he bows
           Mouthing a green bon-bon.

Has no more memory than rubber. Stands
Waist-deep in heavy mud of thought and broods
At his own wetness. When he would get out,
To his surprise he lifts in air a phrase
As whole and clean and silvery as a fish
Which jumps and dangles on his damned hooked grin,
But like a name-card on a man's lapel
           Calls him a conscious fool.

And child-like he remembers all his life
And cannily constructs it, fact by fact,
As boys paste postage stamps in careful books,
Denoting pence and legends and profiles,
Nothing more valuable.—And like a thief,
His eyes glassed over and congealed with guilt,
Fondles his secrets like a case of tools,
           And waits in empty doors.

By men despised for knowing what he is,
And by himself. But he exists for women.
As dolls to girls, as perfect wives to men,
So he to women. And to himself a thing,
All ages, epicene, without a trade.
To girls and wives always alive and fated;
To men and scholars always dead like Greek
    And always mistranslated.

Towards exile and towards shame he lures himself,
Tongue winding on his arm, and thinks like Eve
By biting apple will become most wise.
Sentio ergo sum: he feels his way
And words themselves stand up for him like Braille
And punch and perforate his parchment ear.
All language falls like Chinese on his soul,
    Image of song unsounded.

This is the coward's coward that in his dreams
Sees shapes of pain grow tall. Awake at night
He peers at sounds and stumbles at a breeze.
And none holds life less dear. For as a youth
Who by some accident observes his love
Naked and in some natural ugly act,
He turns with loathing and with flaming hands,
    Seared and betrayed by sight.

He is the business man, on beauty trades,
Dealer in arts and thoughts who, like the Jew,
Shall rise from slums and hated dialects
A tower of bitterness. Shall be always strange,
Hunted and then sought after. Shall be sat
Like an ambassador from another race
At tables rich with music. He shall eat flowers,
Chew honey and spit out gall. They shall all smile
    And love and pity him.

His death shall be by drowning. In that hour
When the last bubble of pure heaven's air
Hovers within his throat, safe on his bed,
A small eternal figurehead in terror,

He shall cry out and clutch his days of straw
Before the blackest wave. Lastly, his tomb
Shall list and founder in the troughs of grass
          And none shall speak his name.

ELEGY FOR A DEAD SOLDIER

I

A white sheet on the tail-gate of a truck
Becomes an altar; two small candlesticks
Sputter at each side of the crucifix
Laid round with flowers brighter than the blood,
Red as the red of our apocalypse,
Hibiscus that a marching man will pluck
To stick into his rifle or his hat,
And great blue morning-glories pale as lips
That shall no longer taste or kiss or swear.
The wind begins a low magnificat,
The chaplain chats, the palmtrees swirl their hair,
The columns come together through the mud.

II

We too are ashes as we watch and hear
The psalm, the sorrow, and the simple praise
Of one whose promised thoughts of other days
Were such as ours, but now wholly destroyed,
The service record of his youth wiped out,
His dream dispersed by shot, must disappear.
What can we feel but wonder at a loss
That seems to point at nothing but the doubt
Which flirts our sense of luck into the ditch?
Reader of Paul who prays beside this fosse,
Shall we believe our eyes or legends rich
With glory and rebirth beyond the void?

III

For this comrade is dead, dead in the war,
A young man out of millions yet to live,
One cut away from all that war can give,

Freedom of self and peace to wander free.
Who mourns in all this sober multitude
Who did not feel the bite of it before
The bullet found its aim? This worthy flesh,
This boy laid in a coffin and reviewed—
Who has not wrapped himself in this same flag,
Heard the light fall of dirt, his wound still fresh,
Felt his eyes closed, and heard the distant brag
Of the last volley of humanity?

IV

By chance I saw him die, stretched on the ground,
A tattooed arm lifted to take the blood
Of someone else sealed in a tin. I stood
During the last delirium that stays
The intelligence a tiny moment more,
And then the strangulation, the last sound.
The end was sudden, like a foolish play,
A stupid fool slamming a foolish door,
The absurd catastrophe, half-prearranged,
And all the decisive things still left to say.
So we disbanded, angrier and unchanged,
Sick with the utter silence of dispraise.

V

We ask for no statistics of the killed,
For nothing political impinges on
This single casualty, or all those gone,
Missing or healing, sinking or dispersed,
Hundreds of thousands counted, millions lost.
More than an accident and less than willed
Is every fall, and this one like the rest.
However others calculate the cost,
To us the final aggregate is *one*,
One with a name, one transferred to the blest;
And though another stoops and takes the gun,
We cannot add the second to the first.

VI

I would not speak for him who could not speak
Unless my fear were true: he was not wronged,
He knew to which decision he belonged

But let it choose itself. Ripe in instinct,
Neither the victim nor the volunteer,
He followed, and the leaders could not seek
Beyond the followers. Much of this he knew;
The journey was a detour that would steer
Into the Lincoln Highway of a land
Remorselessly improved, excited, new,
And that was what he wanted. He had planned
To earn and drive. He and the world had winked.

VII

No history deceived him, for he knew
Little of times and armies not his own;
He never felt that peace was but a loan,
Had never questioned the idea of gain.
Beyond the headlines once or twice he saw
The gathering of a power by the few
But could not tell their names; he cast his vote,
Distrusting all the elected but not law.
He laughed at socialism; *on mourrait
Pour les industriels?* He shed his coat
And not for brotherhood, but for his pay.
To him the red flag marked the sewer main.

VIII

Above all else he loathed the homily,
The slogan and the ad. He paid his bill,
But not for Congressmen at Bunker Hill.
Ideals were few and those there were not made
For conversation. He belonged to church
But never spoke of God. The Christmas tree,
The Easter egg, baptism, he observed,
Never denied the preacher on his perch,
And would not sign Resolved That or Whereas.
Softness he had and hours and nights reserved
For thinking, dressing, dancing to the jazz.
His laugh was real, his manners were homemade.

IX

Of all men poverty pursued him least;
He was ashamed of all the down and out,
Spurned the panhandler like an uneasy doubt,

And saw the unemployed as a vague mass
Incapable of hunger or revolt.
He hated other races, south or east,
And shoved them to the margin of his mind.
He could recall the justice of the Colt,
Take interest in a gang-war like a game.
His ancestry was somewhere far behind
And left him only his peculiar name.
Doors opened, and he recognized no class.

X

His children would have known a heritage,
Just or unjust, the richest in the world,
The quantum of all art and science curled
In the horn of plenty, bursting from the horn,
A people bathed in honey, Paris come,
Vienna transferred with the highest wage,
A World's Fair spread to Phoenix, Jacksonville,
Earth's capital, the new Byzantium,
Kingdom of man—who knows? Hollow or firm,
No man can ever prophesy until
Out of our death some undiscovered germ,
Whole toleration or pure peace is born.

XI

The time to mourn is short that best becomes
The military dead. We lift and fold the flag,
Lay bare the coffin with its written tag,
And march away. Behind, four others wait
To lift the box, the heaviest of loads.
The anesthetic afternoon benumbs,
Sickens our senses, forces back our talk.
We know that others on tomorrow's roads
Will fall, ourselves perhaps, the man beside,
Over the world the threatened, all who walk:
And could we mark the grave of him who died
We would write this beneath his name and date:

EPITAPH

Underneath this wooden cross there lies
A Christian killed in battle. You who read,
Remember that this stranger died in pain;

And passing here, if you can lift your eyes
Upon a peace kept by a human creed,
Know that one soldier has not died in vain.

Dylan Thomas / 1914–1953

THE FORCE THAT THROUGH THE GREEN FUSE DRIVES THE FLOWER

The force that through the green fuse drives the flower
Drives my green age; that blasts the roots of trees
Is my destroyer.
And I am dumb to tell the crooked rose
My youth is bent by the same wintry fever.

The force that drives the water through the rocks
Drives my red blood; that dries the mouthing streams
Turns mine to wax.
And I am dumb to mouth unto my veins
How at the mountain spring the same mouth sucks.

The hand that whirls the water in the pool
Stirs the quicksand; that ropes the blowing wind
Hauls my shroud sail.
And I am dumb to tell the hanging man
How of my clay is made the hangman's lime.

The lips of time leech to the fountain head;
Love drips and gathers, but the fallen blood
Shall calm her sores.
And I am dumb to tell a weather's wind
How time has ticked a heaven round the stars.

And I am dumb to tell the lover's tomb
How at my sheet goes the same crooked worm.

AND DEATH SHALL HAVE NO DOMINION

And death shall have no dominion.
Dead men naked they shall be one
With the man in the wind and the west moon;
When their bones are picked clean and the clean bones
    gone,
They shall have stars at elbow and foot;
Though they go mad they shall be sane,
Though they sink through the sea they shall rise again;
Though lovers be lost love shall not;
And death shall have no dominion.

And death shall have no dominion.
Under the windings of the sea
They lying long shall not die windily;
Twisting on racks when sinews give way,
Strapped to a wheel, yet they shall not break;
Faith in their hands shall snap in two,
And the unicorn evils run them through;
Split all ends up they shan't crack;
And death shall have no dominion.

And death shall have no dominion.
No more may gulls cry at their ears
Or waves break loud on the seashores;
Where blew a flower may a flower no more
Lift its head to the blows of the rain;
Though they be mad and dead as nails,
Heads of the characters hammer through daisies;
Break in the sun till the sun breaks down,
And death shall have no dominion.

ALTARWISE BY OWL-LIGHT

I

Altarwise by owl-light in the half-way house
The gentleman lay graveward with his furies;

Abaddon in the hangnail cracked from Adam,
And, from his fork, a dog among the fairies,
The atlas-eater with a jaw for news,
Bit out the mandrake with to-morrow's scream.
Then, penny-eyed, that gentleman of wounds,
Old cock from nowheres and the heaven's egg,
With bones unbuttoned to the half-way winds,
Hatched from the windy salvage on one leg,
Scraped at my cradle in a walking word
That night of time under the Christward shelter:
I am the long world's gentleman, he said,
And share my bed with Capricorn and Cancer.

II

Death is all metaphors, shape in one history;
The child that sucketh long is shooting up,
The planet-ducted pelican of circles
Weans on an artery the gender's strip;
Child of the short spark in a shapeless country
Soon sets alight a long stick from the cradle;
The horizontal cross-bones of Abaddon,
You by the cavern over the black stairs,
Rung bone and blade, the verticals of Adam,
And, manned by midnight, Jacob to the stars.
Hairs of your head, then said the hollow agent,
Are but the roots of nettles and of feathers
Over these groundworks thrusting through a pavement
And hemlock-headed in the wood of weathers.

III

First there was the lamb on knocking knees
And three dead seasons on a climbing grave
That Adam's wether in the flock of horns,
Butt of the tree-tailed worm that mounted Eve,
Horned down with skullfoot and the skull of toes
On thunderous pavements in the garden time;
Rip of the vaults, I took my marrow-ladle
Out of the wrinkled undertaker's van,
And, Rip Van Winkle from a timeless cradle,
Dipped me breast-deep in the descended bone;
The black ram, shuffling of the year, old winter,
Alone alive among his mutton fold,

We rung our weathering changes on the ladder,
Said the antipodes, and twice spring chimed.

IV

What is the metre of the dictionary?
The size of genesis? the short spark's gender?
Shade without shape? the shape of Pharaoh's echo?
(My shape of age nagging the wounded whisper).
Which sixth of wind blew out the burning gentry?
(Questions are hunchbacks to the poker marrow).
What of a bamboo man among your acres?
Corset the boneyards for a crooked boy?
Button your bodice on a hump of splinters,
My camel's eyes will needle through the shrowd.
Love's reflection of the mushroom features,
Stills snapped by night in the bread-sided field,
Once close-up smiling in the wall of pictures,
Arc-lamped thrown back upon the cutting flood.

V

And from the windy West came two-gunned Gabriel,
From Jesu's sleeve trumped up the king of spots,
The sheath-decked jacks, queen with a shuffled heart;
Said the fake gentleman in suit of spades,
Black-tongued and tipsy from salvation's bottle.
Rose my Byzantine Adam in the night.
For loss of blood I fell on Ishmael's plain,
Under the milky mushrooms slew my hunger,
A climbing sea from Asia had me down
And Jonah's Moby snatched me by the hair,
Cross-stroked salt Adam to the frozen angel
Pin-legged on pole-hills with a black medusa
By waste seas where the white bear quoted Virgil
And sirens singing from our lady's sea-straw.

VI

Cartoon of slashes on the tide-traced crater,
He in a book of water tallow-eyed
By lava's light split through the oyster vowels
And burned sea silence on a wick of words.
Pluck, cock, my sea eye, said medusa's scripture,

Lop, love, my fork tongue, said the pin-hilled nettle;
And love plucked out the stinging siren's eye,
Old cock from nowheres lopped the minstrel tongue
Till tallow I blew from the wax's tower
The fats of midnight when the salt was singing;
Adam, time's joker, on a witch of cardboard
Spelt out the seven seas, an evil index,
The bagpipe-breasted ladies in the deadweed
Blew out the blood gauze through the wound of manwax.

VII

Now stamp the Lord's Prayer on a grain of rice,
A Bible-leaved of all the written woods
Strip to this tree: a rocking alphabet,
Genesis in the root, the scarecrow word,
And one light's language in the book of trees.
Doom on deniers at the wind-turned statement.
Time's tune my ladies with the teats of music,
The scaled sea-sawers, fix in a naked sponge
Who sucks the bell-voiced Adam out of magic,
Time, milk, and magic, from the world beginning.
Time is the tune my ladies lend their heartbreak,
From bald pavilions and the house of bread
Time tracks the sound of shape on man and cloud,
On rose and icicle the ringing handprint.

VIII

This was the crucifixion on the mountain,
Time's nerve in vinegar, the gallow grave
As tarred with blood as the bright thorns I wept;
The world's my wound, God's Mary in her grief,
Bent like three trees and bird-papped through her shift,
With pins for teardrops is the long wound's woman.
This was the sky, Jack Christ, each minstrel angle
Drove in the heaven-driven of the nails
Till the three-coloured rainbow from my nipples
From pole to pole leapt round the snail-waked world.
I by the tree of thieves, all glory's sawbones,
Unsex the skeleton this mountain minute,
And by this blowclock witness of the sun
Suffer the heaven's children through my heartbeat.

IX

From the oracular archives and the parchment,
Prophets and the fibre kings in oil and letter,
The lamped calligrapher, the queen in splints,
Buckle to lint and cloth their natron footsteps,
Draw on the glove of prints, dead Cairo's henna
Pour like a halo on the caps and serpents.
This was the resurrection in the desert,
Death from a bandage, rants the mask of scholars
Gold on such features, and the linen spirit
Weds my long gentleman to dusts and furies;
With priest and pharaoh bed my gentle wound,
World in the sand, on the triangle landscape,
With stones of odyssey for ash and garland
And rivers of the dead around my neck.

X

Let the tale's sailor from a Christian voyage
Atlaswise hold half-way off the dummy bay
Time's ship-racked gospel on the globe I balance:
So shall winged harbours through the rockbirds' eyes
Spot the blown word, and on the seas I image
December's thorn screwed in a brow of holly.
Let the first Peter from a rainbow's quayrail
Ask the tall fish swept from the bible east,
What rhubarb man peeled in her foam-blue channel
Has sown a flying garden round that sea-ghost?
Green as beginning, let the garden diving
Soar, with its two bark towers, to that Day
When the worm builds with the gold straws of venom
My nest of mercies in the rude, red tree.

A REFUSAL TO MOURN THE DEATH,
BY FIRE, OF A CHILD IN LONDON

Never until the mankind making
Bird beast and flower
Fathering and all humbling darkness

Tells with silence the last light breaking
And the still hour
Is come of the sea tumbling in harness

And I must enter again the round
Zion of the water bead
And the synagogue of the ear of corn
Shall I let pray the shadow of a sound
Or sow my salt seed
In the least valley of sackcloth to mourn

The majesty and burning of the child's death.
I shall not murder
The mankind of her going with a grave truth
Nor blaspheme down the stations of the breath
With any further
Elegy of innocence and youth.

Deep with the first dead lies London's daughter,
Robed in the long friends,
The grains beyond age, the dark veins of her mother,
Secret by the unmourning water
Of the riding Thames.
After the first death, there is no other.

DO NOT GO GENTLE INTO THAT GOOD NIGHT

Do not go gentle into that good night,
Old age should burn and rave at close of day;
Rage, rage against the dying of the light.

Though wise men at their end know dark is right,
Because their words had forked no lightning they
Do not go gentle into that good night.

Good men, the last wave by, crying how bright
Their frail deeds might have danced in a green bay,

Rage, rage against the dying of the light.

Wild men who caught and sang the sun in flight,
And learn, too late, they grieved it on its way,
Do not go gentle into that good night.

Grave men, near death, who see with blinding sight
Blind eyes could blaze like meteors and be gay,
Rage, rage against the dying of the light.

And you, my father, there on the sad height,
Curse, bless, me now with your fierce tears, I pray.
Do not go gentle into that good night.
Rage, rage against the dying of the light.

IN MY CRAFT OR SULLEN ART

In my craft or sullen art
Exercised in the still night
When only the moon rages
And the lovers lie abed
With all their griefs in their arms,
I labour by singing light
Not for ambition or bread
Or the strut and trade of charms
On the ivory stages
But for the common wages
Of their most secret heart.

Not for the proud man apart
From the raging moon I write
On these spindrift pages
Nor for the towering dead
With their nightingales and psalms
But for the lovers, their arms
Round the griefs of the ages,
Who pay no praise or wages
Nor heed my craft or art.

VISION AND PRAYER

I

Who
Are   you
Who   is   born
In   the   next   room
So   loud   to   my   own
That   I   can   hear   the   womb
Opening   and   the   dark   run
Over   the   ghost   and   the   dropped   son
Behind   the   wall   thin   as   a   wren's   bone?
In   the   birth   bloody   room   unknown
To   the   burn   and   turn   of   time
And   the   heart   print   of   man
Bows   no   baptism
But   dark   alone
Blessing   on
The   wild
Child.

I

Must   lie
Still   as   stone
By   the   wren   bone
Wall   hearing   the   moan
Of   the   mother   hidden
And   the   shadowed   head   of   pain
Casting   to-morrow   like   a   thorn
And   the   midwives   of   miracle   sing
Until   the   turbulent   new   born
Burns   me   his   name   and   his   flame
And   the   winged   wall   is   torn
By   his   torrid   crown
And   the   dark   thrown
From   his   loin
To   bright
Light.

When
The wren
Bone writhes down
And the first dawn
Furied by his stream
Swarms on the kingdom come
Of the dazzler of heaven
And the splashed mothering maiden
Who bore him with a bonfire in
His mouth and rocked him like a storm
I shall run lost in sudden
Terror and shining from
The once hooded room
Crying in vain
In the caldron
Of his
Kiss

In
The spin
Of the sun
In the spuming
Cyclone of his wing
For I was lost who am
Crying at the man drenched throne
In the first fury of his stream
And the lightnings of adoration
Back to black silence melt and mourn
For I was lost who have come
To dumbfounding haven
And the finding one
And the high noon
Of his wound
Blinds my
Cry.

There
Crouched bare
In the shrine
Of his blazing
Breast I shall waken
To the judge blown bedlam
Of the uncaged sea bottom
The cloud climb of the exhaling tomb
And the bidden dust upsailing
With his flame in every grain.
O spiral of ascension
From the vultured urn
Of the morning
Of man when
The land
And

The
Born sea
Praised the sun
The finding one
And upright Adam
Sang upon origin!
O the wings of the children!
The woundward flight of the ancient
Young from the canyons of oblivion!
The sky stride of the always slain
In battle! the happening
Of saints to their vision!
The world winding home!
And the whole pain
Flows open
And I
Die.

II

In the name of the lost who glory in
The swinish plains of carrion
Under the burial song
Of the birds of burden
Heavy with the drowned
And the green dust
And bearing
The ghost
From
The ground
Like pollen
On the black plume
And the beak of slime
I pray though I belong
Not wholly to that lamenting
Brethren for joy has moved within
The inmost marrow of my heart bone

That he who learns now the sun and moon
Of his mother's milk may return
Before the lips blaze and bloom
To the birth bloody room
Behind the wall's wren
Bone and be dumb
And the womb
That bore
For
All men
The adored
Infant light or
The dazzling prison
Yawn to his upcoming.
In the name of the wanton
Lost on the unchristened mountain
In the centre of dark I pray him

That he let the dead lie though they moan
  For his briared hands to hoist them
    To the shrine of his world's wound
      And the blood drop's garden
        E n d u r e   t h e   s t o n e
          Blind host to sleep
            I n   t h e   d a r k
              A n d   d e e p
                Rock
              A w a k e
            No heart bone
          B u t   l e t   i t   b r e a k
        On the mountain crown
      U n b i d d e n   b y   t h e   s u n
    And the beating dust be blown
  Down to the river rooting plain
Under the night forever falling.

Forever falling night is a known
  Star and country to the legion
    Of sleepers whose tongue I toll
      To mourn his deluging
        Light through sea and soil
          And we have come
            To know all
              P l a c e s
                Ways
              M a z e s
            P a s s a g e s
          Quarters and graves
        Of the endless fall.
      N o w   c o m m o n   lazarus
    Of the charting sleepers prays
  N e v e r   t o   a w a k e   a n d   a r i s e
For the country of death is the heart's size

And the star of the lost the shape of the eyes.
In the name of the fatherless
In the name of the unborn
And the undesirers
Of midwiving morning's
Hands or instruments
O in the name
Of no one
Now or
No
One to
Be I pray
May the crimson
Sun spin a grave grey
And the colour of clay
Stream upon his martyrdom
In the interpreted evening
And the known dark of the earth amen.

I turn the corner of prayer and burn
In a blessing of the sudden
Sun. In the name of the damned
I would turn back and run
To the hidden land
But the loud sun
Christens down
The sky.
I
Am found.
O let him
Scald me and drown
Me in his world's wound.
His lightning answers my
Cry. My voice burns in his hand.
Now I am lost in the blinding
One. The sun roars at the prayer's end.

FERN HILL

Now as I was young and easy under the apple boughs
About the lilting house and happy as the grass was green,
　　　The night above the dingle starry,
　　　　　Time let me hail and climb
　　　　Golden in the heydays of his eyes,
And honoured among wagons I was prince of the apple towns
And once below a time I lordly had the trees and leaves
　　　　　Trail with daisies and barley
　　　　Down the rivers of the windfall light.

And as I was green and carefree, famous among the barns
About the happy yard and singing as the farm was home,
　　　　In the sun that is young once only,
　　　　　Time let me play and be
　　　　Golden in the mercy of his means,
And green and golden I was huntsman and herdsman,
　　　the calves
Sang to my horn, the foxes on the hills barked clear and cold,
　　　　　And the sabbath rang slowly
　　　　In the pebbles of the holy streams.

All the sun long it was running, it was lovely, the hay
Fields high as the house, the tunes from the chimneys,
　　　　it was air
　　　　And playing, lovely and watery
　　　　　And fire green as grass.
　　　　And nightly under the simple stars
As I rode to sleep the owls were bearing the farm away,
All the moon long I heard, blessed among stables, the nightjars
　　　　　Flying with the ricks, and the horses
　　　　　Flashing into the dark.

And then to awake, and the farm, like a wanderer white
With the dew, come back, the cock on his shoulder: it was all
　　　　Shining, it was Adam and maiden,
　　　　　The sky gathered again
　　　　And the sun grew round that very day.

So it must have been after the birth of the simple light
In the first, spinning place, the spellbound horses walking
    warm
      Out of the whinnying green stable
        On to the fields of praise.

And honoured among foxes and pheasants by the gay house
Under the new made clouds and happy as the heart was long,
      In the sun born over and over,
        I ran my heedless ways,
      My wishes raced through the house high hay
And nothing I cared, at my sky blue trades, that time allows
In all his tuneful turning so few and such morning songs
      Before the children green and golden
        Follow him out of grace,

Nothing I cared, in the lamb white days, that time would
    take me
Up to the swallow thronged loft by the shadow of my hand,
      In the moon that is always rising,
        Nor that riding to sleep
    I should hear him fly with the high fields
And wake to the farm forever fled from the childless land.
Oh as I was young and easy in the mercy of his means,
      Time held me green and dying
      Though I sang in my chains like the sea.

Randall Jarrell / 1914–1965

THE SNOW-LEOPARD

His pads furring the scarp's rime,
Weightless in greys and ecru, gliding
Invisibly, incuriously

As the crystals of the cirri wandering
A mile below his absent eyes,
The leopard gazes at the caravan.
The yaks groaning with tea, the burlaps
Lapping and lapping each stunned universe
That gasps like a kettle for its thinning life
Are pools in the interminable abyss
That ranges up through ice, through air, to night.
Raiders of the unminding element,
The last cold capillaries of their kind,
They move so slowly they are motionless
To any eye less stubborn than a man's. . . .
From the implacable jumble of the blocks
The grains dance icily, a scouring plume,
Into the breath, sustaining, unsustainable,
They trade to that last stillness for their death.
They sense with misunderstanding horror, with desire,
Behind the world their blood sets up in mist
The brute and geometrical necessity:
The leopard waving with a grating purr
His six-foot tail; the leopard, who looks sleepily—
Cold, fugitive, secure—at all that he knows,
At all that he is: the heart of heartlessness.

THE DEATH OF THE BALL
TURRET GUNNER

From my mother's sleep I fell into the State,
And I hunched in its belly till my wet fur froze.
Six miles from earth, loosed from its dream of life,
I woke to black flak and the nightmare fighters.
When I died they washed me out of the turret with a hose.

LOSSES

It was not dying: everybody died.
It was not dying: we had died before
In the routine crashes—and our fields
Called up the papers, wrote home to our folks,
And the rates rose, all because of us.
We died on the wrong page of the almanac,
Scattered on mountains fifty miles away;
Diving on haystacks, fighting with a friend,
We blazed up on the lines we never saw.
We died like aunts or pets or foreigners.
(When we left high school nothing else had died
For us to figure we had died like.)

In our new planes, with our new crews, we bombed
The ranges by the desert or the shore,
Fired at towed targets, waited for our scores—
And turned into replacements and woke up
One morning, over England, operational.
It wasn't different: but if we died
It was not an accident but a mistake
(But an easy one for anyone to make).
We read our mail and counted up our missions—
In bombers named for girls, we burned
The cities we had learned about in school—
Till our lives wore out; our bodies lay among
The people we had killed and never seen.
When we lasted long enough they gave us medals;
When we died they said, "Our casualties were low."

They said, "Here are the maps"; we burned the cities.
It was not dying—no, not ever dying;
But the night I died I dreamed that I was dead,
And the cities said to me: "Why are you dying?
We are satisfied, if you are; but why did I die?"

SECOND AIR FORCE

Far off, above the plain the summer dries,
The great loops of the hangars sway like hills.
Buses and weariness and loss, the nodding soldiers
Are wire, the bare frame building, and a pass
To what was hers; her head hides his square patch
And she thinks heavily: My son is grown.
She sees a world: sand roads, tar-paper barracks,
The bubbling asphalt of the runways, sage,
The dunes rising to the interminable ranges,
The dim flights moving over clouds like clouds.
The armorers in their patched faded green,
Sweat-stiffened, banded with brass cartridges,
Walk to the line; their Fortresses, all tail,
Stand wrong and flimsy on their skinny legs,
And the crews climb to them clumsily as bears.
The head withdraws into its hatch (a boy's),
The engines rise to their blind laboring roar,
And the green, made beasts run home to air.
Now in each aspect death is pure.
(At twilight they wink over men like stars
And hour by hour, through the night, some see
The great lights floating in—from Mars, from Mars.)
How emptily the watchers see them gone.

They go, there is silence; the woman and her son
Stand in the forest of the shadows, and the light
Washes them like water. In the long-sunken city
Of evening, the sunlight stills like sleep
The faint wonder of the drowned; in the evening,
In the last dreaming light, so fresh, so old,
The soldiers pass like beasts, unquestioning,
And the watcher for an instant understands
What there is then no need to understand;
But she wakes from her knowledge, and her stare,
A shadow now, moves emptily among
The shadows learning in their shadowy fields
The empty missions.

Remembering,
She hears the bomber calling, *Little Friend!*
To the fighter hanging in the hostile sky,
And sees the ragged flame eat, rib by rib,
Along the metal of the wing into her heart:
The lives stream out, blossom, and float steadily
To the flames of the earth, the flames
That burn like stars above the lands of men.

She saves from the twilight that takes everything
A squadron shipping, in its last parade—
Its dogs run by it, barking at the band—
A gunner walking to his barracks, half-asleep,
Starting at something, stumbling (above, invisible,
The crews in the steady winter of the sky
Tremble in their wired fur); and feels for them
The love of life for life. The hopeful cells
Heavy with someone else's death, cold carriers
Of someone else's victory, grope past their lives
Into her own bewilderment: The years meant *this?*

But for them the bombers answer everything.

THE STATE

When they killed my mother it made me nervous;
I thought to myself, It was *right*:
Of course she was crazy, and how she ate!
And she died, after all, in her way, for the State.
But I minded: how queer it was to stare
At one of them not sitting there.

When they drafted Sister I said all night,
"It's healthier there in the fields";
And I'd think, "Now I'm helping to win the War,"
When the neighbors came in, as they did, with my meals.
And I was, I was; but I was scared
With only one of them sitting there.

When they took my cat for the Army Corps
Of Conservation and Supply,
I thought of him there in the cold with the mice
And I cried, and I cried, and I wanted to die.
They were there, and I saw them, and that is my life.
Now there's nothing. I'm dead, and I want to die.

THE WOMAN AT
THE WASHINGTON ZOO

The saris go by me from the embassies.

Cloth from the moon. Cloth from another planet.
They look back at the leopard like the leopard.

And I. . . .
          this print of mine, that has kept its color
Alive through so many cleanings; this dull null
Navy I wear to work, and wear from work, and so
To my bed, so to my grave, with no
Complaints, no comment: neither from my chief,
The Deputy Chief Assistant, nor his chief—
Only I complain. . . . this serviceable
Body that no sunlight dyes, no hand suffuses
But, dome-shadowed, withering among columns,
Wavy beneath fountains—small, far-off, shining
In the eyes of animals, these beings trapped
As I am trapped but not, themselves, the trap,
Aging, but without knowledge of their age,
Kept safe here, knowing not of death, for death—
Oh, bars of my own body, open, open!

The world goes by my cage and never sees me.
And there come not to me, as come to these,
The wild beasts, sparrows pecking the llamas' grain,
Pigeons settling on the bears' bread, buzzards
Tearing the meat the flies have clouded. . . .
                                        Vulture,
When you come for the white rat that the foxes left,

Take off the red helmet of your head, the black
Wings that have shadowed me, and step to me as man:
The wild brother at whose feet the white wolves fawn,
To whose hand of power the great lioness
Stalks, purring. . . .
                    You know what I was,
You see what I am: change me, change me!

John Berryman / 1914–

WINTER LANDSCAPE

The three men coming down the winter hill
In brown, with tall poles and a pack of hounds
At heel, through the arrangement of the trees,
Past the five figures at the burning straw,
Returning cold and silent to their town,

Returning to the drifted snow, the rink
Lively with children, to the older men,
The long companions they can never reach,
The blue light, men with ladders, by the church
The sledge and shadow in the twilit street,

Are not aware that in the sandy time
To come, the evil waste of history
Outstretched, they will be seen upon the brow
Of that same hill: when all their company
Will have been irrecoverably lost,

These men, this particular three in brown
Witnessed by birds will keep the scene and say
By their configuration with the trees,
The small bridge, the red houses and the fire,
What place, what time, what morning occasion

Sent them into the wood, a pack of hounds
At heel and the tall poles upon their shoulders,
Thence to return as now we see them and
Ankle-deep in snow down the winter hill
Descend, while three birds watch and the fourth flies.

DESIRES OF MEN AND WOMEN

Exasperated, worn, you conjure a mansion,
The absolute butlers in the spacious hall,
Old silver, lace, and privacy, a house
Where nothing has for years been out of place,
Neither shoe-horn nor affection been out of place,
Breakfast in summer on the eastern terrace,
All justice and all grace.

              At the reception
Most beautifully you conduct yourselves—
Expensive and accustomed, bow, speak French,
That Cinquecento miniature recall
The Duke presented to your great-grandmother—

And none of us, my dears, would dream of you
The half-lit and lascivious apartments
That are in fact your goal, for which you'd do
Murder if you had not your cowardice
To prop the law; or dream of you the rooms,
Glaring and inconceivably vulgar,
Where now you are, where now you wish for life,
Whence you project your naked fantasies.

CONVERSATION

Whether the moorings are invisible
Or slipt, we said we could not tell,

But argument held one thing sure
Which none of us that night could well endure:
The ship is locked with fog, no man aboard
Can make out what he's moving toward,
There's little food, few love, less sleep,
The sea is dark and we are told it's deep.

Where is an officer who knows this coast?
If all such men long since have faced
Downward, one summon. Who knows how,
With what fidelity, his voice heard now
Could shout directions from the ocean's floor?
Traditional characters no more
Their learnéd simple parts rehearse
But bed them softly down from the time's curse.

A snapt short log pitched out upon the hearth,
The flaming harbinger come forth
Of holocausts that night and day
Flake from the mind its skinny sovereignty.
We watched the embers cool, embers that brought
To one man there the failing thought
Of cities stripped of knowledge, men,
Our continent a wilderness again.

These are conclusions of the night, we said;
And drank; and were not satisfied.
The fire died down, smoke in the air
Assumed the alarming postures of our fear,—
The overhead horror, in the padded room
The man who will not tell his name,
The guns and subtle friends who face
Into this delicate and dangerous place.

WHETHER THERE IS SORROW
IN THE DEMONS

Near the top a bad turn some dare. Well,
The horse swerves and screams, his eyes pop,

Feet feel air, the firm winds prop
Jaws wide wider until
Through great teeth rider greets the smiles of Hell.

Thick night, where the host's thews crack like thongs
A welcome, curving abrupt on cheek & neck.
No wing swings over once to check
Lick of their fire's tongues,
Whip & chuckle, hoarse insulting songs.

Powers immortal, fixed, intractable.
Only the lost soul jerks whom they joy hang:
Clap of remorse, and tang and fang
More frightful than the drill
An outsize dentist scatters down a skull;

Nostalgia rips him swinging. Fast in malice
How may his masters mourn, how ever yearn
The frore pride wherein they burn?
God's fire. To what *qui tollis*
Stone-tufted ears prick back towards the bright Palace?

Whence Lucifer shone Lucifer's friends hail
The scourge of choice made at the point of light
Destined into eternal night;
Motionless to fulfil
Their least, their envy looks up dense and pale.

.. Repine blackmarket felons; murderers
Sit still their time, till yellow feet go first,
Dies soon in them, and can die, thirst;
Not lives in these, nor years
On years scar their despair—which yet rehearse ...

Their belvedere is black. They believe, and quail.
One shudder racks them only, lonely, and
No mirror breaks at their command.
Unsocketed, their will
Grinds on their fate. So was, so shall be still.

NEW YEAR'S EVE

The grey girl who had not been singing stopped,
And a brave new no-sound blew through acrid air.
I set my drink down, hard. Somebody slapped
Somebody's second wife somewhere,
Wheeling away to long to be alone.
I see the dragon of years is almost done,
Its claws loosen, its eyes
Crust now with tears & lust and a scale of lies.

A whisky-listless and excessive saint
Was expounding his position, whom I hung
Boy-glad in glowing heaven: he grows faint:
Hearing what song the sirens sung,
Sidelong he web-slid and some rich prose spun.
The tissue golden of the gifts undone
Surpassed the gifts. Miss Weirs
Whispers to me her international fears.

Intelligentsia milling. In a semi-German
(Our loss of Latin fractured how far our fate,—
Disinterested once, linkage once like a sermon)
I struggle to articulate
Why it is our promise breaks in pieces early.
The Muses' visitants come soon, go surly
With liquor & mirrors away
In this land wealthy & casual as a holiday.

Whom the Bitch winks at. Most of us are linsey-
woolsey workmen, grandiose, and slack.
On m'analyse, the key to secrets. Kinsey
Shortly will tell us sharply back
Habits we stuttered. How revive to join
(Great evils grieve beneath: eye Caesar's coin)
And lure a while more home
The vivid wanderers, uneasy with our shame?

Priests of the infinite! ah, not for long.
The dove whispers, and diminishes

Up the blue leagues. And no doubt we heard wrong—
Wax of our lives collects & dulls; but was
What we heard hurried as we memorized,
Or brightened, or adjusted? Undisguised
We pray our tongues & fingers
Record the strange word that blows suddenly and lingers.

Imagine a patience in the works of love
Luck sometimes visits. Ages we have sighed,
And cleave more sternly to a music of
Even this sore word 'genocide'.
Each to his own! Clockless & thankless dream
And labour Makers, being what we seem.
Soon soon enough we turn
Our tools in; brownshirt Time Chiefly our works will burn.

I remember: white fine flour everywhere whirled
Ceaselessly, wheels rolled, a slow thunder boomed,
And there were snowy men in the mill-world
With sparkling eyes, light hair uncombed,
And one of them was humming an old song,
Sack upon sack grew portly, until strong
Arms moved them on, by pairs,
And then the bell clanged and they ran like hares.

Scotch in his oxter, my Retarded One
Blows in before the midnight; freezing slush
Stamps off, off. Worth of years! . . no matter, begone;
Your slash and spells (in the sudden hush)
We see now we had to suffer some day, so
I cross the dragon with a blessing, low,
While the black blood slows. Clock-wise,
We clasp upon the stroke, kissing with happy cries.

DREAM SONG 14

Life, friends, is boring. We must not say so.
After all, the sky flashes, the great sea yearns,

we ourselves flash and yearn,
and moreover my mother told me as a boy
(repeatingly) 'Ever to confess you're bored
means you have no

Inner Resources.' I conclude now I have no
inner resources, because I am heavy bored.
Peoples bore me,
literature bores me, especially great literature,
Henry bores me, with his plights & gripes
as bad as achilles,

who loves people and valiant art, which bores me.
And the tranquil hills, & gin, look like a drag
and somehow a dog
has taken itself & its tail considerably away
into mountains or sea or sky, leaving
behind: me, wag.

Robert Lowell / 1917–

NEW YEAR'S DAY

Again and then again . . . the year is born
To ice and death, and it will never do
To skulk behind storm-windows by the stove
To hear the postgirl sounding her French horn
When the thin tidal ice is wearing through.
Here is the understanding not to love
Our neighbor, or tomorrow that will sieve
Our resolutions. While we live, we live

To snuff the smoke of victims. In the snow
The kitten heaved its hindlegs, as if fouled,
And died. We bent it in a Christmas box

And scattered blazing weeds to scare the crow
Until the snake-tailed sea-winds coughed and howled
For alms outside the church whose double locks
Wait for St. Peter, the distorted key.
Under St. Peter's bell the parish sea

Swells with its smelt into the burlap shack
Where Joseph plucks his hand-lines like a harp,
And hears the fearful *Puer natus est*
Of Circumcision, and relives the wrack
And howls of Jesus whom he holds. How sharp
The burden of the Law before the beast:
Time and the grindstone and the knife of God.
The Child is born in blood, O child of blood.

THE QUAKER GRAVEYARD
IN NANTUCKET

for Warren Winslow, dead at sea

*Let man have dominion over the fishes of the sea and the
fowls of the air and the beasts and the whole earth, and
every creeping creature that moveth upon the earth.*

I

A brackish reach of shoal off Madaket,—
The sea was still breaking violently and night
Had steamed into our North Atlantic Fleet,
When the drowned sailor clutched the drag-net. Light
Flashed from his matted head and marble feet,
He grappled at the net
With the coiled, hurdling muscles of his thighs:
The corpse was bloodless, a botch of reds and whites,
Its open, staring eyes
Were lustreless dead-lights
Or cabin-windows on a stranded hulk
Heavy with sand. We weight the body, close
Its eyes and heave it seaward whence it came,

Where the heel-headed dogfish barks its nose
On Ahab's void and forehead; and the name
Is blocked in yellow chalk.
Sailors, who pitch this portent at the sea
Where dreadnaughts shall confess
Its hell-bent deity,
When you are powerless
To sand-bag this Atlantic bulwark, faced
By the earth-shaker, green, unwearied, chaste
In his steel scales: ask for no Orphean lute
To pluck life back. The guns of the steeled fleet
Recoil and then repeat
The hoarse salute.

II

Whenever winds are moving and their breath
Heaves at the roped-in bulwarks of this pier,
The terns and sea-gulls tremble at your death
In these home waters. Sailor, can you hear
The Pequod's sea wings, beating landward, fall
Headlong and break on our Atlantic wall
Off 'Sconset, where the yawing S-boats splash
The bellbuoy, with ballooning spinnakers,
As the entangled, screeching mainsheet clears
The blocks: off Madaket, where lubbers lash
The heavy surf and throw their long lead squids
For blue-fish? Sea-gulls blink their heavy lids
Seaward. The winds' wings beat upon the stones,
Cousin, and scream for you and the claws rush
At the sea's throat and wring it in the slush
Of this old Quaker graveyard where the bones
Cry out in the long night for the hurt beast
Bobbing by Ahab's whaleboats in the East.

III

All you recovered from Poseidon died
With you, my cousin, and the harrowed brine
Is fruitless on the blue beard of the god,
Stretching beyond us to the castles in Spain,
Nantucket's westward haven. To Cape Cod
Guns, cradled on the tide,

Blast the eelgrass about a waterclock
Of bilge and backwash, roil the salt and sand
Lashing earth's scaffold, rock
Our warships in the hand
Of the great God, where time's contrition blues
Whatever it was these Quaker sailors lost
In the mad scramble of their lives. They died
When time was open-eyed,
Wooden and childish; only bones abide
There, in the nowhere, where their boats were tossed
Sky-high, where mariners had fabled news
Of IS, the whited monster. What it cost
Them is their secret. In the sperm-whale's slick
I see the Quakers drown and hear their cry:
"If God himself had not been on our side,
If God himself had not been on our side,
When the Atlantic rose against us, why,
Then it had swallowed us up quick."

IV

This is the end of the whaleroad and the whale
Who spewed Nantucket bones on the thrashed swell
And stirred the troubled waters to whirlpools
To send the Pequod packing off to hell:
This is the end of them, three-quarters fools,
Snatching at straws to sail
Seaward and seaward on the turntail whale,
Spouting out blood and water as it rolls,
Sick as a dog to these Atlantic shoals:
Clamavimus, O depths. Let the sea-gulls wail

For water, for the deep where the high tide
Mutters to its hurt self, mutters and ebbs.
Waves wallow in their wash, go out and out,
Leave only the death-rattle of the crabs,
The beach increasing, its enormous snout
Sucking the ocean's side.
This is the end of running on the waves;
We are poured out like water. Who will dance
The mast-lashed master of Leviathans
Up from this field of Quakers in their unstoned graves?

V

When the whale's viscera go and the roll
Of its corruption overruns this world
Beyond tree-swept Nantucket and Wood's Hole
And Martha's Vineyard, Sailor, will your sword
Whistle and fall and sink into the fat?
In the great ash-pit of Jehoshaphat
The bones cry for the blood of the white whale,
The fat flukes arch and whack about its ears,
The death-lance churns into the sanctuary, tears
The gun-blue swingle, heaving like a flail,
And hacks the coiling life out: it works and drags
And rips the sperm-whale's midriff into rags,
Bobbets of blubber spill to wind and weather,
Sailor, and gulls go round the stoven timbers
Where the morning stars sing out together
And thunder shakes the white surf and dismembers
The red flag hammered in the mast-head. Hide,
Our steel, Jonas Messias, in Thy side.

VI

OUR LADY OF WALSINGHAM

There once the penitents took off their shoes
And then walked barefoot the remaining mile;
And the small trees, a stream and hedgerows file
Slowly along the munching English lane,
Like cows to the old shrine, until you lose
Track of your dragging pain.
The stream flows down under the druid tree,
Shiloah's whirlpools gurgle and make glad
The castle of God. Sailor, you were glad
And whistled Sion by that stream. But see:

Our Lady, too small for her canopy,
Sits near the altar. There's no comeliness
At all or charm in that expressionless
Face with its heavy eyelids. As before,
This face, for centuries a memory,
Non est species, neque decor,
Expressionless, expresses God: it goes

Past castled Sion. She knows what God knows,
Not Calvary's Cross nor crib at Bethlehem
Now, and the world shall come to Walsingham.

VII

The empty winds are creaking and the oak
Splatters and splatters on the cenotaph,
The boughs are trembling and a gaff
Bobs on the untimely stroke
Of the greased wash exploding on a shoal-bell
In the old mouth of the Atlantic. It's well;
Atlantic, you are fouled with the blue sailors,
Sea-monsters, upward angel, downward fish:
Unmarried and corroding, spare of flesh
Mart once of supercilious, wing'd clippers,
Atlantic, where your bell-trap guts its spoil
You could cut the brackish winds with a knife
Here in Nantucket, and cast up the time
When the Lord God formed man from the sea's slime
And breathed into his face the breath of life,
And blue-lung'd combers lumbered to the kill.
The Lord survives the rainbow of His will.

THE DRUNKEN FISHERMAN

Wallowing in this bloody sty,
I cast for fish that pleased my eye
(Truly Jehovah's bow suspends
No pots of gold to weight its ends);
Only the blood-mouthed rainbow trout
Rose to my bait. They flopped about
My canvas creel until the moth
Corrupted its unstable cloth.

A calendar to tell the day;
A handkerchief to wave away
The gnats; a couch unstuffed with storm

Pouching a bottle in one arm;
A whiskey bottle full of worms;
And bedroom slacks: are these fit terms
To mete the worm whose molten rage
Boils in the belly of old age?

Once fishing was a rabbit's foot—
O wind blow cold, O wind blow hot,
Let suns stay in or suns step out:
Life danced a jig on the sperm-whale's spout—
The fisher's fluent and obscene
Catches kept his conscience clean.
Children, the raging memory drools
Over the glory of past pools.

Now the hot river, ebbing, hauls
Its bloody waters into holes;
A grain of sand inside my shoe
Mimics the moon that might undo
Man and Creation too; remorse,
Stinking, has puddled up its source;
Here tantrums thrash to a whale's rage.
This is the pot-hole of old age.

Is there no way to cast my hook
Out of this dynamited brook?
The Fisher's sons must cast about
When shallow waters peter out.
I will catch Christ with a greased worm,
And when the Prince of Darkness stalks
My bloodstream to its Stygian term . . .
On water the Man-Fisher walks.

AS A PLANE TREE BY THE WATER

Darkness has called to darkness, and disgrace
Elbows about our windows in this planned

Babel of Boston where our money talks
And multiplies the darkness of a land
Of preparation where the Virgin walks
And roses spiral her enamelled face
Or fall to splinters on unwatered streets.
Our Lady of Babylon, go by, go by,
I was once the apple of your eye;
Flies, flies are on the plane tree, on the streets.

The flies, the flies, the flies of Babylon
Buzz in my ear-drums while the devil's long
Dirge of the people detonates the hour
For floating cities where his golden tongue
Enchants the masons of the Babel Tower
To raise tomorrow's city to the sun
That never sets upon these hell-fire streets
Of Boston, where the sunlight is a sword
Striking at the withholder of the Lord:
Flies, flies are on the plane tree, on the streets.

Flies strike the miraculous waters of the iced
Atlantic and the eyes of Bernadette
Who saw Our Lady standing in the cave
At Massabielle, saw her so squarely that
Her vision put out reason's eyes. The grave
Is open-mouthed and swallowed up in Christ.
O walls of Jericho! And all the streets
To our Atlantic wall are singing: "Sing,
Sing for the resurrection of the King."
Flies, flies are on the plane tree, on the streets.

MR. EDWARDS AND THE SPIDER

I saw the spiders marching through the air,
   Swimming from tree to tree that mildewed day
      In latter August when the hay
         Came creaking to the barn. But where

The wind is westerly,
Where gnarled November makes the spiders fly
Into the apparitions of the sky,
They purpose nothing but their ease and die
Urgently beating east to sunrise and the sea;

What are we in the hands of the great God?
It was in vain you set up thorn and briar
    In battle array against the fire
    And treason crackling in your blood;
      For the wild thorns grow tame
And will do nothing to oppose the flame;
Your lacerations tell the losing game
You play against a sickness past your cure.
How will the hands be strong? How will the heart endure?

A very little thing, a little worm,
Or hourglass-blazoned spider, it is said,
    Can kill a tiger. Will the dead
    Hold up his mirror and affirm
      To the four winds the smell
And flash of his authority? It's well
If God who holds you to the pit of hell,
Much as one holds a spider, will destroy,
Baffle and dissipate your soul. As a small boy

On Windsor Marsh, I saw the spider die
When thrown into the bowels of fierce fire:
    There's no long struggle, no desire
    To get up on its feet and fly—
      It stretches out its feet
And dies. This is the sinner's last retreat;
Yes, and no strength exerted on the heat
Then sinews the abolished will, when sick
And full of burning, it will whistle on a brick.

But who can plumb the sinking of that soul?
Josiah Hawley, picture yourself cast
    Into a brick-kiln where the blast
    Fans your quick vitals to a coal—
      If measured by a glass,

How long would it seem burning! Let there pass
A minute, ten, ten trillion; but the blaze
Is infinite, eternal: this is death,
To die and know it. This is the Black Widow, death.

THE DEAD IN EUROPE

After the planes unloaded, we fell down
Buried together, unmarried men and women;
Not crown of thorns, not iron, not Lombard crown,
Not grilled and spindle spires pointing to heaven
Could save us. Raise us, Mother, we fell down
Here hugger-mugger in the jellied fire:
Our sacred earth in our day was our curse.

Our Mother, shall we rise on Mary's day
In Maryland, wherever corpses married
Under the rubble, bundled together? Pray
For us whom the blockbusters marred and buried;
When Satan scatters us on Rising-day,
O Mother, snatch our bodies from the fire:
Our sacred earth in our day was our curse.

Mother, my bones are trembling and I hear
The earth's reverberations and the trumpet
Bleating into my shambles. Shall I bear,
(O Mary!) unmarried man and powder-puppet,
Witness to the Devil? Mary, hear,
O Mary, marry earth, sea, air and fire;
Our sacred earth in our day is our curse.

SOFT WOOD

for Harriet Winslow

Sometimes I have supposed seals
must live as long as the Scholar Gypsy.

Even in their barred pond at the zoo they are happy,
and no sunflower turns
more delicately to the sun
without a wincing of the will.

Here too in Maine things bend to the wind forever.
After two years away, one must get used
to the painted soft wood staying bright and clean,
to the air blasting an all-white wall whiter,
as it blows through curtain and screen
touched with salt and evergreen.

The green juniper berry spills crystal-clear gin,
and even the hot water in the bathtub
is more than water,
and rich with the scouring effervescence
of something healing,
the illimitable salt.

Things last, but sometimes for days here
only children seem fit to handle children,
and there is no utility or inspiration
in the wind smashing without direction.
The fresh paint
on the captains' houses hides softer wood.

Their square-riggers used to whiten
the four corners of the globe,
but it's no consolation to know
the possessors seldom outlast the possessions,
once warped and mothered by their touch.
Shed skin will never fit another wearer.

Yet the seal pack will bark past my window
summer after summer.
This is the season
when our friends may and will die daily.
Surely the lives of the old
are briefer than the young.

Harriet Winslow, who owned this house,
was more to me than my mother.

I think of you far off in Washington,
breathing in the heat wave
and air-conditioning, knowing
each drug that numbs alerts another nerve to pain.

FOR THE UNION DEAD

"Relinquunt Omnia Servare Rem Publicam."

The old South Boston Aquarium stands
in a Sahara of snow now. Its broken windows are boarded.
The bronze weathervane cod has lost half its scales.
The airy tanks are dry.

Once my nose crawled like a snail on the glass;
my hand tingled
to burst the bubbles
drifting from the noses of the cowed, compliant fish.

My hand draws back. I often sigh still
for the dark downward and vegetating kingdom
of the fish and reptile. One morning last March,
I pressed against the new barbed and galvanized

fence on the Boston Common. Behind their cage,
yellow dinosaur steamshovels were grunting
as they cropped up tons of mush and grass
to gouge their underworld garage.

Parking spaces luxuriate like civic
sandpiles in the heart of Boston.
A girdle of orange, Puritan-pumpkin colored girders
braces the tingling Statehouse,

shaking over the excavations, as it faces Colonel Shaw
and his bell-cheeked Negro infantry
on St. Gaudens' shaking Civil War relief,
propped by a plank splint against the garage's earthquake.

Two months after marching through Boston,
half the regiment was dead;
at the dedication,
William James could almost hear the bronze Negroes
        breathe.

Their monument sticks like a fishbone
in the city's throat.
Its Colonel is as lean
as a compass-needle.

He has an angry wrenlike vigilance,
a greyhound's gentle tautness;
he seems to wince at pleasure,
and suffocate for privacy.

He is out of bounds now. He rejoices in man's lovely,
peculiar power to choose life and die—
when he leads his black soldiers to death,
he cannot bend his back.

On a thousand small town New England greens,
the old white churches hold their air
of sparse, sincere rebellion; frayed flags
quilt the graveyards of the Grand Army of the Republic.

The stone statues of the abstract Union Soldier
grow slimmer and younger each year—
wasp-waisted, they doze over muskets
and muse through their sideburns . . .

Shaw's father wanted no monument
except the ditch,
where his son's body was thrown
and lost with his "niggers."

The ditch is nearer.
There are no statues for the last war here;
on Boylston Street, a commercial photograph
shows Hiroshima boiling

over a Mosler Safe, the "Rock of Ages"
that survived the blast. Space is nearer.
When I crouch to my television set,
the drained faces of Negro school-children rise like
      balloons.

Colonel Shaw
is riding on his bubble,
he waits
for the blessèd break.

The Aquarium is gone. Everywhere,
giant finned cars nose forward like fish;
a savage servility
slides by on grease.

GRANDPARENTS

They're altogether otherworldly now,
those adults champing for their ritual Friday spin
to pharmacist and five-and-ten in Brockton.
Back in my throw-away and shaggy span
of adolescence, Grandpa still waves his stick
like a policeman;
Grandmother, like a Mohammedan, still wears her thick
lavender mourning and touring veil;
the Pierce Arrow clears its throat in a horse-stall.
Then the dry road dust rises to whiten
the fatigued elm leaves—
the nineteenth century, tired of children, is gone.
They're all gone into a world of light; the farm's my own.

The farm's my own!
Back there alone,
I keep indoors, and spoil another season.
I hear the rattley little country gramophone
racking its five foot horn:
"O Summer Time!"

Even at noon here the formidable
Ancien Régime still keeps nature at a distance. Five
green shaded light bulbs spider the billiards-table;
no field is greener than its cloth,
where Grandpa, dipping sugar for us both,
once spilled his demitasse.
His favorite ball, the number three,
still hides the coffee stain.

Never again
to walk there, chalk our cues,
insist on shooting for us both.
Grandpa! Have me, hold me, cherish me!
Tears smut my fingers. There
half my life-lease later,
I hold an *Illustrated London News*—;
disloyal still,
I doodle handlebar
mustaches on the last Russian Czar.

CENTRAL PARK

Scaling small rocks, exhaling smog,
gasping at game-scents like a dog,
now light as pollen, now as white
and winded as a grounded kite—
I watched the lovers occupy
every inch of earth and sky:
one figure of geometry,
multiplied to infinity,
straps down, and sunning openly . . .
each precious, public, pubic tangle
an equilateral triangle,
lost in the park, half covered by
the shade of some low stone or tree.
The stain of fear and poverty
spread through each trapped anatomy,
and darkened every mote of dust.

All wished to leave this drying crust,
borne on the delicate wings of lust
like bees, and cast their fertile drop
into the overwhelming cup.

Drugged and humbled by the smell
of zoo-straw mixed with animal,
the lion prowled his slummy cell,
serving his life-term in jail—
glaring, grinding, on his heel,
with tingling step and testicle . . .

Behind a dripping rock, I found
a one-day kitten on the ground—
deprived, weak, ignorant and blind,
squeaking, tubular, left behind—
dying with its deserter's rich
Welfare lying out of reach:
milk cartons, kidney heaped to spoil,
two plates sheathed with silver foil.

Shadows had stained the afternoon;
high in an elm, a snagged balloon
wooed the attraction of the moon.
Scurrying from the mouth of night,
a single, fluttery, paper kite
grazed Cleopatra's Needle, and sailed
where the light of the sun had failed.
Then night, the night—the jungle hour,
the rich in his slit-windowed tower . . .
Old Pharaohs starving in your foxholes,
with painted banquets on the walls,
fists knotted in your captives' hair,
tyrants with little food to spare—
all your embalming left you mortal,
glazed, black, and hideously eternal,
all your plunder and gold leaf
only served to draw the thief . . .

We beg delinquents for our life.
Behind each bush, perhaps a knife;

each landscaped crag, each flowering shrub,
hides a policeman with a club.

Howard Nemerov / 1920–

TRUTH

Around, above my bed, the pitch-dark fly
Buzzed in the darkness till in my mind's eye
His blue sound made the image of my thought
An image that his resonance had brought
Out of a common midden of the sun—
A garbage pit, and pile where glittering tin
Cans turned the ragged edges of their eyes
In a mean blindness on mine, where the loud flies
Would blur the summer afternoons out back
Beyond the house. Sleepy, insomniac, black
Remainder of a dream, what house? and when?
Listening now, I knew never again
That winged image as in amber kept
Might come, summoned from darkness where it slept
The common sleep of all such sunken things
By the fly's loud buzzing and his dreaming wings.

I listened in an angry wakefulness;
The fly was bitter. Between dream and guess
About a foundered world, about a wrong
The mind refused, I waited long, long,
And then that humming of the garbage heap
I drew beneath the surface of my sleep
Until I saw the helmet of the king
Of Nineveh, pale gold and glittering
On the king's brow, yet sleeping knew that I
But thought the deepening blue thought of the fly.

B O O M !

SEES BOOM IN RELIGION, TOO

Atlantic City, June 23, 1957 (AP).—*President Eisenhower's pastor said tonight that Americans are living in a period of "unprecedented religious activity" caused partially by paid vacations, the eight-hour day and modern conveniences.*

"These fruits of material progress," said the Rev. Edward L. R. Elson of the National Presbyterian Church, Washington, "have provided the leisure, the energy, and the means for a level of human and spiritual values never before reached."

Here at the Vespasian-Carlton, it's just one
religious activity after another; the sky
is constantly being crossed by cruciform
airplanes, in which nobody disbelieves
for a second, and the tide, the tide
of spiritual progress and prosperity
miraculously keeps rising, to a level
never before attained. The churches are full,
the beaches are full, and the filling-stations
are full, God's great ocean is full
of paid vacationers praying an eight-hour day
to the human and spiritual values, the fruits,
the lesiure, the energy, and the means, Lord,
the means for the level, the unprecedented level,
and the modern conveniences, which also are full.
Never before, O Lord, have the prayers and praises
from belfry and phonebooth, from ballpark and barbecue
the sacrifices, so endlessly ascended.

It was not thus when Job in Palestine
sat in the dust and cried, cried bitterly;
when Damien kissed the lepers on their wounds
it was not thus; it was not thus
when Francis worked a fourteen-hour day
strictly for the birds; when Dante took
a week's vacation without pay and it rained
part of the time, O Lord, it was not thus.

But now the gears mesh and the tires burn
and the ice chatters in the shaker and the priest
in the pulpit, and Thy Name, O Lord,
is kept before the public, while the fruits
ripen and religion booms and the level rises
and every modern convenience runneth over,
that it may never be with us as it hath been
with Athens and Karnak and Nagasaki,
nor Thy sun for one instant refrain from shining
on the rainbow Buick by the breezeway
or the Chris Craft with the uplift life raft;
that we may continue to be the just folks we are,
plain people with ordinary superliners and
disposable diaperliners, people of the stop'n'shop
'n' pray as you go, of hotel, motel, boatel,
the humble pilgrims of no deposit no return
and please adjust thy clothing, who will give to Thee,
if Thee will keep us going, our annual
Miss Universe, for Thy Name's Sake, Amen.

THE GOOSE FISH

On the long shore, lit by the moon
To show them properly alone,
Two lovers suddenly embraced
So that their shadows were as one.
The ordinary night was graced
For them by the swift tide of blood
That silently they took at flood,
And for a little time they prized
    Themselves emparadised.

Then, as if shaken by stage-fright
Beneath the hard moon's bony light,
They stood together on the sand
Embarrassed in each other's sight
But still conspiring hand in hand,
Until they saw, there underfoot,

As though the world had found them out,
The goose fish turning up, though dead,
    His hugely grinning head.

There in the china light he lay,
Most ancient and corrupt and grey
They hesitated at his smile,
Wondering what it seemed to say
To lovers who a little while
Before had thought to understand,
By violence upon the sand,
The only way that could be known
    To make a world their own.

It was a wide and moony grin
Together peaceful and obscene;
They knew not what he would express,
So finished a comedian
He might mean failure or success,
But took it for an emblem of
Their sudden, new and guilty love
To be observed by, when they kissed,
    That rigid optimist.

So he became their patriarch,
Dreadfully mild in the half-dark.
His throat that the sand seemed to choke,
His picket teeth, these left their mark
But never did explain the joke
That so amused him, lying there
While the moon went down to disappear
Along the still and tilted track
    That bears the zodiac.

REDEPLOYMENT

They say the war is over. But water still
Comes bloody from the taps, and my pet cat

In his disorder vomits worms which crawl
Swiftly away. Maybe they leave the house.
These worms are white, and flecked with the cat's blood.

The war may be over. I know a man
Who keeps a pleasant souvenir, he keeps
A soldier's dead blue eyeballs that he found
Somewhere—hard as chalk, and blue as slate.
He clicks them in his pocket while he talks.

And now there are cockroaches in the house,
They get slightly drunk on DDT,
Are fast, hard, shifty—can be drowned but not
Without you hold them under quite some time.
People say the Mexican kind can fly.

The end of the war. I took it quietly
Enough. I tried to wash the dirt out of
My hair and from under my fingernails,
I dressed in clean white clothes and went to bed.
I heard the dust falling between the walls.

THE PHOENIX

The Phoenix comes of flame and dust
He bundles up his sire in myrrh
A solar and unholy lust
Makes a cradle of his bier

In the City of the Sun
He dies and rises all divine
There is never more than one
Genuine

By incest, murder, suicide
Survives the sacred purple bird
Himself his father, son and bride
And his own Word

A SPELL BEFORE WINTER

After the red leaf and the gold have gone,
Brought down by the wind, then by hammering rain
Bruised and discolored, when October's flame
Goes blue to guttering in the cusp, this land
Sinks deeper into silence, darker into shade.
There is a knowledge in the look of things,
The old hills hunch before the north wind blows.

Now I can see certain simplicities
In the darkening rust and tarnish of the time,
And say over the certain simplicities,
The running water and the standing stone,
The yellow haze of the willow and the black
Smoke of the elm, the silver, silent light
Where suddenly, readying toward nightfall,
The sumac's candelabrum darkly flames.
And I speak to you now with the land's voice,
It is the cold, wild land that says to you
A knowledge glimmers in the sleep of things:
The old hills hunch before the north wind blows.

Richard Wilbur / 1921–

T Y W A T E R

Death of Sir Nihil, book the *nth*,
Upon the charred and clotted sward,
Lacking the lily of our Lord,
Alases of the hyacinth.

Could flicker from behind his ear
A whistling silver throwing knife

And with a holler punch the life
Out of a swallow in the air.

Behind the lariat's butterfly
Shuttled his white and gritted grin,
And cuts of sky would roll within
The noose-hole, when he spun it high.

The violent, neat and practiced skill
Was all he loved and all he learned;
When he was hit, his body turned
To clumsy dirt before it fell.

And what to say of him, God knows.
Such violence. And such repose.

"A WORLD WITHOUT OBJECTS IS A SENSIBLE EMPTINESS"

The tall camels of the spirit
Steer for their deserts, passing the last groves loud
With the sawmill shrill of the locust, to the whole honey of
the arid
Sun. They are slow, proud,

And move with a stilted stride
To the land of sheer horizon, hunting Traherne's
Sensible emptiness, there where the brain's lantern-slide
Revels in vast returns.

O connoisseurs of thirst,
Beasts of my soul who long to learn to drink
Of pure mirage, those prosperous islands are accurst
That shimmer on the brink

Of absence; auras, lustres,
And all shinings need to be shaped and borne.

Think of those painted saints, capped by the early masters
    With bright, jauntily-worn

        Aureate plates, or even
    Merry-go-round rings. Turn, O turn
From the fine sleights of the sand, from the long empty
        oven
    Where flames in flamings burn

        Back to the trees arrayed
    In bursts of glare, to the halo-dialing run
Of the country creeks, and the hills' bracken tiaras made
    Gold in the sunken sun,

        Wisely watch for the sight
    Of the supernova burgeoning over the barn,
Lampshine blurred in the steam of beasts, the spirit's right
    Oasis, light incarnate.

JUGGLER

A ball will bounce, but less and less. It's not
A light-hearted thing, resents its own resilience.
Falling is what it loves, and the earth falls
So in our hearts from brilliance,
Settles and is forgot.
It takes a sky-blue juggler with five red balls

To shake our gravity up. Whee, in the air
The balls roll round, wheel on his wheeling hands,
Learning the ways of lightness, alter to spheres
Grazing his finger ends,
Cling to their courses there,
Swinging a small heaven about his ears.

But a heaven is easier made of nothing at all
Than the earth regained, and still and sole within
The spin of worlds, with a gesture sure and noble

He reels that heaven in,
Landing it ball by ball,
And trades it all for a broom, a plate, a table.

Oh, on his toe the table is turning, the broom's
Balancing up on his nose, and the plate whirls
On the tip of the broom! Damn, what a show, we cry:
The boys stamp, and the girls
Shriek, and the drum booms
And all comes down, and he bows and says good-bye.

If the juggler is tired now, if the broom stands
In the dust again, if the table starts to drop
Through the daily dark again, and though the plate
Lies flat on the table top,
For him we batter our hands
Who has won for once over the world's weight.

YEARS-END

Now winter downs the dying of the year,
And night is all a settlement of snow;
From the soft street the rooms of houses show
A gathered light, a shapen atmosphere,
Like frozen-over lakes whose ice is thin
And still allows some stirring down within.

I've known the wind by water banks to shake
The late leaves down, which frozen where they fell
And held in ice as dancers in a spell
Fluttered all winter long into a lake;
Graved on the dark in gestures of descent,
They seemed their own most perfect monument.

There was perfection in the death of ferns
Which laid their fragile cheeks against the stone
A million years. Great mammoths overthrown

Composedly have made their long sojourns,
Like palaces of patience, in the gray
And changeless lands of ice. And at Pompeii

The little dog lay curled and did not rise
But slept the deeper as the ashes rose
And found the people incomplete, and froze
The random hands, the loose unready eyes
Of men expecting yet another sun
To do the shapely thing they had not done.

These sudden ends of time must give us pause.
We fray into the future, rarely wrought
Save in the tapestries of afterthought.
More time, more time. Barrages of applause
Come muffled from a buried radio.
The New-year bells are wrangling with the snow.

STILL, CITIZEN SPARROW

Still, citizen sparrow, this vulture which you call
Unnatural, let him but lumber again to air
Over the rotten office, let him bear
The carrion ballast up, and at the tall

Tip of the sky lie cruising. Then you'll see
That no more beautiful bird is in heaven's height,
No wider more placid wings, no watchfuller flight;
He shoulders nature there, the frightfully free,

The naked-headed one. Pardon him, you
Who dart in the orchard aisles, for it is he
Devours death, mocks mutability,
Has heart to make an end, keeps nature new.

Thinking of Noah, childheart, try to forget
How for so many bedlam hours his saw

Soured the song of birds with its wheezy gnaw,
And the slam of his hammer all the day beset

The people's ears. Forget that he could bear
To see the towns like coral under the keel,
And the fields so dismal deep. Try rather to feel
How high and weary it was, on the waters where

He rocked his only world, and everyone's.
Forgive the hero, you who would have died
Gladly with all you knew; he rode that tide
To Ararat; all men are Noah's sons.

THE DEATH OF A TOAD

A toad the power mower caught,
Chewed and clipped of a leg, with a hobbling hop has got
    To the garden verge, and sanctuaried him
    Under the cineraria leaves, in the shade
        Of the ashen heartshaped leaves, in a dim,
            Low, and a final glade.

The rare original heartsblood goes,
Spends on the earthen hide, in the folds and wizenings,
        flows
    In the gutters of the banked and staring eyes. He lies
    As still as if he would return to stone,
        And soundlessly attending, dies
            Toward some deep monotone,

Toward misted and ebullient seas
And cooling shores, toward lost Amphibia's emperies.
    Day dwindles, drowning, and at length is gone
    In the wide and antique eyes, which still appear
        To watch, across the castrate lawn,
            The haggard daylight steer.

IN THE SMOKING-CAR

The eyelids meet. He'll catch a little nap.
The grizzled, crew-cut head drops to his chest.
It shakes above the briefcase on his lap.
Close voices breathe, "Poor sweet, he did his best."

"Poor sweet, poor sweet," the bird-hushed glades repeat,
Through which in quiet pomp his litter goes,
Carried by native girls with naked feet.
A sighing stream concurs in his repose.

Could he but think, he might recall to mind
The righteous mutiny or sudden gale
That beached him here; the dear ones left behind . . .
So near the ending, he forgets the tale.

Were he to lift his eyelids now, he might
Behold his maiden porters, brown and bare.
But even here he has no appetite.
It is enough to know that they are there.

Enough that now a honeyed music swells,
The gentle, mossed declivities begin,
And the whole air is full of flower-smells.
Failure, the longed-for valley, takes him in.

PART II

A Little Treasury of
Modern Lyrics

Léonie Adams / 1899–

CARYATID

Not at midnight, not at morning, O sweet city,
Shall we come in at your portal, but this girl, your servant,
Bearing on her head a broken stone,
In the body shaped to this, the throat and bosom
Poised no less for the burden now the temple is fallen,
Tells the white Athenian wonder overthrown.

There is no clasp which stays beauty forever.
Time has undone her, from porphyry, from bronze.
She is winged every way and will not rest;
But the gesture of the lover shall remain long after,
Where lovely and imponderable there leans
A weight more grave than marble on the breast.

EARLY WAKING

Four hooves rang out and now are still.
In the dark wall the casements hold
Essential day above each sill,
Just light, and colored like thin gold.
Behind those hooves a drowsy course
All night I rode where hearts were clear,
And wishes blessèd at the source,
And for no shape of time stop here.

No more to raise that lively ghost
Which ran quicksilver to the bone:
By a whim's turn the whole was lost
When all its marrow worth was known.
Ghosts can cast shadows in the breast,
And what was present tears to weep,
Not heart nor mind would bid from rest
As fast as sorrow's, ten years deep.

I travel, not for a ghost's sake,
One step from sleep, and not for one
Left sleeping at my side I wake.
Before bricks rosy with the dawn,
The hooves will sound beyond the light:
There are dark roads enough to go
To last us through the end of night,
And I will make my waking slow.

It was for unconcerning light
That has not fallen on earth, to stare
An instant only out of night
And with night's cloudy character,
Before the laden mind shall slip
Past dream and on to brightmost dream
And fetterless high morning dip
Her two cold sandals in the stream.

COUNTRY   SUMMER

Now the rich cherry, whose sleek wood
And top with silver petals traced,
Like a strict box its gems encased,
Has spilt from out that cunning lid,
All in an innocent green round,
Those melting rubies which it hid;
With moss ripe-strawberry-encrusted,
So birds get half, and minds lapse merry
To taste that deep-red, lark's-bite berry,
And blackcap bloom is yellow-dusted.

The wren that thieved it in the eaves
A trailer of the rose could catch
To her poor droopy sloven thatch,
And side by side with the wren's brood—
O lovely time of beggars' luck—
Opens the quaint and hairy bud;
And full and golden is the yield
Of cows that never have to house,
But all night nibble under boughs,
Or cool their sides in the moist field.

Into the rooms flow meadow airs,
The warm farm baking smell's blown round,
Inside and out, and sky and ground
Are much the same, the wishing star,
Hesperus, kind and early born,
Is risen only finger-far;
All stars stand close in summer air,
And tremble, and look mild as amber,
When wicks are lighted in the chamber,
You might say, stars were settling there.

Now straightening from the flowery hay,
Down the still light the mowers look,
Or turn, because their dreaming shook,
And they waked half to other days,
When left alone in the yellow stubble
The rusty-coated mare would graze.
Yet thick the lazy dreams are born,
Another thought can come to mind,
But like the shivering of the wind,
Morning and evening in the corn.

John Peale Bishop / 1892–1944

ODE

Why will they never sleep
Those great women who sit
Peering at me with parrot eyes?
They sit with grave knees; they keep
Perpetual stare; and their hands move
As though hands could be aware—
Forward and back, to begin again—
As though on tumultous shuttles of wind they wove
Shrouds out of air.

The three are sisters. There is one
Who sits divine in weeping stone
On a small chair of skeleton
And is most inescapable.
I have walked through many mirrors
But always accompanied.
I have been as many men, as many ghosts,
As there are days. The boy was seen
Always at rainfall, mistily, not lost.
I have tried changing shapes
But always, alone, I have heard
Her shadow coming nearer, and known
The awful grasp of striding hands
Goddess! upon
The screaming metamorphosis.

One has a face burned hard
As the red Cretan clay,
Who wears a white torso scarred
With figures like a calendar.
She sits among broken shafts

Of stone; she is and still will be
Who feeds on cities, gods and men
Weapons of bronze and curious ornaments
Reckoning the evens as the odds.
Her least movement recalls the sea.

The last has idiot teeth
And a brow not made
For any thoughts, but suffering.
Tired, she repeats
In idiot singing
A song shaped like a ring:
"Now is now and never Then
Dead Virgins will bear no men
And now that we speak of love, of love,
The woman's beneath
That's burdened with love
And the man's above
While the thing is done and done.
One is one and Three is three
Children may come from a spark in the sun
But One is one and never Three
And never a Virgin shall bear a Son
While the shadow lasts of the gray ashtree!"

Phantasmal marbles!
There was One who might have saved
Me from the grave dissolute stones
And parrot eyes. But He is dead,
Christ is dead. And in a grave
Dark as a sightless skull He lies
And of His bones are charnels made.

THIS DIM AND PTOLEMAIC MAN

For forty years, for forty-one,
Sparing the profits of the sun,
This farmer piled his meagre hoard
To buy at last a rattly Ford.

Now crouched on a scared smile he feels
Motion spurt beneath his heels,
Rheumatically intent shifts gears,
Unloosens joints of rustic years.

Morning light obscures the stars,
He swerves avoiding other cars,
Wheels with the road, does not discern
He eastward goes at every turn.

Nor how his aged limbs are hurled
Through all the motions of the world,
How wild past farms, past ricks, past trees,
He perishes toward Hercules.

THE DREAM

And once again I was within that house
Where light collided with the gloom
And chilled on faces, as though the dawn
Were backward and the stars had gone;
For the long hall was populous
With pale expatriates from the tomb.

The house, deserted, had become a lair,
And all along that hall the dead slid
And tried the doors, one after one,
With hands no longer blest by bone.
They scanned me with a single stare
Because of what that one door hid.

I saw my mother, who had love
Still in her eyes, that did not own
Least light, for they had forfeited
Reflection, having reached the dead.
She spoke: and I was conscious of
An unspoken corruption.

Her speech prevented me from following
Angrily after those famished forms
Who only sought what I had sought
And found. I had been brought,
In the dread time of love's responding,
Undreaming into my young love's arms.

I saw what they were seeking in the gust
That drove them on from door to door
In the long deception of the hall.
They looked: from doors, nothing at all
Looked back at them. Yet though no lust
Awaited them, they must try once more.

I saw the shame that I contemned
Since it was sought by sightless eyes.
I knew what crime would be revealed
If the one door to the dead should yield,
But dreamed that door had been condemned
And in the dream had no surprise.

That none could ever force a look
At incest dangling from a beam
And by a cord all blood attached.
For from the dark I knew there watched
Young eyes too quick with love to mock
The dead in that death-haunted dream.

Edmund Blunden / 1896–

THE PIKE

From shadows of rich oaks outpeer
The moss-green bastions of the weir,
Where the quick dipper forages
In elver-peopled crevices.

And a small runlet trickling down the sluice
Gossamer music tires not to unloose.

    Else round the broad pool's hush
        Nothing stirs.
Unless sometime a straggling heifer crush
Through the thronged spinny whence the pheasant whirs;
    Or martins in a flash
Come with wild mirth to dip their magical wings,
While in the shallow some doomed bulrush swings
    At whose hid root the diver vole's teeth gnash.

And nigh this toppling reed, still as the dead
    The great pike lies, the murderous patriarch,
    Watching the waterpit shelving and dark
Where through the plash his lithe bright vassals thread.

    The rose-finned roach and bluish bream
    And staring ruffe steal up the stream
    Hard by their glutted tyrant, now
    Still as a sunken bough.

    He on the sandbank lies,
        Sunning himself long hours
    With stony gorgon eyes:
        Westward the hot sun lowers.

Sudden the gray pike changes, and quivering poises for
    slaughter;
    Intense terror wakens around him, the shoals scud awry,
    but there chances
A chub unsuspecting; the prowling fins quicken, in fury
    he lances;
And the miller that opens the hatch stands amazed at the
    whirl in the water.

Arna Bontemps / 1902–

SOUTHERN MANSION

Poplars are standing there still as death
And ghosts of dead men
Meet their ladies walking
Two by two beneath the shade
And standing on the marble steps.

There is a sound of music echoing
Through the open door
And in the field there is
Another sound tinkling in the cotton:
Chains of bondmen dragging on the ground.

The years go back with an iron clank,
A hand is on the gate,
A dry leaf trembles on the wall.
Ghosts are walking.
They have broken roses down
And poplars stand there still as death.

LENGTH OF MOON

Then the golden hour
Will tick its last
And the flame will go down in the flower.

A briefer length of moon
Will mark the sea-line and the yellow dune.

Then we may think of this, yet
There will be something forgotten
And something we should forget.

It will be like all things we know:
The stone will fail; a rose is sure to go.

It will be quiet then and we may stay
As long at the picket gate
But there will be less to say.

Rupert Brooke / 1887–1915

THE SOLDIER

If I should die, think only this of me:
    That there's some corner of a foreign field
That is for ever England. There shall be
    In that rich earth a richer dust concealed;
A dust whom England bore, shaped, made aware,
    Gave, once, her flowers to love, her ways to roam,
A body of England's, breathing English air,
    Washed by the rivers, blest by suns of home.

And think, this heart, all evil shed away,
    A pulse in the eternal mind, no less
        Gives somewhere back the thoughts by England given;
Her sights and sounds; dreams happy as her day;
    And laughter, learnt of friends; and gentleness,
        In hearts at peace, under an English heaven.

THE GREAT LOVER

I have been so great a lover: filled my days
So proudly with the splendour of Love's praise,
The pain, the calm, and the astonishment,
Desire illimitable, and still content,
And all dear names men use, to cheat despair,
For the perplexed and viewless streams that bear
Our hearts at random down the dark of life.
Now, ere the unthinking silence on that strife
Steals down, I would cheat drowsy Death so far,
My night shall be remembered for a star
That outshone all the suns of all men's days.
Shall I not crown them with immortal praise
Whom I have loved, who have given me, dared with me
High secrets, and in darkness knelt to see
The inenarrable godhead of delight?
Love is a flame;—we have beaconed the world's night.
A city:—and we have built it, these and I.
An emperor:—we have taught the world to die.
So, for their sakes I loved, ere I go hence,
And the high cause of Love's magnificence,
And to keep loyalties young, I'll write those names
Golden for ever, eagles, crying flames,
And set them as a banner, that men may know,
To dare the generations, burn, and blow
Out on the wind of Time, shining and streaming. . . .

These I have loved:
                White plates and cups, clean-gleaming,
Ringed with blue lines; and feathery, faëry dust;
Wet roofs, beneath the lamp-light; the strong crust
Of friendly bread; and many-tasting food;
Rainbows; and the blue bitter smoke of wood;
And radiant raindrops couching in cool flowers;
And flowers themselves, that sway through sunny hours,
Dreaming of moths that drink them under the moon;
Then, the cool kindliness of sheets, that soon
Smooth away trouble; and the rough male kiss
Of blankets; grainy wood; live hair that is

Shining and free; blue-massing clouds; the keen
Unpassioned beauty of a great machine;
The benison of hot water; furs to touch;
The good smell of old clothes; and other such—
The comfortable smell of friendly fingers,
Hair's fragrance, and the musty reek that lingers
About dead leaves and last year's ferns. . . .
                                    Dear names,
And thousand other throng to me! Royal flames;
Sweet water's dimpling laugh from tap or spring;
Holes in the ground; and voices that do sing;
Voices in laughter, too; and body's pain,
Soon turned to peace; and the deep-panting train;
Firm sands; the little dulling edge of foam
That browns and dwindles as the wave goes home;
And washen stones, gay for an hour; the cold
Graveness of iron; moist black earthen mould;
Sleep; and high places; footprints in the dew;
And oaks; and brown horse-chestnuts, glossy-new;
And new-peeled sticks; and shining pools on grass;—
All these have been my loves. And these shall pass,
Whatever passes not, in the great hour,
Nor all my passion, all my prayers, have power
To hold them with me through the gate of Death.
They'll play deserter, turn with the traitor breath,
Break the high bond we made, and sell Love's trust
And sacramented covenant to the dust.
—Oh, never a doubt but, somewhere, I shall wake,
And give what's left of love again, and make
New friends, now strangers. . . .
                              But the best I've known,
Stays here, and changes, breaks, grows old, is blown
About the winds of the world, and fades from brains
Of living men, and dies.
                              Nothing remains.

O dear my loves, O faithless, once again
This one last gift I give: that after men
Shall know, and later lovers, far-removed,
Praise you, "All these were lovely"; say, "He loved."

HEAVEN

Fish (fly-replete, in depth of June,
Dawdling away their wat'ry noon)
Ponder deep wisdom, dark or clear,
Each secret fishy hope or fear.
Fish say, they have their Stream and Pond;
But is there anything Beyond?
This life cannot be All, they swear,
For how unpleasant, if it were!
One may not doubt that, somehow, Good
Shall come of Water and of Mud;
And, sure, the reverent eye must see
A Purpose in Liquidity.
We darkly know, by Faith we cry,
The future is not Wholly Dry.
Mud unto mud!—Death eddies near—
Not here the appointed End, not here!
But somewhere, beyond Space and Time.
Is wetter water, slimier slime!
And there (they trust) there swimmeth One
Who swam ere rivers were begun,
Immense, of fishy form and mind,
Squamous, omnipotent, and kind;
And under that Almighty Fin,
The littlest fish may enter in.
Oh! never fly conceals a hook,
Fish say, in the Eternal Brook,
But more than mundane weeds are there,
And mud, celestially fair;
Fat caterpillars drift around,
And Paradisal grubs are found;
Unfading moths, immortal flies,
And the worm that never dies.
And in that Heaven of all their wish,
There shall be no more land, say fish.

Countee Cullen / 1903–1946

SATURDAY'S CHILD

Some are teethed on a silver spoon,
With the stars strung for a rattle;
I cut my teeth as the black racoon——
For implements of battle.

Some are swaddled in silk and down,
And heralded by a star;
They swathed my limbs in a sackcloth gown
On a night that was black as tar.

For some, godfather and goddame
The opulent fairies be;
Dame Poverty gave me my name,
And Pain godfathered me.

For I was born on Saturday——
"Bad time for planting a seed,"
Was all my father had to say,
And, "One mouth more to feed."

Death cut the strings that gave me life,
And handed me to Sorrow,
The only kind of middle wife
My folks could beg or borrow.

FROM THE DARK TOWER

We shall not always plant while others reap
The golden increment of bursting fruit,
Not always countenance, abject and mute,
That lesser men should hold their brothers cheap;

Not everlastingly while others sleep
Shall we beguile their limbs with mellow flute,
Not always bend to some more subtle brute;
We were not made eternally to weep.

The night whose sable breast relieves the stark,
White stars is no less lovely being dark,
And there are buds that cannot bloom at all
In light, but crumple, piteous, and fall;
So in the dark we hide the heart that bleeds,
And wait, and tend our agonizing seeds.

W. H. Davies / 1871–1940

LEISURE

What is this life if, full of care,
We have no time to stand and stare.

No time to stand beneath the boughs
And stare as long as sheep or cows.

No time to see, when woods we pass,
Where squirrels hide their nuts in grass.

No time to see, in broad daylight,
Streams full of stars like skies at night.

No time to turn at Beauty's glance,
And watch her feet, how they can dance.

No time to wait till her mouth can
Enrich that smile her eyes began.

A poor life this if, full of care,
We have no time to stand and stare.

SHEEP

When I was once in Baltimore,
    A man came up to me and cried,
'Come, I have eighteen hundred sheep,
    And we will sail on Tuesday's tide.

'If you will sail with me, young man,
    I'll pay you fifty shillings down;
These eighteen hundred sheep I take
    From Baltimore to Glasgow town.'

He paid me fifty shillings down,
    I sailed with eighteen hundred sheep;
We soon had cleared the harbour's mouth,
    We soon were in the salt sea deep.

The first night we were out at sea
    Those sheep were quiet in their mind;
The second night they cried with fear –
    They smelt no pastures in the wind.

They sniffed, poor things, for their green fields,
    They cried so loud I could not sleep:
For fifty thousand shillings down
    I would not sail again with sheep.

H. D. (Hilda Doolittle) / 1886–1961

SONG

You are as gold
as the half-ripe grain
that merges to gold again,
as white as the white rain

that beats through
the half-opened flowers
of the great flower tufts
thick on the black limbs
of an Illyrian apple bough.

Can honey distill such fragrance
as your bright hair—
for your face is as fair as rain,
yet as rain that lies clear
on white honey-comb,
lends radiance to the white wax,
so your hair on your brow
casts light for a shadow.

ORCHARD

I saw the first pear
as it fell—
the honey-seeking, golden-banded,
the yellow swarm
was not more fleet than I,
(spare us from loveliness)
and I fell prostrate,
crying:
you have flayed us
with your blossoms,
spare us the beauty
of fruit-trees.

The honey-seeking
paused not,
the air thundered their song,
and I alone was prostrate.

O rough-hewn
god of the orchard,
I bring an offering—

do you, alone unbeautiful,
son of the god,
spare us from loveliness:

these fallen hazel-nuts,
stripped late of their green sheaths,
grapes, red-purple,
their berries
dripping with wine,
pomegranates already broken,
and shrunken figs
and quinces untouched,
I bring you as offering.

HELEN

All Greece hates
the still eyes in the white face,
the lustre as of olives
where she stands,
and the white hands.

All Greece reviles
the wan face when she smiles,
hating it deeper still
when it grows wan and white,
remembering past enchantments
and past ills.

Greece sees, unmoved,
God's daughter, born of love,
the beauty of cool feet
and slenderest knees,
could love indeed the maid,
only if she were laid,
white ash amid funereal cypresses.

LETHE

Nor skin nor hide nor fleece
    shall cover you,
nor curtain of crimson nor fine
shelter of cedar-wood be over you,
    nor the fir-tree
    nor the pine.

Nor sight of whin nor gorse
    nor river-yew,
nor fragrance of flowering bush,
nor wailing of reed-bird to waken you,
    nor of linnet,
    nor of thrush.

Nor word nor touch nor sight
    of lover, you
shall long through the night but for this:
the roll of the full tide to cover you
    without question,
    without kiss.

John Drinkwater / 1882–1937

SUNRISE ON RYDAL WATER

To E. De S.

Come down at dawn from windless hills
    Into the valley of the lake,
Where yet a larger quiet fills
    The hour, and mist and water make

With rocks and reeds and island boughs
One silence and one element,
Where wonder goes surely as once
It went
    By Galilean prows.

Moveless the water and the mist,
  Moveless the secret air above,
Hushed, as upon some happy tryst
  The poised expectancy of love;
    What spirit is it that adores
    What mighty presence yet unseen?
    What consummation works apace
    Between
      These rapt enchanted shores?

Never did virgin beauty wake
  Devouter to the bridal feast
Than moves this hour upon the lake
  In adoration to the east;
    Here is the bride a god may know,
    The primal will, the young consent,
    Till surely upon the appointed mood
    Intent
      The god shall leap—and, lo,

Over the lake's end strikes the sun,
  White, flameless fire; some purity
Thrilling the mist, a splendour won
  Out of the world's heart. Let there be
    Thoughts, and atonements, and desires,
    Proud limbs, and undeliberate tongue,
    Where now we move with mortal oars
    Among
      Immortal dews and fires.

So the old mating goes apace,
  Wind with the sea, and blood with thought,
Lover with lover; and the grace
  Of understanding comes unsought

When stars into the twilight steer,
Or thrushes build among the may,
Or wonder moves between the hills,
And day
    Comes up on Rydal mere.

James Joyce / 1882–1941

I HEAR AN ARMY CHARGING
UPON THE LAND

I hear an army charging upon the land,
    And the thunder of horses plunging, foam about their
        knees:
Arrogant, in black armour, behind them stand,
    Disdaining the reins, with fluttering whips, the
        charioteers.

They cry unto the night their battle-name:
    I moan in sleep when I hear afar their whirling laughter.
They cleave the gloom of dreams, a blinding flame,
    Clanging, clanging upon the heart as upon an anvil.

They come shaking in triumph their long, green hair:
    They come out of the sea and run shouting by the shore.
My heart, have you no wisdom thus to despair?
    My love, my love, my love, why have you left me alone?

Vachel Lindsay / 1879–1931

GENERAL WILLIAM BOOTH ENTERS INTO HEAVEN

To be sung to the tune of "The Blood of the Lamb"
with indicated instrument

I

(*Bass drum beaten loudly.*)
Booth led boldly with his big bass drum—
(Are you washed in the blood of the Lamb?)
The Saints smiled gravely and they said: "He's come."
(Are you washed in the blood of the Lamb?)
Walking lepers followed, rank on rank,
Lurching bravos from the ditches dank,
Drabs from the alleyways and drug fiends pale—
Minds still passion-ridden, soul-powers frail:—
Vermin-eaten saints with moldy breath,
Unwashed legions with the ways of Death—
(Are you washed in the blood of the Lamb?)

(*Banjos.*)
Every slum had sent its half-a-score
The round world over. (Booth had groaned for more.)
Every banner that the wide world flies
Bloomed with glory and transcendent dyes.
Big-voiced lasses made their banjos bang,
Tranced, fanatical they shrieked and sang:—
"Are you washed in the blood of the Lamb?"
Hallelujah! It was queer to see
Bull-necked convicts with that land make free.
Loons with trumpets blowed a blare, blare, blare
On, on upward thro' the golden air!
(Are you washed in the blood of the Lamb?)

II

(Bass drum slower and softer.)
Booth died blind and still by faith he trod,
Eyes still dazzled by the ways of God.
Booth led boldly, and he looked the chief
Eagle countenance in sharp relief,
Beard a-flying, air of high command
Unabated in that holy land.

(Sweet flute music.)
Jesus came from out the court-house door,
Stretched his hands above the passing poor.
Booth saw not, but led his queer ones there
Round and round the mighty court-house square.
Yet in an instant all that blear review
Marched on spotless, clad in raiment new.
The lame were straightened, withered limbs uncurled
And blind eyes opened on a new, sweet world.

(Bass drum louder.)
Drabs and vixens in a flash made whole!
Gone was the weasel-head, the snout, the jowl!
Sages and sibyls now, and athletes clean,
Rulers of empires, and of forests green!

*(Grand chorus of all instruments. Tambourines to the
    foreground.)*
The hosts were sandalled, and their wings were fire!
(Are you washed in the blood of the Lamb?)
But their noise played havoc with the angel-choir.
(Are you washed in the blood of the Lamb?)
Oh, shout Salvation! It was good to see
Kings and Princes by the Lamb set free.
The banjos rattled and the tambourines
Jing-jing-jingled in the hands of Queens.

(Reverently sung, no instruments.)
And when Booth halted by the curb for prayer
He saw his Master thro' the flag-filled air.
Christ came gently with a robe and crown
For Booth the soldier, while the throng knelt down.

He saw King Jesus. They were face to face,
And he knelt a-weeping in that holy place.
Are you washed in the blood of the Lamb?

Hugh MacDiarmid / 1892–

O WHA'S THE BRIDE?

O wha's the bride that cairries the bunch
O' thistles blinterin' white?
Her cuckold bridegroom little dreids
What he sall ken this nicht.

For closer than gudeman can come
And closer to'r than hersel',
Wha didna need her maidenheid
Has wrocht his purpose fell.

O wha's been here afore me, lass,
And hoo did he get in?
—*A man that deed or was I born
This evil thing has din.*

And left, as it were on a corpse,
Your maidenheid to me?
—*Nae lass, gudeman, sin' Time began
'S hed ony mair to gi'e.*

*But I can gi'e ye kindness, lad,
And a pair o' willin' hands,
And you sall ha'e my breists like stars,
My limbs like willow wands.*

*And on my lips ye'll heed nae mair,
And in my hair forget,
The seed o' a' the men that in
My virgin womb ha'e met.* . . .

WITH THE HERRING FISHERS

"I see herrin'."—I hear the glad cry
And 'gainst the moon see ilka blue jowl
In turn as the fishermen haul on the nets
And sing: "Come, shove in your heids and growl."

"Soom on, bonnie herrin', soom on," they shout,
Or "Come in, O come in, and see me"
"Come gie the auld man something to dae.
It'll be a braw change frae the sea."

O it's ane o' the bonniest sichts in the warld
To watch the herrin' come walkin' on board
In the wee sma' 'oors o' a simmer's mornin'
As if o' their ain accord.

For this is the way that God sees life,
The haill jing-bang o's appearin'
Up owre frae the edge o' naethingness
—It's his happy cries I'm hearin'.

"Left, right—O come in and see me,"
Reid and yellow and black and white
Toddlin' up into Heaven thegither
At peep o' day frae the endless night.

"I see herrin'," I hear his glad cry,
And 'gainst the moon see his muckle blue jowl,
As he handles buoy-tow and bush-raip
Singin': "Come, shove in your heids and growl!"

Ogden Nash / 1902–

PORTRAIT OF THE ARTIST AS
A PREMATURELY OLD MAN

It is common knowledge to every schoolboy and even
     every Bachelor of Arts,
That all sin is divided into two parts.
One kind of sin is called a sin of commission, and that is
     very important,
And it is what you are doing when you are doing something
     you ortant,
And the other kind of sin is just the opposite and is called a
     sin of omission and is equally bad in the eyes of all
     right-thinking people, from Billy Sunday to Buddha,
And it consists of not having done something you shuddha.
I might as well give you my opinion of these two kinds of
     sin as long as, in a way, against each other we are
     pitting them,
And that is, don't bother your head about sins of
     commission because however sinful, they must at
     least be fun or else you wouldn't be committing them.
It is the sin of omission, the second kind of sin,
That lays eggs under your skin.
The way you get really painfully bitten
Is by the insurance you haven't taken out and the checks
     you haven't added up the stubs of and the
     appointments you haven't kept and the bills you
     haven't paid and the letters you haven't written.
Also, about sins of omission there is one particularly
     painful lack of beauty,
Namely, it isn't as though it had been a riotous red-letter
     day or night every time you neglected to do your duty;
You didn't get a wicked forbidden thrill
Every time you let a policy lapse or forgot to pay a bill;

You didn't slap the lads in the tavern on the back and
    loudly cry Whee,
Let's all fail to write just one more letter before we go
    home, and this round of unwritten letters is on me.
No, you never get any fun
Out of the things you haven't done,
But they are the things that I do not like to be amid,
Because the suitable things you didn't do give you a lot
    more trouble than the unsuitable things you did.
The moral is that it is probably better not to sin at all, but
    if some kind of sin you must be pursuing,
Well, remember to do it by doing rather than by not doing.

REFLECTIONS ON
ICE-BREAKING

Candy
Is dandy
But liquor
Is quicker.

Frederic Prokosch / 1908–

THE CONSPIRATORS

And if the dead, and the dead
Of spirit now join, and in their horrifying ritual
Proceed till at last with oriental grace
End their concluding dance with the candles guttering,
The cymbals sobbing, the wind harassing the curtains,
The chill from the flood embracing the golden stairway,
The scent devoured and the bowls blown clean of incense:

Ah then, farewell, sweet northern music;
No longer the flight of the mind across the continents,
The dazzling flight of our words across the tempestuous
Black, or the firelit recital of a distant battle.

No. All that we loved is lost, if the intricate
Languor of recollected centuries
Descends in its terrible sweetness on our limbs.
No shot will echo; no fire; no agonizing
Cry will resound in the city's thickets: only,
The ivy falling gently across the bridges,
The larches piercing the roofs, the reclining steeples,
The cellars rich with the agony of the reptiles,
The contemplative worms, the victorious rodents,
And at last, the climax entrancingly serene,
The inconclusive note drowned on the ascendant:

Our lovely shapes in marble still shine through the greenery,
Our exquisite silver bones still glide with the glaciers
That split our familiar hills, still fall with the avalanche
And weaving their vast wing's thunder over the Indies
The birds, the birds, sob for the time of man.

Peter Quennell / 1905–

THE FLIGHT INTO EGYPT

Within Heaven's circle I had not guessed at this,
I had not guessed at pleasure such as this,
So sharp a pleasure,
That, like a lamp burning in foggy night,
Makes its own orb and sphere of flowing gold
And tents itself in light.

Going before you, now how many days,
Thoughts, all turned back like birds against the wind,
Wheeled sullenly towards my Father's house,

Considered his blind presence and the gathered, bustling
    paean,
The affluence of his sweetness, his grace and unageing
    might.

My flesh glowed then in the shadow of a loose cloak
And my brightness troubled the ground with every pulse of
    the blood,
My wings lax on the air, my eyes open and grave,
With the vacant pride of hardly less than a god.

We passed thickets that quaked with hidden deer,
And wide shallows dividing before my feet,
Empty plains threaded, and between stiff aloes
I took the ass's bridle to climb into mountain pathways.

When cold bit you, through your peasant's mantle,
And my Father filled the air with meaningless stars,
I brought dung and dead white grass for fuel,
Blowing a fire with the breath of the holy word.

Your drudge, Joseph, slept; you would sit unmoving,
In marble quiet, or by the unbroken voice of a river,
Would sometimes bare your maiden breast to his mouth,
The suckling, to the conscious God balanced upon your
    knees.

Apart I considered the melodious names of my brothers,
As again in my Father's house, and the even spheres
Slowly, nightlong recalled the splendour of numbers;
I heard again the voluptuous measure of praise.

Sometimes pacing beneath clarity immeasurable
I saw my mind lie open and desert,
The wavering streams frozen up and each coppice quieted,
A whole valley in starlight with leaves and waters.

Coming at last to these farthest Syrian hills,
Attis or Adon, some abushed lust looked out;
My skin grows pale and smooth, shrunken as silk,
Without the rough effulgence of a God.

And here no voice has spoken;
There is no shrine of any godhead here;
No grove or hallowed fires,
And godhead seems asleep.

Only the vine has woven
Strange houses and blind rooms and palaces,
Into each hollow and crevice continually
Dropped yearlong irrecoverable flowers.

The sprawling vine has built us a close room;
Obedient Hymen fills the air with mist;
And to make dumb our theft
The white and moving sand that will not bear a print.

PROCNE

So she became a bird and bird-like danced
On a long sloe-bough, treading the silver blossom
With a bird's lovely feet,
And shaken blossoms fell into the hands
Of sunlight, and he held them for a moment
And let them drop.
And in the autumn Procne came again
And leapt upon the crooked sloe-bough singing
And the dark berries winked like earth-dimmed beads,
As the branch swung beneath her dancing feet.

Herbert Read / 1889–

SUMMER RAIN

Against the window pane
against the temple of my brain
beat the muffled taps of rain.

Upon the scorch'd and mottled leaves
upon the blench'd and pented sheaves
the land receives

the liquid flood:
water like a blush of blood
returns to the parch'd rood.

The fox has left his fetid hovel
to lick the drench'd blades of sorrel;
odours rise from thyme and fennel.

The worm in his retreat deep under
the earth's insipid crust
hearing a distant drumming thunder

blindly renews his upward undulation.
The soil respires as if in emulation
of living things. All elements their maculation

desire and achieve. A warm breath
issues from the nostrils beneath
the mask of death.

TO A CONSCRIPT OF 1940

Qui n'a pas une fois désespéré de l'honneur,
ne sera jamais un héros.
                                    GEORGE BERNANOS

A soldier passed me in the freshly fallen snow
His footsteps muffled, his face unearthly gray;
And my heart gave a sudden leap
As I gazed on a ghost of five-and-twenty years ago.

I shouted Halt! and my voice had the old accustom'd ring
And he obeyed it as it was obeyed
In the shrouded days when I too was one
Of an army of young men marching

Into the unknown. He turned towards me and I said:
'I am one of those who went before you
Five-and-twenty years ago: one of the many who never
    returned,
Of the many who returned and yet were dead.

We went where you are going, into the rain and the mud;
We fought as you will fight
With death and darkness and despair;
We gave what you will give—our brains and our blood.

We think we gave in vain. The world was not renewed.
There was hope in the homestead and anger in the streets
But the old world was restored and we returned
To the dreary field and workshop, and the immemorial feud

Of rich and poor. Our victory was our defeat.
Power was retained where power had been misused
And youth was left to sweep away
The ashes that the fires had strewn beneath our feet.

But one thing we learned: there is no glory in the deed
Until the soldier wears a badge of tarnish'd braid;
There are heroes who have heard the rally and have seen
The glitter of a garland round their head.

Theirs is the hollow victory. They are deceived.
But you, my brother and my ghost, if you can go
Knowing that there is no reward, no certain use
In all your sacrifice, then honour is reprieved.

To fight without hope is to fight with grace,
The self reconstructed, the false heart repaired.'
Then I turned with a smile, and he answered my salute
As he stood against the fretted hedge, which was like white
    lace.

Michael Roberts / 1902–1948

ST. URSANNE

Leaving the viaduct on the left, and coming over the hill,
We came to a small town, four towers at the corners,
The streets narrow and not dark,
The children playing in green gardens by the waterside.

Was it at the Swan or the White Horse that we stopped?
We walked up to the church and the stone cloister,
Grass growing among the tangle of votive ribbons,
The wax flowers and the twisted wire.

We heard the town-crier ringing a bell under the town
        clock—
Something about a wandering cow and a job for a
        waggoner—
Then we looked at the watermill by the stone bridge,
And went back for a Rossi or a Cinzano.

That was at Eastertide, and the fields and meadows
Mellow with cowslips: there were boys on bicycles
With bandoliers of jonquils, and there was an old lady
With a basket of primroses and violets.

It was a quiet town, and not yet broken,
The people kindly, and the priest 'a good one as priests go',
There was a football team, and a lad who enters from the
        country in the morning,
Singing: Ohé Oh, Ohé Oh!

Isaac Rosenberg / 1890–1918

DEAD MAN'S DUMP

The plunging limbers over the shattered track
Racketed with their rusty freight,
Stuck out like many crowns of thorns,
And the rusty stakes like sceptres old
To stay the flood of brutish men
Upon our brothers dear.

The wheels lurched over sprawled dead
But pained them not, though their bones crunched,
Their shut mouths made no moan.
They lie there huddled, friend and foeman,
Man born of man, and born of woman,
And shells go crying over them
From night till night and now.

Earth has waited for them,
All the time of their growth
Fretting for their decay:
Now she has them at last!
In the strength of their strength
Suspended—stopped and held.

What fierce imaginings their dark souls lit?
Earth! have they gone into you!
Somewhere they must have gone,
And flung on your hard back
Is their soul's sack
Emptied of God-ancestralled essences.
Who hurled them out?   Who hurled?

None saw their spirits' shadow shake the grass,
Or stood aside for the half used life to pass

Out of those doomed nostrils and the doomed mouth,
When the swift iron burning bee
Drained the wild honey of their youth.

What of us who, flung on the shrieking pyre,
Walk, our usual thoughts untouched,
Our lucky limbs as on ichor fed,
Immortal seeming ever?
Perhaps when the flames beat loud on us,
A fear may choke in our veins
And the startled blood may stop.

The air is loud with death,
The dark air spurts with fire,
The explosions ceaseless are.
Timelessly now, some minutes past,
These dead strode time with vigorous life,
Till the shrapnel called 'An end!'
But not to all. In bleeding pangs
Some borne on stretchers dreamed of home,
Dear things, war-blotted from their hearts.

Maniac Earth! howling and flying, your bowel
Seared by the jagged fire, the iron love,
The impetuous storm of savage love.
Dark Earth! dark Heavens! swinging in chemic smoke,
What dead are born when you kiss each soundless soul
With lightning and thunder from your mined heart,
Which man's self dug, and his blind fingers loosed?

A man's brains splattered on
A stretcher-bearer's face;
His shook shoulders slipped their load,
But when they bent to look again
The drowning soul was sunk too deep
For human tenderness.

They left this dead with the older dead,
Stretched at the cross roads.

Burnt black by strange decay
Their sinister faces lie,
The lid over each eye,

The grass and coloured clay
More motion have than they,
Joined to the great sunk silences.

Here is one not long dead;
His dark hearing caught our far wheels,
And the choked soul stretched weak hands
To reach the living word the far wheels said,
The blood-dazed intelligence beating for light,
Crying through the suspense of the far torturing wheels
Swift for the end to break
Or the wheels to break,
Cried as the tide of the world broke over his sight.

Will they come?   Will they ever come?
Even as the mixed hoofs of the mules,
The quivering-bellied mules,
And the rushing wheels all mixed
With his tortured upturned sight.
So we crashed round the bend,
We heard his weak scream,
We heard his very last sound,
And our wheels grazed his dead face.

Carl Sandburg / 1878–1967

CHICAGO

Hog Butcher for the World,
Tool Maker, Stacker of Wheat,
Player with Railroads and the Nation's Freight
    Handler;
Stormy, husky, brawling,
City of the Big Shoulders:

They tell me you are wicked and I believe them, for I have
    seen your painted women under the gas lamps
    luring the farm boys.
And they tell me you are crooked and I answer: Yes, it is
    true I have seen the gunman kill and go free to kill
    again.
And they tell me you are brutal and my reply is: On the
    faces of women and children I have seen the marks
    of wanton hunger.
And having answered so I turn once more to those who
    sneer at this my city, and I give them back the sneer
    and say to them:
Come and show me another city with lifted head singing
    so proud to be alive and coarse and strong and
    cunning.
Flinging magnetic curses amid the toil of piling job on job,
    here is a tall bold slugger set vivid against the little
    soft cities;
Fierce as a dog with tongue lapping for action, cunning as
    a savage pitted against the wilderness,
        Bareheaded,
        Shoveling,
        Wrecking,
        Planning,
        Building, breaking, rebuilding,
Under the smoke, dust all over his mouth, laughing with
    white teeth,
Under the terrible burden of destiny laughing as a young
    man laughs,
Laughing even as an ignorant fighter laughs who has never
    lost a battle,
Bragging and laughing that under his wrist is the pulse,
    and under his ribs the heart of the people,
                Laughing!
Laughing the stormy, husky, brawling laughter of Youth,
    half-naked, sweating, proud to be Hog Butcher, Tool
    Maker, Stacker of Wheat, Player with Railroads and
    Freight Handler to the Nation.

Siegfried Sassoon / 1887–1967

THE DEATH-BED

He drowsed and was aware of silence heaped
Round him, unshaken as the steadfast walls;
Aqueous like floating rays of amber light,
Soaring and quivering in the wings of sleep.
Silence and safety; and his mortal shore
Lipped by the inward, moonless waves of death.

Someone was holding water to his mouth.
He swallowed, unresisting; moaned and dropped
Through crimson gloom to darkness; and forgot
The opiate throb and ache that was his wound.
   Water—calm, sliding green above the weir.
   Water—a sky-lit alley for his boat,
   Bird-voiced, and bordered with reflected flowers
   And shaken hues of summer; drifting down,
   He dipped contented oars, and sighed, and slept.

Night, with a gust of wind, was in the ward,
Blowing the curtain to a glimmering curve.
Night. He was blind; he could not see the stars
Glinting among the wraiths of wandering cloud;
Queer blots of colour, purple, scarlet, green,
Flickered and faded in his drowning eyes.

Rain—he could hear it rustling through the dark;
Fragrance and passionless music woven as one;
Warm rain on drooping roses; pattering showers
That soak the woods; not the harsh rain that sweeps
Behind the thunder, but a trickling peace,
Gently and slowly washing life away.

He stirred, shifting his body; then the pain
Leapt like a prowling beast, and gripped and tore
His groping dreams with grinding claws and fangs.
　　But someone was beside him; soon he lay
　　Shuddering because that evil thing had passed.
　　And death, who'd stepped toward him, paused and
　　　　stared.

Light many lamps and gather round his bed.
Lend him your eyes, warm blood, and will to live.
Speak to him; rouse him; you may save him yet.
He's young; he hated War; how should he die
When cruel old campaigners win safe through?

But death replied: 'I chose him.' So he went,
And there was silence in the summer night;
Silence and safety; and the veils of sleep.
Then, far away, the thudding of the guns.

THE GENERAL

'Good-morning; good-morning!' the General said
When we met him last week on our way to the line.
Now the soldiers he smiled at are most of 'em dead,
And we're cursing his staff for incompetent swine.
'He's a cheery old card,' grunted Harry to Jack
As they slogged up to Arras with rifle and pack.

.　.　.

But he did for them both by his plan of attack.

Marshall Schacht / 1905–

NOT TO FORGET MISS DICKINSON

Flavor the speaking of this one,
The jointed quatrains like a bird's,
The language of Miss Dickinson,
Trapeze performer, dancer of words.

See how the sprightly squirrel mind
Resolves to the kernel love so great
The looking on it sets you blind
An instant, as if in sun or hate.

Observe the "gypsy face transfigured"
Go through the magic burning act
Of singing in a room beleaguered
Up to its sills by the gnawing fact.

Edith Sitwell / 1887–1964

STILL FALLS THE RAIN

The Raids, 1940. Night and Dawn

Still falls the Rain—
Dark as the world of man, black as our loss—
Blind as the nineteen hundred and forty nails
Upon the Cross.

Still falls the Rain
With a sound like the pulse of the heart that is changed to
the hammer-beat
In the Potter's Field, and the sound of the impious feet

On the Tomb:
Still falls the Rain
In the Field of Blood where the small hopes breed and the
human brain
Nurtures its greed, that worm with the brow of Cain.

Still falls the Rain
At the feet of the Starved Man hung upon the Cross.
Christ that each day, each night, nails there, have mercy on
us—
On Dives and on Lazarus:
Under the Rain the sore and the gold are as one.

Still falls the Rain—
Still falls the Blood from the Starved Man's wounded Side:
He bears in His Heart all wounds—those of the light that
died,
The last faint spark
In the self-murdered heart, the wounds of the sad
uncomprehending dark,
The wounds of the baited bear—
The blind and weeping bear whom the keepers beat
On his helpless flesh . . . the tears of the hunted hare.

Still falls the Rain—
Then—O Ile leape up to my God: who pulles me doune—
See, see where Christ's blood streames in the firmament:
It flows from the Brow we nailed upon the tree
Deep to the dying, to the thirsting heart
That holds the fires of the world—dark-smirched with pain
As Caesar's laurel crown.

Then sounds the voice of One who like the heart of man
Was once a child who among beasts has lain—
'Still do I love, still shed my innocent light, my Blood, for
thee.'

LULLABY

Though the world has slipped and gone,
Sounds my loud discordant cry
Like the steel birds' song on high:
'Still one thing is left—the Bone!'
Then out danced the Babioun.

She sat in the hollow of the sea—
A socket whence the eye's put out—
She sang to the child a lullaby
(The steel birds' nest was thereabout).

'Do, do, do, do—
Thy mother's hied to the vaster race:
The Pterodactyl made its nest
And laid a steel egg in her breast—
Under the Judas-colored sun.
She'll work no more, nor dance, nor moan,
And I am come to take her place
Do, do.

There's nothing left but earth's low bed—
(The Pterodactyl fouls its nest):
But steel wings fan thee to thy rest,
And wingless truth and larvae lie
And eyeless hope and handless fear—
All these for thee as toys are spread,
Do—do—

Red is the bed of Poland, Spain,
And thy mother's breast, who has grown wise
In that fouled nest. If she could rise.
Give birth again,
In wolfish pelt she'd hide thy bones
To shield thee from the world's long cold,
And down on all fours shouldst thou crawl
For thus from no height canst thou fall—
Do, do.

She'd give no hands: there's nought to hold
And nought to make: there's dust to sift,
But no food for the hands to lift.
Do, do.

Heed my ragged lullaby,
Fear not living, fear not chance;
All is equal—blindness, sight,
There is no depth, there is no height:
Do, do.

The Judas-colored sun is gone,
And with the Ape thou art alone—
Do,
       Do.'

Bernard Spencer / 1909-1963

PART OF PLENTY

When she carries food to the table and stoops down
—Doing this out of love—and lays soup with its good
Tickling smell, or fry winking from the fire
And I look up, perhaps from a book I am reading
Or other work: there is an importance of beauty
Which can't be accounted for by there and then,
And attacks me, but not separately from the welcome
Of the food, or the grace of her arms.

When she puts a sheaf of tulips in a jug
And pours in water and presses to one side
The upright stems and leaves that you hear creak,
Or loosens them, or holds them up to show me,
So that I see the tangle of their necks and cups
With the curls of her hair, and the body they are held
Against, and the stalk of the small waist rising
And flowering in the shape of breasts;

Whether in the bringing of the flowers or the food
She offers plenty, and is part of plenty,
And whether I see her stooping, or leaning with the flowers,
What she does is ages old, and she is not simply,
No, but lovely in that way.

Edward Thomas / 1878–1917

OLD MAN

Old Man, or Lad's-love,—in the name there's nothing
To one that knows not Lad's-love, or Old Man,
The hoar-green feathery herb, almost a tree,
Growing with rosemary and lavender.
Even to one that knows it well, the names
Half decorate, half perplex, the thing it is:
At least, what that is clings not to the names
In spite of time. And yet I like the names.

The herb itself I like not, but for certain
I love it, as some day the child will love it
Who plucks a feather from the door-side bush
Whenever she goes in or out of the house.
Often she waits there, snipping the tips and shrivelling
The shreds at last on to the path,
Thinking, perhaps of nothing, till she sniffs
Her fingers and runs off. The bush is still
But half as tall as she, though it is as old;
So well she clips it. Not a word she says;
And I can only wonder how much hereafter
She will remember, with that bitter scent,
Of garden rows, and ancient damson trees
Topping a hedge, a bent path to a door,
A low thick bush beside the door, and me
Forbidding her to pick. As for myself,

Where first I met the bitter scent is lost.
I, too, often shrivel the grey shreds,
Sniff them and think and sniff again and try
Once more to think what it is I am remembering,
Always in vain. I cannot like the scent,
Yet I would rather give up others more sweet,
With no meaning, than this bitter one.

I have mislaid the key. I sniff the spray
And think of nothing; I see and I hear nothing;
Yet seem, too, to be listening, lying in wait
For what I should, yet never can, remember:
No garden appears, no path, no hoar-green bush
Of Lad's-love, or Old Man, no child beside,
Neither father nor mother, nor any playmate;
Only an avenue, dark, nameless, without end.

OUT IN THE DARK

Out in the dark over the snow
The fallow fawns invisible go
With the fallow doe;
And the winds blow
Fast as the stars are slow.

Stealthily the dark haunts round
And, when the lamp goes, without sound
At a swifter bound
Than the swiftest hound,
Arrives, and all else is drowned;

And star and I and wind and deer,
Are in the dark together,—near,
Yet far,—and fear
Drums on my ear
In that sage company drear.

How weak and little is the light,
All the universe of sight,
Love and delight,
Before the might,
If you love it not, of night.

Francis Thompson / 1859–1907

THE HOUND OF HEAVEN

I fled Him, down the nights and down the days;
I fled Him, down the arches of the years;
I fled Him, down the labyrinthine ways
    Of my own mind; and in the mist of tears
I hid from Him, and under running laughter.
            Up vistaed hopes I sped;
            And shot, precipitated,
Adown Titanic glooms of chasmèd fears,
    From those strong Feet that followed, followed after.
            But with unhurrying chase,
            And unperturbèd pace,
        Deliberate speed, majestic instancy,
            They beat—and a Voice beat
            More instant than the Feet—
    'All things betray thee, who betrayest Me.'

        I pleaded, outlaw-wise,
By many a hearted casement, curtained red,
    Trellised with intertwining charities;
(For, though I knew His love Who followèd,
        Yet was I sore adread
Lest, having Him, I must have naught beside.)
But, if one little casement parted wide,
    The gust of His approach would clash it to:
    Fear wist not to evade, as Love wist to pursue.

Across the margent of the world I fled,
  And troubled the gold gateways of the stars,
    Smiting for shelter on their clangèd bars;
      Fretted to dulcet jars
And silvern chatter the pale ports o' the moon.
I said to Dawn: Be sudden—to Eve: Be soon;
  With thy young skiey blossoms heap me over
    From this tremendous Lover—
Float thy vague veil about me, lest He see!
  I tempted all His servitors, but to find
My own betrayal in their constancy,
In faith to Him their fickleness to me,
  Their traitorous trueness, and their loyal deceit.
To all swift things for swiftness did I sue;
  Clung to the whistling mane of every wind.
    But whether they swept, smoothly fleet,
      The long savannahs of the blue;
        Or whether, Thunder-driven,
        They clanged his chariot 'thwart a heaven,
Plashy with flying lightnings round the spurn o' their feet:—
  Fear wist not to evade as Love wist to pursue.
        Still with unhurrying chase,
        And unperturbèd pace,
      Deliberate speed, majestic instancy,
        Came on the following Feet,
        And a Voice above their beat—
      'Naught shelters thee, who wilt not shelter Me.'

I sought no more that after which I strayed
        In face of man or maid;
But still within the little children's eyes
      Seems something, something that replies,
They at least are for me, surely for me!
I turned me to them very wistfully;
But just as their young eyes grew sudden fair
      With dawning answers there,
Their angel plucked them from me by the hair.
'Come then, ye other children, Nature's—share
With me' (said I) 'your delicate fellowship;
      Let me greet you lip to lip,
      Let me twine with your caresses,
        Wantoning

With our Lady-Mother's vagrant tresses,
      Banqueting
With her in her wind-walled palace,
Underneath her azured daïs,
Quaffing, as your taintless way is,
      From a chalice
Lucent-weeping out of the dayspring.'
      So it was done:
I in their delicate fellowship was one—
Drew the bolt of Nature's secrecies.
      I knew all the swift importings
      On the wilful face of skies;
      I knew how the clouds arise
      Spumèd of the wild sea-snortings;
         All that's born or dies
      Rose and drooped with; made them shapers
Of mine own moods, or wailful or divine;
      With them joyed and was bereaven.
      I was heavy with the even,
      When she lit her glimmering tapers
      Round the day's dead sanctities.
      I laughed in the morning's eyes.
I triumphed and I saddened with all weather,
      Heaven and I wept together,
And its sweet tears were salt with mortal mine;
Against the red throb of its sunset-heart
      I laid my own to beat,
      And share commingling heat;
But not by that, by that, was eased my human smart.
In vain my tears were wet on Heaven's grey cheek.
For ah! we know not what each other says,
      These things and I; in sound *I* speak—
Their sound is but their stir, they speak by silences.
Nature, poor stepdame, cannot slake my drouth;
      Let her, if she would owe me,
Drop yon blue bosom-veil of sky, and show me
      The breasts o' her tenderness:
Never did any milk of hers once bless
      My thirsting mouth.
      Nigh and nigh draws the chase,
      With unperturbèd pace,

Deliberate speed, majestic instancy;
     And past those noisèd Feet
     A voice comes yet more fleet—
'Lo! naught contents thee, who content'st not Me.'

Naked I wait Thy love's uplifted stroke!
My harness piece by piece Thou hast hewn from me,
     And smitten me to my knee;
     I am defenceless utterly.
     I slept, methinks, and woke,
And, slowly gazing, find me stripped in sleep.
In the rash lustihead of my young powers,
     I shook the pillaring hours
And pulled my life upon me; grimed with smears,
I stand amid the dust o' the mounded years—
My mangled youth lies dead beneath the heap.
My days have crackled and gone up in smoke,
Have puffed and burst as sun-starts on a stream.
     Yea, faileth now even dream
The dreamer, and the lute the lutanist;
Even the linked fantasies, in whose blossomy twist
I swung the earth a trinket at my wrist,
Are yielding; cords of all too weak account
For earth with heavy griefs so overplussed.
     Ah! is Thy love indeed
A weed, albeit an amaranthine weed,
Suffering no flowers except its own to mount?
     Ah! must—
     Designer infinite!—
Ah! must Thou char the wood ere Thou canst limn with it?
My freshness spent its wavering shower i' the dust;
And now my heart is as a broken fount,
Wherein tear-drippings stagnate, spilt down ever
     From the dank thoughts that shiver
Upon the sighful branches of my mind.
     Such is; what is to be?
The pulp so bitter, how shall taste the rind?
I dimly guess what Time in mists confounds;
Yet ever and anon a trumpet sounds
From the hid battlements of Eternity;
Those shaken mists a space unsettle, then

Round the half-glimpsèd turrets slowly wash again.
    But not ere him who summoneth
    I first have seen, enwound
With glooming robes purpureal, cypress-crowned;
His name I know, and what his trumpet saith.
Whether man's heart or life it be which yields
        Thee harvest, must Thy harvest-fields
        Be dunged with rotten death?

        Now of that long pursuit
        Comes on at hand the bruit;
    That Voice is round me like a bursting sea:
        'And is thy earth so marred,
        Shattered in shard on shard?
    Lo, all things fly thee, for thou fliest Me!
    Strange, piteous, futile thing!
Wherefore should any set thee love apart?
Seeing none but I makes much of naught' (He said),
'And human love needs human meriting:
        How hast thou merited—
Of all man's clotted clay the dingiest clot?
        Alack, thou knowest not
How little worthy of any love thou art!
Whom wilt thou find to love ignoble thee,
        Save Me, save only Me?
All which I took from thee I did but take,
        Not for thy harms,
But just that thou might'st seek it in My arms.
        All which thy child's mistake
Fancies as lost, I have stored for thee at home:
        Rise, clasp My hand, and come!'
    Halts by me that footfall:
    Is my gloom, after all,
Shade of His hand, outstretched caressingly?
    'Ah, fondest, blindest, weakest,
    I am He Whom thou seekest!
Thou dravest love from thee, who dravest Me.'

Mark Van Doren / 1894–

THE DISTANT RUNNERS

Six great horses of Spain, set free after his death by
De Soto's men, ran West and restored to America
the wild race lost there some thousands of years ago.

LEGEND

Ferdinand De Soto lies
Soft again in river mud.
Birds again, as on the day
Of his descending, rise and go
Straightly West, and do not know
Of feet beneath that faintly thud.

If I were there in other time,
Between the proper sky and stream;
If I were there and saw the six
Abandoned manes, and ran along,
I could sing the fetlock song
That now is chilled within a dream.

Ferdinand De Soto, sleeping
In the river, never heard
Four-and-twenty Spanish hooves
Fling off their iron and cut the green,
Leaving circles new and clean
While overhead the wing-tips whirred.

Neither I nor any walker
By the Mississippi now
Can see the dozen nostrils open
Half in pain for death of men;
But half in gladness, neighing then
As loud as loping would allow.

On they rippled, tail and back,
A prairie day, and swallows knew
A dark, uneven current there.
But not a sound came up the wind,
And toward the night their shadow thinned
Before the black that flooded through.

If I were there to bend and look,
The sky would know them as they sped
And turn to see. But I am here,
And they are far, and time is old.
Within my dream the grass is cold;
The legs are locked; the sky is dead.

John Hall Wheelock / 1886–

THE BLACK PANTHER

There is a panther caged within my breast,
    But what his name, there is no breast shall know
    Save mine, nor what it is that drives him so,
Backward and forward, in relentless quest—
That silent rage, baffled but unsuppressed,
    The soft pad of those stealthy feet that go
    Over my body's prison to and fro,
Trying the walls forever, without rest.

All day I feed him with my living heart,
    But when the night puts forth her dreams and stars,
        The inexorable frenzy re-awakes:
    His wrath is hurled upon the trembling bars,
The eternal passion stretches me apart,
        And I lie silent—but my body shakes.

SILENCE

There is a mystery too deep for words;
The silence of the dead comes nearer to it,
Being wisest in the end. What word shall hold
The sorrow sitting at the heart of things,
The majesty and patience of the truth!
Silence will serve; it is an older tongue:
The empty room, the moonlight on the wall,
Speak for the unreturning traveller.

EARTH

with apologies to The New Yorker

"A planet doesn't explode of itself," said drily
The Martian astronomer, gazing off into the air—
"That they were able to do it is proof that highly
Intelligent beings must have been living there."

SLOW SUMMER TWILIGHT

Slow summer twilight. Darkening branches loom
Beyond the window. Your belovèd head
Bends over the pale page by lamplight, shed
Like a soft aureole round it in the gloom.
Kind destiny holds back the stroke of doom;
We are together, though no word is said,
We are together, and are comforted—
A peace, stronger than joy, fills all the room.

Outside, the darkness deepens, and I guess
What darker things the years may hold in store—
Watching your face, even lovelier than before

Age had given it this grave tenderness
Love stretches hands toward, that would shield and bless
A face, once young, in age loved all the more.

Yvor Winters / 1900–1967

A SUMMER COMMENTARY

When I was young, with sharper sense,
The farthest insect cry I heard
Could stay me; through the trees, intense,
I watched the hunter and the bird.

Where is the meaning that I found?
Or was it but a state of mind,
Some old penumbra of the ground,
In which to be but not to find?

Now summer grasses, brown with heat,
Have crowded sweetness through the air;
The very roadside dust is sweet;
Even the unshadowed earth is fair.

The soft voice of the nesting dove,
And the dove in soft erratic flight
Like a rapid hand within a glove,
Caress the silence and the light.

Amid the rubble, the fallen fruit,
Fermenting in its rich decay,
Smears brandy on the trampling boot
And sends it sweeter on its way.

Richard Wright / 1908–1960

BETWEEN THE WORLD AND ME

And one morning while in the woods I stumbled suddenly
    upon the thing,
Stumbled upon it in a grassy clearing guarded by scaly oaks
    and elms.
And the sooty details of the scene rose, thrusting themselves
    between the world and me. . . .

There was a design of white bones slumbering forgottenly
    upon a cushion of ashes.
There was a charred stump of a sapling pointing a blunt
    finger accusingly at the sky.

There were torn tree limbs, tiny veins of burnt leaves, and
    a scorched coil of greasy hemp;
A vacant shoe, an empty tie, a ripped shirt, a lonely hat,
    and a pair of trousers stiff with black blood.
And upon the trampled grass were buttons, dead matches,
    butt-ends of cigars and cigarettes, peanut shells, a
    drained gin-flask, and a whore's lipstick;
Scattered traces of tar, restless arrays of feathers, and the
    lingering smell of gasoline.
And through the morning air the sun poured yellow
    surprise into the eye sockets of a stony skull. . . .
And while I stood my mind was frozen with a cold
    pity for the life that was gone.
The ground gripped my feet and my heart was circled by
    icy walls of fear—
The sun died in the sky; a night wind muttered in the grass
    and fumbled the leaves in the trees; the woods poured
    forth the hungry yelping of hounds; the darkness
    screamed with thirsty voices; and the witnesses rose
    and lived:

The dry bones stirred, rattled, lifted, melting themselves
    into my bones.
The grey ashes formed flesh firm and black, entering into
    my flesh.
The gin-flask passed from mouth to mouth; cigars and
    cigarettes glowed, the whore smeared the lipstick red
    upon her lips,
And a thousand faces swirled around me, clamoring that
    my life be burned. . . .

And then they had me, stripped me, battering my teeth
    into my throat till I swallowed my own blood.
My voice was drowned in the roar of their voices, and
    my black wet body slipped and rolled in their hands
    as they bound me to the sapling.
And my skin clung to the bubbling hot tar, falling from me
    in limp patches.
And the down and quills of the white feathers sank into
    my raw flesh, and I moaned in my agony.
Then my blood was cooled mercifully, cooled by a baptism
    of gasoline.
And in a blaze of red I leaped to the sky as pain rose like
    water, boiling my limbs.

Panting, begging I clutched childlike, clutched to the hot
    sides of death.
Now I am dry bones and my face a stony skull staring in
    yellow surprise at the sun. . . .

PART III

A Little Treasury of
Poetry in Progress

Margaret Avison / 1918–

BUTTERFLY BONES; OR SONNET AGAINST SONNETS

The cyanide jar seals life, as sonnets move
towards final stiffness. Cased in a white glare
these specimens stare for peering boys, to prove
strange certainties. Plane dogsled and safari
assure continuing range. The sweep-net skill,
the patience, learning, leave all living stranger.
Insect—or poem—waits for the fix, the frill
precision can effect, brilliant with danger.
What law and wonder the museum spectres
bespeak is cryptic for the shivery wings,
the world cut-diamond-eyed, those eyes' reflectors,
or herbal grass, sunned motes, fierce listening.
Might sheened and rigid trophies strike men blind
like Adam's lexicon locked in the mind?

NEW YEAR'S POEM

The Christmas twigs crispen and needles rattle
Along the windowledge.
        A solitary pearl
Shed from the necklace spilled at last week's party
Lies in the suety, snow-luminous plainness
Of morning, on the windowledge beside them.

And all the furniture that circled stately
And hospitable when these rooms were brimmed
With perfumes, furs, and black-and-silver
Crisscross of seasonal conversation, lapses
Into its previous largeness.
                    I remember
Anne's rose-sweet gravity, and the stiff grave
Where cold so little can contain;
I mark the queer delightful skull and crossbones
Starlings and sparrows left, taking the crust,
And the long loop of winter wind
Smoothing its arc from dark Arcturus down
To the bricked corner of the drifted courtyard,
And the still windowledge.
                    Gentle and just pleasure
It is, being human, to have won from space
This unchill, habitable interior
Which mirrors quietly the light
Of the snow, and the new year.

Wendell Berry / 1934–

NOVEMBER TWENTY-SIXTH
NINETEEN HUNDRED AND
SIXTY-THREE

We know
the winter earth
upon the body
of the young
    president,
    and the early dark
    falling;

We know
the veins
grown quiet
in his temples and
   wrists, and his hands
   and eyes
   grown quiet;

We know
his name written
in the black capitals
   of his death,
   and the mourners
   standing in the rain,
   and the leaves
   falling;

We know
his death's horses
and drums;
the roses, bells,
   candles, crosses;
   the faces
   hidden in veils;

We know
the children
who begin
the youth of loss
   greater than
   they can dream
   now;

We know
the nightlong coming
of faces
into the candle-
   light
   before his coffin,
   and their passing;

We know
the mouth of the grave
waiting,
the bugle and rifles,
   the mourners
   turning
   away;

We know
the young dead body
carried
in the earth
   into the first
   deep night
   of its absence;

We know
our streets and days
slowly opening
into the time
   he is not alive,
   filling with
   our footsteps
   and voices;

We know
ourselves,
the bearers
of the light
of the earth
   he is given to,
   and the light of
   all his lost days;

We know
the long approach
of summers toward the
   healed ground
   where he will be
   waiting,
   no longer the keeper
   of what he was.

Gwendolyn Brooks / 1917–

from TWO DEDICATIONS

I

THE CHICAGO PICASSO

August 15, 1967

*"Mayor Daley tugged a white ribbon, loosing the blue percale
wrap. A hearty cheer went up as the covering slipped off the big
steel sculpture that looks at once like a bird and a woman."*
CHICAGO Sun-Times

(Seiji Ozawa leads the Symphony.
The Mayor smiles.
And 50,000 See.)

Does man love Art? Man visits Art, but squirms.
Art hurts. Art urges voyages—
and it is easier to stay at home,
the nice beer ready.
          In commonrooms
we belch, or sniff, or scratch.
Are raw.

But we must cook ourselves and style ourselves for Art, who
is a requiring courtesan.
We squirm.
We do not hug the Mona Lisa.
We
may touch or tolerate
an astounding fountain, or a horse-and-rider.

At most, another Lion.

Observe the tall cold of a Flower
which is as innocent and as guilty,
as meaningful and as meaningless as any
other flower in the western field.

THE SERMON ON THE WARPLAND

"The fact that we are black is our ultimate reality."
                                        RON KARENGA

And several strengths from drowsiness campaigned
but spoke in Single Sermon on the warpland.

And went about the warpland saying No.
"My people, black and black, revile the River.
Say that the River turns, and turn the River.

Say that our Something in doublepod contains
seeds for the coming hell and health together.
Prepare to meet
(sisters, brothers) the brash and terrible weather;
the pains;
the bruising; the collapse of bestials, idols.
But then oh then!—the stuffing of the hulls!
the seasoning of the perilously sweet!
the health! the heralding of the clear obscure!

Build now your Church, my brothers, sisters. Build
never with brick nor Corten nor with granite.
Build with lithe love. With love like lion-eyes.
With love like morningrise.
With love like black, our black—
luminously indiscreet;
complete; continuous."

Charles Causley / 1917–

ON SEEING A POET OF THE FIRST WORLD WAR ON THE STATION AT ABBEVILLE

Poet, cast your careful eye
Where the beached songs of summer lie,
   White fell the wave that splintered
   The wreck where once you wintered,
White as the snows that lair
Your freezing hair.

Captain, here you took your wine,
The trees at ease in the orchard-line,
   Bonny the errand-boy bird
   Whistles the songs you once heard,
While you traverse the wire,
Autumn will hold her fire.

Through the tall wood the thunder ran
As when the gibbering guns began,
   Swift as a murderer by the stack
   Crawled the canal with fingers black,
Black with your brilliant blood
You lit the mud.

Two grey moths stare from your eyes,
Sharp is your sad face with surprise.
   In the stirring pool I fail
   To see the drowned of Passchendaele,
Where all day drives for me
The spoiling sea.

AUTOBIOGRAPHY

Now that my seagoing self-possession wavers
I sit and write the letter you will not answer.
The razor at my wrist patiently severs
Passion from thought, of which the flesh is censor.
I walk by the deep canal where moody lovers
Find their Nirvana on each other's tongues,
And in my naked bed the usual fevers
Invade the tropic sense, brambling the lungs.
I am drowned to the sound of seven flooding rivers
The distant Bombay drum and the ghazel dancer,
But the English Sunday, monstrous as India, shivers,
And the voice of the muezzin is the voice of the station
        announcer.
The wet fields blot the bitterness of the cry,
And I turn from the tactful friend to the candid sky.

John Ciardi / 1916–

ODE FOR THE BURIAL OF
A CITIZEN

Recorder, tax collector, landlord, friends,
This man is past his obligation.
Salesman, he is no market to be won:
The index of his power to pay descends
On graphs of strata, closes on a stone.
Like all of us he was a business risk,
Sustained a level after starting brisk,
Finally failed to displace his own depreciation.

He is marketable nowhere, auctioneer:
His liabilities zero, his assets zero.

His card has been removed from the credit bureau.
He is off the mailing list of the fiscal year.
His final real investment was to borrow
Courage from courage on the day's receipts
And so by petty cash and small deceits
To contrive one more contrivance for tomorrow.

His ballot is not collectible, public saints:
His politics are simplified and sound.
He has his ear forever to the ground
To hear the perfect congress of his silence.
Weep for him, learned men. I pass around
The hat of sentiment, drop him your tears,
For you are in the contract of his years:
All that he did not find, you have not found.

TO JUDITH ASLEEP

My dear, darkened in sleep turned from the moon
that riots on curtain-stir with every breeze,
leaping in moths of light across your back . . .
far off, then soft and sudden as petals shower
down from wired roses—silently, all at once—
you turn, abandoned and naked, all let down
in ferny streams of sleep and petaled thighs
rippling into my flesh's buzzing garden.

Far and familiar your body's myth-map lights,
traveled by moon and dapple. Sagas were curved
like scimitars to your hips. The raiders' ships
all sailed to your one port. And watchfires burned
your image on the hills. Sweetly you drown
male centuries in your chiaroscuro tide
of breast and breath. And all my memory's shores
you frighten perfectly, washed familiar and far.

Ritual wars have climbed your shadowed flank
where bravos dreaming of fair women tore
rock out of rock to have your cities down

in loot of hearths and trophies of desire.
And desert monks have fought your image back
in a hysteria of mad skeletons.
Bravo and monk (the heads and tails of love)
I stand, a spinning coin of wish and dread,

counting our life, our chairs, our books and walls,
our clock whose radium eye and insect voice
owns all our light and shade, and your white shell
spiraled in moonlight on the bed's white beach;
thinking, I might press you to my ear
and all your coils fall out in sounds of surf
washing a mystery sudden as you are
a light on light in light beyond the light.

Child, child, and making legend of my wish
fastened alive into your naked sprawl—
stir once to stop my fear and miser's panic
that time shall have you last and legendry
undress to old bones from its moon brocade.
Yet sleep and keep our prime of time alive
before that death of legend. My dear of all

saga and century, sleep in familiar-far.
Time still must tick *this is, I am, we are.*

THE GIFT

In 1945, when the keepers cried *kaput,*
Josef Stein, poet, came out of Dachau
like half a resurrection, his other
eighty pounds still in their invisible grave.

Slowly then the mouth opened and first
a broth, and then a medication, and then
a diet, and all in time and the knitting mercies,
the showing bones were buried back in flesh,

and the miracle was finished. Josef Stein,
man and poet, rose, walked, and could even
beget, and did, and died later of other causes
only partly traceable to his first death.

He noted—with some surprise at first—
that strangers could not tell he had died once.
He returned to his post in the library, drank his beer,
published three poems in a French magazine,

and was very kind to the son who at last was his.
In the spent of one night he wrote three propositions:
That Hell is the denial of the ordinary. That nothing lasts.
That clean white paper waiting under a pen

is the gift beyond history and hurt and heaven.

Alex Comfort / 1920–

THE ATOLL IN THE MIND

Out of what calms and pools the cool shell grows
dumb teeth under clear waters, where no currents
fracture the coral's porous horn
grows up the mind's stone tree, the honeycomb,
the plump brain-coral breaking the pool's mirror,
the ebony antler, the cold sugared fan.

All these strange trees stand downward through the water,
the mind's grey candied points tend to the surface—
the greater part is out of sight below:

but when on the island's whaleback spring green blades,
new land on water wavers, birds bring seeds
and tides plant slender trunks by the lagoon

I see the image of the mind's two trees cast downward,
one tilting leaves to catch the sun's bright pennies,
one dark as water, its root among the bones.

HOC EST CORPUS

I who am nothing, and this tissue
steer, find in my servant still my maker
rule and obey, as flame to candle mated.

Whom bone has conjured, Banquo shall the bard
command, the marble rule Pygmalion—
did this tower build me then, who am its garrison?

Strange that in me the shadow
moving the substance speaks—strange that such air
pulls the grey sinew—whom the blood maintains,
whom the heart's coming, slight defection
shall spill, speaks now and holds
time like a permanent stone, its cold weight judging.

NOTES FOR MY SON

Remember when you hear them beginning to say Freedom
Look carefully—see who it is that they want you to butcher.

Remember, when you say that the old trick would not have
        fooled you for a moment
That every time it is the trick which seems new.

Remember that you will have to put in irons
Your better nature, if it will desert to them.

Remember, remember their faces—watch them carefully:
For every step you take is on somebody's body

And every cherry you plant for them is a gibbet
And every furrow you turn for them is a grave

Remember, the smell of burning will not sicken you
If they persuade you that it will thaw the world

Beware. The blood of a child does not smell so bitter
If you have shed it with a high moral purpose.

So that because the woodcutter disobeyed
they will not burn her today or any day

So that for lack of a joiner's obedience
the crucifixion will not now take place

So that when they come to sell you their bloody corruption
you will gather the spit of your chest
and plant it in their faces.

Gregory Corso / 1930–

MARRIAGE

Should I get married? Should I be good?
Astound the girl next door with my velvet suit and faustus
     hood?
Don't take her to movies but to cemeteries
tell all about werewolf bathtubs and forked clarinets
then desire her and kiss her and all the preliminaries
and she going just so far and I understanding why
not getting angry saying You must feel! It's beautiful to feel!
Instead take her in my arms lean against an old crooked
     tombstone
and woo her the entire night the constellations in the sky—

When she introduces me to her parents
back straightened, hair finally combed, strangled by a tie,
should I sit knees together on their 3rd degree sofa
and not ask Where's the bathroom?
How else to feel other than I am,
often thinking Flash Gordon soap—
O how terrible it must be for a young man
seated before a family and the family thinking
We never saw him before! He wants our Mary Lou!
After tea and homemade cookies they ask What do you
    do for a living?
Should I tell them? Would they like me then?
Say All right get married, we're losing a daughter
but we're gaining a son—
And should I then ask Where's the bathroom?

O God, and the wedding! All her family and her friends
and only a handful of mine all scroungy and bearded
just wait to get at the drinks and food—
And the priest! he looking at me as if I masturbated
asking me Do you take this woman for your lawful wedded
    wife?
And I trembling what to say say Pie Glue!
I kiss the bride all those corny men slapping me on the back
She's all yours, boy! Ha-ha-ha!
And in their eyes you could see some obscene honeymoon
    going on—
Then all that absurd rice and clanky cans and shoes
Niagara Falls! Hordes of us! Husbands! Wives! Flowers!
    Chocolates!
All streaming into cozy hotels
All going to do the same thing tonight
The indifferent clerk he knowing what was going to happen
The lobby zombies they knowing what
The whistling elevator man he knowing
The winking bellboy knowing
Everybody knowing! I'd be almost inclined not to do
    anything!
Stay up all night! Stare that hotel clerk in the eye!
Screaming: I deny honeymoon! I deny honeymoon!
running rampant into those almost climactic suites

yelling Radio belly! Cat shovel!
O I'd live in Niagara forever! in a dark cave beneath the
      Falls
I'd sit there the Mad Honeymooner
devising ways to break marriages, a scourge of bigamy
a saint of divorce—

But I should get married I should be good
How nice it'd be to come home to her
and sit by the fireplace and she in the kitchen
aproned young and lovely wanting my baby
and so happy about me she burns the roast beef
and comes crying to me and I get up from my big papa
      chair
saying Christmas teeth! Radiant brains! Apple deaf!
God what a husband I'd make! Yes, I should get married!
So much to do! like sneaking into Mr Jones' house late at
      night
and cover his golf clubs with 1920 Norwegian books
Like hanging a picture of Rimbaud on the lawnmower
like pasting Tannu Tuva postage stamps all over the picket
      fence
like when Mrs Kindhead comes to collect for the
      Community Chest
grab her and tell her There are unfavorable omens in the
      sky!
And when the mayor comes to get my vote tell him
When are you going to stop people killing whales!
And when the milkman comes leave him a note in the
      bottle
Penguin dust, bring me penguin dust, I want penguin dust—

Yet if I should get married and it's Connecticut and snow
and she gives birth to a child and I am sleepless, worn,
up for nights, head bowed against a quiet window, the past
      behind me,
finding myself in the most common of situations a
      trembling man
knowledged with responsibility not twig-smear nor Roman
      coin soup—
O what would that be like!

Surely I'd give it for a nipple a rubber Tacitus
For a rattle a bag of broken Bach records
Tack Della Francesca all over its crib
Sew the Greek alphabet on its bib
And build for its playpen a roofless Parthenon

No, I doubt I'd be that kind of father
not rural not snow no quiet window
but hot smelly tight New York City
seven flights up, roaches and rats in the walls
a fat Reichian wife screeching over potatoes Get a job!
And five nose running brats in love with Batman
And the neighbors all toothless and dry haired
like those hag masses of the 18th century
all wanting to come in and watch TV
The landlord wants his rent
Grocery store Blue Cross Gas & Electric Knights of
      Columbus
Impossible to lie back and dream Telephone snow, ghost
      parking—
No! I should not get married I should never get married!
But—imagine If I were married to a beautiful sophisticated
      woman
tall and pale wearing an elegant black dress and long black
      gloves
holding a cigarette holder in one hand and a highball in
      the other
and we lived high up in a penthouse with a huge window
from which we could see all of New York and even farther
      on clearer days
No, can't imagine myself married to that pleasant prison
      dream—

O but what about love? I forget love
not that I am incapable of love
it's just that I see love as odd as wearing shoes—
I never wanted to marry a girl who was like my mother
And Ingrid Bergman was always impossible
And there's maybe a girl now but she's already married
And I don't like men and—
but there's got to be somebody!

Because what if I'm 60 years old and not married,
all alone in a furnished room with pee stains on my
    underwear
and everybody else is married! All the universe married
    but me!

Ah, yet well I know that were a woman possible as I am
    possible
the marriage would be possible—
Like SHE in her lonely alien gaud waiting her Egyptian
    lover
so I wait—bereft of 2,000 years and the bath of life.

Robert Creeley / 1926–

THE IMMORAL PROPOSITION

If you never do anything for anyone else
you are spared the tragedy of human relation-

ships. If quietly and like another time
there is the passage of an unexpected thing:

to look at it is more
than it was. God knows

nothing is competent nothing is
all there is. The unsure

egoist is not
good for himself.

THE RHYTHM

It is all a rhythm,
from the shutting
door, to the window
opening,

the seasons, the sun's
light, the moon,
the oceans, the
growing of things,

the mind in men
personal, recurring
in them again,
thinking the end

is not the end, the
time returning,
themselves dead but
someone else coming.

If in death I am dead,
then in life also
dying, dying . . .
And the women cry and die.

The little children
grow only to old men.
The grass dries,
the force goes.

But is met by another
returning, oh not mine,
not mine, and
in turn dies.

The rhythm which projects
from itself continuity

bending all to its force
from window to door,
from ceiling to floor,
light at the opening,
dark at the closing.

THE WAY

My love's manners in bed
are not to be discussed by me,
as mine by her
I would not credit comment upon gracefully.

Yet I ride by the margin of that lake in
the wood, the castle,
and the excitement of strongholds;
and have a small boy's notion of doing good.

Oh well, I will say here,
knowing each man,
let you find a good wife too,
and love her as hard as you can.

A MARRIAGE

The first retainer
he gave to her
was a golden
wedding ring.

The second—late at night
he woke up,
leaned over on an elbow,
and kissed her.

The third and the last—
he died with
and gave up loving
and lived with her.

Donald Davie / 1922–

THE WIND AT PENISTONE

The wind meets me at Penistone.
                              A hill
Curves empty through the township, on a slope
Not cruel, and yet steep enough to be,
Were it protracted, cruel.
                          In the street,
A plain-ness rather meagre than severe,
Affords, though quite unclassical, a vista
So bald as to be monumental.
                            Here
A lean young housewife meets me with the glance
I like to think that I can recognize
As dour, not cross.
                   And all the while the wind,
A royal catspaw, toying easily,
Flicks out of shadows from a tufted wrist,
Its mane, perhaps, this lemon-coloured sun.

The wind reserves, the hill reserves, the style
Of building houses on the hill reserves
A latent edge;
              which we can do without
In Pennine gradients and the Pennine wind,
And never miss or, missing it, applaud
The absence of the aquiline;

which in her
Whose style of living in the wind reserves
An edge to meet the wind's edge, we may miss
But without prejudice.
                    And yet in art
Where all is patent, and a latency
Is manifest or nothing, even I,
Liking to think I feel these sympathies,
Can hardly praise this clenched and muffled style.

For architecture asks a cleaner edge,
Is open-handed.
                    And close-fisted people
Are mostly vulgar; only in the best,
Who draw, inflexible, upon reserves,
Is there a stern game that they play with life,
In which the rule is not to show one's hand
Until compelled.
                    And then the lion's paw!
Art that is dour and leonine in the Alps
Grows kittenish, makes curios and clocks,
Giant at play.
                    Here, nothing. So the wind
Meets me at Penistone, and, coming home,
The poet falls to special pleading, chilled
To find in Art no fellow but the wind.

GARDENS NO EMBLEMS

Man with a scythe: the torrent of his swing
Finds its own level; and is not hauled back
But gathers fluently, like water rising
Behind the watergates that close a lock.

The gardener eased his foot into a boot;
Which action like the mower's had its mould,
Being itself a sort of taking root,
Feeling for lodgment in the leather's fold.

But forms of thought move in another plane
Whose matrices no natural forms afford
Unless subjected to prodigious strain:
Say, light proceeding edgewise, like a sword.

Gene Derwood / 1900–1954

WITH GOD CONVERSING

Red paths that wander through the gray, and cells
Of strangeness, rutted mouldings in the brain,
Untempered fevers heated by old kills,
By the pampered word, by the pat printed rune,
Unbalanced coil under glaucous blooms of thought,
A turning mind, unmitigated thinking that
Feeds human hunger and eats us alive
While cringing to the death, expecting love,—
Such make the self we are. And do you make it?
And practice on us? For we cannot take it.

Listen. Grow mild before the flicking lash
Seems welded to your hand, self-wounder.
What are we, cry we, while our pain leaps lush,
Too jungle thick: the jungle where we wander,
No seeded faith before, nor after, miracle,
Of bidden faith in things unseen, no particle.
For we think only through our troubled selves,
We note the worm that in the apple delves,
See gibbous moons and spots upon the sun,
Speak gibberish, and keep the poor in sin.

Plus birth and death must war-lash winnow
While every pod-burst leaf of May sucks life?
Because we think shall we be less than minnow,
Cat, carrot, rat, bat and such from sense aloof?

What doorless maze is this we wander through
With fuming souls parched of our morning dew?
Reason confounds as it presents to NAUGHT:
Earth worn, man moving into self-made night.
Reason-begotten science sets war's pace
And, civil-mouthed, makes civilization pass.

Created in your image, made up of words,
Till words reduce you to a zero-o,
We, then, reflecting you, are less than birds,
Bugs, or empty dugs, still less than minus no.
There must be something wrong with being wise—
Talking we go, wondering and wandering with woes.
Big thoughts have got us, hence we organize,
Govern our heroes with unmeant yeas and nays,
And breathe in dungeons of our nervous mesh
An air too blank to snare meandering flesh.

Night melting dawn shall turn the renewed sky,
Aurora Borealis and Australis
Fanfaring leap the poles, the moon fall by;
But if our science does not quickly fail us
How long for us will space blue light the dun
Of populaces, while wonderers eye the sun?
The gloomy silhouettes of wings we forged
With reason reasonless, are now enlarged,
The falsified subconscious, beast a-woken?
We-you? Post-suicides, shall we awaken?

E L E G Y

*On Gordon Barber, Lamentably Drowned
in his Eighteenth Year*

When in the mirror of a permanent tear
Over the iris of your mother's eye
I beheld the dark tremor of your face, austere
With space of death, spun too benign for youth,
Icicle of the past to pierce her living sigh—

I saw you wish the last kiss of mother's mouth,
Who took the salted waters rather in the suck
Of seas, sighing yourself to fill and drench
With water the plum-rich glory of your breast
Where beat the heart escaping from war's luck.
Gordon, I mourn your wrist, your running foot,
Your curious brows, your thigh, your unborn daughters,
Yet mourn more deep the drought-caught war dry boy
Who goes a killer, to join you in your sleep
And envy you what made you blench
Taking your purple back to drought-less waters.
What choke of terror filled you in the wet
What fierce surprise caught you when play turned fate
And all the rains you loved became your net,
Formlessly yielding, yet stronger than your breath?
Then did you dream of mother or hopes hatched
When the cold cramp held you from nape to foot
And time dissolved, promise dissolved, in Death?
Did you cry 'cruel' to all the hands that stretched
Not near, but played afar, when you sank down
Your sponge of lungs hurt to the quick
Till you had left the quick to join the dead,
Whom, now, your mother mourns grief-sick.
You were too young to drown.

Never will you take bride to happy bed,
Who lay awash in water yet no laving
Needed, so pure so young for sudden leaving.

Gone, gone is Gordon, tall and brilliant lad
Whose mind was science. Now hollow his skull
A noble sculpture, is but sunken bone,
His cells from water come by water laid
Grave-deep, to water gone.
Lost, lost the hope he had
Washed to a cipher his splendour and his skill.

But Gordon's gone, it's other boys who live afraid.

Two years, and lads have grown to hold a gun.
In dust must splendid lads go down and choke,

Red dry their hands and dry their one day's sun
From which they earthward fall to fiery tomb
Bomb-weighted, from bloodying children's hair.
Never a boy but takes as cross Cain's crime
And goes to death by making death, to pass
Death's gate distorted with the dried brown grime—
Better the watery death than death by air
Or death by sand
Where fall hard fish of fear
Loud in unwetted dust.

Spun on a lucky wave, O early boy!
Now ocean's fish you are
As heretofore.
Perhaps you had sweet mercy's tenderness
To win so soon largesse of choice
That you, by grace, went gayly to the wave
And all our mourning should be to rejoice.

AFTER READING ST. JOHN
THE DIVINE

Moon's glow by seven fold multiplied, turned red,
Burned fierce by the coronal limbs at last
Out-leaping insulating space, a-blast
The searing heat sheeting round earth ahead
Of the scorched geoid's course; and I a-bed
Watching that increased flame and holding fast
To pulse and pillow. Worse! No shadow cast
By chair or cat. All people waking dead . . .

Earth lurches spacial waste; my room is hot;
That moon waxes her monstrous, brimstone disk;
Thick fear stretches before the febrile light;
Green fires pierce at my clenching eye's blind spot . . .
My buried soul, rising to face the risk,
With one pure deed restores the natural night.

RIDES

So we ride, and ride through milked heaven
        Above earth.
No more for us the housed and fatted standing still.
The train is carrier of us on the two-striped road-bed;
We sit in thunder over miles, calm as chairs,
        At will?
Look again; we zoom in planes over the hill's head;
Motion, motion, our motion, up, down, and on,
        World's girth.

And laughing under the town-world's crust,
        Thus riding
At the open and rushed dark subway doors;
Swung singing and talking with the unnoticed horses;
Or unfoamed by the spray, on liners,
        Changing lores
Of bored speed; or rivalling winds in their (our?) courses
In the air we flight, to air-pressure-up
        Confiding.

Sometimes on the tumbled skin of laced seas,
        Thus cresting
With staunch legs and opened hallooing, of surf
Making a race-shot thrill, on board with pair of reins,
Lengthened freedom of running covering the inland
        Fraught turf. . . .
Ah, from riding, and the riding, who abstains?
In the cars, to the stars, waves, wars, riding
        And questing.

James Dickey / 1923–

THE HEAVEN OF ANIMALS

Here they are. The soft eyes open.
If they have lived in a wood
It is a wood.
If they have lived on plains
It is grass rolling
Under their feet forever.

Having no souls, they have come,
Anyway, beyond their knowing.
Their instincts wholly bloom
And they rise.
The soft eyes open.

To match them, the landscape flowers,
Outdoing, desperately
Outdoing what is required:
The richest wood,
The deepest field.

For some of these,
It could not be the place
It is, without blood.
These hunt, as they have done,
But with claws and teeth grown perfect,

More deadly than they can believe.
They stalk more silently,
And crouch on the limbs of trees,
And their descent
Upon the bright backs of their prey

May take years
In a sovereign floating of joy.
And those that are hunted
Know this as their life,
Their reward: to walk

Under such trees in full knowledge
Of what is in glory above them,
And to feel no fear,
But acceptance, compliance.
Fulfilling themselves without pain

At the cycle's center,
They tremble, they walk
Under the tree,
They fall, they are torn,
They rise, they walk again.

THE PERFORMANCE

The last time I saw Donald Armstrong
He was staggering oddly off into the sun,
Going down, of the Philippine Islands.
I let my shovel fall, and put that hand
Above my eyes, and moved some way to one side
That his body might pass through the sun,

And I saw how well he was not
Standing there on his hands,
On his spindle-shanked forearms balanced,
Unbalanced, with his big feet looming and waving
In the great, untrustworthy air
He flew in each night, when it darkened.

Dust fanned in scraped puffs from the earth
Between his arms, and blood turned his face inside out,
To demonstrate its suppleness
Of veins, as he perfected his role.
Next day, he toppled his head off
On an island beach to the south,

And the enemy's two-handed sword
Did not fall from anyone's hands
At that miraculous sight,
As the head rolled over upon
Its wide-eyed face, and fell
Into the inadequate grave

He had dug for himself, under pressure.
Yet I put my flat hand to my eyebrows
Months later, to see him again
In the sun, when I learned how he died,
And imagined him, there,
Come, judged, before his small captors,

Doing all his lean tricks to amaze them—
The back somersault, the kip-up—
And at last, the stand on his hands,
Perfect, with his feet together,
His head down, evenly breathing,
As the sun poured up from the sea

And the headsman broke down
In a blaze of tears, in that light
Of the thin, long human frame
Upside down in its own strange joy,
And, if some other one had not told him,
Would have cut off the feet

Instead of the head,
And if Armstrong had not presently risen
In kingly, round-shouldered attendance,
And then knelt down in himself
Beside his hacked, glittering grave, having done
All things in this life that he could.

THE DUSK OF HORSES

Right under their noses, the green
Of the field is paling away
Because of something fallen from the sky.

They see this, and put down
Their long heads deeper in grass
That only just escapes reflecting them

As the dream of a millpond would.
The color green flees over the grass
Like an insect, following the red sun over

The next hill. The grass is white.
There is no cloud so dark and white at once;
There is no pool at dawn that deepens

Their faces and thirsts as this does.
Now they are feeding on solid
Cloud, and, one by one,

With nails as silent as stars among the wood
Hewed down years ago and now rotten,
The stalls are put up around them.

Now if they lean, they come
On wood on any side. Not touching it, they sleep.
No beast ever lived who understood

What happened among the sun's fields,
Or cared why the color of grass
Fled over the hill while he stumbled,

Led by the halter to sleep
On his four taxed, worthy legs.
Each thinks he awakens where

The sun is black on the rooftop,
That the green is dancing in the next pasture,
And that the way to sleep

In a cloud, or in a risen lake,
Is to walk as though he were still
In the drained field standing, head down,

To pretend to sleep when led,
And thus to go under the ancient white
Of the meadow, as green goes

And whiteness comes up through his face
Holding stars and rotten rafters,
Quiet, fragrant, and relieved.

Alan Dugan / 1923–

THE MIRROR PERILOUS

I guess there is a garden named
"Garden of Love." If so, I'm in it:
I am the guesser in the garden.
There is a notice by the central pond
that reads: "Property of Narcissus.
Trespass at your own risk,"
so I went there. That is where,
having won but disdained a lady,
he fell for his own face and died,
rightly, "not having followed through,"
as the sentence read, read by the lady:
Oh you could hear her crying all about
the wilderness and wickedness of law.
I looked in that famous mirror perilous
and it wasn't much: my own face,
beautiful, and at the bottom,
bone, a rusty knife, two beads,
and something else I cannot name.
I drank my own lips on the dare
but could not drink the lips away.
The water was heavy, cool, and clear,
but did not quench. A lady laughed
behind my back; I learned the worst:
I could take it or leave it, go or stay,
and went back to the office drunk,
possessed of an echo but not a fate.

PLAGUE OF DEAD SHARKS

Who knows whether the sea heals or corrodes?
The wading, wintered pack-beasts of the feet
slough off, in spring, the dead rind of the shoes'
leather detention, the big toes' yellow horn
shines with a natural polish, and the whole
person seems to profit. The opposite appears
when dead sharks wash up along the beach
for no known reason. What is more built
for winning than the swept-back teeth,
water-finished fins, and pure bad eyes
these old, efficient forms of appetite
are dressed in? Yet it looks as if the sea
digested what it wished of them with viral ease
and threw up what was left to stink and dry.
If this shows how the sea approaches life
in its propensity to feed as animal entire,
then sharks are comforts, feet are terrified,
but they vacation in the mystery and why not?
Who knows whether the sea heals or corrodes?:
what the sun burns up of it, the moon puts back.

Lawrence Durrell / 1912–

IN CRISIS

My love on Wednesday letting fall her body
From upright walking won by weariness,
As on a bed of flesh by ounces counted out,
Softer than snuff or snow came where my body was.

So in the aboriginal waterways of the mind,
No word being spoken by a familiar girl,

One may have a clear apprehension of ghostly matters,
Audible, as perhaps in the sea-shell's helix.

The Gulf Stream can rub soft music from a pebble
Like quiet rehearsal of the words 'Kneel down':
And cool on the inner corridors of the ear
Can blow on memory and conscience like a sin.

The inner man is surely a native of God
And his wife a brilliant novice of nature.
The woman walks in the dark like a lantern swung,
A white spark blown between points of pain.

We do not speak, embracing with the blood,
The tolling heart marking its measures in darkness
Like the scratch of a match or the fire-stone
Struck to a spark in the dark by a colder one.

So, lying close, the enchanted boy may hear
Soon from Tokio the crass drum sounding,
From the hero's hearth the merry crotchet of war.
Flame shall swallow the lady.

Tall men shall come to cool the royal bush,
Over the grey waters the bugler's octaves
Publish aloud a new resurrection of terror.
Many will give suck at the bomb's cold nipple.

Empty your hearts: or fill from a purer source.
That what is in men can weep, having eyes:
That what is in Truth can speak from the responsible dust
And O the rose grow in the middle of the great world.

ON SEEMING TO PRESUME

On seeming to presume
Where earth and water plan
No place for him, no home
Outside the confining womb,

Mistake him if you can.
The rubber forceps do their job
And here at last stands man.

Refined by no technique
Beyond the great 'I will',
They pour the poison in,
Confuse the middle ear
Of his tormented dust,
Before the brute can speak
'I will' becomes 'I must'.

Excluded from the true
Participating love
His conscience takes its due
From this excluding sense
His condemnation brought.
From past to future tense
He mutters on 'I ought'.

He mutters on 'I ought'

Yet daring to presume
He follows to the stews
His sense of loathsomeness,
Frustration, daily news.
A scholarship in hate
Endows him limb by limb.
'My mother pushed me from behind,
And so I learned to swim.'

The bunsen's head of hair,
All fancy free and passion,
Till iron circumstance
Confirms him in his lies,
To walk the Hamlet fashion.
He wrings his hands and cries
'I want to live', but dies.

He wants to live but dies.

Return, return and find
Beneath what bed or table
The lovers first in mind
Composed this poor unstable
Derivative of clay,
By passion or by play,
That bears the human label.

What king or saint could guide
This caliban of gloom
So swaddled in despair
To breathe the factory's air,
Or locked in furnished room
Weep out his threescore there
For seeming to presume,

For seeming to presume?

ON FIRST LOOKING INTO
LOEB'S HORACE

I found your Horace with the writing in it;
Out of time and context came upon
This lover of vines and slave to quietness,
Walking like a figure of smoke here, musing
Among his high and lovely Tuscan pines.

All the small-holder's ambitions, the yield
Of wine-bearing grape, pruning and drainage
Laid out by laws, almost like the austere
Shell of his verses—a pattern of Latin thrift;
Waiting so patiently in a library for
Autumn and the drying of the apples;
The betraying hour-glass and its deathward drift.

Surely the hard blue winterset
Must have conveyed a message to him—
The premonitions that the garden heard

Shrunk in its shirt of hair beneath the stars,
How rude and feeble a tenant was the self,
An Empire, the body with its members dying—
And unwhistling now the vanished Roman bird?

The fruit-trees dropping apples; he counted them,
The soft bounding fruit on leafy terraces,
And turned to the consoling winter rooms
Where, facing south, began the great prayer,
With his reed laid upon the margins
Of the dead, his stainless authors,
Upright, severe on an uncomfortable chair.

Here, where your clear hand marked up
'The hated cypress' I added 'Because it grew
On tombs, revealed his fear of autumn and the urns',
Depicting a solitary at an upper window
Revising metaphors for the winter sea: 'O
Dark head of storm-tossed curls'; or silently
Watching the North Star which like a fever burns

Away the envy and neglect of the common,
Shining on this terrace, lifting up in recreation
The sad heart of Horace who must have seen it only
As a metaphor for the self and its perfection—
A burning heart quite constant in its station.

Easy to be patient in the summer,
The light running like fishes among the leaves,
Easy in August with its cones of blue
Sky uninvaded from the north; but winter
With its bareness pared his words to points
Like stars, leaving them pure but very few.

He will not know how we discerned him, disregarding
The pose of sufficiency, the landed man,
Found a suffering limb on the great Latin tree
Whose roots live in the barbarian grammar we
Use, yet based in him, his mason's tongue;
Describing clearly a bachelor, sedentary,
With a fond weakness for bronze-age conversation,
Disguising a sense of failure in a hatred for the young,

Who built in the Sabine hills this forgery
Of completeness, an orchard with a view of Rome;
Who studiously developed his sense of death
Till it was all around him, walking at the circus,
At the baths, playing dominoes in a shop—
The escape from self-knowledge with its tragic
Imperatives: *Seek, suffer, endure.* The Roman
In him feared the Law and told him where to stop.

So perfect a disguise for one who had
Exhausted death in art—yet who could guess
You would discern the liar by a line,
The suffering hidden under gentleness
And add upon the flyleaf in your tall
Clear hand: 'Fat, human and unloved,
And held from loving by a sort of wall,
Laid down his books and lovers one by one,
Indifference and success had crowned them all.'

A BALLAD OF THE GOOD
LORD NELSON

The Good Lord Nelson had a swollen gland,
Little of the scripture did he understand
Till a woman led him to the promised land
       Aboard the Victory, Victory O.

Adam and Evil and a bushel of figs
Meant nothing to Nelson who was keeping pigs,
Till a woman showed him the various rigs
       Aboard the Victory, Victory O.

His heart was softer than a new laid egg,
Too poor for loving and ashamed to beg,
Till Nelson was taken by the Dancing Leg
       Aboard the Victory, Victory O.

Now he up and did up his little tin trunk
And he took to the ocean on his English junk,
Turning like the hour-glass in his lonely bunk
       Aboard the Victory, Victory O.

The Frenchman saw him a-coming there
With the one-piece eye and the valentine hair,
With the safety-pin sleeve and occupied air
        Aboard the Victory, Victory O.

Now you all remember the message he sent
As an answer to Hamilton's discontent—
There were questions asked about it in the Parliament
        Aboard the Victory, Victory O.

Now the blacker the berry, the thicker comes the juice,
Think of Good Lord Nelson and avoid self-abuse,
For the empty sleeve was no mere excuse
        Aboard the Victory, Victory O.

'England Expects' was the motto he gave
When he thought of little Emma out on Biscay's wave,
And remembered working on her like a galley-slave
        Aboard the Victory, Victory O.

The first Great Lord in our English land
To honour the Freudian command,
For a cast in the bush is worth two in the hand
        Aboard the Victory, Victory O.

Now the Frenchman shot him there as he stood
In the rage of battle in a silk-lined hood
And he heard the whistle of his own hot blood
        Aboard the Victory, Victory O.

Now stiff on a pillar with a phallic air
Nelson stylites in Trafalgar Square
Reminds the British what once they were
        Aboard the Victory, Victory O.

If they'd treat their women in the Nelson way
There'd be fewer frigid husbands every day
And many more heroes on the Bay of Biscay
        Aboard the Victory, Victory O.

Kenneth Fearing / 1902–1961

CONFESSION OVERHEARD
IN A SUBWAY

You will ask how I came to be eavesdropping, in the first
    place.
The answer is, I was not.
The man who confessed to these several crimes (call him
    John Doe) spoke into my right ear on a crowded
    subway train, while the man whom he addressed (call
    him Richard Roe) stood at my left.
Thus, I stood between them, and they talked, or sometimes
    shouted, quite literally straight through me.
How could I help but overhear?
Perhaps I might have moved away to some other strap.
    But the aisles were full.
Besides, I felt, for some reason, curious.

"I do not deny my guilt," said John Doe. "My own, first,
    and after that my guilty knowledge of still further guilt.
I have counterfeited often, and successfully.
I have been guilty of ignorance, and talking with conviction.
    Of intolerable wisdom, and keeping silent.
Through carelessness, or cowardice, I have shortened the
    lives of better men. And the name for that is murder.
All my life I have been a receiver of stolen goods."

"Personally, I always mind my own business," said
    Richard Roe. "Sensible people don't get into those
    scrapes."

I was not the only one who overheard this confession.
Several businessmen, bound for home, and housewives and
    mechanics, were within easy earshot.

A policeman sitting in front of us did not lift his eyes, at
    the mention of murder, from his paper.
Why should I be the one to report these crimes?
You will understand why this letter to your paper is
    anonymous. I will sign it: Public Spirited Citizen, and
    hope that it cannot be traced.
But all the evidence, if there is any clamor for it, can be
    substantiated.
I have heard the same confession many times since, in
    different places.
And now that I think of it, I had heard it many times
    before.

"Guilt," said John, "is always and everywhere nothing less
    than guilt.
I have always, at all times, been a willing accomplice of the
    crass and the crude.
I have overheard, daily, the smallest details of conspiracies
    against the human race, vast in their ultimate scope,
    and conspired, daily, to launch my own.
You have heard of innocent men who died in the chair. It
    was my greed that threw the switch.
I helped, and I do not deny it, to nail that guy to the cross,
    and shall continue to help.
Look into my eyes, you can see the guilt.
Look at my face, my hair, my very clothing, you will see
    guilt written plainly everywhere.
Guilt of the flesh. Of the soul. Of laughing, when others do
    not. Of breathing and eating and sleeping.
I am guilty of what? Of guilt. Guilty of guilt, that is all, and
    enough."

Richard Roe looked at his wristwatch and said: "We'll be
    twenty minutes late.
After dinner we might take in a show."

Now, who will bring John Doe to justice for his measureless
    crimes?
I do not, personally, wish to be involved.
Such nakedness of the soul belongs in some other province,
    probably the executioner's.

And who will bring the blunt and upright Richard Roe to
    the accuser's stand, where he belongs?
Or will he deny and deny his partnership?

I have done my duty, as a public spirited citizen, in any case.

Lawrence Ferlinghetti / 1919–

from A CONEY ISLAND OF THE MIND

1

In Goya's greatest scenes we seem to see
                    the people of the world
    exactly at the moment when
        they first attained the title of
                 'suffering humanity'
      They writhe upon the page
              in a veritable rage
                    of adversity
      Heaped up
            groaning with babies and bayonets
                  under cement skies
    in an abstract landscape of blasted trees
        bent statues bats wings and beaks
            slippery gibbets
    cadavers and carnivorous cocks
and all the final hollering monsters
      of the
           'imagination of disaster'
they are so bloody real
           it is as if they really still existed

    And they do

      Only the landscape is changed

They still are ranged along the roads
            plagued by legionaires
                        false windmills and demented roosters

They are the same people
                        only further from home
        on freeways fifty lanes wide
                        on a concrete continent
                            spaced with bland billboards
                        illustrating imbecile illusions of happiness
        The scene shows fewer tumbrils
                        but more maimed citizens
                                    in painted cars
            and they have strange license plates
        and engines
                    that devour America

3

The poet's eye obscenely seeing
sees the surface of the round world
                with its drunk rooftops
                and wooden oiseaux on clotheslines
                and its clay males and females
                with hot legs and rosebud breasts
                in rollaway beds
and its trees full of mysteries
and its Sunday parks and speechless statues
and its America
                with its ghost towns and empty Ellis Islands
and its surrealist landscape of
                            mindless prairies
                            supermarket suburbs
                            steamheated cemeteries
                            cinerama holy days
                            and protesting cathedrals
a kissproof world of plastic toiletseats tampax and taxis
                drugged store cowboys and las vegas virgins
                disowned indians and cinemad matrons
                unroman senators and conscientious non-objectors
and all the other fatal shorn-up fragments

of the immigrant's dream come too true
      and mislaid
           among the sunbathers

15
      Constantly risking absurdity
                   and death
        whenever he performs
                above the heads
                      of his audience
  the poet like an acrobat
             climbs on rime
                to a high wire of his own making
and balancing on eyebeams
                above a sea of faces
      paces his way
            to the other side of day
  performing entrechats
            and slight-of-foot tricks
and other high theatrics
            and all without mistaking
      any thing
           for what it may not be
  For he's the super realist
            who must perforce perceive
    taut truth
         before the taking of each stance or step
in his supposed advance
          toward that still higher perch
where Beauty stands and waits
            with gravity
              to start her death-defying leap

     And he
       a little charleychaplin man
             who may or may not catch
       her fair eternal form
            spreadeagled in the empty air
    of existence

Roy Fuller / 1912–

JANUARY 1940

Swift had pains in his head.
Johnson dying in bed
Tapped the dropsy himself.
Blake saw a flea and an elf.
Tennyson could hear the shriek
Of a bat. Pope was a freak.
Emily Dickinson stayed
Indoors for a decade.
Water inflated the belly
Of Hart Crane, and of Shelley.
Coleridge was a dope.
Southwell died on a rope.
Byron had a round white foot.
Smart and Cowper were put
Away. Lawrence was a fidget.
Keats was almost a midget.
Donne, alive in his shroud,
Shakespeare, in the coil of a cloud,
Saw death very well as he
Came crab-wise, dark and massy.
I envy not only their talents
And fertile lack of balance
But the appearance of choice
In their sad and fatal voice.

SPRING 1942

Once as we were sitting by
The falling sun, the thickening air,
The chaplain came against the sky
And quietly took a vacant chair.

And under the tobacco smoke:
'Freedom,' he said, and 'Good' and 'Duty.'
We stared as though a savage spoke.
The scene took on a singular beauty.

And we made no reply to that
Obscure, remote communication,
But only looked out where the flat
Meadow dissolved in vegetation.

And thought: O sick, insatiable
And constant lust; O death, our future;
O revolution in the whole
Of human use of man and nature!

SPRING 1943

I

The skies contain still groves of silver clouds,
The land is low and level, and the buzzards
Rise from a dead and stiff hyena. Hazards
Of war and seas divide me from the crowds
Whose actions alone give numbers to the years;
But all my emotions in this savage place
This moment have a pale and hungry face:
The vision metropolitan appears.
And as I leave the crawling carcase, turning
Into the scrub, I think of rain upon
Factories and banks, the shoulders of a meeting:
And thoughts that always crouch in wait come burning—
Slim naked legs of fabulous and fleeting
Dancers, and rooms where everyone has gone.

II

Always it is to you my thoughts return
From harrowing speculation on the age,
As though our love and you were fictional
And could not ever burn as cities burn,
Nor die as millions, but upon a page
Rested delightful, moving and immortal.
This momentary vision fades. Again
You join the sheeted world whose possible death
Is also ours, and our nostalgic breath
Expires across two continents of pain.
And clearly I see the organizations of
The oppressed, their dangerous and tiny actions,
The problematic serum of the factions,
In these decayed and crucial times, as love.

III

Intelligent, fair and strictly moral as
A heroine of Jane's; here where the hill
Is in another country and shadows pass
Like towns, I think of you so civilized still.
And in that chaos of Europe which surrounds
Your little calm I see those leaping, rising,
Almost engendered by the times, the hounds
of courage, hawks of vision, and the surprising
Gazelles of love. And so I run through all
The virtues, and this hopeless, barbarous space,
Which sometimes I think the future's self, can fall
Into its ancient and forgotten place.
No, I will not believe that human art
Can fail to make reality its heart.

THE   TRIBES

I think of the tribes: the women prized for fatness
Immovable, and by a sympathetic
    Magic sustaining the herds,
    On whose strange humps sit birds;

And those with long dung-stiffened capes of hair,
And those that ceremonially eat their dead;
   The ornamental gashes
   Festered and raised with ashes;

The captured and dishonoured king compelled
To straddle a vertical and sharpened stake,
   Until, his legs hauled at,
   The point burst from his throat;

And all the prohibitions and the cheapness
Of life so hardly got, where it is death
   Even to touch the palace
   And poison expresses malice.

Now in the white men's towns the tribes are gathered
Among the corrugated iron and
   The refuse bins where rats
   Dispute with them for scraps.

Truly, civilisation is for them
The most elemental struggle for bread and love;
   For all the tabus have gone,
   It is man against man alone.

On waste plots and in the decrepit shanties
They begin to discover the individual,
   And, with the sense in time
   Of Adam, perpetuate crime.

The most horrible things you can imagine are
Happening in the towns and the most senseless:
   There are no kings or poison,
   Are laws but no more reason.

VERSIONS OF LOVE

'My love for you has faded' – thus the Bad
Quarto, the earliest text, whose midget page
Derived from the imperfect memories
Of red-nosed, small-part actors
Or the atrocious shorthand of the age.

However, the far superior Folio had
'My love for you was fated' – thus implying
Illicit passion, a tragic final act.

And this was printed from the poet's own
Foul papers, it was reckoned;
Supported by the reading of the Second
Quarto, which had those sombre words exact.

Such evidence was shaken when collation
Showed that the Folio copied slavishly
The literals of that supposedly
Independent Quarto. Thus one had to go
Back to the first text of all.

'My love for you has faded' – quite impossible.
Scholars produced at last the emendation:
'My love for you fast endured.'
Our author's ancient hand that must have been
Ambiguous and intellectual
Foxed the compositors of a certainty.
And so the critical editions gave
Love the sound status that she ought to have
In poetry so revered.

But this conjecture cannot quite destroy
The question of what the poet really wrote
In the glum middle reaches of his life:
Too sage, too bald, too fearful of fiasco
To hope beyond his wife,
Yet aching almost as promptly as a boy.

Jean Garrigue / 1914–

THE STRANGER

Now upon this piteous year
I sit in Denmark beside the quai
And nothing that the fishers say
Or the children carrying boats
Can recall me from that place
Where sense and wish departed me
Whose very shores take on
The whiteness of anon.
For I beheld a stranger there
Who moved ahead of me
So tensile and so dancer made
That like a thief I followed her
Though my heart was so alive
I thought it equal to that beauty.
But when at last a turning came
Like the branching of a river
And I saw if she walked on
She would be gone forever,
Fear, then, so wounded me
As fell upon my ear
The voice a blind man dreams
And broke on me the smile
I dreamed as deaf men hear,
I stood there like a spy,
My tongue and eyelids taken
In such necessity.
Now upon this piteous year
The rains of Autumn fall.
Where may she be?
I suffered her to disappear
Who hunger in the prison of my fear.

That lean and brown, that stride,
That cold and melting pride,
For whom the river like a clear
Melodic line and the distant carrousel
Where lovers on their beasts of play
Rose and fell,
That wayfare where the swan adorned
With every wave and eddy
The honor of his sexual beauty,
Create her out of sorrow
That, never perishing,
Is a stately thing.

FOREST

There is the star bloom of the moss
And the hairy chunks of light between the conifers;
There are alleys of light where the green leads to a funeral
Down the false floor of needles.
There are rocks and boulders that jut, saw-toothed and
     urine-yellow.
Other stones in a field look in the distance like sheep
     grazing,
Grey trunk and trunklike legs and lowered head.
There are short-stemmed forests so close to the ground
You would pity a dog lost there in the spore-budding
Blackness where the sun has never struck down.
There are dying ferns that glow like a gold mine
And weeds and sumac extend the Sodom of color.
Among the divisions of stone and the fissures of branch
Lurk the abashed resentments of the ego.
Do not say this is pleasurable!
Bats, skittering on wires over the lake,
And the bug on the water, bristling in light as he measures
     forward his leaps,
The hills holding back the sun by their notched edges
(What volcanoes lie on the other side
Of heat, light, burning up even the angels)

And the mirror of forests and hills drawing nearer
Till the lake is all forests and hills made double,
Do not say this is kindly, convenient,
Warms the hands, crosses the senses with promise,
Harries our fear.
Uneasy, we bellow back at the tree frogs
And, night approaching like the entrance of a tunnel,
We would turn back and cannot, we
Surprise our natures; the woods lock us up
In the secret crimes of our intent.

FALSE COUNTRY OF THE ZOO

We are large with pity, slow and awkward
In the false country of the zoo.
For the beasts our hearts turn over and sigh,
With the gazelle we long to look eye to eye,
Laughter at the stumbling, southern giraffes
Urges our anger, righteous despair.
As the hartebeest plunges, giddy, eccentric,
From out of the courtyard into his stall,
We long to seize his forehead's steep horns
Which are like the staves of a lyre.
Fleeter than greyhounds the hartebeest
Long-muzzled, small-footed, and shy.
Another runner, the emu, is even better
At kicking. Oh, the coarse chicken feet
Of this bird reputed a fossil!
His body, deep as a table,
Droops gracelessly downwise,
His small head shakes like an old woman's eye.
The emu, the ostrich, the cassowary
Continue to go on living their lives
In conditions unnatural to them
And in relations most strange
Remain the same.
As for the secretary bird,
Snake-killer, he suggests

A mischievous bird-maker.
Like a long-legged boy in short pants
He runs teetering, legs far apart,
On his toes, part gasping girl.
What thought him up, this creature
Eminently equipped by his nervous habits
To kill venomous snakes with his strong
Horny feet, first jumping on them
And then leaping away?
At the reptile and monkey houses
Crowds gather to enjoy the ugly
But mock the kangaroo who walks like a cripple.

In the false country of the zoo,
Where Africa is well represented
By Australia,
The emu, the ostrich and cassowary
Survive like kings, poor antiquated strays,
Deceased in all but vestiges,
Who did not have to change, preserved
In their peculiarities by rifts,
From emigration barred.
Now melancholy, like old continents
Unmodified and discontinued, they
Remain by some discreet permission
Like older souls too painfully handicapped.
Running birds who cannot fly,
Whose virtue is their liability,
Whose stubborn very resistance is their sorrow.
See, as they run, how we laugh
At the primitive, relic procedure.

In the false country of the zoo
Grief is well represented there
By those continents of the odd
And outmoded, Africa and Australia.
Sensation is foremost at a zoo—
The sensation of gaping at the particular:
The striped and camouflaged,
The bear, wallowing in his anger,
The humid tiger wading in a pool.

As for those imports
From Java and India,
The pale, virginal peafowl,
The stork, cracking his bill against a wall,
The peacock, plumes up, though he walks as if weighted
—All that unconscionable tapestry—
Till a wind blows the source of his pride
And it becomes his embarrassment,
The eye, plunged in sensation, closes.
Thought seizes the image. This shrieking
Jungle of spot, stripe, orange
Blurs. The oil from the deer's eye
That streaks like a tear his cheek
Seems like a tear, is, is,
As our love and our pity are, are.

David Gascoyne / 1916–

A WARTIME DAWN

Dulled by the slow glare of the yellow bulb;
As far from sleep still as at any hour
Since distant midnight; with a hollow skull
In which white vapours seem to reel
Among limp muddles of old thought; till eyes
Collapse into themselves like clams in mud . . .
Hand paws the wall to reach the chilly switch;
Then nerve-shot darkness gradually shakes
Throughout the room. *Lie still* . . . Limbs twitch;
Relapse to immobility's faint ache. And time
A while relaxes; space turns wholly black.

But deep in the velvet crater of the ear
A chip of sound abruptly irritates.

A second, a third chirp; and then another far
Emphatic trill and chirrup shrills in answer; notes
From all directions round pluck at the strings
Of hearing with frail finely-sharpened claws.
And in an instant, every wakened bird
Across surrounding miles of air
Outside, is sowing like a scintillating sand
Its throat's incessantly replenished store
Of tuneless singsong, timeless, aimless, blind.

Draw now with prickling hand the curtains back;
Unpin the blackout-cloth; let in
Grim crack-of-dawn's first glimmer through the glass.
All's yet half sunk in Yesterday's stale death,
Obscurely still beneath a moist-tinged blank
Sky like the inside of a deaf mute's mouth . . .
Nearest within the window's sight, ash-pale
Against a cinder coloured wall, the white
Pear-blossom hovers like a stare; rain-wet
The further housetops weakly shine; and there,
Beyond, hangs flaccidly a lone barrage-balloon.

An incommunicable desolation weighs
Like depths of stagnant water on this break of day.—
Long meditation without thought.—Until a breeze
From some pure Nowhere straying, stirs
A pang of poignant odour from the earth, an unheard sigh
Pregnant with sap's sweet tang and raw soil's fine
Aroma, smell of stone, and acrid breath
Of gravel puddles. While the brooding green
Of nearby gardens' grass and trees, and quiet flat
Blue leaves, the distant lilac mirages, are made
Clear by increasing daylight, and intensified.

Now head sinks into pillows in retreat
Before this morning's hovering advance;
(Behind loose lids, in sleep's warm porch, half hears
White hollow clink of bottles,—dragging crunch
Of milk-cart wheels,—and presently a snatch
Of windy whistling as the newsboy's bike winds near,
Distributing to neighbour's peaceful steps
Reports of last-night's battles); at last sleeps.

While early guns on Norway's bitter coast
Where faceless troops are landing, renew fire:
And one more day of War starts everywhere.

ECCE HOMO

Whose is this horrifying face,
This putrid flesh, discoloured, flayed,
Fed on by flies, scorched by the sun?
Whose are these hollow red-filmed eyes
And thorn-spiked head and spear-stuck side?
Behold the Man: He is Man's Son.

Forget the legend, tear the decent veil
That cowardice or interest devised
To make their mortal enemy a friend,
To hide the bitter truth all His wounds tell,
Lest the great scandal be no more disguised:
He is in agony till the world's end,

And we must never sleep during that time!
He is suspended on the cross-tree now
And we are onlookers at the crime,
Callous contemporaries of the slow
Torture of God. Here is the hill
Made ghastly by His spattered blood

Whereon He hangs and suffers still:
See, the centurions wear riding-boots,
Black shirts and badges and peaked caps,
Greet one another with raised-arm salutes;
They have cold eyes, unsmiling lips;
Yet these His brothers know not what they do.

And on his either side hang dead
A labourer and a factory hand,
Or one is maybe a lynched Jew
And one a Negro or a Red,
Coolie or Ethiopian, Irishman,
Spaniard or German democrat.

Behind His lolling head the sky
Glares like a fiery cataract
Red with the murders of two thousand years
Committed in His name and by
Crusaders, Christian warriors
Defending faith and property.

Amid the plain beneath His transfixed hands,
Exuding darkness as indelible
As guilty stains, fanned by funereal
And lurid airs, besieged by drifting sands
And clefted landslides our about-to-be
Bombed and abandoned cities stand.

He who wept for Jerusalem
Now sees His prophecy extend
Across the greatest cities of the world,
A guilty panic reason cannot stem
Rising to raze them all as He foretold;
And He must watch this drama to the end.

Though often named, He is unknown
To the dark kingdoms at His feet
Where everything disparages His words,
And each man bears the common guilt alone
And goes blindfolded to his fate,
And fear and greed are sovereign lords.

The turning point of history
Must come. Yet the complacent and the proud
And who exploit and kill, may be denied—
Christ of Revolution and of Poetry—
The resurrection and the life
Wrought by your spirit's blood.

Involved in their own sophistry
The black priest and the upright man
Faced by subversive truth shall be struck dumb,
Christ of Revolution and of Poetry,
While the rejected and condemned become
Agents of the divine.

Not from a monstrance silver-wrought
But from the tree of human pain
Redeem our sterile misery,
Christ of Revolution and of Poetry,
That man's long journey through the night
May not have been in vain.

A TOUGH GENERATION

To grow unguided at a time when none
Are sure where they should plant their sprig of trust;
When sunshine has no special mission to endow
With gold the rustic rose, which will run wild
And ramble from the garden to the wood
To train itself to climb the trunks of trees
If the old seedsman die and suburbs care
For sentimental cottage-flowers no more;
To grow up in a wood of rotted trees
In which it is not known which tree will be
First to disturb the silent sultry grove
With crack of doom, dead crackling and dread roar—
Will be infallibly to learn that first
One always owes a duty to oneself;
This much at least is certain: one must live.
And one may reach, without having to search
For much more lore than this, a shrewd maturity,
Equipped with adult aptitude to ape
All customary cant and current camouflage;
Nor be a whit too squeamish where the soul's concerned,
But hold out for the best black market price for it
Should need remind one that one has to live.
Yet just as sweetly, where no markets are,
An unkempt rose may for a season still
Trust its own beauty and disclose its heart
Even to the woodland shade, and as in sacrifice
Renounce its ragged petals one by one.

Allen Ginsberg / 1926–

A SUPERMARKET IN CALIFORNIA

What thoughts I have of you tonight, Walt Whitman, for
I walked down the sidestreets under the trees with a head-
ache self-conscious looking at the full moon.

In my hungry fatigue, and shopping for images, I went
into the neon fruit supermarket, dreaming of your enumer-
ations!

What peaches and what penumbras! Whole families shopping at night! Aisles full of husbands! Wives in the avocados,
babies in the tomatoes!—and you, Garcia Lorca, what were
you doing down by the watermelons?

I saw you, Walt Whitman, childless, lonely old grubber,
poking among the meats in the refrigerator and eyeing the
grocery boys.

I heard you asking questions of each: Who killed the pork
chops? What price bananas? Are you my Angel?

I wandered in and out of the brilliant stacks of cans following you, and followed in my imagination by the store
detective.

We strode down the open corridors together in our solitary
fancy tasting artichokes, possessing every frozen delicacy,
and never passing the cashier.

Where are we going, Walt Whitman? The doors close in
an hour. Which way does your beard point tonight?

(I touch your book and dream of our odyssey in the
supermarket and feel absurd.)

Will we walk all night through solitary streets? The trees
add shade to shade, lights out in the houses, we'll both be
lonely.

Will we stroll dreaming of the lost America of love past
blue automobiles in driveways, home to our silent cottage?

Ah, dear father, graybeard, lonely old courage-teacher,

what America did you have when Charon quit poling his
ferry and you got out on a smoking bank and stood watching
the boat disappear on the black waters of Lethe?

TO AUNT ROSE

Aunt Rose—now—might I see you
with your thin face and buck tooth smile and pain
              of rheumatism—and a long black heavy shoe
                   for your bony left leg
   limping down the long hall in Newark on the running
                                            carpet
              past the black grand piano
                   in the day room
                        where the parties were
              and I sang Spanish loyalist songs
                   in a high squeaky voice
                        (hysterical) the committee listening
                   while you limped around the room
                        collected the money—
   Aunt Honey, Uncle Sam, a stranger with a cloth arm
                   in his pocket
                        and huge young bald head
                             of Abraham Lincoln Brigade

—your long sad face
              your tears of sexual frustration
                        (what smothered sobs and bony hips
                             under the pillows of Osborne Terrace)
         —the time I stood on the toilet seat naked
                   and you powdered my thighs with Calomine
                        against the poison ivy—my tender
                             and shamed first black curled hairs
   what were you thinking in secret heart then
                   knowing me a man already—
   and I an ignorant girl of family silence on the thin pedstal
              of my legs in the bathroom—Museum of
                                            Newark.

Aunt Rose

Hitler is dead, Hitler is in Eternity; Hitler is with
Tamburlane and Emily Brontë

Though I see you walking still, a ghost on Osborne Terrace
down the long dark hall to the front door
limping a little with a pinched smile
in what must have been a silken
flower dress
welcoming my father, the Poet, on his visit to Newark
—see you arriving in the living room
dancing on your crippled leg
and clapping hands his book
had been accepted by Liveright

Hitler is dead and Liveright's gone out of business
The Attic of the Past and *Everlasting Minute* are out of print
Uncle Harry sold his last silk stocking
Claire quit interpretive dancing school
Buba sits a wrinkled monument in Old
Ladies Home blinking at new babies

last time I saw you was the hospital
pale skull protruding under ashen skin
blue veined unconscious girl
in an oxygen tent
the war in Spain has ended long ago
Aunt Rose

W. S. Graham / 1917–

LISTEN. PUT ON MORNING

Listen. Put on morning.
Waken into falling light.
A man's imagining

Suddenly may inherit
The handclapping centuries
Of his one minute on earth.
And hear the virgin juries
Talk with his own breath
To the corner boys of his street.
And hear the Black Maria
Searching the town at night.
And hear the playropes caa
The sister Mary in.
And hear Willie and Davie
Among bracken of Narnain
Sing in a mist heavy
With myrtle and listeners.
And hear the higher town
Weep a petition of fears
At the poorhouse close upon
The public heartbeat.
And hear the children tig
And run with my own feet
Into the netting drag
Of a suiciding principle.
Listen. Put on lightbreak.
Waken into miracle.
The audience lies awake
Under the tenements
Under the sugar docks
Under the printed moments.
The centuries turn their locks
And open under the hill
Their inherited books and doors
All gathered to distil
Like happy berry pickers
One voice to talk to us.
Yes listen. It carries away
The second and the years
Till the heart's in a jacket of snow
And the head's in a helmet white
And the song sleeps to be wakened
By the morning ear bright.
Listen. Put on morning.
Waken into falling light.

Thom Gunn / 1929–

A MIRROR FOR POETS

It was a violent time. Wheels, racks and fires
In every writer's mouth, and not mere rant.
Certain shrewd herdsmen, between twisted wires
Of penalty folding the realm, were thanked
For organizing spies and secret police
By richness in the flock, which they could fleece.

Hacks in the Fleet and nobles in the Tower
Shakespeare must keep the peace, and Jonson's thumb
Be branded (for manslaughter), in the power
Of irons lay the admired Southampton.
Above all swayed the diseased and doubtful queen:
Her state canopied by the glamour of pain.

In the society the boundaries met
Of living, danger, death, leaving no space
Between, except where might be set
That mathematical point whose time and place
Could not exist. Yet at this point they found
Arcadia, a fruitful permanent land.

The faint and stumbling crowds were dim to sight
Who had no time for pity or for terror:
Here moved the Forms, flooding like moonlight
In which might act or thought perceive its error.
The dirty details, calmed and relevant.
Here mankind could behold its whole extent.

Here in a cave the Paphlagonian King
Crouched, waiting for his greater counterpart
Who one remove from likelihood may seem

But several nearer to the human heart.
In exile from dimension, change by storm
Here his huge magnanimity was born.

Yet the historians tell us, life meant less.
It was a violent time, and evil-smelling.
Jonson howled 'Hell's a grammar-school to this',
But found renunciation well worth telling.
Winnowing with his flail of comedy
He showed coherence in society.

In street, in tavern, happening would cry
'I am myself, but part of something greater,
Find poets what that is, do not pass by
For feel my fingers in your pia mater.
I am a cruelly insistent friend
You cannot smile at me and make an end.'

ON THE MOVE

'Man, you gotta Go.'

The blue jay scuffling in the bushes follows
Some hidden purpose, and the gust of birds
That spurts across the field, the wheeling swallows,
Have nested in the trees and undergrowth.
Seeking their instinct, or their poise, or both,
One moves with an uncertain violence
Under the dust thrown by a baffled sense
Or the dull thunder of approximate words.

On motorcycles, up the road, they come:
Small, black, as flies hanging in heat, the Boys,
Until the distance throws them forth, their hum
Bulges to thunder held by calf and thigh.
In goggles, donned impersonality,
In gleaming jackets trophied with the dust,
They strap in doubt—by hiding it, robust—
And almost hear a meaning in their noise.

Exact conclusion of their hardiness
Has no shape yet, but from known whereabouts
They ride, direction where the tires press.
They scare a flight of birds across the field:
Much that is natural, to the will must yield.
Men manufacture both machine and soul,
And use what they imperfectly control
To dare a future from the taken routes.

It is a part solution, after all.
One is not necessarily discord
On earth; or damned because, half animal,
One lacks direct instinct, because one wakes
Afloat on movement that divides and breaks.
One joins the movement in a valueless world,
Choosing it, till, both hurler and the hurled,
One moves as well, always toward, toward.

A minute holds them, who have come to go:
The self-defined, astride the created will
They burst away; the towns they travel through
Are home for neither bird nor holiness,
For birds and saints complete their purposes.
At worst, one is in motion; and at best,
Reaching no absolute, in which to rest,
One is always nearer by not keeping still.

INNOCENCE

for Tony White

He ran the course and as he ran he grew,
And smelt his fragrance in the field. Already,
Running he knew the most he ever knew,
The egotism of a healthy body.

Ran into manhood, ignorant of the past:
Culture of guilt and guilt's vague heritage,

Self-pity and the soul; what he possessed
Was rich, potential, like the bud's tipped rage.

The Corps developed, it was plain to see,
Courage, endurance, loyalty and skill
To a morale firm as morality,
Hardening him to an instrument, until

The finitude of virtues that were there
Bodied within the swarthy uniform
A compact innocence, child-like and clear,
No doubt could penetrate, no act could harm.

When he stood near the Russian partisan
Being burned alive, he therefore could behold
The ribs wear gently through the darkening skin
And sicken only at the Northern cold,

Could watch the fat burn with a violet flame
And feel disgusted only at the smell,
And judge that all pain finishes the same
As melting quietly by his boots it fell.

CONSIDERING   THE   SNAIL

The snail pushes through a green
night, for the grass is heavy
with water and meets over
the bright path he makes, where rain
has darkened the earth's dark. He
moves in a wood of desire,

pale antlers barely stirring
as he hunts. I cannot tell
what power is at work, drenched there
with purpose, knowing nothing.
What is a snail's fury? All
I think is that if later

I parted the blades above
the tunnel and saw the thin
trail of broken white across
litter, I would never have
imagined the slow passion
to that deliberate progress.

MY SAD CAPTAINS

One by one they appear in
the darkness: a few friends, and
a few with historical
names. How late they start to shine!
but before they fade they stand
perfectly embodied, all

the past lapping them like a
cloak of chaos. They were men
who, I thought, lived only to
renew the wasteful force they
spent with each hot convulsion.
They remind me, distant now.

True, they are not at rest yet,
but now that they are indeed
apart, winnowed from failures,
they withdraw to an orbit
and turn with disinterested
hard energy, like the stars.

Donald Hall / 1928–

AN AIRSTRIP IN ESSEX, 1960

It is a lost road into the air.
It is a desert
among sugar beets.
The tiny wings
of the Spitfires of nineteen-forty-one
flake in the mud of the Channel.

Near the road a brick pillbox
totters under a load of grass,
where Home Guards waited
in the white fogs of the invasion winter.

Goodnight, old ruined war.

In Poland the wind rides on a jagged wall.
Smoke rises from the stones; no, it is mist.

THE FARM

Standing on top of the hay
in a good sweat,
I felt the wind from the lake,
dry on my back,
where the chaff
grew like the down on my face.

At night on the bare boards
of the kitchen,
we stood while the old man

in his nightshirt gummed
the stale crusts
of his bread and milk.

Up on the gray hill
behind the barn, the stones
had fallen away
where the Pennacook marked
a way to go
south from the narrow river.

By the side of the lake
my dead uncle's rowboat rots
in heavy bushes.
Slim pickerel glint
in the water. Black horned pout
doze on the bottom.

Anthony Hecht / 1923–

JAPAN

It was a miniature country once
To my imagination; Home of the Short,
And also the academy of stunts
        Where acrobats are taught
    The famous secrets of the trade:
    To cycle in the big parade
While spinning plates upon their parasols,
Or somersaults that do not touch the ground,
        Or tossing seven balls
In Most Celestial Order round and round.

A child's quick sense of the ingenious stamped
All their invention: toys I used to get

At Christmastime, or the peculiar, cramped
  Look of their alphabet.
 Fragile and easily destroyed,
 Those little boats of celluloid
Driven by camphor round the bathroom sink,
And delicate the folded paper prize
  Which, dropped into a drink
Of water, grew up right before your eyes.

Now when we reached them it was with a sense
Sharpened for treachery compounding in their brains
Like mating weasels; our Intelligence
  Said: The Black Dragon reigns
 Secretly under yellow skin,
 Deeper than dyes of atabrine
And deadlier. The War Department said:
Remember you are Americans; forsake
  The wounded and the dead
At your own cost; remember Pearl and Wake.

And yet they bowed us in with ceremony,
Told us what brands of Sake were the best,
Explained their agriculture in a phony
  Dialect of the West,
 Meant vaguely to be understood
 As a shy sign of brotherhood
In the old human bondage to the facts
Of day-to-day existence. And like ants,
  Signaling tiny pacts
With their antennae, they would wave their hands.

At last we came to see them not as glib
Walkers of tightropes, worshipers of carp,
Nor yet a species out of Adam's rib
  Meant to preserve its warp
 In Cain's own image. They had learned
 That their tough eye-born goddess burned
Adoring fingers. They were very poor.
The holy mountain was not moved to speak.
  Wind at the paper door
Offered them snow out of its hollow peak.

Human endeavor clumsily betrays
Humanity. Their excrement served in this;
For, planting rice in water, they would raise
    Schistosomiasis
   Japonica, that enters through
   The pores into the avenue
And orbit of the blood, where it may foil
The heart and kill, or settle in the brain.
    This fruit of their nightsoil
Thrives in the skull, where it is called insane.

Now the quaint early image of Japan
That was so charming to me as a child
Seems like a bright design upon a fan,
    Of water rushing wild
   On rocks that can be folded up,
   A river which the wrist can stop
With a neat flip, revealing merely sticks
And silk of what had been a fan before,
    And like such winning tricks,
It shall be buried in excelsior.

SAMUEL SEWALL

Samuel Sewall, in a world of wigs,
Flouted opinion in his personal hair;
For foppery he gave not any figs,
But in his right and honor took the air.

Thus in his naked style, though well attired,
He went forth in the city, or paid court
To Madam Winthrop, whom he much admired,
Most godly, but yet liberal with the port.

And all the town admired for two full years
His excellent address, his gifts of fruit,
Her gracious ways and delicate white ears,
And held the course of nature absolute.

But yet she bade him suffer a peruke,
"That One be not distinguished from the All;"
Delivered of herself this stern rebuke
Framed in the resonant language of St. Paul.

"Madam," he answered her, "I have a Friend
Furnishes me with hair out of His strength,
And He requires only I attend
Unto His charity and to its length."

And all the town was witness to his trust:
On Monday he walked out with the Widow Gibbs,
A pious lady of charm and notable bust,
Whose heart beat tolerably beneath her ribs.

On Saturday he wrote proposing marriage,
And closed, imploring that she be not cruel,
"Your favorable answer will oblige,
Madam, your humble servant, Samuel Sewall."

THE END OF THE WEEKEND

A dying firelight slides along the quirt
Of the cast-iron cowboy where he leans
Against my father's books. The lariat
Whirls into darkness. My girl, in skin-tight jeans,
Fingers a page of Captain Marryat,
Inviting insolent shadows to her shirt.

We rise together to the second floor.
Outside, across the lake, an endless wind
Whips at the headstones of the dead and wails
In the trees for all who have and have not sinned.
She rubs against me and I feel her nails.
Although we are alone, I lock the door.

The eventual shapes of all our formless prayers,
This dark, this cabin of loose imaginings,

Wind, lake, lip, everything awaits
The slow unloosening of her underthings.
And then the noise. Something is dropped. It grates
Against the attic beams.
                I climb the stairs,

Armed with a belt.
              A long magnesium strip
Of moonlight from the dormer cuts a path
Among the shattered skeletons of mice.
A great black presence beats its wings in wrath.
Above the boneyard burn its golden eyes.
Some small grey fur is pulsing in its grip.

John Hollander / 1929–

THE LADY'S-MAID'S SONG

When Adam found his rib was gone
    He cursed and sighed and cried and swore
And looked with cold resentment on
    The creature God had used it for.
All love's delights were quickly spent
    And soon his sorrows multiplied:
He learned to blame his discontent
    On something stolen from his side.

And so in every age we find
    Each Jack, destroying every Joan,
Divides and conquers womankind
    In vengeance for his missing bone.
By day he spins out quaint conceits
    With gossip, flattery, and song,
But then at night, between the sheets,
    He wrongs the girl to right the wrong.

Though shoulder, bosom, lip, and knee
    Are praised in every kind of art,
Here is love's true anatomy:
    His rib is gone; he'll have her heart.
So women bear the debt alone
    And live eternally distressed,
For though we throw the dog his bone
    He wants it back with interest.

For The Man of Mode

THE GREAT BEAR

Even on clear nights, lead the most supple children
Out onto hilltops, and by no means will
They make it out. Neither the gruff round image
From a remembered page nor the uncertain
Finger tracing that image out can manage
To mark the lines of what ought to be there,
Passing through certain bounding stars, until
The whole massive expanse of bear appear
Swinging, across the ecliptic; and, although
The littlest ones say nothing, others respond,
Making us thankful in varying degrees
For what we would have shown them: "There it is!"
"I see it now!" Even "Very like a bear!"
Would make us grateful. Because there is no bear

We blame our memory of the picture: trudging
Up the dark, starlit path, stooping to clutch
An anxious hand, perhaps the outline faded
Then; perhaps could we have retained the thing
In mind ourselves, with it we might have staged
Something convincing. We easily forget
The huge, clear, homely dipper that is such
An event to reckon with, an object set
Across the space the bear should occupy;
But even so, the trouble lies in pointing

At any stars. For one's own finger aims
Always elsewhere: the man beside one seems
Never to get the point. "No! The bright star
Just above my fingertip." The star,

If any, that he sees beyond one's finger
Will never be the intended one. To bring
Another's eye to bear in such a fashion
On any single star seems to require
Something very like a constellation
That both habitually see at night;
Not in the stars themselves, but in among
Their scatter, perhaps, some old familiar sight
Is always there to take a bearing from.
And if the smallest child of all should cry
Out on the wet, black grass because he sees
Nothing but stars, though claiming that there is
Some bear not there that frightens him, we need
Only reflect that we ourselves have need

Of what is fearful (being really nothing)
With which to find our way about the path
That leads back down the hill again, and with
Which to enable the older children standing
By us to follow what we mean by "This
Star," "That one," or "The other one beyond it."
But what of the tiny, scared ones?—Such a bear,
Who needs it? We can still make do with both
The dipper that we always knew was there
And the bright, simple shapes that suddenly
Emerge on certain nights. To understand
The signs that stars compose, we need depend
Only on stars that are entirely there
And the apparent space between them. There

Never need be lines between them, puzzling
Our sense of what is what. What a star does
Is never to surprise us as it covers
The center of its patch of darkness, sparkling
Always, a point in one of many figures.
One solitary star would be quite useless,

A frigid conjecture, true but trifling;
And any single sign is meaningless
If unnecessary. Crab, bull, and ram,
Or frosty, irregular polygons of our own
Devising, or finally the Great Dark Bear
That we can never quite believe is there—
Having the others, any one of them
Can be dispensed with. The bear, of all of them,

Is somehow most like any one, taken
At random, in that we always tend to say
That just because it might be there; because
Some Ancients really traced it out, a broken
And complicated line, webbing bright stars
And fainter ones together; because a bear
Habitually appeared—then even by day
It is for us a thing that should be there.
We should not want to train ourselves to see it.
The world is everything that happens to
Be true. The stars at night seem to suggest
The shapes of what might be. If it were best,
Even, to have it there (such a great bear!
All hung with stars!), there still would be no bear.

Ted Hughes / 1930–

HAWK ROOSTING

I sit in the top of the wood, my eyes closed.
Inaction, no falsifying dream
Between my hooked head and hooked feet:
Or in sleep rehearse perfect kills and eat.

The convenience of the high trees!
The air's buoyancy and the sun's ray

Are of advantage to me;
And the earth's face upward for my inspection.

My feet are locked upon the rough bark.
It took the whole of Creation
To produce my foot, my each feather:
Now I hold Creation in my foot

Or fly up, and revolve it all slowly—
I kill where I please because it is all mine.
There is no sophistry in my body:
My manners are tearing off heads—

The allotment of death.
For the one path of my flight is direct
Through the bones of the living.
No arguments assert my right:

The sun is behind me.
Nothing has changed since I began.
My eye has permitted no change.
I am going to keep things like this.

THE JAGUAR

The apes yawn and adore their fleas in the sun.
The parrots shriek as if they were on fire, or strut
Like cheap tarts to attract the stroller with the nut.
Fatigued with indolence, tiger ánd lion

Lie still as the sun. The boa-constrictor's coil
Is a fossil. Cage after cage seems empty, or
Stinks of sleepers from the breathing straw.
It might be painted on a nursery wall.

But who runs like the rest past these arrives
At a cage where the crowd stands, stares, mesmerized,
As a child at a dream, at a jaguar hurrying enraged
Through prison darkness after the drills of his eyes

On a short fierce fuse. Not in boredom—
The eye satisfied to be blind in fire,
By the bang of blood in the brain deaf the ear—
He spins from the bars, but there's no cage to him

More than to the visionary his cell:
His stride is wildernesses of freedom:
The world rolls under the long thrust of his heel.
Over the cage floor the horizons come.

FAMOUS POET

Stare at the monster: remark
How difficult it is to define just what
Amounts to monstrosity in that
Very ordinary appearance. Neither thin nor fat,
Hair between light and dark,

And the general air
Of an apprentice—say, an apprentice house-
Painter amid an assembly of famous
Architects: the demeanour is of mouse,
Yet is he monster.

First scrutinize those eyes
For the spark, the effulgence: nothing. Nothing there
But the haggard stony exhaustion of a near-
Finished variety artist. He slumps in his chair
Like a badly hurt man, half life-size.

Is it his dreg-boozed inner demon
Still tankarding from tissue and follicle
The vital fire, the spirit electrical
That puts the gloss on a normal hearty male?
Or is it women?

The truth—bring it on
With black drapery, drums, and funeral tread
Like a great man's coffin—no, no, he is not dead

But in this truth surely half-buried:
  Once, the humiliation

  Of youth and obscurity,
The autoclave of heady ambition trapped,
The fermenting of a yeasty heart stopped—
Burst with such pyrotechnics the dull world gaped
  And "Repeat that!" still they cry.

  But all his efforts to concoct
The old heroic bang from their money and praise,
From the parent's pointing finger and the child's amaze,
Even from the burning of his wreathed bays,
  Have left him wrecked: wrecked,

  And monstrous, so,
As a Stegosaurus, a lumbering obsolete
Arsenal of gigantic horn and plate
From a time when half the world still burned, set
  To blink behind bars at the zoo.

VIEW OF A PIG

The pig lay on a barrow dead.
It weighed, they said, as much as three men.
Its eyes closed, pink white eyelashes.
Its trotters stuck straight out.

Such weight and thick pink bulk
Set in death seemed not just dead.
It was less than lifeless, further off.
It was like a sack of wheat.

I thumped it without feeling remorse.
One feels guilty insulting the dead,
Walking on graves. But this pig
Did not seem able to accuse.

It was too dead. Just so much
A poundage of lard and pork.
Its last dignity had entirely gone.
It was not a figure of fun.

Too dead now to pity.
To remember its life, din, stronghold
Of earthly pleasure as it had been,
Seemed a false effort, and off the point.

Too deadly factual. Its weight
Oppressed me—how could it be moved?
And the trouble of cutting it up!
The gash in its throat was shocking, but not pathetic.

Once I ran at a fair in the noise
To catch a greased piglet
That was faster and nimbler than a cat,
Its squeal was the rending of metal.

Pigs must have hot blood, they feel like ovens.
Their bite is worse than a horse's—
They chop a half-moon clean out.
They eat cinders, dead cats.

Distinctions and admirations such
As this one was long finished with.
I stared at it a long time. They were going to scald it,
Scald it and scour it like a doorstep.

PIKE

Pike, three inches long, perfect
Pike in all parts, green tigering the gold.
Killers from the egg: the malevolent aged grin.
They dance on the surface among the flies.

Or move, stunned by their own grandeur,
Over a bed of emerald, silhouette

Of submarine delicacy and horror.
A hundred feet long in their world.

In ponds, under the heat-struck lily pads—
Gloom of their stillness:
Logged on last year's black leaves, watching upwards.
Or hung in an amber cavern of weeds

The jaws' hooked clamp and fangs
Not to be changed at this date;
A life subdued to its instrument;
The gills kneading quietly, and the pectorals.

Three we kept behind glass,
Jungled in weed: three inches, four,
And four and a half: fed fry to them—
Suddenly there were two. Finally one

With a sag belly and the grin it was born with.
And indeed they spare nobody.
Two, six pounds each, over two feet long,
High and dry and dead in the willow-herb—

One jammed past its gills down the other's gullet:
The outside eye stared: as a vice locks—
The same iron in this eye
Though its film shrank in death.

A pond I fished, fifty yards across,
Whose lilies and muscular tench
Had outlasted every visible stone
Of the monastery that planted them—

Stilled legendary depth:
It was as deep as England. It held
Pike too immense to stir, so immense and old
That past nightfall I dared not cast

But silently cast and fished
With the hair frozen on my head
For what might move, for what eye might move.
The still splashes on the dark pond,

Owls hushing the floating woods
Frail on my ear against the dream
Darkness beneath night's darkness had freed,
That rose slowly towards me, watching.

Elizabeth Jennings / 1926–

THE COUNTERPART

Since clarity suggests simplicity
And since the simple thing is here inapt,
    I choose obscurities of tongue and touch,
The shadow side of language and the dark
    Hinted in conversations close to quarrel,
Conceived within the mind in aftermaths.
    The intellect no crystal is but swarming
Darkness on darkness, gently ruffled by
    The senses as they draw an image home.

If art must be abstract that needs to speak
In honesty, in painful honesty,
    Then every scene must be composed likewise,
Familiar objects turn to careful shapes,
    Gestures be stiff, emotions emblematic.
So art makes peace with honesty and we
    Detect a blazing, a Byzantine world,
A formal image shining from the dark
    But no less enigmatic than the dark.

Only in such decorum can our pain
Survive without dilution or pretence.
    The agony of loss, the potent thrust
Of seed that never will become a child
    Need the severity of metaphor,

The symbol on the shield, the dove, the lion
    Fixed in a stillness where the darkness folds
In pleated curtains, nothing disarranged:
    And only then the eye begins to see.

NOT IN THE GUIDE-BOOKS

Nobody stays here long;
    Deliberate visitors know
There is nothing here the guide-books show,
    No ruin or statue to sustain
Some great emotion in their stone.
    So visitors soon go.

Some travellers stay a little
    To collect wine or corn
And here breathe in the over-subtle
    Smell of places worn
Not by a marvellous death or battle
    But by their insignificance brought down.

Yet good, a place like this,
    For one grown tired of histories
To shape a human myth,
    A story but for his
Delight, where he might make the place
    His own success
Building what no one else had bothered with—
    A simple life or death.

LeRoi Jones / 1934–

AN AGONY. AS NOW.

I am inside someone
who hates me. I look
out from his eyes. Smell
what fouled tunes come in
to his breath. Love his
wretched women.

Slits in the metal, for sun. Where
my eyes sit turning, at the cool air
the glance of light, or hard flesh
rubbed against me, a woman, a man,
without shadow, or voice, or meaning.

This is the enclosure (flesh,
where innocence is a weapon. An
abstraction. Touch. (Not mine.
Or yours, if you are the soul I had
and abandoned when I was blind and had
my enemies carry me as a dead man
(if he is beautiful, or pitied.

It can be pain. (As now, as all his
flesh hurts me.) It can be that. Or
pain. As when she ran from me into
that forest.
       Or pain, the mind
silver spiraled whirled against the
sun, higher than even old men thought
God would be. Or pain. And the other. The
yes. (Inside his books, his fingers. They
are withered yellow flowers and were never

beautiful.) The yes. You will, lost soul, say
'beauty.' Beauty, practiced, as the tree. The
slow river. A white sun in its wet sentences.

Or, the cold men in their gale. Ecstasy. Flesh
or soul. The yes. (Their robes blown. Their bowls
empty. They chant at my heels, not at yours.) Flesh
or soul, as corrupt. Where the answer moves too quickly.
Where the God is a self, after all.)

Cold air blown through narrow blind eyes. Flesh,
white hot metal. Glows as the day with its sun.
It is a human love, I live inside. A bony skeleton
you recognize as words or simple feeling.

But it has no feeling. As the metal, is hot, it is not,
given to love.

It burns the thing
inside it. And that thing
screams.

THE INVENTION OF COMICS

I am soul in the world: in
the world of my soul the whirled
light / from the day
the sacked land
of my father.

In the world, the sad
nature of
myself. In myself
nature is sad. Small
prints of the day. Its
small dull fires. Its
sun, like a greyness
smeared on the dark.

The day of my soul, is
the nature of that
place. It is a landscape. Seen
from the top of a hill. A
grey expanse; dull fires
throbbing on its seas.

The man's soul, the complexion
of his life. The menace
of its greyness. The
fire, throbs, the sea
moves. Birds shoot
from the dark. The edge
of the waters lit
darkly for the moon.

And the moon, from the soul. Is
the world, of the man. The man
and his sea, and its moon, and
the soft fire throbbing. Kind
death. O,
my dark and sultry
love.

Galway Kinnell / 1927–

FIRST SONG

Then it was dusk in Illinois, the small boy
After an afternoon of carting dung
Hung on the rail fence, a sapped thing
Weary to crying. Dark was growing tall
And he began to hear the pond frogs all
Calling on his ear with what seemed their joy.

Soon their sound was pleasant for a boy
Listening in the smoky dusk and the nightfall
Of Illinois, and from the fields two small
Boys came bearing cornstalk violins
And they rubbed the cornstalk bows with resins
And the three sat there scraping of their joy.

It was now fine music the frogs and the boys
Did in the towering Illinois twilight make
And into dark in spite of a shoulder's ache
A boy's hunched body loved out of a stalk
The first song of his happiness, and the song woke
His heart to the darkness and into the sadness of joy.

THE AVENUE BEARING
THE INITIAL OF CHRIST
INTO THE NEW WORLD

Was diese kleine Gasse doch für ein Reich an sich war . . .

for Gail

1

pcheek pcheek pcheek pcheek pcheek
They cry. The motherbirds thieve the air
To appease them. A tug on the East River
Blasts the bass-note of its passage, lifted
From the infra-bass of the sea. A broom
Swishes over the sidewalk like feet through leaves.
Valerio's pushcart Ice Coal Kerosene
Moves   clack
                        clack
                                    clack
On a broken wheelrim. Ringing in its chains
The New Star Laundry horse comes down the street
Like a roofleak whucking in a pail.
At the redlight, where a horn blares,

The Golden Harvest Bakery brakes on its gears,
Squeaks, and seethes in place. A propane-
gassed bus makes its way with big, airy sighs.

Across the street a woman throws open
Her window,
She sets, terribly softly,
Two potted plants on the windowledge
                tic   tic
And bangs shut her window.

A man leaves a doorway tic toc tic toc tic toc tic hurrah
        toc splat on Avenue C tic etc and turns the corner.

Banking the same corner
A pigeon coasts 5th Street in shadows,
Looks for altitude, surmounts the rims of buildings,
And turns white.

The babybirds pipe down. It is day.

2

In sunlight on the Avenue
The Jew rocks along in a black fur shtraimel,
Black robe, black knickers, black knee-stockings,
Black shoes. His beard like a sod-bottom
Hides the place where he wears no tie.
A dozen children troop after him, barbels flying,
In skullcaps. They are Reuben, Simeon, Levi, Judah,
        Issachar, Zebulun, Benjamin, Dan, Naphtali, Gad,
        Asher.
With the help of the Lord they will one day become
Courtiers, thugs, rulers, rabbis, asses, adders, wrestlers,
        bakers, poets, cartpushers, infantrymen.

The old man is sad-faced. He is near burial
And one son is missing. The women who bore him sons
And are past bearing, mourn for the son
And for the father, wondering if the man will go down
Into the grave of a son mourning, or if at the last
The son will put his hands on the eyes of his father.

The old man wades towards his last hour.
On 5th Street, between Avenues A and B,
In sunshine, in his private cloud, Bunko Certified
    Embalmer,
Cigar in his mouth, nose to the wind, leans
At the doorway of Bunko's Funeral Home & Parlour,
Glancing west towards the Ukrainians, eastward idly
Where the Jew rocks towards his last hour.

Sons, grandsons at his heel, the old man
Confronts the sun. He does not feel its rays
Through his beard, he does not understand
Fruits and vegetables live by the sun.
Like his children he is sallow-faced, he sees
A blinding signal in the sky, he smiles.

Bury me not Bunko damned Catholic I pray you in Egypt.

Abraham Klein / 1909–

INDIAN RESERVATION:
CAUGHNAWAGA

Where are the braves, the faces like autumn fruit,
who stared at the child from the coloured frontispiece?
And the monosyllabic chief who spoke with his throat?
Where are the tribes, the feathered bestiaries?—
Rank Aesop's animals erect and red,
with fur on their names to make all live things kin'—
Chief Running Deer, Black Bear, Old Buffalo Head?

Childhood, that wished me Indian, hoped that
one afterschool I'd leave the classroom chalk,
the varnish smell, the watered dust of the street,
to join the clean outdoors and the Iroquois track.

Childhood; but always,—as on a calendar,—
there stood that chief, with arms akimbo, waiting
the runaway mascot paddling to his shore.

With what strange moccasin stealth that scene is changed!
With French names, without paint, in overalls,
their bronze, like their nobility expunged,—
the men. Beneath their alimentary shawls
sit like black tents their squaws; while for the tourist's
brown pennies scattered at the old church door,
the ragged papooses jump, and bite the dust.

Their past is sold in a shop: the beaded shoes,
the sweetgrass basket, the curio Indian,
burnt wood and gaudy cloth and inch-canoes—
trophies and scalpings for a traveller's den.
Sometimes, it's true, they dance, but for a bribe;
after a deal don the bedraggled feather
and welcome a white mayor to the tribe.

This is a grassy ghetto, and no home.
And these are fauna in a museum kept.
The better hunters have prevailed. The game,
losing its blood, now makes these grounds its crypt.
The animals pale, the shine of the fur is lost,
bleached are their living bones. About them watch
as through a mist, the pious prosperous ghosts.

Stanley Kunitz / 1905–

A CHOICE OF WEAPONS

Reviewing me without undue elation
A critic who has earned his reputation
By being always Johnny-on-the-spot
Where each contemporary starts to rot

Conceded me integrity and style
And stamina to walk a measured mile,
But wondered why a gang of personal devils
Need clank their jigging bones as public evils:

"The times are suited for the gay empiric,
The witty ironist, the casual lyric;
Apparently it's gristle-fare, not fat,
At certain tables: must we weep at that?
Though poets seem to rail at bourgeois ills
It is their lack of audience that kills.
Their metaphysics but reflects a folly:
'Read me or I'll be damned and melancholy.'
This poet suffers: that's his right, of course,
But we don't have to watch him beat his horse."

Sir, if appreciation be my lack,
You may appreciate me, front and back—
I won't deny that vaguely vulgar need:
But do not pity those whose motives bleed
Even while strolling in a formal garden.
Observe that tears are bullets when they harden;
The triggered poem's no water-pistol toy,
But shoots its cause, and is a source of joy.

FOREIGN AFFAIRS

We are two countries girded for the war,
Whisking our scouts across the pricked frontier
To ravage in each other's fields, cut lines
Along the lacework of strategic nerves,
Loot stores; while here and there,
In ambushes that trace a valley's curves,
Stark witness to the dangerous charge we bear,
A house ignites, a train's derailed, a bridge
Blows up sky-high, and water floods the mines.
Who first attacked? Who turned the other cheek?
Aggression perpetrated is as soon

Denied, and insult rubbed into the injury
By cunning agents trained in these affairs,
With whom it's touch-and-go, don't-tread-on-me,
I-dare-you-to, keep-off, and kiss-my-hand.
Tempers could sharpen knives, and do; we live
In states provocative
Where frowning headlines scare the coffee cream
And doomsday is the eighth day of the week.

Our exit through the slammed and final door
Is twenty times rehearsed, but when we face
The imminence of cataclysmic rupture,
A lesser pride goes down upon its knees.
Two countries separated by desire!—
Whose diplomats speed back and forth by plane,
Portmanteaus stuffed with fresh apologies
Outdated by events before they land.
Negotiations wear them out: they're driven mad
Between the protocols of tears and rapture.

Locked in our fated and contiguous selves,
These worlds that too much agitate each other,
Interdependencies from hip to head,
Twin principalities both slave and free,
We coexist, proclaiming Peace together.
Tell me no lies! We are divided nations
With malcontents by thousands in our streets,
These thousands torn by inbred revolutions.
A triumph is demanded, not moral victories
Deduced from small advances, small retreats.
Are the gods of our fathers not still daemonic?
On the steps of the Capitol
The outraged lion of our years roars panic,
And we suffer the guilty cowardice of the will,
Gathering its bankrupt slogans up for flight
Like gold from ruined treasuries.
And yet, and yet, although the murmur rises,
We are what we are, and only life surprises.

Joseph Langland / 1917–

A SEA-CHANGE: FOR HAROLD

Across the swamps and marshlands of the hours,
Over the cloud-banked air and under the dark
Hills of fog where lamps
Float incandescent caves in drowsy streets,
The drowned sound of the sea wells up in foghorns
Blowing out of their watery towns.
That chilled gray groan
Rises on sunken mountains, upon
Oceanic rain-eroded shores, under
Hollow crystal gongs in icy poles,
And rides through cabled water-years of sound
To echo upward over the rusty buoys,
Bobbing and clanging in a blind mist
Along our inward bays,
To cry an old sad song in the soggy bones
Under our chalky shores.

The cold ache and dull blue sound of the sea
Fades in the foaming crests,
Whispers at rocks
Jutting their gray-green heads from the gray-green sea,
And sleeps in the world's great valleys.
There the riding ocean sighs
Over the shoals of continental shelves
Down to submerged kingdoms
Where drowned soldiers, logged in the sound,
Dream that their salt-encrusted eyes
Glow in the weeds and corals of their skulls.

Across broad rivered deltas and crumbling cliffs
That long gray sound
Faintly vibrates over the ocean floor

And rises under our surface solitudes
As if a huge volcano, muffled under the sea,
Erupted with no sound.

HUNTERS IN THE SNOW: BRUEGHEL

Quail and rabbit hunters with tawny hounds,
Shadowless, out of late afternoon
Trudge toward the neutral evening of indeterminate form.
Done with their blood-annunciated day
Public dogs and all the passionless mongrels
Through deep snow
Trail their deliberate masters
Descending from the upper village home in hovering light.
Sooty lamps
Glow in the stone-carved kitchens.

This is the fabulous hour of shape and form
When Flemish children are gray-black-olive
And green-dark-brown
Scattered and skating informal figures
On the mill ice pond.
Moving in stillness
A hunched dame struggles with her bundled sticks,
Letting her evening's comfort cudgel her
While she, like jug or wheel, like a wagon cart
Walked by lazy oxen along the old snowlanes,
Creeps and crunches down the dusky street.
High in the fire-red dooryard
Half unhitched the sign of the Inn
Hangs in wind
Tipped to the pitch of the roof.
Near it anonymous parents and peasant girl,
Living like proverbs carved in the alehouse walls,
Gather the country evening into their arms
And lean to the glowing flames.

Now in the dimming distance fades
The other village; across the valley

Imperturbable Flemish cliffs and crags
Vaguely advance, close in, loom
Lost in nearness. Now
The night-black raven perched in branching boughs
Opens its early wing and slipping out
Above the gray-green valley
Weaves a net of slumber over the snow-capped homes.
And now the church, and then the walls and roofs
Of all the little houses are become
Close kin to shadow with small lantern eyes.
And now the bird of evening
With shadows streaming down from its gliding wings
Circles the neighboring hills
Of Hertogenbosch, Brabant.

Darkness stalks the hunters,
Slowly sliding down,
Falling in beating rings and soft diagonals.
Lodged in the vague vast valley the village sleeps.

Philip Larkin / 1922–

CHURCH GOING

Once I am sure there's nothing going on
I step inside, letting the door thud shut.
Another church: matting, seats, and stone,
And little books; sprawlings of flowers, cut
For Sunday, brownish now; some brass and stuff
Up at the holy end; the small neat organ;
And a tense, musty, unignorable silence,
Brewed God knows how long. Hatless, I take off
My cycle-clips in awkward reverence,

Move forward, run my hand around the font.
From where I stand, the roof looks almost new—

Cleaned, or restored? Someone would know: I don't.
Mounting the lectern, I peruse a few
Hectoring large-scale verses, and pronounce
'Here endeth' much more loudly than I'd meant.
The echoes snigger briefly. Back at the door
I sign the book, donate an Irish sixpence,
Reflect the place was not worth stopping for.

Yet stop I did: in fact I often do,
And always end much at a loss like this,
Wondering what to look for; wondering, too,
When churches fall completely out of use
What we shall turn them into, if we shall keep
A few cathedrals chronically on show,
Their parchment, plate and pyx in locked cases,
And let the rest rent-free to rain and sheep.
Shall we avoid them as unlucky places?

Or, after dark, will dubious women come
To make their children touch a particular stone;
Pick simples for a cancer; or on some
Advised night see walking a dead one?
Power of some sort or other will go on
In games, in riddles, seemingly at random;
But superstition, like belief, must die,
And what remains when disbelief has gone?
Grass, weedy pavement, brambles, buttress, sky,

A shape less recognisable each week,
A purpose more obscure. I wonder who
Will be the last, the very last, to seek
This place for what it was; one of the crew
That tap and jot and know what rood-lofts were?
Some ruin-bibber, randy for antique,
Or Christmas-addict, counting on a whiff
Of gown-and-bands and organ-pipes and myrrh?
Or will he be my representative,

Bored, uninformed, knowing the ghostly silt
Dispersed, yet tending to this cross of ground
Through suburb scrub because it held unspilt
So long and equably what since is found

Only in separation—marriage, and birth,
And death, and thoughts of these—for whom was built
This special shell? For, though I've no idea
What this accoutred frowsty barn is worth,
It pleases me to stand in silence here;

A serious house on serious earth it is,
In whose blent air all our compulsions meet,
Are recognised, and robed as destinies.
And that much never can be obsolete,
Since someone will forever be surprising
A hunger in himself to be more serious,
And gravitating with it to this ground,
Which, he once heard, was proper to grow wise in,
If only that so many dead lie round.

IF, MY DARLING

If my darling were once to decide
Not to stop at my eyes,
But to jump, like Alice, with floating skirt into my head,

She would find no tables and chairs,
No mahogany claw-footed sideboards,
No undisturbed embers;

The tantalus would not be filled, nor the fender-seat cosy,
Nor the shelves stuffed with small-printed books for the
        Sabbath,
Nor the butler bibulous, the housemaids lazy:

She would find herself looped with the creep of varying
        light,
Monkey-brown, fish-grey, a string of infected circles
Loitering like bullies, about to coagulate;

Delusions that shrink to the size of a woman's glove
Then sicken inclusively outwards. She would also remark
The unwholesome floor, as it might be the skin of a grave,

From which ascends an adhesive sense of betrayal,
A Grecian statue kicked in the privates, money,
A swill-tub of finer feelings. But most of all

She'd be stopping her ears against the incessant recital
Intoned by reality, larded with technical terms,
Each one double-yolked with meaning and meaning's
    rebuttal:

For the skirl of that bulletin unpicks the world like a knot,
And to hear how the past is past and the future neuter
Might knock my darling off her unpriceable pivot.

Laurie Lee / 1914–

FIELD OF AUTUMN

Slow moves the acid breath of noon
over the copper-coated hill,
slow from the wild crab's bearded breast
the palsied apples fall.

Like coloured smoke the day hangs fire,
taking the village without sound;
the vulture-headed sun lies low
chained to the violet ground.

The horse upon the rocky height
rolls all the valley in his eye,
but dares not raise his foot or move
his shoulder from the fly.

The sheep, snail-backed against the wall,
lifts her blind face but does not know
the cry her blackened tongue gives forth
is the first bleat of snow.

Each bird and stone, each roof and well,
feels the gold foot of autumn pass;
each spider binds with glittering snare
the splintered bones of grass.

Slow moves the hour that sucks our life,
slow drops the late wasp from the pear,
the rose tree's thread of scent draws thin—
and snaps upon the air.

SUNKEN EVENING

The green light floods the city square—
   A sea of fowl and feathered fish,
   Where squalls of rainbirds dive and splash
And gusty sparrows chop the air.

Submerged, the prawn-blue pigeons feed
   In sandy grottoes round the Mall,
   And crusted lobster-buses crawl
Among the fountains' silver weed.

There, like a wreck, with mast and bell,
   The torn church settles by the bow,
   While phosphorescent starlings stow
Their mussel shells along the hull.

The oyster-poet, drowned but dry,
   Rolls a black pearl between his bones;
   The mermaid, trapped by telephones,
Gazes in bubbles at the sky.

Till, with the dark, the shallows run,
   And homeward surges tide and fret—
   The slow night trawls its heavy net
And hauls the clerk to Surbiton.

Denise Levertov / 1923–

THE GODDESS

She in whose lipservice
I passed my time,
whose name I knew, but not her face,
came upon me where I lay in Lie Castle!

Flung me across the room, and
room after room (hitting the walls, re-
bounding—to the last
sticky wall—wrenching away from it
pulled hair out!)
till I lay
outside the outer walls!

There in cold air
lying still where her hand had thrown me,
I tasted the mud that splattered my lips:
the seeds of a forest were in it,
asleep and growing! I tasted
her power!

The silence was answering my silence,
a forest was pushing itself
out of sleep between my submerged fingers.

I bit on a seed and it spoke on my tongue
of day that shone already among stars
in the water-mirror of low ground,
and a wind rising ruffled the lights:
she passed near me returning from the encounter,
she who plucked me from the close rooms,

without whom nothing
flowers, fruits, sleeps in season,
without whom nothing
speaks in its own tongue, but returns
lie for lie!

OBSESSIONS

Maybe it is true we have to return
to the black air of ashcan city
because it is there the most life was burned,

as ghosts or criminals return?
But no, the city has no monopoly
of intense life. The dust burned

golden or violet in the wide land
to which we ran away, images
of passion sprang out of the land

as whirlwinds or red flowers, your hands
opened in anguish or clenched in violence
under that sun, and clasped my hands

in that place to which we will not return
where so much happened that no one else noticed,
where the city's ashes that we brought with us
flew into the intense sky still burning.

TO THE SNAKE

Green Snake, when I hung you round my neck
and stroked your cold, pulsing throat
                as you hissed to me, glinting

arrowy gold scales, and I felt
                the weight of you on my shoulders,
and the whispering silver of your dryness
                sounded close at my ears—

Green Snake—I swore to my companions that certainly
                you were harmless! But truly
I had no certainty, and no hope, only desiring
                to hold you, for that joy,
                                which left
a long wake of pleasure, as the leaves moved
and you faded into the pattern
of grass and shadows, and I returned
smiling and haunted, to a dark morning.

SCENES FROM THE LIFE OF
THE PEPPERTREES

I

The peppertrees, the peppertrees!

Cats are stretching in the doorways,
sure of everything. It is morning.
                But the peppertrees
stand aside in diffidence, with berries
of modest red.
                Branch above branch, an air
of lightness; of shadows
scattered lightly.
                A cat
closes upon its shadow.
Up and up goes the sun,
sure of everything.
                The peppertrees
                        shiver a little.
Robust
and soot-black, the cat
leaps to a low branch. Leaves
close about him.

II

The yellow moon dreamily
tipping buttons of light
down among the leaves. Marimba,
marimba — from beyond the
black street.
                    Somebody dancing,
somebody
            getting the hell
outta here. Shadows of cats
weave round the tree trunks,
the exposed knotty roots.

III

The man on the bed sleeping
defenseless. Look —
his bare long feet together
sideways, keeping each other
warm. And the foreshortened shoulders,
the head
barely visible. He is good.
Let him sleep.
                    But the third peppertree
        is restless, twitching
thin leaves in the light
of afternoon. After a while
it walks over and taps
on the upstairs window with a bunch
of red berries. Will he wake?

Alun Lewis / 1915–1944

SONG

On seeing dead bodies floating off the Cape

The first month of his absence
I was numb and sick
And where he'd left his promise
Life did not turn or kick.
The seed, the seed of love was sick.

The second month my eyes were sunk
In the darkness of despair,
And my bed was like a grave
And his ghost was lying there.
And my heart was sick with care.

The third month of his going
I thought I heard him say
"Our course deflected slightly
On the thirty-second day—"
The tempest blew his words away.

And he was lost among the waves,
His ship rolled helpless in the sea,
The fourth month of his voyage
He shouted grievously
"Beloved, do not think of me."

The flying fish like kingfishers
Skim the sea's bewildered crests,
The whales blow steaming fountains,
The seagulls have no nests
Where my lover sways and rests.

We never thought to buy and sell
This life that blooms or withers in the leaf,
And I'll not stir, so he sleeps well,
Though cell by cell the coral reef
Builds an eternity of grief.

But oh! the drag and dullness of my Self;
The turning seasons wither in my head;
All this slowness, all this hardness,
The nearness that is waiting in my bed,
The gradual self-effacement of the dead.

THE PEASANTS

The dwarf barefooted, chanting
Behind the oxen by the lake,
Stepping lightly and lazily among the thorntrees
Dusky and dazed with sunlight, half awake;

The women breaking stones upon the highway,
Walking erect with burdens on their heads,
One body growing in another body,
Creation touching verminous straw beds.

Across scorched hills and trampled crops
The soldiers straggle by.
History staggers in their wake.
The peasants watch them die.

John Manifold / 1915–

FIFE TUNE

for Sixth Platoon, 308th I.T.C.

One morning in spring
We marched from Devizes
All shapes and all sizes
Like beads on a string,
But yet with a swing
We trod the bluemetal
And full of high fettle
We started to sing.

She ran down the stair
A twelve-year-old darling
And laughing and calling
She tossed her bright hair;
Then silent to stare
At the men flowing past her—
There were all she could master
Adoring her there.

It's seldom I'll see
A sweeter or prettier;
I doubt we'll forget her
In two years or three,
And lucky he'll be
She takes for a lover
While we are far over
The treacherous sea.

THE SIRENS

Odysseus heard the sirens; they were singing
Music by Wolf and Weinberger and Morley
About a region where the swans go winging,
Vines are in colour, girls are growing surely

Into nubility, and pylons bringing
Leisure and power to farms that live securely
Without a landlord. Still, his eyes were stinging
With salt and sea blink, and the ropes hurt sorely.

Odysseus saw the sirens; they were charming,
Blonde, with snub breasts and little neat posteriors,
But could not take his mind off the alarming

Weather report, his mutineers in irons,
The radio failing; it was bloody serious.
In twenty minutes he forgot the sirens.

NIGHT PIECE

Three men came talking up the road
And still "tomorrow" was the word.

The night was clear with the lamps' glitter.
The first man spoke and his voice was bitter:

"Tomorrow like another day
I draw the dole and rust away."

The second one said scared and low,
"Tomorrow I may have to go."

And the two spoke never another word
But drew together and looked at the third.

And the third man said, "If tomorrow exists,
It's a day of streets like rivers of fists,

"It's the end of crawling, the end of doles,
And men are treated as human souls."

I stood in the doorway and heard these things
As the three came past with the step of kings.

W. S. *Merwin* / 1927–

THE BONES

It takes a long time to hear what the sands
Seem to be saying, with the wind nudging them,
And then you cannot put it in words nor tell
Why these things should have a voice. All kinds
Of objects come in over the tide-wastes
In the course of a year, with a throaty
Rattle: weeds, drift-wood, the bodies of birds
And of fish, shells. For years I had hardly
Considered shells as being bones, maybe
Because of the sound they could still make, though
I knew a man once who could raise a kind
Of wailing tune out of a flute he had,
Made from a fibula: it was much the same
Register as the shells'; the tune did not
Go on when his breath stopped, though you thought it
    would.
Then that morning, coming on the wreck,
I saw the kinship. No recent disaster
But an old ghost from under a green buoy,
Brought in by the last storm, or one from which
The big wind had peeled back the sand grave
To show what was still left: the bleached, chewed-off

Timbers like the ribs of a man or the jaw-bone
Of some extinct beast. Far down the sands its
Broken cage leaned out, casting no shadow
In the veiled light. There was a man sitting beside it
Eating out of a paper, littering the beach
With the bones of a few more fish, while the hulk
Cupped its empty hand high over him. Only he
And I had come to those sands knowing
That they were there. The rest was bones, whatever
Tunes they made. The bones of things; and of men too
And of man's endeavors whose ribs he had set
Between himself and the shapeless tides. Then
I saw how the sand was shifting like water,
That once could walk. Shells were to shut out the sea,
The bones of birds were built for floating
On air and water, and those of fish were devised
For their feeding-depths, while a man's bones were framed
For what? For knowing the sands are here,
And coming to hear them a long time; for giving
Shapes to the sprawled sea, weight to its winds,
And wrecks to plead for its sands. These things are not
Limitless: we know there is somewhere
An end to them, though every way you look
They extend farther than a man can see.

GRANDFATHER IN THE
OLD MEN'S HOME

Gentle, at last, and as clean as ever,
He did not even need drink any more,
And his good sons unbent and brought him
Tobacco to chew, both times when they came
To be satisfied he was well cared for.
And he smiled all the time to remember
Grandmother, his wife, wearing the true faith
Like an iron nightgown, yet brought to birth
Seven times and raising the family
Through her needle's eye while he got away
Down the green river, finding directions

For boats. And himself coming home sometimes
well-heeled but blind drunk, to hide all the bread
And shoot holes in the bucket while he made
His daughters pump. Still smiled as kindly in
His sleep beside the other clean old men
To see Grandmother, every night the same,
Huge in her age, with her thumbed-down mouth, come
Hating the river, filling with her stare
His gliding dream, while he turned to water,
While the children they both had begotten,
With old faces now, but themselves shrunken
To child-size again, stood ranged at her side,
Beating their little Bibles till he died.

THE DRUNK IN THE FURNACE

       For a good decade
The furnace stood in the naked gulley, fireless
And vacant as any hat. Then when it was
No more to them than a hulking black fossil
To erode unnoticed with the rest of the junk-hill
By the poisonous creek, and rapidly to be added
       To their ignorance,

       They were afterwards astonished
To confirm, one morning, a twist of smoke like a pale
Resurrection, staggering out of its chewed hole,
And to remark then other tokens that someone,
Cosily bolted behind the eye-holed iron
Door of the drafty burner, had there established
       His bad castle.

       Where he gets his spirits
It's a mystery. But the stuff keeps him musical:
Hammer-and-anvilling with poker and bottle
To his jugged bellowings, till the last groaning clang
As he collapses onto the rioting
Springs of a litter of car-seats ranged on the grates,
       To sleep like an iron pig.

In their tar-paper church
On a text about stoke-holes that are sated never
Their Reverend lingers. They nod and hate trespassers.
When the furnace wakes, though, all afternoon
Their witless offspring flock like piped rats to its siren
Crescendo, and agape on the crumbling ridge
Stand in a row and learn.

Robert Mezey / 1935–

S T R E E T   S C E N E

Afternoon.
Teacher and nun, bleak refugee, a stone
Splinters with the cold, and the vacant streets
Await you.
Tattered, and driven by the wind,
A sheet of newspaper borne in a swarm of snow
Scrapes on the curb and pavement.

The parish children,
Home from school and church, escaped and safe,
Stand at the windows. With expressionless eyes
They scan
Lonely slope and parapet,
A purity of contour in the gulleys,
A terrain bare of soldiers.

Hour after hour
The strange light persists. Snow dawdles down.
It is a violet haze in which the snow
Seems grey,
And a solitary nun becomes
A slim black hill possessing empty lands.
Her hood is peaked with snow.

The first crystals
Blazed in constellations on her gown,
And then that somber gown relaxed its bald
          Silhouette,
    And merged with the densely pointed air.
It must be grave compliance that lets her move
          Without seeming to move.

          Teacher and nun,
You are the heiress of warm, refused embraces,
Who now in the sisterless twilight mutely tread
          In drifts
    Through the buried paper, the splintered stone;
In whose infinite midnight hover the small flakes
          Inseparable from stars.

THE FUNERAL HOME

In the environs of the funeral home
The smell of death was absent. All I knew
Were flowers rioting and odors blown
Tangible as a blossom into the face,
To be inhaled and hushed—and where they grew
Smothered the nostrils in the pungent grass.

Hyacinths of innocence, and yellow-hammers,
That beat the air at dawn, at dusk, to metal
Immortality, that flush where a bee clamors
For wine, are blooms of another color. See
How the flush fades as it descends the petal,
How deep the insect drinks, how quietly.

And curious, that among these ferns and rocks,
The violets flying a modest and blue elation,
And flapping ruffles of the white lilacs,
Shaking the air to tempt the golden bee,
Stiffen at the moment of consummation,
Swayed with guilt and weight of the bee's body.

These flowers, when cut and used, will remain ruddy,
As though made deathless in the very way
Their cutter kept the hue in the human body
That they were cut to celebrate and mourn.
The coffin has sprouted in dark mahogany
Out of them—edged, and shining like a thorn.

Josephine Miles / 1911–

MONKEY

God, a man at Yale, adopted a monkey
In order to raise him up in his own image,
But only in some respects could the monk identify,
Could learn manners, but not the word of God.

Ah, always it was so, meditated the monkey dazzled and
        befuddled,
Out of my tree I fell in the forest of Eden,
Or if I mannerly ate, it was the wrong apple,
Or if I climbed I died.

And this is all, I guess, a semantical series
Of my ascent and fall.
His tree is not my tree, His word, my word;
His Yale, my Yale.

THE SAVAGES

As we rowed from our ships and set foot on the shore
In the still coves,
We met our images.

Our brazen images emerged from the mirrors of the wood
Like yelling shadows,
So we searched our souls,

And in that hell and pit of everyman
Placed the location of their ruddy shapes.
We must be cruel to ourselves.

Then through the underbrush we cut our hopes
Forest after forest to within
The inner hush where Mississippi flows

And were in ambush at the very source,
Scalped to the cortex. Yet bought them off.
It was an act of love to seek their salvation.

　　President Jackson asked,
　　What good man would prefer a forested country ranged
　　　　with savages
　　To our extensive republic studded with cities
　　With all the improvements art can devise or industry
　　　　execute?

　　Pastor Smiley inquired,
　　What good man would allow his sins or his neighbors'
　　To put on human dress and run in the wilds
　　To leap out on innocent occasions?

　　Miss Benedict proposed,
　　The partial era of enlightenment in which we live
　　Brings Dionysus to the mesa and the cottonwood grove,
　　And floats Apollo to the barrows of the civic group
　　To ratify entreaties and to harp on hope.

　　Professor Roy Harvey Pearce quoted,
　　These savages are outlandish Tartars and Cain's children,
　　Though someone reported once, "They do not withhold
　　　　assent
　　From the truth set forth in a credible manner."
　　Is it possible?

Henry David Thoreau,
The most popular highbrow overseas reading-material
For our armed forces, because while they work and wait
They see before them in the green shade
His ruddy image, said, as his last word when he died,
    Indians.

Reading today this manual of wisdom,
In the still coves
We meet our images

And, in ambush at the very source,
Would buy them off. It is an act of love
To seek their salvation.

One party to the purchase
Receipts the purchase price and hands us back
His token of negotiation which redeems:

   We cannibals must help these Christians.

VOYAGE

From his small city Columbus
Set sail in the floodtide of sunlight.
The boxes of buildings
Basked in secular light.

The damp interiors
Of shops on the hill streets
Dried in the golden heat,
The stairways dry and bright.

The hills stepped down in ranks
To the spacious harbor,
The whole town afforded
The patient splendor

Of the widest sundry sunshine
Over rank and section
Over room and apartment
Over court and altar.

What had then to do Columbus
With a Spanish ocean
Seamews and curlews
In a brisk brine?

But that he envisioned at its far golden
Corner another
Such a tiered city
High and dry?

Vassar Miller / 1924–

THE FINAL HUNGER

Hurl down the nerve-gnarled body hurtling head-
Long into sworls of shade-hush. Plummeting, keep
The latch of eyelids shut to so outleap
Care's claws. Arms, legs, abandon grace and spread
Your spent sprawl—glutton ravening to be fed
With fats, creams, fruits, meats, spice that heavy-heap
The hands, that golden-gloss the flesh, of sleep,
Sleep, the sole lover that I take to bed.

But they couch crouching in the darkness, city
Of wakefulness uncaptured by assaulting—
Senses by sleep unravished and unwon.
Sun-sword night-sheathed, lie never between (have pity!)
Between me and my love, between me and the vaulting
Down the dense sweetness of oblivion.

BOUT WITH BURNING

I have tossed hours upon the tides of fever,
Upon the billows of my blood have ridden,
Where fish of fancy teem as neither river
Nor ocean spawns from India to Sweden.
Here while my boat of body burnt has drifted
Along her sides crawled tentacles of crabs
Sliming her timbers; on the waves upwafted
Crept water rats to gnaw her ropes and ribs.
Crashing, she has dived, her portholes choking
With weed and ooze, the swirls of black and green
Gulping her inch by inch, the seagulls' shrieking
Sieved depth through depth to silence. Till blast-blown,
I in my wreck beyond storm's charge and churning
Have waked marooned upon the coasts of morning.

Howard Moss / 1922–

THE LIE

Some bloodied sea-bird's hovering decay
Assails us where we lie, and lie
To make that symbol go away,
To mock the true north of the eye.
But lie to me, lie next to me;
The world is an infirmity.

Too much of sun's been said, too much
Of sea, and of the lover's touch,
Whole volumes that old men debauch.
But we, at the sea's edge curled,
Hurl back their bloody world.
Lie to me, lie next to me,

For there is nothing here to see
But the mirror of ourselves, the day,
Clear with the odors of the sea.
Lie to me. And lie to me.

ELEGY FOR MY FATHER

Father, whom I murdered every night but one,
That one, when your death murdered me,
Your body waits within the wasting sod.
Clutching at the straw-face of your God,
Do you remember me, your morbid son,
Curled in a death, all motive unbegun,
Continuum of flesh, who never thought to be
The mourning mirror of your potency?

All you had battled for the nightmare took
Away, as dropping from your eyes, the sea-
Salt tears, with messages that none could read,
Impotent, pellucid, were the final seeds
You sowed. Above you, the white night nurse shook
His head, and moaning on the moods of luck,
We knew the double-dealing enemy:
From pain you suffered, pain had set you free.

Down from the ceiling, father, circles came:
Angels, perhaps, to bear your soul away.
But tasting the persisting salt of pain,
I think my tears created them, though in vain,
Like yours, they fell. All losses link: the same
Creature marred us both to stake his claim.
Shutting my eyelids, barring night and day,
I saw, and see, your body borne away.

Two months dead, I wrestle with your name
Whose separate letters make a paltry sum
That is not you. If still you harbor mine,
Think of the house we had in summertime,
When in the sea-light every early game
Was played with love, and if death's waters came,

You'd rescue me. How I would take you from,
Now, if I could, its whirling vacuum.

Charles Olson / 1910–

I, MAXIMUS OF GLOUCESTER,
TO YOU

Off-shore, by islands hidden in the blood
jewels & miracles, I, Maximus
a metal hot from boiling water, tell you
what is a lance, who obeys the figures of
the present dance

1

the thing you're after
may lie around the bend
of the nest (second, time slain, the bird! the bird!

And there! (strong) thrust, the mast! flight

(of the bird
o kylix, o
Antony of Padua
sweep low, o bless

the roofs, the old ones, the gentle steep ones
on whose ridge-poles the gulls sit, from which they depart,

And the flake-racks
of my city!

2

love is form, and cannot be without
important substance (the weight
say, 58 carats each one of us, perforce
our goldsmith's scale

feather to feather added
(and what is mineral, what
is curling hair, the string
you carry in your nervous beak, these

make bulk, these, in the end, are
the sum
(o my lady of good voyage
in whose arm, whose left arm rests
no boy but a carefully carved wood, a painted face, a schooner!
a delicate mast, as bow-sprit for

forwarding

3

the underpart is, though stemmed, uncertain
is, as sex is, as moneys are, facts!
facts, to be dealt with, as the sea is, the demand
that they be played by, that they only can be, that they must
be played by, said he, coldly, the
ear!

By ear, he sd.
But that which matters, that which insists, that which will
     last,
that! o my people, where shall you find it, how, where, where
     shall you listen
when all is become billboards, when, all, even silence, is
     spray-gunned?

when even our bird, my roofs,
cannot be heard

when even you, when sound itself is neoned in?

when, on the hill, over the water
where she who used to sing,
when the water glowed,
black, gold, the tide
outward, at evening

when bells came like boats
over the oil-slicks, milkweed
hulls

And a man slumped,
attentionless,
against pink shingles

o sea city)

4

one loves only form,
and form only comes
into existence when
the thing is born

        born of yourself, born
        of hay and cotton struts,
        of street-pickings, wharves, weeds
        you carry in, my bird

                of a bone of a fish
                of a straw, or will
                of a color, of a bell
                of yourself, torn

5

love is not easy
but how shall you know,
New England, now
that pejorocracy is here, how
that street-cars, o Oregon, twitter
in the afternoon, offend
a black-gold loin?

        how shall you strike,
        o swordsman, the blue-red back
        when, last night, your aim
        was mu-sick, mu-sick, mu-sick
        And not the cribbage game?

(o Gloucester-man,
weave
your birds and fingers
new, your roof-tops,
clean shit upon racks
sunned on
American
braid
with others like you, such
extricable surface
as faun and oral,
satyr lesbos vase

o kill kill kill kill kill
those
who advertise you
out)

6

in! in! the bow-sprit, bird, the beak
in, the bend is, in, goes in, the form
that which you make, what holds, which is
the law of object, strut after strut, what you are, what you
        must be, what
the force can throw up, can, right now hereinafter erect,
the mast, the mast, the tender
mast!

The nest, I say, to you, I Maximus, say
under the hand, as I see it, over the waters
from this place where I am, where I hear,
can still hear

from where I carry you a feather
as though, sharp, I picked up,
in the afternoon delivered you
a jewel,
        it flashing more than a wing,
than any old romantic thing,
than memory, than place,
than anything other than that which you carry

than that which is,
call it a nest, around the head of, call it
the next second

than that which you
can do!

P. K. Page / 1916–

THE STENOGRAPHERS

After the brief bivouac of Sunday,
their eyes, in the forced march of Monday to Saturday,
hoist the white flag, flutter in the snow storm of paper,
haul it down and crack in the midsun of temper.

In the pause between the first draft and the carbon
they glimpse the smooth hours when they were children—
the ride in the ice-cart, the ice-man's name,
the end of the route and the long walk home;

remember the sea where floats at high tide
were sea marrows growing on the scatter-green vine
or spools of grey toffee, or wasps' nests on water;
remember the sand and the leaves of the country.

Bell rings and they go and the voice draws their pencil
like a sled across snow; when its runners are frozen
rope snaps and the voice then is pulling no burden
but runs like a dog on the winter of paper.

Their climates are winter and summer—no wind
for the kites of their hearts—no wind for a flight;
a breeze at the most, to tumble them over
and leave them like rubbish—the boy-friends of blood.

In the inch of the noon as they move they are stagnant.
The terrible calm of the noon is their anguish;
the lip of the counter, the shapes of the straws
like icicles breaking their tongues are invaders.

Their beds are their oceans—salt water of weeping
the waves that they know—the tide before sleep;
and fighting to drown they assemble their sheep
in columns and watch them leap desks for their fences
and stare at them with their own mirror-worn faces.

In the felt of the morning the calico minded,
sufficiently starched, insert papers, hit keys,
efficient and sure as their adding machines;
yet they weep in the vault, they are taut as net curtains
stretched upon frames. In their eyes I have seen
the pin men of madness in marathon trim
race round the track of the stadium pupil.

THE PERMANENT TOURISTS

Somnolent through landscapes and by trees
nondescript, almost anonymous,
they alter as they enter foreign cities—
the terrible tourists with their empty eyes
longing to be filled with monuments.

Verge upon statues in the public squares
remembering the promise of memorials
yet never enter the entire event
as dogs, abroad in any kind of weather,
move perfectly within their rainy climate.

Lock themselves into snapshots on the steps
of monolithic bronze as if suspecting
the subtle mourning of the photograph
might later, conjure in the memory
all they are now incapable of feeling.

And track all heroes down: the boy who gave
his life to save a town: the stolid queen;
forgotten politicians minus names;
the plunging war dead, permanently brave,
forever and ever going down to death.

Look, you can see them nude in any café
reading their histories from the bill of fare,
creating futures from a foreign teacup.
Philosophies like ferns bloom from the fable
that travel is broadening at the café table.

Yet, somehow beautiful, they stamp the plaza.
Classic in their anxiety they call
all the memorials of naked stone
into their passive eyes, as placid rivers
are always calling to the ruined columns.

Kenneth Patchen / 1911–

AT THE NEW YEAR

In the shape of this night, in the still fall of snow, Father
In all that is cold and tiny, these little birds and children
In everything that moves tonight, the trolleys and the
        lovers, Father
In the great hush of country, in the ugly noise of our cities
In this deep throw of stars, in those trenches where the
        dead are, Father
In all the wide land waiting, and in the liners out on the
        black water
In all that has been said bravely, in all that is mean
        anywhere in the world, Father
In all that is good and lovely, in every house where sham
        and hatred are

In the name of those who wait, in the sound of angry
    voices, Father
Before the bells ring, before this little point in time has
    rushed us on
Before this clean moment has gone, before this night turns
    to face tomorrow, Father
There is this high singing in the air
Forever this sorrowful human face in eternity's window
And there are other bells that we would ring, Father
Other bells that we would ring.

THE CONSTANT BRIDEGROOMS

Far down the purple wood
Coats of a company
Of silent soldiers
Flap idly in the wind.
There they have stood
Since early day—
Faces turned incuriously to the sound
Of the dry rustling
Of leaves in the wind.
No command has reached
Them there;
All silent have they stood
As
Though they were asleep—
Now night darkens their coats.
Far away
Their names are spoken

Somewhere at world's end

WHERE ?

There's a place the man always say
Come in here, child
No cause you should weep
Wolf never catch the rabbit
Golden hair never turn white with grief
Come in here, child
No cause you should moan
Brother never hurt his brother
Nobody here ever wander without a home
There must be some such place somewhere
But I never heard of it

ALL THE ROARY NIGHT

It's dark out, Jack
The stations out there don't identify themselves
We're in it raw-blind, like burned rats
It's running out
All around us
The footprints of the beast, one nobody has any notion of
The white and vacant eyes
Of something above there
Something that doesn't know we exist
I smell heartbreak up there, Jack
A heartbreak at the center of things—
And in which we don't figure at all

Sylvia Plath / 1932–1963

THE COLOSSUS

I shall never get you put together entirely,
Pieced, glued, and properly jointed.
Mule-bray, pig-grunt and bawdy cackles
Proceed from your great lips.
It's worse than a barnyard.

Perhaps you consider yourself an oracle,
Mouthpiece of the dead, or of some god or other.
Thirty years now I have laboured
To dredge the silt from your throat.
I am none the wiser.

Scaling little ladders with gluepots and pails of lysol
I crawl like an ant in mourning
Over the weedy acres of your brow
To mend the immense skull-plates and clear
The bald, white tumuli of your eyes.

A blue sky out of the Oresteia
Arches above us. O father, all by yourself
You are pithy and historical as the Roman Forum.
I open my lunch on a hill of black cypress.
Your fluted bones and acanthine hair are littered

In their old anarchy to the horizon-line.
It would take more than a lightning-stroke
To create such a ruin.
Nights, I squat in the cornucopia
Of your left ear, out of the wind,

Counting the red stars and those of plum-colour.
The sun rises under the pillar of your tongue.
My hours are married to shadow.

No longer do I listen for the scrape of a keel
On the blank stones of the landing.

BLACK ROOK IN RAINY WEATHER

On the stiff twig up there
Hunches a wet black rook
Arranging and rearranging its feathers in the rain.
I do not expect miracle
Or an accident

To set the sight on fire
In my eye, nor seek
Any more in the desultory weather some design,
But let spotted leaves fall as they fall,
Without ceremony, or portent.

Although, I admit, I desire,
Occasionally, some backtalk
From the mute sky, I can't honestly complain:
A certain minor light may still
Leap incandescent

Out of kitchen table or chair
As if a celestial burning took
Possession of the most obtuse objects now and then—
Thus hallowing an interval
Otherwise inconsequent

By bestowing largesse, honour,
One might say love. At any rate, I now walk
Wary (for it could happen
Even in this dull, ruinous landscape); sceptical,
Yet politic; ignorant

Of whatever angel may choose to flare
Suddenly at my elbow. I only know that a rook
Ordering its black feathers can so shine
As to seize my senses, haul
My eyelids up, and grant

A brief respite from fear
Of total neutrality. With luck,
Trekking stubborn through this season
Of fatigue, I shall
Patch together a content

Of sorts. Miracles occur,
If you care to call those spasmodic
Tricks of radiance miracles. The wait's begun again,
The long wait for the angel,
For that rare, random descent.

DADDY

You do not do, you do not do
Any more, black shoe
In which I have lived like a foot
For thirty years, poor and white,
Barely daring to breathe or Achoo.

Daddy, I have had to kill you.
You died before I had time——
Marble-heavy, a bag full of God,
Ghastly statue with one grey toe
Big as a Frisco seal

And a head in the freakish Atlantic
Where it pours bean green over blue
In the waters off beautiful Nauset.
I used to pray to recover you.
Ach, du.

In the German tongue, in the Polish town
Scraped flat by the roller
Of wars, wars, wars.
But the name of the town is common.
My Polack friend

Says there are a dozen or two.
So I never could tell where you

Put your foot, your root,
I never could talk to you.
The tongue stuck in my jaw.

It stuck in a barb wire snare.
Ich, ich, ich, ich,
I could hardly speak.
I thought every German was you.
And the language obscene

An engine, an engine
Chuffing me off like a Jew.
A Jew to Dachau, Auschwitz, Belsen.
I began to talk like a Jew.
I think I may well be a Jew.

The snows of the Tyrol, the clear beer of Vienna
Are not very pure or true.
With my gypsy ancestress and my weird luck
And my Taroc pack and my Taroc pack
I may be a bit of a Jew.

I have always been scared of *you*,
With your Luftwaffe, your gobbledygoo.
And your neat moustache
And your Aryan eye, bright blue.
Panzer-man, panzer-man, O You——

Not God but a swastika
So black no sky could squeak through.
Every woman adores a Fascist,
The boot in the face, the brute
Brute heart of a brute like you.

You stand at the blackboard, daddy,
In the picture I have of you,
A cleft in your chin instead of your foot
But no less a devil for that, no not
Any less the black man who

Bit my pretty red heart in two.
I was ten when they buried you.
At twenty I tried to die

And get back, back, back to you.
I thought even the bones would do.

But they pulled me out of the sack,
And they stuck me together with glue.
And then I knew what to do.
I made a model of you,
A man in black with a Meinkampf look

And a love of the rack and the screw.
And I said I do, I do.
So daddy, I'm finally through.
The black telephone's off at the root,
The voices just can't worm through.

If I've killed one man, I've killed two——
The vampire who said he was you
And drank my blood for a year,
Seven years, if you want to know.
Daddy, you can lie back now.

There's a stake in your fat black heart
And the villagers never liked you.
They are dancing and stamping on you.
They always *knew* it was you.
Daddy, daddy, you bastard, I'm through.

Hyam Plutzik / 1911–1962

THE MYTHOS OF
SAMUEL HUNTSMAN

If I should round the corner quickly—
Or suddenly turn my head—
I know I'd catch them preparing the scene,
Painting a tree or hanging the moon,
Arranging houses and streets exactly
In the desperate game which is God's.

For I have seen through their plausible lies—
That of a uniform world,
And cities existing beyond these hills,
Or on rain-wet pampas ferocious bulls,
A logic of morrows and yesterdays
Or real seeds under this field.

The surface is thin as a gilding of oil
Upon an enormous lake
Deep as infinity, void as a gas,
On which they plant the lying rose
To delude the sniffing child or the fool.
But me they cannot expect

To wink forever, never to turn
And look at their empty stage
Of space starless and planetless
Where they swarm to cover some nakedness,
A ravaged fruit tree perhaps, some sin
That calls to me to judge.

One question has to be wrestled down
Before I smash this façade:
Are they worlds, these other men, Thomas or Roger,
Like me, with their plague of conjurers
Or but lesser dolls in the scene of one
Who will deal alone with God?

THE KING OF AI

They hanged the King of Ai at eventide
On a high tree at the gates of the gutted city,

And the smoke rose out of the ruck of the city
Where the fierce captains shouted at eventide.

Now on the tree the rope was heavy at eventide
Where the gods lay broken under the ash of the city.

He turned once more toward the ravished city
And the head swung slow toward the eventide.

Ah, the smell of the blossoms at eventide
From the almond trees beyond the gates of the city:

But the tightened rope on the tree at the gates of the city
And the swaying shape in the air at eventide.

God, God, for the evil done at eventide,
For the bloody knife and the torch on the doomed city,

And the girls who screamed on the sand by the gates of the
     city,
With the strange seed within them at eventide—

O God be merciful at eventide:
Remember him you condemned by the flaming city,

Where he lies under his cairn at the gates of the city,
And the vultures circle the sky at eventide.

F. T. Prince / 1912–

SOLDIERS BATHING

The sea at evening moves across the sand.
Under a reddening sky I watch the freedom of a band
Of soldiers who belong to me. Stripped bare
For bathing in the sea, they shout and run in the warm air;
Their flesh worn by the trade of war, revives
And my mind towards the meaning of it strives.

All's pathos now. The body that was gross,
Rank, ravenous, disgusting in the act or in repose,

All fever, filth and sweat, its bestial strength
And bestial decay, by pain and labour grows at length
Fragile and luminous. 'Poor bare forked animal,'
Conscious of his desires and needs and flesh that rise and
    fall,
Stands in the soft air, tasting after toil
The sweetness of his nakedness: letting the sea-waves coil
Their frothy tongues about his feet, forgets
His hatred of the war, its terrible pressure that begets
A machinery of death and slavery,
Each being a slave and making slaves of others: finds that
    he
Remembers his old freedom in a game
Mocking himself, and comically mimics fear and shame.

He plays with death and animality;
And reading in the shadows of his pallid flesh, I see
The idea of Michelangelo's cartoon
Of soldiers bathing, breaking off before they were half
    done
At some sortie of the enemy, an episode
Of the Pisan wars with Florence. I remember how he showed
Their muscular limbs that clamber from the water,
And heads that turn across the shoulder, eager for the
    slaughter,
Forgetful of their bodies that are bare,
And hot to buckle on and use the weapons lying there.
—And I think too of the theme another found
When, shadowing men's bodies on a sinister red ground,
Another Florentine, Pollaiuolo,
Painted a naked battle: warriors, straddled, hacked the foe,
Dug their bare toes into the ground and slew
The brother-naked man who lay between their feet and
    drew
His lips back from his teeth in a grimace.

They were Italians who knew war's sorrow and disgrace
And showed the thing suspended, stripped: a theme
Born out of the experience of war's horrible extreme
Beneath a sky where even the air flows
With lacrimae Christi. For that rage, that bitterness, those
    blows,

That hatred of the slain, what could they be
But indirectly or directly a commentary
On the Crucifixion? And the picture burns
With indignation and pity and despair by turns,
Because it is the obverse of the scene
Where Christ hangs murdered, stripped, upon the Cross.
    I mean,
That is the explanation of its rage.

And we too have our bitterness and pity that engage
Blood, spirit, in this war. But night begins,
Night of the mind: who nowadays is conscious of our sins?
Though every human deed concerns our blood,
And even we must know, what nobody has understood,
That some great love is over all we do,
And that is what has driven us to this fury, for so few
Can suffer all the terror of that love:
The terror of that love has set us spinning in this groove
Greased with our blood.

                  These dry themselves and dress,
Combing their hair, forget the fear and shame of nakedness.
Because to love is frightening we prefer
The freedom of our crimes. Yet, as I drink the dusky air,
I feel a strange delight that fills me full,
Strange gratitude, as if evil itself were beautiful,
And kiss the wound in thought, while in the west
I watch a streak of red that might have issued from Christ's
    breast.

TO A FRIEND ON HIS MARRIAGE

A beautiful girl said something in your praise.
And either because in a hundred ways
I had heard of her great worth and had no doubt
To find her lovelier than I thought
And found her also cleverer, or because
Although she had known you well it was
For her too as it had once been for me

Thinking of her: I thought that she
Had spoken of you as rare and legendary.
Now again, hearing that you marry,
My insatiable sense of glory and
My passion for the gay and grand
Deliver you up to fiction. A beautiful
Girl might once have played the fool
If you had called the tune, and I would too,
If anything that I might do
Could ruffle up your rose or flush your glass.
Because you are all things, and because
You show the world the glitter in the face
Of that all-but-extinguished race
Of creatures who delight in and desire
Much less the fuel than the fire;
I wish that when you call for supper, when
You sit down, guests and serving-men
May seem light-bearers planted on the stair,
Lights in the roof, lights everywhere:
So that as if you were a salamander,
Your sensuality may wander
In a community of flames, and breathe
Contentment, savouring wine and wreath.

Henry Reed / 1914–

NAMING OF PARTS

To-day we have naming of parts. Yesterday,
We had daily cleaning. And to-morrow morning,
We shall have to do after firing. But to-day,
To-day we have naming of parts. Japonica
Glistens like coral in all of the neighbouring gardens,
    And to-day we have naming of parts.

This is the lower sling swivel. And this
Is the upper sling swivel, whose use you will see,
When you are given your slings. And this is the piling swivel,
Which in your case you have not got. The branches
Hold in the gardens their silent, eloquent gestures,
     Which in our case we have not got.

This is the safety-catch, which is always released
With an easy flick of the thumb. And please do not let me
See anyone using his finger. You can do it quite easy
If you have any strength in your thumb. The blossoms
Are fragile and motionless, never letting anyone see
     Any of them using their finger.

And this you can see is the bolt. The purpose of this
Is to open the breech, as you see. We can slide it
Rapidly backwards and forwards: we call this
Easing the spring. And rapidly backwards and forwards
The early bees are assaulting and fumbling the flowers:
     They call it easing the Spring.

They call it easing the Spring: it is perfectly easy
If you have any strength in your thumb: like the bolt,
And the breech, and the cocking-piece, and the point of
     balance,
Which in our case we have not got; and the almond-blossom
Silent in all of the gardens and the bees going backwards
     and forwards,
     For to-day we have naming of parts.

CHARD WHITLOW

Mr. Eliot's Sunday Evening Postscript

As we get older we do not get any younger.
Seasons return, and to-day I am fifty-five,
And this time last year I was fifty-four,
And this time next year I shall be sixty-two.
And I cannot say I should care (to speak for myself)

To see my time over again – if you can call it time,
Fidgeting uneasily under a draughty stair,
Or counting sleepless nights in the crowded Tube.

There are certain precautions – though none of them very
         reliable –
Against the blast from bombs, or the flying splinter,
But not against the blast from Heaven, *vento dei venti*,
The wind within a wind, unable to speak for wind;
And the frigid burnings of purgatory will not be touched
By any emollient.
                    I think you will find this put,
Far better than I could ever hope to express it,
In the words of Kharma: 'It is, we believe,
Idle to hope that the simple stirrup-pump
Can extinguish hell.'

                    Oh, listeners,
And you especially who have switched off the wireless,
And sit in Stoke or Basingstoke, listening appreciatively to
         the silence
(Which is also the silence of hell), pray not for yourselves
         but your souls.

And pray for me also under the draughty stair.
As we get older we do not get any younger.

And pray for Kharma under the holy mountain.

Kenneth Rexroth / 1905–

A LIVING PEARL

At sixteen I came West, riding
Freights on the Chicago, Milwaukee
And St. Paul, the Great Northern,
The Northern Pacific. I got

A job as helper to a man
Who gathered wild horses in the
Mass drives in the Okanogan
And Horse Heaven country. The best
We culled out as part profit from
The drive, the rest went for chicken
And dog feed. We took thirty head
Up the Methow, up the Twisp,
Across the headwaters of Lake
Chelan, down the Skagit to
The Puget Sound country. I
Did the cooking and camp work.
In a couple of weeks I
Could handle the stock pretty well.
Every day we saddled and rode
A new horse. Next day we put a
Packsaddle on him. By the
Time we reached Marblemount
We considered them well broken.
The scissorbills who bought them
Considered them untamed mustangs
Of the desert. In a few weeks
They were peacefully pulling
Milk wagons in Sedro-Wooley.
We made three trips a season
And did well enough for the
Postwar depression.
Tonight,
Thirty years later, I walk
Out of the deserted miner's
Cabin in Mono Pass, under
The full moon and the few large stars.
The sidehills are piebald with snow.
The midnight air is suffused
With moonlight. As Dante says,
"It is as though a cloud enclosed
Me, lucid, dense, solid, polished,
Like a diamond forged by the sun.
We entered the eternal pearl,
Which took us as water takes
A ray of light, itself uncleft."
Fifteen years ago, in this place,

I wrote a poem called "Toward
An Organic Philosophy."
Everything is still the same,
And it differs very little
From the first mountain pass I
Crossed so long ago with the
Pintos and zebra duns and
Gunmetal roans and buckskins
And spattered lallapaloosas,
The stocky wild ponies whose
Ancestors came with Coronado.
There are no horse bells tonight,
Only the singing of frogs
In the snow wet meadows, the shrill
Single bark of a mountain
Fox, high in the rocks where the
Wild sheep move silently through the
Crystal moonlight. The same feelings
Come back. Once more all the awe
Of a boy from the prairies where
Lanterns move through the comfortable
Dark, along a fence, through a field,
Home; all the thrill of youth
Suddenly come from the flat
Geometrical streets of
Chicago, into the illimitable
And inhuman waste places
Of the Far West, where the mind finds
Again the forms Pythagoras
Sought, the organic relations
Of stone and cloud and flower
And moving planet and falling
Water. Marthe and Mary sleep
In their down bags, cocoons of
Mutual love. Half my life has
Been passed in the West, much of it
On the ground beside lonely fires
Under the summer stars, and in
Cabins where the snow drifted through
The pines and over the roof.
I will not camp here as often

As I have before. Thirty years
Will never come for me again.
"Our campfire dies out in the
Lonely mountains. The transparent
Moonlight stretches a thousand miles.
The clear peace is without end."
My daughter's deep blue eyes sleep
In the moon shadow. Next week
She will be one year old.

Adrienne Rich / 1929–

AFTER DARK

I

You are falling asleep and I sit looking at you
old tree of life
old man whose death I wanted
I can't stir you up now.

Faintly a phonograph needle
whirs round in the last groove
eating my heart to dust.
That terrible record! how it played

down years, wherever I was
in foreign languages even
over and over, *I know you better
than you know yourself   I know*

*you better than you know
yourself   I know
you*   until, self-maimed,
I limped off, torn at the roots,

stopped singing for a whole year,
got a new body, new breath,

got children, croaked for words,
forgot to listen

or read your *mene tekel* fading on the wall,
woke up one morning
and knew myself your daughter.
Blood is a sacred poison.

Now, unasked, you give ground.
We only want to stifle
what's stifling us already.
Alive now, root to crown, I'd give

—oh,—something—not to know
our struggles now are ended.
I seem to hold you, cupped
in my hands, and disappearing.

When your memory fails—
no more to scourge my inconsistencies—
the sashcords of the world fly loose.
A window crashes

suddenly down. I go to the woodbox
and take a stick of kindling
to prop the sash again.
I grow protective toward the world.

II

Now let's away from prison—
Underground seizures!
I used to huddle in the grave
I'd dug for you and bite

my tongue for fear it would babble
—Darling—
I thought they'd find me there
someday, sitting upright, shrunken,

my hair like roots and in my lap
a mess of broken pottery—
wasted libation—
and you embalmed beside me.

No, let's away. Even now
there's a walk between doomed elms
(whose like we shall not see much longer)
and something—grass and water—

and old dream-photograph.
I'll sit with you there and tease you
for wisdom, if you like,
waiting till the blunt barge

bumps along the shore.
Poppies burn in the twilight
like smudge pots.
I think you hardly see me

but—this is the dream now—
your fears blow out,
off, over the water.
At the last, your hand feels steady.

FACE TO FACE

Never to be lonely like that—
the Early American figure on the beach
in black coat and knee-breeches
scanning the didactic storm in privacy,

never to hear the prairie wolves
in their lunar hilarity
circling one's little all, one's claim
to be Law and Prophets

for all that lawlessness,
never to whet the appetite
weeks early, for a face, a hand
longed-for and dreaded—

How people used to meet!
starved, intense, the old
Christmas gifts saved up till spring,
and the old plain words,

and each with his God-given secret,
spelled out through months of snow and silence,
burning under the bleached scalp; behind dry lips
a loaded gun.

Anne Ridler / 1912–

FOR A CHILD EXPECTED

Lovers whose lifted hands are candles in winter,
Whose gentle ways like streams in the easy summer,
Lying together
For secret setting of a child, love what they do,
Thinking they make that candle immortal, those streams
        forever flow,
And yet do better than they know.

So the first flutter of a baby felt in the womb,
Its little signal and promise of riches to come,
Is taken in its father's name;
Its life is the body of his love, like his caress,
First delicate and strange, that daily use
Makes dearer and priceless.

Our baby was to be the living sign of our joy,
Restore to each the other's lost infancy;
To a painter's pillaging eye
Poet's coiled hearing, add the heart we might earn
By the help of love; all that our passion would yield
We put to planning our child.

The world flowed in; whatever we liked we took:
For its hair, the gold curls of the November oak
We saw on our walk;
Snowberries that make a Milky Way in the wood
For its tender hands; calm screen of the frozen flood
For our care of its childhood.

But the birth of a child is an uncontrollable glory;
Cat's cradle of hopes will hold no living baby,
Long though it lay quietly.
And when our baby stirs and struggles to be born
It compels humility: what we began
Is now its own.

For *as the sun that shines through glass*
So Jesus in His Mother was.
Therefore every human creature,
Since it shares in His nature,
In candle-gold passion or white
Sharp star should show its own way of light.
May no parental dread or dream
Darken our darling's early beam:
May she grow to her right powers
Unperturbed by passion of ours.

Muriel Rukeyser / 1913–

BOY WITH HIS HAIR CUT SHORT

Sunday shuts down on this twentieth-century evening.
The El passes. Twilight and bulb define
the brown room, the overstuffed plum sofa,
the boy, and the girl's thin hands above his head.
A neighbor radio sings stocks, news, serenade.

He sits at the table, head down, the young clear neck
        exposed,
watching the drugstore sign from the tail of his eye;
tattoo, neon, until the eye blears, while his
solicitous tall sister, simple in blue, bending
behind him, cuts his hair with her cheap shears.

The arrow's electric red always reaches its mark,
successful neon! He coughs, impressed by that precision.
His child's forehead, forever protected by his cap,
is bleached against the lamplight as he turns head
and steadies to let the snippets drop.

Erasing the failure of weeks with level fingers,
she sleeks the fine hair, combing: "You'll look fine
          tomorrow!
You'll surely find something, they can't keep turning you
          down;
the finest gentleman's not so trim as you!" Smiling, he raises
the adolescent forehead wrinkling ironic now.

He sees his decent suit laid out, new-pressed,
his carfare on the shelf. He lets his head fall, meeting
her earnest hopeless look, seeing the sharp blades splitting,
the darkened room, the impersonal sign, her motion,
the blue vein, bright on her temple, pitifully beating.

AJANTA

I. THE JOURNEY

Came in my full youth to the midnight cave
Nerves ringing; and this thing I did alone.
Wanting my fulness and not a field of war,
For the world considered annihilation, a star
Called Wormwood rose and flickered, shattering
Bent light over the dead boiling up in the ground,
The biting yellow of their corrupted lives
Streaming to war, denying all our words.
Nothing was left among the tainted weather
But world-walking and shadowless Ajanta.
Hallucination and the metal laugh
In clouds, and the mountain-spectre riding storm.
Nothing was certain but a moment of peace,
A hollow behind the unbreakable waterfall.
All the way to the cave, the teeming forms of death,

And death, the price of the body, cheap as air.
I blessed my heart on the expiation journey
For it had never been unable to suffer:
When I met the man whose face looked like the future,
When I met the whore with the dying red hair,
The child myself who is my murderer.
So came I between heaven and my grave
Past the serene smile of the *voyeur*, to
This cave where the myth enters the heart again.

II. THE CAVE

Space to the mind, the painted cave of dream.
This is not a womb, nothing but good emerges:
This is a stage, neither unreal nor real,
Where the walls are the world, the rocks and palaces
Stand on a borderland of blossoming ground.
If you stretch your hand, you touch the slope of the world
Reaching in interlaced gods, animals, and men.
There is no background.   The figures hold their peace
In a web of movement.   There is no frustration,
Every gesture is taken, everything yields connections.
The heavy sensual shoulders, the thighs, the blood-born
        flesh
And earth turning into color, rocks into their crystals,
Water to sound, fire to form; life flickers
Uncounted into the supple arms of love.
The space of these walls is the body's living space;
Tear open your ribs and breathe the color of time
Where nothing leads away, the world comes forward
In flaming sequences.   Pillars and prisms.   Riders
And horses and the figures of consciousness,
Red cow grows long, goes running through the world.
Flung into movement in carnal purity,
These bodies are sealed—warm lip and crystal hand
In a jungle of light.   Color-sheeted, seductive
Foreboding eyelid lowered on the long eye,
Fluid and vulnerable.   The spaces of the body
Are suddenly limitless, and riding flesh
Shapes constellations over the golden breast,
Confusion of scents and illuminated touch—
Monster touch, the throat printed with brightness,

Wide outlined gesture where the bodies ride.
Bells, and the spirit flashing.   The religious bells,
Bronze under the sunlight like breasts ringing,
Bronze in the closed air, the memory of walls,
Great sensual shoulders in the web of time.

III. LES TENDRESSES BESTIALES

A procession of caresses alters the ancient sky
Until new constellations are the body shining:
There's the Hand to steer by, there the horizon Breast,
And the Great Stars kindling the fluid hill.
All the rooms open into magical boxes,
Nothing is tilted, everything flickers
Sexual and exquisite.
The panther with its throat along my arm
Turns black and flows away.
Deep in all streets passes a faceless whore
And the checkered men are whispering one word.
The face I know becomes the night-black rose.
The sharp face is now an electric fan
And says one word to me.
The dice and the alcohol and the destruction
Have drunk themselves and cast.
Broken bottle of loss, and the glass
Turned bloody into the face.
Now the scene comes forward, very clear.
Dream-singing, airborne, surrenders the recalled,
The gesture arrives riding over the breast,
Singing, singing, tender atrocity,
The silver derelict wearing fur and claws.
O love, I stood under the apple branch,
I saw the whipped bay and the small dark islands,
And night sailing the river and the foghorn's word.
My life said to you: I want to love you well.
The wheel goes back and I shall live again,
But the wave turns, my birth arrives and spills
Over my breast the world bearing my grave,
And your eyes open in earth.   You touched my life.
My life reaches the skin, moves under your smile,
And your throat and your shoulders and your face and
    your thighs

Flash.
       I am haunted by interrupted acts,
Introspective as a leper, enchanted
By a repulsive clew,
A gross and fugitive movement of the limbs.
Is this the love that shook the lights to flame?
Sheeted avenues thrash in the wind,
Torn streets, the savage parks.
I am plunged deep.   Must find the midnight cave.

IV. BLACK BLOOD

A habit leading to murder, smoky laughter
Hated at first, but necessary later.
Alteration of motives.   To stamp in terror
Around the deserted harbor, down the hill
Until the woman laced into a harp
Screams and screams and the great clock strikes,
Swinging its giant figures past the face.
The Floating Man rides on the ragged sunset
Asking and asking.   Do not say, Which loved?
Which was beloved? Only, Who most enjoyed?
Armored ghost of rage, screaming and powerless.
Only find me and touch my blood again.
Find me.   A girl runs down the street
Singing Take me, yelling Take me Take
Hang me from the clapper of a bell
And you as hangman ring it sweet tonight,
For nothing clean in me is more than cloud
Unless you call it.   —As I ran I heard
A black voice beating among all that blood:
"Try to live as if there were a God."

V. THE BROKEN WORLD

Came to Ajanta cave, the painted space of the breast,
The real world where everything is complete,
There are no shadows, the forms of incompleteness.
The great cloak blows in the light, rider and horse arrive,
The shoulders turn and every gift is made.
No shadows fall.   There is no source of distortion.
In our world, a tree casts the shadow of a woman,
A man the shadow of a phallus, a hand raised

The shadow of a whip.
Here everything is itself,
Here all may stand
On summer earth.
Brightness has overtaken every light,
And every myth netted itself in flesh.
New origins, and peace given entire
And the spirit alive.
In the shadowless cave
The naked arm is raised.
Animals arrive,
Interlaced, and gods
Interlaced, and men
Flame-woven.
I stand and am complete.
Crawls from the door,
Black at my two feet
The shadow of the world.

World, not yet one,
Enters the heart again.
The naked world, and the old noise of tears,
The fear, the expiation and the love,
A world of the shadowed and alone.

The journey, and the struggles of the moon.

W. T. Scott / 1910–1968

SWEDISH ANGEL

The Swedish angel is nine inches high and shaped all of
    blond straw.
All of blond straw is her little body and her great
    seven-inch wings.

Her small head is of painted wood and she stands in a slim
    wood base.
Shining and shining in the Christmas candles, shines her
    golden halo.

Even all round her is a kind of shining, circle on circle,
    because
She has—as if—lighted upon a round lake of clear glass
Surrounded by ground-pine and red berries which gleam
    also
In the candlelight that moves on her stilled blond wings.

In this immaculate doll of heaven has been conceived, as
    though
No hands had shaped her, an uninvented innocence
    bequeathing grace
Ring upon ring in halos all around her, and not remote nor
    kind
But only there, dispensing of all the brought light a total
    larger light.

Even now her wings have assumed such shields of glory
    and the pool beneath
Wheels with such wreaths of shining, the room is gathered
    and filled
By her tall and burning stillness and, an actual angel, her
    suspension wars
For a whole minute against all the dark, as if I were a child.

ANNUAL LEGEND

A million butterflies rose up from South America,
All together, and flew in a gold storm toward Spain:
Eastward, the annual legend, a shining amber cloud
Driven homeward as it had been and would be again
Since the conquerors searching the harder shining
Brought for the bargain a handful of wings of flame.

Balboa lies dead somewhere and Pizarro's helmet
Is a spider's kingdom; yet here was the arrogant breath
And the dangerous plume burning across the foreign air
That danced like an ancient Andalusian noon:
A blaze, it rose leaving the jungle dark and the leaves
Heavy with silence, and the wheeltracks folding to doom
Where majesty wandered:

> A million butterflies,
Wheeling eastward from the soil where the nugget lies lost,
Turned homeward in vast diurnal fire that marched one
    day
Burning toward Spain; and after that, for a while,
Spread like a field of death, gold on the sea.

THE U.S. SAILOR WITH THE
JAPANESE SKULL

Bald-bare, bone-bare, and ivory yellow: skull
Carried by a thus two-headed U.S. sailor
Who got it from a Japanese soldier killed
At Guadalcanal in the ever-present war: our

Bluejacket, I mean, aged 20, in August strolled
Among the little bodies on the sand and hunted
Souvenirs: teeth, tags, diaries, boots; but bolder still
Hacked off this head and under a Ginkgo tree skinned it:

Peeled with a lifting knife the jaw and cheeks, bared
The nose, ripped off the black-haired scalp and gutted
The dead eyes to these thoughtful hollows: a scarred
But bloodless job, unless it be said brains bleed.

Then, his ship underway, dragged this aft in a net
Many days and nights—the cold bone tumbling
Beneath the foaming wake, weed-worn and salt-cut
Rolling safe among fish and washed with Pacific;

Till on a warm and level-keeled day hauled in
Held to the sun and the sailor, back to a gun-rest,
Scrubbed the cured skull with lye, perfecting this:
Not foreign as he saw it first: death's familiar cast.

Bodiless, fleshless, nameless, it and the sun
Offend each other in strange fascination
As though one of the two were mocked; but nothing is in
This head, or it fills with what another imagines

As: here were love and hate and the will to deal
Death or to kneel before it, death emperor,
Recorded orders without reasons, bomb-blast, still
A child's morning, remembered moonlight on Fujiyama:

All scoured out now by the keeper of this skull
Made elemental, historic, parentless by our
Sailor boy who thinks of home, voyages laden, will
Not say, "Alas! I did not know him at all."

Anne Sexton / 1928–

HER KIND

I have gone out, a possessed witch,
haunting the black air, braver at night;
dreaming evil, I have done my hitch
over the plain houses, light by light:
lonely thing, twelve-fingered, out of mind.
A woman like that is not a woman, quite.
I have been her kind.

I have found the warm caves in the woods,
filled them with skillets, carvings, shelves,
closets, silks, innumerable goods;
fixed the suppers for the worms and the elves:

whining, rearranging the disaligned.
A woman like that is misunderstood.
I have been her kind.

I have ridden in your cart, driver,
waved my nude arms at villages going by,
learning the last bright routes, survivor
where your flames still bite my thigh
and my ribs crack where your wheels wind.
A woman like that is not ashamed to die.
I have been her kind.

THE FORTRESS

while taking a nap with Linda

Under the pink quilted covers
I hold the pulse that counts your blood.
I think the woods outdoors
are half asleep,
left over from summer
like a stack of books after a flood,
left over like those promises I never keep.
On the right, the scrub pine tree
waits like a fruit store
holding up bunches of tufted broccoli.

We watch the wind from our square bed.
I press down my index finger—
half in jest, half in dread—
on the brown mole
under your left eye, inherited
from my right cheek: a spot of danger
where a bewitched worm ate its way through our soul
in search of beauty. My child, since July
the leaves have been fed
secretly from a pool of beet-red dye.

And sometimes they are battle green
with trunks as wet as hunters' boots,

smacked hard by the wind, clean
as oilskins. No,
the wind's not off the ocean.
Yes, it cried in your room like a wolf
and your pony tail hurt you. That was a long time ago.
The wind rolled the tide like a dying
woman. She wouldn't sleep,
she rolled there all night, grunting and sighing.

Darling, life is not in my hands;
life with its terrible changes
will take you, bombs or glands,
your own child at
your breast, your own house on your own land.
Outside the bittersweet turns orange.
Before she died, my mother and I picked those fat
branches, finding orange nipples
on the gray wire strands.
We weeded the forest, curing trees like cripples.

Your feet thump-thump against my back
and you whisper to yourself. Child,
what are you wishing? What pact
are you making?
What mouse runs between your eyes? What ark
can I fill for you when the world goes wild?
The woods are underwater, their weeds are shaking
in the tide; birches like zebra fish
flash by in a pack.
Child, I cannot promise that you will get your wish.

I cannot promise very much.
I give you the images I know.
Lie still with me and watch.
A pheasant moves
by like a seal, pulled through the mulch
by his thick white collar. He's on show
like a clown. He drags a beige feather that he removed,
one time, from an old lady's hat.
We laugh and we touch.
I promise you love. Time will not take away that.

THE FARMER'S WIFE

From the hodge porridge
of their country lust,
their local life in Illinois,
where all their acres look
like a sprouting broom factory,
they name just ten years now
that she has been his habit;
as again tonight he'll say
honey bunch let's go
and she will not say how there
must be more to living
than this brief bright bridge
of the raucous bed or even
the slow braille touch of him
like a heavy god grown light,
that old pantomime of love
that she wants although
it leaves her still alone,
built back again at last,
mind's apart from him, living
her own self in her own words
and hating the sweat of the house
they keep when they finally lie
each in separate dreams
and then how she watches him,
still strong in the blowzy bag
of his usual sleep while
her young years bungle past
their same marriage bed
and she wishes him cripple, or poet,
or even lonely, or sometimes,
better, my lover, dead.

Louis Simpson / 1923–

TO THE WESTERN WORLD

A siren sang, and Europe turned away
From the high castle and the shepherd's crook.
Three caravels went sailing to Cathay
On the strange ocean, and the captains shook
Their banners out across the Mexique Bay.

And in our early days we did the same.
Remembering our fathers in their wreck
We crossed the sea from Palos where they came
And saw, enormous to the little deck,
A shore in silence waiting for a name.

The treasures of Cathay were never found.
In this America, this wilderness
Where the axe echoes with a lonely sound,
The generations labor to possess
And grave by grave we civilize the ground.

WALT WHITMAN AT BEAR MOUNTAIN

". . . life which does not give the preference to any other life, of any previous period, which therefore prefers its own existence . . ."
                                                                ORTEGA Y GASSET

Neither on horseback nor seated,
But like himself, squarely on two feet,
The poet of death and lilacs
Loafs by the footpath. Even the bronze looks alive
Where it is folded like cloth. And he seems friendly.

"Where is the Mississippi panorama
And the girl who played the piano?
Where are you, Walt?
The Open Road goes to the used-car lot.

"Where is the nation you promised?
These houses built of wood sustain
Colossal snows,
And the light above the street is sick to death.

"As for the people—see how they neglect you!
Only a poet pauses to read the inscription."

"I am here," he answered.
"It seems you have found me out.
Yet, did I not warn you that it was Myself
I advertised? Were my words not sufficiently plain?

"I gave no prescriptions,
And those who have taken my moods for prophecies
Mistake the matter."
Then, vastly amused—"Why do you reproach me?
I freely confess I am wholly disreputable.
Yet I am happy, because you have found me out."

A crocodile in wrinkled metal loafing . . .
Then all the realtors,
Pickpockets, salesmen, and the actors performing
Official scenarios,
Turned a deaf ear, for they had contracted
American dreams.

But the man who keeps a store on a lonely road,
And the housewife who knows she's dumb,
And the earth, are relieved.

All that grave weight of America
Cancelled! Like Greece and Rome.
The future in ruins!
The castles, the prisons, the cathedrals
Unbuilding, and roses
Blossoming from the stones that are not there . . .

The clouds are lifting from the high Sierras,
The Bay mists clearing.
And the angel in the gate, the flowering plum,
Dances like Italy, imagining red.

W. D. Snodgrass / 1926–

APRIL INVENTORY

The green catalpa tree has turned
All white; the cherry blooms once more.
In one whole year I haven't learned
A blessed thing they pay you for.
The blossoms snow down in my hair;
The trees and I will soon be bare.

The trees have more than I to spare.
The sleek, expensive girls I teach,
Younger and pinker every year,
Bloom gradually out of reach.
The pear tree lets its petals drop
Like dandruff on a tabletop.

The girls have grown so young by now
I have to nudge myself to stare.
This year they smile and mind me how
My teeth are falling with my hair.
In thirty years I may not get
Younger, shrewder, or out of debt.

The tenth time, just a year ago,
I made myself a little list
Of all the things I'd ought to know,
Then told my parents, analyst,
And everyone who's trusted me
I'd be substantial, presently.

I haven't read one book about
A book or memorized one plot.
Or found a mind I did not doubt.
I learned one date. And then forgot.
And one by one the solid scholars
Get the degrees, the jobs, the dollars.

And smile above their starchy collars.
I taught my classes Whitehead's notions;
One lovely girl, a song of Mahler's.
Lacking a source-book or promotions,
I showed one child the colors of
A luna moth and how to love.

I taught myself to name my name,
To bark back, loosen love and crying;
To ease my woman so she came,
To ease an old man who was dying.
I have not learned how often I
Can win, can love, but choose to die.

I have not learned there is a lie
Love shall be blonder, slimmer, younger;
That my equivocating eye
Loves only by my body's hunger;
That I have forces, true to feel,
Or that the lovely world is real.

While scholars speak authority
And wear their ulcers on their sleeves,
My eyes in spectacles shall see
These trees procure and spend their leaves.
There is a value underneath
The gold and silver in my teeth.

Though trees turn bare and girls turn wives,
We shall afford our costly seasons;
There is a gentleness survives
That will outspeak and has its reasons.
There is a loveliness exists,
Preserves us, not for specialists.

THE CAMPUS ON THE HILL

Up the reputable walks of old established trees
They stalk, children of the *nouveaux riches;* chimes
Of the tall Clock Tower drench their heads in blessing:
'I don't wanna play at your house;
I don't like you any more.'
My house stands opposite, on the other hill,
Among meadows, with the orchard fences down and falling;
Deer come almost to the door.
You cannot see it, even in this clearest morning.
White birds hang in the air between
Over the garbage landfill and those homes thereto adjacent,
Hovering slowly, turning, settling down
Like the flakes sifting imperceptibly onto the little town
In a waterball of glass.
And yet, this morning, beyond this quiet scene,
The floating birds, the backyards of the poor,
Beyond the shopping plaza, the dead canal, the hillside
        lying tilted in the air,
Tomorrow has broken out today:
Riot in Algeria, in Cyprus, in Alabama;
Aged in wrong, the empires are declining,
And China gathers, soundlessly, like evidence.
What shall I say to the young on such a morning?—
Mind is the one salvation?—also grammar?—
No; my little ones lean not toward revolt. They
Are the Whites, the vaguely furiously driven, who resist
Their souls with such passivity
As would make Quakers swear. All day, dear Lord, all day
They wear their godhead lightly.
They look out from their hill and say,
To themselves, 'We have nowhere to go but down;
The great destination is to stay.'
Surely the nations will be reasonable;
They look at the world—don't they?—the world's way?
The clock just now has nothing more to say.

A FLAT ONE

Old Fritz, on this rotating bed
For seven wasted months you lay
Unfit to move, shrunken, gray,
No good to yourself or anyone
But to be babied—changed and bathed and fed.
        At long last, that's all done.

Before each meal, twice every night,
We set pads on your bedsores, shut
Your catheter tube off, then brought
The second canvas-and-black-iron
Bedframe and clamped you in between them, tight,
        Scared, so we could turn

You over. We washed you, covered you,
Cut up each bite of meat you ate;
We watched your lean jaws masticate
As ravenously your useless food
As thieves at hard labor in their chains chew
        Or insects in the wood.

Such pious sacrifice to give
You all you could demand of pain:
Receive this haddock's body, slain
For you, old tyrant; take this blood
Of a tomato, shed that you might live.
        You had that costly food.

You seem to be all finished, so
We'll plug your old recalcitrant anus
And tie up your discouraged penis
In a great, snow-white bow of gauze.
We wrap you, pin you, and cart you down below,
        Below, below, because

Your credit has finally run out.
On our steel table, trussed and carved,

You'll find this world's hardworking, starved
Teeth working in your precious skin.
The earth turns, in the end, by turn about
     And opens to take you in.

Seven months gone down the drain; thank God
That's through. Throw out the four-by-fours,
Swabsticks, the thick salve for bedsores,
Throw out the diaper pads and drug
Containers, pile the bedclothes in a wad,
     And rinse the cider jug

Half-filled with the last urine. Then
Empty out the cotton cans,
Autoclave the bowls and spit pans,
Unhook the pumps and all the red
Tubes—catheter, suction, oxygen;
     Next, wash the empty bed.

—All this Dark Age machinery
On which we had tormented you
To life. Last, we collect the few
Belongings: snapshots, some odd bills,
Your mail, and half a pack of Luckies we
     Won't light you after meals.

Old man, these seven months you've lain
Determined—not that you would live—
Just to not die. No one would give
You one chance you could ever wake
From that first night, much less go well again,
     Much less go home and make

Your living; how could you hope to find
A place for yourself in all creation?—
Pain was your only occupation.
And pain that should content and will
A man to give it up, nerved you to grind
     Your clenched teeth, breathing, till

Your skin broke down, your calves went flat
And your legs lost all sensation. Still,

You took enough morphine to kill
A strong man. Finally, nitrogen
Mustard: you could last two months after that;
      It would kill you then.

Even then you wouldn't quit.
Old soldier, yet you must have known
Inside the animal had grown
Sick of the world, made up its mind
To stop. Your mind ground on its separate
      Way, merciless and blind,

Into these last weeks when the breath
Would only come in fits and starts
That puffed out your sections like the parts
Of some enormous, damaged bug.
You waited, not for life, not for your death,
      Just for the deadening drug

That made your life seem bearable.
You still whispered you would not die.
Yet in the nights I heard you cry
Like a whipped child; in fierce old age
You whimpered, tears stood on your gun-metal
      Blue cheeks shaking with rage

And terror. So much pain would fill
Your room that when I left I'd pray
That if I came back the next day
I'd find you gone. You stayed for me—
Nailed to your own rapacious, stiff self-will.
      You've shook loose, finally.

They'd say this was a worthwhile job
Unless they tried it. It is mad
To throw our good lives after bad;
Waste time, drugs, and our minds, while strong
Men starve. How many young men did we rob
      To keep you hanging on?

I can't think we did *you* much good.
Well, when you died, none of us wept.

You killed for us, and so we kept
You, because we need to earn our pay.
No. We'd still have to help you try. We would
    Have killed for you today.

William Stafford / 1914–

AT COVE ON THE CROOKED RIVER

At Cove at our camp in the open canyon
it was the kind of place where you might look out
some evening and see trouble walking away.

And the river there meant something
always coming from snow and flashing around boulders
after shadow-fish lurking below the mesa.

We stood with wet towels over our heads for shade,
looking past the Indian picture rock and the kind of trees
that act out whatever has happened to them.

Oh civilization, I want to carve you like this,
decisively outward the way evening comes
over that kind of twist in the scenery

When people cramp into their station wagons
and roll up the windows, and drive away.

WEST OF YOUR CITY

West of your city into the fern
sympathy, sympathy rolls the train

all through the night on a lateral line
where the shape of game fish tapers down
from a reach where cougar paws touch water.

Corn that the starving Indians held
all through moons of cold for seed
and then they lost in stony ground
the gods told them to plant it in—
west of your city that corn still lies.

Cocked in that land tactile as leaves
wild things wait crouched in those valleys
west of your city outside your lives
in the ultimate wind, the whole land's wave.
Come west and see; touch these leaves.

TRAVELING THROUGH THE DARK

Traveling through the dark I found a deer
dead on the edge of the Wilson River road.
It is usually best to roll them into the canyon:
that road is narrow; to swerve might make more dead.

By glow of the tail-light I stumbled back of the car
and stood by the heap, a doe, a recent killing;
she had stiffened already, almost cold.
I dragged her off; she was large in the belly.

My fingers touching her side brought me the reason—
her side was warm; her fawn lay there waiting,
alive, still, never to be born.
Beside that mountain road I hesitated.

The car aimed ahead its lowered parking lights;
under the hood purred the steady engine.
I stood in the glare of the warm exhaust turning red;
around our group I could hear the wilderness listen.

I thought hard for us all—my only swerving—,
then pushed her over the edge into the river.

AT THE BOMB TESTING SITE

At noon in the desert a panting lizard
waited for history, its elbows tense,
watching the curve of a particular road
as if something might happen.

It was looking for something farther off
than people could see, an important scene
acted in stone for little selves
at the flute end of consequences.

There was just a continent without much on it
under a sky that never cared less.
Ready for a change, the elbows waited.
The hands gripped hard on the desert.

May Swenson / 1919–

LION

In the bend of your mouth soft murder
    in the flints of your eyes
        the sun-stained openings of caves
Your nostrils breathe the ordained air
    of chosen loneliness

Magnificently maned as the lustrous pampas
   your head heavy with heraldic curls
   wears a regal frown between the brows

The wide bundle of your chest
   your loose-skinned belly frilled with fur
   you carry easily sinuously pacing on suede paws

Between tight thighs
   under the thick root of your tufted tail
   situated like a full-stoned fruit beneath a bough
   the quiver of your never-used malehood is slung

You pace in dung on cement
   the bars flick past your eyeballs
   fixed beyond the awestruck stares of children

Watching you they remember their fathers
   the frightening hairs in their fathers' ears

Young girls remember lovers too timid and white
   and I remember how I played lion with my brothers
   under the round yellow-grained table
   the shadow our cave in the lamplight

Your beauty burns the brain
   though your paws slue on foul cement
   the fetor of captivity you do right to ignore
   the bars too an illusion

Your heroic paranoia plants you in the Indian jungle
   pacing by the cool water-hole as dawn streaks the sky
   and the foretaste of the all-day hunt
   is sweet as yearling's blood
   in the corners of your lips

QUESTION

Body my house
my horse my hound
what will I do
when you are fallen

Where will I sleep
How will I ride
What will I hunt

Where can I go
without my mount
all eager and quick
How will I know
in thicket ahead
is danger or treasure
when Body my good
bright dog is dead

How will it be
to lie in the sky
without roof or door
and wind for an eye

With cloud for shift
how will I hide?

Charles Tomlinson / 1927–

WINTER ENCOUNTERS

House and hollow; village and valley-side:
    The ceaseless pairings, the interchange
In which the properties are constant
    Resumes its winter starkness. The hedges' barbs

Are bared. Lengthened shadows
 Intersecting, the fields seem parcelled smaller
As if by hedgerow within hedgerow. Meshed
 Into neighbourhood by such shifting ties,
The house reposes, squarely upon its acre
 Yet with softened angles, the responsive stone
Changeful beneath the changing light:
 There is a riding-forth, a voyage impending
In this ruffled air, where all moves
 Towards encounter. Inanimate or human,
The distinction fails in these brisk exchanges—
 Say, merely, that the roof greets the cloud,
Or by the wall, sheltering its knot of talkers,
 Encounter enacts itself in the conversation
On customary subjects, where the mind
 May lean at ease, weighing the prospect
Of another's presence. Rain
 And the probability of rain, tares
And their progress through a field of wheat—
 These, though of moment in themselves,
Serve rather to articulate the sense
 That having met, one meets with more
Than the words can witness. One feels behind
 Into the intensity that bodies through them
Calmness within the wind, the warmth in cold.

HOW STILL THE HAWK

How still the hawk
Hangs innocent above
Its native wood:
Distance, that purifies the act
Of all intent, has graced
Intent with beauty.
Beauty must lie
As innocence must harm
Whose end (sited,
Held) is naked

Like the map it cowers on.
And the doom drops:
Plummet of peace
To him who does not share
The nearness and the need,
The shrivelled circle
Of magnetic fear.

Peter Viereck / 1916–

BLINDMAN'S BUFF

Night-watchmen think of dawn and things auroral.
Clerks wistful for Bermudas think of coral.
The poet in New York still thinks of laurel.
(But lovers think of death and touch each other
As if to prove that love is still alive.)

The Martian space-crew, in an earthward dive,
Think of their sweet unearthly earth Up There,
Where darling monsters romp in airless air.
(Two lovers think of death and touch each other,
Fearing the day when only one's alive.)

We think of cash, but cash does not arrive.
We think of fun, but fate will not connive.
We never mention death. Do we survive?
(The lovers think of death and touch each other
To live their love while love is yet alive.)

Prize-winners are so avid when they strive;
They race so far; they pile their toys so high.
Only a cad would trip them. Yet they die.
(The lovers think of death and touch each other;
Of all who live, these are the most alive.)

When all the lemming-realists contrive
To swim—where to?—in life's enticing tide,
Only a fool would stop and wait outside.
(The lovers stop and wait and touch each other.
Who twinly think of death are twice alive.)

Plump creatures smack their lips and think they thrive;
The hibernating bear, but half alive,
Dreams of free honey in a stingless hive.
He thinks of life at every lifeless breath.
(The lovers think of death.)

1 . *Vale* FROM CARTHAGE

for my brother, 1944

I, now at Carthage. He, shot dead at Rome.
Shipmates last May. "And what if one of us,"
I asked last May, in fun, in gentleness,
"Wears doom, like dungarees, and doesn't know?"
He laughed, *"Not see Times Square again?"* The foam,
Feathering across that deck a year ago,
Swept those five words—like seeds—beyond the seas
   Into his future. There they grew like trees;
    And as he passed them there next spring, they
    laid
   Upon his road of fire their sudden shade.
Though he had always scraped his mess-kit pure
And scrubbed redeemingly his barracks floor,
Though all his buttons glowed their ritual-hymn
Like cloudless moons to intercede for him,
No furlough fluttered from the sky. He will
Not see Times Square—he will not see—he will
Not see Times
    change; at Carthage (while my friend,
Living those words at Rome, screamed in the end)
I saw an ancient Roman's tomb and read

"*Vale*" in stone. Here two wars mix their dead:
    Roman, my shipmate's dream walks hand in hand
    With yours tonight ("New York again" and
        "Rome"),
    Like widowed sisters bearing water home
    On tired heads through hot Tunisian sand
    In good cool urns, and says, "I understand."
    Roman, you'll see your Forum Square no more;
    What's left but this to say of any war?

John Wain / 1925–

THIS ABOVE ALL IS PRECIOUS AND REMARKABLE

This above all is precious and remarkable,
How we put ourselves in one another's care,
How in spite of everything we trust each other.

Fishermen at whatever point they are dipping and lifting
On the dark green swell they partly think of as home
Hear the gale warnings that fly to them like gulls.

The scientists study the weather for love of studying it,
And not specially for love of the fishermen,
And the wireless engineers do the transmission for love of
    wireless,

But how it adds up is that when the terrible white malice
Of the waves high as cliffs is let loose to seek a victim,
The fishermen are somewhere else and so not drowned.

And why should this chain of miracles be easier to believe
Than that my darling should come to me as naturally
As she trusts a restaurant not to poison her?

They are simply examples of well-known types of miracle,
The two of them,
That can happen at any time of the day or night.

BROOKLYN HEIGHTS

This is the gay cliff of the nineteenth century,
Drenched in the hopeful ozone of a new day.

Erect and brown, like retired sea-captains,
The houses gaze vigorously at the ocean.

With the hospitable eyes of retired captains
They preside over the meeting of sea and river.

On Sunday mornings the citizens revisit their beginnings.
Whose families walk in the fresh air of the past.

Their children tricycle down the nineteenth century:
America comes smiling towards them like a neighbour.

While the past on three wheels unrolls beneath them,
They hammer in the blazing forge of the future.

Brooklyn Bridge flies through the air on feathers.
The children do not know the weight of its girders.

It is the citizens carry the bridge on their shoulders:
Its overhead lights crackle in their blood vessels.

But now it is Sunday morning, and a sky swept clean.
The citizens put down the bridge and stroll at ease.

They jingle the hopeful change in their pockets.
They forget the tripping dance of the profit motive.

The big ships glide in under the high statue,
The towers cluster like spear-grass on the famous island.

And the citizens dream themselves back in a sparkle of
    morning.
They ride with their children under a sky swept clean.

Dream on, citizens! Dream the true America, the healer,
Drawing the hot blood from throbbing Europe!

Dream the dark-eyed immigrants from the narrow cities:
Dream the iron steamers loaded with prayers and bundles:

Breathe the ozone older than the name of commerce:
Be the citizens of the true survival!

Robert Penn Warren / 1905–

COLDER FIRE

It rained toward day. The morning came sad and white
With silver of sea-sadness and defection of season.
Our joys and convictions are sure, but in that wan light
We moved—your mother and I—in muteness of spirit past
    logical reason.

Now sun, afternoon, and again summer-glitter on sea.
As you to a bright toy, the heart leaps. The heart unlocks
Joy, though we know, shamefaced, the heart's weather
    should not be
Merely a reflex to a solstice, or sport of some aggrieved
    equinox.

No, the heart should be steadfast: I know that.
And I sit in the late-sunny lee of the watch-house,
At the fortress point, you on my knee now, and the late
White butterflies over gold thistle conduct their ritual
    carouse.

In whisperless carnival, in vehemence of gossamer,
Pale ghosts of pale passions of air, the white wings weave.
In tingle and tangle of arabesque, they mount light, pair
    by pair,
As though that tall light were eternal indeed, not merely
    the summer's reprieve.

You leap on my knee, you exclaim at the sun-stung
    gyration.
And the upper air stirs, as though the vast stillness of sky
Had stirred in its sunlit sleep and made a suspiration,
A luxurious languor of breath, as after love, there is a sigh.

But enough, for the highest sun-scintillant pair are gone
Seaward, past rampart and cliff borne, over blue sea-gleam.
Close to my chair, to a thistle, a butterfly sinks now, flight
    done.
By the gold bloom of thistle, white wings pulse under the
    sky's dream.

The sky's dream is enormous, I lift up my eyes.
In sunlight a tatter of mist clings high on the mountain-
    mass.
The mountain is under the sky, and there the gray scarps
    rise
Past paths where on their appointed occasions men
    climb, and pass.

Past grain-patch, last apron of vineyard, last terrace of
    olive,
Past chestnut, past cork grove, where the last carts can go,
Past camp of the charcoal maker, where coals glow in the
    black hive,
The scarps, gray, rise up. Above them is that place I know.

The pines are there, they are large, in a deep recess—
Shelf above scarp, enclave of rock, a glade
Benched and withdrawn in the mountain-mass, under the
    peak's duress.
We came there—your mother and I—and rested in that
    severe shade.

Pine-blackness mist-tangled, the peak black above: the
    glade gives
On the empty threshold of air, the hawk-hung delight
Of distance unspooled and bright space spilled—ah, the
    heart thrives!
We stood in that shade and saw sea and land lift in the far
    light.

Now the butterflies dance, time-tattered and disarrayed.
I watch them. I think how above that far scarp's sunlit wall
Mist threads in silence the darkness of boughs, and in that
    shade
Condensed moisture gathers at a needle-tip. It glitters, will
    fall.

I cannot interpret for you this collocation
Of memories. You will live your own life, and contrive
The language of your own heart, but let that conversation,
In the last analysis, be always of whatever truth you would
    live.

For fire flames but in the heart of a colder fire.
All voice is but echo caught from a soundless voice.
Height is not deprivation of valley, nor defect of desire,
But defines, for the fortunate, that joy in which all joys
    should rejoice.

COUNTRY BURYING (1919)

A thousand times you've seen that scene:
    Oak grove, bare ground, little white church there,
Bone-white in that light, and through dust-pale green
    Of oak leaf, the steeple pokes up in the bright air.

For it is summer, and once I sat
    At grove-edge beyond the disarray
Of cars in the shade-patch, this way and that.
    They stood patient as mules now in the heat of the day.

Chevrolet, T-Model, a Hudson or two,
    They are waiting like me, and the afternoon glares.
Waiting is all they have come to do.
    What goes on inside is no concern of theirs,

Nor of mine, who have lost a boy's afternoon,
    When summer's so short, and half gone, just to bring
My mother to bury someone she'd scarce known.
    "I respect her," she'd said, but was that enough of a
        thing?

Who was she? Who knows? I'd not thought to ask it.
    That kind came to town, in buggy or Ford,
Some butter to swap, clutch of eggs in a basket,
    Gnarled hands in black mittens, old face yellow as a
        gourd.

It's no matter now who lies in the church,
    Where heads bend in duty in sparse rows.
Green miles of tobacco, sun-dazzled, stretch
    Away. Red clay, the road winds, goes on where it goes,

And we, too, now go, down the road, where it goes,
    My mother and I, the hole now filled.
Light levels in fields now, dusk crouches in hedgerows,
    As we pass from what is, toward what will be, fulfilled,

And I passed toward voices and the foreign faces,
    Knew dawn in strange rooms, and the heart gropes for
        center,
But should I come back, come back now where that place is,
    Oak grove, white church, in day-glare a-daze, I might
        enter.

For what? But enter, and find what I'd guess:
    The odor of varnish, hymnals stacked on a chair,
Light religiously dim by painted paper on window glass,
    And the insistent buzz of a fly lost in shadow, somewhere.

Why doesn't that fly stop buzzing—stop buzzing up there!

ORIGINAL SIN: A SHORT STORY

Nodding, its great head rattling like a gourd,
And locks like seaweed strung on the stinking stone,
The nightmare stumbles past, and you have heard
It fumble your door before it whimpers and is gone:
It acts like the old hound that used to snuffle your door and
        moan.

You thought you had lost it when you left Omaha,
For it seemed connected then with your grandpa, who
Had a wen on his forehead and sat on the veranda
To finger the precious protuberance, as was his habit to do,
Which glinted in sun like rough garnet or the rich old brain
        bulging through.

But you met it in Harvard Yard as the historic steeple
Was confirming the midnight with its hideous racket,
And you wondered how it had come, for it stood so
        imbecile,
With empty hands, humble, and surely nothing in pocket:
Riding the rods, perhaps—or Grandpa's will paid the ticket.

You were almost kindly then, in your first homesickness
As it tortured its stiff face to speak, but scarcely mewed.
Since then you have outlived all your homesickness,
But have met it in many another distempered latitude:
Oh, nothing is lost, ever lost! at last you understood.

It never came in the quantum glare of sun
To shame you before your friends, and had nothing to do
With your public experience or private reformation:
But it thought no bed too narrow—it stood with lips askew
And shook its great head sadly like the abstract Jew.

Never met you in the lyric arsenical meadows
When children call and your heart goes stone in the bosom—
At the orchard anguish never, nor ovoid horror,

Which is furred like a peach or avid like the delicious
        plum.
It takes no part in your classic prudence or fondled axiom.

Not there when you exclaimed: "Hope is betrayed by
Disastrous glory of sea-capes, sun-torment of whitecaps
—There must be a new innocence for us to be stayed by."
But there it stood, after all the timetables, all the maps,
In the crepuscular clutter of *always, always,* or *perhaps.*

You have moved often and rarely left an address,
And hear of the deaths of friends with a sly pleasure,
A sense of cleansing and hope which blooms from distress;
But it has not died, it comes, its hand childish, unsure,
Clutching the bribe of chocolate or a toy you used to
        treasure.

It tries the lock. You hear, but simply drowse:
There is nothing remarkable in that sound at the door.
Later you may hear it wander the dark house
Like a mother who rises at night to seek a childhood
        picture;
Or it goes to the backyard and stands like an old horse cold
        in the pasture.

BEARDED OAKS

The oaks, how subtle and marine,
Bearded, and all the layered light
Above them swims; and thus the scene,
Recessed, awaits the positive night.

So, waiting, we in the grass now lie
Beneath the languorous tread of light:
The grasses, kelp-like, satisfy
The nameless motions of the air.

Upon the floor of light, and time,
Unmurmuring, of polyp made,

We rest; we are, as light withdraws,
Twin atolls on a shelf of shade.

Ages to our construction went,
Dim architecture, hour by hour:
And violence, forgot now, lent
The present stillness all its power.

The storm of noon above us rolled,
Of light the fury, furious gold,
The long drag troubling us, the depth:
Dark is unrocking, unrippling, still.

Passion and slaughter, ruth, decay
Descend, minutely whispering down,
Silted down swaying steams, to lay
Foundation for our voicelessness.

All our debate is voiceless here,
As all our rage, the rage of stone;
If hope is hopeless, then fearless is fear,
And history is thus undone.

Our feet once wrought the hollow street
With echo when the lamps were dead
At windows, once our headlight glare
Disturbed the doe that, leaping, fled.

I do not love you less that now
The caged heart makes iron stroke,
Or less that all that light once gave
The graduate dark should now revoke.

We live in time so little time
And we learn all so painfully,
That we may spare this hour's term
To practice for eternity.

Reed Whittemore / 1919–

A DAY WITH THE FOREIGN LEGION

On one of those days with the Legion
When everyone sticks to sofas and itches and bitches—
A day for gin and bitters and the plague—
Down by Mount Tessala, under the plane trees,
Seated at iron tables, cursing the country,
Cursing the times and the natives, cursing the drinks,
Cursing the food and the bugs, cursing the Legion,
Were Kim and Bim and all those brave heroes
Of all those books and plays and poems and movies
The remorseless desert serves.
And as they sat at the iron tables cursing the country,
Some Sergeant or other rushed in from the Fort
Gallantly bearing the news
From which all those the remorseless desert serves
Take their cues:
"Sir"
        "What is it, Sergeant?"
                        "Sir, the hordes
March e'en now across the desert swards."

Just like the movies.

Now in the movies
The Sergeant's arrival touches off bugles and bells,
Emptying bunks and showers, frightening horses,
Pushing up flags and standards, hardening lines
Of unsoldierly softness, and putting farewells
Hastily in the post so two weeks hence
A perfectly lovely lovely in far-off Canada
Will go pale and bite buttons and stare at the air in Canada.
And in the movies,
Almost before the audience spills its popcorn,
The company's formed and away, with Bim or Kim
Solemnly leading them forth into a sandstorm,

Getting them into what is quite clearly a trap,
Posting a double guard,
Sending messengers frantic to Marrakech,
Inadvertently pouring the water away,
Losing the ammunition, horses and food,
And generally carrying on in the great tradition
By making speeches
Which bring back to mind the glorious name of the Legion,
And serve as the turning point,
After which the Arabs seem doped and perfectly helpless,
Water springs up from the ground, the horses come back,
Plenty of food is discovered in some old cave,
And reinforcements arrive led by the girl
From Canada.

But in this instance nothing from *Beau Geste*
Or the Paramount lot was attempted,
It being too hot for dramatics,
Even from Kim and Bim
Aging under the plane trees,
Cursing the food and the bugs, cursing the Sergeant
Who gallantly bore the news because he was young,
Full of oats and ignorance, so damned young
In his pretty khaki; nothing at all
(So late in the day, with everyone crocked)
Was attempted despite the Sergeant,
Who whirled on his heel, his mission accomplished, and
    marched,
Hip hip,
Out of the bar, a true trooper, as if to the wars.

So the lights went on and the audience,
Pleasantly stupid, whistled and clapped at the rarity
Of a film breaking down in this late year of Our Lord.

But of course it was not the film; it was not the projector;
Nor was it the man in the booth, who hastened away
As soon as the feature was over, leaving the heroes
Cursing the food and the bugs as heathendom marched
And the Sergeant whirled, hip hip;
But some other darker cause having to do
With the script perhaps, or the art,

Or simply the time,
The time and the place, and how could one blame them?
Seated at iron tables cursing the country.
What could they do?
Seated under the plane trees watching the Sergeant
Whirl on his heel, hip hip, in his pretty khaki.
What could they say?
Drinking their gin and bitters by Mount Tessala,
What could they say?

For what after all could be said, after all was said,
But that the feature had merely run out, and the lights had
    gone on
Because it was time for the lights to go on, and time
For them not to dash out and get lost in the desert,
But to rage
As befitted their age
At the drinks and the country, letting their audience
Clap, stamp, whistle and hoot as darkness
Settled on Mount Tessala, the lights went on,
The enemy roamed the desert, and everyone itched.

James Wright / 1927–

ON THE SKELETON OF A HOUND

Nightfall, that saw the morning-glories float
Tendril and string against the crumbling wall,
Nurses him now, his skeleton for grief,
His locks for comfort curled among the leaf.
Shuttles of moonlight weave his shadow tall,
Milkweed and dew flow upward to his throat.
Now catbird feathers plume the apple mound,
And starlings drowse to winter up the ground.
Thickened away from speech by fear, I move
Around the body. Over his forepaws, steep

Declivities darken down the moonlight now,
And the long throat that bayed a year ago
Declines from summer. Flies would love to leap
Between his eyes and hum away the space
Between the ears, the hollow where a hare
Could hide; another jealous dog would tumble
The bones apart, angry, the shining crumble
Of a great body gleaming in the air;
Quivering pigeons foul his broken face.
I can imagine men who search the earth
For handy resurrections, overturn
The body of a beetle in its grave;
Whispering men digging for gods might delve
A pocket for these bones, then slowly burn
Twigs in the leaves, pray for another birth.
But I will turn my face away from this
Ruin of summer, collapse of fur and bone.
For once a white hare huddled up the grass,
The sparrows flocked away to see the race.
I stood on darkness, clinging to a stone,
I saw the two leaping alive on ice,
On earth, on leaf, humus and withered vine:
The rabbit splendid in a shroud of shade,
The dog carved on the sunlight, on the air,
Fierce and magnificent his rippled hair,
The cockleburs shaking around his head.
Then, suddenly, the hare leaped beyond pain
Out of the open meadow, and the hound
Followed the voiceless dancer to the moon,
To dark, to death, to other meadows where
Singing young women dance around a fire,
Where love reveres the living.

                                        I alone
Scatter this hulk about the dampened ground;
And while the moon rises beyond me, throw
The ribs and spine out of their perfect shape.
For a last charm to the dead, I lift the skull
And toss it over the maples like a ball.
Strewn to the woods, now may that spirit sleep
That flamed over the ground a year ago.
I know the mole will heave a shinbone over,

The earthworm snuggle for a nap on paws,
The honest bees build honey in the head;
The earth knows how to handle the great dead
Who lived the body out, and broke its laws,
Knocked down a fence, tore up a field of clover.

A GESTURE BY A LADY WITH
AN ASSUMED NAME

Letters she left to clutter up the desk
Burned in the general gutter when the maid
Came in to do the room and take the risk
Of slipping off the necklace round her head.

Laundry she left to clutter up the floor
Hung to rachitic skeletons of girls
Who worked the bars or labored up the stair
To crown her blowsy ribbons on their curls.

Lovers she left to clutter up the town
Mourned in the chilly morgue and went away,
All but the husbands sneaking up and down
The stairs of that apartment house all day.

What were they looking for? The cold pretense
Of lamentation offered in a stew?
A note? A gift? A shred of evidence
To love when there was nothing else to do?

Or did they rise to weep for that unheard-
Of love, whose misery cries and does not care
Whether or not the madam hears a word
Or skinny children watch the trodden stair?

Whether or not, how could she love so many,
Then turn away to die as though for none?
I saw the last offer a child a penny
To creep outside and see the cops were gone.

PART IV

Appendix

I *On Poets and Poetry*

   PROSE STATEMENTS BY MODERN POETS

II *On Society and Poetry*

    EZRA POUND AND THE BOLLINGEN PRIZE

    POETS ON SOCIETY AND POETRY

III *A Bibliography of Modern Poetic Criticism*

IV *Photographs of the Poets*

PART IV

Appendix

I. On Poem and Poetry
PROSE STATEMENTS BY MODERN POETS

II. On Seeing and Poetry
EZRA POUND AND THE DOLEHOUSE POEM
PORTISON SOCIETY AND POETRY

III. A Bibliography of Modern Poetic Criticism

IV. Photographs of the Poets

I

On Poets and Poetry

PROSE STATEMENTS BY MODERN POETS

CONRAD AIKEN

Poetry has always kept easily abreast with the utmost man can do in extending the horizon of his consciousness, whether outward or inward. It has always been the most flexible, the most comprehensive, the most farseeing, and hence the most successful, of the modes by which he has accepted the new in experience, realized it, and adjusted himself to it. Whether it is a change in his conception of the heavens, or of the law of gravity, or of morality, or of the nature of consciousness, it has always at last been in poetry that man has given his thought its supreme expression— which is to say that most of all, in this, he succeeds in making real for himself the profound myth of personal existence and experience.

from *Poets on Poetry*, 1966

W. H. AUDEN

The concern of the Primary Imagination, its only concern, is with sacred beings and sacred events. The sacred is that to which it is obliged to respond; the profane is that to which it cannot respond and therefore does not know. The profane is known to other faculties of the mind, but not to the Primary Imagination. A sacred being cannot be anticipated; it must be encountered. On encounter the imagination has no option but to respond. All imaginations do not recognize the same sacred beings or events, but every imagination responds to those it recognizes in the same way. The impression made upon the imagination by any sacred being is of an overwhelming but undefinable importance—an unchangeable quality, an Identity, as Keats said: I-am-that-I-am is what every sacred being seems to say. The impression made by a sacred event is of an overwhelming but undefinable significance. . . .

The response of the imagination to such a presence or significance is a passion of awe. This awe may vary greatly in intensity and range in tone from joyous wonder to panic dread. A sacred being may be attractive or repulsive—a swan or an octopus—beautiful or ugly—a toothless hag or a fair young child—good or evil—a Beatrice or a Belle Dame Sans Merci—historical fact or fiction—a person met on the road or an image encountered in a story or a dream—it may be noble or something unmentionable in a drawing room, it may be anything it likes on condition, but this condition is absolute, that it arouse awe. The realm of the Primary Imagination is without freedom, sense of time or humor. Whatever determines this response or lack of response lies below consciousness and is of concern to psychology, not art.

Some sacred beings seem to be sacred to all imaginations at all times. The Moon, for example, Fire, Snakes and those four important beings which can only be defined in terms of nonbeing: Darkness, Silence, Nothing, Death. Some, like kings, are only sacred to all within a certain culture; some only to members of a social group—the Latin language among humanists—and some are only sacred to a single imagination. Many of us have sacred landscapes which probably all have much in common, but there will almost certainly be details which are peculiar to each. An imagination can acquire new sacred beings and it can lose old ones to the profane. Sacred beings can be acquired by social contagion but not consciously. One cannot be taught to recognize a sacred being, one has to be converted. As a rule, perhaps, with advancing age sacred events gain in importance over sacred beings.

A sacred being may also be an object of desire but the imagination does not desire it. A desire can be a sacred being but the imagination is without desire. In the presence of the sacred, it is self-forgetful; in its absence the very type of the profane, "The most unpoetical of all God's creatures." A sacred being may also demand to be loved or obeyed, it may reward or punish, but the imagination is unconcerned: a law can be a sacred being, but the imagination does not obey. To the imagination a sacred being is self-sufficient, and like Aristotle's God can have no need of friends.

The Secondary Imagination is of another character and at another mental level. It is active not passive, and its categories are not the sacred and the profane, but the beautiful and ugly. Our dreams are full of sacred beings and events—indeed, they may well contain nothing else, but we cannot distinguish in dreams—or so it seems to me, though I may be wrong—between the beautiful and the ugly. Beauty and ugliness pertain to Form not to Being. The Primary Imagination only recognizes one kind of being, the sacred, but the Secondary Imagination recognizes both beautiful and ugly forms. To the Primary Imagination a sacred being is that which it is. To the Secondary Imagination a beautiful form is as it ought to be, an ugly form as it ought not to be. Observing the beautiful, it has the feeling of satisfaction, pleasure, absence of conflict; observing the ugly, the contrary feelings. It does not desire the beautiful, but an ugly form arouses in it a desire that its ugliness be corrected and made beautiful. It does not worship the beautiful; it approves of it and can give reasons for its approval. The Secondary Imagination has, one might say, a bourgeois nature. It approves of regularity, of spatial symmetry and temporal repetition, of law and order: it disapproves of loose ends, irrelevance and mess.

Lastly, the Secondary Imagination is social and craves agreement with other minds. If I think a form beautiful and you think it ugly, we cannot both help agreeing that one of us must be wrong, whereas if I think something is sacred and you think it is profane, neither of us will dream of arguing the matter.

Both kinds of imagination are essential to the health of the mind. Without the inspiration of sacred awe, its beautiful forms would soon become banal, its rhythms mechanical; without the activity of the Secondary Imagination the passivity of the Primary would be the mind's undoing; sooner or later its sacred beings would possess it, it would come to think of itself as sacred, exclude the outer world as profane and so go mad.

The impulse to create a work of art is felt when, in certain persons, the passive awe provoked by sacred beings or events is transformed into a desire to express that awe in a rite of worship or homage, and to be fit homage, this rite must be beautiful. This rite has no magical or idolatrous intention; nothing is expected in return. Nor is it, in a Christian sense, an act of devotion. If it praises the Creator, it does so indirectly by praising His creatures —among which may be human notions of the Divine Nature. With God as Redeemer, it has, so far as I can see, little if anything to do.

In poetry the rite is verbal; it pays homage by naming. I suspect that the predisposition of a mind towards the poetic medium may have its origin in an error. A nurse, let us suppose, says to a child, "Look at the moon!" The child looks and for him this is a sacred encounter. In his mind the word "moon" is not a name of a sacred object but one of its most important properties and, therefore, numinous. The notion of writing poetry cannot occur to him, of course, until he has realized that names and things are not identical and that there cannot be an intelligible sacred language, but I wonder if, when he has discovered the social nature of language, he would attach such importance to one of its uses, that of naming, if he had not previously made this false identification.

The pure poem, in the French sense of *la poésie pure* would be, I suppose, a celebration of the numinous-in-itself in abstraction from all cases and devoid of any profane reference whatsoever—a sort of *sanctus, sanctus, sanctus*. If it could be written, which is doubtful, it would not necessarily be the best poem.

A poem is a rite; hence its formal and ritualistic character. Its use of language is deliberately and ostentatiously different from talk. Even when it employs the diction and rhythms of conversation, it employs them as a deliberate informality, presupposing the norm with which they are intended to contrast.

The form of a rite must be beautiful, exhibiting, for example, balance, closure and aptness to that which it is the form of. It is over this last quality of aptness that most of our aesthetic quarrels arise, and must arise, whenever our sacred and profane worlds differ.

> To the Eyes of a Miser, a Guinea is far more beautiful than the Sun & a bag worn with the use of Money has more beautiful proportions than a Vine filled with Grapes.

Blake, it will be noticed, does not accuse the Miser of lacking imagination.

The value of a profane thing lies in what it usefully does, the value of a sacred thing lies in what it *is:* a sacred thing may also have a function but it does not have to. The apt name for a profane being, therefore, is the word or words that accurately describe his function—a Mr. Smith, a Mr. Weaver. The apt name for a sacred being is the word or words which worthily express his importance—Son of Thunder, The Well-Wishing One.

. . .

But it is from the sacred encounters of his imagination that a poet's impulse to write a poem arises. Thanks to the language, he need not name them directly unless he wishes; he can describe one in terms of another and translate those that are private or irrational or socially unacceptable into such as are acceptable to reason and society. Some poems are directly *about* the sacred beings they were written *for:* others are not, and in that case no reader can tell what was the original encounter which provided the impulse for the poem.

. . .

Whatever its actual content and overt interest, every poem is rooted in imaginative awe. Poetry can do a hundred and one things, delight, sadden, disturb, amuse, instruct—it may express every possible shade of emotion, and describe every conceivable kind of event, but there is only one thing that all poetry must do; it must praise all it can for being and for happening.

from *The Dyer's Hand*, 1962

PAUL BLACKBURN

Mine [his poetry] is probably closer to modern music or, partly, even to the concept of modern jazz. A lot of pieces feel like several instruments or voices—they should, anyway. The point is that a poem has to be resolved musically as well as in terms of its content. Very few people have very consistently good ears.

. . .

[In answer to a question about the use of common speech] Yes, I think that's probably, in one degree or another, what anyone who is doing anything at all is doing—actually using the language that we use every day to make their poems with. I think that is one reason why readings in coffee shops and bars and to friends have become so much more common in the last five years. Poetry is less removed from its audience, if you like.

. . .

[About four letter words] If one is writing a violent poem, one uses violent words . . . these words are honest words and they don't really shock you. They shock only if you are willing to be shocked. The words and the parts and functions exist, and if they are out there in the text they are much cleaner and more open, with no suppression and no veiling. The hiding of it and the skirting of it can be more suggestive than the outright statement.

from *The Sullen Art*, 1963

JOHN CIARDI

Every poet, I think, dredges himself in hope of bringing to song and form or to saying and form some shape of his own life, a shape brought up from so deep a level in himself that it will suggest to a good reader his own shapes and his own depths. My theory goes one step further: if the shape is truly caught into a poem and if it is from deep enough in me, it cannot help being a shape from everyone else's depths. That, I suppose, is really a Jungian idea.

. . .

It is a mistake of course to like a poem because the experience from which it took off is a dear one. It could be too easy to confuse the personal experience with the experience the poem makes. . . .

I like both poems that sing and poems that say. Singing and saying both have their rhythms, and any good rhythm is a joy to find. Basically, I think, I am a "saying" poet.

from *Poet's Choice*, 1962

E. E. CUMMINGS

From Rilke "Works of art are of an infinite loneliness and with nothing to be so little reached as with criticism. Only love can grasp and hold and fairly judge them."

In my proud and humble opinion, these two sentences are worth all the soi-disant criticism of the arts which has ever existed or will ever exist. Disagree with them as much as you like, but never forget them; for if you do, you will have forgotten the mystery which you have been, the mystery which you shall be, and the mystery which you are.

. . .

Art is a mystery.

A mystery is something immeasurable.

In so far as every child and woman and man may be immeasurable, art is the mystery of every man and woman and child. In so far as a human being is an artist, skies and mountains and oceans and thunderbolts and butterflies are immeasurable; and art is every mystery of nature. Nothing measurable can be alive; nothing which is not alive can be art; nothing which cannot be art is true: and everything untrue doesn't matter a very good God damn.

. . .

Art is a mystery; all mysteries have their source in a mystery-of-mysteries who is love: and if lovers may reach eternity directly through love herself, their mystery remains essentially that of the loving artist whose way must lie through his art, and of the loving worshipper whose aim is oneness with his god. From another point of view, every human being is in and of himself or herself illimitable; but the essence of his or of her illimitability is precisely its uniqueness—nor could all poetry (past present and future) begin to indicate the varieties of selfhood; and consequently of selftranscendence.

. . .

I am someone who proudly and humbly affirms that love is the mystery-of-mysteries, and that nothing measurable matters "a very good God damn": that "an artist, a man, a failure" is no mere whenfully accreting mechanism, but a givingly eternal complexity—neither some soulless and heartless ultrapredatory infra-animal nor any un-understandingly knowing and believing and thinking automation, but a naturally and miraculously whole human being—a feelingly illimitable individual; whose only happiness is to transcend himself, whose every agony is to grow.

from *Six Non Lectures*, 1953

C. DAY-LEWIS

This has always been, up to a point, the way poetry comes to be written: the poet 'has an idea,' and in the course of contemplating it he draws up from his subconscious a string of associated ideas and images. But there are two important differences which affect the poet and the reader today. In the first place, the poet is almost bound to have accepted the psychological hypothesis of the unconscious, and is therefore bound to be partly aware of the process of poetic creation. This self-consciousness, whether it is a genuine insight into the workings of his own mind or only a false explanation of them, is a source of grave embarrassment to him. Modern poets have tended to dealing with this embarrassment by a kind of jujitsu trick; they give way to free association, using their adversary's own strength to overcome him: whereas poets till recently have fought the stream from the unconscious by direct methods, so to speak, imposing their personality upon it, dividing its forces and typing them up together with logical connections. The former process makes things difficult for the reader, because his associations with any given idea or image are probably different from those of the poet, and he is likely to feel as puzzled and uncomfortable as if he was listening to someone talking in their sleep.

. . .

Poetry was born from magic: it grew up with religion: it lived through the age of reason: is it to die in the century of propaganda?

. . .

Poetry is based on the principle of free individual interpretation; you must create the meaning of each poem out of your private experience. But life for the average child of the twentieth century becomes an endless series of extension-lectures on everything under the sun. . . . Who is he, then, to claim an individual interpretation of anything, let alone poetry?

. . .

It is the nature of the poetic vision to perceive those invisible truths which are like electrons the basis of reality; the nature of the poetic imagination to become aware of the cryptic links that bind our universe together, to find similarity in difference and to make coherence out of contradiction. If the poet is not clairvoyant, he is nothing. And this clairvoyancy is particularly directed towards discovering the 'supernatural' in nature and the 'superhuman' in humanity. There can be no such thing as realist poetry.

. . .

That is as much as we can ever know of the nature of poetry—the angel seen at the window, the air of glory. Whence these visitors come the poet cannot say, whether out of the upper air, influences from the source of all light; or are daimons, the lords of energy alive in all matter, or from the dark continent in his own mind where mankind's past is stored, an Atlantis lost beneath the waves of consciousness. If this last is so . . . then we might predict that the gradual extension of self-consciousness will after many centuries be the death of poetry. . . . Yet if a thousand years is to the poet but as yesterday, his to-morrow has a like span to run. That is a hope for poetry. The voices are vigorous still, not dead.

from *A Hope for Poetry*, 1945

JAMES DICKEY

As a writer of poetry I began comparatively late, around my twenty-fourth year. I came to poetry with no particular qualifications. I had begun to suspect, however, that there is a poet—or a kind of poet—buried in every human being like Ariel in his tree, and that the people whom we are pleased to call poets are only those who have felt the need and contrived the means to release this spirit from its prison. As soon as I began writing I knew that I had the need, but that the means were not immediately forthcoming. I knew nothing whatever of poetic technique, of metrics, prosody, stanzaic construction, and to a certain extent I still consider those things—all the things that Herbert Read calls "the bag of monkey-tricks of English poetry"—as secondary to something else which I can only define, using one of the words I most despised in my younger days, as the spirit of poetry: the individually imaginative or visionary quality.

The first poem I wrote that had anything good in it—anything that I had seen for myself—was, I think, a description of football players dressing in a locker room. It seemed to me that their body-hair was *dry*—very dry-looking—and I put this into the poem, although against my better judgment, since it was a decidedly unbeautiful detail and at that time I wanted very much to write "beautiful" poems. When I looked at what I had put down on paper, I could see immediately that this line, poor as it was, had a quality of observation and of immediacy not to be found in the rest of the poem, which was derived from half a dozen other poets I had been reading. At that unlikely time I began to see what poetry would have to be for me and came by the idea that words, once placed in a certain order, will stay where they have been put and say what one tells them to say.

But what did I want to tell them to say? Very slowly I gravitated toward another idea which, like the other, has never left me: the belief in the inexhaustible fecundity of individual memory. When I examined my own memory, I found that certain images stood out in my mind and recurred to me at odd times, as if seeking something, perhaps some act of understanding, from me. Some recollections seemed more important than others, without my being able to tell why. Later, I saw that these incidents, the more important ones, not only were potential raw material for the kind of poetry I wanted to write, but were in fact the principal incidents in my life: those times when I felt most strongly and was most aware of the intense reality of the objects and people I moved among.

. . .

All poetry, I suspect, is nothing more or less than an attempt to discover or invent conditions under which one can live with oneself. I have been called a mystic, a vitalist, a pantheist, an antirationalist, and a good many other things. I have not been conscious of the applicability of any of these labels, although they very well may all apply. At any rate, what I have always striven for is to find some way to incarnate my best moments—those which in memory are most persistent and obsessive. I find that most of these moments have an element of danger, an element of repose, and an element of joy. I should like now to develop a writing instrument which would be capable of embodying these moments and their attendant states of mind, and I would be most pleased if readers came away from my poems not at all sure as to where the danger and the repose separate, where joy ends and longing begins. Strongly mixed emotions are what I usually have and what I usually remember from the events of my life. Strongly mixed, but giving the impression of being one emotion, impure and overwhelming—that is the condition I am seeking to impose on my readers, whoever they may be. The doing, of course, is another thing.

from *Poets on Poetry*, 1966

ROBERT DUNCAN

It is not that poetry imitates but that poetry enacts in its order the order of first things, as just here in this consciousness, they may exist, and the poet desires to penetrate the seeming of style and subject matter to that most real where there is no form that is not content, no content that is not form. . . .

We begin to imagine a cosmos in which the poet and the poem are one in a moving process, not only here the given Creation and the Exodus or Fall, but also here the immanence of the Creator in Creation. The most real is given and we have fallen away, but the most real is in the falling revealing itself in what is happening. Between the god *in* the story and the god *of* the story, the form, the realization of what is happening, stirs the poet. To answer that call, to become the poet, means to be aware of creation, creature and creator coinherent in the one event. . . .

Central to and defining the poetics I am trying to suggest here is the conviction that the order man may contrive or impose upon the things about him or upon his own language is trivial beside the divine order or natural order he may discover in them.

from *Poets on Poetry*, 1966

LAWRENCE DURRELL

To write a poem is like trying to catch a lizard without its tail falling off. Did you know that? In India when I was a boy they had great big green lizards there, and if you shouted or shot them their tails would fall off. There was only one boy in the school who could catch lizards intact. No one knew quite how he did it. He had a special soft way of going up to them and he'd bring them back with their tails on. That strikes me as the best analogy I can give you. To try and catch your poem without its tail falling off.

. . .

The theme of art is the theme of life itself. This artificial distinction between artists and human beings is precisely what we are all suffering from. An artist is only someone unrolling and digging out and excavating the areas normally accessible to normal people everywhere, and exhibiting them as a sort of scarecrow to show people what can be done with themselves . . . and what we as artists are trying to do is to sum up in a sort of metaphor the cosmology of a particular moment in which we are living. When an artist does that completely and satisfactorily he creates a crisis in the form. The artists immediately following him become dissatisfied with the existing forms and try to invent or grope around for new forms.

from Paris Review Interviews, *Writers at Work*, 1965

RICHARD EBERHART

Two theories about the complex and ancient art of poetry have specially impressed me. They are opposite, yet each seems true, and I can subscribe to both. One is that poetry comes from an excess of *élan vital*. It is an overflowing of powerful feelings from a healthy psyche. A poet is a normal man with superabundant creative powers. The other is that poetry comes from a sick soul and is to heal or make up for psychic deficiencies. One can name poets in either category. I can never find one theory or definition sufficient for all of poetry, and have felt both these points of view as realities within myself, as well as many realities in between.

The problem of time in poetry has always fascinated me. Does a poet mate with his times or transcend his times? What are, or can be, his principles when writing? It would seem that a poet, even the greatest, speaks for a few decades, maybe only one or two. I have the idea of a time-spirit in the air which the poet seizes, mysteriously, out of the air to give his truth to the world. Each time-spirit differs from every other. . . . What makes poems survive, what unique qualities poems which survive possess, are matters of the deepest interest to truth-seeking critics.

In the final analysis, although there is no final analysis, the deepest things about poetry seem to me to be mysterious. They go beyond the mind into the vast reservoir and region of the spirit and appear to be not entirely accountable to reason. I cannot go so far as to say that the deepest things about poetry are irrational, but I would include irrational perception and components in my view of poetry. Poetry is a confrontation of the whole being with reality. It is a basic struggle of the soul, the mind, and the body to comprehend life; to bring order to chaos or to phenomena; and by will and insight to create communicable verbal forms for the pleasure of mankind.

from *Poets on Poetry,* 1966

T. S. ELIOT

I always feel it's not wise to violate rules until you know how to observe them.

from Paris Review Interviews, *Writers at Work,* 1965

. . .

As for "free verse," I expressed my view twenty-five years ago by saying that no verse is free for the man who wants to do a good job. . . . Forms have to be broken and remade: but I believe that any language, so long as it remains the same language, imposes its laws and restrictions and permits its own licence, dictates its own speech rhythms and sound patterns. And a language is always changing . . . even, in the long run, its deterioration— must be accepted by the poet and made the best of. He in turn has the privilege of contributing to the development and maintaining the quality, the capacity of the language to express a wide range, and subtle gradation of feeling and emotion; his task is both to respond to change and make it conscious, and to battle against degradation below the standards which he has learnt from the past. The liberties that he may take are for the sake of order.

. . .

For myself, I can only say that a knowledge of the springs which released a poem is not necessarily a help towards understanding the poem: too much information about the origins of the poem may even break my contact with it. I feel no need for any light upon the Lucy poems beyond the radiance shed by the poems themselves. . . . I am even prepared to suggest that there is, in all great poetry, something which must remain unaccountable, however complete might be our knowledge of the poet, and that that is what matters most. When the poem has been made, something new has happened, something that cannot be wholly explained by *anything that went before.* That, I believe, is what we mean by 'creation.'

from *On Poetry and Poets,* 1957

ROBERT FROST: *The Figure a Poem Makes*

Just as the first mystery was how a poem could have a tune in such a straightness as meter, so the second mystery is how a poem can have wildness and at the same time a subject that shall be fulfilled.

It should be of the pleasure of a poem itself to tell how it can. The figure a poem makes. It begins in delight and ends in wisdom. The figure is the same as for love. No one can really hold that the ecstasy should be static and stand still in one place. It begins in delight, it inclines to the impulse, it assumes direction with the first line laid down, it runs a course of lucky events, and ends in a clarification of life—not necessarily a great clarification, such as sects and cults are founded on, but in a momentary stay against confusion. It has its denouement. It has an outcome that though unforeseen was predestined from the first image of the original mood—and indeed from the very mood.
. . .

The artist must value himself as he snatches a thing from some previous order in time and space into a new order with not so much as a ligature clinging to it of the old place where it was organic. . . . For myself the originality need be no more than the freshness of a poem run in the way I have described it: from delight to wisdom. The figure is the same as for love. Like a piece of ice on a hot stove the poem must ride on its own melting. A poem may be worked over once it is in being, but may not be worried into being.

from Introduction, *Complete Poems of Robert Frost*, 1939

The Constant Symbol

There are many other things I have found myself saying about poetry, but the chiefest of these is that it is metaphor, saying one thing and meaning another, saying one thing in terms of another, the pleasure of ulteriority. Poetry is simply made of metaphor. . . .

Every single poem written regular is a symbol small or great of the way the will has to pitch into commitments deeper and deeper to a rounded conclusion and then be judged for whether any original intention it had has been strongly spent or weakly lost; be it in art, politics, school, church, business, love, or marriage—in a piece of work or in a career. Strongly spent is synonymous with kept.

from *Selected Prose of Robert Frost*, 1946

Education by Poetry

How shall a man go through college without having been marked for taste and judgment. What will become of him? What will his

end be? . . . (college graduates) have not been educated enough
to find their way around in contemporary literature. They don't
know how to judge an editorial when they see one. They don't
know how to judge a political campaign. They don't know when
they are being fooled by a metaphor, an analogy, a parable. And
metaphor is, of course, what we are talking about. Education by
poetry is education by metaphor.

from *Selected Prose of Robert Frost*, 1946

ROBERT GRAVES

Here I must distinguish, as I have done before, between devotees
of Apollo and those of the Muse. Apollonian poetry is composed
in the forefront of the mind: wittily, should the occasion serve,
always reasonably, always on a preconceived plan, and derived
from a close knowledge of rhetoric, prosody, Classical example,
and contemporary fashion. It may, of course, disguise simple statement in masquerade dress, but if so, observes all masquerade con-
ventions; whether the dress chosen be mediaeval doublet and
hose, Roman toga, or pseudo-Homeric armour. The Apollonian
allows no personal emotion to obtrude, and no unexpected incident
to break the smooth musical flow of his verse. The pleasure he
offers is consciously aesthetic.

Muse poetry is composed at the back of the mind: an unaccountable product of a trance in which the emotions of love,
fear, anger, or grief are profoundly engaged, though at the same
time powerfully disciplined; in which intuitive thought reigns
supralogically, and personal rhythm subdues metre to its purposes.
The effect on readers of Muse poetry, with its opposite poles of
ecstasy and melancholia, is what the French call a *frisson*, and
the Scots call a "grue"—meaning the shudder provoked by fearful or supernatural experiences.

from *Oxford Addresses on Poetry*, 1962

JOHN HOLLOWAY

Every work of art, every poem, is a thing in the world. A thing
that reflects more like a river than a mirror: there is a being and
movement which it has of its own. Among the funiture of the
world, it stands with its own shape and obscure otherness, real
as a stone, strange as a meteor, the dumb witness of high tem-
peratures and giant journeys. Its first link with men is to lay a
claim on them: the claim that they take it for itself, strange and
separate thing. No key, no tool, no index merely, but before any
of these things its self. A new thisness made of the substance of
the earth in clay or stone or paint; coming from reverberating
string or column of air, into a placeless reality that touches the
ear alone; or made from the atoms of our speech. It is itself,

its own grain and texture and difference, shape and bias, convolution, resolution.

· · ·

Everyone knows—though many hate to have to say—that poetry does not come from planning and calculating. It draws on these—of course it does, it is art—on its route from birth to full development. But it comes from the imagination. Which, everyone also knows, feeds not on recipes and remedies, but on the food itself: the whole deep crust and mantle of the senses. And what parts of experience will kindle a writer's mind to the uninsistent luminosity, the glimmering explosion when sperm strikes egg for a poem, is beyond prediction or control. It is the writer himself who will sense, by intuition or his finest intelligence as men like to call it, what to begin work on, and what not.

· · ·

A live language grows, also shrinks, all the time; loses, gains. But for English, the powers of growth have largely passed to the powers of evil: to those who make us employees, taxees, above all payees. The university student is taught the skills of the critic (though he cannot win the critic's maturity except by a lapse of years perhaps five times the span of a university course) so as to care for what is strong and reject what is sham. Later, in his advertisement-copy office, he turns those skills to writing what he must still know is trash (at fifty he will have forgotten) but thinks will sell. Just so, the power to coin words, the right of mintage, has now passed to those backers of Gresham whose concern is not to maintain, but exploit, the currency of our tongue. Even in the nasty names that duroglit their fluorescent dyes from shop-windows, the great creative principles of English continue to show clear. Its magisterial lack of syntactical suffixes is what, as in no other western tongue, permits the twist of noun to verb and adjective and back again. It is largely this which makes possible the Shakespearean style and thus our whole poetry; for his is the largest and most 'accidentée' *pente douce* of all. In the shops there is a fat called *Spry*, a cake mixture called *Whisk*. The spider love of the language, that transubstantiates all to monosyllable (coz, 'flu, and those flowers) appears once more in *Daz*. Its strength with hybrids (courtship, 1588; talkative, late medieval) in names like *Farex*, and Duroglit itself. A language in which the compound also flourishes: *Mixmaster, Thunderbird*. But all these are doomed by their parents to be tossed aside almost at birth, in an uninterrupted charade of staggering the customer with the next world-breaking, epoch-shaking, market-making nonentity. Can art flourish in a world of craft?

· · ·

As I said before . . . our generation is one of poets and critics who swear blind that poetry is language, poetry is language, but who stay blind to what our language now is, what it has been, how others differ, what are its innermost powers. It lies before us in ruins . . . the language lies before us in ruins, and we close our eyes to that grandiose and lamentable Palmyra.

. . .

Yet in this splitter of dictions, Palmyra, yes, of a once integrated and imperial language, may lie the potency of poetry truly to reflect the very age and body of the time his form and pressure. Our reality is a great disruptive openness where many realities, from archaic to newfangle, jostle together, and our language of today is the same. In it too, through it, runs this harsh rainbow of broken order, scattered energy, restless change, creative vulgarity, violent potential. In its fulness, our language is already the waiting mirror of the world we have. Mirror of language, waiting to be fused, released, as river of poem.

from *The Lion Hunt*, 1964

DENISE LEVERTOV

First of all, I believe that the gift of being able to write poetry must always be considered *as* a gift. It's a responsibility, whether one considers it given by God or Nature. It's something which the poet must take seriously. His responsibility is not to himself, not to his career, but to poetry itself. Therefore I believe in craftsmanship and care. And, as a craftsman, I feel that every piece of punctuation, every comma, and every colon, is a serious matter and must be duly considered. Punctuation is a tool, all the parts of punctuation and of grammar are tools, and one must use them efficiently. . . . But I do believe in the use of the "objective correlative," as Eliot called it. I don't believe that poetry is the raw expression of personal emotion.

from *The Sullen Art*, 1963

ROBERT LOWELL

The ideal modern form seems to be the novel and certain short stories. Maybe Tolstoi would be the perfect example—his work is imagistic, it deals with all experience, and there seems to be no conflict of the form and content. So one thing is to get into poetry that kind of human richness in rather simple descriptive language. Then there's another side of poetry: compression, something highly rhythmical and perhaps wrenched into a small space. I've always been fascinated by both these things. But getting it all on one page in a few stanzas, getting it all done in as little space as possible, revising and revising so that each word and rhythm though not perfect is pondered and wrestled with—you can't do that in prose very well, you'd never get your book written.

. . .

Poets of my generation and particularly younger ones have gotten terribly proficient at these forms. They write a very musical, difficult poem with tremendous skill, perhaps there's never been such skill. Yet the writing seems divorced from culture somehow. It's become too much something specialized that can't handle much experience. It's become a craft, purely a craft, and there must be some breakthrough back into life. It's hard to think of a young poet who has the vitality, say, of Salinger or Saul Bellow. Yet prose tends to be very diffuse. . . . Yet on the whole prose is less cut off from life than poetry is. Now, some of this Alexandrian poetry is very brilliant, you could not have it changed at all. But I thought it was getting increasingly stifling. I couldn't get my experience into tight metrical forms.

. . .

. . . it's such a miracle if you get lines that are halfway right; it's not just a technical problem. The lines must mean a good deal to you. All your poems are in a sense one poem, and there's always the struggle of getting something that balances and comes out right, in which all parts are good, and that has experience that you value. And so if you have a few lines that shine in a poem or are beginning to shine, and they fail and get covered over and drowned, maybe their real form is in another poem. Maybe you've mistaken the real inspiration in the original poem and they belong in something else entirely. I don't think that violates experience.

. . .

Almost the whole problem of writing poetry is to bring it back to what you really feel, and that takes an awful lot of maneuvering. You may feel the doorknob more strongly than some big personal event, and the doorknob will open into something that you can use as your own. A lot of poetry seems to me very good in the tradition but just doesn't move me very much because it doesn't have personal vibrance to it. I probably exaggerate the value of it, but it's precious to me. Some little image, some detail you've noticed—you're writing about a little country shop, just describing it, and your poem ends up with an existentialist account of your experience. But it's the shop that started it off. You didn't know why it meant a lot to you. Often images and often the sense of the beginning and end of a poem are all you have— some journey to be gone through between those things; you know that, but you don't know the details. And that's marvelous; then you feel the poem will come out. It's a terrible struggle, because what you really feel hasn't got the form, it's not what you can put down in a poem. And the poem you're equipped to write concerns nothing that you care very much about or have much to say on. Then the great moment comes when there's enough resolution of your technical equipment, your way of constructing things, and what you can make a poem out of, to hit something you really want to say. You may not know you have it to say.

from Paris Review Interviews, *Writers at Work*, 1965

VASSAR MILLER

. . . a poet is someone who falls in love with whatever and whomever he likes, and no one, not even all the Mrs. Grundys of the world, has cause for a single complaint. . . .

With what, then, am I (as a poet, of course) in love?
. . .

Some of this poem [Trimming the Sails] implies that I am in love with God myself, at least a little . . . the poet cannot be a pure mystic. . . . The poet has good news to tell, in Richard Wilbur's phrase, of "the things of this world"—even if it is only bad news, because in poetry, as indeed in all art, the ugly, the painful, even the obscene, becomes transmuted. A transubstantiation takes place as in the Holy Eucharist when we give thanks for the Bread and the Wine, the symbols and the sacraments of what were once agony and death.
. . . .

I have also fought a battle against abstraction, which, to my mind, is death to poetry. I have won it insofar as I have dared to let my poems grow out of me, out of my flesh and bones, and not merely out of my ideas about something. For although a poem may have meanings hidden from its author, no artistic creation has any life that has not come from its creator.

from *Poets on Poetry*, 1966

MARIANNE MOORE

Interviewer: One time I heard you give a reading, and I think you said that you didn't like "In Distrust of Merits," which is one of your most popular poems.

Moore: I do like it; it is sincere, but I wouldn't call it a poem. It's truthful; it is testimony—to the fact that war is intolerable, and unjust.

Interviewer: How can you call it not a poem, on what basis?

Moore: Haphazard; as form, what has it? It is just a protest—disjointed, exclamatory. Emotion overpowered me. First this thought and then that.
. . .

It never occurred to me that what I wrote was something to define. I am governed by the pull of the sentence as the pull of a fabric is governed by gravity. I like the end-stopped line and dislike the reversed order of words; like symmetry.

Interviewer: How do you plan the shape of your stanzas . . . ?

Moore: Never, I never "plan" a stanza. Words cluster like chromosomes, determining the procedure. I may influence an arrangement or thin it, then try to have successive stanzas identical with the first. Spontaneous initial originality—say, impetus— seems difficult to reproduce consciously later. As Stravinsky said about pitch, "If I transpose it for some reason, I am in danger of losing the freshness of first contact and will have difficulty in recapturing its attractiveness."

from Paris Review Interviews, *Writers at Work*, 1965

EDWIN MUIR

To examine a poem curiously, arresting it every now and then to scrutinize a line, a phrase, or a word, and slowing down its move- ment, may bring fresh knowledge, and the knowledge may gen- erate a new emotion, but the new emotion may not be the emotion of the poem itself. Too thoroughly applied, this method may sometimes elicit from the poem a set of meanings quite different from those which strike the reader when he first comes to it. Some of those meanings may really throw light on the poem . . . but if this does not happen, if the poem, having been submitted to analysis, does not assume a new yet natural shape, what remains is merely the analysis with its own internal interest; and the poem has been replaced by the criticism.

. . . .

By imagination I mean that power by which we apprehend living beings and living creatures in their individuality, as they live and move, and not as ideas or categories. The knowledge which it gives of Priam and Hecuba is of a different kind from that which his- tory and archaeology can provide. . . . Consequently it is for human living that imagination is indispensable. Exact knowledge is only a fragment of the knowledge we need in order to live.

from *The Estate of Poetry*, 1962

CHARLES OLSON

PROJECTIVE   VERSE

(projectile   (percussive   (prospective

vs.

The NON-Projective

(or what a French critic calls "closed" verse, that verse which print bred and which is pretty much what we have had, in English & American, and have still got, despite the work of Pound & Williams:

it led Keats, already a hundred years ago, to see it (Words- worth's, Milton's) in the light of "the Egotistical Sublime";

*and it persists, at this latter day, as what you might call the
private-soul-at-any-public-wall)*

Verse now, 1950, if it is to go ahead, if it is to be of *essential*
use, must, I take it, catch up and put into itself certain laws and
possibilities of the breath, of the breathing of the man who writes
as well as of his listenings. (The revolution of the ear, 1910, the
trochee's heave, asks it of the younger poets.)

I want to do two things: first, try to show what projective or
OPEN verse is, what it involves, in its act of composition, how,
in distinction from the non-projective, it is accomplished; and II,
suggest a few ideas about what stance toward reality brings such
verse into being, what that stance does, both to the poet and to
his reader. (The stance involves, for example, a change beyond,
and larger than, the technical, and may, the way things look, lead
to new poetics and to new concepts from which some sort of
drama, say, or of epic, perhaps, may emerge.)

I

First, some simplicities that a man learns, if he works in OPEN,
or what can also be called COMPOSITION BY FIELD, as opposed to inherited line, stanza, over-all form, what is the "old"
base of the non-projective.

(1) the *kinetics* of the thing. A poem is energy transferred
from where the poet got it (he will have some several causations),
by way of the poem itself to, all the way over to, the reader. Okay.
Then the poem itself must, at all points, be a high energy-construct
and, at all points, an energy-discharge. So: how is the poet to
accomplish same energy, how is he, what is the process by which
a poet gets in, at all points energy at least the equivalent of the
energy which propelled him in the first place, yet an energy which
is peculiar to verse alone and which will be, obviously, also different from the energy which the reader, because he is a third
term, will take away?

This is the problem which any poet who departs from closed
form is specially confronted by. And it involves a whole series of
new recognitions. From the moment he ventures into FIELD
COMPOSITION—puts himself in the open—he can go by no
track other than the one the poem under hand declares, for itself.
Thus he has to behave, and be, instant by instant, aware of some
several forces just now beginning to be examined. (It is much
more, for example, this push, than simply such a one as Pound
put, so wisely, to get us started: "the musical phrase," go by it,
boys, rather than by, the metronome.)

(2) is the *principle*, the law which presides conspicuously over
such composition, and, when obeyed, is the reason why a projective poem can come into being. It is this: FORM IS NEVER

MORE THAN AN EXTENSION OF CONTENT. (Or so it got phrased by one, R. Creeley, and it makes absolute sense to me, with this possible corollary, that right form, in any given poem, is the only and exclusively possible extension of content under hand.) There it is, brothers, sitting there, for USE.

Now (3) the *process* of the thing, how the principle can be made so to shape the energies that the form is accomplished. And I think it can be boiled down to one statement (first pounded into my head by Edward Dahlberg): ONE PERCEPTION MUST IMMEDIATELY AND DIRECTLY LEAD TO A FURTHER PERCEPTION. It means exactly what it says, is a matter of, at *all* points (even, I should say, of our management of daily reality as of the daily work) get on with it, keep moving, keep in, speed, the nerves, their speed, the perceptions, theirs, the acts, the split second acts, the whole business, keep it moving as fast as you can, citizen. And if you also set up as a poet, USE USE USE the process at all points, in any given poem always, always one perception must must must MOVE, INSTANTER, ON ANOTHER!

from *The New American Poetry*, 1960

EZRA POUND

Interviewer: Your work includes a great range of experience, as well as of form. What do you think is the greatest quality a poet can have? Is it formal, or is it a quality of thinking?

Pound: I don't know that you can put the needed qualities in hierarchic order, but he must have a continuous curiosity, which of course does not make him a writer, but if he hasn't got that he will wither. And the question of doing anything about it depends on a persistent energy. A man like Agassiz is never bored, never tired. The transit from the reception of stimuli to the recording, to the correlation, that is what takes the whole energy of a lifetime.

from Paris Review Interviews, *Writers at Work*, 1965

Credo

Rhythm. I believe in an 'absolute rhythm,' a rhythm, that is, in poetry which corresponds exactly to the emotion or shade of emotion to be expressed. A man's rhythm must be interpretative, it will be, therefore, in the end, his own, uncounterfeiting, uncounterfeitable.

Symbols. I believe that the proper and perfect symbol is the natural object, that if a man use 'symbols' he must so use them that their symbolic quality does not obtrude; so that *a* sense, and the poetic quality of the passage, is not lost to those who do not understand the symbol as such, to whom, for instance, a hawk is a hawk.

Technique. I believe in technique as the test of a man's sincerity; in law when it is ascertainable; in the trampling down of every convention that impedes or obscures the determination of the law, or the precise rendering of the impulse.

Form. I think there is a 'fluid' as well as a 'solid' content, that some poems may have form as a tree has form, some as water poured into a vase. That most symmetrical forms have certain uses. That a vast number of subjects cannot be precisely, and therefore not properly, rendered in symmetrical forms.

from *Literary Essays of Ezra Pound,* 1954

JOHN PRESS

Theories of inspiration which assume that the Muse endows her votaries with the gift of song have one great merit, however rudimentary and clumsy they seem to a sophisticated audience. They recognize that, in the poetic process, there is a mystery which cannot be airily dismissed and which must be humbly accepted before any theorizing can be attempted. To ignore the depth and magnitude of the enigma is to stultify all one's thinking about poetry, however ingenious and logical it may appear. The ancient belief in some form of inspiration and the persistence of this doctrine throughout the centuries are the tribute of rational man to the imaginative truths that are the ground of all his speculative inquiries.

. . .

D. H. Lawrence "I always feel as though I stood naked for the fire of almighty God to go through me. One has to be so terribly religious to be an artist." Such testimony is worth at least as much as the assertions of men who pride themselves on their obtuseness, disguised as common sense. Plato, Isaiah, Shakespeare, Milton, Shelley and Yeats, to name only a few poets, have recorded their convictions and experiences in such a way as to make it clear that inspiration plays a part in the creation of poetry, and that no theory of poetry or of prophecy is valid if it ignores this basic truth.

. . .

The truth seems to be that poetry enlarges and purifies the imaginative vision that lies dormant within us. It does not attempt to solve the riddles of the universe, but it demonstrates, more clearly than any other form of communication, that these riddles exist. . . . The poet reveals something of the power and vitality that streams through the universe and animates all creation. . . . A poem's imagery, rhythm, tone, texture and shape all bear witness to the nature of the poet's experience. A poem can never be satisfactorily paraphrased, because the message that is thereby extracted is merely a report about the poem and not even an accurate report. The question: what is the poem's message? is radically misconceived, for the message does not exist except in the imagery, rhythm, tone, texture, and shape which the paraphrase deliberately ignores. The poem, then, has no plain message, but it has a meaning that speaks to the reader who will try to understand it. 'By logic and reason we die hourly; by imagination we live.' (W. B. Yeats)

from *The Fire and the Fountain*, 1955

KENNETH REXROTH

. . . I try to say as simply as I can, the simplest and most profound experiences of my life, which I think will be of significance to others on a similar level—that is, which will touch them in significant regions of their experience. And, I suppose that my whole attitude toward poetry—toward my own poetry— is to keep always before myself an objective of clarity and depth, and hope that out of this you'll get exaltation.

from *The Sullen Art*, 1963

THEODORE ROETHKE

Suddenly, in the early evening, the poem "The Dance" started and finished itself in a very short time—say thirty minutes, maybe in the greater part of an hour it was all done. I felt, I knew, I had hit it. I walked around, and I wept; and I knelt down—I always do after I've written what I know is a good piece. But at the same time I had, as God is my witness, the actual sense of a Presence— as if Yeats himself were in that room. The experience was in a way terrifying, for it lasted at least half an hour. That house, I repeat, was charged with a psychic presence: the very walls seemed to shimmer. I wept for joy. At last I was somebody again. He, they— the poets dead—were with me.

Now I know there are any number of cynical explanations for this phenomenon: auto-suggestion, the unconscious playing an elaborate trick, and so on. But I accept none of them. It was one of the most profound experiences of my life.

. . .

The novel, that secondary form can teach us how to act; the poem, and music, how to feel: and the feeling is vastly more important. And the "creativity" may be vicarious. Once we feel deeply, to paraphrase Marianne Moore, we begin to behave.

When I was young, to make something in language, a poem that was all of a piece, a poem that could stand for what I was at the time—that seemed to be the most miraculous thing in the world. Most scholarship seemed irrelevant rubbish; most teachers seemed lacking in wisdom, in knowledge they had proved on their pulses. Certain writers called out to me: I believed them implicitly. I still do.

"We think by feeling. What is there to know?" This in its essence, is a description of the metaphysical poet who thinks with his body: An idea for him can be as real as the smell of a flower or a blow on the head. And those so lucky as to bring their whole sensory equipment to bear on the process of thought grow faster, jump more frequently from one plateau to another more often.

And it is one of the ways man at least approaches the divine— in this comprehensive human act, the really good poem.

. . .

It's nonsense, of course, to think that memorableness in poetry comes solely from rhetorical devices, or the following of certain sound patterns, or contrapuntal rhythmical effects. We all know that poetry is shot through with appeals to the unconscious, to the fears and desires that go far back into our childhood, into the imagination of the race. And we know that some words, like *hill, plow, mother, window, bird, fish,* are so drenched with human association, they sometimes can make even bad poems evocative.

. . .

There are areas of experiences in modern life that simply cannot be rendered by either the formal lyric or straight prose. We need the catalogue in our time. We need the eye close on the object, and the poem about the single incident—the animal, the child. We must permit poetry to extend consciousness as far, as deeply, as particularly as it can, to recapture, in Stanley Kunitz's phrase, what it has lost to some extent to prose.

from *On the Poet and His Craft,* 1965

KARL SHAPIRO

The dictatorship of intellectual "modernism," the sanctimonious ministry of "the Tradition," the ugly programmatic quality of twentieth century criticism have maimed our poetry and turned it into a monstrosity of literature. This criticism and the poetry it purveys have corrupted the curriculum of literature at every level in our schools and universities and have effected a complete blackout of public opinion in the art of poetry.

. . .

Textbooks designed for the "understanding" or "exploration" of poetry have probably done more to warp the literary judgment of college students than the Collected Comic Books of the Twentieth Century. Because they are based on the "depersonalized" view of literature and life, they all tend toward the extinction of the faculty of judgment, one of man's most vital characteristics. My experience with students who have been subjected to these dry and terrible tomes, the very paper of which seems impregnated with lead, is that they are utterly and permanently stunned into literary insensibility.

. . .

"What is not Poetry" I firmly believe that whatever good poetry I have written was written because of my ignorance of criticism; I just as firmly believe that every poet of our age who has been too close to criticism has either given up poetry completely or has ruined his work because of it.

. . .

The rational person is least able to understand poetry. . . . He does not perceive, as all other people perceive, including children and savages, that poetry is a way of seeing things, not a way of saying things. Poetry is "different," not because of meters and figures of speech and symbols (these things exist in advertisements), but because it is a way of seeing a thing differently. The reaction of an audience to good poetry is laughter—the laughter of delight and discovery, not of derision. In fact, the basic emotion aroused by any work of art, however somber or tragic, is joy, even hilarity.

. . .

But what the poet sees with his always new vision is not what is "imaginary"; he sees what others have forgotten how to see. The poet is always inadvertently stripping away the veils and showing us his reality.

from *In Defense of Ignorance*, 1952

Someone has said that poetry is everywhere at its goal. That is so. Many of the disagreements of critics throughout history over what poetry is results from their approach to poetry. Most critics come to poetry with a split consciousness: they are as interested in the cause of the poem (which they call its meaning) as they are in the poem itself, or they are interested in the poem's effect on history, or they are interested in the mechanics of the poem and will not approach it until they have put on the white overalls of analytical criticism.

To say that poetry is everywhere at its goal is to say that poetry gives us knowledge of its own kind, a unique, unrepeatable, intelligible form. Poetic knowledge is neither intuitive, nor provable, nor ordered, nor consistent, but self-contradictory, beyond demonstration, beyond proof. We accept it by conviction or not at all. We accept it as we accept the belief in another's pain or pleasure, or we reject it as unconvincing, not sincere, or a symptom of disorder. How much bad poetry is only pitiful bravado, a falsetto cry of self-assertion! Poetic truth is in fact personal truth itself, that which comes out of the experience of life, and *only* out of the experience itself. Poetry is not universal, nor is its knowledge; it is not the truth for all, nor the whole truth, nor the real truth, nor the truth in a flash. Above all, it is not the truth of the Outside, of the State, or of Nature, or of God, or of the Cosmos. It is the personal particular human truth which cannot be ordered or reasoned or preconceived. It can only be lived in life and it can only be *made* in art. Poetic knowledge shows no development and cannot be pieced together like rational knowledge, nor even made consistent, like knowledge of the gods. Nor are there any absolutes in poetry, except the absolutes of the particular poet. It is as though there were an infinite number of atomic systems, all mutually contradictory, all provable, all believable. With poetry it is never a question of true and false but only of the credibility of the work. Natural knowledge tells us that the world turns; religion tells us to forgive; poetry tells us that my love is like a red, red rose. Poetry tells us that ripeness is all, and it tells us that nothing is so beautiful as spring (two truths which "contradict" each other). We call a poem a true poem when we do not hesitate to believe it—when it is impossible in its artfulness not to believe it.

Poetic knowledge differs from other knowledge in this also: it does not seek, it does not ask; it affirms. But poetic affirmation is neither for better nor for worse, and we must not be deceived into thinking, as poets sometimes are, that poetry is praise. It is sometimes praise, sometimes damnation, sometimes neither. Almost all youthful poetry does ask the philosophical questions, Who am I? and What am I? But the poet who writes this is still outside poetic knowledge and trying to approach it.

from *A Primer for Poets*, 1953

GILBERT SORRENTINO

The poet's job is to delineate the objects in the world. The poet's job is not to take that door over there and lay on that door what his idea of that door is. The poet's job is to reveal the door in its essence. Everything has its signature, everything is as important as everything else to the poet—or should be. Once the poet believes that he is more important than the other objects that walk or stand upon the earth, he begins writing "I" poems, which are of interest to no one . . . you've got to know your place as a poet in the world—all you are is someone who reveals the essence of things. If you feel that your essence is worth revealing, then that's got to be done with absolute artistry, or its a failure. . . . Pound spoke of things before the eye. He brought things back to the concrete, which the poem has always been, or should be. The poem should deal with the concrete—what one can see, what one can touch, what one can hold. If it doesn't, it usually will fail, because a poet's job is not to talk about the abstract— the poet's job is to talk about the world he lives in.

from *The Sullen Art*, 1963

STEPHEN SPENDER

There is no doubt that writing poetry, when a poem appears to succeed, results in an intense physical excitement, a sense of release and ecstasy. On the other hand, I dread writing poetry, for, I suppose, the following reasons: a poem is a terrible journey, a painful effort of concentrating the imagination; words are an extremely difficult medium to use, and sometimes when one has spent days trying to say a thing clearly one finds that one has only said it dully; above all, the writing of a poem brings one face to face with one's own personality with all its familiar and clumsy limitations. In every other phase of existence, one can exercise the orthodoxy of a conventional routine: one can be polite to one's friends, one can get through the day at the office, one can pose, one can draw attention to one's position in society, one is—in a word—dealing with men. In poetry, one is wrestling with a god.

from *The Making of a Poem*, 1962

MAY SWENSON

The poet is the great antispecialist. . . . I said earlier that a point of contiguity between the poet and the scientist is that both employ *language* to communicate what they find. At this point there is also a crucial departure, for language is not only a tool in poetry, it is its very being. In a poem, subject is not presented by means of language, but language is the thing presented with the aid of subject. (A scientific treatise can be restated and not lose its point.) But tamper with, or reconstruct the tissue of a poem and you deal death to its cells and molecules. The poet reaches for a vision of reality that is whole, seamless, and undivided; if he succeeds in that, his product need not suffer obsolescence. True art combines the properties of change *and* endurance.

. . . .

More plain than ever before is the potent fact that we are human particles in a culture of living change. We must either master the Great Whirl or become victims of it. Science is unavoidably reshaping our environment and in the future will prominently influence the next development of individual man and his species. Art, more intimately, deals with and forms the emotional and spiritual climate of our experience. Poetry can help man to stay human.

from *Poets on Poetry*, 1966

ALLEN TATE

On reading my essays over, I found that I was talking most of the time about what poetry cannot be expected to do to save mankind from the disasters in which poetry itself must be involved: that, I suppose, is a "limit" of poetry. Lessing says that poetry is not painting or sculpture; I am saying in this book, with very little systematic argument, that it is neither religion nor social engineering.

. . .

For a political poetry, or a poetical politics, of whatever denomination is a society of two members living on each other's washing. They devour each other in the end. It is the heresy of spiritual cannibalism. . . . For poetry does not explain our experience. If we begin by thinking that it ought to "explain" the human predicament, we shall quickly see that it does not, and we shall end up thinking that therefore it has no meaning at all. . . . But poetry is at once more modest and, in the great poets, more profound. It is the art of apprehending and concentrating our experience in the mysterious limitations of form.

. . .

The poet had better write his poetry first; examine it; then decide what he thinks. The poetry may not reveal all that he thinks; it will reveal all he thinks that is any good—for poetry. Poetry is one test of ideas; it is ideas tested by experience, by the act of direct apprehension.

What I am saying, of course, is that the meaning of poetry is its "tension," the full organized body of all the extension and intension that we can find in it. The remotest figurative significance that we can derive does not invalidate the extensions of the literal statement. Or we may begin with the literal statement and by stages develop the complications of metaphor: at every stage we may pause to state the meaning so far apprehended, and at every stage the meaning will be coherent.

. . .

Since I have not set out to prove an argument, but to look into arguments that seem to me to be wrong, I will state a conclusion as briefly as possible: that poetry finds its true usefulness in its perfect inutility, a focus of repose for the will-driven intellect that constantly shakes the equilibrium and persons and societies with its unremitting imposition of partial formulas. When the will and its formulas are put back into an implicit relation with the whole of our experience, we get the true knowledge which is poetry.

from *Essays of Four Decades*, 1968

WILLIAM CARLOS WILLIAMS

I was in my stride now [1948]. I thought I had found my form. I said what I had to say, using the American idiom; I felt free with it. The rhythmical construction of a poem was determined for me by the language as it is spoken. Word of mouth language, not classical English. That feeling of the language was the fountainhead of what I wanted to do. If I could make that distinguished I would have accomplished my purpose. . . .

. . .

Paterson II is a milestone for me. One of the most successful things in it is a passage in section three of the poem which brought about—without realizing it at the time of writing—my final conception of what my own poetry should be; a passage which, sometime later, brought all my thinking about free verse to a head.

. . .

Several years afterward in looking over the thing I realized I had hit upon a device (that is, the practical focus of a device) which I could not name when I wrote it. My dissatisfaction with free verse came to a head in that I always wanted a verse that was ordered, so it came to me that the concept of the foot itself would have to be altered in our new relativistic world. It took me several years to get the concept clear. I had a feeling that there was somewhere an exact way to define it; the task was to find the word to describe it, to give it an epitaph, and I finally hit upon it. The foot not being fixed is only to be described as variable. If the foot is variable it allows order in so-called free verse. Thus the verse becomes not free at all but just simply variable, as all things in life properly are. From the time I hit on this I knew what I was going to do.

from *I Wanted to Write a Poem*, 1958

. . .

"Poetry is a dangerous subject for a boy to fool with, for the dreams of the race are involved in it." The impractical dreams of men least able to advise those just reaching adulthood were my constant diet. I was caught up by the fascination of it and forgot the warning—for my father warned me to give poetry a wide berth. But I knew best what was good for me.

The trace of these beginnings remains in all I have said subsequently on the subject of verse—because it is principally about the poem that I have written critically all my life. All the emotion that is involved in the making and defining of a poem is brought out. It shows how much I am involved and how my judgment has been twisted in the defense of what I have wanted to defend.

We are a half-mad race, and what we say is not to be trusted.

In this morass of feeling began to be born an idea. It wasn't at first much of an idea and didn't come in a burst of revelation. It was a gradual conviction that writing, and especially verse, has parts precisely as the human body has also of which it is made up and if a man is to know it, it behooves him to become familiar with those parts.

That took the whole field out of the realm of the emotions for their own sakes and made it a study of means to an end. Such a move was risky—it seemed to involve a contradiction in terms. If the emotions do not control the poem, what in Heaven's name does? The answer is the mind, which drives and selects among them as though they were a pack of trained hounds. Not that I was up to the task that I had chosen for myself, but at least, win or lose, I saw the way that lay ahead. Or rather I did not see it at all but was convinecd that the way, a way, was there had I the ability to find it.

.   .   .

Yet the artist is limited to the range of his contact with the objective world. True, in begetting his poem he takes parts from the imagination, but it is simply that working among stored memories his mind has drawn parallels, completed progressions, transferred units from one category to another, clipped here, modified there. But it is inconceivable that, no matter how circuitously, contact with an immediate objective world of actual experience has not been rigorously maintained. By "artist" is meant nearly this thing alone.

from *Selected Essays*, 1954

W. B. YEATS

The purpose of rhythm, it has always seemed to me, is to prolong the moment of contemplation, the moment when we are both asleep and awake, which is the one moment of creation, by hushing us with an alluring monotony, while it holds us waking by variety, to keep us in that state of perhaps real trance, in which the mind liberated from the pressure of the will is unfolded in symbols. If certain sensitive persons listen persistently to the ticking of a watch, or gaze persistently on the monotonous flashing of a light, they fall into the hypnotic trance; and rhythm is but the ticking of a watch made softer, that one must needs listen, and various, that one may not be swept beyond memory or grow weary of listening; while the patterns of the artist are but the monotonous flash woven to take the eyes in a subtler enchantment. I have heard in meditation voices that were forgotten the moment they had spoken; and I have been swept, when in more profound meditation, beyond all memory but of those things that came from beyond the threshold of waking life. I was writing once at a very symbolical and abstract poem, when my pen fell on the ground; and as I stooped to pick it up, I remembered some phantastic adventure that yet did not seem phantastic, and then another like adventure, and when I asked myself when these things had happened, I found that I was remembering my dreams for many nights. I tried to remember what I had done the day before, and then what I had done that morning; but all my waking life had perished from me, and it was only after a struggle that I came to remember it again, and as I did so that more powerful and startling life perished in its turn. Had my pen not fallen on the ground and so made me turn from the images that I was weaving into verse, I would never have known that meditation had become trance, for I would have been like one who does not know that he is passing through a wood because his eyes are on the pathway. So I think that in the making and in the understanding of a work of art, and the more easily if it is full of patterns and symbols and music, we are lured to the threshold of sleep, and it may be far beyond it, without knowing that we have ever set our feet upon the steps of horn or of ivory.

from The Symbolism of Poetry, 1900

II

On Society and Poetry

EZRA POUND AND THE BOLLINGEN PRIZE

Is poetry a private world, far removed from war, social struggle, politics? Is the poet a "loner" whose views on practical matters are irrelevant to his poetry? Does society have anything to learn—or fear—from the poet and his poetry?

These questions have been debated at least from the time of Plato. They were brought into focus by the Ezra Pound controversy when a great many poets, as well as general citizens, found themselves taking vehement sides in a dispute that sharply divided the literary world.

The controversy began when Pound was awarded the $1000 annual Bollingen prize for his *Pisan Cantos*, a book of poetry reflecting the author's admiration for Mussolini's fascist state as well as a persistent antisemitism. The jury, which was not unanimous, consisted of Conrad Aiken, W. H. Auden, Louise Bogan, Katherine Garrison Chapin, T. S. Eliot, Paul Green, Robert Lowell, Katherine Anne Porter, Karl Shapiro, Theodore Spencer, Allen Tate, Willard Thorp and Robert Penn Warren, as well as Léonie Adams, then (1948) Consultant in Poetry in English at the Library of Congress.

The announcement of the prize in 1949 ignited a controversy which raged for years afterwards and dramatized many of the paradoxes involved in the poet-and-society relation. The variety of reaction is illustrated by the following statements:

STATEMENT OF JURY

"The fellows are aware that objections may be made to awarding a prize to a man situated as is Mr. Pound. In their view, however, the possibility of such objection did not alter the responsibility assumed by the Jury of Selection. This was to make a choice for the award among the eligible books, provided any one merited such recognition, according to the stated terms of the Bollingen Prize. To permit other considerations than that of poetic achievement to sway the decision would destroy the significance of the award and would in principle deny the validity of that objective perception of value on which civilized society must rest."

Library of Congress, Press Release No. 542, February 20, 1949

ROBERT LOWELL

I thought it was a very simple problem of voting for the best book of the year; and it seemed to me Pound's was. I thought the *Pisan Cantos* was the best writing Pound had ever done, though it included some of his worst. It is a very mixed book: that was the question. But the consequences of not giving the best book of the year a prize for extraneous reasons, even terrible ones in a sense—I think that's the death of art. Then you have Pasternak suppressed and everything becomes stifling. Particularly in a strong country like ours you've got to award things objectively and not let the beliefs you'd like a man to have govern your choice. It was very close after the war, and anyone must feel that the poetry award was a trifling thing compared with the concentration camps. I actually think they were very distant from Pound. He had no political effect whatsoever and was quite eccentric and impractical. Pound's social credit, his Fascism, all these various things, were a tremendous gain to him; he'd be a very Parnassian poet without them. Even if they're bad beliefs—and some were bad, some weren't, and some were just terrible, of course—they made him more human and more to do with life, more to do with the times. They served him. Taking what interested him in these things gave a kind of realism and life to his poetry that it would not have had otherwise.

from Paris Interviews, *Writers at Work*, 1965

ARCHIBALD MAC LEISH

Mr. Bollingen: You seem to imply that because Pound's perception of our time and place is contemptuous of both it must lack justness. But is that true? From Baudelaire on down, poetry has thought it saw in our industrial civilization not an eternal, or even a temporal, order but a tragic disorder which made meaningless the very heart of meaning. Some poets, it is true, used the art of poetry as Rimbaud used it to press through the disorder and the incoherence to an experience of private rapture which a worldly and ambitious church was unable either to give or to remember. Others, like Yeats, used the art to erect, beyond fear and beyond faith and beyond remorse, the tower of a stoical and tragic joy. Others still, like Mallarmé, attempted, by the incarna-

ON SOCIETY AND POETRY 881

tion of the metaphor, to construct a paradise safe even from the
hopes of men. But few poets of our age indeed, and they by no
means the greatest, considered that it lay within the honest practice of their art to present the central meaning of our time in
terms of order and of beauty and of virtue. Loyalty to the art of
poetry has not been synonymous, in other words, with loyalty to
the society and the values it accepts.

Mr. Saturday: But *dis*loyalty to these values! Disloyalty to the
fundamental decencies of human life! Disloyalty to human life
itself! a perverse and sniggering celebration of the ultimate evil—
the evil which rejects not only good but the possibility of good!
Which despises not only charity and love but the human mind
itself with its need of charity; its necessity of love!

Mr. Bollingen: I agree that fascism is precisely such a disloyalty.
And I agree that nothing like Pound's addiction to fascism—
nothing so infantile or so distorted—has accompanied the perception of the great disorder of our time in other poets. Baudelaire
and Rimbaud and Yeats had their occultism. Rilke had his self-
pity and his fears. But none of them committed the fascist's crime
of treason against humanity itself. Nevertheless the question is not
one of the childishness and perversity of Pound's political beliefs
as they are expressed in this poem. The question is whether their
expression here deprives the poem's insights of their meaning. If
it is true that poetry is an instrument of intuitive knowledge, does
it not follow that the presence of opinions in a poem destroys the
poem only when the opinions predetermine the intuitions—when
they, and not the poet's sensibility, supply the insights? No one
would trust the insights of a Communist poet or a Franco-fascist.
With them the opinions come first and the poetry—if you can
call it that—comes after. But it is possible, as Dante proves, for
the most dogmatic opinions—opinions hateful to multitudes of
human beings—to live in a poem beside the most profound and
enduring insights, where the poet's overriding loyalty is to his
poet's perception of the world. With Pound, as this poem itself
demonstrates and as the earlier Cantos make abundantly clear,
the loyalty is not to dogmas of fascism but to the poet's vision
of a tragic disorder which lies far deeper in our lives and in our
time.

Mr. Saturday: And yet the dogma does involve the poet. Granted
that the vision of disorder is the central preoccupation—and I
agree that it is—the fact that Pound himself was attracted to
fascism, to put it no more forcefully than that, is relevant to a
judgment of the poem. If the function of poetry is to reveal, by
the insights of the art, the coherence or the incoherence which
life, in the poet's time, possesses, then the poet's power to perceive
true things truly is very much in issue.

Mr. Bollingen: I think the poem, with all its evil and its ignorance about it, accomplishes in some measure what a poem should accomplish. I think it accomplishes this because its poet, for all the childishness of his opinions, is loyal in the end not to his opinions but his art.

Mr. Saturday: So that the upshot of the whole matter is that Pound's poem is good in spite of its evil. . . .

Mr. Bollingen: Not in spite of its evil: including its evil. It is only with its evil about it that this poem can give this poet's vision of hell. For he himself is damned in it and speaks.

from *Poetry and Opinion*, 1950

KARL SHAPIRO

I voted against Pound in the balloting for the Bollingen Prize. My first and more crucial reason was that I am a Jew and cannot honor antisemites. My second reason I stated in a report which was circulated among the Fellows: "I voted against Pound in the belief that the poet's political and moral philosophy ultimately vitiates his poetry and lowers its standards as literary work." This statement of principle I would place against the official statement of the Fellows, which seems to me evasive, historically untrue and illogical.

from *Partisan Review*, May 1949

POETS ON SOCIETY AND POETRY

W. H. AUDEN

The integrity of a writer is more threatened by appeals to his social conscience, his political or religious convictions, than by appeals to his cupidity. It is morally less confusing to be goosed by a travelling salesman than by a bishop.

.   .   .

The relation of a poet or any artist, to society and politics is, except in Africa or still backward semi-feudal countries, more difficult than it has ever been because, while he cannot but approve of *everybody* getting enough food to eat and enough leisure, this problem has nothing whatever to do with art, which is concerned with *singular persons*, as they are alone and as they are in their personal relations. Since these interests are not the predominate ones in his society; indeed in so far as one thinks about them at all, it is with suspicion and latent hostility—it secretly or openly thinks that the claim that one is a singular person, or a demand for privacy, is putting on airs, a claim to be superior to other folk—every artist feels himself at odds with modern civilization.

. . .

I sometimes wonder if there is not something a bit questionable, from a Christian point of view, about all works of art which make overt Christian references. They seem to assert that there is such a thing as a Christian culture, which there cannot be. Culture is one of Caesar's things. One cannot help noticing that the great period of "religious" painting coincided with the period when the Church was a great temporal power.

from *The Dyer's Hand*, 1962

JOHN BRINNIN

[Of the Beats and hortatory poets in general:] I share their discontent and impatience, and their hunger for a realization, in our lifetime, of those potentialities for man that the twentieth century tends inexcusably to curb and to corrode. I meet these poets on common ground in the realm of ideas, but I cannot believe that their deliberate impoverishment of poetry as an art, their deliberate turning away from the marvelous poetic inventions of the late-nineteenth and early-twentieth century does anything, finally, but muffle the voice of poetry at a time when its resonance is most urgently needed. When a poet leaves his study to mount a platform he makes a noise that will soon be spent. When he must deny the infinite richness and complexity of his art to make what he thinks is a necessary communication, he dishonors his calling and betrays the inadequacy of his gifts. Poets cannot save the world, but they can contribute to the civilizing process that might make the world more worthy of salvation. . . . The greatest need we all have, I think, is to keep alive the sense of wonder that will enable us to overcome the brutalizing forces of expediency and conformity in the mass societies of which we are a part. Only man wonders; only man imagines. When the sense of wonder is allowed to diminish, poetry becomes, inevitably, a matter of assertion and thus loses all of its Orphic power to enchant, beguile, and otherwise extend the range of our attention. Assertion is an impulse of the ego; wonder is a faculty of the soul.

from *Poets on Poetry*, 1966

GREGORY CORSO

I am the substance of my poetry. If you honor poetry, you honor me; if you damn me, you damn poetry. I am the poetry I write. . . . The times demand that the poet—that is, man—be as true as a poem. And this is happening. Poets are their poems.

I'd say these poets are extremely different from the poets of old, first, because of their stress on the psyche rather than on the poem. They wholly believe that if the poet's being is of a good shape so the poem will be of a good shape. It is impossible for a crooked poet to create a straight poem. And second, the poet today has to cope with a changing world and a changing common consciousness; he has to deal with the unpoetic rather than the poetic; this goes completely contrary to his entire make-up, his whole being; yet he must himself change or else die.

. . .

My concern is not just with American poets but with the poets of the world because a poet is first of all a universal being—that is why it is impossible for a true poet to be nationalistic. To write poems for the state and not from his heart is death to the poet.

from *Poets on Poetry*, 1966

T. S. ELIOT

People sometimes are suspicious of any poetry that has a particular purpose: poetry in which the poet is advocating social, moral, political or religious views. And they are much more inclined to say it isn't poetry when they dislike the particular views; just that other people often think that something is real poetry because it happens to express a point of view which they like. I should say that the question of whether the poet is using his poetry to advocate or attack a social attitude does not matter.

. . .

Now if we are to find the essential social function of poetry we must look first at its more obvious functions, those which it must perform if it is to perform any. The first, I think, that we can be sure about is that poetry has to give pleasure. If you ask what kind of pleasure then I can only answer, the kind of pleasure that poetry gives: simply because any other answer would take us far afield into aesthetics, and the general question of the nature of art.

. . .

. . . there is always the communication of some new experience, or some fresh understanding of the familiar, or the expression of something we have experienced but have no words for, which enlarges our consciousness or refines our sensibility.

. . .

We observe that poetry differs from every other art in having a value for the people of the poet's race and language which it can have for no other.

. . .

The impulse toward the literary use of the languages of the peoples began with poetry. . . . It is easier to think in a foreign language than it is to feel in it. Therefore no art is more stubbornly national than poetry.

. . .

And when a civilization is healthy, the great poet will have something to say to his fellow countrymen at every level of education.

We may say that the duty of the poet, as poet, is only indirectly to his people: his direct duty is to his *language*, first to preserve, and second to extend and improve. In expressing what other people feel he is also changing the feeling by making it more conscious; he is making people more aware of what they feel already, and therefore teaching them something about themselves. But he is not merely a more conscious person than the others; he is also individually different from other people, and from other poets too, and can make his readers share consciously in new feelings which they had not experienced before. This is the difference between the writer who is merely eccentric or mad and the genuine poet. The former may have feelings which are unique but which cannot be shared, and are therefore useless; the latter discovers new variations of sensibility which can be appropriated by others.

from *On Poetry and Poets,* 1957

ROBERT FROST

It has been said that recognition in art is all. Better say correspondence is all. Mind must convince mind that it can uncurl and wave the same filaments of subtlety, soul convince soul that it can give off the same shimmers of eternity . . . a distinction must be made between griefs and grievances. Grievances are probably more useful than griefs. . . . I had it from one of the youngest lately: "Whereas we once thought literature should be without content, we now know it should be charged full of propaganda." Wrong twice, I told him. Wrong twice and of theory prepense. But he returned to his position after a moment out for reassembly: "Surely art can be considered good only as it prompts to action." How soon, I asked him. But there is danger of undue levity in teasing the young. . . .

But for me, I don't like grievances. I find I gently let them alone wherever published. What I like is griefs and I like them Robinsonianly profound. I suppose there is no use in asking but I should think we might be indulged to the extent of having grievances restricted to prose if prose would accept the imposition, and leaving poetry free to go its way in tears.

from Introduction, *King Jasper* by A. E. Robinson, 1935

ALLEN GINSBERG

A word on Academies; poetry has been attacked by an ignorant & frightened bunch of bores who don't understand how it's made, & the trouble with these creeps is they wouldn't know Poetry if it came up and buggered them in broad daylight.

A word on the Politicians: my poetry is Angelical Ravings, & has nothing to do with dull materialistic vagaries about who should shoot who. The secrets of individual imagination—which are transconceptual & non-verbal—I mean unconditioned Spirit —are not for sale to this consciousness, are of no use to this world, except perhaps to make it shut its trap & listen to the music of the Spheres. Who denies the music of the spheres denies poetry, denies man, & spits on Blake, Shelley, Christ & Buddha. Meanwhile have a ball. The universe is a new flower. America will be discovered. Who wants a war against roses will have it. Fate tells big lies, & the gay Creator dances on his own body in Eternity.

from *The New American Poetry*, 1960

RANDALL JARRELL

Art matters not merely because it is the most magnificent orna-ment and the most nearly unfailing occupation of our lives, but because it is life itself. From Christ to Freud we have believed that, if we knew the truth, the truth will set us free: art is indispensable because so much of this truth can be learned through works of art and through works of art alone—for which of us could have learned for himself what Proust and Chekhov, Hardy and Yeats and Rilke, Shakespeare and Homer learned for us? and in what other way could they have made us see the truths which they themselves saw, those differing and contradictory truths which seem nevertheless, to the mind which contains them, in some sense a single truth? And all these things, by their very nature, demand to be shared; if we are satisfied to know these things ourselves, and to look with superiority or indifference at those who do not have that knowledge, we have made a refusal that corrupts us as surely as anything can.
. . .
Poetry does not need to be defended, any more than air or food needs to be defended; poetry—using the word in its widest sense, the only sense in which it is important—has been an in-dispensable part of any culture we know anything about. Human life without some form of poetry is not human life but animal existence.

from *Poetry and the Age*, 1953

ROBERT LOWELL

Interviewer: So you end up saying that the poem does have some integrity and can have some beauty apart from the beliefs expressed in the poem.
Lowell: I think it can only have integrity apart from the beliefs; that no political position, religious position, postion of generosity, or what have you, can make a poem good. It's all to the good if

a poem *can* use politics, or theology, or gardening, or anything that has its own validity aside from poetry. But these things will never *per se* make a poem.

from Paris Review Interviews, *Writers at Work*, 1965

ARCHIBALD MAC LEISH

But poetry, despite the almost magical powers of the greatest poets, is a human labor and what humanity most desperately needs is not the creation of new worlds, but the re-creation, in terms of human comprehension, of the world we have, and it is to this task that all the arts are committed. Indeed it is for this reason that the arts go on from generation to generation in spite of the fact that Phidias has already carved and Homer has already sung. The Creation, we are informed, was accomplished in seven days with Sunday off, but the re-creation will never be accomplished because it is always to be accomplished anew for each new generation of living men.

. . .

We are deluged with facts, but we have lost, or are losing, our human ability to feel them. Which means that we have lost or are losing our ability to comprehend the facts of our experience as poetry comprehends them, recreated and made real in the imagination. Poetry still survives with us: survives with vigor and inventiveness, throwing up new masters capable of standing with the old. But the poem has lost its power in men's minds. We have not discarded the art . . . but we have impaired the practice of the skill the art can give, the skill of feeling truly and so truly knowing. We know with the head now, by the facts, by the abstractions. We seem unable to know as Shakespeare knew who made King Lear cry out to blinded Gloucester on the heath: ". . . you see how this world goes," and Gloucester answer: "I see it feelingly."

. . .

The real defense of freedom is imagination, that feeling-life of the mind which actually knows because it involves itself in its knowing, puts itself in the place where its thought goes. . . . The man who knows with his heart knows himself to be a man, feels as himself, cannot be silenced.

To me,—not many others think so—the real crisis in the life of our society is the crisis of the life of the imagination. Far more than we need an intercontinental missile or a moral rearmament or a religious revival, we need to come alive again, to recover the virility of the imagination on which all earlier civilizations have been based: Coleridge's "synthetic and magical power" by which "the whole soul of man" may be brought to activity and knowledge may be known.

from *Poetry and Journalism*, 1958

EDWIN MUIR

Poetry has no quarrel with pure science, with the disinterested inquiry into the nature of things; for poetry is concerned in a different way with the same inquiry. But, if you have two great powers, both of them serviceable to human life, and one of them develops at a great speed while the other marks time, the result is bound to be dangerous . . . during the past three centuries, slowly at first, then more and more rapidly, the balance between the poetic imagination and the scientific intellect has been lost.

. . .

What can the imagination do with this world? . . . Hugo von Hofmannsthal once said that true imagination is always conservative. By this he may have meant that it keeps intact the bond which unites us with the past of mankind, so that we can still understand Odysseus and Penelope and the people of the Old Testament. Or he may have meant something more: that imagination is able to do this because it sees the life of everyone as the endless repetition of a single pattern. . . . Applied science shows us a world of consistent, mechanical progress. . . . But in the world of imagination and of human beings all is different. There you find no consistent progress, no starting where the previous generation left off; instead there is continuity.

. . .

Poetry too has its object, which is not knowledge in the scientific or philosophical sense, but the creation of a true image of life. We all help to create that image, for imagination is a faculty as natural to us as the desire to see and to know; it is the most common form of the same faculty. . . . The supreme expression of imagination is in poetry, and so like philosophy and science it has a responsibility to itself; the responsibility to preserve a true image of life. If the image is true, poetry fulfills its end. Anything that distorts the image, any tendency to over-simplify or soften it so that it may be more acceptable to a greater number of people, falsifies it, degrades those for whom it is intended, and cannot set us free. This means that the first allegiance of any poet is to imaginative truth, and that if he is to serve mankind, that is the only way in which he can do it.

from *The Estate of Poetry*, 1962

. . .

Where I disagree with Mr. Daiches is where he says that the 'real' work is discovered by investigating the book's genesis in the civilization which produced it; for he seems to imply that our first actual experience of it—whatever it may be . . . is in some way less real than these same books after the historical excavator has done with them. He implies this because he regards an understanding of the relation of the book to its period and its

society not only as a help in understanding it more fully, but as a first interpretative principle which, by explaining both the novel and our response to it in a new way, turns them into something else. . . . Mr. Daiches' insistence on this is merely another form of his insistence that the political interpretation is not merely one among several interpretations, but the only real one.
. . .

But the nature of poetry has not changed, and in our own time has resurrected, for instance, the myths which Leopardi thought were gone forever; they have been brought back in order that the imagination might see farther into the life of things, and past the flat image which the life of the contemporary world gives us. The contemporary image cannot be ignored; simply because it is the world in which we live; but it takes on a deeper significance when we see it as rooted in a past whose extent we cannot measure, and perhaps never will be able to measure. Imagination unites us with humanity in time and space. . . . So that to treat a poem scientifically, to analyze a poem as if it were a curious object, or simply a problem, and not a mysterious mode of apprehension natural and necessary to mankind, is to approach it from the blind side. . . . Besides, the strain of standing outside a poem while this prolonged scrutiny is carried on is an unnatural strain.

from *Essays on Literature and Society*, 1965

EZRA POUND

Has literature a function in the state, in the aggregation of humans, in the republic, in the *res publica*, which ought to mean the public convenience (despite the slime of bureaucracy, and the execrable taste of the populace in selecting its rulers)? It has.

And this function is *not* the coercing or emotionally persuading, or bullying or suppressing people into the acceptance of any one set or any six sets of opinions as opposed to any other one set or half-dozen sets of opinions.

It has to do with the clarity and vigour of 'any and every' thought and opinion. It has to do with maintaining the very cleanliness of the tools, the health of the very matter of thought itself. Save in the rare and limited instances of invention in the plastic arts, or in mathematics, the individual cannot think and communicate his thought, the governor and legislator cannot act effectively or frame his laws, without words, and the solidity and validity of these words is in the care of the damned and despised *litterati*. When their work goes rotten—by that I do not mean when they express indecorous thoughts—but when their very medium, the very essence of their work, the application of word to thing goes rotten, i.e. becomes slushy and inexact, or excessive or bloated, the whole machinery of social and of individual thought and order goes to pot. This is a lesson of history, and a lesson not yet half learned.

. . . .

If an artist falsifies his report as to the nature of man, as to his own nature, as to the nature of his ideal of the perfect, as to the nature of his ideal of this, that or the other, of god, if god exists, of the life force, of the nature of good and evil, if good and evil exist, of the force with which he believes or disbelieves this, that or the other, of the degree in which he suffers or is made glad; if the artist falsifies his reports on these matters or on any other matter in order that he may conform to the taste of his time, to the proprieties of a sovereign, to the conveniences of a preconceived code of ethics, then that artist lies. If he lies out of deliberate will to lie, if he lies out of carelessness, out of laziness, out of cowardice, out of any sort of negligence whatsoever, he nevertheless lies and he should be punished or despised in proportion to the seriousness of his offense. His offense is of the same nature as the physician's and according to his position and the nature of his lie he is responsible for future oppressions and for future misconceptions. Albeit his lies are known to only a few. Albeit he may pass without censure for one and without praise for the other. Albeit he can only be punished on the plane of his crime and by nothing save the contempt of those who know of his crime. Perhaps it is caddishness rather than crime. However there is perhaps nothing worse for a man than to know that he is a cur, and to know that someone else, if only one person, knows it.

from *Literary Essays of Ezra Pound*, 1954

KARL SHAPIRO

All true poetry is absolutely amoral. What is the moral of Mozart's Twentieth Piano Concerto? These are nonsense questions. . . . Poetry is eternally out of favor with all forms of authority, not because it is antagonistic to authority (only inferior poetry battles against society) but because it does not recognize the reality of authority as it is practiced in society. . . . Poetry dedicated to the "elites," the authorities, is degenerate, moralistic, authoritarian poetry.

. . . .

The uses of poetry are always self-limiting, however, and bear no relationship to society. . . . Poetry exists in a dimension outside civilization, as Plato said or seemed to say. Everything shows progress except poetry. The reason is that the poet exists in past, present and future together. History to the poet is a fairy tale. Nor does the poet recognize Literature; he sees this poem and that poem, but not in time, in sequence.

from *In Defense of Ignorance*, 1952

The artifice of poetry is without science, without philosophy, without religion. You cannot write or understand a poem philosophically, you cannot write or understand a poem religiously, you cannot write or understand a poem scientifically. The uniqueness of a work of art is its primary characteristic. Outside the work of art there is no rationale which can shed light on it. The poet therefore has no obligation to "explain" his poem in other terms, for there is nothing to explain unless something has gone wrong.

. . .

Myth is easily changed into culture propaganda, as was the case in Russia and also in countries where the artist changed to the seer. It makes no difference whether the poetry is supposed to be for the peasants or for the aristocracy: as soon as poetry becomes *for* something or somebody, it is doomed. A poetry that distills values or sets standards or projects myths is at once official poetry.

from *A Primer for Poets*, 1953

STEPHEN SPENDER

. . . there are examples enough to show—the effect on Coleridge's poetry of his delving into abstract philosophy is one—that the poetic imagination is harmed by absorbing more intellectual knowledge than it can digest. The poet can use no more knowledge than he can transform into his poetry. . . . When one is talking about the beauty of a poem, one means something quite different from the beauty of the second law of thermodynamics.

For the beauty of the poem consists of the fact that when the poet operates upon the object of his experience to make the poem, the poem is penetrated with the subjective qualities of his being. . . . Precisely what is beautiful about the scientific law is that if another scientist had discovered it, it would have been the same law. It is objective truth. Precisely what is beautiful about the poem is that if another poet had written about the same subject, it would have been entirely different.

. . .

I am brought back to considering once again Shelley's sweeping generalizations. Although the role of poet as saviour of humanity which these suggest is extravagant, what is not absurd is the idea that poetry should imaginatively dramatize the intellectual and historic forces of the time.

. . .

Art expresses the truth that despite all our systems of knowledge and analysis, to grasp, to get the feeling of our world, we are driven back on to ourselves, our own feelings. . . . There is no doubt that Shelley was wrong in thinking that poetry could legislate for the social world. . . . But he would not have been wrong if he had said that it can order inside worlds. And if it can order inside ones, it may, in the long run, at least influence outside ones.

from *The Struggle of the Modern*, 1963

ALLEN TATE

In literature as in life nothing reaches us pure. The task of the civilized intelligence is one of perpetual slavage. We cannot decide that our daily experience must be either aesthetic or practical—art or life. It is never, as it comes to us, either/or; it is always both/and. But as persons of a particular *ethos*, of a certain habit and character, we discharge our responsibilities to society from the point of view of the labors in which we are placed. We are placed in the profession of letters. We cannot expect the businessman and the politician, the men who run the state, to know that our particular responsibility exists; we cannot ask them to understand the more difficult fact that our responsibility to them is for the language which they themselves use for the general welfare. They are scarcely aware of language at all; what one is not aware of one almost always abuses. But the medium cannot be extricated from the material, the how from the what: part of our responsibility is to correct the monism of the statesman who imagines that what he says is scarcely said in language at all, that it exists apart from the medium in a "purity" of action which he thinks of a "practicality." If men of letters do not look after the medium, nobody else will. We need never fear that the practical men will fail to ignore our concern for the health of language: this he has already done by indicting Pound as if Pound, like himself, were a monist of action. Pound's language remains our particular concern. If he were a convicted traitor, I should still think that, in another direction which complicates the problem ultimately beyond our comprehension, he had performed an indispensable duty to society."

from *Essays of Four Decades*, 1968

PETER VIERECK

I believe that beauty is life-enhancing and not life-indifferent. I believe that greatness is more often found inside this area of overlapping than outside it. I believe that the *realness of values* underlies art and it underlies politics, though more often semiconsciously than consciously and far more effectively when implied than when stated. . . . But primarily these pages do not deal with Pound personally, nor with political implications. They deal with the impersonal ethical and aesthetic implications raised for poetry as a whole by the Pound controversy. . . . The position which I took in the public Pound controversy of 1949–51, and which is here elaborated and broadened, is to subordinate so-called "pure" art to ethics—or more precisely, to subordinate "pure" art to an admittedly unpure art in which the two realms of ethics and aesthetics overlap to each other's mutual benefit.

. . .

For us the issue is whether, as some of the school of "new critics" believe, form and technique can be considered apart from content and meaning. The sympathies of the committee were not with Pound's politics. Judging by their much debated press release, their sympathies were with the widely held belief—a belief I consider unhistorical and psychologically false but not at all "fascist"—that artistic form can be considered apart from its content and moral meaning.

. . .

Anti-fascist admirers of Pound, writing in honest bewilderment, have asked me personally why Pound's fascism, though admittedly evil, should spoil his poetry for me when the anti-democratic views and alleged "bad politics" of Dante or Shakespeare obviously do not spoil their poetry for me in the slightest. The answer is that genocidal anti-Semitism is not, except ephemerally and superficially, politics at all but a uniquely obscene anti-ethics, a metaphysics of satanism. There is no such metaphysics, no such ethical obscenity basic to Dante or Shakespeare; one may disagree with their monarchism, but this disagreement does not affect the value of their poetry; no basic challenge to civilization is involved in it.

. . .

The famous "new criticism's" method of analysis tends to treat a poem by itself, like a self-created airtight-sealed object, outside cause and effect. By discarding a poem's *irrelevant* historical, psychological, and "moralizing" encrustations, the "new critics" have splendidly taught us to read the text itself. But by also discarding the *relevant* historical, psychological, and ethical aspects, they are often misreading the text itself.

. . .

To Archibald MacLeish's splendid statement about poetry ("a poem should not mean but be") must be added the belief that a poem should both mean and be. Only to be, leads to hermetic "new critic" formalism. Only to mean leads to demagogy, the wrong kind of popularity, and ultimately to the fatal exploitation by literature by Agitprop, which is not really "democratic," as claimed, but either commercial (in America) or totalitarian (in Soviet and fellow-traveler circles).

. . .

A "patriotic propagandist" has ceased to be an artist or serious writer; he has become a hack.

. . .

What characterizes the free spirit? The earth is a freer place to breathe in, every time you love without asking or calculating any return. It is freer everytime you feel spontaneous sympathy for strangers. It is freer every time you make your drudgeries and routines still more inefficient by taking plenty of time out to experience the shock of beauty, whether in nature, poetry, music, or the fine arts. Admittedly this becomes impractical in a short-run crisis. But in the long-run, whatever enriches your inner sensibility with the unguessed surprises of beauty and love, is a moral act and even a political act. It is a liberating political gesture— precisely because *not* intended politically.

. . . There is no intellectual gesture, no matter how intimate, which is not by implication a moral and political act. The Soviets recognize this in reverse. They condemn the lyric poetry of Akhmatova and Pasternak for the crime of expressing private love and loneliness . . . from their viewpoint, the Soviets are right in resenting and hating this. Whatever expresses ethics, beauty and love with genuine human individuality, is thereby a blow against tyrants (whether communists, fascists, or domestic American thought-controllers). For it aspires beyond the propagandistic, the expedient, and the temporary to the true and lasting aspect of things.

. . .

Potentially, mechanization is a means to freedom of spirit. It is a means which the unrealistic aesthete dares not grasp and which the over-realistic materialist grasps too eagerly and too grossly. The world of spirit gives us certain aspirations upon which all creeds and nations can in part agree. The world of machinery gives us certain energies which men of all creeds and nations like to manipulate. Unless these two worlds can be united, our road to hell will be paved with good intentions.

The unifying artist sees beauty in both and not merely one of these worlds. Let him be as *l'art-pour-l'art* as ever he likes. Yet by seeing simultaneously the beauty of both worlds, his vision becomes an act of mediation between them. *He who mediates is also a healer.*

from *Dream and Responsibility*, 1953

RICHARD WILBUR

There are risks of corruption, then, in becoming a poet-citizen, rather than an alienated artist, but I myself would consider them risks well taken, because it seems to me that poetry is sterile unless it arises from a sense of community or, at least, from the hope of community.

. . .

I don't think poetry can be healthy if it derives its attitudes from any authority. On the other hand, I don't think that society should look to poetry for new philosophies, new religions, and synoptic intellectual structures. . . . Poets are often intelligent men and they are entitled to their thoughts; but intellectual pioneering and the construction of new thought-systems are not their special function. . . .

What poetry does with ideas is to redeem them from abstraction and submerge them in sensibility; it embodies them in persons and things and surrounds them with a weather of feeling; it thereby tests the ability of any ideas to consort with human nature in its contemporary condition.

from *Poets on Poetry*, 1966

WILLIAM CARLOS WILLIAMS   *The Wedge*, 1944

The war is the first and only thing in the world today.

The arts generally are not, nor is this writing a diversion from that for relief, a turning away. It *is* the war or part of it, merely a different sector of the field.

Critics of rather better than average standing have said in recent years that after socialism has been achieved it's likely there will be no further use for poetry, that it will disappear. This comes from nothing else than a faulty definition of poetry—and the arts generally. I don't hear anyone say that mathematics is likely to be outmoded, to disappear shortly. Then why poetry?

It is an error attributable to the Freudian concept of the thing, that the arts are a resort from frustration, a misconception still entertained in many minds.

They speak as though action itself in all its phases were not compatible with frustration. All action the same. But Richard Coeur de Lion wrote at least one of the finest lyrics of his day. Take Don Juan for instance. Who isn't frustrated and does not prove it by his actions—if you want to say so? But through art the psychologically maimed may become the most distinguished man of his age. Take Freud for instance.

The making of poetry is no more an evidence of frustration than is the work of Henry Kaiser or of Timoshenko. It's the war, the driving forward of desire to a complex end. And when that shall have been achieved, mathematics and the arts will turn elsewhere—beyond the atom if necessary for their reward and let's all be frustrated together.
. . .

The arts have a *complex* relation to society. The poet isn't a fixed phenomenon, no more is his work. *That* might be a note on current affairs, a diagnosis, a plan for procedure, a retrospect— all in its own peculiarly enduring form. There need be nothing limited or frustrated about that. It may be a throw-off from the most violent and successful action or run parallel to it, a saga. It may be the picking out of an essential detail for memory, something to be set aside for further study, a sort of shorthand of emotional significances for later reference.

Let the metaphysical take care of itself, the arts have nothing to do with it. They will concern themselves with it if they please, among other things. To make two bald statements: There's nothing sentimental about a machine, and: A poem is a small (or large) machine made of words. When I say there's nothing sentimental about a poem I mean that there can be no part, as in any other machine, that is redundant.

Prose may carry a load of ill-defined matter like a ship. But poetry is the machine which drives it, pruned to a perfect economy. As in all machines its movement is intrinsic, undulant, a physical more than a literary character. In a poem this movement is distinguished in each case by the character of the speech from which it arises.

. . .

When a man makes a poem, makes it, mind you, he takes words as he finds them interrelated about him and composes them—without distortion which would mar their exact significances—into an intense expression of his perceptions and ardors that they may constitute a revelation in the speech that he uses. It isn't what he *says* that counts as a work of art, it's what he makes, with such intensity of perception that it lives with an intrinsic movement of its own to verify its authenticity. Your attention is called now and then to some beautiful line or sonnet-sequence because of what is said there. So be it. To me all sonnets say the same thing of no importance. What does it matter what the line "says"?

There is no poetry of distinction without formal invention, for it is in the intimate form that works of art achieve their exact meaning, in which they most resemble the machine, to give language its highest dignity, its illumination in the environment to which it is native. Such war, as the arts live and breathe by, is continuous.

It may be that my interests as expressed here are pre-art. If so I look for a development along these lines and will be satisfied with nothing else.

from *Selected Essays*, 1954

III

A Bibliography of
Modern Poetic Criticism

ALLEN, DONALD, ed. *New American Poetry, 1945–1960*. New York, 1960.

AUDEN, W. H. *The Dyer's Hand*. New York, 1962.

BODKIN, MAUD. *Archetypal Patterns in Poetry: Psychological Studies in Imagination*. New York, 1934.

BOGAN, LOUISE. *Achievement in American Poetry*. Chicago, 1951.

BROOKS, CLEANTH. *Modern Poetry and the Tradition*. Chapel Hill, 1939.

————. *The Well Wrought Urn*. New York, 1956.

CUMMINGS, E. E. *i: Six Nonlectures*. Cambridge, Mass., 1953.

DAY-LEWIS, C. *A Hope for Poetry*. Oxford, 1945.

————. *The Lyric Impulse*. Cambridge, Mass., 1965.

DEUTSCH, BABETTE. *Poetry in Our Time*, 2nd ed. New York, 1963.

DICKEY, JAMES. *Babel to Byzantium*. New York, 1968.

DREW, ELIZABETH and G. CONNOR. *Discovering Modern Poetry*. New York, 1963.

DURRELL, LAWRENCE. *A Key to Modern British Poetry*. Norman, 1952.

ELIOT, T. S. *Selected Essays*, rev. ed. New York, 1950.

————. *On Poetry and Poets*. New York, 1957.

EMPSON, WILLIAM. *Seven Types of Ambiguity*. New York, 1953.

ENGLE, PAUL and JOSEPH LANGLAND, eds. *Poet's Choice*. New York, 1962.

FROST, ROBERT. *Selected Prose*, ed. Hyde Cox and Edward Lathem. New York, 1966.

GRAVES, ROBERT. *Oxford Addresses on Poetry*. London, 1962.

————. *The White Goddess: A Historical Grammar of Poetic Myth*, rev. ed. New York, 1966.

HALL, DONALD and ROBERT PACK, eds. *New Poets of England and America*, Vol. 2, Second Selection. Cleveland, 1962.

HOLLOWAY, JOHN. *The Lion Hunt: A Pursuit of Poetry and Reality*. Hamden, Conn., 1964.

HOUSMAN, A. E. *The Name and Nature of Poetry*. New York, 1933.

HYMAN, STANLEY EDGAR. *The Armed Vision: A Study in the Method of Modern Literary Criticism*, abridged ed. New York, 1955.

──────. *Poetry and Criticism: Four Revolutions in Literary Taste*. New York, 1961.

JARRELL, RANDALL. *Poetry and the Age*. New York, 1953.

LEARY, PARIS and ROBERT KELLY, eds. *Controversy of Poets: An Anthology of Contemporary American Poetry*. New York, 1965.

MAC LEISH, ARCHIBALD. *Poetry and Opinion*. Urbana, 1950.

──────. *Poetry and Journalism*. Minneapolis, 1958.

MUIR, EDWIN. *The Estate of Poetry*. Cambridge, Mass., 1962.

──────. *Essays on Literature and Society*, rev. ed. Cambridge, Mass., 1965.

NEMEROV, HOWARD, ed. *Poets on Poetry*. New York, 1965.

O'CONNOR, WILLIAM VAN and EDWARD STONE, eds. *A Casebook on Ezra Pound*. New York, 1959.

OSSMAN, DAVID. *The Sullen Art*. New York, 1962.

POUND, EZRA. *Literary Essays*, ed. T. S. Eliot. New York, 1968.

PRESS, JOHN. *The Chequer'd Shade*. New York, 1958.

──────. *Rule and Energy*. New York, 1963.

──────. *The Fire and the Fountain*, 2nd ed. New York, 1966.

RANSOM, JOHN CROWE. *The World's Body*. New York, 1938.

RICHARDS, I. A. *Principles of Literary Criticism*. New York, 1925.

──────. *Practical Criticism*. New York, 1929.

ROETHKE, THEODORE. *On the Poet and His Craft: Selected Prose of Theodore Roethke*, ed. R. J. Mills, Jr. Seattle, 1965.

ROSENTHAL, MYRON L., ed. *One Hundred Postwar Poems: British and American*. New York, 1968.

SHAPIRO, KARL. *In Defense of Ignorance*. New York, 1960.

──────. *A Primer for Poets*. Lincoln, Nebr., 1965.

SPENDER, STEPHEN. *The Making of a Poem*. New York, 1962.

──────. *The Struggle of the Modern*. Berkeley, 1963.

STAUFFER, DONALD A. *The Nature of Poetry*. New York, 1962.

STEPANCHEV, STEPHEN. *American Poetry Since 1945*. New York, 1965.

STEVENS, WALLACE. *The Necessary Angel*. New York, 1951.

TATE, ALLEN, ed. *The Language of Poetry*. New York, 1942.

──────. *On the Limits of Poetry: Selected Essays*. Chicago, 1948.

TRILLING, LIONEL. *The Liberal Imagination*. New York, 1953.

VIERECK, PETER. *Dream and Responsibility: Tension between Poetry and Society*. Washington, D. C., 1953.

WAGGONER, HYATT H. *American Poets 1650–1968*. Boston, 1968.

WALSH, CHAD. *Today's Poets*. New York, 1964.

WILLIAMS, WILLIAM CARLOS. *Selected Essays*. New York, 1954.

————. *I Wanted to Write a Poem*, ed. Edith Heal. Boston, 1958.

WILSON, EDMUND. *The Wound and the Bow: Seven Studies in Literature*. New York, 1947.

WINTERS, YVOR. *In Defense of Reason*. Chicago, 1947.

Writers at Work: Paris Review Interviews, 2nd Series, ed. Malcolm Cowley. New York, 1963.

I V

Photographs of the Poets

EZRA POUND

DYLAN THOMAS

ROBERT PENN WARREN

WALTER DE LA MARE

ARCHIBALD MAC LEISH

T. S. ELIOT

ARIANNE MOORE

GERARD MANLEY HOPKINS

GREGORY CORSO

ROBERT MEZEY

H. D. (HILDA DOOLITTLE)

ROBERT GRAVES

THOM GUNN

KENNETH REXROTH

JAMES WRIGHT

LAURIE LEE

GWENDOLYN BROOKS

STANLEY KUNITZ

PETER VIERECK

DONALD HALL

MAY SWENSON

CHARLES OLSON

STEPHEN SPENDER

VASSAR MILLER

VERNON WATKINS

CONRAD AIKEN

OGDEN NASH

RICHARD EBERHART

KARL SHAPIRO

GALWAY KINNELL

ANNE SEXTON

HOWARD NEMEROV

DELMORE SCHWARTZ

COUNTEE CULLEN

LOUIS MAC NEICE

ADRIENNE RICH

TED HUGHES

CHARLES CAUSLEY

THEODORE ROETHKE

EDWIN MUIR   DENISE LEVERTOV

ROBERT CREELEY

LAWRENCE DURRELL

W. D. SNODGRASS

JAMES DICKEY

P. K. PAGE

HOWARD MOSS

CHARLES TOMLINSON

JOHN WAIN

LE ROI JONES

LOUIS SIMPSON

SIR HERBERT READ

W. H. AUDEN

A. E. HOUSMAN

EMILY DICKINSON

WILLIAM CARLOS WILLIAMS

KENNETH PATCHEN

LAWRENCE FERLINGHETTI

D. H. LAWRENCE

JAMES JOYCE

WILFRED OWEN

MARK VAN DOREN

JOHN HALL WHEELOCK

EDITH SITWELL

Index of Authors and Titles

ADAMS, LÉONIE
Caryatid, 603
Early Waking, 603
Country Summer, 604

AIKEN, CONRAD
From Discordants, 325
From Senlin: A Biography, 325
Tetélestai, 327
Sea Holly, 331
The Room, 332
Preludes for Memnon, 333
   I
   LII
   LVI

AUDEN, W. H.
From Five Songs, 465
As I Walked Out One Evening, 465
Musée des Beaux Arts, 467
In Memory of W. B. Yeats, 468
Voltaire at Ferney, 470
The Unknown Citizen, 471
From Twelve Songs, 472
Mundus et Infans, 474
From "For the Time Being," 476

AVISON, MARGARET
Butterfly Bones; or Sonnet Against Sonnets, 661
New Year's Poem, 661

BARKER, GEORGE
The Crystal, 523
Resolution of Dependence, 524
From Pacific Sonnets, 526
   V
   VI
   VII
   XII
From Secular Elegies, 527
   V
To My Mother, 528
To Any Member of My Generation, 529
News of the World III, 529
Dog, Dog, in My Manger, 531

BERRY, WENDELL
November Twenty-Sixth Nineteen Hundred and Sixty-Three, 662

BERRYMAN, JOHN
Winter Landscape, 566
Desires of Men and Women, 567
Conversation, 567
Whether There Is Sorrow in the Demons, 568
New Year's Eve, 570
Dream Song 14, 571

BISHOP, ELIZABETH
The Imaginary Iceberg, 503
The Man-Moth, 504

BISHOP, ELIZABETH (*Cont.*)
Roosters, 506
The Fish, 510
At the Fishhouses, 512
The Prodigal, 514

BISHOP, JOHN PEALE
Ode, 606
This Dim and Ptolemaic Man, 607
The Dream, 608

BLUNDEN, EDMUND
The Pike, 609

BOGAN, LOUISE
Men Loved Wholly Beyond Wisdom, 379
The Sleeping Fury, 380
Putting to Sea, 381
The Dream, 382

BONTEMPS, ARNA
Southern Mansion, 611
Length of Moon, 611

BRIDGES, ROBERT
I Heard a Linnet Courting, 51
A Passer-by, 52
London Snow, 52
On a Dead Child, 54
The Philosopher to His Mistress, 55
The Idle Life I Lead, 56
The Storm Is Over, the Land Hushes to Rest, 56
Nightingales, 57

BROOKE, RUPERT
The Soldier, 612
The Great Lover, 613
Heaven, 615

BROOKS, GWENDOLYN
The Chicago Picasso, 665
The Sermon on the Warpland, 666

CAUSLEY, CHARLES
On Seeing a Poet of the First World War on the Station at Abbeville, 667
Autobiography, 668

CIARDI, JOHN
Ode for the Burial of a Citizen, 668
To Judith Asleep, 669
The Gift, 670

COMFORT, ALEX
The Atoll in the Mind, 671
Hoc Est Corpus, 672
Notes for My Son, 672

CORSO, GREGORY
Marriage, 673

CRANE, HART
To Brooklyn Bridge, 383
The Dance, 385
National Winter Garden, 388
Quaker Hill, 389
Atlantis, 391
Emblems of Conduct, 394
Praise for an Urn, 394
Chaplinesque, 395
Repose of Rivers, 396
From For the Marriage of Faustus and Helen, 397
From Voyages, 398
The Broken Tower, 399

CRANE, STEPHEN
In the Desert, 117
I Saw a Man Pursuing the Horizon, 118
War Is Kind, 118
On the Desert, 119
A Slant of Sun on Dull Brown Walls, 120
A Man Said to the Universe, 120
The Trees in the Garden Rained Flowers, 121

CREELEY, ROBERT
The Immoral Proposition, 677
The Rhythm, 678
The Way, 679
A Marriage, 679

CULLEN, COUNTEE
Saturday's Child, 616
From the Dark Tower, 616

CUMMINGS, E. E.
All in green went my love riding, 357
my love, 358
nobody loses all the time, 359
a man who had fallen among thieves, 360
"next to of course god america i, 361
i sing of olaf glad and big, 362
somewhere i have never travelled, gladly beyond, 363
as freedom is a breakfastfood, 364
anyone lived in a pretty how town, 365
it was a goodly co, 366
pity this busy monster,manunkind, 367
what if a much of a which of a wind, 368

DAVIE, DONALD
The Wind at Penistone, 680
Gardens No Emblems, 681

DAVIES, W. H.
Leisure, 617
Sheep, 618

DAY-LEWIS, C.
It Is Becoming Now to Declare My Allegiance, 425
As One Who Wanders into Old Workings, 426
Do Not Expect Again a Phoenix Hour, 427

Consider These, for We Have Condemned Them, 428
The Conflict, 429

DE LA MARE, WALTER
The Listeners, 131
An Epitaph, 132
The Ghost, 132
In the Dock, 133
Sunk Lyonesse, 133
Nostalgia, 134

DERWOOD, GENE
With God Conversing, 682
Elegy, 683
After Reading St. John the Divine, 685
Rides, 686

DICKEY, JAMES
The Heaven of Animals, 687
The Performance, 688
The Dusk of Horses, 689

DICKINSON, EMILY
Success Is Counted Sweetest, 3
I Taste a Liquor Never Brewed, 3
There's a Certain Slant of Light, 4
Before I Got My Eye Put Out, 5
A Bird Came Down the Walk, 5
The First Day's Night Had Come, 6
'Twas Like a Maelstrom, with a Notch, 7
Much Madness Is Divinest Sense, 8
Undue Significance a Starving Man Attaches, 8
I Died for Beauty—But Was Scarce, 9
I Heard a Fly Buzz—When I Died, 9
I Started Early—Took My Dog, 10

DICKINSON, EMILY (*Cont.*)

I Had Been Hungry, All the Years, *11*

I Like to See It Lap the Miles, *11*

Our Journey Had Advanced, *12*

Pain—Has an Element of Blank, *12*

Because I Could Not Stop for Death, *13*

A Narrow Fellow in the Grass, *14*

I Never Saw a Moor, *14*

Tell All the Truth but Tell It Slant, *15*

As Imperceptibly As Grief, *15*

My Life Closed Twice Before Its Close, *16*

H. D. (HILDA DOOLITTLE)

Song, *618*

Orchard, *619*

Helen, *620*

Lethe, *621*

DRINKWATER, JOHN

Sunrise on Rydal Water, *621*

DUGAN, ALAN

The Mirror Perilous, *691*

Plague of Dead Sharks, *692*

DURRELL, LAWRENCE

In Crisis, *692*

On Seeming to Presume, *693*

On First Looking into Loeb's Horace, *695*

A Ballad of the Good Lord Nelson, *697*

EBERHART, RICHARD

For a Lamb, *430*

The Groundhog, *430*

'In a Hard Intellectual Light,' *432*

Rumination, *433*

'If Only I Could Live at the Pitch That Is Near Madness,' *433*

On Shooting Particles Beyond the World, *434*

The Cancer Cells, *435*

Seals, Terns, Time, *436*

The Horse Chestnut Tree, *437*

The Fury of Aerial Bombardment, *438*

New Hampshire, February, *438*

On a Squirrel Crossing the Road in Autumn, in New England, *439*

Marrakech, *440*

ELIOT, T. S.

The Love Song of J. Alfred Prufrock, *278*

Gerontion, *282*

Sweeney among the Nightingales, *285*

The Waste Land, *286*

The Hollow Men, *302*

Journey of the Magi, *305*

Burnt Norton, *306*

EMPSON, WILLIAM

The Scales, *441*

Legal Fiction, *442*

The Last Pain, *442*

Homage to the British Museum, *444*

Ignorance of Death, *444*

Missing Dates, *445*

Just a Smack at Auden, *446*

Sonnet, *447*

FEARING, KENNETH

Confession Overheard in a Subway, *699*

FERLINGHETTI, LAWRENCE

From A Coney Island of the Mind, *701*

1

3

15

FROST, ROBERT
Mending Wall, *164*
The Road Not Taken, *165*
Birches, *166*
The Hill Wife, *167*
The Witch of Coös, *170*
Fire and Ice, *174*
Stopping by Woods on a Snowy
    Evening, *174*
Once by the Pacific, *175*
Bereft, *175*
Acquainted with the Night, *176*
Two Tramps in Mud Time, *177*
The Span of Life, *179*
Come In, *179*
The Gift Outright, *179*
The Lesson for Today, *180*
A Semi-Revolution, *184*
Directive, *185*
Pod of the Milkweed, *186*
Forgive, O Lord, My Little
    Jokes on Thee, *188*

FULLER, ROY
January 1940, *704*
Spring 1942, *705*
Spring 1943, *705*
The Tribes, *706*
Versions of Love, *708*

GARRIGUE, JEAN
The Stranger, *709*
Forest, *710*
False Country of the Zoo, *711*

GASCOYNE, DAVID
A Wartime Dawn, *713*
Ecce Homo, *715*
A Tough Generation, *717*

GINSBERG, ALLEN
A Supermarket in California,
    718
To Aunt Rose, *719*

GRAHAM, W. S.
Listen. Put on Morning, *720*

GRAVES, ROBERT
The Bards, *368*
Traveller's Curse after Misdi-
    rection, *369*
The Legs, *369*
Flying Crooked, *371*
The Devil's Advice to Story-
    Tellers, *371*
Interruption, *372*
Recalling War, *373*
Down, Wanton, Down!, *374*
Time, *375*
Ogres and Pygmies, *376*
The Thieves, *377*
To Juan at the Winter Solstice,
    377
The Persian Version, *379*

GUNN, THOM
A Mirror for Poets, *722*
On the Move, *723*
Innocence, *724*
Considering the Snail, *725*
My Sad Captains, *726*

HALL, DONALD
An Airstrip in Essex, 1960, *727*
The Farm, *727*

HARDY, THOMAS
In Tenebris II, *16*
The Darkling Thrush, *17*
The Man He Killed, *18*
The Convergence of the Twain,
    19
The Blinded Bird, *20*
The Oxen, *21*
For Life I Had Never Cared
    Greatly, *22*
The Pity of It, *23*
In Time of "The Breaking of
    Nations," *23*
Afterwards, *24*
The Contretemps, *25*
And There Was a Great Calm,
    26
An Ancient to Ancients, *28*

HECHT, ANTHONY
Japan, *728*
Samuel Sewall, *730*
The End of the Weekend, *731*

HODGSON, RALPH
Time, You Old Gipsy Man, *122*
Eve, *123*
Stupidity Street, *125*
The Bells of Heaven, *125*
The Bull, *125*

HOLLANDER, JOHN
The Lady's-Maid's Song, *732*
The Great Bear, *733*

HOPKINS, GERARD MANLEY
The Wreck of the Deutschland, *30*
God's Grandeur, *40*
The Starlight Night, *40*
Spring, *41*
The Windhover, *41*
Pied Beauty, *42*
The Caged Skylark, *42*
The Candle Indoors, *43*
Felix Randal, *43*
Spring and Fall, *44*
Inversnaid, *45*
As Kingfishers Catch Fire, Dragonflies Dráw Fláme, *45*
The Leaden Echo and the Golden Echo, *46*
Spelt from Sibyl's Leaves, *48*
No Worst, There Is None. Pitched Past Pitch of Grief, *49*
My Own Heart Let Me More Have Pity On, *49*
Thou Art Indeed Just, Lord, if I Contend, *50*

HOUSMAN, A. E.
Loveliest of Trees, the Cherry Now, *58*
Reveille, *59*

When I Was One-and-Twenty, *59*
To an Athlete Dying Young, *60*
Is My Team Ploughing, *61*
Into My Heart an Air That Kills, *62*
With Rue My Heart Is Laden, *62*
Terence, This Is Stupid Stuff, *63*
I Hoed and Trenched and Weeded, *65*
Could Man Be Drunk for Ever, *65*
The Night Is Freezing Fast, *66*
Tell Me Not Here, It Needs Not Saying, *66*
I Did Not Lose My Heart in Summer's Even, *67*

HUGHES, LANGSTON
Harlem Sweeties, *420*
Cross, *421*
Dream Deferred, *422*
American Heartbreak, *422*
Slave, *423*
Undertow, *423*
Impasse, *424*
Go Slow, *424*

HUGHES, TED
Hawk Roosting, *735*
The Jaguar, *736*
Famous Poet, *737*
View of a Pig, *738*
Pike, *739*

JARRELL, RANDALL
The Snow-Leopard, *560*
The Death of the Ball Turret Gunner, *561*
Losses, *562*
Second Air Force, *563*
The State, *564*
The Woman at the Washington Zoo, *565*

JEFFERS, ROBINSON
Shine, Perishing Republic, 257
Promise of Peace, 258
Hurt Hawks, 258
The Stars Go over the Lonely
Ocean, 259
Battle, 260
The Bloody Sire, 261
Black-Out, 262
I Shall Laugh Purely, 263
The Eye, 266
Cassandra, 266

JENNINGS, ELIZABETH
The Counterpart, 741
Not in the Guide-Books, 742

JONES, LE ROI
An Agony. As Now., 743
The Invention of Comics, 744

JOYCE, JAMES
I Hear an Army Charging upon
the Land, 623

KINNELL, GALWAY
First Song, 745
The Avenue Bearing the Initial
of Christ into the New
World, 746

KLEIN, ABRAHAM
Indian Reservation: Caughnawaga, 748

KUNITZ, STANLEY
A Choice of Weapons, 749
Foreign Affairs, 750

LANGLAND, JOSEPH
A Sea-Change: For Harold, 752
Hunters in the Snow: Brueghel,
753

LARKIN, PHILIP
Church Going, 754
If, My Darling, 756

LAWRENCE, D. H.
Moonrise, 211
The Song of a Man Who Has
Come Through, 212
Snake, 212
Tortoise Shout, 215
Humming-Bird, 218
How Beastly the Bourgeois Is,
219
Don'ts, 220
The Elephant Is Slow to Mate,
221

LEE, LAURIE
Field of Autumn, 757
Sunken Evening, 758

LEVERTOV, DENISE
The Goddess, 759
Obsessions, 760
To the Snake, 760
Scenes from the Life of the Pep-
pertrees, 761

LEWIS, ALUN
Song, 763
The Peasants, 764

LINDSAY, VACHEL
General William Booth Enters
into Heaven, 624

LOWELL, ROBERT
New Year's Day, 572
The Quaker Graveyard in Nan-
tucket, 573
The Drunken Fisherman, 577
As a Plane Tree by the Water,
578
Mr. Edwards and the Spider,
579
The Dead in Europe, 581
Soft Wood, 581
For the Union Dead, 583
Grandparents, 585
Central Park, 586

MAC DIARMID, HUGH
O Wha's the Bride?, 626
With the Herring Fishers, 627

MAC LEISH, ARCHIBALD
The Silent Slain, 340
L'an Trentiesme de Mon Eage, 340
The End of the World, 341
Ars Poetica, 341
You, Andrew Marvell, 342
Invocation to the Social Muse, 344

MAC NEICE, LOUIS
Turf-Stacks, 455
August, 456
Perseus, 457
Snow, 458
Bagpipe Music, 458
The British Museum Reading Room, 460
Jehu, 460
Alcohol, 462
From The Kingdom, 463
   I
   II

MANIFOLD, JOHN
Fife Tune, 765
The Sirens, 766
Night Piece, 766

MASEFIELD, JOHN
The West Wind, 188
Cargoes, 189
C.L.M., 190
Flesh, I Have Knocked at Many a Dusty Door, 191
Is There a Great Green Commonwealth of Thought, 191
I Could Not Sleep for Thinking of the Sky, 192
Night Is on the Downland, on the Lonely Moorland, 192
On Growing Old, 193

MASTERS, EDGAR LEE
The Hill, 113
Carl Hamblin, 114
Henry C. Calhoun, 115
Anne Rutledge, 116
Lucinda Matlock, 116
Davis Matlock, 117

MERWIN, W. S.
The Bones, 767
Grandfather in the Old Men's Home, 768
The Drunk in the Furnace, 769

MEZEY, ROBERT
Street Scene, 770
The Funeral Home, 771

MILES, JOSEPHINE
Monkey, 772
The Savages, 772
Voyage, 774

MILLAY, EDNA ST. VINCENT
Recuerdo, 337
Elegy Before Death, 338
On Hearing a Symphony of Beethoven, 339
Oh, Sleep Forever in the Latmian Cave, 339

MILLER, VASSAR
The Final Hunger, 775
Bout with Burning, 776

MOORE, MARIANNE
Poetry, 267
Roses Only, 268
Spenser's Ireland, 269
A Carriage from Sweden, 271
In Distrust of Merits, 272
His Shield, 275
Tell Me, Tell Me, 276
The Mind, Intractable Thing, 277

MOSS, HOWARD
The Lie, 776
Elegy for My Father, 777

MUIR, EDWIN
The Road, 246
The Human Fold, 247
The Grove, 249
The Gate, 250
The Trophy, 251
The Voyage, 251
The Rider Victory, 254
The Window, 255
In Love for Long, 256

NASH, OGDEN
Portrait of the Artist as a Pre-
    maturely Old Man, 628
Reflections on Ice-Breaking, 629

NEMEROV, HOWARD
Truth, 588
Boom!, 589
The Goose Fish, 590
Redeployment, 591
The Phoenix, 592
A Spell before Winter, 593

OLSON, CHARLES
I, Maximus of Gloucester, to
    You, 778

OWEN, WILFRED
Insensibility, 345
Apologia Pro Poemate Meo, 347
Greater Love, 348
Arms and the Boy, 349
Anthem for Doomed Youth, 350
The Show, 350
Dulce et Decorum Est, 351
À Terre, 352
Disabled, 354
From My Diary, July 1914, 356

PAGE, P. K.
The Stenographers, 782
The Permanent Tourists, 783

PATCHEN, KENNETH
At the New Year, 784
The Constant Bridegrooms, 785
Where?, 786
All the Roary Night, 786

PLATH, SYLVIA
The Colossus, 787
Black Rook in Rainy Weather,
    788
Daddy, 789

PLUTZIK, HYAM
The Mythos of Samuel Hunts-
    man, 791
The King of Ai, 792

POUND, EZRA
Ballad for Gloom, 222
Ballad of the Goodly Fere, 223
An Immorality, 225
Ancient Music, 226
Near Perigord, 226
Hugh Selwyn Mauberley, 232
Canto XLV, 244

PRINCE, F. T.
Soldiers Bathing, 793
To a Friend on His Marriage,
    795

PROKOSCH, FREDERIC
The Conspirators, 629

QUENNELL, PETER
The Flight into Egypt, 630
Procne, 632

RANSOM, JOHN CROWE
Bells for John Whiteside's
    Daughter, 311
Here Lies a Lady, 312
Judith of Bethulia, 313
Captain Carpenter, 314
Her Eyes, 316
Man without Sense of Direction,
    317

RANSOM, JOHN CROWE (*Cont.*)
The Equilibrists, *319*
Little Boy Blue, *321*
Painted Head, *321*
Address to the Scholars of New
    England, *323*

READ, HERBERT
Summer Rain, *632*
To a Conscript of 1940, *633*

REED, HENRY
Naming of Parts, *796*
Chard Whitlow, *797*

REXROTH, KENNETH
A Living Pearl, *798*

RICH, ADRIENNE
After Dark, *801*
Face to Face, *803*

RIDLER, ANNE
For a Child Expected, *804*

ROBERTS, MICHAEL
St. Ursanne, *635*

ROBINSON, EDWIN ARLINGTON
Luke Havergal, *99*
Richard Cory, *100*
George Crabbe, *100*
Credo, *101*
The Master, *101*
Miniver Cheevy, *103*
For a Dead Lady, *104*
Flammonde, *105*
Cassandra, *108*
Eros Turannos, *109*
The Dark Hills, *111*
Mr. Flood's Party, *111*

RODGERS, W. R.
Directions to a Rebel, *488*
Snow, *491*
White Christmas, *492*

Awake!, *493*
Neither Here nor There, *495*

ROETHKE, THEODORE
My Papa's Waltz, *478*
Dolor, *478*
The Lost Son, *479*
A Field of Light, *484*
Elegy for Jane, *486*
The Waking, *487*
I Knew a Woman, *487*

ROSENBERG, ISAAC
Dead Man's Dump, *636*

RUKEYSER, MURIEL
Boy with His Hair Cut Short,
    805
Ajanta, *806*

SANDBURG, CARL
Chicago, *338*

SASSOON, SIEGFRIED
The Death-Bed, *640*
The General, *641*

SCHACHT, MARSHALL
Not to Forget Miss Dickinson,
    642

SCHWARTZ, DELMORE
In the Naked Bed, in Plato's
    Cave, *515*
Tired and Unhappy, You Think
    of Houses, *516*
For the One Who Would Take
    Man's Life in His Hands,
    517
Socrates' Ghost Must Haunt Me
    Now, *518*
Calmly We Walk Through This
    April's Day, *519*
The Heavy Bear Who Goes
    with Me, *520*
A Dog Named Ego, the Snow-
    flakes as Kisses, *521*

The Sequel, *522*
I Did Not Know the Truth of Growing Trees, *522*

SCOTT, W. T.
Swedish Angel, *810*
Annual Legend, *811*
The U. S. Sailor with the Japanese Skull, *812*

SEXTON, ANNE
Her Kind, *813*
The Fortress, *814*
The Farmer's Wife, *816*

SHAPIRO, KARL
The Dome of Sunday, *532*
The Fly, *533*
Auto Wreck, *535*
Scyros, *536*
Hollywood, *537*
Poet, *539*
Elegy for a Dead Soldier, *541*

SIMPSON, LOUIS
To the Western World, *817*
Walt Whitman at Bear Mountain, *817*

SITWELL, EDITH
Still Falls the Rain, *642*
Lullaby, *644*

SNODGRASS, W. D.
April Inventory, *819*
The Campus on the Hill, *821*
A Flat One, *822*

SPENCER, BERNARD
Part of Plenty, *645*

SPENDER, STEPHEN
I Think Continually of Those Who Were Truly Great, *496*
After They Have Tired of the Brilliance of Cities, *497*
The Express, *498*
The Landscape Near an Aerodrome, *499*
Not Palaces, an Era's Crown, *500*
Ultima Ratio Regum, *501*
The Double Shame, *502*

STAFFORD, WILLIAM
At Cove on the Crooked River, *825*
West of Your City, *825*
Traveling Through the Dark, *826*
At the Bomb Testing Site, *827*

STEVENS, WALLACE
Le Monocle de Mon Oncle, *135*
Sunday Morning, *139*
Peter Quince at the Clavier, *142*
Thirteen Ways of Looking at a Blackbird, *144*
Connoisseur of Chaos, *146*
The Sense of the Sleight-of-Hand Man, *147*
From Extracts from Addresses to the Academy of Fine Ideas, *148*
So-and-So Reclining on Her Couch, *149*
Crude Foyer, *150*
Esthétique du Mal, *151*
Continual Conversation with a Silent Man, *160*
The Prejudice against the Past, *161*
From Notes toward a Supreme Fiction—It Must Change, *162*
Soldier, There Is a War between the Mind, *163*

SWENSON, MAY
Lion, *827*
Question, *829*

TATE, ALLEN
The Mediterranean, *401*
Ode to the Confederate Dead, *402*
Sonnets at Christmas, *405*
More Sonnets at Christmas, *406*
The Traveller, *407*
The Oath, *408*
The Wolves, *409*
A Pauper, *410*

THOMAS, DYLAN
The Force That Through the Green Fuse Drives the Flower, *545*
And Death Shall Have No Dominion, *546*
Altarwise by Owl-Light, *546*
A Refusal to Mourn the Death, by Fire, of a Child in London, *550*
Do Not Go Gentle into That Good Night, *551*
In My Craft or Sullen Art, *552*
Vision and Prayer, *553*
Fern Hill, *559*

THOMAS, EDWARD
Old Man, *646*
Out in the Dark, *647*

THOMPSON, FRANCIS
The Hound of Heaven, *648*

TOMLINSON, CHARLES
Winter Encounters, *829*
How Still the Hawk, *830*

VAN DOREN, MARK
The Distant Runners, *653*

VIERECK, PETER
Blindman's Buff, *831*
Vale from Carthage, *832*

WAIN, JOHN
This Above All Is Precious and Remarkable, *833*
Brooklyn Heights, *834*

WARREN, ROBERT PENN
Colder Fire, *835*
Country Burying (1919), *837*
Original Sin: A Short Story, *839*
Bearded Oaks, *840*

WATKINS, VERNON
The Dead Words, *448*
Discoveries, *448*
The Song of the Good Samaritan, *450*
Music of Colours—White Blossom. . . , *453*
The Fire in the Snow, *454*

WHEELOCK, JOHN HALL
The Black Panther, *654*
Silence, *655*
Earth, *655*
Slow Summer Twilight, *655*

WHITTEMORE, REED
A Day with the Foreign Legion, *842*

WILBUR, RICHARD
Tywater, *593*
"A World without Objects Is a Sensible Emptiness," *594*
Juggler, *595*
Years-End, *596*
Still, Citizen Sparrow, *597*
The Death of a Toad, *598*
In the Smoking-Car, *599*

WILLIAMS, OSCAR
The Last Supper, *411*
I Sing an Old Song, *412*
The Mirage, *413*
By Fiat of Adoration, *414*
Dwarf of Disintegration, *415*

The Praying Mantis Visits a Penthouse, *417*
The Leg in the Subway, *418*
Shopping for Meat in Winter, *420*

WILLIAMS, WILLIAM CARLOS
The Yachts, *194*
Tract, *195*
The Widow's Lament in Springtime, *197*
Spring and All, *198*
The Red Wheelbarrow, *199*
The Bull, *199*
The Dance, *200*
Burning the Christmas Greens, *200*
To a Dog Injured in the Street, *203*

WINTERS, YVOR
A Summer Commentary, *656*

WRIGHT, JAMES
On the Skeleton of a Hound, *844*
A Gesture by a Lady with an Assumed Name, *846*

WRIGHT, RICHARD
Between the World and Me, *657*

WYLIE, ELINOR
The Eagle and the Mole, *205*

Wild Peaches, *206*
Let No Charitable Hope, *207*
Address to My Soul, *208*
Hymn to Earth, *209*

YEATS, WILLIAM BUTLER
The Lake Isle of Innisfree, *68*
When You Are Old, *68*
To a Friend Whose Work Has Come to Nothing, *69*
A Coat, *69*
An Irish Airman Forsees His Death, *70*
Easter 1916, *70*
The Second Coming, *72*
A Prayer for My Daughter, *73*
Sailing to Byzantium, *75*
The Tower, *76*
Leda and the Swan, *82*
Among School Children, *82*
A Dialogue of Self and Soul, *84*
For Anne Gregory, *86*
Byzantium, *87*
Crazy Jane and the Bishop, *88*
After Long Silence, *89*
Lapis Lazuli, *89*
News for the Delphic Oracle, *91*
Long-Legged Fly, *92*
John Kinsella's Lament for Mrs. Mary Moore, *93*
The Apparitions, *94*
Cuchulain Comforted, *95*
Under Ben Bulben, *96*